CW01500188

DISCARD

ISBN 1-9015810-0-4 ISSN 1362-5241
©1998 Carlton Publishing and Printing Limited, part of The Carlton Group.
All Rights Reserved.

The Carlton Group
410-420 Rayners Lane
Pinner, Middlesex, HA5 5DY
England
Telephone: + 44 (0) 181 429 0056
Facsimile: + 44 (0) 181 429 3977
E-mail: carltongroup@compuserve.com
Web: www.carlton-group.co.uk

Published by: Carlton Publishing and Printing Limited, part of The Carlton Group, England.
The contents of this book are believed correct at the time of printing. Nevertheless, the publisher can accept no responsibility for errors or omissions or changes in the details given.

Illustrations by: Jeanette Sutton Design.
Typeset and Produced by: Carlton Publishing and Printing Limited and Printed in England.

The Guide to the

House of Lords

●

1998

BROADCASTING

BBC

BBC PUBLIC AFFAIRS

Ground Floor, 4 Millbank, Westminster,

London SW1P 3JA

Telephone (0171) 973 6361/6
Fax: (0171) 973 6368/9

Contact: Michael Hastings – *Head - UK Public Affairs*

BBC Public Affairs aims to serve MPs and Peers in their desire to understand the BBC's public service remit in radio, television and through new media services and to access BBC programmes and policy as desired.

HUNTING AND BLOOD SPORTS

The League Against Cruel Sports is the leading organisation in the UK working for the abolition of hunting wild animals for sport. The League works with MPs of all political parties providing research, information and expertise on all aspects of hunting. In addition to the political objective of outlawing hunting and coursing the League runs in the West Country where all wildlife is protected.

Contacts:
Graham Sirl, Chief Officer
David Coulthread, Head of Political Affairs
Samantha Arditti, Political Officer

Address:
League Against Cruel Sports Ltd
Sparling House, 83/87 Union Street,
London, SE1 1SG
Telephone (0171) 403 6155/(0171) 407 0979
Fax (0171) 403 4532

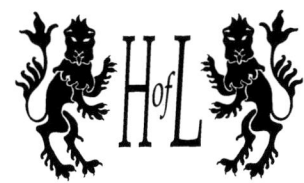

Contents

Introduction

The format of this book, The Guide to the House of Lords, reflects that of its companion publications – The Directory of Westminster and Whitehall, and The Guide to the Governance of Britain in Europe.

This publication aims to make the House of Lords more accessible. It provides information on the workings of the House, including details of Government Ministers, Opposition Spokesmen, Lords Spiritual, Law Lords and Committee Structures. It also details relevant information on individual peers. We are most grateful to those who have contributed articles, and to members of the House of Lords. We would also like to thank the staff of the House of Lords Journal and Information Office for their help.

Finally, I should like to thank our research and production team, and also in particular Mr Tim Lamport for his advice and assistance in the preparation of this publication.

Imogen Carlton
(Editor)

A CHAPEL IN A ROYAL PALACE

The Chapel of St Mary Undercroft serves both Houses of Parliament. It is situated immediately beneath what was previously the first floor of the Collegiate Chapel of St Stephen and is now St Stephen's Hall. In fact it was part of a "double-decker" chapel within the Royal Palace of Westminster.

St Stephen's Chapel was conceived by Edward I, almost certainly in imitation of the prestigious *Sainte Chapelle* in Paris, in which his royal cousin worshiped. Work began on 20 April 1291, but the Chapel was not completed until Edward III's reign in 1348. Why "double-decker"? Because the upper part of the Chapel was reserved for the Royal Family, while the Royal Household at large worshiped in the undercroft, which is what remains still in use today.

In architectural terms, it is known as S*eigneurial style* – an arrangement which can be seen to derive from the long-standing custom of living on the upper storey of a farm house, while stalling your animals underneath. Thus the Seigneur and his family occupied the upper storey and the animals and servants lived beneath. It also conveniently provided a primitive form of central heating!

On 6th August 1348 Edward III, fresh from victories abroad at Calais and Crécy, founded two college of priests to pray for him and his family. One was in Windsor Castle (now known as St George's Chapel and the home of the Order of the Garter), the other at Westminster in St Stephen's Chapel. Each college consisted of a Dean and 12 canons, with other priests and assistants. The Dean and canons of St Stephen's had the custody of the Palace Clock Tower (predecessor of the present one and its bell, 'Big Ben'). Many of them were eminent civil servants, or members of the Royal Household – the last Dean was Henry VIII's personal physician.

The Chapel, both as it once stood and as it now survives in the shape of the undercroft, is of considerable significance in the history of English architecture. The vaulted roof of the Chapel is a key example of a transitional style, where patterns extend beyond the structural into the purely decorative. These are possibly the first 'lierne' vaults in England: ornamental non-structural ribs joined between main ribs of the vault to form star-like and other geometrical patterns. This design, dating from the fourteenth century, is a tribute to the architects of that time.

There is probably no truth in the often repeated story that Cromwell kept his horses here. The number of places claiming that particular act of desecration seems vastly to exceed the Puritans' need for stabling. Certainly it was not used again as a chapel until the end of the last century and was for a time the Speaker's Dining Room.

The fire of 1834 completely devastated the main part (first floor) of the Chapel of St Stephen. Since 1574 this had been where the House of Commons had met. The Undercroft Chapel, not anything like as badly damaged, was restored by Sir Charles Barry, the architect of the New Palace, and then later, by his son, E M Barry did the internal restoration between 1860 and 1870. The Chapel of St Mary Undercroft now stands as an unmistakable and rich example of High Victorian decoration applied to one of the significant ecclesiastical buildings of medieval Gothic. The work was done by J G Crace & Sons who had executed Pugin's designs in the Palace.

These days the Chapel is used regularly for baptisms, weddings and memorial services for Members and Officers of both Houses.

While Parliament is in session there is a weekly Anglican Eucharist on Wednesdays at 12.45pm (On Holy Days of Obligation there is a Roman Catholic Mass). There are also annual services for the Church of Scotland and the Methodists.

So although you have to go down stairs to enter the Chapel, it is not a "crypt" – indeed, it is at medieval ground level and it is the rest of the world that has gone up! Its ancient title was Santa Maria Sub Volta – for which St Mary Undercroft seems an adequate enough translation.

[signature]

Rev Canon Donald Gray TD PhD
Chaplain to the Speaker

If you wish to use the Chapel, bookings should be made in the first place with the Clerk to the Lord Great Chamberlain in Black Rod's Office: (0171) 219 3100. The Chaplain to the Speaker is always available to discuss the details of services: (0171) 219 3768 or (0171) 222 4027.

RT HON LORD RICHARD OF AMMANFORD QC

On behalf of the House as a whole, may I extend a warm welcome to readers of this Guide.

Since the Election, Labour peers have formed the Government side in the Lords. The two Houses are mirror opposites of one another. In the Commons, Labour has 418 MPs to the Conservatives' 165. In the Lords, just 158 Labour peers are opposed by no fewer than 496 Conservatives.

Notwithstanding this, Labour peers are playing an important role in helping to deliver the Government's programme. The Lords performs an important range of activities. All Bills, except financial measures, go through the Lords in the same way as the Commons and receive rigorous scrutiny. Our procedures mean that the Government has few formal weapons with with which to secure its business and everything has to depend on co-operation within the House.

Scrutiny extends to statutory instruments and daily Parliamentary Questions, with an average of nearly eight minutes for each topic; far longer than in the Commons.

The House has a distinctive role on policy issues. Experts abound, and Ministers find themselves responding to debates on an enormous range of topics. The Select Committees of the House, organised on cross-departmental lines and specialising in European and scientific matters, regularly produce reports which are widely read.

Sixteen Ministers and seven Whips between them cover the whole range of the Government's business in the House. I am especially pleased that nearly one third of our frontbench are women peers. They have all performed with elan and distinction.

Because Departments have fewer Ministers in the Lords that the Commons (or in some cases none at all) the frontbench has to work harder to represent the Government in Parliament. Ministers and Whips can frequently expect to be at the Despatch Box several times in a week, doubling-up to cover Departments without a Minister or assisting Ministers steering major Bills.

The Government has a major programme. In the first session this includes bills on Devolution, Education, the European Convention of Human Rights, a Minimum Wage, Crime and Disorder, PR for European elections, a referendum on London government, Data Protection, the People's Lottery and development agencies in the regions.

The Labour Party manifesto gave a clear commitment to reform of the Lords. The hereditary element must go. In due course we will bring forward our proposals for a modern second chamber. We have made a start with proposals to modernise the ceremony by which we introduce life peers, retaining the best of tradition while enhancing the standing of the House.

The House can look forward in the coming time to an absorbing and important period in its history.

Rt Hon Lord Richard of Ammanford QC
Leader of the   House of Lords

RT HON LORD MACKAY OF ARDBRECKNISH

At the simplest the difference between the House of Commons and the House of Lords is that in the Commons you can lose the argument, yet win the vote, whereas in the Lords if you lose the argument you are very likely to lose the vote as well.

This means the Lords is well placed to examine legislation, to expose difficulties and to ask the Government and eventually the Commons to think again. It does so, not in spite of its composition, but because of it.

In the Lords the Government does not have the same command and control as it does in the Commons. The existence of a large group of crossbench peers, and the Government's lack of control over its own backbenchers mean that poorly drafted or poorly argued legislation is more likely to be defeated.

In the last Parliament if Labour, Liberal Democrats and Crossbenchers came together, the Government's majority was in trouble. And only a few rebel peers on its own benches would change trouble into almost certain defeat. I know; I was at the receiving end of a few such defeats!

As an Opposition we will be mindful of our numerical advantage but we will also be mindful that the Executive's control of the Commons is so overwhelming that proper scrutiny of legislation may not happen.

During the passage of any Bill we will be looking to interested organisations outside the House to bring their concerns to us so that we can put them to the Government. It is only through exploring the aims of a piece of legislation, checking to see if these aims are achieved, and guarding against unintended consequences that we can subject Legislation to proper scrutiny. With no gulliotine in the Lords, and the whole House involved at each stage, we are in an excellent position to ensure proper detailed scrutiny.

That we will do, and we will not be deflected by threats from the Government to behave or else!

Reform of the Lords should not be treated as a stick to beat us into uncritical acceptance of the Government's legislative programme. Nor should reform just address the composition. That would be like balancing only one of the wheels on your car.

As Enoch Powell and Michael Foot argued the last time a proposal for the abolition of the hereditary peers was discussed, any change in the composition of the Lords inevitably increases its powers in relation to the Commons. It would not be any wiser today to abolish the hereditaries or reduce their numbers without addressing the wider issues of the powers of the Lords.

There are some simple principals which should guide any reform. The Lords must have a different basis for its composition than the Commons which must remain the ultimate authority. There must continue to be a significant independent element in the House, and the Prime Minister's patronage ought not to predominate. The revising nature of the House must be retained and strengthened, and the relationship between the two Houses of Parliament should be clear, including method, to resolve significant disagreements.

Above all, in any reformed House, the Government must continue to have to win the argument before it wins the vote.

Rt Hon Lord Mackay of Ardbrecknish

The House of Lords

The House of Lords is one of two Houses of Parliament. Together with the House of Commons it is responsible for passing and revising legislation and is also a forum for public debate. It also acts as the highest court of appeal for most legal cases. Unlike the House of Commons, its members are not elected.

MEMBERSHIP

The present House of Lords (as at 1st March 1998) comprises 1,271 peers. It comprises:
   a. 750 peers by succession; that is peers who have succeeded to a peerage following the death of an ancestor who was an hereditary peer;
   b. 9 peers of first creation who themselves have been granted an hereditary peerage;
   c. 460 life peers, created under the 1958 Life Peerages Act;
   d. 26 life peers created Law Lords under the Appellate Jurisdiction Act;
   e. 26 Lords Spiritual - The Archbishops of Canterbury and York, plus 24 bishops of the Church of England.

There are:
   a. 68 peers who have not received a Writ of Summons, including two who are under 21 years old, and so for the time being ineligible to attend the House of Lords;
   b. 55 peers who are on Leave of Absence from the House of Lords.

The potentially active membership is therefore 1,148.

Under the Peerages Acts 1963, people who inherit a peerage have the right to disclaim it for life. Currently there are 10 peerages that have been so disclaimed (although three of the individuals concerned sit in the House of Lords by virtue of other titles).

Although the legal age of majority in the United Kingdom is 18, a peer may not take his/her seat in the House of Lords until the age of 21. At the moment two holders of peerages are unable to sit for this reason.

Awarding of Peerages

Peerages are normally awarded by the Crown, acting on the advice of the Prime Minister of the day, although the Queen may, on occasion, make a personal award. They are usually published in Honours Lists, which are issued twice a year – at New Year and on the Queen's Official Birthday. Occasionally, special Honours Lists may be announced at other times (eg. the Queen's Silver Jubilee in 1977); and, from time to time, separate lists of new "working peers" may be issued – as, for instance, in August 1996 when 14 were announced; and again in August 1997, when 46 were announced. (This unusually high number may be due, at least in part, to a wish by the incoming Labour government to begin to redress party political imbalance and also to increase the proportion of non-hereditary peers). In this context, the peerages are awarded to individuals on the understanding that they will be active in the House of Lords on behalf of their respective political parties, rather than simply as an honour. In practice, however, this distinction is often blurred; and, formally, these peerages are no different from any other.

It is also customary for an outgoing Prime Minister to draw up a "Resignation Honours List"; and a "Dissolution Honours List" may also be issued at, or following, the end of a Parliament. By their nature, such lists may be drawn up by one Prime Minister but published during the term of office of his/her successor. (For instance, publication of John Major's "Resignation Honours", which included 10 peerages, coincided with Tony Blair's list of working peers in August 1997).

Prime Ministers have tended to recommend peerages particularly for members of their own political party; but people with no political allegiance and members of other parties also appear on Honours Lists. Some peers may have had distinguished careers outside politics; for instance, in the law, business, industry, the trade unions, local government or public service. Nominations may be put forward to the Prime Minister's Office by others, including by leaders of other political parties. However, since peerages are formally conferred by the Crown on the advice of the Prime Minister, there is no guarantee that nominations by others will always be accepted.

THE HOUSE OF LORDS

Candidates for peerages may be examined for their suitability by the Honours Scrutiny Committee. This committee aims to ensure that awards are not made to individuals who could cause embarrassment because of activities such as crime, potential bankruptcy or other scandal, or directly in return for financial return. It can report any objections to both the Prime Minister and the Queen.

Many of the individuals granted peerages were once members of the House of Commons. Peers who are former MPs have special privileges within the Palace of Westminster; they can, for example, use the House of Commons' library and refreshment facilities, as well as those in the House of Lords.

It is common practice for peerages to be awarded to former Cabinet ministers and Chief Whips and to some other former ministers; and the same is true for former Speakers of the House of Commons and Archbishops (as well as former Chiefs of the Defence Staff, the Lord Chief Justice, former Private Secretaries to the Queen and former heads of the Civil Service). The House of Lords thus includes many Privy Counsellors among its members.

Of course, members of the House of Lords cannot at the same time be members of the House of Commons; and any sitting MP awarded or succeeding to a peerage must resign his seat. Sometimes ensuing by-elections may be lost, as at Leyton in 1965 and Workington in 1976, so Prime Ministers may tend to be cautious in this respect.

Members of the House of Lords are not permitted to vote in Parliamentary elections, but may vote in elections to the European Parliament and in local elections.

Hereditary Peers

Hereditary peers (that is to say peers by succession and peers of first creation granted an hereditary peerage), form the largest group of peers in the House of Lords. The categories of hereditary peerages are in order of precedence:
    Duke
    Marquess
    Earl/Countess
    Viscount
    Baron/Lord/Baroness/Lady
The order of precedence has no significance for the work of the House of Lords.

Most hereditary peerages are passed solely to male heirs and women cannot inherit them. However, this depends on the terms by which the peerage was created; and some do allow for succession to pass to a female where there is no male heir (although male heirs always take precedence). Any such women were not allowed to take their seats until this was changed by the Peerage Act 1963. Nevertheless, there are still relatively few women hereditary peers.

Following the introduction of life peerages under the Life Peerages Act 1958, the practice of granting hereditary peerages diminished. On election as Prime Minister in 1964, Harold Wilson announced that he would not in future be recommending the creation of any hereditary peers. This policy was also followed by Edward Heath and James Callaghan. However, a small number of hereditary peerages were created on the advice of Margaret Thatcher. These were:

1983 - Viscount Whitelaw (previously Conservative Chief Whip, Secretary of State for Northern Ireland and Home Secretary, William Whitelaw)
1983 - Viscount Tonypandy (previously Labour Secretary of State for Wales and Speaker of the House of Commons, George Thomas)
1984 - Earl of Stockton (previously Conservative Foreign Secretary, Chancellor of the Exchequer and Prime Minister, Harold Macmillan)

Neither Viscount Whitelaw nor Viscount Tonypandy had any direct heir, which meant that, in practice, their peerages would not continue beyond their lifetimes. However, the first Earl of Stockton was succeeded by his grandson in 1987.

In addition to the above, the Queen's second son, Prince Andrew, was created Duke of York in 1986, joining four other members of the Royal Family who are entitled to sit in the House of Lords. *(See section entitled Members of the Royal Family at page 16)* No hereditary peerages have been created since then.

THE HOUSE OF LORDS

Life Peers

The vast majority of peerages awarded in recent years have been life peerages, conferred under the powers contained in the Life Peerages Act 1958. Prior to this all peerages were hereditary, with the exception of these conferred on Law Lords under the Appellate Jurisdiction Act 1876. *(See section entitled Law Lords below.)*

Life peerages, as their name implies, cease with the death of the holder and do not pass to his/her heirs. All life peerages carry the rank of baron or baroness.

There is no formal limit under the 1958 Act on the number of peerages which can be created, but usually the number of creations in a year is relatively small. Honours Lists usually contain between two and five life peerages; and other lists of working peers, announced every year or two, usually contain between 10 and 15 life peerages. A total of almost 800 Letters Patent have been issued for new peerages under the Act since its inception. However, since life peerages end with the death of the individual holder, and a limited number of peerages are granted annually, the total number of life peers in the House of Lords continues to be exceeded by the total number of hereditary peers.

Law Lords

Lords of Appeal in Ordinary are created under the Appellate Jurisdiction Act 1876, as subsequently amended. They are created by the Crown on the advice of the Lord Chancellor. The maximum number has been increased over the years from two to twelve. Initially, individuals held the peerages only until their retirement, but this was changed in 1887 and they are now held for life.

The Lords of Appeal in Ordinary sit to hear appeals in civil cases, and (except from Scotland) in criminal cases; and they may be joined by other holders or former holders of senior legal positions who are members of the House of Lords.

The Law Lords may also speak and participate in debates and votes in the House of Lords, although not all necessarily choose to do so. They may choose to participate especially in debates and legislation on crime and the penal system, when their legal expertise and experience is likely to be heard with particular interest. This experience may also be drawn on to advise on legal points and interpretation of proposed legislation *(See also section entitled Judicial Role at page 33, and list of Law Lords at page 78)*

Lords Spiritual

The term 'Lords' Spiritual' is used to describe the archbishops and bishops of the Church of England who sit in the House of Lords. Their membership of the House of Lords which dates back to before the Reformation, can be seen as a reflection of the position of the Church of England as the established church.

The Lords Spiritual comprise:
    a. The Archbishop of Canterbury;
    b. The Archbishop of York;
    c. The Bishops of London, Durham and Winchester;
    d. 21 other English diocesan bishops. These are chosen on the basis of their length of service as diocesan bishops, (including any years in a previous episcopal see).

When any of the 21 bishops without an automatic seat retires or is promoted to one of the more senior posts, the longest serving diocesan bishop outside the Lords then joins the bench of bishops.

Until 1847 all diocesan bishops sat in the House of Lords, but with the creation of new sees – there are now over 40 – it was felt necessary to limit the numbers. The Bishop of Sodor and Man does not sit in the House of Lords, but instead has a seat in the Manx Parliament.

THE HOUSE OF LORDS

When a bishop who is already a member of the House of Lords changes his see or becomes an archbishop, he has to be reintroduced to the House as the representative of that particular see. For example, the present Archbishop of York, Dr David Hope, has been introduced to the House of Lords three times: as Bishop of Wakefield, then Bishop of London, and most recently as Archbishop of York.

Bishops and archbishops sit as such in the House of Lords only until they retire. The retirement age is now set at 70, but any bishop appointed to his office before the retirement age was laid down is not obliged to retire. (There are currently two bishops to whom this applies). It has become common practice when Archbishops of Canterbury and York retire to award them life peerages. Former Archbishops Coggan, Runcie and Habgood are all now life peers.

The Lords Spiritual sit together on benches on the government side of the House. This position is in accordance with an Act passed by Parliament in 1539. Because the bishops sit together in this way they are sometimes collectively referred to as "the bench of bishops". The bishops wear robes (rochet and chimere) when in the Chamber.

The attendance of the Lords Spiritual is variable. Obviously they have other duties; and attendance may depend on a range of factors, including the personal interests of the individual concerned, the perceived spiritual and social importance of issues being debated on a particular day, the proximity of a bishop's see to London, and the coincidence of a bishop having other engagements in London on any particular day.

The House of Lords occasionally debates issues which directly affect the Church of England and certain measures affecting the church still have to go through Parliament. Such occasions normally see a relatively high attendance of bishops. A fairly recent example was the issue of whether women could become Church of England priests. Other matters may also affect the Church's interest directly. Examples include education debates, because the Church of England manages a large number of schools, and major property legislation, because the Church of England, through the Church Commissioners, is a major property owner.

Members of the Bench of Bishops try to ensure that, whenever a matter which might be considered as raising moral issues is debated, at least one bishop is present and speaks during the debate. An official at Lambeth Palace has the job of briefing the Archbishop of Canterbury and other bishops as necessary and co-ordinating their response, where appropriate. A duty bishop is, in any case, present each day the House is sitting in order to lead prayers.

Representatives of other churches and religions do not sit as of right in the House of Lords. However, some individuals prominent in such churches or religions have been awarded life peerages. Examples include Lord Soper (Methodist), Lord Eames (Primate, Church of Ireland), and Lord Jakobovits (former Chief Rabbi). *(For a list of current Lords Spiritual see page 68)*

Members of the Royal Family

Certain members of the Royal Family are members of the House of Lords as Royal Dukes. They are:
    The Prince of Wales
    The Duke of York
    The Duke of Edinburgh
    The Duke of Gloucester
    The Duke of Kent

In modern times members of the Royal Family rarely speak in the House of Lords; indeed, the Dukes of Edinburgh, Kent and York have never spoken. At the time of writing, the Prince of Wales, Duke of Edinburgh and Duke of York had not taken the Oath; but the Duke of Gloucester and the Duke of Kent had done so.

Although in past centuries royal peers spoke regularly and were sometimes outspoken in voicing political views, there is now an expectation that members of the Royal Family will avoid becoming involved in matters of political controversy.

THE HOUSE OF LORDS

Women Peers

There were no women members of the House of Lords until the passing in 1958 of the Life Peerage Act That Act did not discriminate between men and women; under it both could be created life peers.

The 1963 Peerage Act allowed women who inherited peerages by succession to take their seat in the Lords, but they are relatively few in number, and the great majority of peerages are inherited by men *(See also section entitled Hereditary Peers at page 57)*.

There are currently (March 1998) 97 women peers in the House of Lords, of whom 16 are peers by succession and 81 are life peers. *(For a list of women peers see page 69)*.

Renouncing a Peerage

Under the Peerage Act 1963, individual peers by succession (hereditary peers) may renounce their peerages for their lifetime.

This constitutional change followed the controversy which arose in 1960 when the then MP for Bristol South East, Anthony Wedgwood Benn (now known as Tony Benn), inherited a peerage (the Viscountcy of Stansgate). He wished to continue as an MP, but was debarred from so doing, since peers cannot also be MPs. No individual is permitted to be a member of both Houses of Parliament but, at that time, there was no constitutional provision to allow an individual to renounce a peerage.

When, on the death of his father, Benn automatically inherited the peerage, he was disqualified from membership of the House of Commons and a by-election was called. Benn then stood as a candidate in that by-election and actually increased his majority; but an election court declared his election void and the Conservative candidate to be the MP.

Subsequently a Select Committee of both Houses of Parliament was established to consider the constitutional implications of the issues involved. Following its report, Parliament passed the Peerage Act 1963. Under it, hereditary peers have a year from succeeding to a title in which to decide whether or not they wish to disclaim it. However, if the individual concerned is an MP, he or she has to decide within a month. Once an individual has disclaimed a title, that person cannot reclaim the same peerage. However, the same person may subsequently accept another peerage if it is offered, although not, of course, while sitting in the House of Commons. The peerage is only renounced for the lifetime of the individual concerned. After his death, his heirs may revive use of the title and take their seats in the House of Lords.

After the passing of the Peerage Act 1963, Tony Benn renounced his peerage; and the Conservative who had been serving as MP for Bristol South East resigned his seat, thus creating another by-election, in which Benn again topped the poll. This time he was allowed to take his seat and serve as MP for the constituency.

In addition to allowing newly succeeded peers to disclaim, the 1963 Peerage Act also gave the same opportunity to all existing peers by succession at that particular time. This coincided with the contest to succeed the then Conservative Prime Minister, Harold Macmillan. Two of the leading contenders resigned their peerages using the provisions of the 1963 Act, and sought House of Commons seats. Lord Home, as Sir Alec Douglas Home, became MP for Kinross and West Perthshire – and Prime Minister; and Lord Hailsham, as Quintin Hogg, became MP for St Marylebone. Eventually both returned to the House of Lords with life peerages, when they retired from the House of Commons.
(See page 70 for a list of peerages currently disclaimed.)

THE HOUSE OF LORDS

Peers who do not sit

Not all members of the House of Lords attend regularly and some do not attend at all. Those peers who are on Leave of Absence and those who have not received a Writ of Summons are not active members of the House of Lords.

Peers are not allowed to take their seat in the House of Lords until they have received a _Writ of Summons_ from the Queen. The Writ of Summons has to be applied for; it is not issued automatically. The application is made to the Lord Chancellor by the peer concerned. If they do not want to take part in the proceedings of the House, peers may choose not to apply for a Writ of Summons. Peers who are bankrupts, minors or aliens are disqualified from receiving a Writ of Summons. Detention in prison does not initself disqualify a peer from holding a Writ of Summons, although individual is obviously unable to attend proceedings.

Peers on _Leave of Absence_ are peers who have received a Writ of Summons, but have subsequently applied for Leave of Absence from the House. Although members of the House of Lords, these peers are expected not to attend sittings of the House of Lords. A peer can apply to have his/her Leave of Absence terminated so he/she can take part in the proceedings of the House, but must give a month's notice. Unless a request for termination is made, Leave of Absence lasts for the length of a Parliament. Consequently, after a general election, peers who wish to continue on Leave of Absence are invited to reapply for it. The House grants Leave to those who reapply. The system of Leave of Absence is relatively recent and was brought in by an amendment made in the late 1950s to the Standing Orders of the House.

Application for Leave of Absence indicates formally an intention by that individual not to play an active part in the proceedings of the House of Lords. However, there is no formal attendance requirement, and there may be other peers who, for whatever reason, do not in practice play an active part in the affairs of the House.

(For lists of peers without Writ of Summons or on Leave of Absence, see page 70)

Working Peers and Attendance

The term "working peer" has no official definition; but is often used to describe a peer who has been granted a life peerage on the understanding that he/she will attend and play an active part in the House of Lords on a regular basis. These peers have usually been recommended for appointment by the Prime Minister or the leaders of the other parties on that assumption, and are generally recognised as political appointments.

In practice, some peers who have been appointed on a "working peer" basis may, in the event, attend the House comparatively rarely, for one reason or another. Conversely, there are also individuals who have been awarded life peerages in the twice yearly Honours Lists, (as opposed to "working peers") who, in practice, attend the House on a regular basis and play an active part in its work, as also do some hereditary peers.

The Labour Government's 1968 White Paper on the Reform of the House of Lords defined "regular" attenders as those present on more than one-third of sitting days. On that basis, in the 1996-97 Session, 457 out of a potentially active membership of 1,087 could be described as regular attenders. The numbers of regular attenders divided roughly equally between the life and hereditary peers (although, of course, overall there are many more hereditary peers who could attend). The average daily attendance was 381. There were some 232 peers potentially able to attend but who did not put in a single appearance.

Of course, simple attendance is not, in itself, the only yardstick which may be used to judge the contribution made by individual peers. Some may attend regularly, but not speak; others may attend comparatively rarely, but make a significant or authoritative contribution when they do so. The Law Lords and Lords Spiritual have major commitments outside the House; and so do other peers who hold important positions in industry, commerce or public life.

Although the number of peers attending the House is in the range of 300 to 400 a day, the actual figure varies according to the nature of the business and peers' other commitments. Sometimes attendance can be low; and sometimes, if the issue being debated is particularly controversial, the House can be crowded. The highest attendances in recent sessions were 470 on 19th March 1996 for the Third Reading of the Broadcasting Bill (in the 1995-96 Session), and 482 on 18th March 1997 for the Report Stage of the Criminal Sentences Bill (1996-7 Session).

THE HOUSE OF LORDS

Peers' Backgrounds

Although many former MPs have been granted life peerages since they were introduced in 1958, the House of Lords includes people from a wide range of occupational backgrounds other than that of professional politicians. Indeed this is sometimes said to be to the advantage of the House which, it is argued, can call upon a breadth of experience and expertise in its debates. Individuals with experience – sometimes ongoing – of business and industry, the universities and education, the civil and diplomatic services, local government, the military, trade unions, the law and the media are all represented.

The House is, nevertheless, dominated numerically by hereditary peers and, according to the academic Donald Shell (*The House of Lords* 2nd edition 1992, published by Harvester Wheatsheaf), over half of these could be described as landowners. Another academic study by Nicholas Baldwin (unpublished PhD thesis, Exeter University, 1985), found that in 1981, 86 per cent of peers were drawn from the business and professional classes and just 2 per cent from the working classes. This also showed that 86 per cent of peers by succession and 45 per cent of life peers were educated at public school (compared with 5 per cent of the general population).

However, the existence of hereditary peers helps ensure the presence of some relatively young individuals. In 1997 the average age of all peers eligible to sit was 65, but for created peers the average age was 71, compared with 61 for hereditary peers. The youngest attending member was the Earl of Hardwicke (b1971) and the oldest was Lord Denning (b1899). The Father of the House is Lord Oranmore and Browne, who succeeded to his title in 1927, but who is on Leave of Absence and no longer active.

POLITICAL ORGANISATION IN THE HOUSE OF LORDS

Political Composition

The present party political composition of the House of Lords is:

	Hereditary	*Life*
Conservative	323	173
Labour	17	141
Liberal Democrat	24	44
Cross Bench	204	118
Other Independent	73	31

Note:
(i) The above figures do not include peers without Writ of Summons or on Leave of Absence.
(ii) The 26 Lords Spiritual are included in the 31 Other Independent Life Peers.
(iii) The figures were correct as of 1st March 1998.

It can be seen that the Conservatives are the largest party in both categories, but that their predominance is much greater amongst the hereditary peers than amongst the life peers. This does not mean that a Conservative government can always take a majority for granted in the House of Lords. For instance, Margaret Thatcher's Conservative Government was defeated 155 times between 1979 and 1990, although this compared with 350 defeats suffered by the Labour Government between 1974 and 1979.

Not all such defeats are on major items of legislation and the House of Commons may often subsequently overturn a defeat or reach a compromise. There have been complaints, particularly by opposition parties, that a Conservative government could call in "backwoodsmen" who rarely attend, in order to secure a majority in crucial divisions. One such example was a vote on the community charge ("poll tax") in 1988, when more than 500 peers voted. More recently, in 1996, similar criticisms were voiced concerning votes on the sale of army housing and on the Asylum Bill.

THE HOUSE OF LORDS

The Labour Party argued during the 1997 general election the party strengths should reflect more accurately votes cast; and that no party should seek an overall majority in the House of Lords. The present Labour Government has indicated its intention to end the right of hereditary peers to sit and vote in the House of Lords, which would reduce considerably the party inbalance.

Party organisation is, perhaps, more relaxed in the House of Lords than in the Commons, since governments do not depend for their existence on the Lords. Nevertheless, governments need to get their legislation through both Houses of Parliament – Lords as well as Commons – and opposition parties seek to amend it or to ensure the government has to reconsider its actions. Each party employs back up staff, researchers and secretaries, and has offices on the premises of the House. Most significantly, perhaps, each party has its whips.

(For lists of peers by political party see page 48)

Party Whips

All the political parties appoint whips in order to ensure a good attendance and vote by their supporters on issues they regard as important. The whips aim to keep track of their party's members in the House of Lords, to know of their interests and concerns in order to maximise attendances for important votes and ensure that the views of their party are put forward in debates.

The whipping system in the House of Lords is in some respects similar to that operating in the House of Commons. A written weekly whip is issued to those peers who have a party political allegiance, whether Conservative, Labour or Liberal Democrat. This is a piece of paper giving details of the following week's business in the House. The number of lines under each subject for debate indicate the importance that party's Parliamentary leadership attaches to each item to be debated during the week. One thick line typed under a subject means the vote is regarded as relatively unimportant; two that it is fairly important and three lines that it is very important. For a three line whip, a party will expect as many of its peers to attend as humanly possible.

However, party political competition in the Lords is less intense than in the Commons. Not only are there many members with no political affiliation; even those who are identified with a party and accept the whip may feel more free of party political constraints than do MPs. Membership of the House of Lords is a lifetime honour which, once granted, is not taken away. Thus peers do not face the practical, personal disciplines which tend to ensure MPs normally toe their party's political line. They do not have to worry about reselection by their parties between elections, or about rejection by the electorate; and they may be less susceptible to pressure from party leaders, less concerned with political promotion. Even some peers who were once government ministers, but who are no longer seeking office may feel less constrained to toe the party line than in the House of Commons.

Members of the House of Lords thus tend to be more willing to express views which are not in accord with their party's policies than are MPs in the House of Commons. The whips have to rely on persuasion rather than coercion.

Government whips are members of the government and may speak in the House on its behalf. They are also appointed to positions in the Royal Household.

The Government Chief Whip and Opposition Chief Whip receive a salary paid by the public purse; so too do the other government whips.

THE HOUSE OF LORDS

Cross Bench Peers

Many peers have no party political affiliation and are known as "Cross Bench" peers. This term derives from the location of the benches across the chamber, rather than on one side or the other. The Cross Bench peers do have a degree of organisation, including a Convenor – currently Lord Weatherill, the former Speaker of the House of Commons – regular meetings and an advice note on forthcoming business

Numerically, the Cross Bench peers are larger than any party grouping except the Conservatives, but they are not an homogeneous group and Cross Bench peers decide individually how to vote, if at all. Since they receive no party whip to encourage them to vote, Cross Benchers tend to be less likely to do so than peers with party affiliations.

Nevertheless, since no party can be sure of an absolute majority in the House of Lords, the votes of Cross Bench peers can often be important. Also, contributions by distinguished individuals with no political axe to grind may sometimes be quite influential. When governments have been defeated in the Lords, this has usually been with the assistance of a significant number of Cross Bench votes.

Strictly speaking, the term "Cross Bencher" does not apply to all peers without party political affiliation, but only to those who have registered as such. At 1st March 1998 there were 322 such peers. There are a further 227 independent peers (including 123 without Writ or on Leave of Absence) who have not registered in this way.

(For lists of Cross Bench and independent peers see page 53)

Government Ministers in the House of Lords

Governments have to get their business through both Houses of Parliament. Most government ministers sit in the House of Commons, but there are a number in the House of Lords, with responsibility for making statements, answering debates and questions and handling legislation there. Currently there are 23 members of the Government in the House of Lords, including Government Whips *(See section entitled Government Ministers in the House of Lords at page 72)*

As far as members of the Cabinet are concerned, the Lord Chancellor and the Leader of the House of Lords are necessarily peers. Occasionally members of the House of Lords are appointed to other Cabinet posts, sometime senior ones – notable examples being Lord Carrington and Lord Young of Graffham in Margaret Thatcher's Government, who served as Foreign Secretary and Trade and Industry Secretary respectively. In such cases a more junior minister would deal with business in the Commons, but this was not popular with some MPs, who argued that senior ministers should be answerable directly to the elected House.

For the same reasons it is now expected that the Prime Minister will sit in the House of Commons. The last Prime Minister to serve his term in the Lords was the third Marquess of Salisbury, between 1895 and 1902. The 14th Earl of Home, who was Prime Minister from 1963 to 1964, disclaimed his peerage and was elected to the House of Commons, although he was later given a separate life peerage (as Lord Home of the Hirsel) in 1974.

Strictly speaking, a government minister does not have to be a member of either House, but this would mean that he/she could not then speak or be answerable in Parliament, nor deal with legislation there. It is therefore a rare occurrence, and then usually only temporary. Creating a peerage allows the Prime Minister to appoint an individual who has not hitherto been in Parliament to a ministerial post, as in the case of Lord Young of Graffham, who was appointed a Cabinet Minister in 1984, or more recently in the case of Lord Falconer of Thoroton who was appointed Solicitor General (a post more usually held by a member of the Commons) in 1997; or it can allow an individual who has lost a Parliamentary seat to continue in office, as in the case of Baroness Chalker of Wallasey, who continued as Minister of State for Overseas Development after losing her seat in 1992.

THE HOUSE OF LORDS

As of 1st March 1998, there are 23 peers who are members of the Government. They are:

a. the Lord Chancellor;

b. the Leader of the House of Lords who holds the office of Lord Privy Seal;

c. the Lord Advocate for Scotland;

d. the Solicitor General;

e. 5 Government Ministers who are Ministers of State in Government Departments;

f. 7 Government Ministers who are Parliamentary Under Secretaries of State in Government Departments;

g. the Government Chief Whip (who holds the post of Captain of the Gentlemen-at-Arms);

h. the Government Deputy Chief Whip (who holds the post of Captain of the Yeoman of the Guard);

i. 5 Government Whips (who hold the posts of Lord/Baroness in Waiting).

Not every government department has a Minister who is a member of the House of Lords operating within it. However, legislation from all departments must pass through the Lords as well as the Commons, and peers can ask questions and debate issues involving all departments. To ensure that, when needed, there is a peer present in the Chamber to put the government's case or to pilot legislation, ministers attached to one department are charged with covering other subjects. Government whips also act as spokesmen and answer questions on behalf of government departments.

Ministers in the House of Lords receive an official salary in their capacity as Ministers.

(For a full list of individual Government Ministers and spokesmen in the Lords see pages 72 and 74)

Opposition Front Benches

The main opposition parties also need to make arrangements to ensure that their views are represented in the House of Lords. Members speaking officially on behalf of the main opposition party speak from the front bench opposite the government. This comprises the leader, deputy leader, chief whip and other whips, and spokesmen shadowing various subjects and/or departments. The Leader of the Opposition and the Opposition Chief Whip receive salaries from public funds.

The third party, currently the Liberal Democratic Party, also has a leader, deputy leader, chief whip and other whips in the House of Lords, along with other nominated spokesmen.

The opposition parties in the Lords receive a limited amount of public funding to support their activities, under a scheme approved by Resolution of the House of Lords. In the year beginning 1st April 1997, a maximum of £102,600 was available for the official Opposition and £30,780 for the second largest opposition party.

(For membership of opposition Front Benches see page 75)

THE STATE OPENING OF PARLIAMENT

The State Opening of Parliament is an annual event. It is usually held at the beginning of each Parliamentary session in October or November, and also soon after a general election at the beginning of a new Parliament, in whichever month that should be. It is centred on the Chamber of the House of Lords. After various traditional ceremonies, the Sovereign reads the Queen's Speech from the throne in the House of Lords' Chamber.

While she reads the Speech, the peers sit, attired in their red robes, on the benches of their House. Meanwhile MPs, who have been summoned to the House of Lords to hear the Speech, stand behind the Bar of the Chamber.

The Queen's Speech is, in fact, written by the Cabinet. Its contents outline the government's proposals for legislation which will be put before Parliament by government ministers, and then considered by Parliament during the coming Parliamentary session.

Parliamentary sessions usually last a year and start in October or November. However, if a general election takes place earlier in a particular year, the Queen's Speech is brought forward and the Parliamentary Session on that occasion may be lengthened, as in the case in 1997-98.

THE HOUSE OF LORDS

THE CONDUCT OF BUSINESS IN THE HOUSE OF LORDS

Hours and Sessions

The sittings of the House of Lords are divided into sessions. A session usually lasts from October/November to the following October. Exceptions to this occur when there is a general election earlier in a year. Then the State Opening will be held soon after the general election and a longer Parliamentary session, extending to October the following year, is the norm.

There are breaks within a session when the House does not sit and when it is described as being "in recess". Recesses normally take place at Christmas, Easter, spring bank holiday and summer. The summer recess is usually the longest and can last between seven and twelve weeks, depending on the pressure of Parliamentary business. In recent years the House has sat for 140 days in the year; and daily sittings have lasted an average of just under seven hours.

The House of Lords sits regularly during the middle of the week (Tuesday to Thursday inclusive). It also sits on many Mondays and occasionally on Fridays. Business on the floor of the House of Lords starts at 2.30pm on Mondays, Tuesdays, and Wednesdays; at 3pm on Thursdays; and at 11am if the House sits on a Friday. Sitting hours in the House of Lords vary greatly because there are no cut-off points (such as 7pm and 10pm in the House of Commons) and few limitations on the right to speak. Thus the House sometimes rises early in the evenings, especially in the early part of the session, but may sit well into the night, especially on controversial legislation. (When the House sits late there is sometimes a break in proceedings for dinner). All night sittings are unusual but not unknown. The average time of rising in the last session (1996-7) was 9:10pm, but 30 of the 79 sittings went beyond 10.00pm, the latest finishing just after 3:00am.

Neither House of Parliament sits at weekends unless there is a major crisis. For instance, when Argentina invaded the Falklands Islands, both the Houses met on Saturday 3rd April 1982. In the case of the House of Lords, notice was given by the Lord Chancellor the previous day that the House would meet on the Saturday. The Foreign Secretary at the time, Lord Carrington, was a member of the House of Lords (although he resigned from the Government two days later).

On certain days at the start of each Parliament the House sits only for peers to take the Oath. These are called "Swearing-in Days" and no other business is conducted.

Hansard

Hansard is the printed verbatim record of the proceedings in Parliament. The House of Lords Hansard is printed daily when the House of Lords sits. It also details any written questions which have received a reply on the particular day, giving the full text of both the question asked and the reply received. A separate Hansard is published for the House of Commons.

Hansard is available the following day from Stationery Office Ltd and can be obtained from the Parliamentary Bookshop, 12 Bridge Street, Parliament Square, Westminster, London, SW1A 2JX. Tel: (0171) 219 3890. The House of Lords Hansard costs £2.50p a copy.

Broadcasting of Proceedings

The proceedings of the House may be broadcast on radio and television. Television broadcasting was introduced in the House of Lords before the the House of Commons, experimentally in 1985, with the arrangement made permanent in 1986. Proceedings can be broadcast live, but more usually extracts from proceedings are included in news and current affairs programmes on the main channels. A cable channel – The Parliamentary Channel – gives wide coverage of House of Lords debates. Broadcasting is governed by Resolutions of the House of 28th July 1977 and 15th May 1986.

THE HOUSE OF LORDS

Prayers before Proceedings

Prayers are said before proceedings begin in both Houses of Parliament. In the House of Lords they are read by a Lord Spiritual. The bishops operate a rota to ensure that one of them is always there at the start of a day's proceedings *(See Article by Canon Donald Gray on page 10)*

Introduction of Peers

Any newly created peers are usually introduced at the beginning of the day's business. They are presented to the Lord Chancellor by two supporters, each of them robed for the occasion. Most peers, with the exception of the Lord Chancellor and the Lords Spiritual, do not otherwise wear their robes, apart from at the State Opening. Peers who have inherited their titles do not need to be formally introduced. The present Leader of the House has indicated the Government's intention to look at ways of speeding up the procedure of introduction, which currently lasts about 11 minutes; and a Select Committee of the House was set up in December 1997 to consider alternatives.

Procedure and Conduct of Debates

The Lord Chancellor acts as the Speaker of the House of Lords. Unlike the Speaker of the House of Commons, he is not politically neutral, but is a member of the Cabinet. A number of other peers are designated to deputise in his absence. *(See section entitled Officers of the House at page 34)* The Leader of the House of Lords (who is also a member of the Cabinet), in addition to having responsibilities for government business management, advises the House on matters of procedure and order. However, unique amongst national parliaments, the House of Lords is a self-regulating chamber and the maintenance of order and the control of debates are the responsibility of the House itself, according to practice and standing orders.

Business is set out on the order paper, which is published daily. Starred Questions are taken first and, except on Wednesdays, proceedings on Bills come before general debates. There is no limit on the number of peers who may speak in a debate. However, for some debates, a list of speakers is prepared, based on those who have given notification of their intention to speak, and these are then given priority ahead of any others who may wish to do so.

Whilst there are very few constraints on a peer's right to speak in the Chamber, the House of Lords does now time limit several of its debates. There is a general expectation that peers will exercise self-restraint in the length of their speeches. *The Companion to the Standing Orders and Guide to the Proceedings of the House of Lords* states:

"In debates not formally time-limited, Lords opening or winding up from either side are expected to keep within 20 minutes. Other speakers are expected to keep within 15 minutes. These are only guidelines and, on occasion, a speech of outstanding importance, or a Ministerial speech winding up an exceptionally long debate, may exceed the limit."

Peers are normally only permitted to speak once in a debate, although they may intervene in other speeches. This limitation does not apply when the House is in committee.

If a peer is thought to be offending against accepted practice, then it is possible to move that he/she be no longer heard. If that motion is agreed, that individual would be prevented from speaking on the particular motion under debate. This procedure is rarely used.

It is also possible for a peer to move next business. This could be used to curtail debate and /or avoid the House recording an opinion; but the motion would itself have to be debated and voted on. It is also possible to move the closure, but this is considered to be a most exceptional procedure.

Whereas in the House of Commons much debate on legislation takes place in Committees sitting in Committee Rooms away from the Chamber, in the House of Lords the Committee stage of legislation usually takes place in a Committee of the whole House, sitting in the Chamber itself *(See section entitled Legislation at page 25 opposite)*

Voting in the House of Lords is recorded on the basis of "Contents" and "Not-Contents", the former being in favour of any particular proposal and the latter opposed to it. As in the Commons, peers vote in division lobbies on either side of the Chamber.

THE HOUSE OF LORDS

LEGISLATION

Legislation can be divided into two categories: Public Bills containing measures which, if enacted, will have a general effect throughout the United Kingdom or one of its constituent countries; and Private Bills which affect only one particular area, organisation or group of people.

Public Bills

Consideration of Public Bills forms an important part of the work of the House of Lords. In recent Parliamentary Sessions, this has occupied more than 50 per cent of the Lords' working time. A Public Bill must pass through all its stages in both the House of Commons and the House of Lords, before it receives the Royal Assent. Only then does it become an Act of Parliament. Legislation can be presented either by the government or by individual members of either House, in which case it is known as a Private Member's Bill *(See section entitled Private Members Bills at page 27)*

Although most important and politically contentious legislation is usually introduced first in the House of Commons, Bills can be introduced in either House. In fact, in the 1995-96 Session, 40 Public Bills were brought to the Lords from the House of Commons (25 of them Government Bills) and 32 Public Bills (13 of them Government Bills) were introduced in the House of Lords. In the short 1996-97 Session, 37 Public Bills (22 of them Government Bills) were brought to the Lords from the Commons; and 28 Public Bills (7 of them Government Bills) were introduced in the Lords. These figures do not include Consolidation Bills. *(See section entitled Consolidation Legislation at page 27)* Although Bills introduced in the Lords tend to be less contentious, this is not invariably the case. For instance, in the 1995-96 Session, the Broadcasting Bill was introduced there. An earlier example was the Shops Bill in the 1985-86 Session, which was subsequently defeated in the Commons. Bills for which the Lord Chancellor has responsibility are also normally introduced in the House of Lords. These, too, are usually uncontentious, but again not always, as in the case of the Family Law Bill in the 1995-96 Session.

The process by which legislation goes through in the House of Lords is similar to that in the House of Commons. It has a formal First Reading; and then a Second Reading, when there is a general debate. This is usually followed by Committee Stage, where there can be detailed discussion and amendments; and then a Report Stage, at which the Bill as amended is reported back to the House, and at which further amendments may be made. Finally there is a Third Reading, which is sometimes, but not always, a formality. In the Lords (unlike the Commons) amendments can also be made at the Third Reading.

Unlike the Commons, there is little machinery for curtailing debate or for the selection of amendments to Bills, so all may be debated. In the Lords, the Committee stage normally takes place in the Chamber itself, in a "Committee of the Whole House". However, other procedures may be adopted; and Bills can instead be referred at this stage to particular Lords' Committees. These are:

A <u>Grand Committee</u> (formerly known as a Committee off the Floor) in which all peers can attend and participate, but there are no divisions;

A <u>Public Bill Committee,</u> in which only those peers selected as members may vote but all peers may participate. (This may be used for Government Bills of a technical and non-controversial nature);

A <u>Special Public Bill Committee,</u> which is similar to the former, but which may take evidence before considering a Bill in detail (This may be used for any Bill).

In addition to these a *Select Committee* may be established to take evidence and recommend whether or not a Bill should proceed; and it may make amendments before recommitting it to the whole House if it does so proceed. As an experiment, for certain items of Scottish legislation, *Scottish Select Committees* have been established, able to take evidence in Scotland and present this to the House before the legislation goes to another Committee.

THE HOUSE OF LORDS

The House of Lords may amend legislation or reject it completely, although it is extremely rare for it to reject outright legislation which has been passed by the House of Commons. When it has amended a Bill brought from the Commons, the Bill is returned to the Commons, which may accept or reject the Lords' amendments, or itself amend them further. The Bill is then returned to the House of Lords which, can agree or disagree to the Commons' amendments or amend them further; or insist or not insist on any of its amendments which the Commons has rejected. This process, often known as "ping pong", can continue until final agreement is reached by both Houses, or (most unusually) until deadlock is reached.

If agreement is not reached by the end of the Parliamentary session and a Bill fails to complete all its stages, then it is lost and will have to be re-introduced, if so desired, in the following session. This happened in the case of the Labour Government's Trade Union and Labour Relations Bill in 1975 and its Aircraft and Shipbuilding Industries Bill in 1976.

Limitations on Powers of the House of Lords

The powers of the House of Lords over public legislation are restricted by the Parliament Acts of 1911 and 1949. If the House of Lords rejects or fails to pass a Bill passed by the House of Commons, the Bill may be re-introduced in the following session. If again passed by the Commons but rejected or amended by the Lords, it is enacted in the form in which it left the Commons. There must, however, be an interval of at least one year between the Second Reading in the Commons of the original Bill and the Third Reading in the Commons of the further identical Bill. There is an important exception to this provision relating to a Bill to extend the life of a Parliament. Any such Bill must be passed by both Houses of Parliament and, thus, the Lords retain an absolute power of veto in this instance.

Since the 1949 Parliament Act itself, the only legislation to be enacted using its provisions was the War Crimes Bill, which had been defeated in the Lords on Second Reading in 1989-90 Session and again in 1990-91, but which received the Royal Assent under the Parliament Acts in May 1991.

The "Salisbury Doctrine"

For most of the period since the Second World War, the House of Lords has observed what is known as the "Salisbury Doctrine". This convention was put forward by the 5th Marquess of Salisbury, the Leader of the Conservative Party in the House of Lords, following the Labour party's victory in the 1945 General Election. Under it any measure which was in the government party's election manifesto should be regarded as having been approved by the people. Accordingly the House of Lords would not refuse a Second Reading to any such Bill.

However, even though the House of Lords may not refuse a Second Reading, may still amend legislation. For instance, it made significant and substantive amendments to important legislation passed by the Commons during the period of the 1974-79 Labour Government. Thus the Aircraft and Shipbuilding Industries Bill, while not defeated at Second Reading, was nevertheless lost at the end of the 1975-76 Session. The Government at the time argued that, since it had been in its election manifesto, the Salisbury Doctrine had been breached.

Revision of Legislation

The House of Lords makes a large number of amendments to Bills. In some Parliamentary sessions, these have exceeded 2,000. In 1995-96 there were a total of 1,705 amendments to legislation of all types (1,555 of them to Government Bills); and in the shorter 1996-97 Session the respective figures were 963 (898). Very few were subsequently rejected by the House of Commons.

Many amendments are of a technical or tidying up nature. Indeed they are often moved by the government itself. In addition to tidying up, such amendments may be designed to take account of practical considerations raised following publication of the Bill, to give effect to undertakings made at an earlier stage, or as a result of a rethink in response to outside pressure or representations. The House of Lords is thus often referred to as a "revising chamber", although in fact, a significant number of Bills are introduced there. In the 1994-95 Session, the Commons actually made 753 amendments to Lords' Bills, (of all types); and in 1996-97 the total was 265.

THE HOUSE OF LORDS

By no means all amendments made in the Lords are unimportant or politically insignificant. While governments with a majority are rarely defeated in the Commons, they do sometimes suffer defeats in the Lords. In the 1992-97 Parliament, the then Conservative government was defeated in a total of 62 divisions, an average of 12 times per Parliamentary session. Sometimes a government will accept the defeats and the amendments. On other occasions it may seek to compromise. Then again it may seek to reverse the amendments and hope to persuade the Lords to accept the re-affirmed wishes of the Commons. All this may depend on the strength of a government's position in the Commons. When a government has only a small or no majority in the Commons, it may find it harder to reverse the Lords' amendments.

Money Bills

The powers of the House of Lords over the raising and spending of public funds are strictly limited. The Parliament Act 1911 (which resulted partly from the actions of the House of Lords in attempting to block an earlier Budget) provides that, if the Speaker of the House of Commons certifies a Commons Bill as a "Money Bill" dealing only with national taxation or public expenditure, then it may receive Royal Assent within a month, whether or not the House of Lords has passed it; and that the Commons can disregard any Lords' amendments.

It is the practice that Supply Bills (Bills to raise taxes or to authorise expenditure, usually referred to as Finance Bills and Consolidated Fund Bills) originate in the Commons and are not amended by the Lords. If the House of Lords amends any other Bill in a way which the Commons considers to breach its financial privilege, the Commons draw attention to this in their reasons for disagreement and the Lords are expected to back down.

There is also a technical procedure involving a Bill originating in the Lords which involves charges and expenditure, whereby the Lords make what is known as a "privilege amendment" in a sub-section stating that nothing in the Bill involves charges and expenditure. This is then removed by amendment in the Commons, thus maintaining the Commons' privilege in matters financial.

Private Members Bills

These are Bills which are Public Bills which are introduced by individual peers in the Lords (as by individual MPs in the Commons), rather than by the government. They should not be confused with Private Bills (see below). Many Private Members Bills introduced in the House of Lords do not reach the statute book, since they also have to get through the House of Commons, where time is limited. In the 1995-96 Session, for example, only three out of 19 Private Members Bills introduced in the Lords went on to receive the Royal Assent, although in the 1996-97 Session seven out of 21 did so. Whether or not Private Members Bills reach the statute book, they can nevertheless be a useful means of promoting debate.

Private Members Bills originated and passed by the Commons subsequently have to go through the House of Lords. In the 1995-96 Session there were 14 such Bills, four of which went on to receive the Royal Assent, and in the 1996-97 Session there were 15, all of which went on to receive the Royal Assent.

Consolidation Legislation

Consolidation Bills consolidate earlier legislation (i.e. assemble it together in one Bill with the aim of making the law more intelligible), or repeal obscure or obsolete provisions of earlier legislation. Consolidation legislation may have been prompted by recommendations of the Law Commission, which is charged with revising legislation to ensure it is up-to-date and comprehensible. The *Joint Committee on Consolidation Bills*, chaired by a Law Lord, and comprising members of both the House of Commons and the House of Lords, undertakes much of the work on such Bills, which consequently occupy little time on the floor of either the Commons or the Lords.

Consolidation Bills are usually sponsored by the Lord Chancellor and so begin their passage in the House of Lords.

THE HOUSE OF LORDS

Private Bills

Private Bills originate outside Parliament and are usually promoted by bodies – often local authorities – which are seeking extra powers which are not available to them under general legislation. Certain firms of solicitors specialise in the drafting of Private Bills, for which they are known as Parliamentary Agents.

Private Bills may be introduced in either the House of Commons or the House of Lords. The powers of the House of Lords are not restricted in respect of these Bills and it thus has the same powers as the Commons. Private Bills in the House of Lords are mostly considered in Committee rather than on the floor of the House. They are scrutinised first by the Chairman of Committees and, if they are opposed, they are committed to a Select Committee. Otherwise they are sent to an *Unopposed Bill Committee.*

Interested parties can petition against private legislation. Petitions are heard by a Select Committee, which usually comprises five peers, who listen to the arguments from both petitioners and sponsors of the Bill. It may amend a Bill or recommend that it proceeds no further.

Private Bills may be carried over from one Parliamentary session to the next, if both Lords and Commons agree.

There are also procedures for *Personal Bills,* relating to matters that are not in conflict with public policy, and conferring benefits which are peculiar to the petitioner and so do not affect the interests of the general public. Such Bills must be consented to by all the people principally concerned in the consequences of the Bill, must safeguard the interests of any infants affected, and involve objects which cannot be achieved by any other legal means. The *Personal Bills Committee* considers petitions for such Bills relating to the affairs of individuals.

Hybrid Bills

Hybrid Bills contain elements of both Public and Private Bills. They are public and general in nature, but they also affect particular local or private interests. If a Bill is declared to be hybrid, then interested parties have the right to petition, as with a Private Bill. Only if there are no petitions, can it proceed as a Public Bill. Otherwise, after Second Reading, it goes on to a Select Committee which, as with a Private Bill, receives evidence and can amend it or recommend it proceeds no further. If the Bill does proceed from this, it then goes to a Committee of the Whole House, following the normal Public Bill procedure.

Delegated Legislation

Delegated powers are an increasingly common feature of British legislation. Delegated powers are given to ministers under Acts of Parliament, to make regulations or orders on matters arising from the particular Act.

Most delegated legislation is in the form of Statutory Instruments, of which there are four types:

(i)   **Negative Instruments:** These come into force unless they are annulled by resolution of either the House of Commons or the House of Lords within a certain time limit, usually 40 days from the date of publication;

(ii)   **Affirmative Instruments:** These are Statutory Instruments which require a positive vote by Parliament (in both Houses, except in the case of financial legislation) before they can become law;

(iii)   **General Instruments:** These are Statutory Instruments which may be issued by ministers, but which are not subject to Parliamentary proceedings;

(iv)   **Hybrid Instruments:** These are Affirmative Instruments which affect defined private or local interests in a special way, akin to a Private Bill. The House of Lords has a special Committee dealing with these, called the *Hybrid Instruments Committee,* which considers any petitions from interested parties and can recommend further inquiry by a select committee. There is no equivalent to this procedure in the House of Commons.

THE HOUSE OF LORDS

The powers of the House of Lords over delegated legislation are not restricted. Thus they enjoy potentially the same powers in respect of this as the Commons. In practice, the Lords have never annulled a negative instrument; and there is only one occasion on which they have rejected an affirmative instrument. This was in the case of the Southern Rhodesia (United Nations Sanctions) Order in 1968, although this was itself later re-introduced and passed.

Delegated legislation cannot be amended. The House of Lords can, however, make known any criticism or reservations, either through an "Unstarred Question" to debate the matter *(see sub-section entitled Unstarred Questions at page 30)*, or through what is called a "Non-Fatal Critical Motion", which may criticise the instrument or call on the government to withdraw it. This would not, however, force the government to respond.

Most Statutory Instruments are examined by the *Joint Committee on Statutory Instruments*, comprising members of both Houses of Parliament, to ensure that they are properly drafted and are within the authority of the Act under which they are issued. Under the Lords' Standing Orders, the House cannot approve an affirmative instrument before this Committee has reported on it.

It has been argued that the increased use of delegated legislation could limit the exercise of the democratic process, since delegated powers are, by their very nature, not as open to public scrutiny and debate as are actual Bills. Concern about the growth in delegated legislation led the House of Lords to establish a Delegated Powers Scrutiny Committee in 1992-93. In 1996 this Committee changed its name to the Delegated Powers and De-regulation Committee.

The *Delegated Powers and Deregulation Committee* is unique to the House of Lords. There is no similar body in the House of Commons. Its terms of reference are "to report on whether the provisions of any bill inappropriately delegate legislative power" or "whether they subject the exercise of legislative power to an appropriate degree of Parliamentary scrutiny". If the Committee is concerned about any proposal for delegated powers contained within a Bill, it can draw this to the attention of the House. Amendments may then be made to the Bill to provide for greater Parliamentary scrutiny than would otherwise have been the case (for instance, by making an instrument affirmative rather than negative). Such amendments have been accepted on many occasions. The Committee may also ask the House – and the government – to consider whether in a particular instance, a power should be delegated at all.

The Committee also considers proposed deregulation orders put forward under the Deregulation and Contracting Out Act 1994.

The Committee issued a report in March 1997 proposing an extension of its remit, or the appointment of another committee, to facilitate the involvement of Parliament in public consultation over legislation.

NON-LEGISLATIVE BUSINESS

General Debates

Much time in the House of Lords is taken up with legislation and government business, but general debates are also held regularly. These usually take place on motions for papers. Such a motion draws attention to a particular subject. It is then normally withdrawn, without a vote, at the end of the debate. Motions may also be moved to "take note", but this is more usually done when a particular report or situation is being debated.

The business of the House on Wednesdays during the session before the Spring Bank Holiday Recess is normally devoted mainly to these debates rather than to legislative business. After this, most Parliamentary time is taken up with government legislation, since governments are always anxious to get their legislation through both Houses of Parliament before the end of the session.

THE HOUSE OF LORDS

One of these Wednesdays each month is set aside for two debates on motions chosen by backbench peers by ballot. These are limited to 2½ hours each. Other Wednesdays are allocated to the party grouping, including the Cross Bench peers, or the subject may be determined through the "usual channels". (The latter is a Parliamentary term to describe the behind the scenes way in which the leading figures of government and opposition, particularly the whips, talk to each other privately in order to agree, as far as possible, on how to arrange the details of Parliamentary life and thus ensure the smooth running of the House.) Increasingly, the parties are deciding to hold two time limited debates on their respective Wednesdays.

Although individual peers can put down motions on the order paper without prior agreement by the "usual channels", in practice this rarely happens.

Questions in the House

In the House of Lords there are four types of questions: Starred Questions, Unstarred Questions, Questions for Written Answer and Private Notice Questions, Questions in the House of Lords, unlike in the House of Commons, are normally addressed to the government generally, rather than to a particular minister. They may also sometimes be addressed to individual peers holding official positions, in relation to the affairs of the House itself.

Starred Questions
On every sitting day in the House of Lords, except Friday, Parliamentary business starts with up to four Starred Questions from peers to the government. These must be tabled at least 24 hours in advance. A peer normally must be present to ask his/her question which appears in writing on the order paper, and is marked with an asterisk (although another peer may ask the question, if given the leave of the House to do so). Supplementary questions may be asked by any peer. A maximum of half an hour is allocated to Starred Questions which usually see the highest attendance in the Chamber. In the 1995-96 Session a total of 498 Starred Questions were asked, and in the short 1996-97 Session the total was 262.

Unstarred Questions
Unstarred Questions can be asked usually at the end of a day's business. They are similar to adjournment debates in the House of Commons and provide an opportunity for a peer to raise issues of concern, with a short debate and reply from the government. During 1995-96 Session there were 26 such Unstarred Questions, and in 1996-97 there were 27.

Private Notice Questions
Just as MPs can ask Private Notice Questions as matters of urgency, so too can peers. The question to be asked must be submitted to the Leader of the House in writing by noon on the day when it is proposed to ask it. The Leader of the House can rule that a Private Notice Question does not raise matters of sufficient urgency. but if the peer disagrees, he may appeal to the whole House, to be heard. If accepted, Private Notice Questions are taken after Starred Questions. They are rarely asked; only one such was answered in the 1996-97 Session, and none at all in the previous 1995-96 Session.

Questions for Written Answer
Peers may also put down Questions for Written Answer by the government. Replies are sent to the questioner and printed in Hansard. The time between question and answer may depend on the complexity of the subject involved, but should not be longer than two weeks. Since not all government departments have ministers in the Lords, the answer may not always be supplied directly by a minister in the relevant department.

Statements

The government regularly makes statements to Parliament. Most statements are made by the responsible minister, and so are made in the House of Commons. If they are judged to be important they may be repeated in the House of Lords by a junior minister. If the responsible minister is in the Lords, then he or she will make the statement there. Peers can question whoever makes the statement there on behalf of the government; but quite often government statements are merely printed in the House of Lords Hansard.

THE HOUSE OF LORDS

COMMITTEES OF THE HOUSE

The House of Lords does not have a range of select committees shadowing the work of particular Whitehall departments in the way the House of Commons does. It does, however, have its own select committees, including some which do work not covered by the House of Commons' committees.

The House has two select committees which are re-appointed every session:
   a. The European Communities Committee;
   b. The Science and Technology Committee.

As can be seen from their titles, each of these committees covers the functions of a range of Government departments in its deliberations.

European Communities Committee

This was established in 1974 to examine all Community proposals, including draft proposals; and to report on those which it considers raise important matters of principle or policy. It can also consider other questions which it thinks should be drawn to the attention of the House. The first Chairman of the Committee was Baroness White, a former Foreign Office Minister. The Chairman of the Committee for the 1997-98 Session is Lord Tordoff.

Much of the Committee's work is carried on through sub-committees. The sub-committees for the 1997-98 Session are:
   Economic and Financial Affairs, Trade and External Relations
   Energy, Industry and Transport
   Environment, Public Health and Consumer Protection
   Agriculture, Fisheries and Food
   Law and Institutions
   Social Affairs, Education and Home Affairs

The Sub-Committee on Law and Institutions is charged with considering the legal implications of legislative proposals and is usually chaired by a Law Lord (currently Lord Hoffman). It also has a legal adviser.

Additional ad-hoc sub-committees of the European Communities Committee may be established as necessary.

The European Communities Committee and its Sub-Committees are able to appoint special advisers, and regularly take evidence in public. (This is also the case with the Science and Technology Committee.)

When proposals are put forward from the European Commission, they are subject to examination by select committees in the Lords and the Commons. These committees report to their respective Houses and may recommend that the reports be debated. The government has undertaken not normally to agree to any proposals until both Houses of Parliament have had the opportunity to express an opinion. The Lords' opinion is expressed primarily through its European Communities Committee. It tends to have more time at its disposal than does the Commons to investigate proposals thoroughly, and the Committee's reports have been noted for the depth of their coverage. The government gives a written response to the reports. On average there are about 20 such reports each year and about half are debated on the floor of the House of Lords.

In the 1996-97 Session it produced reports on the following subjects: Freedom of Access to Information on the Environment; Preparations for EMU; Third Country Fisheries Agreements; Review of EC Merger Regulations. It also reported on Correspondence with Ministers.

Science and Technology Committee

Following the successful establishment of the European Communities Committee, the House of Lords decided in 1980 to set up another permanent select committee, with terms of reference simply "to consider science and technology". The Committee on Science and Technology is currently chaired by Lord Phillips of Ellesmere.

THE HOUSE OF LORDS

It works mainly through two sub-committees, which conduct in-depth enquiries, lasting up to six months. During the 1996-97 Session it published the following reports: Towards Zero Emissions for Road Transport: EU Framework for Research and Technological Development; The Innovation - Exploitation Barrier; Sustainable Management of North Sea Fisheries. At the time of writing (February 1998) there were sub-committees looking at Resistance to Antimicrobial Agents and at the Management of Nuclear Waste. Reports are normally debated in the House and receive a written response from the government. It was in response to one of the Committee's earlier reports that the then Government established an Advisory Council on Science and Technology.

Ad-hoc Select Committees

Additionally, the House of Lords regularly appoints *ad hoc* select committees to consider particular subjects. These have recently included committees on Medical Ethics (1993-4), Sustainable Development (1994-5), and Relations between Central and Local Government (1995-6). The latter published a report 'Rebuilding Trust' in July 1996.

The Select Committee on the *Public Service* was established in April 1996, with Lord Slynn of Hadley as Chairman. In July 1996 it published a report on the Government proposals for the privatisation of Recruitment and Assessment Services (RAS). Re-appointed for the following session, it made a interim report on the condition and future development of public service in Britain in March 1997. It has since been re-appointed further to continue this work. Its terms of reference are "to consider the present and future development of the Public Service in Great Britain with particular regard to the effectiveness of recent and continuing changes and their impact on standards of conduct and service in the public interest." Its remit exclude local government, the NHS, schools and higher/further education institutions; but include all Government Departments, trusts and other organisations created by or working for the public service.

The most recently established Committee is that on the <u>*Ceremony of Introduction,*</u> to consider alterations and recommendations It was appointed in December 1997, under the chairmanship of Lord Marsh.

A select committee may also be established to consider a specific item of legislation at Committee Stage, as in the case of the Dangerous Dogs (Amendment) Bill (HL) in 1995.

Other Committees

The roles of other ad hoc committees handling legislation and of the Personal Bills Committee, the Hybrid Instruments Committee, the Delegated Powers and De-regulation Committee, the Joint Committees (with the Commons) on Consolidation Bills and the Joint Committee on Statutory Instruments are noted in the section on 'Legislation' *(see above page 25)*

Other Committees not noted elsewhere include the following, which deal mainly with procedural or administrative matters:

<u>Procedure Committee</u> - this reviews the procedures of the House and issues reports which may suggest changes in procedure or re-affirm support for existing procedures.

<u>Liaison Committee</u> - to allocate resources to Committees, to co-ordinate the committee work of the House and to recommend the appointment of ad hoc Select Committees.

<u>Committee of Selection</u> - to propose the names of peers for membership of most other Committees of the House.

<u>Standing Orders (Private Bills) Committee</u> - to consider Standing Orders relating to the handling of Private Bills.

<u>Committee for Privileges</u> - to consider matters referred to it relating to the privileges of the House, claims of peerage and precedence. This also has a *Sub-Committee on Lords' Interests*, which oversees the operation of the Register of Lords' Interests, including allegations of failure to register or abide by the rules. There is also a *Joint Committee* (with the House of Commons) on *Parliamentary Privilege*, set up "to review Parliamentary Privilege and make recommendations thereon."

THE HOUSE OF LORDS

<u>House of Lords Offices Committee</u> - to consider and report on the domestic affairs of the House It has four sub committees - Administration and Works, Finance and Staff, Library and Computers, Refreshment. There is also an Advisory Panel on Works of Art.

<u>Ecclesiastical Committee</u> - a joint Committee with the House of Commons to deal with measures submitted by the General Synod of the Church of England.

(For membership of the above mentioned committees see page 83)

JUDICIAL ROLE

The House of Lords acts as the ultimate court of appeal for civil cases throughout the United Kingdom and also for criminal cases, apart from Scotland. This role is exercised mainly by the Lords of Appeal in the Ordinary ("Law Lords"), of whom there are a maximum of twelve (This number may be increased by Affirmative Instrument). Two are normally from Scotland.

In addition to these, the Lord Chancellor and other peers who hold or have held high judicial office are entitled to sit and hear appeals. These peers may include former Lord Chancellors, the Lord Chief Justice of Northern Ireland and other senior figures, including Scottish judges, who have been awarded life peerages.

Since 1995, those appointed Lords of Appeal in the Ordinary must retire at the age of 70; and no other Lords (with the exception of the Lord Chancellor) may sit judicially after they have reached the age of 75. (Lords of Appeal in the Ordinary may, like other life peers, continue as members of the House of Lords for their lifetime).

Appeals are not normally heard in the House of Lords Chamber. Instead, the Law Lords usually meet to hear appeals in an Appellate Committee, usually comprising five Law Lords. However, the final judgement on any appeal is given in the Chamber, usually on a Thursday before the start of public business. Leave, given either by a lower court or the House itself (by the Appellate Committee), is required to appeal to the House of Lords.

The Lord Chancellor, who is a member of the Cabinet, is also head of the judiciary. He is in charge of a Government department responsible for administration of the legal system. He has important responsibilities in respect of the courts and the judiciary, including the appointment of judges, as well as acting as the speaker of the House of Lords.
(See page 78 for names of Lords eligible to hear appeals.)

OFFICERS OF THE HOUSE

The Lord Chancellor, currently Lord Irvine of Lairg, effectively acts as Speaker of the House of Lords.

The Chairman of Committees, currently Lord Boston of Faversham, takes the chair when the House deals with legislation in committee and can also deputise for the Lord Chancellor in the House. He also supervises the work of and appointments to certain committees, including those dealing with private legislation. There is, in addition, a Principal Deputy Chairman of Committees, currently Lord Tordoff, who also acts as Chairman of the European Communities Committee. Both are appointed by the House itself and paid a salary. They have the assistance of counsel.

There is also a panel of Deputy Speakers, currently comprising some 28 peers, (including the two mentioned above), who may take the chair when necessary; and a panel of 30 Deputy Chairmen of Committees, who may perform the duties of the Chairman of Committees or, if necessary, deputise as Speaker by sitting on the Woolsack. Members of these panels do not receive a salary. *(see page 34 below)*

THE HOUSE OF LORDS

OFFICIALS OF THE HOUSE

The senior official of the House of Lords is the Clerk of the Parliaments. The current holder of the post is Mr J M Davies. He is the Accounting Officer of the House and is responsible for most aspects of administration; including the Public Bill Office, the Private Bill Office, the Committee Office, the Judicial Office, the Journal and Information Office, the Library, the Official Report (Hansard), the Overseas Office, the Record Office, the Establishment Office, the Accountant's Office, and the Refreshment Department.

Clerks responsible to the Clerk of Parliaments service Committees, advise on procedure and prepare order papers. The Clerk Assistant and Clerk of Legislation, currently Mr P D G Harper, is responsible for minutes of proceedings and the preparation of Order Papers containing future business, and for the Public and Private Bill Office.

The Reading Clerk, currently Mr M G Pownall, is also Principal Finance Officer. Both of these are know as 'Clerks at the Table.' The fourth Clerk at the Table (Judicial), currently Mr J A Vallance White, heads the Judicial Office and also acts as Registrar of Lords' Interests. The Clerk of Committees, currently Mr D R Beamish heads the Committee Office which is responsible for administering and advising the Lords' select committees, including the Clerks to those committees and sub-committees. The Clerk of the Journals, currently Mr B P Keith, is responsible for information services and also acts as Clerk to the Procedure Committee.

The Gentleman Usher of the Black Rod has ceremonial duties, including that of summoning the Commons to hear the Queen's Speech at the beginning of each Parliamentary Session. He is also Serjeant at Arms for the House of Lords and he has administrative responsibility for accommodation, security and services, including the admission of visitors. The post is usually held by a retired senior military figure and the present incumbent is General Sir Edward Jones. His deputy, the Yeoman Usher of the Black Rod and Deputy Serjeant at Arms is Air Vice-Marshal David Hawkins.

The House of Lords' administration employees 328 staff. (This figure does not include those employed by political parties or individual peers.) It is divided into two departments – the Parliament Office (under the Clerk of Parliaments) and Black Rod's Department. Total expenditure on all House of Lords' administration and services estimated to £38.5 million in 1996/97. *(For a list of senior officials see page 80)*

The Clerk of the Crown in Chancery is also Permanent Secretary to the Lord Chancellor (and his office is not formally part of the House of Lords' administration). Amongst other duties he is responsible for issuing writs of summons and preparing certain other documents, including letters patent creating peerages. The current holder of this office is Sir Thomas Legg.

EXPENSES AND SALARIES

Allowances

With a few exceptions *(see immediately opposite page 35)* peers are not paid a salary; nor, unlike members of the House of Commons, do they have a system of free postage. They are entitled to recover the costs of certain expenses within specified daily maxima. These are currently limited to £75.50 for overnight accommodation; £33.50 a day subsistence; plus £32.50 a day for secretarial expenses. The cost of travel between home and London when attending sittings of the House, or otherwise on Parliamentary business, may be claimed by peers (and the cost of two return journeys per year by spouses may also be claimed).

THE HOUSE OF LORDS

Salaries

The following members of the House of Lords receive salaries which are paid from public funds in respect of the Parliamentary/Government office they hold:

  a. Lord Chancellor
  b. Leader of the House of Lords
  c. Other Government Ministers
  d. Government Whips
  e. Leader of the Opposition
  f. Opposition Chief Whip
  g. The Chairman of Committees
  h. The Deputy Chairman of Committees

In addition, the Lords of Appeal in Ordinary receive a salary from public funds.

REGISTER OF INTERESTS

Resolutions passed on November 1995 require peers to register consultancies, or similar arrangements, involving payment or other incentive or reward for providing Parliamentary advice or services, and financial interests in businesses involved in Parliamentary lobbying on behalf of clients. They are not allowed to speak, vote or lobby in respect of such interests. They may also register other particulars relating to matters which they consider may affect the public perception of the way they discharge their Parliamentary duties. (This is monitored by a Sub-Committee of the Committee for Privileges).

THE HOUSE OF LORDS CHAMBER

The Chamber of the House of Lords is rectangular in shape. Its decor is very ornate and the predominant colour, like much else in the House of Lords, is red.

On three sides of the Chamber there are benches on which peers sit. On the fourth side is the Throne which stands on a dais below a gilded canopy. The Queen sits on the Throne when she comes to the House to give the Queen's Speech at the start of each new Session of Parliament.

In front of the Throne, below the dais is the Woolsack. This is the Lord Chancellor's seat. It is a large square bag, backless and armless, and is covered in red cloth. When a new Lord Chancellor is appointed he is said to be "appointed to the Woolsack".

The Woolsack is so called because the seat is stuffed with wool. The present content of the Woolsack is wool from the various Commonwealth countries; but the tradition of stuffing with wool goes back to the days of Edward III (reigned 1327-1377) who was an enthusiastic promoter of the woollen industry. Edward III felt that a sack of wool would remind the English nobility of wool as the country's staple commodity.

In front of the Lord Chancellor's Woolsack, are two smaller woolsacks. These are called the Judges' Woolsacks, which are used by the Judges at the State Opening of Parliament. Apart from that time, any Peer may sit on, but not speak from, these Woolsacks during a sitting.

In front of these and in the centre of the Chamber is a large table: the Table of the House.

On each side of the House there are four rows of seats. The benches on the Lord Chancellor's left hand are mostly occupied by supporters of the opposition parties. Government ministers, whips and oppositions spokesmen normally occupy the front benches of their respective sides, and when they address the House in these capacities they speak from a despatch box placed on the Table.

THE HOUSE OF LORDS

The benches opposite the Throne and Woolsack are known as Cross Benches, and are normally occupied by these peers not affiliated to any political party. The Bishops, however, while not politically affiliated, always sit on the government side of the House, on the benches closest to the Lord Chancellor.

The Clerks sit on duty at the Table in the centre of the Chamber, and behind them are the shorthand writers taking copy for Hansard.

Visitors are normally confined to the galleries when the House is sitting; but certain distinguished persons, such as the sons of peers and Privy Counsellors, may sit on the steps of the throne (although not, of course during the State Opening).

CONTACTING THE LORDS

The address of the House of Lords is:
    The House of Lords
    London, SW1A 0PW

The main telephone number for the House of Lords is: Tel: (0171) 219 3000

Bulk mailshots for members of the House of Lords should be taken or sent to the Sorting Office, 9 Howick Place, London, SW1P 1AA. Each mailshot to each individual peer must be addressed to an individually named peer and be in a stamped first or second class envelope. Further information on this can be obtained from telephone (0171) 219 3366.

HOUSE OF LORDS JOURNAL AND INFORMATION OFFICE

The House of Lords Journal and Information Office is open Monday to Friday between the hours of 10:00am–5:00pm. Fact Sheets are available free of charge covering various different subject areas from the Information Office (Tel: (0171) 219 3107; Web site address http://www.parliament.uk).

Schools can obtain tickets to visit the House of Lords from the Education Unit in the House of Commons (which serves both Houses of Parliament – Tel: (0171) 219 4750). Members of the general public need to queue up outside St Stephen's entrance to Parliament and will get a seat in the gallery; alternatively if they know a peer or MP personally they may be able to obtain a ticket through them. It should be born in mind that at times when particularly controversial issues are being debated there may be some delay in gaining access to the Gallery.

HOUSE OF LORDS RECORD OFFICE

The records of both Houses are preserved in the Victoria Tower and are in the charge of the Clerk of the Records (currently David Johnson). The office is open to the public by prior arrangement (Tel: (0171) 219 3074).

A BRIEF HISTORY OF THE HOUSE OF LORDS

The origins of Parliament may be found in the Councils summoned by medieval kings. These began to be called 'Parliaments' from the 13th century onwards. Those attending them included bishops, abbots, earls, barons and the king's ministers. From the late 13th century, representatives from counties, boroughs etc. also began to be summoned and by the end of the 14th century they formed a separate House of Commons. At this time the Lords, or "Upper House", also acquired a separate identity as a House of Parliament, and from the 16th century was commonly referred to as the "House of Lords".

THE HOUSE OF LORDS

This was and still is made up of the Lords Spiritual and the Lords Temporal. The Lords Spiritual originally comprised archbishops, bishops, abbots and some priors. The latter two categories ceased to be represented after the dissolution of the monasteries in the 16th century. The Lords Temporal became almost entirely hereditary. They were known as peers, the term deriving from the Latin word 'pares' which means equal. Although there is a formal order of precedence, so far as business in the House of Lords is concerned, all ranks of peer have equal standing.

The Act of Union with Scotland in 1707 and that with Ireland in 1800 provided for peers from each of those countries to elect a limited number of representatives from among themselves to sit in the House of Lords. After Irish self-government in 1922, their representative peers continued to sit but were not replaced. Irish peers may now sit only if they also have an English, British or United Kingdom title. Since 1963, all Scottish peers have had the right to sit in the House of Lords.

Since 1847 there has been a limitation on the number of bishops entitled to sit in the House of Lords. Irish and Welsh bishops ceased to sit following the disestablishment of their churches. The bishops sit only from the date they enter the House to the end of their term of office. The first Law Lords were created in 1876, initially sitting only for their term of office, but later given the right to sit for their lifetime.

Restrictions on the legislative powers of the House of Lords were introduced in the 1911 Parliament Act and these powers were limited further by the 1949 Parliament Act.

Life peerages for individuals (other than Law Lords) and including women were introduced from 1958. The 1963 Peerage Act allowed hereditary peeresses in their own right to sit and allowed individuals to disclaim hereditary peerages for their lifetime.

(More details of these recent changes affecting composition and powers are given in the following sections.)

REFORM OF THE HOUSE OF LORDS

There have been four major legislative changes this century affecting the House of Lords.

Parliament Act 1911

This was passed by Parliament during the period of the Liberal Government headed by Herbert Asquith and followed the rejection in 1909 by the House of Lords of the Finance Bill to complement the proposals in the Budget introduced by the Chancellor of the Exchequer, David Lloyd George. The House of Lords had the power at this time to reject the legislation and the Parliament Act 1911 was only passed when backed up by a threat to create sufficient peers to ensure its passage. Its main provisions were that:

(a) Bills certified as Money Bills would receive the Royal Assent one month after being sent to the House of Lords, with or without its consent.

(b) Other Public Bills (except to extend the life of a Parliament) passed by the Commons in three successive sessions and rejected by the Lords would nevertheless receive the Royal Assent, provided that there was a minimum period of two years between the Commons Second Reading in the first session and Third Reading in the third session. The preamble to the Act stated that it was intended to substitute for the existing hereditary chamber one constituted on a popular basis, and that it was thus a transitional measure. However, these further changes did not in the event materialise.

THE HOUSE OF LORDS

Parliament Act 1949

This was passed during the period of the Labour Government under Clement Attlee. It reduced the period of delay required by the 1911 Act for the passage of Public Bills without the agreement of the Lords to two successive sessions and one year between Second Reading in the first session and Third Reading in the second session.

Life Peerages Act 1958

Passed under the Conservative Government of Harold Macmillan, this provided for the creation of life peerages (other than those already provided for Law Lords). These were available to men or women and, following this, women sat for the first time in the House of Lords.

Peerage Act 1963

Passed during the period of the same Government, this allowed peers by succession to disclaim a peerage for their own lifetime. The Act also included provisions to allow women succeeding to hereditary peerages to sit in the House of Lords, and also for all Scottish peers to sit in the House. (Previously they had only elected a limited number from among themselves).

Other measures affecting the House of Lords have been brought in at various times without the need for separate legislation – for instance, the introduction of travelling expenses in 1946, subsistence allowances in 1957 and provision for Leave of Absence in 1958.

Other Proposals for Reform of the House of Lords

There have been many proposals for reform of the House of Lords this century, which have not been implemented. The most important of these include the following:

1908 - The Roseberry Committee recommended reform and restructuring of the House of Lords. It proposed that possession of a peerage would not in itself carry with it the right to participate in the House of Lords; and that it should instead comprise a smaller number of hereditary peers, elected from their own number, together with hereditary peers who had held high office and some life peers.

1918 - The Bryce Commission, whose proposals were published in a White Paper, recommended new arrangements for joint consultation between the two Houses to resolve differences. Composition should be made up of 246 members indirectly elected by members of the House of Commons on a regional basis, together with 81 existing members elected by a committee of both Houses.

1922 - In place of the Bryce proposals, the Coalition Government proposed a House of 350 members, comprising mainly members elected directly or indirectly from outside, plus some hereditary peers elected from among themselves and some nominated by the Crown. Further similar proposals were put forward in 1927, but were then dropped.

1948 - After the Labour Government had introduced its Parliament Bill, all-party talks were held in an attempt to reach consensus. Agreement was reached on a number of principles and issued as an agreed statement in a White Paper. Amongst these were that the second chamber should be complementary to rather than rival the House of Commons, that it should not be constituted so as to provide a permanent majority for one party, and that women should be eligible for membership. However, the talks broke down over the period of the Lords' delaying powers, and the Government went ahead with its legislation, which was passed as the 1949 Parliament Act.

1968 - The Labour Government published a White Paper proposing what was in effect a two tier chamber, comprising around 230 nominated voting peers, with a retirement age, and a second tier of non-voting peers who could participate but not vote. Existing hereditary peers would be non voting peers (unless themselves created voting peers), but their successors would have no such rights. The government should have a majority over opposition parties, but not necessarily an overall majority. Delaying powers would be reduced to six months. The White Paper followed all party talks, which had been broken off following the Lords' rejection of the Southern Rhodesia Sanctions Order. Its proposals were embodied in the Parliament (No2) Bill 1969, but this made slow and difficult progress through the House of Commons and was withdrawn before it had completed its committee stage.

THE HOUSE OF LORDS

1977 - The Labour Party published a statement entitled "The Machinery of Government and the House of Lords" recommending abolition of the House of Lords, with no replacement second chamber. This was approved by the Party's annual conference which also passed overwhelmingly a resolution calling for abolition of the House of Lords, and the reform of Parliament into a single chamber legislating body. Although officially Labour party policy, this was not included in the party's 1979 election manifesto. Later the policy was dropped; and in its 1992 General Election Manifesto advocated an elected second chamber with special papers to safeguard individual constitutional rights. In 1993 the Labour Party Conference voted to support a regional list system of proportional representation for the second chamber.

1978 - The Conservative Party published a report by a Review Committee chaired by Lord Home of the Hirsel, which recommended either a wholly elected chamber or a partly elected chamber (with two thirds of its members elected and one third nominated), the latter being its preferred option. It was not adopted as official Conservative policy and subsequent governments did not implement it.

Policies of the Political Parties

Labour
The Labour Party's objective of an elected chamber has not been finally abandoned, but the policy has been significantly modified at least in the short-to-medium term. The Labour Party's 1997 General Election Manifesto stated that, as an initial self contained reform," the right of hereditary peers to sit and vote in the House of Lords would be ended by statute. This would be "the first stage in a process of reform to make the House of Lord more democratic and representative." The Lords' legislative powers would remain unaltered. The system of appointment of life peers would be reviewed, with the objective of ensuring that party appointees "more accurately reflect the proportion of votes cast the the previous general election." Labour was, however, committed to maintaining a Cross Bench presence; and "no one political party should seek a majority in the House of Lords." A committee of both Houses of Parliament would be appointed to undertake "a wide ranging review of possible further change" and bring forward proposals of reform.

No proposals for the reform of the House of Lords were included in the Queen's Speech for the first legislative session under the Labour Government. However, it was repeated early in 1998 that a Cabinet Committee had been established on reform of the House of Lords and that legislation to implement the first stage would probably feature in the 1998 - 99 Session.

Conservative
The last Conservative government broadly supported the House of Lords as it is presently constituted; and its 1997 General Election Manifesto laid emphasis on the need to preserve the stability of our constitution "woven over the centuries". More specifically it stated that "fundamental charges which have not been fully thought through - such as opposition proposals on the House of Lords - would be extremely damaging We will oppose change for change's sake." At the time of writing there had been no further policy statement, although there were reports early in 1988 which suggested that the Conservative Party was reviewing its position.

Liberal Democrat
The Liberal Democrats' 1997 General Election Manifesto stated their intention "over two Parliaments" to transform the House of Lords into a predominantly elected second chamber, capable of representing the nations and regions of the UK and of playing a key role in scrutinising European legislation. Proposals issued prior to the election in a draft "Great Reform Bill" envisaged in the longer term a senate of 300 members: three-quarters directly elected by the single transferable vote system of proportional representation and the remainder indirectly elected by a joint committee of both Houses of Parliament. As an interim measure, it proposed a second chamber of 500 members indirectly elected (200 by existing peers and 300 by the Commons) to reflect party strengths at the previous general election, but also with cross-benchers. Existing peers would retain their titles but would not sit unless themselves elected. The new chamber (both in the interim and the long term) would have special responsibilities to represent the regions and nations of the UK, act as constitutional watchdog, oversee quangos and scrutinise proposed European Union legislation.

MEMBERS OF THE HOUSE OF LORDS IN ALPHABETICAL ORDER

Notes: In this list and the following lists:
(i) Information is as at 1st March 1998.
(ii) These abbreviations are used to denote titles:

Abp . . . . *Archbishop*	D . . . . *Duke*	M . . . . *Marquess*
Bp . . . . *Bishop*	E . . . . *Earl*	P . . . . *Prince*
Bs . . . . *Baroness*	L . . . . *Baron/Lord*	V . . . . *Viscount*
C . . . . *Countess*	Ly . . . . *Lady*	

A

Aberconway, L
Abercorn, D
Aberdare, L
Aberdeen and Temair, M
Abergavenny, M
Abinger, L
Ackner, L
Acton, L
Addington, L
Addison, V
Ailesbury, M
Ailsa, M
Airlie, E
Alanbrooke, V
Albemarle, E
Aldenham, L
Alderdice, L
Aldington, L
Alexander of Tunis, E
Alexander of Weedon, L
Allen of Abbeydale, L
Allenby of Megiddo, V
Allendale, V
Alport, L
Alton of Liverpool, L
Alvingham, L
Amherst of Hackney, L
Amos, B
Ampthill, L
Amwell, L
Anelay of St Johns, Bs
Anglesey, M
Annaly, L
Annan, L
Annandale and Hartfell, E
Arbuthnott, V
Archer of Sandwell, L
Archer of Weston-Super-Mare, L
Argyll, D
Armstrong of Ilminster, L
Arran, E
Ashbourne, L
Ashburton, L
Ashcombe, L
Ashley of Stoke, L
Ashton of Hyde, L
Astor, V
Astor of Hever, L
Atholl, D

Attenborough, L
Attlee, E
Auckland, L
Avebury, L
Aylesford, E

B

Baden-Powell, L
Bagot, L
Bagri, L
Baillieu, L
Baker of Dorking, L
Baldwin of Bewdley, E
Balfour, E
Balfour of Burleigh, L
Balfour of Inchrye, L
Banbury of Southam, L
Barber, L
Barber of Tewkesbury, L
Barnard, L
Barnett, L
Basing, L
Bassam of Brighton, L
Bath, M
Bath and Wells, Bp
Bathurst, E
Bauer, L
Bearsted, V
Beatty, E
Beaufort, D
Beaumont of Whitley, L
Beaverbrook, L
Bedford, D
Belhaven and Stenton, L
Bellwin, L
Beloff, L
Belper, L
Belstead, L
Berkeley, L
Berners, Bs
Bessborough, E
Bethell, L
Bicester, L
Biddulph, L
Biffen, L
Bingham of Cornhill, L
Birdwood, L
Birkett, L
Birmingham, Bp
Blackburn, Bp

Blackstone, Bs
Blackwell, L
Blake, L
Blakenham, V
Blaker, L
Blatch, Bs
Blease, L
Bledisloe, V
Blyth, L
Blyth of Rowington, L
Boardman, L
Bolingbroke and St John, V
Bolton, L
Borrie, L
Borthwick, L
Borwick, L
Boston, L
Boston of Faversham, L
Bowness, L
Boyd of Merton, V
Boyd-Carpenter, L
Boyne, V
Brabazon of Tara, L
Brabourne, L
Bradbury, L
Bradford, Bp
Bradford, E
Brain, L
Braine of Wheatley, L
Bramall, L
Brandon of Oakbrook, L
Brassey of Apethorpe, L
Braybrooke, L
Braye, Bs
Brentford, V
Bridge of Harwich, L
Bridgeman, V
Bridges, L
Bridport, V
Briggs, L
Brightman, L
Brigstocke, Bs
Bristol, Bp
Bristol, M
Broadbridge, L
Brocket, L
Brooke and Warwick, E
Brooke of Alverthorpe, L
Brooke of Ystradfellte, Bs
Brookeborough, V
Brookes, L

MEMBERS OF THE HOUSE OF LORDS IN ALPHABETICAL ORDER

Brooks of Tremorfa, L
Brougham and Vaux, L
Broughshane, L
Browne-Wilkinson, L
Brownlow, L
Bruce of Donington, L
Bruntisfield, L
Buccleuch and Queensberry, D
Buchan, E
Buckinghamshire, E
Buckmaster, V
Bullock, L
Burden, L
Burgh, L
Burlison, L
Burnham, L
Burton, L
Bute, M
Butterfield, L
Butterworth, L
Buxton of Alsa, L
Byford, BS
Byron, L

C

Cadman, L
Cadogan, E
Cairns, E
Caithness, E
Caldecote, V
Callaghan of Cardiff, L
Calverley, L
Camden, M
Cameron of Lochbroom, L
Camoys, L
Campbell of Alloway, L
Campbell of Croy, L
Canterbury, Abp
Carew, L
Carlisle, Bp
Carlisle, E
Carlisle of Bucklow, L
Carmichael of Kelvingrove, L
Carnarvon, E
Carnegy of Lour, Bs
Carnock, L
Carr of Hadley, L
Carrick, E
Carrington, L
Carter, L
Carver, L
Castle of Blackburn, Bs
Cathcart, E
Catto, L
Cavendish of Furness, L
Cawdor, E

Cawley, L
Cayzer, L
Chadlington, L
Chalfont, L
Chalker of Wallasey, Bs
Chandos, V
Chapple, L
Charteris of Amisfield, L
Chatfield, L
Chelmsford, V
Chesham, L
Chetwode, L
Chichester, Bp
Chichester, E
Chilston, V
Chilver, L
Chitnis, L
Cholmondeley, M
Chorley, L
Churchill, V
Churston, L
Citrine, L
Clancarty, E
Clanwilliam, E
Clarendon, E
Clark of Kempston, L
Cledwyn of Penrhos, L
Clifford of Chudleigh, L
Clinton, L
Clinton-Davis, L
Clitheroe, L
Clwyd, L
Clyde, L
Clydesmuir, L
Cobbold, L
Cobham, V
Cochrane of Cults, L
Cockfield, L
Cocks of Hartcliffe, L
Coggan, L
Coleraine, L
Coleridge, L
Colgrain, L
Colville of Culross, V
Colwyn, L
Colyton, L
Combermere, V
Congleton, L
Constantine of Stanmore, L
Conyngham, M
Cooke of Islandreagh, L
Cooke of Thorndon, L
Cope of Berkeley, L
Cork and Orrery, E
Cornwallis, L
Cottenham, E
Cottesloe, L

Courtown, E
Coventry, E
Cowdray, V
Cowdrey of Tonbridge, L
Cowley, E
Cox, Bs
Craig of Radley, L
Craigavon, V
Craigmyle, L
Cranborne, V
Cranbrook, E
Cranworth, L
Crathorne, L
Craven, E
Crawford and Balcarres, E
Crawshaw, L
Crickhowell, L
Croft, L
Croham, L
Cromartie, E
Cromer, E
Cromwell, L
Crook, L
Cross, V
Cuckney, L
Cudlipp, L
Cullen of Ashbourne, L
Cumberlege, Bs
Cunliffe, L
Currie of Marylebone, L

D

Dacre, Bs
Dacre of Glanton, L
Dahrendorf, L
Dainton, L
Dalhousie, E
Darcy de Knayth, Bs
Daresbury, L
Darling, L
Darnley, E
Dartmouth, E
Darwen, L
Daventry, V
David, Bs
Davidson, V
Davies, L
Davies of Coity, L
Davies of Oldham, L
de Clifford, L
De Freyne, L
De La Warr, E
De L'Isle, V
De Mauley, L
De Ramsey, L
De Ros, L

MEMBERS OF THE HOUSE OF LORDS IN ALPHABETICAL ORDER

De Saumarez, L
de Villiers, L
Dean of Beswick, L
Dean of Harptree, L
Dean of Thornton-le-Fylde, Bs
Deedes, L
Delacourt-Smith of Alteryn, Bs
Delamere, L
Denbigh, E
Denham, L
Denington, Bs
Denman, L
Denning, L
Denton of Wakefield, Bs
Deramore, L
Derby, E
Derwent, L
Desai, L
Devon, E
Devonport, V
Devonshire, D
Dholakia, L
Diamond, L
Dickinson, L
Digby, L
Dilhorne, V
Dinevor, L
Dixon, L
Dixon-Smith, L
Donaldson of Kingsbridge, L
Donaldson of Lymington, L
Donegall, M
Donoughmore, E
Donoughue, L
Dormand of Easington, L
Dormer, L
Dowding, L
Downe, V
Downshire, M
Drogheda, E
Dubs, L
Ducie, E
Dudley, Bs
Dudley, E
Dulverton, L
Dundee, E
Dundonald, E
Dunleath, L
Dunmore, E
Dunn, Bs
Dunrossil, V
Durham, Bp
Dysart, C

E

Eames, L
Eatwell, L

Ebury, L
Eccles, V
Eccles of Moulton, Bs
Eden of Winton, L
Edinburgh, D
Effingham, E
Eglinton, E
Egmont, E
Eldon, E
Elgin and Kincardine, E
Elibank, L
Elis-Thomas, L
Ellenborough, L
Elles, Bs
Elliott of Morpeth, L
Elphinstone, L
Elton, L
Ely, Bp
Ely, M
Elystan-Morgan, L
Emerton, Bs
Emslie, L
Enniskillen, E
Erne, E
Erroll, E
Erroll of Hale, L
Esher, V
Essex, E
Evans of Parkside, L
Ewing of Kirkford, L
Exeter, Bp
Exeter, M
Exmouth, V
Ezra, L

F

Fairfax of Cameron, L
Fairhaven, L
Falconer of Thoroton, L
Falkender, Bs
Falkland, V
Falmouth, V
Fanshawe of Richmond, L
Faringdon, L
Farrington of Ribbleton, Bs
Feldman, L
Ferrers, E
Feversham, L
Fife, D
Fisher, L
Fisher of Rednal, Bs
Fitt, L
FitzWalter, L
Flather, Bs
Flowers, L
Foley, L

Fookes, Bs
Foot, L
Forbes, L
Forester, L
Forres, L
Forte, L
Fortescue, E
Forteviot, L
Fraser of Carmyllie, L
Freeman, L
Freyberg, L

G

Gage, V
Gainford, L
Gainsborough, E
Gallacher, L
Galloway, E
Gardner of Parkes, Bs
Garel-Jones, L
Geddes, L
Geraint, L
Gerard, L
Gibson, L
Gibson-Watt, L
Gifford, L
Gilbert, L
Gillmore of Thamesfield, L
Gilmour of Craigmillar, L
Gisborough, L
Gladwin of Clee, L
Gladwyn, L
Glanusk, L
Glasgow, E
Glenamara, L
Glenarthur, L
Glenconner, L
Glendevon, L
Glendyne, L
Glentoran, L
Gloucester, Bp
Gloucester, D
Goff of Chieveley, L
Goodhart, L
Gordon of Strathblane, L
Gorell, L
Gormanston, V
Goschen, V
Gosford, E
Gough, V
Gould of Potternewton, Bs
Gowrie, E
Grade, L
Grafton, D
Graham of Edmonton, L
Granard, E

MEMBERS OF THE HOUSE OF LORDS IN ALPHABETICAL ORDER

Grantchester, L
Grantley, L
Granville, E
Gray, L
Gray of Contin, L
Greene of Harrow Weald, L
Greenhill, L
Greenhill of Harrow, L
Greenway, L
Greenwood, V
Gregson, L
Grenfell, L
Gretton, L
Grey, E
Grey of Codnor, L
Grey of Naunton, L
Gridley, L
Griffiths, L
Griffiths of Fforestfach, L
Grimston of Westbury, L
Grimthorpe, L
Guilford, E

H
Habgood, L
Hacking, L
Haddington, E
Haden-Guest, L
Haig, E
Hailsham of Saint Marylebone, L
Halifax, E
Halsbury, E
Hambleden, V
Hambro, L
Hamilton and Brandon, D
Hamilton of Dalzell, L
Hampden, V
Hampton, L
Hamwee, Bs
Hankey, L
Hanson, L
Hanworth, V
Hardie, L
Harding of Petherton, L
Hardinge, V
Hardinge of Penshurst, L
Hardwicke, E
Hardy of Wath, L
Harewood, E
Harlech, L
Harmar-Nicholls, L
Harmsworth, L
Harrington, E
Harris, L
Harris of Greenwich, L
Harris of High Cross, L

Harris of Peckham, L
Harrowby, E
Hartwell, L
Harvey of Tasburgh, L
Haskel, L
Haslam, L
Hastings, L
Hatherton, L
Hattersley, L
Hawke, L
Hayhoe, L
Hayman, Bs
Hayter, L
Hazlerigg, L
Head, V
Headfort, M
Healey, L
Hemingford, L
Hemphill, L
Henderson of Brompton, L
Henley, L
Henniker, L
Hereford, Bp
Hereford, V
Herries, Ly
Herschell, L
Hertford, M
Hesketh, L
Heytesbury, L
Higgins, L
Hill, V
Hill-Norton, L
Hilton of Eggardon, Bs
Hindlip, L
Hives, L
Hoffman, L
Hogg, Bs
Hogg of Cumbernauld, L
Holderness, L
Hollenden, L
Hollick, L
Hollis of Heigham, Bs
Holme of Cheltenham, L
HolmPatrick, L
Home, E
Hood, V
Hooper, Bs
Hooson, L
Hope of Craighead, L
Hothfield, L
Howard de Walden, L
Howard of Penrith, L
Howe, E
Howe of Aberavon, L
Howell, L
Howell of Guildford, L
Howick of Glendale, L

Howie of Troon, L
Hoyle, L
Hughes, L
Hughes of Woodside, L
Hunt, L
Hunt of King's Heath, L
Hunt of Tanworth, L
Hunt of Wirral, L
Huntingdon, E
Huntly, M
Hurd of Westwell, L
Hussey of North Bradley, L
Hutchinson of Lullington, L
Hutton, L
Hylton, L
Hylton-Foster, Bs

I
Iddesleigh, E
Ilchester, E
Iliffe, L
Inchcape, E
Inchyra, L
Inge, L
Ingleby, V
Inglewood, L
Ingrow, L
Inverforth, L
Ironside, L
Irvine of Lairg, L
Islwyn, L
Iveagh, E

J
Jacobs, L
Jakobovits, L
James of Holland Park, Bs
Janner of Braunstone, L
Jauncey of Tullichettle, L
Jay of Paddington, Bs
Jeffreys, L
Jeger, Bs
Jellicoe, E
Jenkin of Roding, L
Jenkins of Hillhead, L
Jenkins of Putney, L
Jersey, E
Johnston of Rockport, L
Joicey, L
Jopling, L
Judd, L

MEMBERS OF THE HOUSE OF LORDS IN ALPHABETICAL ORDER

K

Keith of Castleacre, L
Keith of Kinkel, L
Kelvedon, L
Kemsley, V
Kenilworth, L
Kennedy of the Shaws, Bs
Kennet, L
Kensington, L
Kenswood, L
Kent, D
Kenyon, L
Kershaw, L
Keyes, L
Kilbracken, L
Killanin, L
Killearn, L
Kilmarnock, L
Kilpatrick of Kincraig, L
Kimball, L
Kimberley, E
Kindersley, L
King of Wartnaby, L
Kingsdown, L
Kingsland, L
Kinloss, Ly
Kinnoull, E
Kinross, L
Kintore, E
Kirkhill, L
Kirkwood, L
Kitchener, E
Knight of Collingtree, Bs
Knights, L
Knollys, V
Knutsford, V

L

Laing of Dunphail, L
Lambert, V
Lane, L
Lane of Horsell, L
Lang of Monkton, L
Lansdowne, M
Latham, L
Latymer, L
Lauderdale, E
Lawrence, L
Lawson of Blaby, L
Layton, L
Leathers, V
Leconfield and Egremont, L
Leicester, Bp
Leicester, E
Leigh, L
Leighton of Saint Mellons, L

Leinster, D
Lester of Herne Hill, L
Lestor of Eccles, Bs
Leven and Melville, E
Levene of Portsoken, L
Leverhulme, V
Levy, L
Lewin, L
Lewis of Newnham, L
Lichfield, Bp
Lichfield, E
Lilford, L
Limerick, E
Lincoln, Bp
Lincoln, E
Lindsay, E
Lindsay of Birker, L
Lindsey and Abingdon, E
Linklater of Butterstone, Bs
Linlithgow, M
Listowel, E
Liverpool, E
Lloyd of Berwick, L
Lloyd of Highbury, Bs
Lloyd-George of Dwyfor, E
Lloyd-Weber, L
Lockwood, Bs
Lofthouse of Pontefract, L
Londesborough, L
London, Bp
Londonderry, M
Long, V
Longford, E
Lonsdale, E
Lothian, M
Loudoun, C
Lovat, L
Lovelace, E
Lovell-Davis, L
Lowry, L
Lucan, E
Lucas, L
Lucas of Chilworth, L
Ludford, Bs
Luke, L
Lyell, L
Lytton, E
Lyveden, L

M

McAlpine of West Green, L
MacAndrew, L
Macaulay of Bragar, L
McCarthy, L
Macclesfield, E
McCluskey, L

McColl of Dulwich, L
McConnell, L
Macdonald of Gwaenysgor, L
Macfarlane of Bearsden, L
McFarlane of Llandaff, Bs
McGowan, L
McIntosh of Haringey, L
Mackay of Ardbrecknish, L
Mackay of Clashfern, L
Mackay of Drumadoon, L
Mackenzie-Stuart, L
Mackie of Benshie, L
Mackintosh of Halifax, V
MacLaurin of Knebworth, L
Maclay, L
MacLehose of Beoch, L
Macleod of Borve, Bs
McNair, L
McNally, L
Macpherson of Drumochter, L
Maddock, Bs
Mallalieu, Bs
Malmesbury, E
Malvern, V
Manchester, Bp
Manchester, D
Mancroft, L
Manners, L
Mansfield, E
Manton, L
Mar, C
Mar and Kellie, E
Marchamley, L
Marchwood, V
Margadale, L
Margesson, V
Marks of Broughton, L
Marlborough, D
Marlesford, L
Marsh, L
Martonmere, L
Masham of Ilton, Bs
Mason of Barnsley, L
Massereene and Ferrard, V
May, L
Mayhew of Twysden, L
Meath, E
Melchett, L
Mellish, L
Melville, V
Menuhin, L
Merlyn-Rees, L
Merrivale, L
Mersey, V
Meston, L
Methuen, L
Middleton, L

MEMBERS OF THE HOUSE OF LORDS IN ALPHABETICAL ORDER

Midleton, V
Milford, L
Milford Haven, M
Miller of Hendon, Bs
Mills, V
Milne, L
Milner of Leeds, L
Milverton, L
Minto, E
Mishcon, L
Molloy, L
Molyneux of Killhead, L
Monck, V
Monckton of Brenchley, V
Moncreiff, L
Monk Bretton, L
Monkswell, L
Monro of Langholm, L
Monson, L
Montagu of Beaulieu, L
Montague of Oxford, L
Monteagle of Brandon, L
Montgomery of Alamein, V
Montrose, D
Moore of Lower Marsh, L
Moore of Wolvercote, L
Moran, L
Moray, E
Morley, E
Morris, L
Morris of Castle Morris, L
Morris of Kenwood, L
Morris of Manchester, L
Morton, E
Mostyn, L
Mottistone, L
Mount Edgcumbe, E
Mountbatten of Burma, C
Mountevans, L
Mountgarret, V
Mowbray and Stourton, L
Moyne, L
Moynihan, L
Moyola, L
Munster, E
Murray of Epping Forest, L
Murton of Lindisfarne, L
Mustill, L

N

Napier and Ettrick, L
Napier of Magdâla, L
Naseby, L
Nathan, L
Neill of Bladen, L
Nelson, E

Nelson of Stafford, L
Netherthorpe, L
Newall, L
Newby, L
Newton, L
Newton of Braintree, L
Nicholls of Birkenhead, L
Nicholson of Winterbourne, Bs
Nickson, L
Nicol, Bs
Noel-Buxton, L
Nolan, L
Norfolk, D
Normanby, M
Normanton, E
Norrie, L
Northampton, M
Northbourne, L
Northbrook, L
Northesk, E
Northfield, L
Northumberland, D
Norton, L
Norwich, Bp
Norwich, V
Nunburnholme, L

O

O'Cathain, Bs
Ogmore, L
O'Hagan, L
Oliver of Aylmerton, L
O'Neill, L
Onslow, E
Onslow of Woking, L
Oppenheim-Barnes, Bs
Oram, L
Oranmore and Browne, L
Orkney, E
Orr-Ewing, L
Owen, L
Oxford, Bp
Oxford and Asquith, E
Oxfuird, V

P

Palmer, L
Palumbo, L
Park of Monmouth, Bs
Parkinson, L
Parmoor, L
Parry, L
Patten, L
Paul, L
Pearson of Rannoch, L
Peel, E

Pembroke and Montgomery, E
Pender, L
Penrhyn, L
Perry of Southwark, Bs
Perry of Walton, L
Perth, E
Peston, L
Petre, L
Peyton of Yeovil, L
Phillimore, L
Phillips of Ellesmere, L
Piercy, L
Pike, Bs
Pilkington of Oxenford, L
Pitkeathley, Bs
Plant of Highfield, L
Platt of Writtle, Bs
Plowden, L
Plumb, L
Plummer of St Marylebone, L
Plunket, L
Plymouth, E
Poltimore, L
Polwarth, L
Ponsonby of Shulbrede, L
Poole, L
Porter of Luddenham, L
Portland, E
Portman, V
Portsmouth, E
Powerscourt, V
Powis, E
Prentice, L
Prior, L
Prys-Davies, L
Puttnam, L
Pym, L

Q

Queensberry, M
Quinton, L
Quirk, L

R

Radnor, E
Raglan, L
Ramsay of Cartvale, Bs
Randall of St Budeaux, L
Ranfurly, E
Rankeillour, L
Rathcavan, L
Rathcreedan, L
Ravensdale, L
Ravensworth, L
Rawlings, Bs

MEMBERS OF THE HOUSE OF LORDS IN ALPHABETICAL ORDER

Rawlinson of Ewell, L
Rayleigh, L
Rayne, L
Rayner, L
Razzall, L
Rea, L
Reading, M
Reay, L
Redesdale, L
Rees, L
Rees-Mogg, L
Remnant, L
Rendell of Baburgh,
Renfrew of Kaimsthorn, L
Rennell, L
Renton, L
Renton of Mount Harry, L
Renwick, L
Renwick of Clifton, L
Revelstoke, L
Richard, L
Richardson, L
Richardson of Duntisbourne, L
Richmond Lennox and Gordon, D
Ridley, V
Ripon, Bp
Ritchie of Dundee, L
Riverdale, L
Rix, L
Robens of Woldingham, L
Roberts of Conwy, L
Robertson of Oakridge, L
Roborough, L
Robson of Kiddington, Bs
Rochdale, V
Rochester, L
Rockley, L
Rodger of Earlsferry, L
Rodgers of Quarry Bank, L
Rodney, L
Rogers of Riverside, L
Roll of Ipsden, L
Rollo, L
Romney, E
Rootes, L
Rosebery, E
Rosslyn, E
Rossmore, L
Rothermere, V
Rotherwick, L
Rothes, E
Rothschild, L
Rowallan, L
Roxburghe, D
Rugby, L
Runcie, L
Runciman of Doxford, V

Russell, E
Russell of Liverpool, L
Russell-Johnston, L
Rutland, D
Ryder of Eaton Hastings, L
Ryder of Warsaw, Bs
Ryder of Wensum, L

S

Saatchi, L
Sackville, L
Sainsbury, L
Sainsbury of Preston Candover, L
Sainsbury of Turville, L
Saint Albans, D
St Aldwyn, E
St Davids, V
St Germans, E
St Helens, L
St John of Bletso, L
St John of Fawsley, L
Saint Levan, L
Saint Oswald, L
St Vincent, V
Salisbury, M
Saltoun of Abernethy, Ly
Samuel, V
Sandberg, L
Sanderson of Bowden, L
Sandford, L
Sandhurst, L
Sandwich, E
Sandys, L
Savile, L
Savile of Newdigate, L
Saye and Sele, L
Scanlon, L
Scarbrough, E
Scarman, L
Scarsdale, V
Scotland of Asthal, L
Seafield, E
Seccombe, Bs
Sefton of Garston, L
Selborne, E
Selby, V
Selkirk of Douglas, L
Selsdon, L
Sempill, L
Serota, Bs
Sewel, L
Shaftesbury, E
Shannon, E
Sharples, Bs
Shaughnessy, L
Shaw of Northstead, L

Shawcross, L
Shepherd, L
Sheppard of Didgemere, L
Sherfield, L
Shore of Stepney, L
Shrewsbury, E
Shuttleworth, L
Sidmouth, V
Sieff of Brimpton, L
Silsoe, L
Simon, V
Simon of Glaisdale, L
Simon of Highbury, L
Simon of Wythenshawe, L
Simpson of Dunkeld, L
Sinclair, L
Sinclair of Cleeve, L
Sinha, L
Skelmersdale, L
Skidelsky, L
Sligo, M
Slim, V
Slynn of Hadley, L
Smith, L
Smith of Clifton, L
Smith of Gilmorehill, Bs
Snowdon, E
Somerleyton, L
Somers, L
Somerset, D
Soper, L
Soulbury, V
Soulsby of Swaffham Prior, L
Southampton, L
Southwark, Bp
Southwell, Bp
Spencer, E
Spens, L
Stafford, L
Stair, E
Stallard, L
Stamp, L
Stanley of Alderley, L
Steel of Aikwood, L
Sterling of Plaistow, L
Stevens of Ludgate, L
Stewartby, L
Steyn, L
Stockton, E
Stodart of Leaston, L
Stoddart of Swindon, L
Stokes, L
Stone of Blackheath, L
Strabolgi, L
Stradbroke, E
Strafford, E
Strang, L

MEMBERS OF THE HOUSE OF LORDS IN ALPHABETICAL ORDER

Strange, Bs
Strathalmond, L
Strathcarron, L
Strathclyde, L
Strathcona and Mount Royal, L
Stratheden and Campbell, L
Strathmore and Kinghorne, E
Strathspey, L
Stuart of Findhorn, V
Sudeley, L
Suffield, L
Suffolk and Berkshire, E
Sutherland, D
Sutherland, C
Swansea, L
Swaythling, L
Swinfen, L
Swinton, E
Symons of Vernham Dean, L
Sysonby, L

T

Tankerville, E
Tanlaw, L
Taverne, L
Taylor of Blackburn, L
Taylor of Gryfe, L
Taylor of Warwick, L
Tebbit, L
Tedder, L
Temple of Stowe, E
Templeman, L
Tenby, V
Tennyson, L
Terrington, L
Teviot, L
Teynham, L
Thatcher, Bs
Thomas of Gresford, L
Thomas of Gwydir, L
Thomas of Macclesfield
Thomas of Swynnerton, L
Thomas of Walliswood, Bs
Thomson of Fleet, L
Thomson of Monifieth, L
Thurlow, L
Thurso, V
Tollemache, L
Tombs, L
Tope, L
Tordoff, L
Torphichen, L
Torrington, V
Townshend, M
Trefgarne, L
Trenchard, V

Trevethin and Oaksey, L
Trevor, L
Trumpington, Bs
Tryon, L
Tugendhat, L
Turner of Camden, Bs
Tweeddale, M
Tweedsmuir, L

U

Ullswater, V

V

Varley, L
Vaux of Harrowden, L
Vernon, L
Verulam, E
Vestey, L
Vincent of Coleshill, L
Vinson, L
Vivian, L

W

Waddington, L
Wade of Chorlton, L
Wakefield, Bp
Wakeham, L
Wakehurst, L
Waldegrave, E
Wales, P
Walker of Doncaster, L
Walker of Worcester, L
Wallace of Coslany, L
Wallace of Saltaire, L
Walpole, L
Walsingham, L
Walton of Detchant, L
Wardington, L
Warnock, Bs
Waterford, M
Watson of Invergowrie, L
Waverley, V
Weatherill, L
Wedderburn of Charlton, L
Wedgwood, L
Weidenfeld, L
Weinstock, L
Weir, V
Wellington, D
Wemyss and March, E
Westbury, L
Westminster, D
Westmorland, E
Westwood, L

Whaddon, L
Wharncliffe, E
Wharton, Bs
White, Bs
Whitelaw, V
Whitty, L
Wigoder, L
Wigram, L
Wilberforce, L
Wilcox, Bs
Williams of Crosby, Bs
Williams of Elvel, L
Williams of Mostyn, L
Willoughby de Broke, L
Willoughby de Eresby, Bs
Wilson, L
Wilson of Tillyorn, L
Wilton, E
Wimborne, V
Winchester, Bp
Winchester, M
Winchilsea and Nottingham, E
Windlesham, L
Winston, L
Wise, L
Wolfson, L
Wolfson of Sunningdale, L
Wolverton, L
Woolf, L
Woolton, E
Wraxall, L
Wrenbury, L
Wright of Richmond, L
Wrottesley, L
Wyfold, L
Wynford, L

Y

Yarborough, E
York, D
York, Abp
Young, Bs
Young of Dartington, L
Young of Graffham, L
Young of Old Scone, Bs
Younger of Leckie, V

Z

Zetland, M
Zouche of Haryngworth, L

MEMBERS OF THE HOUSE OF LORDS BY PARTY

Note: The following list also includes peers of no political party affiliation – those who have registered as Cross Benchers and others.

Conservative

A

Aberconway, L
Abercorn, D
Aberdare, L
Abinger, L
Addison, V
Ailsa, M
Aldenham, L
Aldington, L
Alexander of Tunis, E
Alexander of Weedon, L
Allendale, V
Anelay of St Johns, Bs
Annaly, L
Annandale and Hartfell, E
Archer of Weston-Super-Mare, L
Argyll, D
Arran, E
Ashbourne, L
Astor, V
Astor of Hever, L
Attlee, E
Aylesford, E

B

Bagri, L
Baker of Dorking, L
Balfour, E
Banbury of Southam, L
Barber, L
Bathurst, E
Bauer, L
Bearsted, V
Beaufort, D
Beaverbrook, L
Belhaven and Stenton, L
Bellwin, L
Beloff, L
Belstead, L
Berners, Bs
Bethell, L
Biddulph, L
Biffen, L
Birdwood, L
Blackwell, L
Blake, L
Blakenham, V
Blaker, L
Blatch, Bs
Blyth of Rowington, L
Boardman, L
Bolton, L
Boston, L
Bowness, L
Boyd-Carpenter, L
Brabazon of Tara, L

Bradbury, L
Bradford, E
Braine of Wheatley, L
Brassey of Apethorpe, L
Braybrooke, L
Brentford, V
Bridgeman, V
Brigstocke, Bs
Brougham and Vaux, L
Bruntisfield, L
Buccleuch and Queensberry, D
Buckinghamshire, E
Burnham, L
Burton, L
Butterfield, L
Butterworth, L
Buxton of Alsa, L
Byford, Bs
Byron, L

C

Cadman, L
Cadogan, E
Caithness, E
Caldecote, V
Camden, M
Campbell of Alloway, L
Campbell of Croy, L
Carlisle of Bucklow, L
Carnegy of Lour, Bs
Carnock, L
Carr of Hadley, L
Carrington, L
Cathcart, E
Cavendish of Furness, L
Cawley, L
Cayzer, L
Chadlington, L
Chalker of Wallasey, Bs
Chelmsford, V
Chesham, L
Chichester, E
Chilston, V
Chilver, L
Churston, L
Clanwilliam, E
Clark of Kempston, L
Clinton, L
Clitheroe, L
Cochrane of Cults, L
Cockfield, L
Coleraine, L
Coleridge, L
Colwyn, L
Constantine of Stanmore, L
Cope of Berkeley, L
Cork and Orrery, E
Cottenham, E
Courtown, E
Coventry, E

Cowdrey of Tonbridge, L
Cowley, E
Cox, Bs
Craigmyle, L
Cranborne, V
Cranbrook, E
Cranworth, L
Crathorne, L
Crawford and Balcarres, E
Crickhowell, L
Cromer, E
Cross, V
Cuckney, L
Cullen of Ashbourne, L
Cumberlege, Bs

D

Dacre of Glanton, L
Darnley, E
Daventry, V
Davidson, V
De Freyne, L
De La Warr, E
De L'Isle, V
De Ramsey, L
De Saumarez, L
Dean of Harptree, L
Deedes, L
Denbigh, E
Denham, L
Denman, L
Denton of Wakefield, Bs
Derwent, L
Digby, L
Dilhorne, V
Dixon-Smith, L
Donegall, M
Donoughmore, E
Downshire, M
Dudley, E
Dundee, E
Dundonald, E

E

Eccles, V
Eccles of Moulton, B
Eden of Winton, L
Elgin and Kincardine, E
Elibank, L
Ellenborough, L
Elles, Bs
Elliott of Morpeth, L
Elton, L
Erne, E
Erroll of Hale, L

MEMBERS OF THE HOUSE OF LORDS BY PARTY

F

Fairfax of Cameron, L
Fairhaven, L
Falmouth, V
Fanshawe of Richmond, L
Feldman, L
Ferrers, E
Flather, Bs
Fookes, Bs
Forbes, L
Forester, L
Forte, L
Fortescue, L
Forteviot, L
Fraser of Carmyllie, L
Freeman, L

G

Gage, V
Gainford, L
Galloway, E
Gardner of Parkes, Bs
Garel-Jones, L
Geddes, L
Gibson-Watt, L
Gilmour of Craigmillar, L
Gisborough, L
Glenarthur, L
Glendyne, L
Glentoran, L
Gormanston, V
Goschen, V
Gowrie, E
Grafton, D
Granard, E
Gray, L
Gray of Contin, L
Griffiths of Fforestfach, L
Grimston of Westbury, L
Grimthorpe, L

H

Hacking, L
Haddington, E
Haig, E
Hailsham of Saint Marylebone, L
Halifax, E
Hambleden, V
Hambro, L
Hamilton of Dalzell, L
Hanson, L
Harding of Petherton, L
Hardwicke, E
Harlech, L
Harmar-Nicholls, L
Harmsworth, L
Harris of Peckham, L
Harrowby, E
Harvey of Tasburgh, L
Haslam, L
Hastings, L
Hawke, L

Hayhoe, L.
Hemphill, L
Henley, L
Hesketh, L
Higgins, L
Hindlip, L
Hogg, B
Holderness, L
HolmPatrick, L
Home, E
Hood, V
Hooper, Bs
Hothfield, L
Howe, E
Howe of Aberavon, L
Howell of Guildford, L
Hunt of Wirral, L
Huntly, M
Hurd of Westwell, L

I

Inchcape, E
Inglewood, L
Ingrow, L
Ironside, L

J

James of Holland Park, Bs
Jeffreys, L
Jellicoe, E
Jenkin of Roding, L
Johnston of Rockport, L
Jopling, L

K

Keith of Castleacre, L
Kelvedon, L
Kemsley, V
Kenilworth, L
Kenyon, L
Keyes, L
Killearn, L
Kimball, L
Kimberley, E
King of Wartnaby, L
Kingsland, L
Kinnoull, E
Kitchener, E
Knight of Collingtree, Bs
Knollys, V
Knutsford, V

L

Laing of Dunphail, L
Lane of Horsell, L
Lang of Monkton, L
Lauderdale, E
Lawson of Blaby, L
Layton, L
Leconfield and Egremont, L
Leigh, L
Leverhulme, V

Lichfield, E
Limerick, E
Lindsay, E
Lindsey and Abingdon, E
Liverpool, E
Lloyd-Webber, L
Long, V
Lonsdale, E
Lothian, M
Lucas, L
Lucas of Chilworth, L
Luke, L
Lyell, L

M

MacAndrew, L
McColl of Dulwich, L
Macfarlane of Bearsden, L
Mackay of Ardbrecknish, L
Mackay of Clashfern, L
Mackay of Drumadoon, L
Mackintosh of Halifax, V
MacLaurin of Knebworth, L
Macleod of Borve, Bs
Macpherson of Drumochter, L
Malmesbury, E
Mancroft, L
Manners, L
Mansfield, E
Manton, L
Marchwood, V
Marlborough, D
Marlesford, L
Massereene and Ferrard, V
May, L
Mayhew of Twysden, L
Melville, V
Merrivale, L
Mersey, V
Middleton, L
Milford Haven, M
Miller of Hendon, Bs
Mills, V
Milverton, L
Monk Bretton, L
Monro of Langholm, L
Montagu of Beaulieu, L
Monteagle of Brandon, L
Montgomery of Alamein, V
Montrose, D
Moore of Lower Marsh, L
Morley, E
Mostyn, L
Mottistone, L
Mountevans, L
Mowbray and Stourton, L
Moyne, L
Moynihan, L
Moyola, L
Munster, E
Murton of Lindisfarne, L

MEMBERS OF THE HOUSE OF LORDS BY PARTY

N
Naseby, L
Newall, L
Newton, L
Newton of Braintree, L
Nickson, L
Noel-Buxton, L
Norfolk, D
Norrie, L
Northbrook, L
Northesk, E

O
O'Cathain, Bs
O'Hagan, L
Onslow, E
Onslow of Woking, L
Oppenheim-Barnes, Bs
Orkney, E
Orr-Ewing, L
Oxfuird, V

P
Palumbo, L
Park of Monmouth, Bs
Parkinson, L
Patten, L
Pearson of Rannoch, L
Peel, E
Pembroke and Montgomery, E
Pender, L
Penrhyn, L
Perry of Southwark, Bs
Peyton of Yeovil, L
Phillimore, L
Pike, Bs
Pilkington of Oxenford, L
Platt of Writtle, Bs
Plumb, L
Plummer of St Marylebone, L
Plunket, L
Poltimore, L
Polwarth, L
Poole, L
Portman, V
Prentice, L
Prior, L
Pym, L

Q
Quinton, L

R
Radnor, E
Rankeillour, L
Rawlings, Bs
Rawlinson of Ewell, L
Rayleigh, L
Reading, M
Reay, L
Rees, L
Remnant, L

Renfrew of Kaimsthorn, L
Rennell, L
Renton, L
Renton of Mount Harry, L
Renwick, L
Roberts of Conwy, L
Rockley, L
Rodney, L
Romney, E
Rotherwick, L
Rowallan, L
Roxburghe, D
Ryder of Wensum, L

S
Saatchi, L
Sackville, L
Sainsbury of Preston Candover, L
Saint Albans, D
St Aldwyn, E
St Davids, V
St Germans, E
St John of Fawsley, L
Saint Levan, L
Saint Oswald, L
Salisbury, M
Sanderson of Bowden, L
Sandford, L
Sandys, L
Savile, L
Seafield, E
Seccombe, Bs
Selborne, E
Selkirk of Douglas, L
Selsdon, L
Shaftesbury, E
Sharples, Bs
Shaw of Northstead, L
Sheppard of Didgemere, L
Shrewsbury, E
Shuttleworth, L
Sieff of Brimpton, L
Skelmersdale, L
Skidelsky, L
Soulsby of Swaffham Prior, L
Stafford, L
Stanley of Alderley, L
Sterling of Plaistow, L
Stevens of Ludgate, L
Stewartby, L
Stockton, E
Stodart of Leaston, L
Strange, Bs
Strathcarron, L
Strathclyde, L
Strathcona and Mount Royal, L
Strathmore and Kinghorne, E
Sudeley, L
Suffield, L
Suffolk and Berkshire, E
Swaythling, L
Swinfen, L
Swinton, E

T
Taylor of Warwick, L
Tebbit, L
Teviot, L
Teynham, L
Thatcher, Bs
Thomas of Gwydir, L
Tollemache, L
Torphichen, L
Torrington, V
Townshend, M
Trefgarne, L
Trenchard, V
Trevethin and Oaksey, L
Trumpington, Bs
Tugendhat, L

U
Ullswater, V

V
Vaux of Harrowden, L
Vestey, L
Vinson, L
Vivian, L

W
Waddington, L
Wade of Chorlton, L
Wakeham, L
Wakehurst, L
Waldegrave, E
Walker of Worcester, L
Wardington, L
Waterford, M
Wedgwood, L
Weir, V
Wemyss and March, E
Westbury, L
Westminster, D
Whitelaw, V
Wigram, L
Wilcox, Bs
Willoughby de Broke, L
Windlesham, L
Wise, L
Wolfson, L
Wolfson of Sunningdale, L
Woolton, E
Wrottesley, L
Wynford, L

Y
Yarborough, E
Young, Bs
Young of Graffham, L
Younger of Leckie, L

Z
Zetland, M
Zouche of Haryngworth, L

MEMBERS OF THE HOUSE OF LORDS BY PARTY

Labour

A
Acton, L
Amos, L
Archer of Sandwell, L
Ashley of Stoke, L
Attenborough, L

B
Barnett, L
Bassam of Brighton, L
Berkeley, L
Blackstone, Bs
Blease, L
Borrie, L
Brooke of Alvethorpe, L
Brooks of Tremorfa, L
Bruce of Donington, L
Burlison, L

C
Callaghan of Cardiff, L
Carmichael of Kelvingrove, L
Carter, L
Castle of Blackburn, B
Chandos, V
Cledwyn of Penrhos, L
Clinton-Davis, L
Cocks of Hartcliffe, L
Currie of Marylebone L

D
David, Bs
Davies of Coity, L
Davies of Oldham, L
Dean of Beswick, L
Dean of Thornton-le-Fylde, Bs
Delacourt-Smith of Alteryn, Bs
Denington, Bs
Desai, L
Diamond, L
Dixon, L
Donoughue, L
Dormand of Easington, L
Dubs, L

E
Eatwell, L
Evans of Parkside, L
Ewing of Kirkford, L

F
Falconer of Thoroton, L
Falkender, Bs
Farrington of Ribbleton, Bs
Fisher of Rednal, Bs

G
Gallacher, L
Gifford, L
Gilbert, L
Gladwin of Clee, L
Glenamara, L
Gordon of Strathblane, L
Gould of Potternewton, Bs
Graham of Edmonton, L
Grantchester, L

Greene of Harrow Weald, L
Gregson, L
Grenfell, L

H
Hanworth, V
Hardie, L
Hardy of Wath, L
Haskel, L
Hattersley, L
Hayman, B
Healey, L
Hilton of Eggardon, Bs
Hogg of Cumbernauld, L
Hollick, L
Hollis of Heigham, Bs
Howell, L
Howie of Troon, L
Hoyle, L
Hughes, L
Hughes of Woodside, L
Hunt of Kings Health, L

I
Irvine of Lairg, L
Islwyn, L

J
Janner of Braunstone, L
Jay of Paddington, Bs
Jeger, Bs
Jenkins of Putney, L
Judd, L

K
Kennedy of the Shaws, Bs
Kennet, L
Kilbracken, L
Kirkhill, L

L
Lestor of Eccles, B
Levy, L
Lockwood, Bs
Lofthouse of Pontefract, L
Longford, E
Lovell-Davis, L

M
Macaulay of Bragar, L
McCarthy, L
McIntosh of Haringey, L
Mallalieu, Bs
Mason of Barnsley, L
Merlyn-Rees, L
Milner of Leeds, L
Mishcon, L
Molloy, L
Monkswell, L
Montague of Oxford, L
Morris of Castle Morris, L
Morris of Manchester, L
Murray of Epping Forest, L

N
Nicol, Bs
Northfield, L

O
Oram, L
Orme, L

P
Parry, L
Paul, L
Peston, L
Pitkeathley, Bs
Plant of Highfield, L
Ponsonby of Shulbrede, L
Prys-Davies, L
Puttnam, L

R
Ramsay, of Cartvale, B
Randall of St Budeaux, L
Rendell of Baberg, Bs
Rea, L
Renwick of Clifton, L
Richard, L
Rogers of Riverside, L

S
Sainsbury of Turville
Scanlon, L
Scotland of Asthall, Bs
Sefton of Garston, L
Serota, Bs
Sewel, L
Shepherd, L
Shore of Stepney, L
Simon, V
Simon of Highbury, L
Simpson of Dunkeld, L
Smith of Gilmorehill, Bs
Soper, L
Stallard, L
Stoddart of Swindon, L
Stone of Blackheath, L
Strabolgi, L
Symons of Vernham Dean, Bs

T
Taylor of Blackburn, L
Taylor of Gryfe, L
Thomas of Macclesfield, L
Turner of Camden, B

V
Varley, L

W
Walker of Doncaster, L
Wallace of Campsie, L
Wallace of Coslany, L
Watson of Invergowrie, L
Wedderburn of Charlton, L
Whaddon, L
White, Bs
Whitty, L
Williams of Elvel, L
Williams of Mostyn, L
Winston, L

Y
Young of Dartington, L
Young of Old Scone, Bs

MEMBERS OF THE HOUSE OF LORDS BY PARTY

Liberal Democrat

A

Addington, L
Alderdice, L
Avebury, L

B

Bath, M
Beaumont of Whitley, L

C

Calverley, L
Carlisle, E
Cudlipp, L

D

Dahrendorf, L
Davies, L
Dhokalia, L
Donaldson of Kingsbridge, L

E

Ezra, L

F

Falkland, V
Foot, L

G

Geraint, L
Glasgow, E
Glenconner, L
Goodhart, L
Grey, E
Gridley, L

H

Hampton, L
Hamwee, Bs
Harris of Greenwich, L
Holme of Cheltenham, L
Hooson, L
Hunt, L
Hutchinson of Lullington, L

J

Jacobs, L
Jenkins of Hillhead, L

K

Kirkwood, L

L

Lester of Herne Hill, L
Linklater of Butterstone, Bs
Ludford, Bs

M

Mackie of Benshie, L
McNair, L
McNally, L
Maddock, Bs
Mar and Kellie, E
Meston, L
Methuen, L

N

Newby, L
Nicholson of Winterbourne, Bs

O

Ogmore, L

P

Perry of Walton, L

R

Razzall, L
Redesdale, L
Ritchie of Dundee, L
Robson of Kiddington, B
Rochester, L
Rodgers of Quarry Bank, L
Russell, E
Russell-Johnston, L

S

Sandberg, L
Smith of Clifton, L
Steel of Aikwood, L

T

Taverne, L
Thomas of Gresford, L
Thomas of Swynnerton, L
Thomas of Walliswood, Bs
Thomson of Monifieth, L
Thurso, V
Tope, L
Tordoff, L

W

Wallace of Saltaire, L
Wigoder, L
Williams of Crosby, Bs
Winchilsea and Nottingham, E

MEMBERS OF THE HOUSE OF LORDS BY PARTY

Cross Bench

A

Aberdeen and Temair, M
Abergavenny, M
Ackner, L
Ailesbury, M
Airlie, E
Alanbrooke, V
Albemarle, E
Allen of Abbeydale, L
Allenby of Megiddo, V
Alton of Liverpool, L
Amherst of Hackney, L
Ampthill, L
Amwell, L
Anglesey, M
Annan, L
Arbuthnott, V
Armstrong of Ilminster, L
Ashburton, L
Ashton of Hyde, L

B

Baldwin of Bewdley, E
Balfour of Burleigh, L
Balfour of Inchrye, L
Barber of Tewkesbury, L
Barnard, L
Bingham of Cornhill, L
Birkett, L
Bledisloe, V
Blyth, L
Borthwick, L
Boston of Faversham, L
Boyne, V
Brabourne, L
Brain, L
Bramall, L
Brandon of Oakbrook, L
Bridge of Harwich, L
Bridges, L
Briggs, L
Brightman, L
Broadbridge, L
Brookeborough, L
Brookes, L
Broughshane, L
Browne-Wilkinson, L
Buchan, E
Buckmaster, V
Bullock, L

C

Cairns, E
Cameron of Lochbroom, L
Camoys, L
Carew, L
Carnarvon, E
Carrick, E
Carver, L
Cawdor, E

Chalfont, L
Chapple, L
Charteris of Amisfield, L
Chitnis, L
Cholmondeley, M
Chorley, L
Clancarty, E
Clifford of Chudleigh, L
Clwyd, L
Clyde, L
Cobbold, L
Coggan, L
Colgrain, L
Colville of Culross, V
Combermere, V
Congleton, L
Cooke of Islandreagh, L
Cooke of Thorndon, L
Cornwallis, L
Cottesloe, L
Cowdray, V
Craig of Radley, L
Craigavon, V
Croham, L
Cromartie, E
Cromwell, L
Crook, L
Cunliffe, L

D

Dacre, Bs
Darcy de Knayth, B
Denning, L
Derby, E
Devonport, V
Devonshire, D
Dickinson, L
Donaldson of Lymington, L
Dowding, L
Drogheda, E
Dulverton, L
Dunn, Bs
Dunrossil, V

E

Eames, L
Edinburgh, D
Effingham, E
Eldon, E
Elis-Thomas, L
Emerton, Bs
Emslie, L
Enniskillen, E
Erroll, E
Essex, E
Exeter, M
Exmouth, V

F

Faringdon, L
Feversham, L
Flowers, L

Forres, L
Freyberg, L

G

Gainsborough, E
Gerard, L
Gibson, L
Gillmore of Thamesfield, L
Gladwyn, L
Gloucester, D
Goff of Chieveley, L
Gorell, L
Gosford, E
Gough, V
Grade, L
Grantley, L
Greenhill of Harrow, L
Greenway, L
Grey of Naunton, L
Griffiths, L

H

Habgood, L
Halsbury, E
Hamilton and Brandon, D
Hampden, V
Hankey, L
Hardinge, V
Harris of High Cross, L
Hartwell, L
Hayter, L
Head, V
Headfort, M
Hemingford, L
Henderson of Brompton, L
Henniker, L
Hill-Norton, L
Hoffman, L
Hope of Craighead, L
Hunt of Tanworth, L
Huntingdon, E
Hussey of North Bradley, L
Hutton, L
Hylton, L
Hylton-Foster, Bs

I

Iddesleigh, E
Ilchester, E
Inchyra, L
Inge, L
Ingleby, V
Iveagh, E

J

Jakobovits, L
Jauncey of Tullichettle, L
Joicey, L

K

Keith of Kinkel, L
Kent, D

MEMBERS OF THE HOUSE OF LORDS BY PARTY

Killanin, L
Kilmarnock, L
Kilpatrick of Kincraig, L
Kindersley, L
Kingsdown, L
Kinloss, Ly
Kintore, E
Knights, L

L

Lane, L
Lawrence, L
Leathers, V
Leicester, E
Levene of Portsoken, L
Lewin, L
Lewis of Newnham, L
Lindsay of Birker, L
Lloyd of Berwick, L
Lloyd of Highbury, Bs
Lloyd-George of Dwyfor, E
Loudoun, C
Lovelace, E
Lowry, L
Lytton, E

M

Macclesfield, E
McCluskey, L
McConnell, L
McFarlane of Llandaff, Bs
Mackenzie-Stuart, L
MacLehose of Beoch, L
Manchester, D
Mar, C
Marks of Broughton, L
Marsh, L
Martonmere, L
Masham of Ilton, B
Menuhin, L
Midleton, V
Milne, L
Minto, E
Molyneaux of Killead, L
Monckton of Brenchley, V
Monson, L
Moore of Wolvercote, L
Moran, L
Morris of Kenwood, L
Morton, E
Mount Edgcumbe, E
Mountbatten of Burma, C
Mountgarret, V
Mustill, L

N

Napier and Ettrick, L
Napier of Magdala, L
Nathan, L
Neill of Bladen, L
Nelson, E
Nelson of Stafford, L

Netherthorpe, L
Nicholls of Birkenhead, L
Nolan, L
Normanby, M
Northbourne, L
Northumberland, D
Norton, L

O

Oliver of Aylmerton, L
Owen, L
Oxford and Asquith, E

P

Palmer, L
Perth, E
Petre, L
Phillips of Ellesmere, L
Plowden, L
Porter of Luddenham, L
Portland, E
Powis, E

Q

Quirk, L

R

Raglan, L
Ranfurly, E
Rathcavan, L
Rathcreedan, L
Ravensdale, L
Rayne, L
Rees-Mogg, L
Richardson, L
Richardson of Duntiobourne, L
Richmond Lennox and Gordon, D
Ridley, V
Rix, L
Robertson of Oakridge, L
Roborough, L
Rodger of Earlsferry, L
Roll of Ipsden, L
Roskill, L
Rosslyn, E
Rothschild, L
Rugby, L
Runcie, L
Runciman of Doxford, V
Russell of Liverpool, L
Ryder of Warsaw, Bs

S

St John of Bletso, L
Saltoun of Abernethy, Ly
Samuel, V
Sandhurst, L
Sandwich, E
Saville of Newdigate, Bs
Scarman, L
Sempill, L
Shannon, E

Shaughnessy, L
Shawcross, L
Sidmouth, V
Simon of Glaisdale, L
Slim, V
Slynn of Hadley, L
Smith, L
Snowdon, E
Somerleyton, L
Somerset, D
Soulbury, V
Spencer, E
Spens, L
Stamp, L
Steyn, L
Stokes, L
Strafford, E
Strathalmond, L
Stratheden and Campbell, L
Swansea, L

T

Tanlaw, L
Temple of Stowe, E
Templeman, L
Tenby, V
Tennyson, L
Terrington, L
Thurlow, L
Tombs, L
Tryon, L
Tweeddale, M
Tweedsmuir, L

V

Vincent of Coleshill, L

W

Wales, P
Walpole, L
Walton of Detchant, L
Warnock, Bs
Waverley, V
Weatherill, L
Weidenfeld, L
Weinstock, L
Wellington, D
Westmorland, E
Wharton, Bs
Wilberforce, L
Willoughby de Eresby, Bs
Wilson of Tillyorn, L
Wimborne, V
Wolverton, L
Woolf, L
Wrenbury, L
Wright of Richmond, L

Y

York, D

MEMBERS OF THE HOUSE OF LORDS BY PARTY

Other

A

Alport, L
Alvingham, L
Ashcombe, L
Atholl, D
Auckland, L

B

Baden-Powell, L
Bagot, L
Baillieu, L
Basing, L
Bath and Wells, Bp
Beatty, E
Bedford, D
Belper, L
Bessborough, E
Bicester, L
Birmingham, Bp
Blackburn, Bp
Bolingbroke and St John, V
Borwick, L
Boyd of Merton, V
Bradford, Bp
Braye, Bs
Bridport, V
Bristol, M
Bristol, Bp
Brocket, L
Brooke and Warwick, E
Brooke of Ystradfellte, Bs
Brownlow, L
Burden, L
Burgh, L
Bute, M

C

Canterbury, Abp
Carlisle, Bp
Catto, L
Chatfield, L
Chetwode, L
Chichester, Bp
Churchill, V
Citrine, L
Clarendon, E
Clydesmuir, L
Cobham, V
Colyton, L
Conyngham, M
Craven, E

Crawshaw, L
Croft, L

D

Dalhousie, E
Daresbury, L
Darling, L
Dartmouth, E
Darwen, L
de Clifford, L
De Mauley, L
De Ros, L
de Villiers, L
Delamere, L
Deramore, L
Devon, E
Dinevor, L
Dormer, L
Downe, V
Ducie, E
Dudley, B
Dunleath, L
Dunmore, E
Durham, Bp
Dysart, C

E

Ebury, L
Eglinton, E
Egmont, E
Elphinstone
Ely, Bp
Ely, M
Elystan-Morgan, L
Esher, V
Exeter, Bp

F

Fife, D
Fisher, L
Fitt, L
FitzWalter, L
Foley, L

G

Glanusk, L
Glendevon, L
Gloucester, Bp
Greenhill, L
Greenwood, V
Gretton, L
Grey of Codnor, L
Guilford, E

H

Haden-Guest, L
Hardinge of Penshurst, L
Harewood, E
Harrington, E
Harris, L
Hatherton, L
Hazlerigg, L
Hereford, Bp
Hereford, V
Herries, Ly
Herschell, L
Hertford, M
Heytesbury, L
Hill, V
Hives, L
Hollenden, L
Howard de Walden, L
Howard of Penrith, L
Howick of Glendale, L

I

Iliffe, L
Inverforth, L

J

Jersey, E

K

Kensington, L
Kenswood, L
Kershaw, L
Kinross, L

L

Lambert, V
Lansdowne, M
Latham, L
Latymer, L
Leicester, Bp
Leighton of Saint Mellons, L
Leinster, D
Leven and Melville, E
Lichfield, Bp
Lilford, L
Lincoln, Bp
Lincoln, E
Linlithgow, M
Listowel, E
Londesborough, L
London, Bp

MEMBERS OF THE HOUSE OF LORDS BY PARTY

Londonderry, M
Lovat, L
Lucan, E
Lyveden, L

M

McAlpine of West Green, L
Macdonald of Gwaenysgor, L
McGowan, L
Maclay, L
Malvern, V
Manchester, Bp
Marchamley, L
Margadale, L
Margesson, V
Meath, E
Melchett, L
Mellish, L
Milford, L
Monck, V
Moncreiff, L
Moray, E
Morris, L

N

Normanton, E
Northampton, M
Norwich, V
Norwich, Bp
Nunburnholme, L

O

O'Neill, L
Oranmore and Browne, L
Oxford, Bp

P

Parmoor, L
Piercy, L
Plymouth, E
Portsmouth, E
Powerscourt, V

Q

Queensberry, M

R

Ravensworth, L
Rayner, L
Revelstoke, L
Ripon, Bp
Riverdale, L
Robens of Woldingham, L
Rochdale, V
Rollo, L
Rootes, L
Rosebery, E
Rossmore, L
Rothermere, V
Rothes, E
Rutland, D
Ryder of Eaton Hastings, L

S

Sainsbury, L
St Helens, L
St Vincent, V
Salisbury, Bp
Saye and Sele, L
Scarborough, E
Scarsdale, V
Selby, V
Sheffield, Bp
Sherfield, L
Silsoe, L
Simon of Wythenshawe, L
Sinclair, L
Sinclair of Cleeve, L
Sinha, L
Sligo, M
Somers, L
Southampton, L
Southwell, Bp
Stair, E
Stradbroke, E
Strang, L
Strathspey, L
Stuart of Findhorn, V
Sutherland, D
Sutherland, C
Sysonby, L

T

Tankerville, E
Tedder, L
Thomson of Fleet, L
Trevor, L

V

Vernon, L
Verulam, E

W

Wakefield, Bp
Walsingham, L
Westwood, L
Wharncliffe, E
Wilson, L
Wilton, E
Winchester, Bp
Winchester, M
Wraxall, L
Wyfold, L

Y

York, Abp

HEREDITARY PEERS BY PARTY

Note: (i) The following list includes peers of no party affiliation – those who have registered as Cross Benchers and Other.

Conservative

A
Aberconway, L
Abercorn, D
Aberdare, L
Abinger, L
Addison, V
Ailsa, M
Aldenham, L
Aldington, L
Alexander of Tunis, E
Allendale, V
Annaly, L
Annandale and Hartfell, E
Argyll, D
Arran, E
Ashbourne, L
Astor, V
Astor of Hever, L
Aylesford, E

B
Balfour, E
Banbury of Southam, L
Bathurst, E
Bearsted, V
Beaufort, D
Beaverbrook, L
Belhaven and Stenton, L
Belstead, L
Berners, Bs
Bethell, L
Biddulph, L
Birdwood, L
Blakenham, V
Bolton, L
Boston, L
Brabazon of Tara, L
Bradbury, L
Bradford, E
Brassey of Apethorpe, L
Braybrooke, L
Brentford, V
Bridgeman, V
Brougham and Vaux, L
Bruntisfield, L
Buccleuch and Queensberry, D
Buckinghamshire, E
Burnham, L
Burton, L
Byron, L

C
Cadman, L
Cadogan, E
Caithness, E
Caldecote, V
Camden, M
Carnock, L
Carrington, L
Cathcart, E
Cawley, L
Chelmsford, V
Chesham, L
Chichester, E
Chilston, V
Churston, L
Clanwilliam, E
Clinton, L
Clitheroe, L
Cochrane of Cults, L
Coleraine, L
Coleridge, L
Colwyn, L
Cork and Orrery, E
Cottenham, E
Courtown, E
Coventry, E
Cowley, E
Craigmyle, L
Cranborne, V
Cranbrook, E
Cranworth, L
Crathorne, L
Crawford and Balcarres, E
Cromer, E
Cross, V
Cullen of Ashbourne, L

D
Darnley, E
Daventry, V
Davidson, V
De Freyne, L
De La Warr, E
De L'Isle, V
De Ramsey, L
De Saumarez, L
Denbigh, E
Denham, L
Denman, L
Derwent, L
Digby, L

Dilhorne, V
Donegall, M
Donoughmore, E
Downshire, M
Dudley, E
Dundee, E
Dundonald, E

E
Eccles, V
Elgin and Kincardine, E
Elibank, L
Ellenborough, L
Elton, L
Erne, E
Erroll of Hale, L

F
Fairfax of Cameron, L
Fairhaven, L
Falmouth, V
Ferrers, E
Forbes, L
Forester, L
Fortescue, E
Forteviot, L

G
Gage, V
Gainford, L
Galloway, E
Geddes, L
Gisborough, L
Glenarthur, L
Glendyne, L
Glentoran, L
Gormanston, V
Goschen, V
Gowrie, E
Grafton, D
Granard, E
Gray, L
Grimston of Westbury, L
Grimthorpe, L

H
Hacking, L
Haddington, E
Haig, E

HEREDITARY PEERS BY PARTY

Halifax, E
Hambleden, V
Hamilton of Dalzell, L
Harding of Petherton, L
Hardwicke, E
Harlech, L
Harmsworth, L
Harrowby, E
Harvey of Tasburgh, L
Hastings, L
Hawke, L
Hemphill, L
Henley, L
Hesketh, L
Hindlip, L
HolmPatrick, L
Home, E
Hood, V
Hothfield, L
Howe, E
Huntly, M

I

Inchcape, E
Inglewood, L
Ironside, L

J

Jeffreys, L
Jellicoe, E

K

Kemsley, V
Kenilworth, L
Kenyon, L
Keyes, L
Killearn, L
Kimberley, E
Kinnoull, E
Kitchener, E
Knollys, V
Knutsford, V

L

Lauderdale, E
Layton, L
Leconfield and Egremont, L
Leigh, L
Leverhulme, V
Lichfield, E
Limerick, E

Lindsay, E
Lindsey and Abingdon, E
Linlithgow, M
Liverpool, E
Long, V
Lonsdale, E
Lothian, M
Lucas, L
Lucas of Chilworth, L
Luke, L
Lyell, L

M

MacAndrew, L
Mackintosh of Halifax, V
Macpherson of Drumochter, L
Malmesbury, E
Mancroft, L
Manners, L
Mansfield, E
Manton, L
Marchwood, V
Marlborough, D
Massereene and Ferrard, V
May, L
Melville, V
Merrivale, L
Mersey, V
Middleton, L
Milford Haven, M
Mills, V
Milverton, L
Monk Bretton, L
Montagu of Beaulieu, L
Monteagle of Brandon, L
Montgomery of Alamein, V
Montrose, D
Morley, E
Mostyn, L
Mottistone, L
Mountevans, L
Mowbray and Stourton, L
Moyne, L
Moynihan, L
Munster, E

N

Newall, L
Newton, L
Noel-Buxton, L
Norfolk, D
Norrie, L
Northbrook, L
Northesk, E

O

O'Hagan, L
Onslow, E
Orkney, E
Oxfuird, V

P

Peel, E
Pembroke and Montgomery, E
Pender, L
Penrhyn, L
Phillimore, L
Plunket, L
Poltimore, L
Polwarth, L
Poole, L
Portman, V

R

Radnor, E
Rankeillour, L
Rayleigh, L
Reading, M
Reay, L
Remnant, L
Rennell, L
Renwick, L
Rockley, L
Rodney, L
Romney, E
Rotherwick, L
Rowallan, L
Roxburghe, D

S

Sackville, L
Saint Albans, D
St Aldwyn, E
St Davids, V
St Germans, E
Saint Levan, L
Saint Oswald, L
Salisbury, M
Sandford, L
Sandys, L
Savile, L
Seafield, E
Selborne, E
Selsdon, L
Shaftesbury, E
Shrewsbury, E
Shuttleworth, L

HEREDITARY PEERS BY PARTY

Skelmersdale, L
Stafford, L
Stanley of Alderley, L
Stockton, E
Strange, Bs
Strathcarron, L
Strathclyde, L
Strathcona and Mount Royal, L
Strathmore and Kinghorne, E
Sudeley, L
Suffield, L
Suffolk and Berkshire, E
Swaythling, L
Swinfen, L
Swinton, E

T
Teviot, L
Teynham, L
Tollemache, L
Torphichen, L
Torrington, V
Townshend, M
Trefgarne, L
Trenchard, V
Trevethin and Oaksey, L

U
Ullswater, V

V
Vaux of Harrowden, L
Vestey, L
Vivian, L

W
Wakehurst, L
Waldegrave, E
Wardington, L
Waterford, M
Wedgwood, L
Weir, V
Wemyss and March, E
Westbury, L
Westminster, D
Whitelaw, V
Wigram, L
Willoughby de Broke, L
Windlesham, L
Wise, L
Woolton, E
Wrottesley, L
Wynford, L

Y
Yarborough, E
Younger of Leckie, L

Z
Zetland, M
Zouche of Haryngworth, L

Labour

A
Acton, L

B
Berkeley, L

C
Chandos, V

G
Gifford, L
Granchester, L
Grenfell, L

H
Hanworth, V

K
Kennet, L
Kilbracken, L

L
Longford, E

M
Milner of Leeds, L
Monkswell, L

P
Ponsonby of Shulbrede, L

R
Rea, L

S
Shepherd, L
Simon, V
Strabolgi, L

Liberal Democrat

A
Addington, L
Avebury, L

B
Bath, M

C
Calverley, L
Carlisle, E

D
Davies, L

F
Falkland, V

G
Glasgow, E
Glenconner, L
Grey, E
Gridley, L

H
Hampton, L

K
Kirkwood, L

M
McNair, L
Mar and Kellie, E
Meston, L
Methuen, L

O
Ogmore, L

R
Redesdale, L
Ritchie of Dundee, L
Rochester, L
Russell, E

T
Thurso, V

W
Winchilsea and Nottingham, E

HEREDITARY PEERS BY PARTY

Cross Bench

A

Aberdeen and Temair, M
Abergavenny, M
Ailesbury, M
Airlie, E
Alanbrooke, V
Albemarle, E
Allenby of Megiddo, V
Amherst of Hackney, L
Ampthill, L
Amwell, L
Arbuthnott, V
Ashburton, L
Ashton of Hyde, L

B

Baldwin of Bewdley, E
Balfour of Burleigh, L
Balfour of Inchrye, L
Barnard, L
Birkett, L
Bledisloe, V
Blyth, L
Borthwick, L
Boyne, V
Brabourne, L
Brain, L
Bridges, L
Broadbridge, L
Broughshane, L
Buchan, E
Buckmaster, V

C

Cairns, E
Camoys, L
Carew, L
Carnarvon, E
Carrick, E.
Cawdor, E
Cholmondeley, M
Chorley, L
Clancarty, E
Clifford of Chudleigh, L
Clwyd, L
Cobbold, L
Colgrain, L
Colville of Culross, V
Combermere, V
Congleton, L

Cornwallis, L
Cottesloe, L
Cowdray, V
Craigavon, V
Cromartie, E
Cromwell, L
Crook, L
Cunliffe, L

D

Dacre, Bs
Darcy de Knayth, Bs
Derby, E
Devonport, V
Devonshire, D
Dickinson, L
Dowding, L
Drogheda, E
Dulverton, L
Dunrossil, V

E

Edinburgh, D
Effingham, E
Eldon, E
Enniskillen, E
Erroll, E
Essex, E
Exeter, M
Exmouth, V

F

Faringdon, L
Feversham, L
Forres, L
Freyberg, L

G

Gainsborough, E
Gerard, L
Gloucester, D
Gorell, L
Gosford, E
Gough, V
Grantley, L
Greenway, L

H

Halsbury, E
Hamilton and Brandon, D
Hampden, V
Hankey, L
Hardinge, V
Hayter, L
Head, V
Headfort, M
Hemingford, L
Henniker, L
Huntingdon, E
Hylton, L

I

Iddesleigh, E
Ilchester, E
Inchyra, L
Ingleby, V
Iveagh, E

J

Joicey, L

K

Kent, D
Killanin, L
Kilmarnock, L
Kindersley, L
Kinloss, Ly
Kintore, E

L

Lawrence, L
Leathers, V
Leicester, E
Lindsay of Birker, L
Lloyd-George of Dwyfor, E
Loudoun, C
Lovelace, E
Lytton, E

M

Macclesfield, E
Manchester, D
Mar, C
Marks of Broughton, L
Martonmere, L
Midleton, V
Milne, L

HEREDITARY PEERS BY PARTY

Minto, E
Monckton of Brenchley, V
Monson, L
Moran, L
Morris of Kenwood, L
Morton, E
Mount Edgcumb, E
Mountbatten of Burma, C
Mountgarret, V

N
Napier and Ettrick, L
Napier of Magdâla, L
Nathan, L
Nelson, E
Nelson of Stafford, L
Netherthorpe, L
Normanby, M
Northbourne, L
Northumberland, D
Norton, L

O
Oxford and Asquith, E

P
Palmer, L
Perth, E
Petre, L
Portland, E
Powis, E

R
Raglan, L
Ranfurly, E
Rathcavan, L
Rathcreedan, L
Richmond, Lennox and Gordon, D
Ridley, V
Robertson of Oakridge, L
Roborough, L
Rosslyn, E
Rothschild, L
Rugby, L
Runciman of Doxford, V
Russell of Liverpool, L

S
St John of Bletso, L
Saltoun of Abernethy, Ly
Samuel, V
Sandhurst, L
Sandwich, E
Sempill, L
Shannon, E
Shaughnessy, L
Sidmouth, V
Slim, V
Snowdon, E
Somerleyton, L
Somerset, D
Soulbury, V
Spencer, E
Spens, L
Stamp, L
Strafford, E
Strathalmond, L
Stratheden and Campbell, L
Swansea, L

T
Temple of Stowe, E
Tenby, V
Tennyson, L
Terrington, L
Thurlow, L
Tryon, L
Tweeddale, M
Tweedsmuir, L

W
Wales, P
Walpole, L
Waverley, V
Wellington, D
Westmorland, E
Wharton, Bs
Willoughby de Eresby, Bs
Wimborne, V
Wolverton, L
Wrenbury, L

Y
York, D

Other

A
Alvingham, L
Anglesey, M
Ashcombe, L
Atholl, D
Auckland, L

B
Baden-Powell, L
Bagot, L
Baillieu, L
Basing, L
Beatty, E
Bedford, D
Belper, L
Berners, Bs
Bessborough, E
Bicester, L
Bolingbroke and St John, V
Borwick, L
Boyd of Merton, V
Braye, Bs
Bridport, V
Bristol, M
Brocket, L
Brooke and Warwick, E
Brownlow, L
Burden, L
Burgh, L
Bute, M

C
Catto, L
Chatfield, L
Chetwode, L
Churchill, V
Citrine, L
Clarendon, E
Clydesmuir, L
Cobham, V
Colyton, L
Conyngham, M
Craven, E
Crawshaw, L
Croft, L

HEREDITARY PEERS BY PARTY

D

Dalhousie, E
Daresbury, L
Darling, L
Dartmouth, E
Darwen, L
de Clifford, L
De Mauley, L
De Ros, L
de Villiers, L
Delamere, L
Deramore, L
Devon, E
Dinevor, L
Dormer, L
Downe, V
Ducie, E
Dudley, Bs
Dunleath, L
Dunmore, E
Dysart, C

E

Ebury, L
Eglinton, E
Egmont, E
Elphinstone, L
Ely, M
Esher, V

F

Fife, D
Fisher, L
FitzWalter, L
Foley, L
Fortescue, E

G

Glanusk, L
Glendevon, L
Granville, E
Greenhill, L
Greenwood, V
Gretton, L
Grey of Codnor, L
Guilford, E

H

Haden-Guest, L
Hardinge of Penshurst, L
Harewood, E
Harrington, E
Harris, L
Hatherton, L
Hazlerigg, L
Hereford, V
Herries, Ly
Herschell, L
Hertford, M
Heytesbury, L
Hill, V
Hives, L
Hollenden, L
Howard de Walden, L
Howard of Penrith, L
Howick of Glendale, L

I

Iliffe, L
Inverforth, L

J

Jersey, E

K

Kensington, L
Kenswood, L
Kershaw, L
Kinross, L

L

Lambert, V
Lansdowne, M
Latham, L
Latymer, L
Leathers, V
Leighton of Saint Mellons, L
Leinster, D
Leven and Melville, E
Lilford, L
Lincoln, E

Linlithgow, M
Listowell, E
Londesborough, L
Londonderry, M
Lovat, L
Lucan, E
Lyveden, L

M

Macdonald of Gwaenysgor, L
McGowan, L
Maclay, L
Malvern, V
Marchamley, L
Margadale, L
Margesson, V
Meath, E
Melchett, L
Milford, L
Monck, V
Moncreiff, L
Moray, E
Morrison, L

N

Normanton, E
Northampton, M
Norwich, V
Nunburnholme, L

O

O'Neill, L
Oranmore and Browne, L

P

Parmoor, L
Piercy, L
Plymouth, E
Portsmouth, E
Powerscourt, V

HEREDITARY PEERS BY PARTY

Q

Queensberry, M

R

Ravensworth, L
Revelstoke, L
Riverdale, L
Rochdale, V
Rollo, L
Rootes, L
Rosebery, E
Rossmore, L
Rothermere, V
Rothes, E
Rutland, D

S

St Helens, L
St Vincent, V
Saye and Sele, L
Scarborough, E
Scarsdale, V
Selby, V
Sherfield, L
Silsoe, L
Simon of Wythenshawe, L
Sinclair, L
Sinclair of Cleeve, L
Sinha, L
Sligo, M
Somers, L
Southampton, L
Stair, E
Stradbroke, E
Strang, L
Strathspey, L
Stuart of Findhorn, V
Sutherland, D
Sutherland, C
Sysonby, L

T

Tankerville, E
Tedder, L
Thomson of Fleet, L
Trevor, L

V

Vernon, L
Verulam, E

W

Walsingham, L
Westwood, L
Wharncliffe, E
Wilson, L
Wilton, E
Winchester, M
Wraxall, L
Wyfold, L

LIFE PEERS BY PARTY

Note: The following list of life peers excludes Lords/Spiritual (serving Bishops/Archbishops) who are listed separately on page 68. For a separate list of law lords currently able to hear appeals see page 78.

Conservative

A

Alexander of Weedon, L
Anelay of St Johns, Bs
Archer of Weston-Super-Mare, L

B

Bagri, L
Baker of Dorking, L
Barber, L
Bauer, L
Bellwin, L
Beloff, L
Biffen, L
Blackwell, L
Blake, L
Blaker, L
Blatch, Bs
Blyth of Rowington, L
Boardman, L
Bowness, L
Boyd-Carpenter, L
Braine of Wheatley, L
Brigstocke, Bs
Butterfield, L
Butterworth, L
Buxton of Alsa, L
Byford, Bs

C

Campbell of Alloway, L
Campbell of Croy, L
Carlisle of Bucklow, L
Carnegy of Lour, Bs
Carr of Hadley, L
Cavendish of Furness, L
Cayzer, L
Chadlington, L
Chalker of Wallasey, Bs
Chelmer, L
Chilver, L
Clark of Kempston, L
Cockfield, L
Constantine of Stanmore, L
Cope of Berkeley, L
Cowdrey of Tonbridge, L
Cox, Bs
Crickhowell, L
Cuckney, L
Cumberlege, Bs

D

Dacre of Glanton, L
Dean of Harptree, L
Deedes, L

Denton of Wakefield, Bs
Dixon-Smith, L

E

Eccles of Moulton, Bs
Eden of Winton, L
Elles, Bs
Elliott of Morpeth, L

F

Fanshawe of Richmond, L
Feldman, L
Flather, Bs
Fookes, Bs
Forte, L
Fraser of Carmyllie, L
Freeman, L

G

Gardner of Parkes, Bs
Garel-Jones, L
Gibson-Watt, L
Gilmour of Craigmillar, L
Gray of Contin, L
Griffiths of Fforestfach, L

H

Hailsham of Saint Marylebone, L
Hambro, L
Hanson, L
Harmar-Nicholls, L
Harris of Peckham, L
Harvington, L
Haslam, L
Hayhoe, L
Higgins, L
Hogg, Bs
Holderness, L
Hooper, Bs
Howe of Aberavon, L
Howell of Guildford, L
Hunt of Guildford, L
Hunt of Wirral, L
Hurd of Westwell, L

I

Ingrow, L

J

James of Holland Park, Bs
Jenkin of Roding, L
Johnston of Rockport, L
Jopling, L

K

Keith of Castleacre, L
Kelvedon, L
Kimball, L
King of Wartnaby, L
Kingsland, L
Knight of Collingtree, Bs

L

Laing of Dunphail, L
Lane of Horsell, L
Lang of Monckton, L
Lawson of Blaby, L
Lloyd-Webber, L

M

McColl of Dulwich, L
Macfarlane of Bearsden, L
Mackay of Ardbrecknish, L
Mackay of Clashfern, L
Mackay of Drumadoon, L
MacLaurin of Knebworth, L
Macleod of Borve, Bs
Marlesford, L
Mayhew of Twysden, l
Miller of Hendon, Bs
Monro of Langholm, L
Moore of Lower Marsh, L
Moyola, L
Murton of Lindisfarne, L

N

Naseby, L
Newton of Braintree, L
Nickson, L

LIFE PEERS BY PARTY

O
O'Cathain, Bs
Onslow of Woking, L
Oppenheim-Barnes, Bs
Orr-Ewing, L

P
Palumbo, L
Park of Monmouth, Bs
Parkinson, L
Patten, L
Pearson of Rannoch, L
Perry of Southwark, Bs
Peyton of Yeovil, L
Pike, Bs
Pilkington of Oxenford, L
Platt of Writtle, Bs
Plumb, L
Plummer of St Marylebone, L
Prentice, L
Prior, L
Pym, L

Q
Quinton, L

R
Rawlings, Bs
Rawlinson of Ewell, L
Rees, L
Renfrew of Kaimsthorn, L
Renton, L
Renton of Mount Harry, L
Roberts of Conwy, L
Ryder of Wensum, L

S
Saatchi, L
Sainsbury of Preston Candover, L
St John of Fawsley, L
Sanderson of Bowden, L
Seccombe, Bs
Selkirk of Douglas, L
Sharples, Bs
Shaw of Northstead, L
Sheppard of Didgemere, L
Sieff of Brimpton, L
Skidelsky, L
Soulsby of Swaffham Prior, L
Sterling of Plaistow, L

Stevens of Ludgate, L
Stewartby, L
Stodart of Leaston, L

T
Taylor of Warwick, L
Tebbit, L
Thatcher, Bs
Thomas of Gwydir, L
Trumpington, Bs
Tugendhat, L

V
Vinson, L

W
Waddington, L
Wade of Chorlton, L
Wakeham, L
Walker of Worcester, L
Wilcox, Bs
Wolfson, L
Wolfson of Sunningdale, L

Y
Young, Bs
Young of Graffham, L

Labour

A
Amos, Bs
Archer of Sandwell, L
Ashley of Stoke, L
Attenborough, L

B
Barnett, L
Bassam of Brighton, L
Blackstone, Bs
Blease, L
Borrie, L
Brooke of Alverthorpe, L
Brooks of Tremorfa, L
Bruce of Donington, L
Burlison, L

C
Callaghan of Cardiff, L
Carmichael of Kelvingrove, L
Carter, L
Castle of Blackburn, Bs
Cledwyn of Penrhos, L
Clinton-Davis, L
Cocks of Hartcliffe, L
Currie of Marylebone, L

D
David, Bs
Davies of Coity, L
Davies of Oldham, L
Dean of Beswick, L
Dean of Thornton-le-Flyde, Bs
Delacourt-Smith of Alteryn, Bs
Denington, Bs
Desai, L
Diamond, L
Dixon, L
Donoughue, L
Dormand of Easington, L
Dubs, L

E
Eatwell, L
Evans of Parkside, L
Ewing of Kirkford, L

F
Falconer of Thoroton, L
Falkender, Bs
Farrington of Ribbleton, Bs
Fisher of Rednal, Bs

G
Gallacher, L
Gilbert, L
Gladwin of Clee, L
Glenamara, L
Gordon of Strathblane, L
Gould of Potternewton, Bs
Graham of Edmonton, L
Greene of Harrow Weald, L
Gregson, L

LIFE PEERS BY PARTY

H
Hardie, L
Hardy of Wath, L
Haskel, L
Hattersley, L
Hayman, Bs
Healey, L
Hilton of Eggardon, Bs
Hogg of Cumbernauld, L
Hollick, L
Hollis of Heigham, Bs
Howell, L
Howie of Troon, L
Hoyle, L
Hughes, L
Hughes of Woodside, L
Hunt of Kingsheath, L

I
Irvine of Lairg, L
Islwyn, L

J
Janner of Braunstone, L
Jay of Paddington, Bs
Jeger, Bs
Jenkins of Putney, L
Judd, L

K
Kennedy of the Shaws, L
Kennet, L
Kilbracken, L
Kirkhill, L

L
Lestor of Eccles, Bs
Levy, L
Llewelyn-Davies of Hastoe, Bs
Lockwood, Bs
Lofthouse of Pontefract, L
Lovell-Davis, L

M
Macaulay of Bragar, L
McCarthy, L
McIntosh of Haringey, L
Mallalieu, Bs
Mason of Barnsley, L
Merlyn-Rees, L

Mishcon, L
Montague of Oxford, L
Molloy, L
Morris of Castle Morris, L
Morris of Manchester L
Murray of Epping Forest, L

N
Nicol, Bs
Northfield, L

O
Oram, L
Orme, L

P
Parry, L
Paul, L
Peston, L
Pitkeathley, L
Plant of Highfield, L
Prys-Davies, L
Puttnam, L

R
Ramsay of Cartvale, Bs
Randall of St Budeaux, L
Rendell of Babergh, L
Renwick of Clifton, L
Richard, L
Rogers of Riverside, L

S
Sainsbury of Turville
Scanlon, L
Scotland of Asthal, Bs
Sefton of Garston, L
Serota, Bs
Sewel, L
Shore of Stepney, L
Simon of Highbury, L
Simpson of Dunkeld, L
Smith of Gilmorehill, Bs
Soper, L
Stallard, L
Stoddart of Swindon, L
Stone of Blackheath, L
Symons of Vernham Dean, Bs

T
Taylor of Blackburn, L
Taylor of Gryfe, L
Turner of Camden, Bs
Thomas of Macclesfield, L

V
Varley, L

W
Walker of Doncaster, L
Wallace of Campsie, L
Wallace of Coslany, L
Watson of Invergowrie, L
Wedderburn of Charlton, L
Whaddon, L
White, Bs
Whitty, L
Williams of Elvel, L
Williams of Mostyn, L
Winston, L

Y
Young of Dartington, L
Young of Old Scone, Bs

Liberal Democrat

A
Alderdice, L

B
Beaumont of Whitley, L

C
Cudlipp, L

D
Dahrendorf, L
Dhakolia, L
Donaldson of Kingsbridge, L

E
Ezra, L

LIFE PEERS BY PARTY

F

Foot, L

G

Geraint, L
Goodhart, L

H

Hamwee, Bs
Harris of Greenwich, L
Holme of Cheltenham, L
Hooson, L
Hunt, L
Hutchinson of Lullington, L

J

Jacobs, L
Jenkins of Hillhead, L

L

Lester of Herne Hill, L
Linklater of Butterstone, Bs
Ludford, Bs

M

Mackie of Benshie, L
McNally, L
Maddock, Bs

N

Newby, L
Nicholston of Winterbourne, Bs

P

Perry of Walton, L

R

Razzall, L
Robson of Kiddington, Bs
Rodgers of Quarry Bank, L
Russell-Johnston, L

S

Sandberg, L
Smith of Clifton, L
Steel of Aikwood, L

T

Taverne, L
Thomas of Gresford, L
Thomas of Swynnerton, L
Thomas of Walliswood, Bs
Thomson of Monifieth, L
Tope, L
Tordoff, L

W

Wallace of Saltaire, L
Wigoder, L
Williams of Crosby, Bs

Cross Bench

A

Ackner, L
Allen of Abbeydale, L
Alton of Liverpoll, L
Annan, L
Armstrong of Ilminster, L

B

Barber of Tewkesbury, L
Bingham of Cornhill, L
Boston of Faversham, L
Bramall, L
Brandon of Oakbrook, L
Bridge of Harwich, L
Briggs, L
Brightman, L
Brookes, L
Browne-Wilkinson, L
Bullock, L

C

Cameron of Lochbroom, L
Carver, L
Chalfont, L
Chapple, L
Charteris of Amisfield, L
Chitnis, L
Coggan, L
Cooke of Islandreagh, L
Cooke of Thorndon, L
Craig of Radley, L
Croham, L

D

Denning, L
Donaldson of Lymington, L
Dunn, Bs

E

Eames, L
Elis-Thomas, L
Emerton, Bs
Emslie, L

F

Flowers, L

G

Gibson, L
Gilllmore of Thamesfield, L
Goff of Chieveley, L
Grade, L
Greenhill of Harrow, L
Grey of Naunton, L
Griffiths, L

H

Habgood, L
Harris of High Cross, L
Hartwell, L
Henderson of Brompton, L
Hill-Norton, L
Hoffman, L
Hope of Craighead, L
Hunt of Tanworth, L
Hussey of North Bradley, L
Hutton, L
Hylton-Foster, Bs

I

Inge, L

J

Jakobovits, L
Jauncey of Tullichettle, L

K

Keith of Kinkel, L
Kilpatrick of Kincraig, L
Kingsdown, L
Knights, L

LIFE PEERS BY PARTY

L

Lane, L
Levene of Portsoken, L
Lewin, L
Lewis of Newnham, L
Lloyd of Berwick, L
Lloyd of Highbury, Bs
Lowry, L

M

McCluskey, L
McConnell, L
McFarlane of Llandaff, Bs
Mackenzie-Stuart, L
MacLehose of Beoch, L
Marsh, L
Masham of Ilton, Bs
Menuhin, L
Molyneaux of Killead, L
Moore of Wolvercote, L
Mustill, L

N

Neill of Bladen, L
Nicholls of Birkenhead, L
Nolan, L

O

Oliver of Aylmerton, L
Owen, L

P

Phillips of Ellesmere, L
Plowden, L
Porter of Luddenham, L

Q

Quirk, L

R

Rayne, L
Rees-Mogg, L
Richardson, L
Richardson of Duntisbourne, L
Rix, L
Rodger of Earlsferry, L
Roll of Ipsden, L
Runcie, L
Ryder of Warsaw, Bs

S

Saville of Newdigate, L
Scarman, L
Shawcross, L
Simon of Glaisdale, L
Slynn of Hadley, L
Smith, L
Steyn, L
Stokes, L

T

Tanlaw, L
Templeman, L
Tombs, L

V

Vincent of Coleshill, L

W

Walton of Detchant, L
Warnock, Bs
Weatherill, L
Weidenfeld, L
Weinstock, L

Cross Bench

Wilberforce, L
Wilson of Tillyorn, L
Woolf, L
Wright of Richmond, L

Other

A

Alport, L

B

Brooke of Ystradfellte, Bs

E

Elystan-Morgan, L

F

Fitt, L

M

McAlpine of West Green, L
Mellish, L

R

Rayner, L
Robens of Woldingham, L
Ryder of Eaton Hastings, L

S

Sainsbury, L

LORDS SPIRITUAL

The following sit in the House of Lords as Lords Spiritual (as at 1st March 1998):

Archbishops	Bradford	Gloucester	Norwich
Canterbury	Bristol	Hereford	Oxford
York	Carlisle	Leicester	Ripon
	Chichester	Lichfield	Salisbury
Bishops	Durham	Lincoln	Southwell
Bath and Wells	Ely	London	Wakefield
Birmingham	Exeter	Manchester	Winchester
Blackburn			

Note: None of the Lords Spiritual has any registered political affiliation.

WOMEN PEERS

There are (as of 1st March 1998) 97 women peers, of whom 16 are hereditary peers and 81 are life peers.

*Note: * Denotes an hereditary peer.*

Amos, Bs
Anelay of St Johns, Bs
Berners, Bs*
Blackstone, Bs
Blatch, Bs
Braye, Bs *
Brigstocke, Bs
Brooke of Ystradfellte, Bs
Byford, Bs
Carnegy of Lour, Bs
Castle of Blackburn, Bs
Chalker of Wallasey, Bs
Cox, Bs
Cumberlege, Bs
Dacre, Bs*
Darcy de Knayth, Bs*
David, Bs
Dean of Thornton-le-Fylde, Bs
Delacourt-Smith of Alteryn, Bs
Denington, Bs
Denton of Wakefield, Bs
Dudley, Bs*
Dunn, Bs
Dysart, C*
Eccles of Moulton, Bs
Elles, Bs
Emerton, Bs
Falkender, Bs
Farrington of Ribbleton, Bs
Fisher of Rednal, Bs
Flather, Bs
Fookes, Bs
Gardner of Parkers, Bs
Gould of Potternewton, Bs
Hamwee, Bs
Hayman, Bs
Herries, Ly*
Hilton of Eggardon, Bs
Hogg, Bs
Hollis of Heigham, Bs
Hooper, Bs
Hylton-Foster, Bs
James of Holland Park, Bs
Jay of Paddington, Bs
Jeger, Bs
Kennedy of the Shaws, Bs
Kinloss, Ly*
Knight of Collingtree, Bs
Lestor of Eccles, Bs

Linklater of Butterstone, Bs
Lloyd of Highbury, Bs
Lockwood, Bs
Loudoun, C*
Ludford, Bs
McFarlane of Llandaff, Bs
Macleod of Borve, Bs
Maddock, Bs
Mallalieu, Bs
Mar, C*
Masham of Ilton, Bs
Miller of Hendon, Bs
Mountbatten of Burma, C*
Nicholson, Bs
Nicol, Bs
O'Cathain, Bs
Oppenheim-Barnes, Bs
Park of Monmouth, Bs
Perry of Southwark, Bs
Pike, Bs
Pitkeathley, Bs
Platt of Writtle, Bs
Ramsay of Cartvale, Bs
Rawlings, Bs
Rendell of Babergh, Bs
Robson of Kiddington, Bs
Ryder of Warsaw, Bs
Saltoun of Abernethy, Ly*
Scotland of Asthall, Bs
Seccombe, Bs
Serota, Bs
Sharples, Bs
Smith of Gilmorehill, Bs
Strange, Bs*
Sutherland, C*
Symons of Vernham Dean, Bs
Thatcher, Bs
Thomas of Walliswood, Bs
Trumpington, Bs
Turner of Camden, Bs
Warnock, Bs
Wharton, Bs*
White, Bs
Wilcox, Bs
Williams of Crosby, Bs
Willoughby de Eresby, Bs*
Young, Bs
Young of Old Scone, Bs

PEERAGES DISCLAIMED

The peerages, listed below are currently disclaimed under the provisions of the 1963 Peerage Act:

Altrincham, L	Reith, L
Camrose, V*	Sanderson of Ayot, L
Durham, E	Selkirk, E*
Hailsham, V*	Silkin, L
Merthyr, L	Stansgate, V

Note:

The individuals who have disclaimed these titles sit in the House of Lords by virtue of holding other (life) peerages – as Lord Hartwell, Lord Hailsham of St Marylebone and Lord Selkirk of Douglas respectively.

PEERS WITHOUT WRIT OF SUMMONS

The following list of peers who have not received a Writ of Summons includes two who are minors and so may not take their seat until the age of 21 (Earl of Craven and Lord Elphinstone). It also include two who are ineligible because of bankruptcy (Lord Morris and Lord Westwood). It does not, however, include:

Atholl, D	Leighton of Saint Mellons, L
Auckland, L	Leven and Melville, E
Basing, L	Lincoln, E
Beatty, E	Listowell, E
Bicester, L	Londonderry, M
Bolingbroke and St John, V	Lovat, L
Burden, L	Lucan, E
Catto, L	Lyveden, L
Churchill, V	Macdonald of Gwaenysgor, L
Citrine, L	Malvern, V
Conyngham, M	Marchamley, L
Craven, E	Monck, V
Crawshaw, L	Morris, L
Croft, L	Orkney, E
Darwen, L	Piercy, L
de Clifford, L	Powerscourt, L
De Ros, L	Revelstoke, L
de Villiers, L	Rochdale, L
Delamere, L	Rollo, L
Ducie, E	Rootes, L
Dunmore, E	Sherfield, L
Dysart, C	Simon of Wythenshawe, L
Elphinstone, L	Sinclair of Cleeve, L
Glendevon, L	Sinha, L
Granville, E	Sligo, M
Greenhill, L	Strang, L
Gretton, L	Strathspey, L
Harris, L	Sysonby, L
Hatherton, L	Tankerville, E
Herries, Ly	Tedder, L
Howick of Glendale, L	Thomson of Fleet, L
Inverforth, L	Westwood, L
Kenswood, L	Wharncliffe, E
Lambert, V	Wilson, L

PEERS ON LEAVE OF ABSENCE

The following is a list of Peers on Leave of Absence (as at 1st March 1998)

Baden-Powell, L
Baillieu, L
Bessborough, E
Borwick, L
Boyd of Merton, L
Bridport, V
Brooke and Warwick, E
Brook of Ystradfellte, Bs
Brownlow, L
Chatfield, L
Cobham, V
Darling, L
De Mauley, L
Deramore, L
Dudley, Bs
Elystan-Morgan, L
Esher, V
Greenwood, V
Harrington, E
Hazlerigg, L
Herschell, L
Hill, V
Hollenden, L
Howard de Walden, L
Howard of Penrith, L
Jersey, E
Kensington, L
Latham, L

Leinster, D
Lilford, L
Maclay, L
Margresson, V
Meath, E
Melchett, L
Milford, L
Moncrieff, L
Norwich, V
Oranmore and Browne, L
Plymouth, E
Queensberry, M
Ravensworth, L
Rayner, L
Riverdale, L
Robens of Woldingham, L
Rossmore, L
Rothes, E
Rutland, D
Ryder of Eaton Hasting, L
St Vincent, L
Saye and Sele, L
Silsoe, L
Sinclair, L
Stuart of Findhorn, V
Vernon, L
Wyfold, L

GOVERNMENT MINISTERS IN THE HOUSE OF LORDS

Notes: 1. In this section and throughout the Guide the term 'Parliamentary Secretary' is used to denote a
'Parliamentary Under Secretary of State'.
2. This list includes Government Whips.

Lord Chancellor . . . . Rt Hon Lord Irvine of Lairg QC

Lord Privy Seal and Leader of the House of Lords . . . . Rt Hon Lord Richard QC

Ministry of Agriculture, Fisheries and Food
Parliamentary Secretary . . . . Lord Donoughue

Ministry of Defence
Minister of State . . . . Rt Hon Lord Gilbert
(Minister for Defence Procurement)

Department for Education and Employment
Minister of State . . . . Baroness Blackstone

Department of the Environment, Transport and the Regions
Parliamentary Secretary . . . . Baroness Hayman *(Minister for Roads)*

Foreign and Commonwealth Office
Parliamentary Secretary . . . . Baroness Symons of Vernham Dean

Department of Health
Minister of State (and Deputy Leader of the House of Lords). . . . . . . Baroness Jay of Paddington

Home Office
Parliamentary Secretary . . . . Lord Williams of Mostyn

Lord Advocate. . . . . Rt Hon Lord Hardie QC

Northern Ireland Office
Parliamentary Secretary . . . . Lord Dubs

Scottish Office
Parliamentary Secretary . . . . Lord Sewel CBE

Department of Social Security
Parliamentary Secretary . . . . Baroness Hollis of Heigham

Solicitor General. . . . . Lord Falconer of Thoroton QC

Department of Trade and Industry
Ministers of State. . . . . Lord Clinton-Davis *(Minister for Trade)*
Lord Simon of Highbury CBE *(Minister for Trade*
and Competitiveness in Europe)

Captain of the Gentleman at Arms
(Chief Whip) . . . . Lord Carter

Captain of the Yeoman of the Guard
(Deputy Chief Whip) . . . . Lord McIntosh of Haringey

Lords in Waiting
(Government Whips) . . . . Lord Haskel
Lord Hoyle
Lord Whitty

Baronesses in Waiting
(Government Whips). . . . . Baroness Farrington of Ribbleton
Baroness Ramsay of Cartvale

LORD CHANCELLOR'S OFFICE

Selborne House, 54-60 Victoria Street, London, SW1E 6QW
Tel: (0171) 210 3000 Fax: (0171) 210 8549

House of Lords, Westminster, London, SW1A 0PW
Tel: (0171) 219 3000

Lord Chancellor . . . . Rt Hon Lord Irvine of Lairg QC
   Principal Private Secretary . . . . Ms Liz Hutchinson . . . . Tel: (0171) 219 3232
   Parliamentary Secretary
   (House of Commons) . . . . Mr Geoff Hoon MP

Permanent Secretary, Lord Chancellor's Department and
   Clerk of the Crown in Chancery . . . . . . Sir Thomas Legg KCB QC
   Private Secretary . . . . Mr L Sullivan . . . . Tel: (0171) 219 6080
Clerk of the Chamber . . . . Mr C I P Denyer . . . . Tel: (0171) 219 4687

LORD PRIVY SEAL'S OFFICE

68 Whitehall, London, SW1A 2AT
Tel: (0171) 270 0501

House of Lords, Westminster, London, SW1A 0PW
Tel: (0171) 219 3200

Lord Privy Seal and Leader of the House of Lords . . . . Rt Hon Lord Richard of
Ammanford QC
Principal Private Secretary . . . . Ms L Bainsfair
Private Secretary *(House of Lords)* . . . . Mr S Burton

Special Advisers . . . . Mr Damian Welfare
Ms Marianne Morris . . . . Tel: (0171) 219 3131/4991

GOVERNMENT SPOKESMEN IN THE HOUSE OF LORDS

The following is a list of government spokesmen by subject, including those members of the government not attached to a specific government department but who speak for it in the House of Lords.

Agriculture . . . . Lord Donoghue
Lord Carter
Lord Hoyle

Constitution . . . . Lord McIntosh of Haringey

Culture, Media and Sport . . . . Lord McIntosh of Haringey
Baroness Ramsay of Cartvale

Defence . . . . Rt Hon Lord Gilbert
Lord Hoyle

Education and Employment . . . . Baroness Blackstone
Lord Whitty

Environment, Transport and Regions . . . . Baroness Hayman
Baroness Farrington of Ribbleton

Europe . . . . Lord Whitty

Foreign and Commonwealth Affairs . . . . Baroness Symons of Vernham Dean
Lord Whitty

Health . . . . Baroness Jay of Paddington
Baroness Ramsay of Cartvale

Home Affairs . . . . Lord Williams of Mostyn
Lord Hoyle

International Development . . . . Baroness Symons of Vernham Dean
Lord Whitty

Legal Affairs . . . . Rt Hon Lord Irvine of Lairg QC
Rt Hon Lord Hardie QC
Lord Falconer of Thoroton QC
Lord McIntosh of Haringey

Northern Ireland . . . . Lord Dubs
Baroness Farrington of Ribbleton

Public Service . . . . Lord McIntosh of Haringey

Scotland . . . . Lord Sewel CBE
Baroness Farrington of Ribbleton
Baroness Ramsay of Cartvale

Social Security . . . . Baroness Hollis of Heigham
Lord Haskel

Trade and Industry . . . . Lord Clinton-Davis
Lord Simon of Highbury CBE
Lord Haskel

Treasury . . . . Lord McIntosh of Haringey
Lord Haskel

Wales . . . . Lord McIntosh of Haringey
Lord Williams of Mostyn

OPPOSITION SPOKESMEN IN THE HOUSE OF LORDS

The following is a list of Conservative Frontbench Spokesman and Whips.
Note: Peers may shadow more than one subject.

Leader . . . . Rt Hon Viscount Cranborne

Deputy Leader . . . . Rt Hon Lord Fraser of Carmyllie QC

Agriculture, Fisheries and Food . . . . Baroness Anelay of St Johns
Earl of Lindsay
Lord Luke

Constitution . . . . Rt Hon Lord Mackay of Ardbrecknish
Rt Hon Lord Fraser of Carmyllie
Rt Hon Lord Roberts of Conwy
Rt Hon Lord Mackay of Drumadoon QC
Earl of Courtown

Culture, Media and Sport . . . . Lord Skidelsky
Baroness Rawlings
Lord Luke

Defence . . . . Lord Burnham
Lord Luke

Education and Employment . . . . Rt Hon Baroness Blatch
Lord Pilkington of Oxenford
Baroness Seccombe

Environment . . . . Lord Bowness
Lord Inglewood
Earl Lindsay
Baroness Miller of Hendon
Baroness Seccombe

Foreign and Commonwealth . . . . Lord Moynihan
Baroness Rawlings

Health . . . . Earl Howe
Lord McColl of Dulwich
Baroness Miller of Hendon

Home Affairs . . . . Lord Henley
Viscount Astor
Rt Hon Lord MacKay of Drumadoon QC

International Development . . . . Lord Lucas
Baroness Rawlings

Legal Affairs . . . . Rt Hon Lord Kingsland
Rt Hon Lord Mackay of Drumadoon QC
Lord Luke

Northern Ireland . . . . Rt Hon Lord Cope of Berkeley
Baroness Seccombe

OPPOSITION SPOKESMEN IN THE HOUSE OF LORDS

Public Service . . . . Rt Hon Viscount Cranborne
Rt Hon Lord Strathclyde

Scotland . . . . Rt Hon Lord Mackay of Ardbrecknish
Rt Hon Lord Mackay of Drumadoon QC
Earl of Courtown

Social Security . . . . Rt Hon Lord Higgins
Baroness Anelay of St Johns

Trade and Industry . . . . Rt Hon Lord Fraser of Carmyllie QC
Earl of Home
Baroness Miller of Hendon

Treasury . . . . Lord Mackay of Ardbrecknish
Lord Henley
Rt Hon Lord Higgins
Earl of Home
Lord Luke

Wales . . . . Rt Hon Lord Roberts of Conwy
Baroness Anelay of St Johns

Chief Whip . . . . Rt Hon Lord Strathclyde

Deputy Opposition Chief Whip . . . . Lord Burnham

Whips . . . . Baroness Anelay of St Johns
Earl of Courtown
Lord Luke
Baroness Miller of Hendon
Baroness Rawlings
Baroness Seccombe

LIBERAL DEMOCRAT SPOKESMEN IN THE HOUSE OF LORDS

The following is a list of Liberal Democrat Front Bench Spokesmen and Whips.

Leader . . . . Rt Hon Lord Rodgers of Quarry Bank

Deputy Leader . . . . Rt Hon Lord Steel of Aikwood

Agriculture . . . . Lord Mackie of Benshie

Culture, Media and Sport . . . . Viscount Falkland

Defence . . . . Lord Wallace of Saltaire

Economic Affairs . . . . Lord Ezra

Education . . . . Lord Tope

Energy . . . . Lord Ezra

Environment
    Conservation and Countryside . . . . Lord Beaumont of Whitley
    Housing . . . . Baroness Maddock
    Local Government and Planning . . . . Baroness Hamwee
    Transport . . . . Baroness Thomas of Walliswood

Foreign Affairs . . . . Rt Hon Baroness Williams of Crosby

Health . . . . Baroness Robson of Kiddington

Home Office . . . . Lord McNally

International Development . . . . Lord Redesdale

Northern Ireland . . . . Lord Holme of Cheltenham

Scotland . . . . Lord Mackie of Benshie

Social Security . . . . Earl Russell
    Disability . . . . Lord Addington

Treasury . . . . Lord Taverne

Wales . . . . Lord Thomas of Gresford

Chief Whip . . . . Lord Harris of Greenwich

Deputy Chief Whip . . . . Viscount Falkland

LAW LORDS

The following are currently (as at 1st March 1998) Lords of Appeal in the Ordinary *(in order of seniority):*

Lord Goff of Chieveley

Lord Browne-Wilkinson

Lord Slynn of Hadley

Lord Lloyd of Berwick

Lord Nolan

Lord Nicholls of Birkenhead

Lord Steyn

Lord Hoffman

Lord Hope of Craighead

Lord Clyde

Lord Hutton

Lord Saville of Newdigate

The following peers are also eligible to hear appeals:

Lord Bingham of Cornhill *(Lord Chief Justice)*

Lord Cameron of Lochbroom

Lord Cooke of Thorndon

Lord Griffiths

Lord Irvine of Lairg *(Lord Chancellor)*

Lord Jauncey of Tullichettle

Lord McCluskey

Lord McKay of Cleshfern

Lord McKenzie-Stuart

Lord Mustill

Lord Rodger of Earlsferry

Lord Woolf *(Master of the Rolls)*

SPEAKER AND DEPUTY SPEAKERS

Speaker and Deputy Speakers

The Lord Chancellor, Rt Hon Lord Irvine of Lairg QC, is effectively the Speaker of the House of Lords.

There is a Panel of Deputy Speakers, comprising the following:

Rt Hon Lord Aberdare
Viscount Allenby of Megiddo
Rt Hon Lord Ampthill
Lord Boston of Faversham
Lord Broadbridge
Lord Brougham and Vaux
Lord Burnham
Rt Hon Lord Cocks of Hartcliffe
Baroness Cox
Rt Hon Lord Dean of Harptree
Lord Elliott of Morpeth
Lord Geraint
Lord Graham of Edmonton
Rt Hon Lord Hailsham of St Marylebone

Baroness Hooper
Lord Inglewood
Rt Hon Earl of Listowell
Baroness Lockwood
Lord Lyell
Lord McColl of Dulwich
Rt Hon Lord Moston of Lindisfarne
Baroness Nicol
Viscount Oxfuird
Viscount St Davids
Baroness Serota
Lord Skelmersdale
Lord Tordoff

Note: The above Panel was commissioned in May 1995. The Earl of Listowell is currently without a Writ of Summons.

Chairman and Deputy Chairmen

The Chairman of Committees is Lord Boston of Faversham. The Principal Deputy Chairman of Committees is Lord Tordoff.

There is also a panel of Deputy Chairmen, comprising the following:

Rt Hon Lord Aberdare
Viscount Allenby of Megiddo
Rt Hon Lord Ampthill
Lord Broadbridge
Lord Brougham and Vaux
Lord Burnham
Lord Carter
Lord Chesham
Rt Hon Lord Cocks of Hartcliffe
Baroness Cox
Rt Hon Lord Dean of Harptree
Lord Elliott of Morpeth
Lord Elton
Lord Geraint
Lord Graham of Edmonton

Baroness Hooper
Baroness Lockwood
Lord Lyell
Lord McColl of Dulwich
Lord McIntosh of Harringey
Countess of Mar
Rt Hon Lord Marton of Lindisfarne
Baroness Nichol
Viscount Oxfuird
Viscount St Davids
Baroness Serota
Lord Skelmersdale
Lord Strabolgi
Rt Hon Lord Strathclyde
Baroness Turner of Camden

HOUSE OF LORDS STAFF

Senior officials of the House of Lords are listed below:

Clerk of the Parliaments . . . . Mr J M Davies
    Personal Assistant . . . . Miss E A Murray

Clerk Assistant and Clerk of Legislation . . . . Mr P D G Hayter

Reading Clerk and Principal Finance Officer . . Mr M G Pownall

Accountant . . . . Mr C Preece

Clerk of Committees . . . . Mr D R Beamish

Computer Executive . . . . Mr J O'Meara

Establishment Officer . . . . Mr R H Walters

Clerk of the Journals . . . . Mr B P Keith

Fourth Clerk at the Table (Judicial) and
    Registrar of Lords' Interests . . . . Mr J A Vallace White

Librarian . . . . Mr D L Jones

Editor of Official Report (Hansard) . . . . Mrs M E E C Villiers

Clerk of Private Bills . . . . Dr F P Tudor

Clerk of Public Bills . . . . Mr E C Ollard

Clerk of the Records . . . . Mr D J Johnson

Gentleman Usher of the Black Rod and
    Serjeant-at-Arms . . . . General Sir Edward Jones

Yeoman Usher of the Black Rod and
    Serjeant-at-Arms . . . . Air Vice-Marshal D R Hawkins

Administration Officer . . . . Brigadier A J Mc D Clark

Staff Superintendent . . . . Major A M Charlesworth

Note: The Office of the Crown in Chancery comes under the Lord Chancellor's Department see page 73.

HOUSE OF LORDS COMMITTEES

EUROPEAN COMMUNITIES COMMITTEE

Lord Tordoff *(Chairman)*
Lord Barnett
Lord Berkeley
Lord Borrie
Lord Bridges
Lord Elis-Thomas
Lord Geddes
Lord Gisborough
Lord Haslam
Baroness Hilton of Eggardon
Lord Hoffman
Lord Hussey of North Bradley
Lord Marsh
Lord Reay
Lord Wallace of Saltaire
Lord Walpole
Baroness Williams of Crosby
Lord Willoughby de Broke

Clerk: Mr D R Beamish

Legal Adviser: Dr C S Kerse

SUB-COMMITTEES OF THE EUROPEAN COMMUNITIES COMMITTEE

Note: Sub-Committees are chaired by a member of the main committee, and include some members of the main committee plus some co-opted members. Further members may be co-opted for particular enquiries.

A. Economic and Financial Affairs, Trade and External Relations

Lord Barnett *(Chairman)*
Lord Ashburton
Lord Boardman
Lord Dahrendorf
Lord Desai
Lord Grenfell
Lord Hussey of North Bradley
Lord Randall of St Budeaux
Lord Renton of Mount Harry
Lord St John of Bletso
Lord Shaw of Northstead
Baroness Williams of Crosby

Clerk: Mr J L Goddard

B. Energy, Industry and Transport

Lord Geddes *(Chairman)*
Lord Berkeley
Baroness Dean of Thornton-le-Fylde
Lord Haslam
Lord Howell of Guildford
Lord Marsh
Lord Methuen
Lord Paul
Lord Skelmersdale
Lord Thomas of Macclesfield

Clerk: Miss K S Ball

C. Environment, Public Health and Consumer Protection

Baroness Hilton of Eggardon *(Chairman)*
Earl of Cranbrook
Lord Elis-Thomas
Lord Hughes of Woodside
Lord Judd
Lord Lewis of Newnham
Earl of Lindsay
Lord Mackie of Benshie
Countess of Mar
Lord Middleton
Lord Walpole
Baroness Wilcox

Clerk: Mr T E Radice

D. Agriculture, Fisheries and Food

Lord Reay *(Chairman)*
Lord Gallacher
Lord Gisborough
Lord Grantchester
Lord Jopling
Lord Moran
Lord Rathcavan
Lord Redesdale
Baroness Robson of Kiddington
Lord Wade of Chorlton
Lord Willoughby de Broke
Baroness Young of Old Scone

Clerk: Mr A J MacKensie

HOUSE OF LORDS COMMITTEES

E. Law and Institutions
Lord Hoffman *(Chairman)*
Baroness Anelay of St Johns
Lord Borrie
Baroness Elles
Lord Goodhart
Lord Hacking
Lord Nathan
Lord Plant of Highfield
Lord Wedderburn of Charlton
Lord Wigoder

Clerk: Mrs T E Radice

Legal Adviser: Dr C S Kerse

F. Social Affairs, Education and Home Affairs
Lord Wallace of Saltaire *(Chairman)*
Baroness Amos
Lord Bridges
Lord Dhakolia
Earl of Dundee
Lord Elibank
Lord Inglewood
Lord Lester of Herne Hill
Lord Pilkington of Oxenford
Lord Rix
Baroness Turner of Camden
Lord Watson of Invergowrie

Clerk: Mrs M B Bloor

SCIENCE AND TECHNOLOGY COMMITTEE
Lord Phillips of Ellesmere *(Chairman)*
Lord Carmichael of Kelvingrove
Lord Craig of Radley
Lord Dixon-Smith
Lord Flowers
Lord Gregson
Baroness Hogg
Lord Howie of Troon
Lord Jenkin of Roding
Lord Kirkwood
Lord Perry of Walton
Baroness Platt of Writtle
Lord Porter of Luddenham
Lord Soulsby of Swaffham Prior
Lord Tombs
Lord Winston

Clerk: Mr A Makower

The Committee has two Sub-committees, comprising some members of the main Committee plus additional co-opted members.

Sub-Committee I: Cannabis

Lord Perry of Walton *(Chairman)*
Lord Butterfield
Lord Carmichael of Kelvingrove
Lord Dixon-Smith
Lord Kirkwood
Lord Nathan
Lord Porter of Luddenham
Lord Rea
Lord Soulsby of Swaffham Prior
Lord Walton of Detchant
Lord Winston

Sub-Committee II: Management of Nuclear Waste

Lord Phillips of Ellesmere *(Chairman)*
Lord Craig of Radley
Lord Cranbrook
Lord Flowers
Lord Gregson
Baroness Hogg
Lord Howie of Troon
Lord Jenkins of Roding
Baroness Nicol
Baroness Platt of Writtle
Lord Tombs

Clerk: Mr D Rolt

HOUSE OF LORDS COMMITTEES

COMMITTEE ON THE PUBLIC SERVICE

Note: The Committee's terms of reference are:
"To consider the present condition and future development of the Public Service in Great Britain with particular regard to the effectiveness of recent and continuing changes and their impact on standards of conduct and service in the public interest. For the purposes of the Select Committee, the Public Service should be deemed to exclude local government, the National Health Service, schools and institution of higher and further education, and to include all Government Departments, trusts and other organisation created by or working for the public service."

Lord Slynn of Hadley *(Chairman)*
Lord Brabazon of Tara
Lord Croham
Lord Cuckney
Lord Gillmore of Thamesfield
Lord Hayhoe
Lord Lane of Horsell
Lord McNally
Lord Merlyn-Rees
Earl Russell
Baroness Serota
Baroness Turner of Camden

Clerk: Mrs M B Bloor

CEREMONY OF INTRODUCTION COMMITTEE
Lord Alexander of Weedon *(Chairman)*
Lord Ampthill
Lord Archer of Sandwell
Lord Dahrendorf
Lord Dean of Harptree
Lord Mayhew of Twysden
Lord Merlyn-Rees
Baroness Perry of Southwark

PERSONAL BILLS COMMITTEE
Lord Boston of Faversham *(Chairman)*
Lord Astor of Hever
Lord Meston
Lord Strabolgi
Lord Templeman
Lord Wilberforce

Clerk: Dr F P Tudor

HYBRID INSTRUMENTS COMMITTEE

Lord Boston of Faversham *(Chairman)*
Lord Brougham and Vaux
Lord Burnham
Lord Carmichael of Kelvingrove
Viscount Craigavon
Viscount Oxfuird
Baroness Thomas of Walliswood

Clerk: Dr F P Tudor

DELEGATED POWERS AND DE-REGULATION COMMITTEE
Lord Alexander of Weedon *(Chairman)*
Lord Ampthill
Lord Archer of Sandwell
Lord Dahrendorf
Lord Dean of Harptree
Lord Mayhew of Twysden
Lord Merlyn-Rees
Baroness Perry of Southwark

Clerk: Dr F P Tudor
Counsel: Sir James Nursaw

JOINT COMMITTEE ON STATUTORY INSTRUMENTS
Note: Joint Committee with House of Commons. Names of members from House of Lords are listed below:

Viscount Addiston
Lord Meston
Lord Prys-Davies
Lord Shaughnessy
Lord Skelmersdale
Lord Vivian
Lord Walker of Doncaster

Clerk: Mr J A Vaughan

HOUSE OF LORDS COMMITTEES

PROCEDURE COMMITTEE

Lord Boston of Faversham (Chairman)
Baroness Anelay of St Johns
Lord Brougham and Vaux
Lord Browne-Wilkinson
Earl of Caithness
Lord Carter
Lord Chesham
Viscount Cranborne
Baroness David
Earl Ferrers
Lord Fraser of Carmyllie
Lord Gladwin of Clee
Baroness Hamwee
Lord Harris of Greenwich
Lord Irvine of Lairg
Baroness Jay of Paddington
Lord Jenkins of Hillhead
Lord Mackay of Clashfern
Lord Richard
Lady Saltoun of Abernethy
Baroness Serota
Lord Skelmersdale
Lord Strathclyde
Viscount Tenby
Lord Tordoff
Lord Weatherill
Baroness Young

Clerk: Mr B P Keith

Note: The Clerk of Parliaments also sits with this Committee.

LIAISON COMMITTEE

Lord Boston of Faversham (Chairman)
Lord Allen of Abbeydale
Lord Belstead
Viscount Cranborne
Lord Jenkins of Hillhead
Lord Kimball
Lord Morris of Castle Morris
Lord Richard
Lord Weatherill
Lord Wigoder

Clerk: Mr D R Beamish

COMMITTEE OF SELECTION

Lord Boston of Faversham (Chairman)
Viscount Allenby of Megiddo
Lord Burnham
Lord Carter
Viscount Cranborne
Lord Harris of Greenwich
Lord Jenkins of Hillhead
Lord McIntosh of Haringey
Lord Richard
Lord Strathclyde
Lord Weatherill

Clerk: Mr D J Batt

STANDING ORDERS (PRIVATE BILLS) COMMITTEE

Lord Boston of Faversham (Chairman)
Lord Bridgeman
Viscount Falkland
Lord Gallacher
Viscount Hood
Earl Lloyd-George of Dwyfor
Lord Monkswell
Lord Wade of Chorlton

Clerk: Dr F P Tudor

JOINT COMMITTEE ON PARLIAMENTARY PRIVILEGE

Note: Joint Committee with the House of Commons. Names of members from the House of Lords are listed below:
Lord Nicholls of Birkenhead (Chairman)
Lord Archer of Sandwell
Lord Mayhew of Twysden
Lord Merlyn-Rees
Lord Waddington
Lord Wigoder

Clerk: Mr B P Keith

HOUSE OF LORDS COMMITTEES

COMMITTEE FOR PRIVILEGES
Lord Boston of Faversham *(Chairman)*
Lord Allen of Abbeydale
Lord Campbell of Alloway
Lord Carter
Lord Cledwyn of Penrhos
Viscount Cranborne
Lord Glenamara
Lord Jenkins of Hillhead
Lord Mowbray and Stourton
Lord Nathan
Lord Richard
Lord Strabolgi
Lord Strathclyde
Lord Weatherill
Viscount Whitelaw
Lord Wigoder

Clerk: Mr B P Keith
Clerk (Peerage Claims): Mr J A Vallance White

Note: In addition to the peers listed above, any four Lords of Appeal may sit with this Committee.

Sub-Committee (of the Committee for Privileges) on Lords Interests
Lord Griffiths *(Chairman)*
Earl Ferrers
Lord Nathan
Baroness Serota
Lord Wigoder

Clerk: Mr J A Vallance White

Note: In addition to the above, any other two Lords of Appeal may sit with this Sub-Committee.

HOUSE OF LORDS OFFICES COMMITTEE
Lord Boston of Faversham *(Chairman)*
Viscount Allenby of Megiddo
Lord Brabazon of Tara
Lord Brougham and Vaux
Lord Bruce of Donington
Earl of Caithness
Lord Carter
Lord Colwyn
Viscount Cranborne
Lord Dean of Beswick
Viscount Falkland
Lord Fraser of Carmyllie
Earl Gowrie
Lord Harris of Greenwich
Lord Irvine of Lairg
Baroness Jay of Paddington
Lord Jenkins of Hillhead
Lord Lane of Horsell
Baroness Nicol
Earl Northesk
Bishop of Oxford
Lord Renfrew of Kaimsthorn
Lord Richard
Viscount Slim
Lord Strathclyde
Lord Thomas of Walliswood
Lord Tordoff
Baroness Turner of Camden
Viscount Ullswater
Lord Weatherill

Clerk: Mr D J Batt

Note: The Clerk of Parliaments and the Gentleman Usher of the Black Rod also sit with this Committee.

HOUSE OF LORDS COMMITTEES

SUB-COMMITTEES OF THE HOUSE OF LORDS' OFFICES COMMITTEE

Administration and Works Sub-Committee
Lord Boston of Faversham *(Chairman)*
Lord Allenby of Megiddo
Lord Barclay
Lord Carter
Lord Colwyn
Baroness David
Viscount Davonport
Earl Gowrie
Lord Hankey
Lord Harris of Greenwich
Lord Methuen
Baroness Rawlings
Lord Renfrew of Kaimsthorn
Lord Strathclyde
Lord Weatherill

Clerk: Mr D J Batt

Note: The Clerk of Parliaments and the Gentleman Usher of the Black Rod also sit with this Committee.

Finance and Staff Sub-Committee
Lord Boston of Faversham *(Chairman)*
Lord Colwyn
Viscount Cranborne
Lord Gladwin of Clee
Lord Harris of Greenwich
Earl of Northesk
Lord Renfrew of Kaimsthorn
Lord Richard
Lord Rodgers of Quarry Bank
Lord Sheppard of Didgemere
Lord Weatherill
Lord Williams of Elvel

Clerk: Mr R H Walters

Note: The Clerk of Parliaments also sits with this Sub-Committee.

Library and Computers Sub-Committee
Lord Renfrew of Kaimsthorn *(Chairman)*
Lord Avebury
Lord Freyberg
Lord Hoffmann
Lord Holderness
Baroness Lockwood
Lord Lucas
Lord McIntosh of Haringey
Baroness Nicol
Baroness Platt of Writtle
Lord St John of Bletso

Clerk: Dr F P Tudor

Note: The Clerk of Parliaments also sits with this Sub-Committee.

Refreshment Sub-Committee
Lord Colwyn *(Chairman)*
Earl of Arran
Lord Burnham
Lord Carter
Baroness David
Lord Graham of Edmonton
Lord Harris of Greenwich
Lord Howell
Lord Lawrence
Lord Palmer
Viscount Thurso

Clerk: Mr R H Walters

Advisory Panel on Works of Art
Earl Gowrie *(Chairman)*
Lord Chorley
Lord Cobbold
Lord Craythorne
Viscount Falkland
Baroness Hilton of Eggardon
Lord Hindlip
Lord Morris of Castle Morris
Lord Palmer
Baroness Trumpington

Clerk: Mr D J Batt

OTHER HOUSE OF LORDS BODIES AND DELEGATIONS

THE HOUSE OF LORDS COLLECTION TRUST

The trust is a registered charity. It collects works of art, books and other material, and aims to enhance public awareness and understanding of the British political systems - past and present; with particular emphasis on the role of the House of Lords and its members.

The following peers act as trustees:
Lord Richard *(Chairman)*
Lord Boston of Faversham
Earl Gowrie

Note: The Clerk of Parliaments and the Clerk of Records are also trustees.

Secretary: Mr D J Batt

BRITISH IRISH INTER-PARLIAMENTARY BODY

This is a joint body comprising members of the House of Commons and House of Lords.

Members from the House of Lords are listed below:
Lord Alderdice *
Lord Blease
Lord Glentoran *
Lord Holme of Cheltenham
Lord Lester of Herne Hill *
Lord Lyell *
Lord Merlyn-Rees
Baroness O'Cathain *
Lord Rathcavan

*Note: * Denotes associate member*

British Clerk: Mr D G Millar

DELEGATIONS TO INTERNATIONAL ASSEMBLIES

The lists below show House of Lords members of UK delegations to international assemblies.

Parliamentary Assembly of the Council of Europe and Assembly of the Western European Union
Representatives:
Lord Kirkhill
Lord Newall
Lord Ponsonby of Shulbrede
Lord Russell-Johnston

Substitutes:
Earl of Dundee
Lord Grenfell
Lord Judd
Lord Steel of Aikwood

Secretary: Mr C A Shaw

Parliamentary Assembly of the Organisation for Security and Co-operation in Europe.
Representatives:
Viscount Montgomery of Alamein
Baroness Ramsay of Cartvale

Substitute:
Lord Jopling

Secretary: Mr C A Shaw

North Atlantic Assembly
Representatives:
Lord Gladwyn of Clee
Lord Kennet

Secretary: Mr M Hennessy

M E M B E R S   O F   T H E   H O U S E   O F   L O R D S

Notes: (i)   *Peers are listed in alphabetical order by title.*

(ii)   *Peers are listed here with their rank of peerage. However, Barons are normally addressed as Lord _____.*

(iii)   *'Succeeded' indicates the year in which the individual concerned succeeded to an hereditary peerage. 'Created' indicates the year in which the individual concerned was created a peer.*

(iv)   *In this section, and throughout the Guide, for Ministerial posts, the term 'Parliamentary Secretary' is used to denote 'Parliamentary Under Secretary of State.' For civil service posts the terms 'Deputy Secretary', 'Permanent Secretary' is used to denote 'Parliamentary Under Secretary of State.' For civil service posts the terms 'Deputy Secretary, 'Permanent Secretary' etc are used to denote 'Deputy Under Secretary of State,' 'Permanent Under Secretary of State' etc.*

(v)   *Not all peers listed are active in Parliament. Where peers have not received a Writ of Summons or are on Leave of Absence, this is indicated.*

(vi)   *For lists of Government and Opposition Spokesmen, Deputy Speakers Chairmen of Committees and peers who are members of Select Committees and other House of Lords Committee's, please see the relevant earlier sections.*

(vii)   *Information is, as far as possible, at end February 1998.*

(viii) *Individual addresses for correspondence are given for peers, where available. Where none is shown, correspondence may be addresses to the House of Lords, London, SW1A 0PW. Individual telephone numbers are also given, where available. The main switchboard number for both the House of Lords and the House of Commons is (0171) 219 3000.*

(ix)   *Where appropriate the category Professional Career also includes significant non-parliamentary/political position held by an individual peer.*

(x)   *Bulk mailshots for members of the House of Lords should be taken or sent to the Sorting Office, 9 Howick Place, London, SW1. Each mailshot to each individual peer must be addressed to an individually named peer and be in a stamped first or second class envelope. Further information on this can be obtained from telephone 0171 219 3366.*

(xi)   *The term "Type of Life Peerage" indicates a peerage created under the 1958 Life Peerages Act, except where the term Law Lord/Former Law Lord is indicated under the Appelate Restriction Act of 1876.*

A

Aberconway of Bodnant, Baron (Charles Melville McLaren)

Type of Peerage . . . . Hereditary
Political Allegiance . . . . . Conservative
Succeeded 1953
Born . . . . 16th April 1913 in London
Educated . . . . Eton
New College, Oxford
Professional Career . . . . . 1935 - 84 Director, English China Clays
(Chairman 1963-84)
1939 - 85 Director, John Brown & Co
(Chairman 1953-78)
1953 - 83 Director, National Provincial,
then National Westminster Bank
1961 - 84 President,
Royal Horticultural Society
1963 - 84 Chairman,
English China Clays Ltd
1976 - 85 Deputy Chairman,
Sun Alliance and London Insurance
Subject Interests . . . . Horticulture
Correspondence Address . . Bodnant Tal-y-Cafn, Colwyn Bay,
Clwyd, LL28 5RE
Tel: (01492) 650 200

Abercorn, Duke of (James Hamilton)

Type of Peerage . . . . Hereditary
Political Allegiance . . . . . Conservative
Born . . . . 4th July 1934
Succeeded 1979

Aberdare, Baron (Rt Hon Morys George Lyndhurst Bruce)

Type of Peerage . . . . Hereditary
Political Allegiance . . . . . Conservative
Succeeded 1957
Born . . . . 16th June 1919 in London
Political Career . . . . 1970 - 74 Minister of State, Department of
Health and Social Security
1970 - 74 Deputy Leader, House of Lords
1974 Minister without Portfolio
1974 - 75 Deputy Opposition Leader,
House of Lords
1976 - 92 Chairman of Committees,
House of Lords
1978 - 92 Chairman, Sound and Television
Broadcasting Committee, House of Lords
Deputy Speaker, House of Lords and
Deputy Chairman of Committees,
House of Lords
Subject Interests . . . . Wales, Sport, Broadcasting
Recreational Interests . . . Real Tennis and Rackets;
Chairman, The Football Trust
Correspondence Address . . House of Lords, Westminster,
London, SW1A 0PW
Tel: (0171) 219 6925

Aberdeen and Temair, Marquess of (Alastair Ninian John Gordon)

Type of Peerage . . . . Hereditary
Political Allegiance . . . . . Cross Bench
Succeeded 1984
Born . . . . 20th July 1920 in London
Educated . . . . Harrow
Camberwell School of Arts and Crafts
Professional Career . . . . . 1948 - Professional Artist
Subject Interests . . . . Visual arts, Architecture, Music,
Model ships, Royal Navy, RNLI, CPRE,
Rehabilitation of difficult school children
Recreational Interests . . . Country life
Correspondence Address . . Quicks Green, Ashampstead,
Berkshire, RG8 8SN
Tel: (01491) 671331

MEMBERS OF THE HOUSE OF LORDS

Abergavenny, Marquess (John Henry Guy Nevill)

Type of Peerage	Hereditary
Political Allegiance.....	Cross Bench
Succeeded............	1954
Born...............	8th November 1914

Abinger, Baron (James Richard Scarlett)

Type of Peerage	Hereditary
Political Allegiance.....	Conservative
Succeeded............	1943
Born...............	28th September 1914 in Datchet, Buckinghamshire
Educated	Eton College Magdalene College, Cambridge
Professional Career.....	1936 - 47 Army Officer (Royal Artillery) 1947 - 93 Farmer and Landowner 1965 - 82 Director, Pen Yr Orsedd Slate Quarries
Subject Interests........	Agriculture, Forestry, Rural conservation, Aviation
Recreational Interests ...	Field sports, Flying
Correspondence Address..	Sheepcot, 23 Queen Street, Castle Hedingham, Halstead, Essex, CO9 3HA Tel: (01787) 460388

Ackner, Baron (Rt Hon Desmond James Conrad Ackner)

Type of Peerage	Life (Former Law Lord)
Political Allegiance.....	Cross Bench
Created.............	1986
Born...............	18th September 1920 in London
Educated	Highgate School Clare College, Cambridge
Professional Career.....	1945 - 61 Barrister (QC 1961) 1968 - 70 Chairman, Bar Council 1971 - 80 High Court Judge 1980 - 86 Lord Justice of Appeal 1986 - 92 Lord of Appeal in Ordinary
Subject Interests.......	Law, Judicial Administration, Penology
Recreational Interests ...	Swimming, Gardening, Travel, Theatre
Correspondence Address..	House of Lords, Westminster, London, SW1A 0PW Tel: (0171) 219 3295 Fax: (0171) 219 2082

Acton, Baron (Richard Gerald Lyon-Dalberg-Acton)

Type of Peerage	Hereditary
Political Allegiance.....	Labour
Succeeded............	1989
Born...............	30th July 1941 in Much Wenlock, Shropshire
Educated	St George's College, Salisbury, South Rhodesia Trinity College, Oxford
Professional Career.....	1964 - 66 Management Trainee, Amalgamated Packaging Industries 1967 - 70 Trainee, Coutts and Co 1970 - 74 Director, Coutts and Co 1977 - 81 Barrister 1981 - 85 Senior Law Officer, Ministry of Justice, Zimbabwe 1986 - Writer
Subject Interests.......	Foreign and Commonwealth affairs, British–American relations, Southern Africa, Penal affairs, Mental health
Recreational Interests ...	Reading, Travel
Correspondence Address..	152 Whitehall Court, London, SW1A 2EL Tel: (0171) 839 3077 Fax: (0171) 839 3077

Addington, Baron (Dominic Bryce Hubbard)

Type of Peerage	Hereditary
Political Allegiance.....	Liberal Democrat
Succeeded............	1982
Born...............	24th August 1963
Political Career.......	1997 - Liberal Democrat Spokesman on Disability

Addison, Viscount (William Matthew Wand Addison)

Type of Peerage	Hereditary
Political Allegiance.....	Conservative
Succeeded............	1992
Born...............	13th June 1945

Ailesbury, Marquess (Michael Sydney Cedric Brudenell Bruce)

Type of Peerage	Hereditary
Political Allegiance.....	Cross Bench
Succeeded............	1974
Born...............	31st March 1926

Ailsa, Marquess of (Archibald Angus Charles Kennedy)

Type of Peerage	Hereditary
Political Allegiance.....	Conservative
Succeeded............	1994
Born...............	13th September 1956

MEMBERS OF THE HOUSE OF LORDS

Airlie, Earl of (Rt Hon David George Coke Patrick Ogilvy)

Type of Peerage	Hereditary
Political Allegiance	Cross Bench
Succeeded	1968
Born	17th May 1926 in London
Professional Career	1944 - 50 Officer, Scots Guards
	1945 Served 2nd Battalion Germany
	1947 - 48 Captain, ADC to
	High Commissioner and C-in-C Australia
	1948 - 49 Captain, ADC to
	High Commissioner and C-in-C Malaya
	1961 - 84 Director, J Henry Schroder
	Wagg and Co Ltd (Chairman 1973 - 77)
	1968 - 82 Chairman,
	Ashdown Investment Trust Ltd
	1969 - 83 Director, Scottish and
	Newcastle Breweries plc
	1977 - 84 Chairman, Schroders plc
	1983 - 93 Director,
	Royal Bank of Scotland Group
	1984 - 97 Lord Chamberlain of
	H M Household
	1984 - 97 Chancellor, Royal Victorian Order
	1985 - 89 Governor,
	Nuffield Nursing Homes Trust
	1986 - Director, Baring Stratton
	Investment Trust
	1987 - 97 Chairman, General Accident
	Fire and Life Assurance Corporation
	1989 - Lord Lieutenant of Angus
	1994 - Chancellor,
	University of Abertay, Dundee

Alanbrooke, Viscount (Albert Victor Harold Brooke)

Type of Peerage	Hereditary
Political Allegiance	Cross Bench
Born	24th November 1932
Succeeded	1972

Albemarle, Earl of (Rufus Arnold Alexis Keppel)

Type of Peerage	Hereditary
Political Allegiance	Cross Bench
Born	16th July 1965
Succeeded	1979

**Aldenham, Baron (Vicary Tyser Gibbs;
also Baron Hunsdon of Hunsdon)**

Type of Peerage	Hereditary
Political Allegiance	Conservative
Succeeded	1986
Born	9th June 1948 in Santiago, Chile
Educated	Eton
	Oriel College, Oxford
	Royal Agricultural College, Cirencester
Professional Career	1975 - 80 Stockbroker
	1980 - Farmer
	1995 - Chairman, Hertfordshire and
	Middlesex, County Landowners Association
	1996 - Chairman,
	Watling Chase Community Forest
Subject Interests	Agriculture, Local history, Wild life
Recreational Interests	Reading, Trees, Fishing, History

Alderdice, Baron (John Thomas Alderdice)

Type of Peerage	Life
Political Allegiance	Liberal Democrat
	(also Alliance Party Northern Ireland)
Created	1996
Born	28th March 1955 in Lurgan,
	Northern Ireland
Educated	Ballymena Academy
	Queen's University of Belfast
Professional Career	1978 - 79 Junior House Officer,
	Lagan Valley Hospital
	1979 - 80 Senior House Officer,
	Belfast City Hospital
	1980 - 81 Registrar,
	Whiteabbey and Holywell Hospitals
	1981 - 82 Registrar,
	Shaftesbury Square Hospital
	1982 - 83 Registrar, Child Psychiatry
	Department, Belfast
	1983 - 87 Senior Registrar in Psychotherapy,
	Belfast City Hospital
	1988 - Consultant Psychotherapist, South
	and East Belfast HSS Trust
	1990 - Hon Lecturer,
	Queen's University Belfast
	1993 - 97 Executive Medical Director,
	South and East Belfast HSS Trust
Political Career	1987 - Vice Chairman,
	Alliance Party (Northern Ireland)
	1989 - 97 Belfast City Councillor
	1992 - Vice President, Liberal International
	1994 - Leader, Alliance Group, Forum for
	Peace and Reconciliation, Dublin Castle
	1995 - Treasurer, European Liberal
	Democrat and Reform Party
	1996 - Leader, Alliance Group,
	Northern Ireland Forum
Subject Interests	Conflict Resolution, (particularly the use of
	psychoanalytic concepts applied to this field)
Recreational Interests	Reading, Music
Correspondence Address	House of Lords, Westminster, London,
	SW1A 0PW
	Tel: (0171) 219 5050
	E-mail: alderdicej@parliament.uk
	55 Knock Road, Belfast,
	Northern Ireland, BT5 6LB
	Tel: (01232) 793097/324274
	Fax: (01232) 796689
Personal Staff	Cllr Richard Good *(Personal Assistant)*
	Tel: (01232) 324274/653663

MEMBERS OF THE HOUSE OF LORDS

**Aldington, Baron (Rt Hon Toby Austin
Richard William Low KCMG, CBE, DSO)**

Type of Peerage . . . . Hereditary (First Creation)
Political Allegiance . . . . . Conservative
Born . . . . 25th May 1914 in London
Created 1962
Educated . . . . Winchester College
New College, Oxford
Professional Career . . . . . 1939 - Barrister
1944 - 45 Brigadier, BGS 5 Corps Italy
1964 - 68 Chairman, GEC
1964 - 76 Chairman, Grindlays Bank plc
1967 - 85 Director, Lloyds Bank
1968 - 84 Deputy Chairman, GEC
1969 - 84 Director, Citicorp
1971 - 77 Chairman,
Port of London Authority
1971 - 85 Chairman, Sun Alliance and
London Insurance Company
1977 - 85 Chairman, Westland Aircraft
1986 - 89 President,
British Standards Institute
Political Career . . . . 1945 - 62 MP (Conservative) for
Blackpool North
1951 - 54 Parliamentary Secretary,
Ministry of Supply
1954 - 57 Minister of State, Board of Trade
1957 - 61 Chairman, Select Committee on
Nationalised Industries, House of Commons
1959 - 63 Deputy Chairman, Conservative
Party Organisation
1984 - 85 Chairman, Select Committee on
Overseas Trade, House of Lords
1990 - 93 Chairman, Sub-Committee A,
European Communities Select Committee,
House of Lords
Correspondence Address . . Knoll Farm, Aldington, Ashford,
Kent, TN25 7BY
Tel: (01233) 720292 Fax: (01233) 721243

Alexander of Tunis, Earl (Shane William Desmond Alexander)

Type of Peerage . . . . Hereditary
Political Allegiance . . . . . Conservative
Born . . . . 30th June 1935 in London
Succeeded 1969

Alexander of Weedon, Baron (Robert Scott Alexander QC)

Type of Peerage . . . . Life
Political Allegiance . . . . . Conservative
Created 1988
Born . . . . 5th September 1936 in
Newcastle-under-Lyme, Staffordshire
Educated . . . . Brighton College
King's College, Cambridge
Professional Career . . . . . 1961 - 89 Barrister (QC 1973)
1985 - 86 Chairman, Bar Council
1987 - 89 Chairman, Panel on
Takeover and Mergers
1989 - Chairman, National
Westminster Bank
Political Career . . . . 1995 - Chairman, Delegated Powers Scrutiny
Committee, House of Lords
Subject Interests . . . . Arts, Finance, Law
Recreational Interests . . . Theatre, Tennis, Gardens, the Arts
Correspondence Address . . Chairman's Office, NatWest Group,
41 Lothbury, London, EC2P 2BP
Tel: (0171) 726 1030 Fax: (0171) 726 1144
28 Blomfield Road, London, W9 1AA
Fax: (0171) 266 1657
Personal Staff . . . . Miss Jane Erith *(Secretary)*
Tel: (0171) 726 1030

Allen of Abbeydale, Baron (Philip Allen)

Type of Peerage . . . . Life
Political Allegiance . . . . . Cross Bench
Created 1976
Born . . . . 8th July 1912 in Sheffield, Yorkshire
Educated . . . . King Edward VII School, Sheffield
Queens' College, Cambridge
Professional Career . . . . . 1934 - 66 Civil Servant, including posts in
the Home Office, the War Cabinet Office
and Ministry of Housing and Local
Government
1963 - 66 Second Permanent Secretary,
H M Treasury
1966 - 72 Permanent Secretary, Home Office
1973 - 77 Chairman, National Council of
Social Service
1973 - 78 Chairman, Occupational
Pensions Board
1973 - 78 Member, Royal Commission on
Liability Compensation for Personal Injury
1973 - 91 Member, Security Commission
1974 - 76 Member, Royal Commission on
Standards of Conduct in Public Life
1975 Chief Counting Officer,
EEC Referendum
1977 - 85 Chairman, Gaming Board
1978 - 82 Member, Tribunal of Inquiry into
Crown Agents
Parliamentary Career . . . 1977 - 78 Chairman, Select Committee on a
Bill of Rights, House of Lords

MEMBERS OF THE HOUSE OF LORDS

Allenby of Megiddo, Viscount
(Michael Jaffray Hynman Allenby)

Type of Peerage . . . . Hereditary
Political Allegiance . . . . . Cross Bench
Succeeded 1984
Born . . . . 20th April 1931 in Camberley, Surrey
Educated . . . . Eton
                                   Royal Military Academy, Sandhurst
Professional Career . . . . . 1956 - 58 ADC to Governor, Cyprus
                                   1967 - 70 Brigade Major, 51 Brigade
                                   1974 - 77 Commanding Office,
                                        Royal Yeomanry, Territorial Army
                                   1977 - 79 CSOI Instructor,
                                        Nigerian Staff College
Political Career . . . . 1992 - Deputy Speaker and Deputy
                                        Chairman of Committees, House of Lords
Subject Interests . . . . Defence, Animal welfare
Recreational Interests . . . Horses, Sailing
Correspondence Address . . House of Lords, Westminster,
                                   London, SW1A 0PW
                                   Tel: (0171) 219 3497/5353
                                   Fax: (0171) 219 5979
                                   Newnham Lodge, Newnham, Hook,
                                   Hampshire, RG27 9AJ
                                   Tel: (01256) 762689 Fax: (01256) 760064

Allendale, Viscount (Wentworth Hubert Charles Beaumont)

Type of Peerage . . . . Hereditary
Political Allegiance . . . . . Conservative
Succeeded 1984
Born . . . . 20th April 1931

Alport, Baron (Rt Hon Cuthbert James McCall Alport TD)

Type of Peerage . . . . Life
Political Allegiance . . . . . None ("Independent Conservative")
Born . . . . 22nd March 1912 in Johannesburg,
                                   South Africa
Created 1961
Educated . . . . Haileybury
                                   Pembroke College, Cambridge
Professional Career . . . . . 1935 - 37 Barrister
                                   1939 - 45 War Service,
                                        (Hon Lieutenant-Colonel)
                                   1953 - 55 Chairman, Joint East and
                                        Central African Board
                                   1954 - 55 Governor, Charing Cross Hospital
                                   1961 - 63 British High Commissioner,
                                        Federation of Rhodesia and Nyasaland
                                   1967 British Government Representative to
                                        Rhodesia
                                   1972 - 79 Pro Chancellor, City University
                                   1978 - 91 President, Minories Art Gallery,
                                        Colchester
Political Career . . . . 1945 - 50 Director, Conservative
                                        Political Centre
                                   1950 - 61 Conservative MP for Colchester
                                   1955 - 57 Assistant Postmaster-General
                                   1957 - 59 Parliamentary Secretary,
                                        Commonwealth Relations Office
                                   1959 - 61 Minister of State,
                                        Commonwealth Relations Office
                                   1971 - 94 Deputy Speaker, House of Lords
Subject Interests . . . . Commonwealth affairs
Correspondence Address . . The Cross House, Layer De La Haye,
                                   Colchester, Essex, CO2 0JG
                                   Tel: (01206) 734217

Alton of Liverpool, Baron (David Patrick Paul Alton)

Type of Peerage . . . . Life
Political Allegiance . . . . . Cross Bench
Created 1997
Born . . . . 15th March 1951 in Bow, London
Educated . . . . St Edmund Campion School, Essex
                                   Christ's College, Liverpool
Professional Career . . . . . 1972 - 74 Teacher,
                                        Lancashire Education Authority
                                   1974 - 79 Teacher of Special Needs
                                        Children, Sefton
                                   1994 President, Liverpool USPCC
                                   1997 - Chairman, Merseyside Council of
                                        Voluntary Service
                                   1997 - Professor of Citizenship,
                                        Liverpool John Moores University
Political Career . . . . 1969 - 72 Chairman South Liverpool
                                        Young Liberals
                                   1972 - 73 Chairman North West
                                        Young Liberals
                                   1972 - 80 Liverpool City Councillor
                                        (Deputy Leader 1978)
                                   1973 - 77 Merseyside County Councillor
                                   1979 - 83 MP (Liberal) for
                                        Liverpool Edge Hill
                                   1983 - 97 MP (Liberal and Liberal
                                        Democrat) for Liverpool Mossley Hill
                                   1986 Liberal Chief Whip
                                   1987 - 88 Liberal Northern Ireland
                                        Spokesman
                                   1995 - 96 Member, Parliamentary
                                        Committee of Privileges
                                   1997 - Treasurer: Land Mines Eradication
                                        Group, Pro-Life Group, and All Party
                                        Church Colleges Group
Subject Interests . . . . Pro-life, Inner cities, Northern Ireland,
                                   Human rights, Citizenship
Recreational Interests . . . Walking, Gardening, Reading
Correspondence Address . . Laund House, 25 North Mossley Hill Road,
                                   Liverpool, L18 8BL
                                   Tel: (0151) 724 6106 Fax: (0151) 231 3853
                                   Foundation for Citizenship, Liverpool
                                   John Moores University, Roscoe Court,
                                   Rodney Street, Liverpool, L5 5UX
                                   Tel: (0151) 231 3852 Fax: (0151) 231 3853
Personal Staff . . . . Mrs Barbara Mare *(Administrator/Secretary)*
                                   Tel: (0151) 231 3852

Alvingham, Baron (Major-General Robert Guy
Eardley Yerburgh CBE)

Type of Peerage . . . . Hereditary
Political Allegiance . . . . . None
Succeeded 1955
Born . . . . 16th December 1926 in Chelsea, London
Professional Career . . . . . 1945 - 81 Regular Soldier
Recreational Interests . . . Golf, Fishing, Shooting, Trees, Music,
                                   Service charities
Correspondence Address . . Bix Hall, Henley-on-Thames,
                                   Oxfordshire, R69 6BW

MEMBERS OF THE HOUSE OF LORDS

Amherst of Hackney, Baron (William Hugh Cecil)

Type of Peerage	Hereditary
Political Allegiance	Cross Bench
Born	28th December 1940 in Norfolk
Succeeded	1980
Educated	Eton College
Professional Career	1968 - Member Baltic Exchange
	1975 - 90 Director, E A Gibson Shipbrokers Ltd
	1994 - 97 Director, Seascope Sale and Purchase Ltd
	1995 - Director, Short Sea Europe Ltd.
Parliamentary Interests	Shipping, Commercial fishing, the New Forest
Recreational Interests	Sailing (Vice-Commodore, Royal Yacht Squadron)
Correspondence Address	Hillside House, Hyde, Near Fordingbridge, Hampshire, GP6 2HD
	Tel: (01425) 654316 Mobile: (0860) 204395
	Fax: (01425) 655483/(0171) 235 2027

Amos, Baroness (Valerie Amos)

Type of Peerage	Life
Political Allegiance	Labour
Born	13th March 1954 in Guyana
Created	1997
Educated	Townley Grammar School for Girls
	University of Warwick
	University of Birmingham
Professional Career	1989 - 94 Chief Executive, Equal Opportunities Commission
	1994 - 95 Managing Director, Quality and Equality
	1995 - Director, Amos Fraser Bernard
Subject Interests	Employment, Health, Human rights, Equal opportunities, International Development, Home Affairs
Correspondence Address	House of Lords, Westminster, London, SW1A 0PW
	Tel: (01444) 400662 Fax: (01444) 400662
Personal Staff	Ms Veronica Stewart (Secretary)

Ampthill, Baron (Rt Hon Geoffrey Denis Erskine Russel CBE)

Type of Peerage	Hereditary
Political Allegiance	Cross Bench
Succeeded	1973
Born	15th October 1921
Educated	Stowe
Professional Career	1941 - 46 Irish Guards (Captain, 1944)
	1947 - 51 General Manager, Fortnum and Mason
	1951 - 64 Chairman, New Providence Hotel Co Ltd
	1953 - 81 Managing Director of various theatre owning and production companies
	1980 - 87 Director, Dualvest plc
	1981 - 96 Director, United Newspapers/ United News and Media (Deputy Chairman 1991 - 96)
	1985 - Director, Express Newspapers
	1991 - 96 Deputy Chairman, United Newspapers
Political Career	1980 - 92 Deputy Chairman of Committees, House of Lords
	1983 - 94 Deputy Speaker, House of Lords
	1987 Chairman, Select Committee on the Channel Tunnel Bill, House of Lords
	1992 - 94 Chairman of Committees, House of Lords
	1996 Chairman, Select Committee on the Channel Tunnel Rail Link
Correspondence Address	6 North Court, Great Peter Street, London, SW1P 3LL

Amwell, Baron (Keith Norman Montague)

Type of Peerage	Hereditary
Political Allegiance	Cross Bench
Succeeded	1990
Born	1st April 1943 in Hanwell, Middlesex
Professional Career	1965 - Consulting Civil Engineer
Subject Interests	Construction, Environment
Recreational Interests	Walking, Gardening, Photography

Anelay of St John, Baroness (Joyce Anne Anelay DBE)

Type of Peerage	Life
Political Allegiance	Conservative
Created	1996
Born	17th July 1947 in London
Educated	Enfield County School
	Bristol University
	University of London Institute of Education
	Brunel University
Professional Career	1969 -74 Teacher, History Department, Welsh Girls School, Ashford
	1976 - 85 Voluntary Adviser, Woking CAB
	1982 - 96 Member, Social Security Appeals Tribunals
	1985 - 87 Magistrate
	1985 - Chairman, then President, Woking CAB
	1989 - 96 Member, Social Security Advisory Committee (UK)
Political Career	1997 Opposition Whip, (Home Affairs and Social Security)
	1997 - Opposition Spokesman on Agriculture, Fisheries and Food
Subject Interests	Social Security, Home affairs
Recreational Interests	Golf, Reading
Correspondence Address	House of Lords, Westminster, London, SW1A 0PW
	Tel: (0171) 219 4858
	E-mail: anelayj@parliament.uk

Anglesey, Marquess of (George Charles Henry Victor Paget)

Type of Peerage	Hereditary
Political Allegiance	Cross Bench
Succeeded	1947
Born	8th October 1922 in London
Educated	Eton College
Professional Career	1946 Major, Royal Horse Guards
	1953 - 92 Member, Historic Buildings Council for Wales (Chairman 1977-92)
	1962 - 68 President, National Museum of Wales
	1964 - 86 Treasurer, Danilo Dolci Trust (Britain)
	1965 - 71 Member, Royal Fine Art Commission
	1966 - 84 President, Friends of Friendless Churches
	1969 - 78 Member, Redundant Churches Fund
	1973 - 89 Divisional Director, (Wales) Nationwide Building Society
	1975 - 85 Vice Chairman, Welsh Committee, National Trust
	1979 - 84 President, Ancient Monuments Society
	1980 - 92 Member, National Heritage Memorial Fund
	1984 - 92 Member, Royal Commission on Historical Manuscripts
	1986 Honorary Professor, University College of Wales
Political Career	1948 - 83 President, Anglesey Conservative Association
Subject Interests	Military history, the National Trust, Historic and ancient monuments/buildings
Recreational Interests	Reading, Classical Music
Correspondence Address	Plas Newydd, Lllanfairpwll, Anglesey, LL61 6DZ

MEMBERS OF THE HOUSE OF LORDS

Annaly, Baron (Luke Richard White)

Type of Peerage	Hereditary
Political Allegiance	Conservative
Succeeded	1990
Born	29th June 1954
Political Career	1994 Government Whip (Lord in Waiting)

Annan, Baron (Noël Gilroy Annan OBE)

Type of Peerage	Life
Political Allegiance	Cross Bench
Created	1965
Born	25th December 1916 in London
Educated	Stowe School
	King's College, Cambridge
Professional Career	1944 - 56 Fellow, King's College, Cambridge
	1956 - 66 Provost, King's College, Cambridge
	1966 - 78 Provost, University College, London
	1978 - 81 Vice-Chancellor, University of London
Subject Interests	Higher Education, the Arts, Media, Foreign affairs, European Union, Censorship, Penal reform, Military intelligence
Correspondence Address	45 Ranelagh Grove, London, SW1W 8PB
	Tel: (0171) 730 4930
Personal Staff	Mrs Anne Pease *(Secretary)*
	Tel: (01235) 850030

Annandale and Hartfell, Earl of
(Patrick Andrew Wentworth Hope Johnstone)

Type of Peerage	Hereditary
Political Allegiance	Conservative
Succeeded	1985
Born	19th April 1941

Arbuthnott, Viscount (John Campbell Arbuthnott KT)

Type of Peerage	Hereditary
Political Allegiance	Cross Bench
Born	26th October 1924 in Montrose, Scotland
Succeeded	1966
Educated	Fettes College, Edinburgh
	Cambridge University
Professional Career	1949 - 79 Chartered Surveyor and Land Agent
	1969 - 75 Chairman, Red Deer Commission
	1979 - 97 Company Director
	1980 - 85 Deputy Chairman, Nature Conservancy Council
	1984 - 87 Chairman, Scottish Widow's Fund and Life Assurance Society
	1986 - 91 Chairman, Aberdeen and Northern Marts
Subject Interests	Land management
Recreational Interests	Countryside activities
Correspondence Address	Arbuthnott House, Laurencekirk, AB30 1PA
	Tel: (01561) 361226 Fax: (01561) 320476

Archer of Sandwell, Baron (Rt Hon Peter Kingsley Archer QC)

Type of Peerage	Life
Political Allegiance	Labour
Created	1992
Born	20th November 1926 in Wednesbury, Sandwell
Educated	Wednesbury High School
	London School of Economics
	University College, London
Professional Career	1953 - Barrister (QC 1971)
	1974 - Bencher, Grays Inn
	1980 - Recorder, Crown Court
	1992 - Chairman, Council on Tribunals
Political Career	1966 - 74 MP (Labour) for Rowley Regis and Tipton
	1974 - 79 Solicitor General
	1974 - 92 MP (Labour) for Warley West
	1981 - 82 Chief Opposition Spokesman on Legal Affairs
	1982 - 83 Chief Opposition Spokesman on Trade
	1983 - 87 Chief Opposition Spokesman on Northern Ireland
Subject Interests	Human rights, Law reform, International affairs, Disarmament
Recreational Interests	Music, Writing, Talking
Correspondence Address	7 Old School Court, Wraysbury, Staines, Middlesex, TW19 5BP
	Tel: (0171) 219 3223 / (01784) 483136
	Fax: (01784) 483136

Archer of Weston-Super-Mare, Baron
(Jeffrey Howard Archer)

Type of Peerage	Life
Political Allegiance	Conservative
Created	1992
Born	15th April 1940 in London
Educated	Wellington School
	Brasenose College, Oxford
Professional Career	1975 - Author
Political Career	1966 - 70 Member, Greater London Council
	1969 - 74 Conservative MP for Louth
	1985 - 86 Deputy Chairman, Conservative Party
Subject Interests	Politics, Writing, Art
Correspondence Address	The Penthouse, 93 Albert Embankment, London, SE1 7JY
Personal Staff	Ms Alison Prince *(Personal Assistant)*

Argyll, Duke of (Ian Campbell)

Type of Peerage	Hereditary
Political Allegiance	Conservative
Succeeded	1973
Born	28th August 1937
Correspondence Address	Inveraray Castle, Argyll, Scotland, PA32 8XF
	Tel: (01499) 302203 Fax: (01499) 302421

MEMBERS OF THE HOUSE OF LORDS

Armstrong of Ilminster, Baron
    (Robert Temple Armstrong GCB)

Type of Peerage . . . . Life
Political Allegiance . . . . . Cross Bench
Created 1988
Born . . . . 30th March 1927 in Oxford
Educated . . . . Eton College
                 Christ Church, Oxford
Professional Career . . . . . 1950 - 64 Civil Service
           (various posts in HM Treasury)
           1964 - 66 Assistant Secretary,
           Cabinet Office
           1967 - 68 Assistant Secretary, H M Treasury
           1968 - 70 Under Secretary, H M Treasury
           1970 - 75 Principal Private Secretary to the
           Prime Minister (Rt Hon Edward Heath MP
           and subsequently Rt Hon Harold
           Wilson MP)
           1975 - 77 Deputy Secretary, Home Office
           1977 - 79 Permanent Secretary, Home Office
           1979 - 87 Cabinet Secretary
           1981 - 87 Head of the Home Civil Service
           1988 - 97 Chairman, Board of Trustees,
           Victoria and Albert Museum
           1988 - Chairman, Royal Academy of
           Music Foundation
           1991 - 95 Director, Carlton Television Ltd
           1994 - Chancellor, Hull University
Subject Interests . . . . Arts, (especially music),
                 Public administration,
                 (particularly the Civil Service)
Recreational Interests . . . Music
Correspondence Address . . House of Lords, Westminster,
                 London, SW1A 0PW

Arran, Earl of (Arthur Desmond Colquhoun Gore)

Type of Peerage . . . . Hereditary
Political Allegiance . . . . . Conservative
Succeeded 1983
Born . . . . 14th July 1938 in London
Educated . . . . Eton College
                 Balliol College, Oxford
Political Career . . . . 1987 - 89 Government Whip,
           (Lord in Waiting)
           1989 - 92 Parliamentary Secretary,
           Ministry of Defence (Minister for the
           Armed Forces)
           1992 - 94 Parliamentary Secretary,
           Northern Ireland Office
           1994 Parliamentary Secretary,
           Department of Environment
           1994 - 95 Government Deputy Chief Whip,
           House of Lords
Recreational Interests . . . Field sports, Tennis, Croquet, Gardening

Ashbourne, Baron (Edward Barry Greynville Gibson)

Type of Peerage . . . . Hereditary
Political Allegiance . . . . . Conservative
Succeeded 1983
Born . . . . 28th January 1933 in Malta
Educated . . . . Rugby School
                 Royal Naval Staff College
Professional Career . . . . . 1951 - 72 Royal Navy
           1972 - 73 Kitcat and Aitken (Stockbrokers)
           1973 - 76 Vickers, da Costa and Co Ltd
           (Stockbrokers)
           1976 - 79 Kitcat and Aitken (Stockbrokers)
           1979 - 81 Save and Prosper Group
           1981 - 88 GT Management
           1989 - 93 Civil Servant, Ministry of Defence
Political Career . . . . 1995 - Chairman, All Party Royal Yacht
           Parliamentary Group
           1997 - Chairman, Lords and Commons
           Family and Child Protection Group
Subject Interests . . . . Defence, Christian/Ethical issues
Recreational Interests . . . Gardening, Sailing
Correspondence Address . . House of Lords, Westminster,
                 London, SW1A 0PW
                 Tel: (0171) 219 5899 Fax: (0171) 219 5979
                 Colebrook Barn, East Harting Farm,
                 Petersfield, GU31 5LV
                 Tel: (01730) 825655
Personal Staff . . . . Francis Pym *(Researcher)*
                 Tel: (01444) 881877

Ashburton, Baron (John Francis Harcourt Baring KG)

Type of Peerage . . . . Hereditary
Political Allegiance . . . . . Cross Bench
Born . . . . 2nd November 1928
Succeeded 1991

Ashcombe, Baron (Henry Edward Cubitt)

Type of Peerage . . . . Hereditary
Born . . . . 31st March 1924 in London
Succeeded 1962
Professional Career . . . . . 1939 - 45 RAF
           1961 - 68 Consul General (London) for
           Principality of Monaco
           1962 - 68 Chairman, Holland,
           Hannen and Cubitts
           1962 - 96 Chairman, Cubitts Estate
Subject Interest . . . . Drugs and Alcohol
Recreational Interests . . . Shooting and Falconry

Ashley of Stoke, Baron (Rt Hon Jack Ashley CH)

Type of Peerage . . . . Life
Political Allegiance . . . . . Labour
Created 1993
Born . . . . 6th December 1922 in Widnes
Professional Career . . . . . 1936 - 41 Labourer
           1941 - 42 Soldier
           1942 - 46 Crane Driver
           1946 - 51 Student, Oxford and
           Cambridge Universities
           1951 - 66 BBC Radio and
           Television Producer
Political Career . . . . 1966 - 92 Labour MP for Stoke-on
           Trent South
           1976 - 78 Member, Labour Party
           National Executive
Subject Interest . . . . Disablement, Disadvantaged people,
                 Women's rights, Health, Overseas aid
Recreational Interests . . . Tennis, Snooker

MEMBERS OF THE HOUSE OF LORDS

Ashton of Hyde, Baron (Thomas John Ashton TD)

Type of Peerage	Hereditary
Political Allegiance	Cross Bench
Born	19th November 1926 in London
Succeeded	1983
Educated	Eton
	New College, Oxford
Correspondence Address	Fir Farm, Upper Slaughter, Cheltenham, Gloucestershire, GL54 2JR
	Tel: (01451) 830652

Astor, Viscount (William Waldorf Astor)

Type of Peerage	Hereditary
Political Allegiance	Conservative
Succeeded	1973
Born	27th December 1951 in Oxford
Educated	Eton
Political Career	1990 - 93 Government Whip, (Lord in Waiting)
	1993 - 94 Parliamentary Secretary, Department of Social Security
	1994 - 95 Parliamentary Secretary, Department of National Heritage
	1997 - Opposition Spokesman on Home Affairs, House of Lords

Astor of Hever, Baron (John Jacob Astor DL)

Type of Peerage	Hereditary
Political Allegiance	Conservative
Born	16th June 1946 in London
Succeeded	1984
Educated	Eton
	Mons Officer Candidates School
Professional Career	1995 - President, Motorsport Industry Association
	1996 - President, Royal Society for the Prevention of Accidents
	1997 - Deputy Lieutenant of Kent
Political Career	1996 - Member, Executive Committee, Association of Conservative Peers
Subject Interests	Defence, Motor industry and motorsport, France, Accident prevention
Correspondence Address	Frenchstreet House, Westerham, Kent, TN16 1PW
	Tel: (01959) 562051 Fax: (01959) 561286
	E-mail: astorjj@parliament.uk
Personal Staff	Mrs Tracy Murrell *(Personal Assistant)*
	Tel: (01959) 562051

Atholl, Duke of (John Murray)

Type of Peerage	Hereditary
Without Writ of Summons	
Succeeded	1996
Born	19th January 1929

Attenborough, Baron (Richard Attenborough CBE)

Type of Peerage	Life
Political Allegiance	Labour
Created	1993
Born	29th August 1923

Attlee, Earl of (John Richard Attlee)

Type of Peerage	Hereditary
Political Allegiance	Conservative
Succeeded	1991
Born	3rd October 1956
Political Career	1997 - Opposition Whip, (Lord in Waiting)

Auckland, Baron (Robert Ian Burnard Eden)

Type of Peerage	Hereditary
Political Allegiance	None
Succeeded	1997
Born	25th June 1962

Avebury, Baron (Eric Reginald Lubbock)

Type of Peerage	Hereditary
Political Allegiance	Liberal Democrat
Succeeded	1971
Born	29th September 1928 in London
Educated	Upper Canada College
	Balliol College, Oxford
Professional Career	1949 - 50 2nd Lieutenant, Welsh Guards
	1950 - 55 Rolls Royce Ltd (Aero Engine Division)
	1958 - 60 PE Ltd (Management Consultants)
	1960 - 62 Charterhouse Group
Political Career	1962 - 70 MP (Liberal) for Orpington
	1963 - 70 Liberal Chief Whip, House of Commons
Subject Interests	Human rights, Prisons
Recreational Interests	Music, Reading
Correspondence Address	House of Lords, Westminster, London, SW1A 0PW
	Tel: (0171) 274 4617 Fax: (0171) 738 7864
	E-mail: 104125.1657@compuserve.com

Aylesford, Earl of (Charles Ian Finch-Knightley)

Type of Peerage	Hereditary
Political Allegiance	Conservative
Born	2nd November 1918 in Melbourne, Australia
Succeeded	1958
Educated	Oundle School
Professional Career	1937 - 39 Sergeant, London Scottish
	1940 - 42 Captain, Royal Scots Fusiliers
	1942 - 46 Captain, Black Watch
	1946 - 58 Secretary to Packington Estates
	1948 - Warwickshire County Magistrate
	1958 - Landowner, Packington Estate
	1964 - 74 Vice-Lieutenant, Warwickshire
	1974 - 94 Lord Lieutenant, West Midlands
Subject Interests	Water, Canals, Waste disposal
Recreational Interests	Nature conservation, Shooting, Fishing, Archery
Correspondence Address	The Old Hall, Packington, Meriden, Coventry, CV7 7HG
	Tel: (01676) 523273
	Office Tel: (01676) 522020

MEMBERS OF THE HOUSE OF LORDS

B

Baden-Powell, Baron (Robert Crause Baden-Powell)

Type of Peerage . . . . Hereditary
On Leave of Absence
Born . . . . 15th October 1936 in Johannesburg,
South Africa
Succeeded 1963
Educated . . . . Bryanston School
Professional Career . . . . . 1964 - 70 Director, City Share Trust
1964 - 84 Money Broker, M W Marshall
1965 - 70 Director, Provincial Unit Trusts
1965 - 82 Chief Scout Commissioner
1972 - 81 President, West Yorkshire
Scout Council
1974 - 88 Director, Bolton Building Society
1985 - Director, Fieldguard
1986 - 95 Director, Highline Estates
1988 - 90 London Director, Cheltenham and
Gloucester Building Society
1992 - President, Camping and
Caravanning Club
Subject Interests . . . . Equine and animal care, Youth,
International finance, Caravans and camping
Recreational Interests . . . Breeding and racing American Quarter
horses, Ballet, Opera
Correspondence Address . . Clandon Manor Farm, Back Lane, East
Clandon, Guildford, Surrey, GU4 7SA
Tel: (01483) 224262 Fax: (01483) 222087

Bagot, Baron (Heneage Charles Bagot)

Type of Peerage . . . . Hereditary
Political Allegiance . . . . . None
Succeeded 1979
Born . . . . 11th June 1914 in Tenbury Wells
Educated . . . . Harrow School
Professional Career . . . . . 1941 - 45 Service with QEO,
6th Gurkha Rifles
Plantation Interests in Sri Lanka
Subject Interests . . . . Conservation
Recreational Interests . . . Skiing, Shooting

Bagri, Baron (Raj Kumar Bagri)

Type of Peerage . . . . Life
Political Allegiance . . . . . Conservative
Created 1997
Born . . . . 24th August 1930 in Calcutta, India
Professional Career . . . . . 1976 - Chairman, Metdist Group
1993 - Non Executive Chairman,
London Metal Exchange Limited
1996 - Member, Advisory Committee,
Prince's Youth Business Trust
1997 - Member, Governing Body of School of
Oriental Studies
Subject Interests . . . . Financial Services, International trade and
industry (in particular metals and
minerals), Ethnic minorities
Recreational Interests . . . Indian classical music, Theatre,
Cricket and other sports
Correspondence Address . . House of Lords, Westminster,
London, SW1A 0AA
Metdist Limited, 80 Cannon Street,
London, EC4N 6EJ
Tel: (0171) 606 8321 Fax: (0171) 606 6650

Baillieu, Baron (James William Latham Baillieu)

Type of Peerage . . . . Hereditary
On Leave Of Absence
Succeeded 1973
Born . . . . 16th November 1950 in Hartfield,
East Sussex
Educated . . . . Radley College
Monash University, Melbourne, Australia
Professional Career . . . . . 1970 - 73 Short Service Commission
Coldstream Guards
1978 - 80 Banque Nationale de Paris
1980 - 88 Assistant Director,
Rothschild Australia Ltd
1988 - 90 Director, Manufacturers
Hanover Australia Ltd
1990 - 92 Director, Standard Chartered
Asia Ltd
1992 - 94 Assistant Director,
Credit Lyonnais Asia Ltd
1992 - Director, Anthony Baillieu and
Associates (Hong Kong) Ltd
1995 Assistant Director, Nomura
International (Hong Kong) Ltd
1996 General Director, Regent
European Securities
1996 - Director, Centre Invest Group,
Moscow
Correspondence Address . . Post International Box 148, 2 Gales
Gardens, Birbeck Street, London, E2 0EJ

Baker of Dorking, Baron (Rt Hon Kenneth Wilfred Baker CH)

Type of Peerage . . . . Life
Political Allegiance . . . . . Conservative
Created 1997
Born . . . . 3rd November 1934 in Newport
Educated . . . . St Paul's School
Magdalen College, Oxford
Political Career . . . . 1968 - 70 MP (Conservative) for Acton
(By-Election)
1970 - 83 MP (Conservative) for
St Marylebone
1972 - 74 Parliamentary Secretary,
Civil Service Department
1974 - 75 PPS to the Leader of the
Opposition, (Rt Hon Edward Heath MP)
1981 - 83 Minister of State, Department of
Industry (Minister for Information
Technology)
1983 - 97 MP (Conservative) for Mole Valley
1984 - 85 Minister for Local Government,
Department of Environment
1985 - 86 Secretary of State for the
Environment
1986 - 89 Secretary of State for Education
and Science
1989 - 90 Chancellor of the Duchy of
Lancaster and Chairman of the
Conservative Party
1990 - 92 Home Secretary
Subject Interests . . . . Communications, Education and Information
Technology
Recreational Interests . . . Reading, Writing anthologies of poetry,
Collecting political prints and cartoons, the
Museum of British History
Personal Staff . . . . Miss Kathy Hibbard
Tel: (0171) 495 0025

MEMBERS OF THE HOUSE OF LORDS

Baldwin of Bewdley, Earl of
(Edward Alfred Alexander Baldwin)

Type of Peerage . . . . Hereditary
Political Allegiance . . . . . Cross Bench
Succeeded 1976
Born . . . . 3rd January 1938 in Martley, Worcestershire
Educated . . . . Eton College
Trinity College, Cambridge
Professional Career . . . . . 1970 - 77 School Teacher
1978 - 87 Local Education Authority Officer
1990 - Chair, British Acupuncture
Accreditation Board
Subject Interests . . . . Complementary medicine, Sport, Education
Recreational Interests . . . Sport, Music
Correspondence Address . . Manor Farm House, Godstow Road,
Oxford, OX2 8AJ
Tel and Fax: (01865) 552683

Balfour, Earl of (Gerald Arthur James Balfour)

Type of Peerage . . . . Hereditary
Political Allegiance . . . . . Conservative
Succeeded 1968
Born . . . . 23rd December 1925 in Whittingehame,
Scotland
Educated . . . . Eton College
HMS Conway
Sir John Cass College, Aldgate
Professional Career . . . . . 1944 - 54 Merchant Navy
1954 - 59 Brunton Wire Mills (Musselburgh)
1959 - 69 Technical Representative in
Building Industry
1970 - Farmer
Subject Interests . . . . Scottish affairs, Meteorology, Seamanship,
Housing
Recreational Interests . . . Shooting, Yachting
Correspondence Address . . Whittingehame Tower, Haddington,
EH41 4QA
Tel: (01368) 850208
Office Tel: (01620) 860254

Balfour of Burleigh, Baron (Robert Bruce)

Type of Peerage . . . . Hereditary
Political Allegiance . . . . . Cross Bench
Succeeded 1967
Born . . . . 6th January 1927

Balfour of Inchrye, Baron (Ian Balfour)

Type of Peerage . . . . Hereditary
Political Allegiance . . . . . Cross Bench
Succeeded 1988
Born . . . . 21st December 1924 in Windsor
Educated . . . . Eton College
Magdalen College, Oxford
Professional Career . . . . . Business Consultant and Composer

Banbury of Southam, Baron (Charles William Banbury)

Type of Peerage . . . . Hereditary
Political Allegiance . . . . . Conservative
Succeeded 1981
Born . . . . 29th July 1953 in Cirencester

Barber, Baron (Rt Hon Anthony Perrinott Lysberg Barber)

Type of Peerage . . . . Life
Political Allegiance . . . . . Conservative
Created 1974
Born . . . . 4th July 1920 in Hessle, Yorkshire
Political Career . . . . 1951 - 64 MP (Conservative) for Doncaster
1955 - 57 Assistant Government Whip,
House of Commons
1957 - 58 Government Whip,
House of Commons
1958 - 59 PPS to the Prime Minister
(Rt Hon Harold MacMillan MP)
1959 - 62 Economic Secretary, HM Treasury
1962 - 63 Financial Secretary, HM Treasury
1963 - 64 Minister of Health
1965 - 74 MP (Conservative) for Altrincham
and Sale
1967 - 70 Chairman, Conservative Party
1970 Chancellor of the Duchy of Lancaster
1970 - 74 Chancellor of the Exchequer

Barber of Tewkesbury, Baron (Derek Coates Barber)

Type of Peerage . . . . Life
Political Allegiance . . . . . Cross Bench
Created 1992
Professional Career . . . . . 1946 - 72 Agricultural Adviser
1972 - 93 Consultant, Humbert Chartered
Surveyors

Barnard, Baron (Harry John Neville Vane TD)

Type of Peerage . . . . Hereditary
Political Allegiance . . . . . Cross Bench
Succeeded 1964
Born . . . . 21st September 1923

Barnett, Baron (Rt Hon Joel Barnett)

Type of Peerage . . . . Life
Political Allegiance . . . . . Labour
Created 1983
Born . . . . 14th October 1923 in Manchester
Educated . . . . Manchester Central High School
Accountancy College
Professional Career . . . . . Accountant
Political Career . . . . 1964 - 83 MP (Labour) for Heywood and
Royton
1970 - 74 Opposition Spokesman on
Treasury Matters, House of Commons
1974 - 79 Chief Secretary, HM Treasury
1979 - 83 Chairman, Public Accounts
Committee (House of Commons)
1983 - 86 Spokesman on Finance and
Economics, House of Lords
1995 - Chairman, Sub-Committee A of the
European Communities Committee,
House of Lords
Correspondence Address . . House of Lords, Westminster,
London, SW1A 0PW
Tel: (0171) 219 5440 Fax: (0161) 219 5979
Personal Staff . . . . Ms Cathy Cave *(Secretary)*
Tel: (01625) 505300

MEMBERS OF THE HOUSE OF LORDS

Basing, Baron (Neil Lutley Slater-Booth)
Type of Peerage . . . . Hereditary
Without Writ of Summons
Political Allegiance . . . . . None
Succeeded 1983
Born . . . . 16th January 1939

Bassam of Brighton, Baron (John Steven Bassam)
Type of Peerage . . . . Life
Political Allegiance . . . . . Labour
Created 1997
Born . . . . 11th June 1953 in Hull
Educated . . . . Clacton Secondary Modern School for Boys
University of Sussex
University of Kent
Professional Career . . . . . 1976 - 77 Social Worker
1979 - 83 Legal Adviser, North Lewisham
Law Centre
1983 - 84 Policy Adviser, Camden Council
1984 - 86 Policy Adviser,
Greater London Council
1986 - 87 Policy Adviser, London
Strategic Policy Unit
1988 - 97 Assistant Secretary,
Association of Metropolitan Authorities
1997 - 98 Head of Environment,
Health and Consumer Affairs,
Local Government Association
Political Career . . . . 1986 - 96 Leader, Brighton Council
1996 - Leader, Brighton and Hove Council
Subject Interests . . . . Housing, Arts, Culture, Local government,
Constitutional reform, Management issues,
Animal welfare, Human rights
Recreational Interests . . . Football, Cricket, Walking, Old churches,
the Railway system
Correspondence Address . . House of Lords, Westminster,
London, SW1A 0PW
Tel: (0171) 219 5353 Fax: (0171) 219 5959
"Longstone", 25 Church Place, Brighton,
Sussex, BN2 5JN
Tel: (01273) 609473 Fax: (01273) 291138
Personal Staff . . . . Mrs Linda Brown *(Secretary)*
Tel: (01273) 291011

Bath, Marquess of (Alexander George Thynn)
Type of Peerage . . . . Hereditary
Political Allegiance . . . . . Liberal Democrat
Succeeded 1992
Born . . . . 6th May 1932 in London
Educated . . . . Eton College
Christ Church College, Oxford
Professional Career . . . . . 1951 - 52 National Service, Life Guards
1953 - Painter and Author
Political Career . . . . 1974 Parliamentary Candidate,
Wessex Regionist Party
1979 Candidate (European Elections),
Wessex Regionist and European
Federal Party
Subject Interests . . . . Art, Music, Writing
Recreational Interests . . . Chess, Collector of Wessex artists' paintings
Correspondence Address . . Longleat House, Warminster, Wiltshire,
Wessex, BA12 7NN
Tel: (01985) 844400/844300
Fax: (01985) 844888
E-mail: lord.bath@btinternet.com
Personal Staff . . . . Mrs Sue Smith *(Secretary)*
Tel: (01985) 845426

Bath and Wells, Bishop of (Rt Rev James Lawton Thompson)
Type of Peerage . . . . Bishop
Political Allegiance . . . . . None
Born . . . . 11th August 1936
Professional Career . . . . . 1966 - 68 Curate, East Ham
1968 - 71 Chaplain, Cuddesdon College
1971 - 78 Rector, Thamesmead
1978 - 91 Bishop of Stepney
1991 - Bishop of Bath and Wells
Correspondence Address . . The Palace, Wells, BA5 2PD
Tel: (01749) 672341 Fax: (01749) 679355

Bathurst, Earl of (Henry Allen John Bathurst)
Type of Peerage . . . . Hereditary
Political Allegiance . . . . . Conservative
Succeeded 1943
Born . . . . 1st May 1927
Professional Career . . . . . 1949 - 57 Captain, Royal Gloucester
Hussars
1959 - 61 Chancellor, Primrose League
1976 - 78 President, Royal Forestry Society
1986 - 92 Director, Forestor Group
1983 - 87, 1995 - President, Association of
Professional Foresters
Political Career . . . . 1957 - 61 Government Whip,
(Lord in Waiting)
1961 - 62 Parliamentary Secretary,
Home Office

Bauer, Baron (Peter Thomas Bauer)
Type of Peerage . . . . Life
Political Allegiance . . . . . Conservative
Created 1982
Professional Career . . . . . 1960 - 83 Professor of Economics, London
School of Economics

Bearsted, Viscount (Nicholas Alan Samuel)
Type of Peerage . . . . Hereditary
Political Allegiance . . . . . Conservative
Succeeded 1966
Born . . . . 22nd January 1950

Beatty, Earl of (David Beatty)
Type of Peerage . . . . Hereditary
Without Writ of Summons
Succeeded 1972
Born . . . . 21st November 1946

Beaufort, Duke of (David Robert Somerset)
Type of Peerage . . . . Hereditary
Political Allegiance . . . . . Conservative
Succeeded 1984
Born . . . . 23rd February 1928

MEMBERS OF THE HOUSE OF LORDS

Beaumont of Whitley, Baron
  (Rev Timothy Wentworth Beaumont)
Type of Peerage . . . . Life
Political Allegiance. . . . . Liberal Democrat
Created. 1967
Born. . . . . 22nd November 1928 in London
Educated . . . . Gordonstoun School
          Christ Church, Oxford
          Westcott House, Cambridge
Professional Career . . . . . 1955 - 56 Assistant Chaplain,
          St John's Cathedral, Hong Kong
          1956 - 58 Vicar, Christ Church,
          Kowloon Tong, Hong Kong
          1960 - 64 Editor, Prism
          1963 - 68 Chairman, Studio Vista Books
          1964, 1972 - 74 Editor, New Outlook
          1965 - 70 Proprietor, New Christian
          1986 - 91 Vicar, St Philip and
          All Saints with St Luke, Kew
Political Career. . . . . . . 1962 - 63 Joint Hon Treasurer, Liberal Party
          1963 - 64 Chairman, Liberal Publications
          Department
          1965 - 66 Head of Organisation,
          Liberal Party
          1967 - 68 Chairman, Liberal Party
          1968 - 86 Liberal Education and Arts
          Spokesman, House of Lords
          1969 - 70 President, Liberal Party
          1978 - 80 Co-ordinator, The Green Alliance
          1992 - 95 Member, Liberal Democrat
          Policy Committee
          1993 - Liberal Democrat Spokesman on
          Conservation and the Countryside,
          House of Lords
Subject Interests. . . . . . . Green issues
Recreational Interests . . . Reading, Writing
Correspondence Address . . House of Lords, Westminster,
          London, SW1A OPW
          Tel: (0171) 300 3121
          40 Elms Road, London, SW4 9EX
          Tel: (0171) 498 8664

Beaverbrook, Baron (Maxwell William Humphrey Aitken)
Type of Peerage . . . . Hereditary
Political Allegiance. . . . . Conservative
Succeeded. 1985
Born. . . . . 29th December 1951 in London
Educated . . . . Charterhouse School
          Pembroke College, Cambridge
Professional Career . . . . . 1972 - 77 Beaverbrook Newspapers
          1985 - Chairman, Beaverbrook Foundation
          1988 - 92 Chairman,
          Ventech Healthcare Corp Inc
          1988 - 92 Chairman, Abbey Foster
          Medical Corp Inc
Political Career. . . . . . . 1986 - 88 Government Whip,
          (Lord in Waiting), Spokesman on
          Treasury, Trade and Industry, House of
          Lords
          1988 - 90 Deputy Treasurer,
          Conservative Party
          1990 - 92 Treasurer, Conservative Party
          1990 - 92 Hon Treasurer,
          European Democratic Union
Correspondence Address . . 11 Old Queen Street, London, SW1H 9JA
          Tel: (0171) 222 7474 Fax: (0171) 222 2198

Bedford, Duke of (John Robert Russell)
Type of Peerage . . . . Hereditary
Political Allegiance. . . . . None
Succeeded. 1953
Born. . . . . 24th May 1917

Belhaven and Stenton, Baron
  (Robert Anthony Carmichael Hamilton)
Type of Peerage . . . . Hereditary
Political Allegiance. . . . . Conservative
Succeeded. 1961
Born. . . . . 27th February 1927

Bellwin, Baron (Irwin Norman Bellow)
Type of Peerage . . . . Life
Political Allegiance. . . . . Conservative
Created. 1979
Born. . . . . 7th February 1923 in Leeds
Educated . . . . Leeds Grammar School
          Leeds University
Professional Career . . . . . 1992 - Chairman,
          North Hull Housing Action Trust
Political Career. . . . . . . 1975 - 79 Leader, Leeds City Council
          1979 - 83 Parliamentary Secretary,
          Department of Environment
          1983 - 84 Minister of State for Local
          Government
Subject Interest . . . . Local government
Recreational Interest . . . . Golf
Correspondence Address. . Woodside Lodge, Ling Lane, Scarcroft,
          Leeds, LS14 3HX
          Tel: (01132) 892908 Fax: (01132) 892213

Beloff, Baron (Max Beloff)
Type of Peerage . . . . Life
Political Allegiance. . . . . Conservative
Created. 1981
Born. . . . . 2nd July 1913 in London
Educated . . . . St Paul's School
          Corpus Christi College, Oxford
Professional Career . . . . . 1939 - 46 Assistant Lecturer in History,
          Manchester University
          1946 - 57 Fellow of Nuffield College, Oxford
          1957 - 74 Gladstone Professor of
          Government and Public Administration,
          Oxford University; Fellow of All Souls
          1974 - 79 Principal,
          University College Buckingham
Subject Interests. . . . . . . Education, Constitutional matters, Defence
Recreational Interests . . . Cricket, Opera
Correspondence Address . . House of Lords, Westminster, London,
          SW1A 0PW
          Tel: (0171) 219 6669 Fax: (0171) 219 5979
          Flat No 9, 22 Lewes Crescent, Brighton,
          BN2 1GB *(Parliamentary Recess)*
          Tel: (01273) 688622

Belper, Baron (Alexander Ronald George Strutt)
Type of Peerage . . . . Hereditary
Succeeded. 1956
Born. . . . . 23rd April 1912

MEMBERS OF THE HOUSE OF LORDS

Belstead, Baron (Rt Hon John Julian Ganzoni)

Type of Peerage	Hereditary
Political Allegiance	Conservative
Succeeded	1958
Born	30th September 1932 in Ipswich
Educated	Eton College
	Christ Church, Oxford
Professional Career	1974 - 79 Chairman, Governing Bodies
	Association of Public Schools
	1992 - 97 Chairman, Parole Board
	1994 - Lord Lieutenant of Suffolk
Political Career	1970 - 73 Parliamentary Secretary,
	Department of Education and Science
	1973 - 74 Parliamentary Secretary,
	Northern Ireland Office
	1979 - 82 Parliamentary Secretary,
	Home Office
	1982 - 83 Minister of State,
	Foreign and Commonwealth Office
	1983 - 88 Deputy Leader, House of Lords
	1983 - 87 Minister of State, Ministry of
	Agriculture, Fisheries and Food
	1987 - 88 Minister of State,
	Department of the Environment
	1988 - 90 Leader of the House of Lords and
	Lord Privy Seal
	1990 - 92 HM Paymaster General, Minister,
	Northern Ireland Office

Berkeley, Baron (Anthony Fitzhardinge Gueterbock OBE)

Type of Peerage	Hereditary
Political Allegiance	Labour
Succeeded	1992
Born	20th September 1939
Professional Career	1962 - 67 Sir Alexander Gibb and Partners
	1968 - 85 George Wimpey plc
	1985 - 96 Eurotunnel plc
	1996 - Chairman, Rail Freight Group

Berners, Baroness (Pamela Vivien Kirkham)

Type of Peerage	Hereditary
Political Allegiance	Conservative
Succeeded	1995
Born	30th September 1929 in Cheltenham
Educated	Stonor School, Melksham, Wiltshire
	Radcliffe Infirmary, Oxford
Professional Career	1951 State Registered Nurse
Subject Interests	Health, Agriculture, Arts
Recreational Interests	Reading, Gardening
Correspondence Address	Ashwellthorpe, 103 Charlton Lane,
	Cheltenham, GL53 9EE
	Tel: (01242) 519595

Bessborough, Earl of (Arthur Mountifort Longfield Ponsonby)

Type of Peerage	Hereditary
On Leave of Absence	
Succeeded	1993
Born	11th December 1912 in London
Educated	Harrow School
	Trinity College, Cambridge
Correspondence Address	Roche Court, Winterslow,
	Wiltshire, SP5 1BG
	Tel: (01980) 862204 Fax: (01980) 862447

Bethell, Baron (Nicholas William Bethell)

Type of Peerage	Hereditary
Political Allegiance	Conservative
Succeeded	1967
Born	19th July 1938
Professional Career	Freelance Writer
	1962 - 64 Editorial Staff,
	Times Literary Supplement
	1964 - 67 Script Editor, BBC Radio Drama
Political Career	1970 - 71 Government Whip,
	(Lord in Waiting)
	1975 - 94 Member of the European
	Parliament (Conservative)

Bicester, Baron (Angus Edward Vivien Smith)

Type of Peerage	Hereditary
Without Writ of Summons	
Succeeded	1968
Born	20th February 1932

Biddulph, Baron (Anthony Nicholas Colin Maitland-Biddulph)

Type of Peerage	Hereditary
Political Allegiance	Conservative
Succeeded	1988
Born	8th April 1959 in London
Educated	Cheltenham College
	Cirencester Agricultural College
	Inchbald School of Interior Design Farmer
Professional Career	1980 - 88 Interior Designer
	1988 - 97 Sporting Manager
Subject Interests	Agriculture, Economics
Recreational Interests	Fishing, Shooting, Skiing, Painting
Correspondence Address	Makerstoun House, Kelso,
	The Borders, TD5 7PA
	Tel: (01573) 460234
	8 Orbel Street, London, SW11 3NZ
	Tel: (0171) 228 9865

MEMBERS OF THE HOUSE OF LORDS

Biffen, Baron (Rt Hon William John Biffen)
Type of Peerage . . . . Life
Political Allegiance . . . . . Conservative
Created 1997
Born . . . . 3rd November 1930 in Bridgwater, Somerset
Educated . . . . Dr Morgan School, Bridgwater
Jesus College, Cambridge
Political Career . . . . 1961 - 83 MP (Conservative) for Oswestry
1965 - 66 Opposition Spokesman on
Technology
1976 Opposition Spokesman on Energy
1976 - 77 Opposition Spokesman on
Industry
1978 - 79 Opposition Spokesman on
Small Businesses
1979 - 81 Chief Secretary to the Treasury
1981 - 82 Secretary of State for Trade
1982 - 83 Lord President of the Council and
Leader of the House of Commons
1983 - 97 MP (Conservative) for
Shropshire North
1983 - 87 Lord Privy Seal and Leader of the
House of Commons
Subject Interests . . . . Economics, Europe
Correspondence Address . . Tanat House, Llanyblodwel,
Oswestry, SY10 8NQ
Tel and Fax: (01691) 828808
31 Anhart Road, London, SW11
Tel and Fax: (0171) 223 0230

Bingham of Cornhill, Baron (Rt Hon Thomas Henry Bingham)
Type of Peerage . . . . Life
Political Allegiance . . . . . Cross Bench
Created 1996
Born . . . . 13th October 1933
Educated . . . . Sedbergh School
Balliol College, Oxford
Professional Career . . . . . 1959 - Barrister (QC 1972)
1975 - 80 Recorder of the Crown Court
1980 - 86 High Court Judge,
Queen's Bench Division
1986 - 92 Lord Justice of Appeal
1992 - 96 Master of the Rolls
1996 - Lord Chief Justice
Correspondence Address . . Royal Courts of Justice, Strand, London,
WC2A 2LL
Tel: (0171) 936 6001

Birdwood, Baron (Mark William Ogilvie Birdwood)
Type of Peerage . . . . Hereditary
Political Allegiance . . . . . Conservative
Succeeded 1963
Born . . . . 23rd November 1938 in Bombay, India
Educated . . . . Radley College
Trinity College, Cambridge
Professional Career . . . . . 1986 - Chairman, Martlet Ltd
1995 - Chairman, Fiortho plc
Subject Interests . . . . Interaction between science and social
change, Industrial design, Political
structures
Correspondence Address . . Russell House, Broadway, Worcestershire,
WR12 7BO
Tel: (01386) 852583
5 Holbein Mews, London, SW1W 8NW
Tel: (0171) 730 0759/6437
Fax: (0171) 823 5962

Birkett, Baron (Michael Birkett)
Type of Peerage . . . . Hereditary
Political Allegiance . . . . . Cross Bench
Succeeded 1962
Born . . . . 22nd October 1929 in London
Educated . . . . Stowe School
Trinity College, Cambridge
Professional Career . . . . . 1953 - 73 Assistant Director, Director and
Producer in the film industry
1973 - 76 Deputy Director, National Theatre
1980 -86 Director for Recreation and the
Arts, Greater London Council
Subject Interests . . . . Arts, Environment
Recreational Interests . . . Music, Gardening
Correspondence Address . . Great Allfields, Balls Cross, Petworth,
West Sussex, GU28 9JR
Tel: (01403) 820226 Fax: (01403) 820035

Birmingham, Bishop of (Rt Rev Mark Santer)
Type of Peerage . . . . Bishop
Political Allegiance . . . . . None
Entered Lords 1994
Born . . . . 29th December 1936 in Bristol
Educated . . . . Marlborough College
Queen's College, Cambridge
Westcott House, Cambridge
Professional Career . . . . . 1963 - 67 Tutor, Cuddesdon College, Oxford
1967 - 72 Fellow and Dean of Clare College,
Cambridge
1968 - 72 Assistant Lecturer in Divinity,
University of Cambridge
1973 - 81 Principal, Westcott House,
Cambridge
1981 - 87 Bishop of Kensington
1987 - Bishop of Birmingham
Subject Interests . . . . Church unity, Health, Justice
Correspondence Address . . Bishop's Croft, Old Church Road, Harborne,
Birmingham, B17 0BG
Tel: (0121) 427 1163 Fax: (0121) 426 1322

Blackburn, Rt Rev, Bishop of (Rt Rev Alan David Chesters)
Type of Peerage . . . . Bishop
Political Allegiance . . . . . None
Entered Lords 1995
Born . . . . 26th August 1937 in Huddersfield,
Yorkshire
Educated . . . . Elland Grammar School
St Chad's College, Durham
St Catherine's College, Oxford
St Stephen's House, Oxford
Professional Career . . . . . 1962 - 66 Assistant Curate, St Anne's,
Wandsworth, London
1966 - 72 Chaplain and Head of Religious
Education, Tiffin School, Kingston-upon-
Thames
1972 - 85 Director of Education, Diocese of
Durham and Rector of Brancepeth
1985 - 89 Archdeacon of Halifax
1989 - Bishop of Blackburn
Subject Interests . . . . Ecclesiastical, Education, Transport,
Countryside
Recreational Interests . . . Railway, Walking, Blackburn Rovers,
Reading biographies
Correspondence Address . . Bishop's House, Ribchester Road,
Blackburn, BB1 9EF
Tel: (01254) 248234 Fax: (01254) 246668

MEMBERS OF THE HOUSE OF LORDS

Blackstone, Baroness (Tessa Blackstone)

Type of Peerage	Life
Political Allegiance	Labour
Created	1987
Born	27th September 1942 in London
Educated	Ware Grammar School
	London School of Economics
Professional Career	1965 - 66 Associate Lecturer, Enfield College
	1966 - 75 Lecturer, London School of Economics
	1972 - 74 Fellow, Centre for Studies in Social Policy
	1975 - 78 Adviser, Central Policy Review Staff, Cabinet Office
	1978 - 83 Professor of Educational Administration, University of London Institute of Education
	1983 - 87 Deputy Education Officer, then Clerk and Director of Education, Inner London Education Authority
	1987 - 91 Chairman, BBC General Advisory Council
	1987 - 97 Master, Birkbeck College, University of London
Political Career	1988 - 92 Opposition Spokesman on Education and Science, House of Lords
	1992 - 97 Opposition Spokesman on Foreign Affairs, House of Lords
	1997 - Minister of State, Department of Education and Science
Subject Interests	Education, Foreign policy, Social policy, the Arts
Recreational Interests	Ballet, Opera, Tennis, Cinema, Walking
Correspondence Address	Department for Education and Employment, Sanctuary Buildings, London, SW1P 3BT
	Tel: (0171) 925 6245 Fax: (0171) 925 5011

Blackwell, Baron (Norman Roy Blackwell)

Type of Peerage	Life
Political Allegiance	Conservative
Created	1997
Born	29th July 1952 in Eastcote
Educated	Latymer Upper School, Hammersmith
	Trinity College, Cambridge
	Wharton Business School, University of Pennsylvania
Professional Career	1976 - 78 Planning Unit, Plessey Co
	1978 - 95 Associate, then Partner, McKinsey & Co
	1997 - Director of Group Development, NatWest Group plc
Political Career	1986 - 87 Member of Prime Minister's Policy Unit (under Rt Hon Margaret Thatcher MP)
	1995 - 97 Head of Prime Minister's Policy Unit (under Rt Hon John Major MP)
Subject Interests	Economics, Industry and technology, Welfare, Urban regeneration
Recreational Interests	Classical Music, Walking
Correspondence Address	House of Lords, Westminster, London, SW1A 0PW
	Tel: (0171) 726 1000

Blake, Baron (Robert Norman William Blake)

Type of Peerage	Life
Political Allegiance	Conservative
Born	23rd December 1916 in Brundall, Norfolk
Created	1971
Educated	King Edward VI School, Norwich
	Magdalen College, Oxford
Professional Career	1947 - 1968 Fellow of Christ Church, Oxford
	1968 - 87 Provost of Queen's College, Oxford
Subject Interests	Political and constitutional history
Recreational Interests	Reading and Writing
Correspondence Address	Riverview House, Brundall, Norwich, NR13 5LA
	Tel: (01603) 712133

Blakenham, Viscount (Michael John Hare)

Type of Peerage	Hereditary
Political Allegiance	Conservative
Succeeded	1982
Born	25th January 1938 in London
Educated	Eton College
	Harvard University
Professional Career	1961 - 63 Lazard Brothers
	1963 - 71 Standard Industrial Group
	1972 - 77 Doulton and Co
	1978 - 83 Chief Executive, Pearson plc
	1983 - 97 Chairman, Pearson plc
	1984 - 93 Chairman, Financial Times
	1984 - 97 Partner, Lazard Partners
	1987 - Director, Sotheby's Holdings Inc
	1990 - 93 Director, MEPC plc
	1993 - Chairman, MEPC plc
	1997 - Director, Lafange SA
Correspondence Address	12 St. James's Square, London, SW1Y 4LB
	Tel: (0171) 911 5487

Blaker, Baron (Rt Hon Peter Allan Renshaw Blaker KCMG)

Type of Peerage	Life
Political Allegiance	Conservative
Created	1994
Born	4th October 1922 in Hong Kong
Educated	Shrewsbury School
	Trinity College, Toronto
	New College, Oxford
Professional Career	1942 - 46 Canadian Army
	1952 - 53 Barrister
	1953 - 64 HM Foreign Service
Political Career	1964 - 92 MP (Conservative) for Blackpool South
	1966 - 67 Opposition Whip, House of Commons
	1970 - 72 PPS to Chancellor of Exchequer (Rt Hon Anthony Barber MP)
	1972 - 74 Parliamentary Secretary, (Army), Ministry of Defence
	1974 - Parliamentary Secretary, Foreign and Commonwealth Office
	1979 - 81 Minister of State, Foreign and Commonwealth Office
	1981 - 83 Minister of State, Ministry of Defence, (Minister for the Armed Forces)
Subject Interests	Foreign affairs, Defence
Recreational Interests	Sailing and Opera
Correspondence Address	Woodsland Farm, Lindfield, Haywards Heath, West Sussex, RH16 2QT
	Tel: (01444) 482381 Fax: (01444) 482264

MEMBERS OF THE HOUSE OF LORDS

Blatch, Baroness (Rt Hon Emily May Blatch CBE)

Type of Peerage	Life
Political Allegiance	Conservative
Created	1987
Born	24th July 1937 in Birkenhead
Educated	Prenton Secondary School for Girls
	Huntingdonshire College, Huntingdon
Professional Career	1955 - 59 WRAF, Air Traffic Control
	1959 - 63 Ministry of Aviation
Political Career	1977 - 87 County Councillor, Cambridgeshire (Leader of Council 1981 - 85)
	1989 - 90 Government Whip (Baroness in Waiting)
	1990 - 91 Parliamentary Secretary, Department of the Environment
	1991 - 92 Minister of State, Department of the Environment
	1992 - 94 Minister of State, Department for Education
	1994 - 97 Minister of State, Home Office
	1997 - Opposition Spokesman on Education, House of Lords
Subject Interests	Education
Recreational Interests	Music, Theatre, Family

Blease, Baron (William John Blease)

Type of Peerage	Life
Political Allegiance	Labour
Created	1978
Born	28th May 1914 in Belfast
Educated	Belfast College of Technology
Professional Career	1946 - 59 Branch Manager, Co-operative Society
	1959 - 78 Trade Union Official, Irish Congress Trade Unions
Political Career	1949 - 59 Executive Member, Northern Ireland Labour Party
	1979 - 82 Opposition Spokesman on Northern Ireland, House of Lords
Parliamentary Interests	Northern Ireland (Political, economic and social affairs)
Recreational Interests	Reading, Gardening
Correspondence Address	House of Lords, Westminster, London, SW1A 0PW
	Tel: (0171) 219 5857/5353
	Fax: (0171) 219 5979

Bledisloe, Viscount (Christopher Hiley Ludlow Bathurst QC)

Type of Peerage	Life
Political Allegiance	Cross Bench
Succeeded	1979
Born	24th June 1934

Blyth, Baron (Anthony Audley Rupert Blyth)

Type of Peerage	Hereditary
Political Allegiance	Cross Bench
Created	1977
Born	3rd June 1931

Blyth of Rowington, Baron (James Blyth)

Type of Peerage	Life
Political Allegiance	Conservative
Created	1995
Born	8th May 1940 in Scotland
Educated	Spiers School
	University of Glasgow
Professional Career	1963 - 69 Mobil Oil Company
	1969 - 71 General Foods Ltd
	1971 - 74 Marketing Manager, Mars UK Ltd
	1974 - 77 Director and General Manager, Lucas Batteries Ltd.
	1977 - 81 Director and General Manager, Lucas Aerospace Ltd
	1981 - 85 Head of Defence Sales, Ministry of Defence
	1985 - 86 Managing Director, Plessey Electronic Systems Ltd
	1986 - 87 Managing Director, The Plessey Co. plc
	1987 - Chief Executive, The Boots Company plc (Deputy Chairman since 1994)
	1991 - 97 Chairman, Prime Minister's Advisory Panel on the Citizen's Charter
Recreational Interests	Tennis, Skiing, Theatre, Modern art, Antiques
Correspondence Address	c/o The Boots Company plc, Group Headquarters, Nottingham, NG2 3AA
	Tel: (0115) 968 7001 Fax: (0115) 968 7155
Personal Staff	Ms Catherine Saunders (*Personal Assistant*)
	Tel: (0115) 968 7003

Boardman, Baron (Rt Hon Thomas Gray Boardman MC, TD)

Type of Peerage	Life
Political Allegiance	Conservative
Created	1980
Born	12th January 1919 at Staverton Hall, Northamptonshire
Educated	Bromsgrove School
Professional Career	1939 - 45 Officer, Northamptonshire Yeomanry
	1947 - Solicitor
	1958 - 72 Director/Chairman of various companies including Chamberlain Phipps, Allied Breweries
	1974 - 89 Director/Chairman of various companies including National Westminster Bank (Chairman 1983 - 89) MEPC, Steetley
	1977 - 80 President, Association of British Chambers of Commerce
	1979 High Sheriff, Northamptonshire
	1981 - 82 Chairman, Committee of London and Scottish Banks
	1990 - 97 Advisory Board, LEK Partnership
	1995 - Editorial Board, Nottingham Evening Post
Political Career	1967 - 74 MP (Conservative) for Leicester South West then Leicester South
	1969 - 72 Member, Executive of 1922 Committee
	1972 - 74 Minister for Industry, Department of Trade and Industry
	1974 Chief Secretary, HM Treasury
	1981 - 82 Honorary Treasurer of the Conservative Party
	1981 - 84, 1991 Member, Executive Committee Association of Conservative Peers
Subject Interests	Finance, Trade and industry, the Countryside
Recreational Interests	Horse Riding, Golf
Correspondence Address	The Manor House, Welford, Northamptonshire, NN6 6HX
	Tel: (01858) 575235 Fax: (01858) 575404
	Flat 29, Tufton Court, Tufton Street, Westminster, London, SW1P 3QH
	Tel: (0171) 222 6793

MEMBERS OF THE HOUSE OF LORDS

Bolingbroke and St John, Viscount
   (Kenneth Oliver Musgrave St John)

Type of Peerage . . . . Hereditary
Without Writ of Summons
Succeeded 1974
Born . . . . 22nd March 1927

Bolton, Baron (Richard William Algar Orde-Powlett)

Type of Peerage . . . . Hereditary
Political Allegiance . . . . . Conservative
Succeeded 1963
Born . . . . 11th July 1929

Borrie, Baron (Gordon Johnson Borrie QC)

Type of Peerage . . . . Life
Political Allegiance . . . . . Labour
Succeeded 1995
Born . . . . 13th March 1931 in Croydon
Educated . . . . John Bright Grammar School, Llandudno
                            Manchester University
Professional Career . . . . . 1965 - 69 Senior Lecturer in Law,
                            University of Birmingham
                            1969 - 76 Professor of English Law,
                            Birmingham University
                            1976 - 92 Director General of Fair Trading
Subject Interests . . . . Competition, Consumer policy, Industry,
                            the Media
Recreational Interests . . . Travel, Theatre, Gastronomy, Piano playing
Correspondence Address . . Manor Farm, Abbots Morton,
                            Worcestershire, WR7 4NA
                            Tel: (01386) 792330
                            1 Plowden Buildings, Temple,
                            London, EC4Y 9BU
                            Tel: (0171) 353 4434

Borthwick, Baron (John Hugh Borthwick of That Ilk)

Type of Peerage . . . . Hereditary
Political Allegiance . . . . . Cross Bench
Succeeded 1996
Born . . . . 14th November 1940

Borwick, Baron (James Hugh Myles Borwick MC)

Type of Peerage . . . . Hereditary
On Leave of Absence
Succeeded 1961
Born . . . . 12th December 1917 in Canterbury, Kent
Educated . . . . Eton College
                            Royal Military College, Sandhurst
Professional Career . . . . . 1937 - 47 Officer, HM Land Forces
                            1947 - 50 Company Director
                            1950 - Farming
Recreational Interests . . . Sailing, Outdoor Sports
Correspondence Address . . Leys Farm, Bircher, Leominster,
                            Hereford, HR6 0AZ
                            Tel: (01568) 780367

Boston, Baron (Timothy George Frank Boteler Irby)

Type of Peerage . . . . Hereditary
Political Allegiance . . . . . Conservative
Succeeded 1978
Born . . . . 27th March 1939 in Kingston upon Thames
Educated . . . . Claysmore School
                            Southampton University
Professional Career . . . . . 1961 - 87 Investment Management and
                            Stockbroking
                            1987 - 90 Landmatch Rural Property
                            1990 - Menai Holiday Cottages
Subject Interests . . . . Rural Pastimes, Recreation, Property,
                            Farming, Field Sports, Self Catering
                            Holidays
Recreational Interests . . . Skiing, Riding, Shooting, Theatre, Cinema
Correspondence Address . . Caer Borth, Moelfre, Anglesey, LL72 8NN
                            Tel: (01248) 717135 Fax: (01248) 717051

Boston of Faversham, Baron (Terence George Boston QC)

Type of Peerage . . . . Life
Political Allegiance . . . . . Cross Bench
Created 1976
Born . . . . 21st March 1930 in Bromley, Kent
Educated . . . . Woolwich Polytechnic
                            King's College, London
Professional Career . . . . . 1950 - 52 Royal Air Force
                            1957 - 64 BBC (Sub-Editor, News; then
                            Senior Producer, Current Affairs)
                            1970 - 83 Barrister (QC 1981)
                            1980 - 90 Chairman, TVS Entertainment
Political Career . . . . 1964 - 70 MP (Labour) for Faversham
                            1969 - 70 Assistant Government Whip,
                            House of Commons
                            1978 - 79 Minister of State, Home Office
                            1992 - 94 Principal Deputy Chairman of
                            Committees and Chairman, Select
                            Committee on the European Communities,
                            House of Lords
                            1994 - Chairman of Committees,
                            House of Lords
Recreational Interests . . . Opera, Fell-walking
Correspondence Address . . House of Lords, Westminster,
                            London, SW1A 0PW
                            Tel: (0171) 219 3324

MEMBERS OF THE HOUSE OF LORDS

Bowness, Baron (Peter Spencer Bowness CBE)

Type of Peerage	Life
Political Allegiance	Conservative
Created	1997
Born	19th May 1943 in Cardiff
Educated	Whitgift School, Croydon
Professional Career	1970 - Partner, Weightman Sadler Solicitors, Purley
	1981 Deputy Lieutenant, Greater London
	1983 - 95 Member, Audit Commission England and Wales
	1989 - 92 Member, National Training Task Force
	1993 - 94 Board Member, London First/London Forum
Political Career	1976 - 79, 1980 - 94 Leader of Council, London Borough of Croydon
	1978 - 94 Chairman, London Boroughs Association
	1978 - 80 Deputy Chairman, Association of Metropolitan Authorities
	1985 - 93 London Residuary Body
	1990 - Member, Congress of Local and Regional Authorities of Europe
	1993 - Member, UK Delegation, EU Committee of the Regions (Bureau Member)
	1994 - 96 Leader of Opposition, Croydon Council
	1997 Opposition Spokesman on Environment, House of Lords
Recreational Interests	Gardening, Theatre
Correspondence Address	Weightman Sadler, 1/2 The Exchange, Purley Road, Purley, CR2 2YY
	Tel: (0181) 660 6455 Fax: (0181) 668 3250
	Three Gables, 10 Westview Road, Warlingham, Surrey, CR6 9JD
	Tel and Fax: (01883) 624546
	E-mail: bowness@globalnet.co.uk

Boyd of Merton, Viscount
(Simon Donald Rupert Neville Lennox-Boyd)

Type of Peerage	Hereditary
Succeeded	1983
Born	7th December 1939
Educated	Eton College
	Christ Church, Oxford
Professional Career	1981 - 86 Chairman, Arthur Guinness and Sons
	1987 - 92 Chairman, SCF
	1992 - Chairman, Stonham Housing Association
Correspondence Address	41 Harrington Gardens, London, SW7 4JU
	Tel: (0171) 373 7261 Fax: (0171) 244 8281

Boyd-Carpenter, Baron
(Rt Hon John Archibald Boyd-Carpenter DL)

Type of Peerage	Life
Political Allegiance	Conservative
Created	1972
Born	2nd June 1908 in Harrogate, Yorkshire
Educated	Stowe School
	Balliol College, Oxford
Professional Career	1934 - 39 Barrister
	1940 - 45 Officer, Scots Guards
	1969 - 72 Chairman, Orion Insurance Co
	1970 - 72 Chairman, CLRP Investment Trust
	1972 - 77 Chairman, Civil Aviation Authority
	1973 - 83 Deputy Lieutenant, Greater London
	1977 - 89 Chairman, Rugby Portland Cement
	1986 - 90 Chairman, Mail Users' Association
Political Career	1945 - 72 MP (Conservative) for Kingston-upon-Thames
	1951 - 54 Financial Secretary, HM Treasury
	1954 - 55 Minister for Transport and Civil Aviation
	1955 - 62 Minister for Pensions and National Insurance
	1962 - 64 Chief Secretary, HM Treasury and Paymaster General
	1964 - 66 Opposition Spokesman, Housing, Local Government and Land
	1964 - 70 Chairman, Public Accounts Committee, House of Commons
	1991 - President, Association of Conservative Peers
Subject Interests	Finance, Constitutional issues, Transport
Recreational Interests	Tennis, Gardening and Travel
Correspondence Address	12 Eaton Terrace, London, SW1 8EZ
	Tel: (0171) 736 7765
	Crux Easton House, Crux Easton, Near Newbury, Berkshire, RG15 9QF
	Tel: (01635) 253037

Boyne, Viscount (Gustavus Michael Stucley Hamilton-Russell)

Type of Peerage	Hereditary
Political Allegiance	Cross Bench
Succeeded	1995
Born	27th May 1965 in London
Educated	Harrow School
	Royal Agricultural College, Cirencester
Professional Career	1992 - 97 Senior Land Agent, John German (Land Agents)
	1997 - Associate, Carter Jonas (Land Agents)
Subject Interests	Conservation, Rural Economy, Farming
Recreational Interests	Travel, Field sports, Tennis, Cricket
Correspondence Address	Dingle Leys, Burwarton, Bridgnorth, Shropshire, WV16 6QG
	Tel and Fax: (01746) 787221

MEMBERS OF THE HOUSE OF LORDS

Brabazon of Tara, Baron (Ivon Anthony Moore-Brabazon)

Type of Peerage	Hereditary
Political Allegiance	Conservative
Succeeded	1974
Born	20th December 1946 in London
Professional Career	1972 - 84 Member, London Stock Exchange
Educated	Harrow School
Political Career	1984 - 86 Government Whip, (Lord in Waiting)
	1986 - 89 Parliamentary Secretary, Department of Transport
	1989 - 90 Minister of State, Foreign and Commonwealth Office
	1990 - 92 Minister of State, Department of Transport
Subject Interests	Transport, Aviation, Shipping, Economy, Sport
Recreational Interests	Golf, Sailing
Correspondence Address	House of Lords, Westminster, London, SW1A 0PW
	Tel: (0171) 219 6796

Brabourne, Baron (John Ulick Knatchbull CBE)

Type of Peerage	Hereditary
Political Allegiance	Cross Bench
Succeeded	1945
Born	9th November 1924 in London
Educated	Eton College
	Brasenose College, Oxford
Professional Career	Film and Television Producer
	1970 - Director, Mersham Productions Ltd
	1977 - Patron, London International Film School
	1978 - 95 Director, Thames Television Ltd (Chairman 1991 - 93)
	1979 - 94 Governor, British Film Institute
	1979 - 95 Director, Euston Films Ltd
	1981 - 86 Director, Thorn EMI plc
	1981 - Governor, National Film and Television School
	1987 - Chairman, then (since 1994) Vice Chairman, Copyright Promotions Group plc
	1988 - Vice President, Royal Society for Nature Conservation
Subject Interests	Films, Arts, Theatre, Television
Recreational Interests	Fishing, Photography
Correspondence Address	Mersham Productions Ltd, Newhouse, Mersham, Ashford, Kent, TN25 6NQ
	Tel: (01233) 503636 Fax: (01233) 502244
Personal Staff	Miss Barbara Tolhurst *(Secretary)*

Bradbury, Baron (John Bradbury)

Type of Peerage	Hereditary
Political Allegiance	Conservative
Succeeded	1994
Born	19th March 1940

Bradford, Bishop of (Rt Rev David James Smith)

Type of Peerage	Bishop
Entered Lords	1997
Born	14th July 1935 in Ware
Educated	Hertford Grammar School
	King's College, London
Professional Career	1959 - 62 Assistant Curate, All Saints, Gosforth
	1962 - 64 Assistant Curate, St Francis, High Heaton
	1964 - 68 Assistant Curate, Longbenton
	1968 - 75 Vicar, Longhirst with Hebron
	1975 - 81 Vicar, St. Mary, Monkseaton
	1980 - 87 Archdeacon of Lindisfarne
	1987 - 92 Bishop of Maidstone
	1990 - 92 Bishop to HM Forces
	1992 - Bishop of Bradford
Subject Interests	Christian Relations with Islam (esp. Sudan and Pakistan) and Other world faiths
Recreational Interests	Watching sport, Walking, Reading, Listening to music
Correspondence Address	Bishopscroft, Ashwell Road, Heaton, Bradford, West Yorkshire, BD9 4AU
	Tel: (01274) 545414 Fax: (01274) 544831
	Web: www.bradford.anglican.org\

Bradford, Earl of (Richard Thomas Orlando Bridgeman)

Type of Peerage	Hereditary
Political Allegiance	Conservative
Succeeded	1981
Born	3rd October 1947

Brain, Baron (Christopher Langdon Brain)

Type of Peerage	Hereditary
Political Allegiance	Cross Bench
Succeeded	1966
Born	30th August 1926 in London
Educated	Leighton Park School, Reading
	New College, Oxford
Professional Career	1946 - 48 Royal Navy
	1951 - 53 Molins Machine Co (Trainee)
	1953 - 69 Ilford Limited (Management posts)
	1970 - 76, 1980 - 96 Management Consultancy (various posts)
	1976 - 80 Avalon Leather Board Ltd (Works Manager)
	1982 Royal Photographic Society (General Manager)
Subject Interests	Copyright, Science and technology, Medicine, Disadvantaged charities
Recreational Interests	Shooting, Fishing, Birdwatching
Correspondence Address	8 Cross Street, Moretonhampstead, Devon, TQ13 8NL

MEMBERS OF THE HOUSE OF LORDS

Braine of Wheatley, Baron (Rt Hon Bernard Richard Braine)

Type of Peerage . . . . Life
Political Allegiance . . . . . Conservative
Created 1992
Born . . . . 24th June 1914 in Ealing, London
Professional Career . . . . . 1980 - 88 President, UK Committee for
Defence of the Unjustly Prosecuted
Political Career . . . . 1950 - 55 MP (Conservative) for Billericay
1955 - 83 MP (Conservative) for
South East Essex
1960 - 61 Parliamentary Secretary, Ministry
of Pensions and National Insurance
1961 - 62 Parliamentary Secretary,
Commonwealth Relations
1962 - 64 Parliamentary Secretary,
Ministry of Health
1967 - 70 Opposition Spokesman on
Commonwealth Affairs and Overseas Aid
1970 - 71 Chairman, Select Committee on
Overseas Aid, House of Commons
1970 - 77 Deputy Chairman, then Treasurer,
Commonwealth Parliamentary Association
(UK Branch)
1970 - 92 Chairman, British–German
Parliamentary Group
1973 - 74 Chairman, Select Committee on
Overseas Development, House of Commons
1979 - 92 Vice-Chairman, Parliamentary
Human Rights Group
1979 - 92 Chairman, British–Greek
Parliamentary Group
1983 - 92 MP (Conservative) for Castle Point
1984 - 88 Chairman, All-Party Misuse of
Drugs Committee
1987 - 92 Father of the House of Commons

Bramall, Baron (Field Marshal
Edwin Noel Westby Bramall KG,GCB, OBE, MC**)**

Type of Peerage . . . . Life
Political Allegiance . . . . . Cross Bench
Created 1987
Born . . . . 18th December 1923
Educated . . . . Eton College
Professional Career . . . . . 1943 - 86 Military (Chief of General Staff,
1979 - 82; Chief of Defence Staff, 1982 - 83)

Brandon of Oakbrook, Baron
(Rt Hon Henry Vivian Brandon MC**)**

Type of Peerage . . . . Life (Former Law Lord)
Political Allegiance . . . . . Cross Bench
Born . . . . 3rd June 1920
Created 1981

Brassey of Apethorpe, Baron (David Henry Brassey)

Type of Peerage . . . . Hereditary
Political Allegiance . . . . . Conservative
Succeeded 1967
Born . . . . 16th September 1932 in London
Educated . . . . Stowe School
Professional Career . . . . . 1951 - 67 Major, Grenadier Guards
1967 - Farmer
Subject Interests . . . . Criminal Justice System
Correspondence Address . . The Manor House, Apethorpe,
Peterborough, PE8 5DL
Tel: (01780) 470231 Fax: (01780) 470224

Braybrooke, Baron (Robin Henry Charles Neville)

Type of Peerage . . . . Hereditary
Political Allegiance . . . . . Conservative
Succeeded 1990
Born . . . . 29th January 1932 in London
Educated . . . . Eton College
Magdalene College, Cambridge
Professional Career . . . . . Farmer and Landowner
1983 - 95 Chairman, Price Trust
1984 - 90 Chairman, Rural Development
Commission for Essex
1992 - Lord Lieutenant of Essex
Political Career . . . . 1959 - 69 Member, Saffron Waldon Rural
District Council
1969 - 72 Member, Essex County Council
Recreational Interests . . . Flying, Railways, Motorcycling
Correspondence Address . . Abbey House, Audley End, Saffron Walden,
Essex, CB11 4JB
Tel: (01799) 541956/541354
Fax: (01799) 42134

Braye, Baroness (Mary Penelope Aubrey-Fletcher)

Type of Peerage . . . . Hereditary
Political Allegiance . . . . . None
Succeeded 1985
Born . . . . 28th September 1941

Brentford, Viscount (Crispin William Joynson-Hicks)

Type of Peerage . . . . Hereditary
Political Allegiance . . . . . Conservative
Succeeded 1983
Born . . . . 7th April 1933 in London
Educated . . . . Eton College
New College, Oxford
Professional Career . . . . . 1961 - 95 Solicitor
Subject Interests . . . . Homelessness, Parenting, Youth, Elderly,
Human rights
Recreational Interests . . . Sport, Gardening
Correspondence Address . . Cousley Place, Wadhurst,
East Sussex, TN5 6HF
Tel: (01892) 783737 Fax: (01892) 784428
E-mail 101563.2113@compuserve.com
14 Westminster Palace Gardens,
London, SW1P 1RL
Tel: (0171) 222 6169 Fax: (0171) 233 2525

Bridge of Harwich, Baron (Rt Hon Nigel Cyprian Bridge)

Type of Peerage . . . . Life (Former Law Lord)
Political Allegiance . . . . . Cross Bench
Created 1980
Born . . . . 26th February 1917 in Codicote,
Hertfordshire
Educated . . . . Marlborough College
Professional Career . . . . . 1947 - 68 Barrister
1964 - 68 Junior Counsel to the Treasury
(Queen's Bench Division)
1968 - 75 High Court Judge
1975 - 80 Lord Justice of Appeal
1980 - 92 Lord of Appeal in Ordinary

MEMBERS OF THE HOUSE OF LORDS

Bridgeman, Viscount (Robin John Orlando Bridgeman)

Type of Peerage . . . . Hereditary
Political Allegiance . . . . . Conservative
Succeeded 1982
Born . . . . 5th December 1930

Bridges, Baron (Thomas Edward Bridges GCMG)

Type of Peerage . . . . Hereditary
Political Allegiance . . . . . Cross Bench
Succeeded 1969
Born . . . . 27th November 1927
Educated . . . . Eton College
New College, Oxford
Professional Career . . . . . 1951 - 87 HM Diplomatic Service
1972 - 74 Private Secretary (Overseas
Affairs) to the Prime Minister
(Rt Hon Edward Heath MP)
1979 - 82 Deputy Secretary, Foreign and
Commonwealth Office
1983 - 87 Ambassador to Italy
Political Career . . . . 1988 - 92, 1994 - Member, Select
Committee on European Communities,
House of Lords
Subject Interests . . . . Europe, Environmental affairs,
the Public service
Correspondence Address . . 56 Church Street, Orford, Woodbridge,
Suffolk, IP12 2NT
Tel and Fax: (01394) 450235
Tel: (0171) 821 1769

Bridport, Viscount (Alexander Nelson Hood)

Type of Peerage . . . . Hereditary
On Leave Of Absence
Succeeded 1979
Born . . . . 17th March 1948 in London
Educated . . . . Eton College
Sorbonne, Paris
Professional Career . . . . . 1967 - 79 Kleinwort Benson Ltd
1982 - 86 Chase Manhattan
1986 - 90 Shearson Lehman
1991 - Bridport and Cie (Managing Partner)
Recreational Interests . . . Skiing, Sailing
Correspondence Address . . 1 Place Longemalle, 1204 Geneva,
Switzerland
Tel: 00 41 22 312 2000
Fax: 00 41 22 312 2190

Briggs, Baron (Asa Briggs)

Type of Peerage . . . . Life
Political Allegiance . . . . . Cross Bench
Created 1976
Born . . . . 7th May 1921 in Keighley, Yorkshire
Educated . . . . Keighley Grammar School
Sidney Sussex College, Cambridge
Professional Career . . . . . 1945 - 55 Fellow, Worcester College, Oxford
1955 - 61 Professor of History,
University of Leeds
1961 - 76 Pro-Vice Chancellor/Vice
Chancellor, Sussex University
1976 - 91 Provost, Worcester College,
Oxford
1978 - 94 Chancellor, Open University
Subject Interests . . . . Health, Education, Social policy,
Communications
Recreational Interests . . . Travel
Correspondence Address . . The Caprons, Keere Street, Lewes,
East Sussex, BN7 1TY
Tel: (01273) 814472 Fax: (01273) 814462
Personal Staff . . . . Ms Veronica Hurchancy *(Secretary)*

Brightman, Baron (Rt Hon John Anson Brightman)

Type of Peerage . . . . Life (former Law Lord)
Political Allegiance . . . . . Cross Bench
Created 1982
Born . . . . 20th June 1911 in St Albans, Hertfordshire
Educated . . . . Marlborough College
St John's College, Cambridge
Professional Career . . . . . 1932 - 70 Barrister (QC 1961)
1970 - 79 High Court Judge
1979 - 82 Lord Justice of Appeal
1982 - 86 Lord of Appeal in Ordinary
Subject Interests . . . . The Arctic
Correspondence Address . . House of Lords, Westminster,
London, SW1A OPW
Tel: (0171) 219 2034 Fax: (0171) 219 5979

Brigstocke, Baroness (Heather Renwick Brigstocke)

Type of Peerage . . . . Life
Political Allegiance . . . . . Conservative
Created 1990
Born . . . . 2nd September 1929 in Birchington, Kent
Professional Career . . . . . 1951 - 53 Classics Mistress, Francis Holland
School, London
1954 - 60 Classics Mistress (Part-Time),
Godolphin and Latymer School, London
1962 - 64 Latin Teacher (Part-Time),
National Cathedral School,
Washington DC, USA
1965 - 74 Head Mistress, Francis Holland
School, London
1974 - 89 High Mistress, St Paul's
Girls School, London

MEMBERS OF THE HOUSE OF LORDS

Bristol, Marquess of
(Frederick William John Augustus Hervey)
Type of Peerage . . . . Hereditary
Political Allegiance . . . . . None
Succeeded 1985
Born . . . . 15th September 1954

Bristol, Bishop of (Rt Rev Barry Rogerson)
Type of Peerage . . . . Bishop
Entered Lords 1990
Born . . . . 25th July 1936 in Timperley, Cheshire
Educated . . . . Magnus Grammar School, Newark
    University of Leeds
    Wells Theological College
Professional Career . . . . . 1952 - 57 Bank Clerk, Midland Bank
    1962 - 65 Curate, St Hilda's with St Thomas,
        South Shields
    1965 - 67 Curate, St Nicholas',
        Bishopswearmouth
    1967 - 71 Lecturer, Lichfield Theological
        College
    1971 - 72 Vice Principal, Lichfield
        Theological College
    1972 - 75 Lecturer, Salisbury and Wells
        Theological College
    1975 - 79 Team Rector, St Thomas',
        Wednesfield
    1979 - 85 Bishop of Wolverhampton
    1985 - Bishop of Bristol
Subject Interests . . . . Homelessness and Housing, Vocational
    Education
Recreational Interests . . . Cinema, Stained glass, Photography, Sailing
Correspondence Address . . Bishop's House, Clifton Hill,
    Bristol, BS8 1BW
    Tel: (0117) 973 0222 Fax: (0117) 923 9670
    E-mail: 106430.1040@compuserve.com

Broadbridge, Baron (Peter Hewett Broadbridge)
Type of Peerage . . . . Hereditary
Political Allegiance . . . . . Cross Bench
Succeeded 1972
Born . . . . 19th August 1938 in London
Educated . . . . Hurstpierpoint College, Sussex
    St Catherine's College, Oxford
Professional Career . . . . . 1963 - 66 Management Trainee,
        Unilever Ltd
    1966 - 67 Marketing Manager,
        Colgate-Palmolive Ltd
    1967 - 70 Marketing Manager, Gallaher Ltd
    1970 - 80 Marketing Consultant,
        Peat Marwick Mitchell Ltd
    1980 - 83 Consultant, Coopers and Lybrand
    1983 - 90 Director, The London Venture
        Capital Market Ltd
Political Career . . . . 1994 - Deputy Speaker, House of Lords
    A Deputy Chairman of Committees,
    House of Lords
Subject Interests . . . . Traffic and Transport, Conservation,
    Local Government, the Arts
Recreational Interests . . . Silversmithing, Painting/Drawing in
    watercolours, Illumination and calligraphy
Correspondence Address . . House of Lords, Westminster,
    London, SW1A 0PW
    Tel: (0171) 219 5353
    21 Bromfield Street, London, N1 0PZ
    Tel: (0171) 354 5312
Personal Staff . . . . Mr Roderick Rugman *(Research Assistant)*

Brocket, Baron (Charles Ronald George Nall-Cain)
Type of Peerage . . . . Hereditary
Political Allegiance . . . . . None
Succeeded 1967
Born . . . . 12th February 1952
Note: At the time of writing Lord Brocket was serving a prison sentence and thus unable to attend the House of Lords.

Brooke, Earl; and Earl of Warwick, (Guy David Greville)
Type of Peerage . . . . Hereditary
On Leave Of Absence
Political Allegiance . . . . . None
Succeeded 1996
Born . . . . 30th January 1957
Educated . . . . Summerfields
    Eton
Correspondence Address . . PO Box 467, Claremont WA, Australia, 6010

Brooke of Alverthorpe, Baron (Clive Brooke)
Type of Peerage . . . . Life
Political Allegiance . . . . . Labour
Created 1997
Born . . . . 21st June 1942 in Alverthorpe, West
    Yorkshire
Educated . . . . Thornes House Grammar School, Wakefield
Professional Career . . . . . 1964 - 65 Deputy General Secretary, then
        (from 1988) General Secretary, Inland
        Revenue Staff Federation
    1996 - Joint General Secretary, Public
        Services Tax and Commerce Union
    1996 - Member, Pensions
        Compensation Board
Subject Interests . . . . Employment, Education, Community affairs
Recreational Interests . . . Travel, Community services, Reading,
    Walking, Politics, Church affairs
Correspondence Address . . House of Lords, Westminster,
    London, SW1A 0PN
    Tel: (0171) 219 5353 Fax: (0171) 228 8982
    37 Whistler's Avenue, Morgans Walk,
    London, SW1 3TS
    Tel: (0171) 228 8982
    Mobile: (0831) 471450

MEMBERS OF THE HOUSE OF LORDS

Brooke of Ystradfellte, Baroness (Barbara Brook DBE)

Type of Peerage . . . . Life
On Leave Of Absence
Born . . . . 14th January 1908
Created 1964

Brookeborough, Viscount (Alan Henry Brooke)

Type of Peerage . . . . Hereditary
Political Allegiance . . . . . Cross Bench
Succeeded 1987
Born . . . . 30th June 1952 in Belfast
Educated . . . . Harrow School
  Millfield School
  Royal Agricultural College, Cirencester
Professional Career . . . . . 1971 - 94 Army
  1994 - Farming and Estate Manager
  1995 High Sherriff, Co Fermagh
Subject Interests . . . . Northern Ireland, Agriculture, Defence,
Tourism
Recreational Interests . . . Outdoor Field sports, Skiing
Correspondence Address . . Colebrooke Park, Brookeborough, Co
  Fermanagh, Northern Ireland, BT94 4DW
  Tel: (01365) 531402

Brookes, Baron (Raymond Pervical Brookes)

Type of Peerage . . . . Life
Political Allegiance . . . . . Cross Bench
Created 1975
Born . . . . 10th April 1909 in West Bromwich
Educated . . . . Kendrick Technical College, West Bromwich
Professional Career . . . . . 1962 - 65 Managing Director, GKN Group
  1965 - 75 Chairman and Chief Executive,
  GKN plc
Subject Interests . . . . Engineering, Manufacturing
Recreational Interests . . . Fly Fishing, Golf
Correspondence Address . . Mallards, Santon, Isle of Man, IM4 1EH
  Tel: (01624) 822451 Fax: (01624) 824707

Brooks of Tremorfa, Baron (Jack Brooks)

Type of Peerage . . . . Life
Political Allegiance . . . . . Labour
Created 1979
Born . . . . 12th April 1927
Educated . . . . Coleg Harlech
Political Career . . . . 1973 - 93 Councillor, South Glamorgan
  County Council (Leader 1973 - 77,
  1986 - 92, Chairman 1981 - 82)
  1978 - 79 Chairman, Labour Party, Wales
  1980 - 81 Opposition Defence Spokesman

Brougham and Vaux, Baron (Michael John Brough CBE)

Type of Peerage . . . . Hereditary
Political Allegiance . . . . . Conservative
Succeeded 1967
Born . . . . 2nd August 1938 in London
Professional Career . . . . . 1986 - 89 President, Royal Society for the
  Prevention of Accidents
  1989 - 91 President, Tax Payers Society
  1992 - Chairman, European Secure
  Vehicle Alliance
  1994 - President, National Health and
  Safety Groups Council
Political Career . . . . 1992 Deputy Chairman of Committees,
  House of Lords
  1995 - Deputy Speaker, House of Lords
Subject Interests . . . . Road Safety, Transport, Motor and Aircraft
  Industry

Broughshane, Baron (William Kensington Davison)

Type of Peerage . . . . Hereditary
Political Allegiance . . . . . Cross Bench
Succeeded 1976
Born . . . . 25th November 1914 in London
Educated . . . . Shrewsbury School
  Magdalen College, Oxford
Professional Career . . . . . 1961 - 89 Barrister Executive at the
  Royal Opera House, Covent Garden
Subject Interests . . . . Music, Ballet, Opera
Recreational Interests . . . Mountain walking
Correspondence Address . . 3 Godfrey Street, London, SW3 3TA
  Tel: (0171) 352 7826

Browne-Wilkinson, Baron
(Rt Hon Nicholas Christopher Henry Browne-Wilkinson)

Type of Peerage . . . . Life (Law Lord)
Political Allegiance . . . . . Cross Bench
Created 1991
Born . . . . 30th March 1930

Brownlow, Baron (Edward John Peregrine Cust)

Type of Peerage . . . . Hereditary
On Leave Of Absence
Succeeded 1978
Born . . . . 25th March 1936

MEMBERS OF THE HOUSE OF LORDS

Bruce of Donington, Baron (Donald William Trevor Bruce)

Type of Peerage	Life
Political Allegiance	Labour
Created	1974
Born	3rd October 1912 in Norbury
Educated	The Grammar School, Donnington, Lincolnshire
Professional Career	Chartered Accountant and Management Consultant
Political Career	1945 - 50 MP (Labour) for North Portsmouth
	1945 - 50 PPS to the Minister of Health, (Rt Hon Aneurin Bevan MP)
	1975 - 79 Member of the European Parliament
	1979 - 91 Opposition Spokesman on Treasury, Trade and Industry and Economic Questions, House of Lords
Subject Interests	Finance, Economics, European Community
Correspondence Address	House of Lords, Westminster, London, SW1A 0PW
	Tel: (0171) 219 3172 Fax: (0171) 219 5979
Personal Staff	Ms Mary Bruce *(Research Assistant)*

Bruntisfield, Baron (John Robert Warrender OBE, MC, TD)

Type of Peerage	Hereditary
Political Allegiance	Conservative
Succeeded	1993
Born	7th February 1921

Buccleuch and Queensbury, Duke of
(Walter Francis John Montagu Douglas Scott KT)

Type of Peerage	Hereditary
Political Allegiance	Conservative
Succeeded	1973
Born	18th September 1923 in London
Educated	Eton College
	Christ Church, Oxford
Parliamentary Career	1957 - 60 Member, Roxburghshire County Council
	1960 - 73 MP (Conservative) for Edinburgh North

Buchan, Earl of (Malcolm Henry Erskine)

Type of Peerage	Hereditary
Political Allegiance	Cross Bench
Succeeded	1984
Born	4th July 1930

Buckinghamshire, Earl of (George Miles Hobart-Hampden)

Type of Peerage	Hereditary
Political Allegiance	Conservative
Born	15th December 1944 in Madras, India
Educated	Clifton College, Bristol
	Exeter University
	Birkbeck College and Institute of Commonwealth Studies, University of London
Professional Career	1970 - 81 Noble Lowndes and Partners
	1981 - 86 Director, HSBC Gibbs
	1986 - 91 Wardley International Services Ltd (Managing Director from 1988)
	1991 - 95 Director, The Wyatt Company (UK) Ltd
	1995 - Partner, Watson Wyatt Partners (Actuaries and Consultants)
Political Career	1990 - President, Buckingham Constituency Conservative Association
Subject Interests	Pensions, Financial, Regulation
Recreational Interests	Real tennis, Rugby, Football, Fly fishing, Reading, Walking
Correspondence Address	c/o Watson Wyatt Partners, PO Box 77, Gate House, Fretherne Road, Welwyn Garden City, Hertfordshire, AL8 6PP
	Tel: (01707) 607503 Fax: (01707) 607563
Personal Staff	Mrs Margaret Earl *(Personal Assistant)*
	Tel: (01707) 607525

Buckmaster, Viscount (Martin Stanley Buckmaster OBE)

Type of Peerage	Hereditary
Political Allegiance	Cross Bench
Succeeded	1974
Born	11th April 1921

Bullock, Baron (Alan Louis Charles Bullock)

Type of Peerage	Life
Political Allegiance	Cross Bench
Created	1976
Born	13th December 1914

Burden, Baron (Andrew Philip Burden)

Type of Peerage	Hereditary
Without Writ of Summons	
Succeeded	1995
Born	20th July 1959

Burgh, Baron (Alexander Peter Willoughby Leith)

Type of Peerage	Hereditary
Political Allegiance	None
Succeeded	1959
Born	20th March 1935

MEMBERS OF THE HOUSE OF LORDS

Burlison, Baron (Tom Burlison)
Type of Peerage . . . . Life
Political Allegiance . . . . . Labour
Created 1997
Born . . . . 23rd May 1936
Professional Career . . . . . 1953 - 65 Professional Footballer
　　　　　　　　　　　1965 - General Municipal and
　　　　　　　　　　　　　Boilermakers Union
　　　　　　　　　　　　　(Deputy General Secretary since 1991)
Political Career . . . . 1991 - 96 Treasurer, Labour Party

Burnham, Baron (Hugh John Frederick Lawson)
Type of Peerage . . . . Hereditary
Political Allegiance . . . . Conservative
Succeeded 1993
Born . . . . 15th August 1931
Professional Career . . . . 1955 - 86 Daily Telegraph
　　　　　　　　　　　(Deputy Managing Director from 1984)
　　　　　　　　　　　1988 - 93 Director General, King George's
　　　　　　　　　　　　　Fund for Sailors
Political Career . . . . 1997 - Opposition Spokesman on Defence,
　　　　　　　　　　　House of Lords
　　　　　　　　　　　Deputy Speaker and Deputy Chairman of
　　　　　　　　　　　Committees, House of Lords
Correspondence Address . . House of Lords, Westminster,
　　　　　　　　　　　London, SW1A 0PW

Burton, Baron (Michael Evan Victor Baillie)
Type of Peerage . . . . Hereditary
Political Allegiance . . . . . Conservative
Succeeded 1962
Born . . . . 27th June 1924 in Burton-on-Trent

Bute, Marquess of (John Colum Chrichton-Stuart)
Type of Peerage . . . . Hereditary
Without Writ of Summons
Succeeded 1993
Born . . . . 26th April 1958

Butterfield, Baron (William John Hughes Butterfield OBE)
Type of Peerage . . . . Life
Political Allegiance . . . . . Conservative
Created 1988
Born . . . . 28th March 1920 in Stechford, Birmingham
Educated . . . . Solihull School
　　　　　　　　　　　Exeter College, Oxford
　　　　　　　　　　　John Hopkins University, Baltimore, USA
Professional Career . . . . . 1946 - 48 Member, Scientific Council,
　　　　　　　　　　　　Medical Research Council
　　　　　　　　　　　1958 - 71 Professor of Medicine,
　　　　　　　　　　　　Guy's Hospital
　　　　　　　　　　　1971 - 75 Vice Chancellor,
　　　　　　　　　　　　Nottingham University
　　　　　　　　　　　1976 - 87 Regius Professor of Physics,
　　　　　　　　　　　　Cambridge University
　　　　　　　　　　　1978 - 87 Master, Downing College,
　　　　　　　　　　　　Cambridge
　　　　　　　　　　　1983 - 85 Vice Chancellor,
　　　　　　　　　　　　Cambridge University
Subject Interests . . . . Education, Medical research
Recreational Interests . . . Cricket, Real tennis
Correspondence Address . . 39 Clarendon Street, Cambridge, CB1 1JX
　　　　　　　　　　　Tel: (01223) 462326/328854
　　　　　　　　　　　Fax: (01223) 328854
Personal Staff . . . . Mrs Jill Hall *(Personal Assistant)*
　　　　　　　　　　　Tel: (01223) 462326

Butterworth, Baron (John Blackstock Butterworth CBE)
Type of Peerage . . . . Life
Political Allegiance . . . . . Conservative
Created 1985
Born . . . . 13th March 1918 in Sutton-in-Ashfield,
　　　　　　　　　　　Nottinghamshire
Educated . . . . Queen Elizabeth's Grammar School,
　　　　　　　　　　　Mansfield
　　　　　　　　　　　Queen's College, Oxford
Professional Career . . . . 1939 - 46 Major, Royal Artillery
　　　　　　　　　　　1946 - 63 Fellow, New College Oxford
　　　　　　　　　　　　(Bursar 1956 - 63)
　　　　　　　　　　　1947 - Barrister
　　　　　　　　　　　1963 - 85 Vice Chancellor,
　　　　　　　　　　　　Warwick University
　　　　　　　　　　　1974 - Deputy Lieutenant, West Midlands
　　　　　　　　　　　1989 Honorary Bencher, Lincoln's Inn
Subject Interests . . . . Law revision, Manufacturing industry and
　　　　　　　　　　　the European Union
Recreational Interests . . . Education, Industry, Industrial relations,
　　　　　　　　　　　Development and Aid
Correspondence Address . . The Barn, Barton, Guiting Power,
　　　　　　　　　　　Gloucestershire, GL54 5US
　　　　　　　　　　　Tel: (01451) 850297 Fax: (01451) 850108
　　　　　　　　　　　727 Nell Gwynn House, Sloane Avenue,
　　　　　　　　　　　London, SW3 3AX
　　　　　　　　　　　Tel: (0171) 581 4838 Fax: (0171) 823 9388

Buxton of Alsa, Baron (Aubrey Leland Oakes Buxton KCVO)
Type of Peerage . . . . Life
Political Allegiance . . . . . Conservative
Created 1978
Born . . . . 15th July 1918 in Oxford
Professional Career . . . . . 1958 - 88 Chairman, Anglia Television
　　　　　　　　　　　1981 - 86 Chairman, ITN

Byford, Baroness (Hazel Byford DBE)
Type of Peerage . . . . Life
Political Allegiance . . . . . Conservative
Created 1996
Born . . . . 14th January 1941 in Leicester
Educated . . . . St Leonard's School
　　　　　　　　　　　St Andrew's, Fife
　　　　　　　　　　　Moulton Agricultural College, Northampton
Professional Career . . . . . 1958 - 61 Poultry Farmer
　　　　　　　　　　　1961 - 96 WRVS Leicestershire
　　　　　　　　　　　　(County Organiser 1972 - 76)
Political Career . . . . 1990 - 93 Chairman, Conservative Women's
　　　　　　　　　　　　National Union
　　　　　　　　　　　1996 - 97 President, National Union of
　　　　　　　　　　　　Conservative and Unionist Associations
　　　　　　　　　　　1997 - Opposition Whip, House of Lords
Subject Interests . . . . Rural affairs, Farming, Voluntary and
　　　　　　　　　　　community projects
Recreational Interests . . . Sport, Bridge and Reading

Byron, Baron (Robert James Bryan)
Type of Peerage . . . . Hereditary
Political Allegiance . . . . . Conservative
Succeeded 1989
Born . . . . 5th April 1950

MEMBERS OF THE HOUSE OF LORDS

C

Cadman, Baron (John Anthony Cadman)

Type of Peerage . . . . Hereditary
Political Allegiance . . . . . Conservative
Succeeded 1967
Born . . . . 3rd July 1938 in Northampton
Educated . . . . Harrow School
   Cambridge University
   Royal Agricultural College, Cirencester
Professional Career . . . . . 1964 - 85 Farmer
   1986 - 93 Restaurateur
Subject Interests . . . . Railway affairs, Transport, Agriculture,
   the Licensed trade
Recreational Interests . . . Caravanning, Travel
Correspondence Address . . 3 Court Farm Road, Willsbridge,
   Bristol, BS30 9AA
   Tel: (0117) 9323552

Cadogan, Earl of (Charles Gerald John Cadogan)

Type of Peerage . . . . Hereditary
Political Allegiance . . . . . Conservative
Succeeded 1997
Born . . . . 24th March 1937
Educated . . . . Eton College
   Magdalen College, Oxford
Professional Career . . . . . 1955 - 57 National Service,
      Commissioned Coldstream Guards
   1958 - 74 Schroders
   1974 - Cadogan Estates
Recreational Interests . . . Country Pursuits, Horseracing, Golf, Soccer,
   Rugby, Cricket, Tennis, Agricultural and
   forestry management
Correspondence Address . . 18 Cadogan Gardens, London, SW3 2RP
   Tel: (0171) 730 4567 Fax: (0171) 823 5514
Personal Staff . . . . Mrs Susan Wizard *(Secretary)*

Cairns, Earl (Simon Dallas Cairns CBE)

Type of Peerage . . . . Hereditary
Political Allegiance . . . . . Cross Bench
Succeeded 1989
Born . . . . 27th May 1939 in Chichester, Sussex
Educated . . . . Eton College
   Trinity College, Cambridge
Professional Career . . . . . 1963 - 1978 J & A Scrimgeour
      (becoming Partner and then Director)
   1978 - SG Warburg & Co Ltd
      (variously Director, Managing Director,
      Vice-Chairman and Joint Chairman
   1985 - SG Warburg Group
      (variously Director, Vice-Chairman,
      Deputy Chairman and Chief Executive)
   1993 - Vice President, Voluntary
      Service Overseas
   1995 - Chairman, Overseas Development
      Institute
   1995 - Chairman, Commonwealth
      Development Corporation
   1996 - Chairman, BAT Industries plc
Correspondence Address . . Windsor House, 50 Victoria Street,
   London, SW1H 6LW
   Tel: (0171) 233 3249 Fax: (0171) 222 4094
   Bolehyde Manor, Allington, near
   Chippenham, Wiltshire, SN14 6LW
   Tel: (01249) 652105 Fax: (01249) 659296

Caithness, Earl of (Rt Hon Malcolm Ian Sinclair)

Type of Peerage . . . . Hereditary
Political Allegiance . . . . . Conservative
Succeeded 1965
Born . . . . 3rd July 1938 in Northampton
Educated . . . . Marlborough College
   Royal Agricultural College, Cirencester
Political Career . . . . 1984 - 85 Government Whip,
      (Lord in Waiting)
   1985 - 96 Parliamentary Secretary,
      Department of Transport
   1986 - 88 Minister of State, Home Office
   1989 - 90 Paymaster General and Minister
      of State, H M Treasury
   1990 - 92 Minister of State, Foreign and
      Commonwealth Office
   1992 - 94 Minister of State,
      Department of Transport

Caldecote, Viscount (Robert Andrew Inskip)

Type of Peerage . . . . Hereditary
Political Allegiance . . . . . Conservative
Succeeded 1947
Born . . . . 8th October 1917 in London
Educated . . . . Eton College
   Kings College, Cambridge
   Royal Naval College, Greenwich
Professional Career . . . . . 1953 - 69 Director, English Electric
      Company
   1960 - 63 Managing Director,
      English Electric Aviation
   1961 - 67 Deputy Managing Director,
      British Aircraft Corporation
   1965 - 72 Chairman, EDC Movement of
      Exports
   1970 - 71 Chairman, Export Council for
      Europe
   1972 - 80 Chairman, Design Council
   1972 - 82 Chairman, Delta Group plc
   1977 - 80 Chairman, Legal and
      General Group
   1980 - 87 Chairman, Investors in Industry
   1980 - 87 Chairman, BBC General
      Advisory Council
   1983 - 92 Chairman, Mary Rose Trust
   1990 Crown Appointments Commission
Subject Interests . . . . Manufacturing, Engineering, Maritime,
   Education, Christianity
Correspondence Address . . Orchard Cottage, South Harting, Petersfield,
   Hampshire, GU31 5NR
   Tel and Fax: (01730) 825763

MEMBERS OF THE HOUSE OF LORDS

Callaghan of Cardiff, Baron
(Rt Hon Leonard James Callaghan KG)

Type of Peerage	Life
Political Allegiance	Labour
Created	1987
Born	27th March 1912 in Portsmouth
Educated	Portsmouth North Secondary School
Political Career	1945 - 50 MP (Labour) for Cardiff South
	1947 - 50 Parliamentary Secretary, Ministry of Transport
	1950 - 51 Parliamentary and Financial Secretary, Admiralty
	1950 - 83 MP (Labour) for Cardiff South East
	1951 - 53 Opposition Spokesman on Transport, House of Commons
	1953 - 55 Opposition Spokesman on Fuel and Power, House of Commons
	1956 - 61 Opposition Spokesman on Colonial Affairs, House of Commons
	1961 - 64 Shadow Chancellor of the Exchequer
	1964 - 67 Chancellor of the Exchequer
	1967 - 70 Home Secretary
	1970 - 71 Shadow Home Secretary
	1971 - 72 Shadow Employment Secretary
	1972 - 74 Shadow Foreign Secretary
	1974 - 76 Foreign Secretary
	1976 - 80 Leader of the Labour Party
	1976 - 79 Prime Minister
	1979 - 80 Leader of HM Opposition
	1983 - 87 MP (Labour) for Cardiff South and Penarth
	1983 - 87 Father of the House of Commons

Calverley, Baron (Charles Rodney Muff)

Type of Peerage	Hereditary
Political Allegiance	Liberal Democrat
Succeeded	1971
Born	2nd October 1946

Camden, Marquess of (David George Edward Henry Pratt)

Type of Peerage	Hereditary
Political Allegiance	Conservative
Succeeded	1983
Born	13th August 1930 in London
Educated	Eton College
Professional Career	1949 - 50 National Service
	1951 - 52 Learner, Land Agent
	1953 - 54 Learner, Merchant Bank
	1955 - 56 Partner, Discount Broker
	1957 - 69 Director, Discount Broker
	1970 - 76 Chairman, Various Private Companies
	1977 - 97 Chairman, Farming Company
Subject Interests	Farming, Forestry, Sport, Motoring
Recreational Interests	Golf, Shooting, Skiing
Correspondence Address	Wherwell House, Andover, Hampshire, SP11 7JP
	Tel: (01264) 860243 Fax: (01264) 860123

Cameron of Lochbroom, Baron
(Rt Hon Kenneth John Cameron QC)

Type of Peerage	Life
Political Allegiance	Cross Bench
Created	1984
Born	11th June 1931 in Edinburgh
Educated	The Edinburgh Academy
	Corpus Christi College, Oxford
	Edinburgh University
Professional Career	1958 - Barrister (QC 1972)
	1981 - 84 Advocate Depute
	1984 - 89 Lord Advocate
	1989 - Senator of the College of Justice, Scotland
	1994 - Chairman, Royal Fine Art Commission for Scotland
Subject Interests	Music, the Arts, Architecture, Education
Recreational Interests	Fishing, Sailing
Correspondence Address	Court of Session, Parliament Square, Edinburgh, EH1 1RF
	Tel: (0131) 225 2595
	House of Lords, Westminster, London, SW1A 0PW

Camoys, Baron
(Ralph Thomas Campion George Sherman Stonor)

Type of Peerage	Hereditary
Political Allegiance	Cross Bench
Succeeded	1976
Born	16th April 1940 in Henley-on-Thames
Educated	Eton College
	Balliol College, Oxford
Professional Career	1968 - 85 Chairman, Jacksons of Piccadilly
	1975 - 78 Rothschild International Bank (Managing Director, then Chairman)
	1978 - 86 Amex Bank Ltd (Managing Director, then Executive Vice-Chairman)
	1987 - Deputy Chairman, Barclays de Zoete Wedd
	1993 - Deputy Chairman, Sotheby's
	1998 - Lord Chamberlain, HM Household
Subject Interests	Heritage, Economy, Financial services, the Arts
Recreational Interests	Arts, Shooting
Correspondence Address	Stonor Park, Henley-on-Thames, Oxford, RG9 6HF

Campbell of Alloway, Baron (Alan Robertson Campbell QC)

Type of Peerage	Life
Political Allegiance	Conservative
Created	1981
Born	24th May 1917
Educated	Aldenham School
Professional Career	1939 - Barrister (QC 1965, Bencher Inner Temple 1972)
Subject Interests	The Constitution, EC Law, Industrial relations, Restrictive trade practices and monopolies

MEMBERS OF THE HOUSE OF LORDS

Campbell of Croy, Baron
(Rt Hon Gordon Thomas Calthrop Campbell MC, DL)

Type of Peerage . . . . Life
Political Allegiance . . . . . Conservative
Created 1974
Born . . . . 8th June 1921 in Quetta, British India
Educated . . . . Wellington College
Professional Career . . . . . 1939 - 46 Regular Army (Major from 1942)
1946 - 57 HM Diplomatic Service
1975 - 92 Non Executive positions –
business/industry
1981 Chairman (Scotland), International
Year of Disabled People
Political Career . . . . 1959 - 74 MP (Conservative) for
Moray and Nairn
1961 - 63 Assistant Government Whip,
House of Commons
1963 - 64 Parliamentary Secretary,
Scottish Office
1967 - 68 Opposition Spokesman on
Defence, House of Commons
1969 - 70 Opposition Spokesman on
Scotland, House of Commons
1970 - 74 Secretary of State for Scotland
1974 - 79 Opposition Front Bench,
House of Lords
Subject Interests . . . . Foreign affairs, Defence, Consumer interests,
Environment, Disability
Recreational Interests . . . Music, Natural History
Correspondence Address . . House of Lords, Westminster,
London, SW1A 0PW
Tel: (0171) 219 5353 Fax: (0171) 219 5979

Canterbury, Archbishop of
(Most Rev and Rt Hon George Leonard Carey)

Type of Peerage . . . . Bishop
Political Allegiance . . . . . None
Entered Lords 1991
Born . . . . 13th November 1935 in Bow, London
Educated . . . . Bifrons Secondary Modern School, Barking
King's College, University of London
London College of Divinity
Professional Career . . . . . 1950 - 58 Clerk, London Electricity Board
1962 - Ordained Deacon
1962 - 66 Assistant Curate,
St Mary's Islington
1966 - 70 Lecturer, Oak Hill Theological
College, Southgate
1970 - 75 Lecturer, St John's Theological
College, Nottingham
1975 - 82 Vicar, St Nicholas' Church,
Durham
1982 - 87 Principal, Trinity College, Bristol
1987 - 91 Bishop of Bath and Wells
1991 - Archbishop of Canterbury
Subject Interests . . . . Theology
Recreational Interests . . . Reading, Listening to music, Writing
Correspondence Address . . Lambeth Palace, London, SE1 7JU
Tel: (0171) 928 8282 Fax: (0171) 261 9836
Web: www.church-of-
england.org/main/lambeth/abchome.htm

Carew, Baron (Patrick Thomas Conolly-Carew)

Type of Peerage . . . . Hereditary
Political Allegiance . . . . . Cross Bench
Succeeded 1994
Born . . . . 6th March 1938 in London
Professional Career . . . . . 1959 - 65 Captain, Royal Horse Guards
1968, 1972, 1976 Irish Equestrian Team,
Olympic Games
1989 - Member, Fédération Equestre
Internationale
Subject Interests . . . . Ireland, Sport

Carlisle, Bishop of (Rt Rev Ian Harland)

Type of Peerage . . . . Bishop
Political Allegiance . . . . . None
Entered Lords 1996
Born . . . . 19th December 1932 in Nottingham
Educated . . . . Haileybury School
Peterhouse College, Cambridge
Wycliffe Hall, Oxford
Professional Career . . . . . 1956 - 58 Teacher, Sunningdale School
1960 - 63 Curate, Melton Mowbray
1963 - 72 Vicar, Oughitbridge, Sheffield
1972 - 75 Vicar, Fir Vale, Sheffield
1975 - 79 Vicar of Rotherham
1979 - 85 Archdeacon of Doncaster
1985 - 89 Bishop of Lancaster
1989 - Bishop of Carlisle
Subject Interests . . . . Constitution, Law reform, Community
Relations, Police, Education, Agriculture,
Youth policy
Recreational Interests . . . Football, Crosswords, Travel
Correspondence Address . . Rose Castle, Dalston, Carlisle,
Cumbria, CA5 7BZ
Tel: (01697) 476274 Fax: (01697) 476550

Carlisle, Earl of (George Howard)

Type of Peerage . . . . Hereditary
Political Allegiance . . . . . Liberal Democrat
Succeeded 1994
Born . . . . 15th February 1949 in London
Educated . . . . Eton College
Balliol College, Oxford
Army Staff College, Camberley
Professional Career . . . . . 1967 - 87 Regular Army Officer
1994 - Teacher in Estonia; Patron,
The Baltic Council of Great Britain
Political Career . . . . Secretary, British Estonian All-Party
Parliamentary Group
Subject Interests . . . . Baltic states, Foreign affairs,
Defence, Hill farming
Recreational Interests . . . Reading, Travel, Walking, Museums
Correspondence Address . . House of Lords, Westminster,
London, SW1A 0PW
Tel: (0171) 219 5353

MEMBERS OF THE HOUSE OF LORDS

Carlisle of Bucklow, Baron (Rt Hon Mark Carlisle QC)

Type of Peerage	Life
Political Allegiance	Conservative
Created	1987
Born	7th July 1929
Educated	Radley College
	Manchester University
Professional Career	1953 - Barrister (QC 1971)
	1976 - 79 Recorder
	1988 - Chairman, Advisory Committee on Business Appointments
	1990 - Chairman, Criminal Injuries Compensation Board
	1990 - Judge of Court of Appeal of the Channel Islands
Political Career	1964 - 83 MP (Conservative) for Runcorn
	1970 - 72 Parliamentary Secretary, Home Office
	1972 - 74 Minister of State, Home Office
	1979 - 81 Secretary of State for Education and Science
	1982 - 85 Treasurer, Commonwealth Parliamentary Association
	1983 - 87 MP (Conservative) for Warrington South
	1996 - Chairman, Society of Conservative Lawyers
Subject Interests	Penal reform, Criminal law, Education
Recreational Interests . . .	Golf
Correspondence Address . .	Criminal Injuries Compensation Board, Morley House, Holborn Viaduct, London
	Tel: (0171) 842 6801

Carmichael of Kelvingrove, Baron (Neil George Carmichael)

Type of Peerage	Life
Political Allegiance	Labour
Born	October 1921 in Scotland
Created	1983
Educated	Estbank Academy
	Royal College of Science and Technology, Glasgow
Political Career	1962 - 74 MP (Labour) for Glasgow Woodside
	1974 - 83 MP (Labour) for Glasgow Kelvingrove
	1967 - 69 Parliamentary Secretary, Ministry of Transport
	1969 - 70 Parliamentary Secretary, Ministry of Technology
	1974 - 75 Parliamentary Secretary, Department of Environment
	1975 - 76 Parliamentary Secretary, Department of Industry
	1987 - 97 Opposition Spokesman on Scotland and Transport, House of Lords

Carnarvon, Earl of
(Henry George Reginald Molyneux Herbert KCVO KBE, DL)

Type of Peerage	Hereditary
Political Allegiance	Cross Bench
Succeeded	1987
Born	19th January 1924 in London
Educated	Eton College
	Royal Agricultural College, Cirencester
Professional Career	1960 - 67 Chairman, Game Research Association
	1963 - 66 Member, Nature Conservancy Council
	1964 - 66 Chairman, Thoroughbred Breeders Association (also President 1969-74, 1986 - 91)
	1967 - 79 Member, Forestry Commission
	1969 - 75 President, Amateur Riders Association
	1971 - 79 Chairman, South East Economic Planning Council
	1975 - President, Hampshire Association for the Care of the Blind
	1978 - 82 Chairman, Agricultural Research Council
	1978 - Chairman, Standing Conference on Countryside Sports
	1980 - 81 President, Royal Agricultural Society
	1981 - Chairman, Basingstoke and North Hampshire Medical Fund
	1985 - Chairman, Newbury Racecourse plc
	1986 - Chairman, Equine Virology Research Foundation
	1987 - 94 President, Hampshire and Isle of Wight Naturalists Trust
	1989 - Chairman, Standing Conference on London and South Regional Planning
Political Career	1954 - 77 Member, Hampshire County Council (Chairman 1973 - 77)
	1968 - 74 Chairman, County Councils Association Planning Committee
	1971 - 74 Vice-Chairman, County Councils Association
	1993 - Chairman, House of Lords All-Party London Group
	1994 - 97 Vice-President, Association of County Councils
	1997 - Vice-President, Local Government Association
Subject Interests	Countryside, Planning, Farming, Thoroughbred breeding
Recreational Interests . . .	Gardening, Cricket
Correspondence Address . .	Milford Lake House, Burghclere, Newbury, Berkshire, RG20 9EL
	Tel: (01635) 253387 Fax: (01635) 253984

MEMBERS OF THE HOUSE OF LORDS

Carnegy of Lour, Baroness
(Elizabeth Patricia Carnegy of Lour)

Type of Peerage . . . . Life
Political Allegiance . . . . . Conservative
Created 1982
Born . . . . 28th April 1925 in London
Educated . . . . Downham School
Professional Career . . . . . 1943 - 46 Cavendish Laboratory, Cambridge
1958 - 89 Farmer
1956 - 63 County Commissioner, Angus Girl Guides Association
1958 - 62 Training Adviser, (Scotland), Girl Guides Association
1963 - 65 Training Adviser, (Commonwealth HQ), Girl Guides Association
1969 - 84 Honorary Sheriff, Forfar
1979 - 83 Member, Manpower Services Commission (Chairman, Scotland, 1980 -83)
1981 - 88 Chairman, Scottish Council for Community Education
1988 Deputy Lieutenant, Angus
Political Career . . . . 1974 - 82 Councillor, Tayside Regional Council
1976 - 82 Chairman, Education Committee, Tayside Regional Council
1990 - 94 Vice Chairman, Association of Conservative Peers
Subject Interests . . . . Scottish affairs, European Union, Agriculture, Local Government , Constitutional affairs, Education
Correspondence Address . . House of Lords, Westminster, London, SW1A OPW
Tel: (0171) 219 5353
Lour, Forfar, Angus, DD8 2LR
Tel: (01307) 820237

Carnock, Baron (David Henry Arthur Nicholson)
Type of Peerage . . . . Hereditary
Political Allegiance . . . . . Conservative
Succeeded 1982
Born . . . . 10th July 1920 in London
Educated . . . . Winchester College
Balliol College, Oxford
Professional Career . . . . . 1946 - 86 Solicitor
Correspondence Address . . Ermewood House, Harford, Ivybridge, Devon, PL21 0JE

Carr of Hadley, Baron (Rt Hon Leonard Robert Carr)
Type of Peerage . . . . Life
Political Allegiance . . . . . Conservative
Created 1976
Born . . . . 11th November 1916 in London
Educated . . . . Westminster School
Gonville and Caius College, Cambridge
Metallurgist
Professional Career . . . . . 1979 - 86 Director, Cadbury Schweppes
1980 - 85 Chairman, Prudential
Political Career . . . . 1950 - 74 MP (Conservative) for Mitcham
1950 - 55 PPS to Foreign Secretary then Prime Minister (Rt Hon Sir Anthony Eden MP)
1955 - 58 Parliamentary Secretary, Ministry of Labour and National Service
1963 - 64 Secretary for Technical Co-operation
1970 - 72 Secretary of State for Employment
1972 Leader of the House of Commons and Lord President of the Council
1972 - 74 Home Secretary
1974 - 75 MP (Conservative) for Sutton/Carshalton
Subject Interests . . . . Industry, Employment, Economic, Home affairs
Recreational Interests . . . Tennis, Gardening, Music
Correspondence Address . . House of Lords, Westminster, London, SW1A OPW
Tel: (0171) 219 4582
14 North Court, Great Peter Street, London, SW1P 3LL
Tel: (0171) 222 4232
Personal Staff . . . . Mrs Margaret Dunster *(Secretary)*
Tel: (01932) 562446

Carrick Earl of (David James Thoeobald Somerset Butler)
Type of Peerage . . . . Hereditary
Political Allegiance . . . . . Cross Bench
Succeeded 1992
Born . . . . 9th January 1953

MEMBERS OF THE HOUSE OF LORDS

Carrington, Rt Hon Baron
(Peter Alexander Rupert Carrington KG, GCMG, CH, MC)

Type of Peerage . . . . Hereditary
Political Allegiance . . . . . Conservative
Succeeded 1938
Born . . . . 6th June 1919 in London
Educated . . . . Eton College
Professional Career . . . . . 1956 - 59 UK High Commissioner to
Australia
1983 - 84 Chairman, GEC
1983 - 88 Chairman, Board of Trustees,
Victoria and Albert Museum
1984 - 88 Secretary-General, NATO
1988 - 93 Chairman, Christie's International
1991 - 92 Chairman, EC Conference on
Yugoslavia
1992 - Chancellor, University of Reading
Political Career . . . . 1951 - 54 Parliamentary Secretary,
Ministry of Agriculture and Fisheries
1954 - 56 Parliamentary Secretary,
Ministry of Defence
1959 - 63 First Lord of the Admiralty
1963 - 64 Leader of the House of Lords and
Minister without Portfolio
1964 - 70, 1974 - 79 Leader of the
Opposition, House of Lords
1970 - 74 Secretary of State for Defence
1972 - 74 Chairman, Conservative Party
1974 Secretary of State for Energy
1979 - 82 Foreign Secretary
Correspondence Address . . 32a Ovington Square, London, SW13 1LR
Tel: (0171) 584 1476/4243
Fax: (0171) 823 9051
Personal Staff . . . . Miss Margaret Howe *(Secretary)*
Tel: (0171) 584 4243

Carter, Baron (Denis Victor Carter)

Type of Peerage . . . . Life
Political Allegiance . . . . . Labour
Created 1987
Born . . . . 17th January 1932 in London
Educated . . . . Xaverian College, Brighton
East Sussex Institute of Agriculture
Essex Institute of Agriculture
Professional Career . . . . . 1949 - 50, 1953 Audit Clerk
1953 - 54 Farmworker
1957 - Director (and Founder), Agricultural
Accounting and Management Co (AKC)
1970 - 72 Ministry of Agriculture, Fisheries
and Food, Senior Fellowship in
Agricultural Marketing, Oxford University
1975 - Farmer
1976 - Partner, Drayton Farms
1988 - 97 Executive Produce, LINK
1992 - Fellow, Institute of Agricultural
Management
1993 - 97 Chairman, UK Co-operative
Council
Political Career . . . . 1987 - Opposition Spokesman on
Agriculture, Fisheries and Food,
House of Lords
1990 - 97 Opposition Deputy Chief Whip,
House of Lords
1997 - Government Chief Whip,
House of Lords (Captain of the
Honourable Corps of Gentlemen at Arms)
Deputy Chairman of Committees, House of
Lords
Recreational Interests . . . Reading, Walking, Southampton
Football Club
Correspondence Address . . House of Lords, Westminster,
London, SW1A 0PW
Tel: (0171) 219 3131 Fax: (0171) 219 6837

Carver, Baron (Field-Marshal
Richard Michael Power Carver GCB, CBE, DSO, MC)

Type of Peerage . . . . Life
Political Allegiance . . . . . Cross Bench
Created 1977
Born . . . . 24th April 1915 in Bletchingley, Surrey
Educated . . . . Winchester College
Royal Military College, Sandhurst
Professional Career . . . . . 1944 - 47 Commander, 4th Armoured
Brigade
1960 - 62 Commander, 6th Infantry Brigade
1962 - 64 GOC 3rd Division
1964 - 66 Director, Army Staff Duties
1966 - 67 Commander, Far East Land
Forces
1967 - 69 Commander in Chief, Far East
1969 - 71 GOC in C, Southern Command
1971 - 73 Chief of the General Staff
1973 - 76 Chief of the Defence Staff
1977 - 78 British Resident Commissioner
(designate), Rhodesia
Subject Interests . . . . Defence, Military history, Science and
technology
Correspondence Address . . Wood End House, Wickham, Fareham,
Hampshire, PO17 6JZ
Tel: (01329) 832143

Castle of Blackburn, Baroness (Rt Hon Barbara Anne Castle)

Type of Peerage . . . . Life
Political Allegiance . . . . . Labour
Created 1990
Born . . . . 6th October 1910 in Chesterfield
Educated . . . . Bradford Girls' Grammar School
St Hugh's College, Oxford
Professional Career . . . . . 1936 - 40 Editor, Town and County
Councillor
1941 - 44 Administrative Officer,
Ministry of Food
1944 - 45 Housing Correspondent,
Daily Mirror
Political Career . . . . 1945 - 50 MP (Labour) for Blackburn
1950 - 55 MP (Labour) for Blackburn East
1950 - 79 Member, Labour Party
National Executive (Chairman 1958 - 59)
1955 - 79 MP (Labour) for Blackburn
1964 - 65 Minister for Overseas
Development
1965 - 68 Minister of Transport
1968 - 70 First Secretary and State and
Secretary of State for Employment and
Productivity
1974 - 76 Secretary of State for
Social Services
1979 - 89 Member of the European
Parliament (Labour) for Greater Manchester
North, then Greater Manchester West
1979 - 85 Leader of British Labour Group,
European Parliament
1984 - 89 Member of the European
Parliament (Labour) for Greater
Manchester North
Subject Interests . . . . Animal welfare
Recreational Interests . . . Poetry, Walking
Correspondence Address . . House of Lords, Westminster,
London, SW1A 0PW
Tel: (0171) 219 5486 Fax: (01491) 638676
Personal Staff . . . . Mrs Joan Woodman *(Secretary)*
Tel: (01491) 638313

MEMBERS OF THE HOUSE OF LORDS

Cathcart, Earl (Alan Cathcart CB, DSO, MC)

Type of Peerage	Hereditary
Political Allegiance	Conservative
Succeeded	1927 (as a minor)
Born	22nd August 1919 in Eastbourne
Educated	Eton College
	Magdelene College, Cambridge
Professional Career	1939 - 74 Army Officer
	GOC, Berlin 1970 -73)
	1974 - 80 Commodore, Royal Yacht Squadron
	1976 - 82 President, Army Cadet Force Association
	1982 - 86 President, Royal Society for the Prevention of Accidents
Political Career	1976 - 89 Deputy Speaker, House of Lords
Subject Interests	Defence, Safety, Prevention of accidents
Correspondence Address	Moor Hatches, West Amesbury, Salisbury, Wiltshire, SP4 7BH

Catto, Baron (Stephen Gordon Catto)

Type of Peerage	Hereditary
Without Writ of Summons	
Succeeded	1959
Born	14th January 1923

Cavendish of Furness, Baron (Richard Hugh Cavendish)

Type of Peerage	Life
Political Allegiance	Conservative
Created	1990
Born	2nd November 1941 in Holker Hall, Cumbria
Professional Career	1961 - 71 International Banking, London
	1971 - Chairman, Holker Estate, Group of Companies
	1992 - Member, Historic Buildings and Monuments Commission for England
	1993 - Director, Nirex Ltd
	1994 - Chairman, Lancashire and Cumbria Foundation for Medical Research
Political Career	1985 - 90 Member, Cumbria County Council
	1990 - 92 Government Whip, (Lord in Waiting)
Subject Interests	Education, Environment, Industry, Foreign Affairs, Treatment of drug and alcohol abuse, Agriculture, Forestry
Recreational Interests	Gardening, National Hunt Racing, Reading, Travel

Cawdor, Earl of (Colin Robert Vaughan Campbell)

Type of Peerage	Hereditary
Political Allegiance	Cross Bench
Succeeded	1993
Born	30th June 1962

Cawley, Baron (Frederick Lee Cawley)

Type of Peerage	Hereditary
Political Allegiance	Conservative
Succeeded	1954
Born	27th July 1913 in Salford, Lancashire
Educated	Eton College
	New College, Oxford
Professional Career	1939 - 73 Barrister (practising in intellectual property law)
Political Career	1958 - 67 Deputy Chairman of Committees, House of Lords
Subject Interests	Intellectual property law, Wildlife
Recreational Interests	Gardening, Natural history
Correspondence Address	Bircher Hall, Leominster, Herefordshire, HR6 0AX
	Tel: (01586) 780218

Cayzer, Baron (William Nicholas Cayzer)

Type of Peerage	Life
Political Allegiance	Conservative
Created	1981
Born	21st January 1910
Professional Career	1938 - 87 Chairman, Clan Line Steamers
	1956 - 87 Chairman, Union-Castle Mail Steamship Company
	1958 - 94 Chairman, Caledonia Investments

Chadlington, Baron (Peter Selwyn Gummer)

Type of Peerage	Life
Political Allegiance	Conservative
Created	1996
Born	24th August 1942 in Bexley, Kent
Educated	King's School, Rochester
	Selwyn College, Cambridge
Professional Career	1964 - 65 Portsmouth and Sunderland Newspaper Group
	1965 - 66 Viyella International Group
	1966 - 67 Public Relations Manager, Hodgkinson and Partners
	1967 - 74 Public Relations Manager, Industrial and Commercial Finance Corporation
	1974 - Chairman, Shandwick International plc
	1996 - 97 Chairman, Royal Opera House
Recreational Interests	Opera, Ballet, Rugby, Cricket
Correspondence Address	61 Grosvenor Street, London, W1X 9DA
	Tel: (0171) 408 2232 Fax: (0171) 493 3048
Personal Staff	Mrs Carolyn Lambert *(Personal Assistant)*

MEMBERS OF THE HOUSE OF LORDS

Chalfont, Rt Hon Baron
(Rt Hon Alun Arthur Gwynne Jones OBE, MC**)**

Type of Peerage . . . . Life

Political Allegiance . . . . . Cross Bench

Created 1964

Born . . . . 5th December 1919 in Llantarnam

Educated . . . . West Monmouth School
School of Slavonic Studies,
University of London

Professional Career . . . . . 1940 - 61 Regular Army Officer
1961 - 64 Defence Correspondent,
The Times
1970 - 71 Foreign Editor, New Statesman
1983 - 90 Chairman, Nottingham
Building Society
1987 - 95 Chairman, VSEL plc
1989 - 90 Deputy Chairman,
Independent Broadcasting Authority
1990 - 94 Chairman, Radio Authority
1994 - Chairman, Marlborough Stirling plc
1997 - Chairman, Southern Mining
Corporation

Political Career . . . . 1964 - 70 Minister of State, Foreign and
Commonwealth Office
1967 - 70 British Permanent Representative
to the Western European Union
Chairman, All Party Media Group,
House of Lords
President, All Party Defence Group,
House of Lords

Subject Interests . . . . Defence, Foreign affairs, Media

Recreational Interests . . . Music

Correspondence Address . . House of Lords, Westminster,
London, SW1A 0PW
Fax: (0171) 828 4654

Personal Staff . . . . Mrs Gail Caskie *(Personal Assistant)*

Chalker of Wallasey, Baroness (Rt Hon Lynda Chalker)

Type of Peerage . . . . Life

Political Allegiance . . . . . Conservative

Created 1992

Born . . . . 29th April 1942 in Hitchin, Hertfordshire

Educated . . . . Roedean School, Brighton
Heidelberg University
University of London

Professional Career . . . . . 1963 - 69 Statistician, RBL (Unilever) Ltd
1969 - 72 Deputy Head of Market Research,
Shell Mex and BP
1972 - 74 Chief Executive, International
Research, Louis Harris International
Research
1976 - 79 Part Time Adviser, Barclays Bank
International
1997 - Independent Consultant on Africa
and Development

Political Career . . . . 1974 - 92 MP (Conservative) for Wallasey
1976 - 79 Opposition Spokesman on
Social Services, House of Commons
1979 - 82 Parliamentary Secretary,
Department of Health and Social Security
1982 - 83 Parliamentary Secretary,
Department of Transport
1983 - 86 Minister of State, Department of
Transport
1986 - 89 Minister of State, Foreign and
Commonwealth Office
1989 - 97 Minister for Overseas Development,
Foreign and Commonwealth Office

Subject Interests . . . . Europe, Africa, Development,
Volunteer and NGO work

Recreational Interests . . . Jazz, Gardening, Driving, Photography,
Environment, Tourism

Correspondence Address . . House of Lords, Westminster,
London, SW1A 0PW
Tel: (0171) 219 5098 Fax: (0118) 947 2835
E-mail: lchalker@btinternet.com

Personal Staff . . . . Mrs Karen Greve *(Adviser/Secretary)*
Tel: (0118) 946 2894
Miss Kate Wilson *(Researcher)*

Chandos, Viscount (Thomas Orlando Lyttleton)

Type of Peerage . . . . Hereditary

Political Allegiance . . . . . Labour

Succeeded 1980

Born . . . . 12th February 1953

MEMBERS OF THE HOUSE OF LORDS

Chapple, Baron (Francis Joseph Chapple)
Type of Peerage .... Life
Political Allegiance ..... Cross Bench
Created 1984
Born .... 8th August 1921 in London
Educated .... Elementary School
Professional Career ..... 1963 - 84 Assistant General Secretary, then
(from 1966) General Secretary, Electrical
Electronic Telecommunications and
Plumbing Union
1971 - 83 Member, General Council, Trades
Union Congress (Chairman 1982 - 83)
Political Career .... 1965 - 71 Member, Labour Party National
Executive Committee
Subject Interests .... Environment, Science and technology
Recreational Interests ... Pigeon racing, Poetry, Classical music

Charteris of Amisfield, Baron
(Rt Hon Martin Michael Charles Charteris GCB, GCVO, OBE)
Type of Peerage .... Life
Political Allegiance ..... Cross Bench
Created 1978
Born .... 13th September 1913 in London
Educated .... Eton College
Royal Military College, Sandhurst
Professional Career ..... 1932 - 50 Regular Army Officer
1950 - 52 Private Secretary to HRH
Princess Elizabeth
1952 - 72 Assistant Private Secretary to
HM The Queen
1972 - 78 Private Secretary to
HM The Queen and Keeper of the Archive
1978 - 91 Provost of Eton College
1980 - 92 Chairman, National Heritage
Memorial Fund
Subject Interests .... Heritage, Education
Recreational Interests ... Sculpture
Correspondence Address .. 11 Kylestrome House, Cundy Street,
London, SW1W 9JT
Tel: (0171) 730 2959
Wood Stanway House, Wood Stanway,
Cheltenham, Gloucestershire, GL54 5PG
Tel: (01386) 584480

Chatfield, Baron (Ernle David Lewis Chatfield)
Type of Peerage .... Hereditary
On Leave of Absence
Succeeded 1967
Born .... 2nd January 1917 in Edinburgh
Correspondence Address .. 535 Island Road, Victoria,
BC V8S 2T7, Canada

Chelmsford, Viscount (Frederic Jan Thesiger)
Type of Peerage .... Hereditary
Political Allegiance ..... Conservative
Succeeded 1970
Born .... 7th March 1931 in London

Chesham, Baron (Nicholas Charles Cavendish)
Type of Peerage .... Hereditary
Political Allegiance ..... Conservative
Succeeded 1989
Born .... 7th November 1941 in Surrey
Political Career .... 1995 -97 Government Deputy Chief Whip,
(Captain of the Yeomen of the Guard)
Deputy Chairman of Committees, House of
Lords

Chetwode, Baron (Philip Chetwode)
Type of Peerage .... Hereditary
Succeeded 1950
Born .... 26th March 1937 in London
Professional Career ..... 1955 - 66 Officer Royal Horse Guards
Farmer and Stockbroker

Chichester, Bishop of (Rt Rev Eric Waldram Kemp)
Type of Peerage .... Bishop
Political Allegiance ..... None
Entered Lords 1979
Born .... 27th April 1915
Educated .... Brigg Grammar School, Lincolnshire
Exeter College Oxford
St Stephen's House, Oxford
Professional Career ..... 1939 - 41 Curate, St Luke's, Southampton
1941 - 46 Librarian, Pusey House, Oxford
1946 - 69 Fellow, Chaplain and Lecturer,
Exeter College, Oxford
1969 - 74 Dean of Worcester
1974 - Bishop of Chichester
Recreational Interests ... Music
Correspondence Address .. The Palace, Chichester,
West Sussex, PO19 1PY
Tel: (01243) 782161

Chichester, Earl of (Nicholas John Pelham)
Type of Peerage .... Hereditary
Political Allegiance ..... Conservative
Succeeded .... 1944 (as a minor)
Born .... 14th April 1944

Chilston, Viscount (Alastair George Akers-Douglas)
Type of Peerage .... Hereditary
Political Allegiance ..... Conservative
Succeeded 1982
Born .... 5th September 1946
Professional Career ..... Film Producer

Chilver, Baron (Henry Chilver)
Type of Peerage .... Life
Political Allegiance ..... Conservative
Created 1987
Born .... 30th October 1926

MEMBERS OF THE HOUSE OF LORDS

Chitnis, Baron (Pratap Chidamber Chitnis)
Type of Peerage . . . . Life
Political Allegiance . . . . . Cross Bench
Created 1977
Born . . . . 1st May 1936

Cholmondeley, Marquess of
 (David George Philip Cholmondeley)
Type of Peerage . . . . Hereditary
Has Not Taken The Oath
Political Allegiance . . . . . Cross Bench
Succeeded 1990
Born . . . . 18th March 1959

Chorley, Baron (Roger Richard Edward Chorley)
Type of Peerage . . . . Hereditary
Political Allegiance . . . . . Cross Bench
Succeeded 1978
Born . . . . 14th August 1930 in London
Educated . . . . Stowe School
 Gonville and Caius College, Cambridge
Professional Career . . . . . 1955 - 89 Coopers and Lybrand
 (Partner 1967 - 89)
 1965 - 68 Accounting Adviser, National
 Board for Prices and Incomes (seconded)
 1974 - 77 Member, Royal Commission on
 the Press
 1979 - 82 Visiting Professor, Imperial
 College of Science and Technology,
 London University
 1981 - 90 Member, Top Salaries Review
 Body
 1983 - 85 Member, Ordnance Survey,
 Advisory Board
 1990 - Deputy Chairman, British Council
 1991 - 96 Chairman, National Trust
Subject Interests . . . . Heritage, Environment, Development
Recreational Interests . . . Mountains
Correspondence Address . . 9 Melbourne House, Kensington Place,
 London, W8 7PW

Churchill, Viscount (Victor George Spencer)
Type of Peerage . . . . Hereditary
Without Writ of Summons
Succeeded 1973
Born . . . . 31st July 1934

Churston, Baron (John Francis Yarde-Buller)
Type of Peerage . . . . Hereditary
Political Allegiance . . . . . Conservative
Succeeded 1991
Born . . . . 29th December 1934 in London
Educated . . . . Eton College
Correspondence Address . . Yowlestone, Puddington, Tiverton,
 Devon, EX16 8LN
 Tel: (01884) 860328

Citrine, Baron (Norman Arthur Citrine)
Type of Peerage . . . . Hereditary
Without Writ of Summons
Succeeded 1983
Born . . . . 27th September 1914

Clancarty, Earl of (Nicholas Paver Ricard Le Poer Trench)
Type of Peerage . . . . Hereditary
Political Allegiance . . . . . Cross Bench
Succeeded 1995
Born . . . . 1st May 1952 in London
Subject Interests . . . . Film and Visual Arts

Clanwilliam, Earl of (John Herbert Meade)
Type of Peerage . . . . Hereditary
Political Allegiance . . . . . Conservative
Succeeded 1989
Born . . . . 27th September 1919

Clarendon, Earl of (George Frederick Laurence Hyde Villiers)
Type of Peerage . . . . Hereditary
Political Allegiance . . . . . None
Succeeded 1955
Born . . . . 2nd February 1933

Clark of Kempston, Baron (Rt Hon William Gibson Clark)
Type of Peerage . . . . Life
Political Allegiance . . . . . Conservative
Created 1992
Born . . . . 18th October 1917 in London
Professional Career . . . . . 1945 - 62 Practising Accountant
Political Career . . . . 1959 - 66 MP (Conservative) for
 Nottingham South
 1964 - 66 Opposition Spokesman on
 Treasury Matters
 1970 - 74 MP (Conservative) for East Surrey
 1970 - 75 Treasurer, Conservative Party
 1973 Chairman, Select Committee on Tax
 Credits, House of Commons
 1974 - 92 MP (Conservative) for
 Croydon South
 1975 - 77 Deputy Chairman,
 Conservative Party
 1979 - 92 Chairman, Conservative Back
 Bench Finance Committee,
 House of Commons
Subject Interests . . . . Finance, Trade
Recreational Interests . . . Tennis
Correspondence Address . . 3 Barton Street, London, SW1P 3NG
 Tel: (0171) 222 5588

MEMBERS OF THE HOUSE OF LORDS

Cledwyn of Penrhos, Baron (Rt Hon Cledwyn Hughes CH)

Type of Peerage	Life
Political Allegiance	Labour
Created	1979
Born	14th September 1916 in Holyhead, Anglesey
Educated	Holyhead Grammar School
	University of Wales, Aberystwyth
Professional Career	1945 - 64 Solicitor in Private Practice
	1974 - 84 President, University of Wales, Aberystwyth
	1984 - 94 Pro-Chancellor, University of Wales
	1995 - President, University of Wales, Bangor
Political Career	1946 - 54 Anglesey County Council
	1951 - 79 MP (Labour) for Anglesey
	1959 - 64 Shadow Minister for Local Government
	1964 - 66 Minister of State for Commonwealth Relations
	1966 - 68 Secretary of State for Wales
	1968 - 70 Minister of Agriculture, Fisheries and Food
	1974 - 79 Chairman, Parliamentary Labour Party
	1981 - 82 Deputy Leader of the Opposition, House of Lords
	1982 - 92 Leader of the Opposition, House of Lords
Subject Interests	Foreign affairs, Agriculture, Welsh affairs, Education
Recreational Interests	Cricket, Tennis, Football
Correspondence Address	House of Lords, Westminster, London, SW1A 0PW
	Tel: (0171) 735 9300
	Penmorfa, Trearddur, Anglesey, LL65 2YU

Clifford of Chudleigh, Baron, (Captain Thomas Hugh Clifford)

Type of Peerage	Hereditary
Political Allegiance	Cross Bench
Succeeded	1988
Born	17th March 1948 in Singapore
Educated	Downside Abbey
	Royal Agricultural College, Cirencester
Professional Career	1967 - 77 Officer, Coldstream Guards
	1979 - 93 Manager, Ugbrooke Home Farm
	1983 - Manager, Ugbrooke Enterprises and Clifford Estate
Subject Interests	Disability, Family law, Military, Countryside protection, Law and order, Environment, Northern Ireland
Recreational Interests	Fishing, Shooting, Croquet
Correspondence Address	Ugbrooke Park, Chudleigh, South Devon, TQ13 0AD
	Tel: (01626) 852179 Fax: (01626) 853322

Clinton, Baron (Gerard Nevile Mark Fane Trefusis DL)

Type of Peerage	Hereditary
Political Allegiance	Conservative
Succeeded	1965
Born	7th October 1934 in London
Educated	Gordonstoun School
Subject Interests	Forestry, Landowning
Recreational Interests	Horse Racing, Fishing, Shooting
Correspondence Address	Heanton Satchville, Okehampton, Devon, EX20 3QE
	Tel: (01805) 804224

Clinton-Davis, Lord (Stanley Clinton-Davis)

Type of Peerage	Life
Political Allegiance	Labour
Created	1990
Born	6th December 1928 in London
Educated	Hackney Downs School
	Mercers School
	King's College, University of London
Professional Career	Solicitor
	1985 - 89 Member of the European Commission
Political Career	1970 - 83 Labour MP for Hackney Central
	1974 - 79 Parliamentary Secretary, Department of Trade
	1979 - 81 Opposition Spokesman on Trade, House of Commons
	1981 - 83 Opposition Spokesman on Foreign Affairs, House of Commons
	1990 - 97 Principal Opposition Spokesman on Transport, House of Lords
	1997 - Minister of State, Department of Trade and Industry
Subject Interests	Europe, Transport, Foreign affairs, Environment (particularly European issues), Civil liberties, Refugee issues, Trade and industry
Recreational Interests	Political Biographies, Golf, Soccer

Clitheroe, Baron (Ralph John Assheton)

Type of Peerage	Hereditary
Political Allegiance	Conservative
Succeeded	1984
Born	3rd November 1929
Professional Career	1990 - Chairman, Yorkshire Bank plc
Subject Interests	Industry, Conservation
Recreational Interests	Skiing, Field Sports, Country Pursuits

Clwyd, Baron (John Anthony Roberts)

Type of Peerage	Hereditary
Political Allegiance	Cross Bench
Succeeded	1987
Born	2nd January 1935
Educated	Harrow School
	Trinity College, Cambridge
Professional Career	1973 - 77 Legal Assistant, ICC
Recreational Interests	Music, Literature
Correspondence Address	24 Salisbury Avenue, Cheam, Sutton, Surrey, SM1 2DJ
	Tel: (0181) 642 2527

MEMBERS OF THE HOUSE OF LORDS

Clyde, Baron (Rt Hon James John Clyde)

Type of Peerage . . . . Life (Law Lord)
Political Allegiance . . . . . Cross Bench
Created 1996
Born . . . . 29th January 1932 in Edinburgh
Educated . . . . The Edinburgh Academy
Corpus Christi College, Oxford
Edinburgh University
Professional Career . . . . . 1959 - Advocate (QC 1971)
1972 - 85 Chancellor to the Bishop of Argyll
and the Isles
1972 - 96 Member, later Chairman,
Scottish Valuation Advisory Council
1973 - 74 Advocate - Depute
1974 - 85 Chairman, Medical Appeal
Tribunal
1979 - 85 Judge, Courts of Appeal of
Jersey and Guernsey
1985 - 96 Senator of the College of
Justice (Scotland)
1991 - 92 Chairman, Orkney
Childrens Inquiry
Subject Interests . . . . Law
Recreational Interests . . . Music, Gardening
Correspondence Address . . House of Lords, Westminster,
London, SW1A 0PW
Tel: (0171) 219 3202

Clydesmuir, Baron (David Ronald Colville)

Type of Peerage . . . . Hereditary
Has Not Taken The Oath
Political Allegiance . . . . . None
Succeeded 1996
Born . . . . 8th April 1949

Cobbold, Baron (David Antony Fromanteel Lytton Cobbold) ·

Type of Peerage . . . . Hereditary
Political Allegiance . . . . . Cross Bench
Succeeded 1987
Born . . . . 14th July 1937 in London
Educated . . . . Eton College
Trinity College, Cambridge
Professional Career . . . . . 1955 - 57 Pilot Officer, Royal Air Force
1962 - 72 Bank of London and South
America Ltd
1972 - Managing Director Lytton
Enterprises Ltd
1974 - 79 Treasurer, Finance for
Industry Ltd
1979 - 87 Treasury Director, British
Petroleum
1987 - 89 Director/General Manager,
TSB – Hill Samuel Bank
1989 - 94 Managing Director,
Gaiacorp (UK) Ltd
Subject Interests . . . . European Union (particularly Economic and
Monetary Union), China, Historic buildings
Correspondence Address . . Knebworth House, Knebworth,
Hertfordshire, SG3 6PY
Tel: (01438) 812661 Fax: (01438) 811908

Cobham, Viscount (John William Leonard Lyttleton)

Type of Peerage . . . . Hereditary
On Leave of Absence
Succeeded 1977
Born . . . . 5th June 1943

Cochrane of Cults, Baron

Type of Peerage . . . . Hereditary
Political Allegiance . . . . . Conservative
Succeeded 1990
Born . . . . 20th September 1926

Cockfield, Baron (Rt Hon Francis Arthur Cockfield)

Type of Peerage . . . . Life
Political Allegiance . . . . . Conservative
Created 1978
Born . . . . 28th September 1916
Political Career . . . . 1979 - 82 Minister of State, HM Treasury
1983 - 84 Chancellor of the
Duchy of Lancaster

Cocks of Hartcliffe, Baron (Rt Hon Michael Frances Loveel Cocks)

Type of Peerage . . . . Life
Political Allegiance . . . . . Labour
Created 1987
Born . . . . 19th August 1929
Educated . . . . Bristol University
Professional Career . . . . . Education (various posts)
1993 - 98 Vice-Chairman,
BBC Board of Governors
Political Career . . . . 1970 - 87 MP (Labour) for Bristol South
1974 - 76 Assistant Government Whip,
House of Commons
1976 - 79 Government Chief Whip,
House of Commons
1979 - 85 Opposition Chief Whip,
House of Commons
Deputy Speaker and
Deputy Chairman of Committees,
House of Lords

Coggan, Baron (Rt Rev and Rt Hon Frederick Donald Coggan)

Type of Peerage . . . . Life
Political Allegiance . . . . . Cross Bench
Created . . . . 1980 (previously in the House of Lords as
Archbishop)
Born . . . . 9th October 1909 in London
Educated . . . . Merchant Taylors School
St John's College, Cambridge
Wycliffe Hall, Oxford
Professional Career . . . . . 1931 - 34 Assistant Lecturer in Semitic
Languages and Literature, Manchester
University
1934 - 37 Curate, St Mary's, Islington,
London
1937 - 44 Professor, Wycliffe College,
Toronto
1944 - 56 Principal, London College of
Divinity
1956 - 61 Bishop of Bradford
1961 - 74 Archbishop of York
1974 - 80 Archbishop of Canterbury
Subject Interests . . . . Ecclesiastical, Moral, Third world
Recreational Interests . . . Travel, Tapestry
Correspondence Address . . 28 Lions Hall, St Swithun Street,
Winchester, Hampshire, SO23 9HW
Tel: (01962) 864289

MEMBERS OF THE HOUSE OF LORDS

Coleraine, Baron (James Martin Bonar Law)
Type of Peerage . . . . Hereditary
Political Allegiance . . . . . Conservative
Succeeded 1981
Born . . . . 8th August 1931 in London

Coleridge, Baron (William Duke Coleridge)
Type of Peerage . . . . Hereditary
Political Allegiance . . . . . Conservative
Succeeded 1984
Born . . . . 18th June 1937 in Ottery St Mary

Colgrain of Everlands, Baron (David Colin Campbell)
Type of Peerage . . . . Hereditary
Political Allegiance . . . . Cross Bench
Born . . . . 24th April 1920 in Bombay, India
Succeeded 1973
Educated . . . . Eton College
　　　　　　　　　　　　Trinity College, Cambridge
Professional Career . . . . . 1940 - 45 Army, 9th Queen's Royal Lancers
　　　　　　　　　　　　1945 - 49 Manager, Grindlays Bank
　　　　　　　　　　　　1949 - 83 Antony Gibbs and Sons Ltd
　　　　　　　　　　　　　　(Director from 1954)
Subject Interests . . . . Farming, Forestry, Music
Recreational Interests . . . Soccer, Cricket, Birdwatching, Music
Correspondence Address . . Bushes Farm, Weald, Sevenoaks,
　　　　　　　　　　　　Kent, TN14 6ND
　　　　　　　　　　　　Tel: (01732) 463279

Colville of Culross, Viscount
(John Mark Alexander Colville QC)
Type of Peerage . . . . Hereditary
Political Allegiance . . . . . Cross Bench
Born . . . . 19th July 1933 in Victoria B.C., Canada
Succeeded 1945
Educated . . . . Rugby School
　　　　　　　　　　　　New College, Oxford
Professional Career . . . . . 1960 - Barrister (QC 1978)
Political Career . . . . 1972 - 74 Minister of State, Home Office
Subject Interests . . . . Law, Human rights

Colwyn, Baron (Ian Anthony Hamilton-Smith CBE)
Type of Peerage . . . . Hereditary
Political Allegiance . . . . . Conservative
Succeeded 1967
Born . . . . 1st January 1942 in Cheltenham
Educated . . . . Cheltenham College
　　　　　　　　　　　　St Bartholomew's Medical School
　　　　　　　　　　　　Royal Dental Hospital, University of London
Professional Career . . . . . 1966 - Dental Surgeon
　　　　　　　　　　　　1990 - President, Natural Medicines Society
　　　　　　　　　　　　1992 - President, Mental Health Foundation
　　　　　　　　　　　　1994 - 97 President, Society of
　　　　　　　　　　　　　　Advancement of Anaesthesia in Dentistry
　　　　　　　　　　　　1996 - Chairman, Dental Protection Ltd
Political Career . . . . 1997 - Chairman, Refreshment
　　　　　　　　　　　　　　Sub Committee, House of Lords
Subject Interests . . . . Health, Pharmaceutical biotechnology,
　　　　　　　　　　　　Alternative/Complementary medicine,
　　　　　　　　　　　　Music, Sport
Recreational Interests . . . Tennis, Golf, Rugby union
Correspondence Address . . 53 Wimpole Street, London, W1M 7DF
　　　　　　　　　　　　Tel: (0171) 935 6809 Fax: (0171) 224 0689
　　　　　　　　　　　　House of Lords, Westminster,
　　　　　　　　　　　　London, SW1A 0PW

Colyton, Baron (Alasdair John Munro Hopkinson)
Type of Peerage . . . . Hereditary
Has Not Taken The Oath
Political Allegiance . . . . . None
Succeeded 1996
Born . . . . 7th May 1958

Combermere, Rt Hon Viscount
(Michael Wellington Stapleton-Cotton)
Type of Peerage . . . . Hereditary
Political Allegiance . . . . . Cross Bench
Succeeded 1968
Born . . . . 8th August 1929 in South Wales
Educated . . . . Eton College
　　　　　　　　　　　　King's College, University of London
Professional Career . . . . . 1947 - 48 Constable, Palestine Police
　　　　　　　　　　　　1948 - 50 Constable, Royal Canadian
　　　　　　　　　　　　　　Mounted Police
　　　　　　　　　　　　1950 - 58 Pilot, RAF
　　　　　　　　　　　　1958 - 61 Representative, Teleflex
　　　　　　　　　　　　　　Products Ltd
　　　　　　　　　　　　1972 - 94 Lecturer, then Senior Lecturer in
　　　　　　　　　　　　　　Religious Studies, Birkbeck College,
　　　　　　　　　　　　　　London
Parliamentary Interests . . Adult education, Religious education,
　　　　　　　　　　　　World religion
Correspondence Address . . Vanners, Bucklebury, near Reading,
　　　　　　　　　　　　Berkshire, RG7 6RU
　　　　　　　　　　　　Tel: (01189) 713336

Congleton, Baron (Christopher Patrick Parnell)
Type of Peerage . . . . Hereditary
Political Allegiance . . . . . Cross Bench
Succeeded 1967
Born . . . . 11th March 1930 in Minstead, Hampshire
Educated . . . . Eton College
　　　　　　　　　　　　New College, Oxford
Professional Career . . . . . 1959 - Farming
　　　　　　　　　　　　1972 - 77 Chairman, Salisbury and South
　　　　　　　　　　　　　　Wiltshire Museum
　　　　　　　　　　　　1981 - 87 Member, Advisory Board for
　　　　　　　　　　　　　　Redundant Churches
　　　　　　　　　　　　1997 - Chairman, Wessex Medical Trust
Political Career . . . . 1964 - 77 Councillor, Salisbury and Wilton
　　　　　　　　　　　　　　Rural District Council (Chairman 1972)
Subject Interests . . . . Local government, Rural economy,
　　　　　　　　　　　　Archaeology
Recreational Interests . . . Skiing, Music, Angling
Correspondence Address . . West End Lodge, Ebbesbourne Wake,
　　　　　　　　　　　　Salisbury, Wiltshire, SP5 5JR
　　　　　　　　　　　　Tel: (01722) 700301

Constantine of Stanmore, Baron (Theodore Constantine CBE)
Type of Peerage . . . . Life
Political Allegiance . . . . . Conservative
Created 1981
Born . . . . 15th March 1910

MEMBERS OF THE HOUSE OF LORDS

Conyngham, Marquess
(Frederick William Henry Francis Conyningham)
Type of Peerage . . . . Hereditary
Without Writ of Summons
Succeeded 1974
Born . . . . 13th March 1924

Cooke of Islandreagh, Baron (Victor Alexander Cooke OBE)
Type of Peerage . . . . Life
Political Allegiance . . . . . Cross Bench
Created 1992
Born . . . . 18th October 1920
Educated . . . . Marlborough College
Trinity College, Cambridge
Professional Career . . . . . 1940 - 46 Royal Navy
1946 - 89 Henry R Ayton Ltd, Belfast
(Chairman 1970 - 89)
1963 Chairman, Belfast Savings Bank
1970 - 85 Director, Northern Ireland
Airports
1974 - 78 Member, Northern Ireland
Economic Council
1970 - 89 Chairman, Henry R Ayton, Belfast
1980 - 81 Chairman, Harland and Wolff
1990 - 92 Chairman, Commissioners of Irish
Lights
Political Career . . . . 1960 - 68 Senator, Northern Ireland
Parliament
Recreational Interests . . . Sailing, Shooting

Cooke of Thorndon, Baron
(Rt Hon Robin Brunskill Cooke KBE)
Type of Peerage . . . . Life
Political Allegiance . . . . . Cross Bench
Created 1996
Born . . . . 9th May 1926 in Wellington, New Zealand
Educated . . . . Wanganui Collegiate School, New Zealand
Victoria University College, Wellington
Clare College, Cambridge
Gonville and Caius College, Cambridge
Professional Career . . . . . 1955 - 72 Barrister
1972 - 76 Judge of Supreme Court of New
Zealand
1976 - 96 Judge of Court of Appeal of New
Zealand (President from 1986)
1981 - 82 President, Court of Appeal of
Cook Islands
1982 , 1994 President, Court of Appeal of
Western Samoa
1995 - Judge of Supreme Court of Fiji
1997 - Judge of Court of Final Appeal of
Hong Kong
Subject Interests . . . . Constitutional and administrative law
(United Kingdom and Commonwealth)
Recreational Interests . . . Theatre, 'The Times" crossword, Watching
cricket
Correspondence Address . . House of Lords, Westminster,
London, SW1A 0PW
Tel: (0171) 219 3202 Fax: (0171) 219 6156
PO Box 1530, Wellington, New Zealand
Tel: 00 64 4 471 5355 ext. 6334
Fax: 00 64 4 495 3295
Personal Staff . . . . Ms Dale Densem *(Secretary)*
Tel: 00 64 4 479 3142

Cope of Berkeley, Baron (Rt Hon John Ambrose Cope)
Type of Peerage . . . . Life
Political Allegiance . . . . . Conservative
Created 1997
Born . . . . 13th May 1937 in Leicester
Educated . . . . Oakham School
Professional Career . . . . Chartered Accountant
Political Career . . . . 1974 - 83 MP (Conservative) for
Gloucestershire South
1979 - 83 Government Whip, House of
Commons
1983 - 97 MP (Conservative) for Northavon
1983 - 87 Government Deputy Chief Whip,
House of Commons
1987 - 89 Minister of State, Department of
Employment
1989 - 91 Minister of State, Northern Ireland
Office
1990 - 92 Deputy Chairman and Joint
Treasurer, Conservative Party
1997 - Opposition Spokesman on Northern
Ireland, House of Lords
1992 - 94 HM Paymaster General
1997 - Opposition Spokesman, on Northern
Ireland, House of Lords
Correspondence Address . . House of Lords, Westminster,
London, SW1A 0PW
Tel: (0171) 219 2249
E-mail: john.cope@email.tory.org.uk

Cork and Orrery, Earl of (John William Boyle DSC, VRD, FICE)
Type of Peerage . . . . Hereditary
Political Allegiance . . . . . Conservative
Succeeded 1995
Born . . . . 12th May 1916 in London
Educated . . . . Harrow School
King's College, University of London
Professional Career . . . . . Chartered Civil Engineer
Subject Interests . . . . Defence, Engineering industry
Recreational Interests . . . Country, Family life
Correspondence Address . . Nether Craigantaggart, Dunkeld,
Perthshire, PH8 0HQ
Tel and Fax: (01738) 710239

Cornwallis, Baron (Fiennes Neil Wykeham Cornwallis OBE)
Type of Peerage . . . . Hereditary
Political Allegiance . . . . . Cross Bench
Succeeded 1982
Born . . . . 29th June 1921 in Winchester
Educated . . . . Eton College
Professional Career . . . . . 1952 - 54 President, British Agricultural
Contractors Association
1957 - 63, 1986 - President, National
Association of Agricultural Contractors
1978 - 81, 1991 - 92 Chairman, Town and
County Building Society
1984 - 86 Vice President, Federation of
Agricultural Co-operatives
1990 - 94 Chairman, English Apples and
Pears Ltd
Subject Interests . . . . Horticulture, Local government,
Environment
Recreational Interests . . . Fishing, Philately
Correspondence Address . . Ruck Farm, Horsmonden, Tonbridge, Kent,
TN12 8DT
Tel: (01892) 722267 Fax: (01892) 722465
25B Queen's Gate Mews, London, SW7 5QL
Tel: (0171) 589 1167

MEMBERS OF THE HOUSE OF LORDS

Cottenham, Earl (Kevin Charles Everard Digby Pepys)
Type of Peerage . . . . Hereditary
Political Allegiance . . . . . Conservative
Succeeded 1968
Born . . . . 27th November 1948

Cottesloe, Baron (Commander John Tapling Fremantle)
Type of Peerage . . . . Hereditary
Political Allegiance . . . . . Cross Bench
Succeeded 1994
Born . . . . 22nd January 1927 in London
Educated . . . . Eton College
Professional Career . . . . . 1944 - 66 Royal Navy
    1969 - 70 High Sheriff of Buckinghamshire
    1984 - 97 Lord Lieutenant of
      Buckinghamshire
Subject Interests . . . . Agriculture, Forestry, Rural Affairs, Steam
    Railways, Sherlock Holmes
Recreational Interests . . . Shooting, Stalking, Crosswords
Correspondence Address . . The Estate Office, Swanbourne, Milton
    Keynes, Buckinghamshire, MK17 0SW
    Tel: (01296) 720256 Fax: (01296) 720302
Personal Staff . . . . Miss Fiona Dowdell *(Secretary)*

Courtown, Earl of
(James Patrick Montagu Burgoyne Winthrop Stopford)
Type of Peerage . . . . Hereditary
Political Allegiance . . . . . Conservative
Succeeded 1975
Born . . . . 19th March 1954
Political Career . . . . 1995 - 97 Government Whip,
    (Lord in Waiting)
    1997 - Opposition Whip, House of Lords

Coventry, Earl of (George William Coventry)
Type of Peerage . . . . Hereditary
Political Allegiance . . . . . Conservative
Succeeded . . . . 1940 (as a minor)
Born . . . . 25th January 1934

Cowdray, Viscount (Michael Orlando Weetman Pearson)
Type of Peerage . . . . Hereditary
Political Allegiance . . . . . Cross Bench
Succeeded 1995
Born . . . . 17th June 1944

Cowdrey of Tonbridge, Baron (Michael Colin Cowdrey CBE)
Type of Peerage . . . . Life
Political Allegiance . . . . . Conservative
Created 1997
Born . . . . 24th December 1932 in Bangalore, South
    India
Educated . . . . Tonbridge School
    Brasenose College, Oxford
Professional Career . . . . . 1951 - 77 Cricketer
    (Captain of Kent and of England)
    1989 - 93 Chairman, International
      Cricket Council
    1991 - Consultant, Barclays Bank plc
    1995 - Director, Bilton plc
Subject Interests . . . . Sport , The Commonwealth
Recreational Interests . . . Cricket, Rugby, Soccer, Golf
Correspondence Address . . Angmering Park, Littlehampton,
    West Sussex, BN16 4EX
    Tel: (01903) 871423 Fax: (01903) 871530
Personal Staff . . . . Miss Virginia Freeland *(Secretary)*

Cowley, Earl (Gareff Graham Wellesely)
Type of Peerage . . . . Hereditary
Political Allegiance . . . . . Conservative
Succeeded 1975
Born . . . . 30th July 1934

Cox of Queensbury, Baroness (Caroline Anne Cox)
Type of Peerage . . . . Life
Political Allegiance . . . . . Conservative
Created 1982
Born . . . . 6th July 1937 in London
Educated . . . . Channing School
    University of London
Professional Career . . . . . 1974 - 77 Head of Sociology Department,
    North London Polytechnic
    1977 - 84 Director, Nursing Education
      Research Unit, Chelsea College,
      London University
    1980 - Co-Director, Education Research
      Trust
    1985 Baroness in Waiting
Political Career . . . . 1986 - A Deputy Speaker, House of Lords
Subject Interests . . . . Human rights, Humanitarian aid, Health,
    Education
Recreational Interests . . . Squash, Campanology, Hill walking
Correspondence Address . . 1 Arnellan House, 146 Slough Lane,
    Kingsbury, London, NW9 8XJ
    Tel: (0181) 204 7336 Fax: (0181) 204 5661
Personal Staff . . . . Mrs Jana Person *(Personal Assistant)*

Craig of Radley, Baron
(Marshal of the RAF David Brownrigg Craig GCB, OBE)
Type of Peerage . . . . Life
Political Allegiance . . . . . Cross Bench
Created 1991
·*Born* . . . . 17th September 1929 in Dublin
Educated . . . . Radley College
    Lincoln College, Oxford
Professional Career . . . . . 1951 - 80 RAF (Staff and Command
    Appointments)
    1980 - 82 Vice-Chief of the Air Staff
    1982 - 85 Air Officer Commanding in Chief,
      RAF Strike Command
    1985 - 88 Chief of the Air Staff
    1988 - 91 Chief of the Defence Staff
    1991 - 92 Director, ML Holdings plc
    1992 - 93 Chairman, Enterprise
      Lottery Co Ltd
Subject Interests . . . . Defence, Science and Technology
    (especially Information Technology)
Recreational Interests . . . Shooting, Woodwork, Golf
Correspondence Address . . House of Lords, Westminster,
    London, SW1A 0PW
    Tel: (0171) 219 5353
    E-mail: craigd@parliament.uk

Craigavon, Viscount (Janric Fraser Craig)
Type of Peerage . . . . Hereditary
Political Allegiance . . . . . Cross Bench
Succeeded 1974
Born . . . . 9th June 1944

MEMBERS OF THE HOUSE OF LORDS

Craigmyle, Baron (Thomas Donald Mackay Shaw)

Type of Peerage	Hereditary
Political Allegiance	Conservative
Succeeded	1944
Born	17th November 1923 in London
Educated	Eton College
	Trinity College, Oxford
Parliamentary Interests	Ethical matters, maintaining Christian values in public life
Correspondence Address	18 The Boltons, London, SW10 9SY
	Tel: (0171) 373 5157/3533
	Fax: (0171) 370 2711

Cranborne, Viscount
(Rt Hon Robert Michael James Gascoyne-Cecil)

Type of Peerage	Hereditary
Political Allegiance	Conservative
Entered Lords	1992 (as Baron Cecil of Essendon)
Born	30th September 1946 in London
Educated	Eton College
	Christ Church, Oxford
Political Career	1979 - 87 MP (Conservative) for Dorset South
	1992 - 94 Parliamentary Secretary, Ministry of Defence
	1994 - 97 Lord Privy Seal and Leader of the House of Lords
	1997 - Leader of The Opposition, House of Lords
Parliamentary Interests	Constitutional, administrative and foreign affairs, Defence
Correspondence Address	House of Lords, Westminster, London, SW1A 0PW
	Tel: (0171) 219 3237

Note: Viscount Cranborne is the heir to the Marquess of Salisbury who continues to sit in the House of Lords. He was introduced to the House of Lords in the name of a subsidiary peerage, under a rarely used procedure.

Cranbrook, Earl of (Gathorne Gathorne-Hardy)

Type of Peerage	Hereditary
Political Allegiance	Conservative
Succeeded	1978
Born	20th June 1933 in London
Professional Career	1961 - 70 Senior Lecturer in Zoology, University of Malaya
	1973 - 80 Editor, Ibis
	1981 - 92 Member, Royal Commission on Environmental Pollution
	1987 - 89 Board Member, Anglian Water Authority
	1989 - Harwich Haven Authority (Vice Chairman from 1995)
	1991 - Chairman, English Nature
Political Career	1980 - 83, 1987 - 90 Chairman, Environment Sub-Committee of European Communities Select Committee, House of Lords

Cranworth, Baron (Philip Bertram Gurdon)

Type of Peerage	Hereditary
Political Allegiance	Conservative
Succeeded	1964
Born	24th May 1940
Educated	Eton College
	Magdalene College, Cambridge
Correspondence Address	Grundisburgh Hall, Woodbridge, Suffolk, IP13 6TW

Crathorne, Baron (Charles James Crathorne)

Type of Peerage	Hereditary
Political Allegiance	Conservative
Succeeded	1977
Born	12th September 1939 in Sutton, Surrey
Educated	Eton College
	Trinity College, Cambridge
Professional Career	1963 - 66 Impressionist Painting Department, Sotheby's
	1966 - 69 Assistant to the President, Parke-Bernet (New York)
	1969 - Fine Art Consultancy
	1979 - 96 Director, Blakeney Hotels
	1990 - Chairman, The Georgian Group
	1996 - Chairman, Joint Committee of National Amenity Societies
	1996 - Director, Cliveden plc
Political Career	1981 - Secretary, All Party Parliamentary Arts and Heritage Group
	1983 - Editorial Board, "House Magazine"
Parliamentary Interests	Visual and performing arts, Heritage
Recreational Interests	Photography, Travel, Country pursuits
Correspondence Address	Crathorne House, Yarm, North Yorkshire, TS15 0AT
	Tel: (01642) 700431 Fax: (01642) 700632

Craven, Earl of (Benjamin Robert Joseph Craven)

Type of Peerage	Hereditary
Without Writ of Summons (a minor)	
Succeeded	1990
Born	13th June 1989

Crawford and Balcarres, Earl of
(Rt Hon Robert Alexander Lindsay KT)

Type of Peerage	Hereditary
Political Allegiance	Conservative
Succeeded	1992 (First entered House of Lords with Life Peerage as Lord Balniel, 1974)
Born	5th March 1927
Political Career	1955 - 74 MP (Conservative) for Hertford
	1970 - 72 Minister of State, Defence
	1972 - 74 Member of State, Foreign and Commonwealth Office

Crawshaw, Baron (William Michael Clifton Brooks)

Type of Peerage	Hereditary
Political Allegiance	None
Succeeded	1997
Born	25th March 1933

MEMBERS OF THE HOUSE OF LORDS

Crickhowell, Baron (Rt Hon Roger Nicholas Edwards)

Type of Peerage . . . . Life
Political Allegiance . . . . . Conservative
Created 1987
Born . . . . 25th February 1934 in London
Educated . . . . Westminster School
      Trinity College, Cambridge
Professional Career . . . . . 1957 - 76 Director/Managing Director,
      William Brandts (Insurance Holdings) Ltd
      and Subsidiaries
      1988 - President, University of Wales,
      Cardiff
      1988 - 89 Chairman, National Rivers
      Advisory Committee
      1989 - 96 Chairman, National Rivers
      Authority
Political Career . . . . 1970 - 87 MP (Conservative) for Pembroke
      1974 - 79 Opposition Spokesman on Welsh
      Affairs, House of Commons
      1979 - 87 Secretary of State for Wales
Subject Interests . . . . Environment, Arts, Welsh affairs
Recreational Interests . . . Fishing, Gardening, Collecting water colours
      and drawings
Correspondence Address . . 4 Henning Street, London, SW11 3DR
      Pontesgob Mill, Fforest Coalpit, near
      Abergavenny, NP7 7LS

Croft, Baron (Bernard William Henry Page Croft)

Type of Peerage . . . . Hereditary
Political Allegiance . . . . . None
Succeeded 1997
Born . . . . 28th August 1949

Croham, Baron (Douglas Albert Vivian Allen GCB)

Type of Peerage . . . . Life
Political Allegiance . . . . . Cross Bench
Created 1978
Born . . . . 15th December 1917 in Wallington, Surrey
Educated . . . . Wallington County School for Boys
      London School of Economics
Professional Career . . . . . 1939 - 77 Civil Service
      1966 - 68 Permanent Secretary,
      Department of Economic Affairs
      1968 - 74 Permanent Secretary,
      H M Treasury
      1974 - 77 Permanent Secretary, Civil
      Service Department and Head of Home
      Civil Service
      1978 - 83 Adviser to Governor,
      Bank of England
      1978 - 86 Deputy Chairman then
      (Chairman from 1982), British National
      Oil Corporation
      1982 - Chairman, Anglo-German Foundation
      1983 - 87 Chairman, Guinness Peat Group
Subject Interests . . . . Energy, Economic policy, Anglo-German
      relations, Civil Service
Recreational Interests . . . Woodwork, Contract bridge
Correspondence Address . . 9 Manor Way, South Croydon,
      Surrey, CR2 7BT
      Tel: (0181) 688 0496

Cromartie, Earl of (John Ruaridh Grant Mackenzie)

Type of Peerage . . . . Hereditary
Political Allegiance . . . . . Cross Bench
Succeeded 1989
Born . . . . 12th June 1948 in Inverness
Educated . . . . Rannoch School, Perthshire
      Strathclyde University, Glasgow
Professional Career . . . . . 1978 - Explosives Consultant
Subject Interests . . . . Land Use in the Highlands, Public access to
      land, Explosives
Recreational Interests . . . Mountaineering, Geology, Art
Correspondence Address . . Cromartie Estate Office, Castle Leod,
      Strathpeffer, Ross-shire, IVI4 9AA
      Tel: (01997) 421264
Personal Staff . . . . Ms B Martin (*Secretary*)

Cromer, Earl of (Evelyn Rowland Esmond Baring)

Type of Peerage . . . . Hereditary
Political Allegiance . . . . . Conservative
Succeeded 1991
Born . . . . 3rd June 1946 in London
Professional Career . . . . . 1979 - 94 Director, Inchcape Pacific Ltd
      1979 - 94 Managing Director, various
      Inchape Companies
      1994 - Chief Executive,
      Cromer Associates Ltd
Recreational Interests . . . Mountain climbing and Deep sea diving

Cromwell, Baron (Geoffrey John Bewicke-Copley)

Type of Peerage . . . . Hereditary
Political Allegiance . . . . . Cross Bench
Succeeded 1982
Born . . . . 4th March 1960

Crook, Baron (Douglas Edwin Crook)

Type of Peerage . . . . Hereditary
Political Allegiance . . . . . Cross Bench
Succeeded 1989
Born . . . . 19th November 1926 in Islington, London
Educated . . . . Whitgift Middle School, Croydon
      Imperial College, London
Professional Career . . . . . 1945 - 93 Consulting Engineer, Halcrow
Recreational Interests . . . Painting and Drawing
Correspondence Address . . Ridgehill Barn, Etchinghill, Folkestone,
      Kent, CT18 8DF
      Tel: (01303) 863353

Cross, Viscount (Assherton Henry Cross)

Type of Peerage . . . . Hereditary
Political Allegiance . . . . . Conservative
Succeeded . . . . 1932 (as a minor)
Born . . . . 7th May 1920

MEMBERS OF THE HOUSE OF LORDS

Cuckney, Baron (John Graham Cuckney)

Type of Peerage . . . . Life
Political Allegiance . . . . . Conservative
Created 1995
Born . . . . 12th July 1925
Educated . . . . Shrewsbury School
St Andrews University
Professional Career . . . . . 1970 - 72 Chairman, Mersey Docks and
Harbour Board
1972 - 74 Chief Executive, Property Service
Agency Department of the Environment)
1974 - 85 Chairman, International
Military Services
1974 - 78 Senior Crown Agent and
Chairman, Crown Agents for Overseas
Governments and Administrations
1976 - 80 Chairman, EDC for Building
1977 - 79 Chairman, Port of London
Authority
1978 - 87 Chairman,
Thomas Cook Group Ltd
1979 - 94 Director/Chairman,
Royal Insurance Holdings plc
1981 - 85 Chairman, International Maritime
Bureau, International Chamber of
Commerce
1981 - 84 Chairman, Brooke Bond Group plc
1983 - 86 Chairman, John Brown plc
1985 - 94 Royal Insurance Holdings plc
1985 - 89 Chairman, Westland Group plc
1987 - 92 Chairman, 3i Group plc
1988 - 91 Chairman, Understanding
Industry Trust
1990 - 95 Vice-Chairman,
Glaxo Wellcome plc
1992 - 95 Adviser to the Secretary of State
for Social Security and Chairman,
Maxwell Pensioners' Trust
1994 - 97 Chairman, Orion Publishing Group
Subject Interests . . . . City matters, Economic and
financial affairs

Cudlipp, Baron (Hugh Cudlipp OBE)

Type of Peerage . . . . Life
Political Allegiance . . . . . Liberal Democrat
Created 1974
Born . . . . 28th August 1913 in Cardiff
Professional Career . . . . . 1932 - 35 Features Editor, Sunday Chronicle
1935 - 37 Features Editor, Daily Mirror
1937 - 40, 1946 - 49 Editor,
Sunday Pictorial
1950 - 52 Managing Editor, Sunday Express
1952 - 63 Editorial Director, Daily Mirror
and Sunday Mirror
1961 - 63 Chairman, Odhams Press Ltd
1963 - 68 Chairman, Daily Mirror
Newspapers Ltd
1968 - 73 Chairman, International
Publishing Corporation

**Cullen of Ashbourne, Baron
(Charles Borlase Marsham Cokayne MBE)**

Type of Peerage . . . . Hereditary
Political Allegiance . . . . . Conservative
Succeeded 1932
Born . . . . 6th October 1912 in Roehampton, Surrey
Educated . . . . Eton College
Professional Career . . . . 1935 - 75 Stockbroker
Political Career . . . . 1977 - 79 Opposition Whip, House of Lords
1979 - 82 Government Whip,
(Lord in Waiting)
1982 - 91 Deputy Speaker, House of Lords
Parliamentary Interests . . Finance, Health, Optics, Sport
Correspondence Address . . 75 Cadogan Gardens, London, SW3 2RB
Tel: (0171) 589 1981

Cumberlege, Baroness (Julia Frances Cumberlege CBE)

Type of Peerage . . . . Life
Political Allegiance . . . . . Conservative
Created 1990
Born . . . . 27th January 1943 in India
Educated . . . . Convent of the Sacred Heart,
Tunbridge Wells
Professional Career . . . . 1981 - 88 Chairman, Brighton Health
Authority
1984 - 88 Vice Chairman, then Chairman,
National Association of Health Authorities
1988 - 92 Chairman, South West Thames
Regional Health Authority
Political Career . . . . 1966 - 79 Member, Lewes District Council
(Leader 1977-78)
1974 - 85 Member, East Sussex County
Council (Chairman, Social Services
Committee, 1979 -80)
1992 - 97 Parliamentary Secretary,
Department of Health
Recreational Interests . . . Bicycling, "Other people's gardens"
Correspondence Address . . Vuggles Farm, Newick, Lewes,
Sussex, BN8 4RU
Tel: (01273) 400453 Fax: (01273) 401084
Personal Staff . . . . Mrs Charlotte Standing *(Secretary)*
Tel: (0181) 877 1528

Cunliffe, Baron (Roger Cunliffe)

Type of Peerage . . . . Hereditary
Political Allegiance . . . . . Cross Bench
Succeeded 1963
Born . . . . 12th January 1932 in Furneux Pelham,
Hertfordshire
Educated . . . . Eton College
Loughborough Technical College
Trinity College, Cambridge
Architectural Association
Open University
Professional Career . . . . . Architect, Planning and Management
Consultant
1969 - 71 Director, Architectural
Association
Subject Interests . . . . Export of consultancy services,
Life-long learning
Recreational Interests . . . Tree Planting, Taxonomy, Photography
Correspondence Address . . The Broadhurst, Brandeston, Woodbridge,
Suffolk, IP13 7AG

Currie of Marylebone, Baron (David Anthony Currie)
Type of Peerage . . . . Life
Political Allegiance . . . . . Labour
Created 1996
Born . . . . 9th December 1946

MEMBERS OF THE HOUSE OF LORDS

D

Dacre, Baroness (Rachel Leila Douglas-Home)
Type of Peerage . . . . Hereditary
Political Allegiance . . . . . Cross Bench
Peerage Revived 1970
Born . . . . 24th October 1929

Dacre of Glanton, Baron (Hugh Redwald Trevor-Roper)
Type of Peerage . . . . Life
Political Allegiance . . . . . Conservative
Created 1979
Born . . . . 15th January 1914 in Glanton,
  Northumberland
Professional Career . . . . . 1957 - 80 Regius Professor of Modern
  History, Oxford University
  1974 - 88 Director, Times Newspapers
  1980 - 87 Master of Peterhouse,
  Cambridge University

Dahrendorf, Baron (Ralf Gustav Dahrendorf)
Type of Peerage . . . . Life
Political Allegiance . . . . . Liberal Democrat
Created 1993
Born . . . . 1st May 1929 in Hamburg, Germany
Educated . . . . University of Hamburg
  London School of Economics
Professional Career . . . . . 1958 - 69 Professor of Sociology, Hamburg,
  then Tubingen and Konstanz Universities
  1970 - 74 European Commissioner
  (Foreign Trade and Foreign Affairs)
  1974 - 84 Director, London School of
  Economics
  1987 - 97 Warden, St Antony's College,
  Oxford
Political Career . . . . 1969 - 70 Parliamentary Secretary of State,
  Foreign Office, West Germany
Subject Interests . . . . Europe, Economic policy, Social policy
Correspondence Address . . Bankgesellschaft Berlin (UK) plc,
  1 Crown Court, Cheapside,
  London, EC2V 6JP
  Tel: (0171) 572 6100 Fax: (0171) 572 6256

Dalhousie, Earl of (Simon Ramsay KT)
Type of Peerage . . . . Hereditary
Political Allegiance . . . . . None
Succeeded 1950
Born . . . . 17th October 1914

Darcy de Knayth, Baroness (Davina Marcia Ingrams DBE)
Type of Peerage . . . . Hereditary
Political Allegiance . . . . . Cross Bench
Succeeded . . . . 1943 (as a minor)
Born . . . . 10th July 1938 in London
Educated . . . . St Mary's School, Wantage
  Sorbonne, Paris
Subject Interests . . . . Disability matters (particularly education,
  transport, mobility and access)
Recreational Interests . . . Theatre, Cinema

Daresbury, Baron (Peter Gilbert Greenall)
Type of Peerage . . . . Hereditary
Political Allegiance . . . . . None
Succeeded 1996
Born . . . . 18th July 1953 in London
Educated . . . . Eton College
  Magdalene College, Cambridge
  London Business School
Professional Career . . . . . 1981 - 1982 Finance and Planning,
  Greenall Whitley
  1982 - 1986 Managing Director,
  Stretton Leisure
  1986 - 1988 Greenalls Retail Management
  1988 - 1992 Managing Director,
  Greenalls Brewery/Greenalls Inns
  1988 - Chairman, Aintree Racecourse
  1992 - Managing Director, then
  Chief Executive, Greenalls Group
Correspondence Address . . The Greenalls Group plc, Wilderspool
  House, Greenalls Avenue, Warrington,
  Cheshire, WA4 6RH
  Tel: (01925) 651234 Fax: (01925) 630110
  Hall Lane Farm, Daresbury, Warrington,
  Cheshire, WA4 4AF
  Tel: (01925) 740212 Fax: (01925) 740884
Personal Staff . . . . Mrs Joanne Burke *(Personal Assistant)*
  Tel: (01925) 651234

Darling, Baron (Robert Charles Henry Darling)
Type of Peerage . . . . Hereditary
Political Allegiance . . . . . Conservative
On Leave of Absence
Succeeded 1936
Born . . . . 15th May 1919 in Lyndhurst, Hampshire
Educated . . . . Wellington College, Berkshire
  Royal Military College, Sandhurst
Professional Career . . . . . 1939 - 54 Army Officer, Somerset
  Light Infantry
  1954 - 79 Assistant Secretary, then
  Secretary, Chief Executive, Royal Bath
  and West Society
Recreational Interests . . . Gardening, Fishing
Correspondence Address . . Puckpits, Limpley Stoke, Bath,
  Somerset, BA3 6JH
  Tel: (01225) 722146

Darnley, Earl of (Adam Ivo Stuart Bligh)
Type of Peerage . . . . Hereditary
Political Allegiance . . . . . Conservative
Succeeded 1980
Born . . . . 8th November 1941

Dartmouth, Earl of (Gerald Humphrey Legge)
Type of Peerage . . . . Hereditary
Political Allegiance . . . . . None
Succeeded 1962
Born . . . . 26th April 1924

MEMBERS OF THE HOUSE OF LORDS

Darwen, Baron (Roger Michael Davies)

Type of Peerage	Hereditary
Without Writ of Summons	
Succeeded	1988
Born	28th June 1938

Daventry, Viscount
(Francis Humphrey Maurice FitzRoy Newdegate)

Type of Peerage	Hereditary
Political Allegiance	Conservative
Succeeded	1986
Born	17th December 1921 in Havant, Hampshire
Subject Interests	Agriculture
Recreational Interests	Shooting, Fishing

David, Baroness (Nora Ratcliff David)

Type of Peerage	Life
Political Allegiance	Labour
Created	1978
Born	23rd September 1913 in Ashby-de-la Zouch, Leicestershire
Educated	Ashby Girls' Grammar School
	St Felix School, Southwold
	Newnham College, Cambridge
Professional Career	1964 - 83 JP, City of Cambridge
Political Career	1964 - 74 Member, Cambridgeshire City Council
	1974 - 78 Member, Cambridgeshire County Council
	1978 - 79 Government Whip (Baroness in Waiting)
	1979 - 82 Opposition Whip, House of Lords
	1980 - 86, 1988 - 90 Opposition Spokesman on Education, House of Lords
	1982 - 87 Opposition Deputy Chief Whip, House of Lords
	1986 - 88 Opposition Spokesman on Local Government, House of Lords
Subject Interests	Environment, Education, Children, Penal affairs, Theatre, the Arts
Recreational Interests	Walking, Theatre, Swimming, Travel, Opera
Correspondence Address	House of Lords, Westminster, London, SW1A 0PW
	Tel: (0171) 219 3159 Fax: (0171) 219 5979
	50 Highsett, Cambridge, CB2 1NZ
	Tel: (01223) 350376

Davidson, Viscount (John Andrew Davidson)

Type of Peerage	Hereditary
Political Allegiance	Conservative
Succeeded	1970
Born	22nd December 1928
Political Career	1985 - 86 Government Whip (Lord in Waiting)
	1986 - 91 Government Deputy Chief Whip (Captain of the Yeomen of the Guard)

Davies, Baron (David Davies)

Type of Peerage	Hereditary
Political Allegiance	Liberal Democrat
Succeeded	1944 (as a minor)
Born	2nd October 1940
Educated	Eton College
	King's College, Cambridge
	Cranfield Institute of Technology
Professional Career	1975 - Chairman, Welsh National Opera Company
Subject Interests	Arts, Construction
Recreational Interests	Sailing, Opera, Countryside
Correspondence Address	Plas Dinam, Llandinam, Powys, SY17 5DG
	Tel and Fax: (01686) 688202

Davies of Coity, Baron (David Garfield Davies)

Type of Peerage	Life
Political Allegiance	Labour
Created	1997
Born	24th June 1935 in Bridgend, Glamorgan
Educated	Heolgam Secondary Modern School, Bridgend
	Bridgend Technical College
Professional Career	1950 - 69 Junior Operative, Apprentice and Electrician, Steel Company of Wales
	1969 - 97 Area Organiser, then Deputy Divisional Officer, National Officer and (from 1986) General Secretary, Union of Shop Distributive and Allied Workers (USDAW)
	1986 - 97 Member, General Council, Trade Union Congress (Spokesman on International Affairs 1991 - 97)
Political Career	1963 - 69 Parish Councillor (Labour)
	1966 - 69 Rural District Councillor (Labour)
Subject Interests	Industrial relations, Education, National Health Service
Recreational Interests	Football, Rugby, Cricket, Golf, Family, Reading
Correspondence Address	64 Dairyground Road, Bramhall, Stockport, Cheshire, SK7 2QW
	Tel: (0161) 439 9548
	House of Lords, Westminster, London, SW1A 0PW
	Tel: (0171) 219 5353/6932

MEMBERS OF THE HOUSE OF LORDS

Denington, Baroness (Evelyn Joyce Denington DBE)
Type of Peerage . . . . Life
Political Allegiance . . . . . Labour *(No longer active in House)*
Created 1978
Born . . . . 9th August 1907

Denman, Baron (Charles Spencer Denman CBE, MC, TD)
Type of Peerage . . . . Hereditary
Political Allegiance . . . . . Conservative
Succeeded 1971
Born . . . . 7th July 1916

Denning, Rt Hon Baron (Rt Hon Alfred Thompson Denning QC)
Type of Peerage . . . . Life (Former Law Lord)
Has Not Taken The Oath
Political Allegiance . . . . . Cross Bench
Created 1957
Born . . . . 23rd January 1899 in Whitchurch,
Hampshire
Educated . . . . Andover Grammar School
Magdalen College, Oxford
Professional Career . . . . . 1923 - 38 Barrister (KC 1938)
1944 - 48 High Court Judge
1948 - 57 Lord Justice of Appeal
1957 - 62 Lord of Appeal in Ordinary
1962 - 82 Master of the Rolls
Correspondence Address . . The Lawn, Whitchurch,
Hampshire, RG28 7AS
Personal Staff . . . . Mr Peter Port *(Agent)*
Tel: (01980) 611380

Denton of Wakefield, Baroness (Jean Denton CBE)
Type of Peerage . . . . Life
Political Allegiance . . . . . Conservative
Created 1991
Born . . . . 29th December 1935
Political Career . . . . 1991 - 92 Government Whip, (Baroness in
Waiting)
1992 - 93 Parliamentary Secretary,
Department of Trade and Industry
1993 - 94 Parliamentary Secretary,
Department of Environment
1994 - 97 Parliamentary Secretary,
Northern Ireland Office

Deramore, Baron (Richard Arthur de Yarburgh-Bateson)
Type of Peerage . . . . Hereditary
On Leave Of Absence
Succeeded 1964
Born . . . . 9th April 1911 in London
Educated . . . . Harrow School
St John's College, Cambridge
Professional Career . . . . . 1932 - 81 Architect
Subject Interests . . . . Architecture, Motoring, Cycling,
Recreational Interests . . . Writing, Watercolour painting and drawing
Correspondence Address . . Heslington House, Aislaby, Pickering,
North Yorkshire, YO18 8PE
Tel: (01751) 473195

Derby, Earl of (Edward Richard William Stanley)
Type of Peerage . . . . Hereditary
Political Allegiance . . . . . Cross Bench
Succeeded 1994
Born . . . . 10th October 1962 in London
Educated . . . . Eton College
Royal Agricultural College, Cirencester
Professional Career . . . . . 1981 - 85 Grenadier Guards
1995 - President, Knowsley
Chamber of Commerce
1995 - President, Liverpool
Chamber of Commerce
1995 - President, Liverpool College
Subject Interests . . . . Merseyside
Recreational Interests . . . Skiing, Shooting, Food and wine
Correspondence Address . . Knowsley, Prescot, Merseyside, L34 4AF
Tel and Fax: (0151) 489 6148
Personal Staff . . . . Miss Margaret Brooks *(Secretary)*

**Derwent, Baron
(Robin Evelyn Leo Vanden-Bempde-Johnstone)**
Type of Peerage . . . . Hereditary
Political Allegiance . . . . . Conservative
Succeeded 1986
Born . . . . 30th October 1930 in London
Educated . . . . Winchester College
Clare College, Cambridge
Professional Career . . . . . 1953 - 69 HM Diplomatic Service
1969 - 85 Director, N M Rothschild and
Sons Ltd
1985 - Managing Director, Hutchinson
Whampoa (Europe) Ltd
Subject Interests . . . . National Parks, Foreign Affairs,
Telecommunications
Recreational Interests . . . Shooting, Fishing
Correspondence Address . . 9 Queen Street, Mayfair, London, W1X 7PH
Tel: (0171) 491 1888

Desai, Baron (Meghnad Jagdishchandra Desai)
Type of Peerage . . . . Life
Political Allegiance . . . . . Labour
Born . . . . 10th July 1940 in Baroda, India
Created 1991
Professional Career . . . . . 1965 - 83 Lecturer, then Senior Lecturer
and Reader in Economics, London
School of Economics
1983 - Professor of Economics,
London School of Economics
1990 - 95 Head of Development Studies
Institute
1992 - Director, Centre for the Study of
Global Governance, London School
of Economics
Correspondence Address . . London School of Economics, Houghton
Street, London, WC2A 2AE

MEMBERS OF THE HOUSE OF LORDS

Devon, Earl of (Charles Christopher Courtenay)

Type of Peerage .... Hereditary
Political Allegiance..... None
Succeeded........... 1935
Born............... 13th July 1916 in Honiton
Educated .... Winchester School
            Royal Military Academy, Sandhurst
Correspondence Address .. The Estate Office, Powderham Castle,
            Kenton, Exeter, Devon, EX6 8JQ
            Tel: Office (01626) 891367 Ext 17
            Fax: (01626) 890729
            E-mail: powderham@eclipse.co.uk
Personal Staff........ Lt Col Cedric Delfonce DSO TD
            (Personal Assistant)

Devonport, Viscount (Terence Kearley)

Type of Peerage .... Hereditary
Political Allegiance..... Cross Bench
Succeeded........... 1973
Born............... 29th August 1944 in Peasmarsh, Sussex
Professional Career..... 1967 - 86 Architect
            1977 - 96 Farmer and Fruit Owner
            1978 - 86 Landscapt Architect
            1984 - 86 Residential Home Owner
            1986 - 96 Property Developer
            1994 - 96 Trustee, Tree Advisory Trust
            1995 - 96 President, Arborticultural
            Association
Subject Interests........ The Arts, Architecture, Landscape,
            Environment, Farming and wildlife
            conservation
Recreational Interests ... Walking, Skiing, Music and Country Sports

Devonshire, Rt Hon Duke of
(Andrew Robert Buxton Cavendish KG)

Type of Peerage .... Hereditary
Political Allegiance..... Cross Bench
Succeeded........... 1950
Born............... 2nd January 1920
Political Career........ 1960 - 62 Parliamentary Secretary,
            Commonwealth Relations Office
            1962 - 64 Minister of State,
            Commonwealth Relations Office
            1963 - 64 Parliamentary Secretary,
            Colonial Office

Dholakia, Baron (Navnit Dholakia OBE)

Type of Peerage .... Life
Created.............. 1997
Political Allegiance..... Liberal Democrat
Born............... 4th March 1937 in Tabora, Tanzania
Educated .... Institute of Science, Bhavnagar,
            Gujarat, India
            Brighton Technical College
Professional Career..... 1960 -66 Medical Laboratory Technician
            1966 - 68 Development Officer, National
            Committee for Commonwealth Immigrants
            1968 - 76 Senior Development Officer,
            then Principal Officer and Secretary,
            Community Relations Commission
            1976 - 81 Principal Officer, Commission for
            Racial Equality
            1984 - 94 Head, Administration of Justice
            Section, Commission for Racial Equality
            1995 - Vice Chairman, National Association
            for Care and Resettlement of Offenders
Political Career........ 1961 - 64 Councillor (Liberal),
            Brighton County Borough Council
            1969 - 74 Secretary, Race and Community
            Relations Panel, Liberal Party
            1996 - Member, Federal Policy and Federal
            Executive Committee, Liberal Democrats
Subject Interests........ Criminal justice
Recreational Interests ... Photography, Travel, Gardening, Cooking
Correspondence Address .. 76 Penland Road, Haywards Heath,
            West Sussex, RH16 1PH
            Tel and Fax: (01444) 450065

Diamond, Baron (Rt Hon John Diamond)

Type of Peerage .... Life
Political Allegiance..... Labour
Born............... 30th April 1907
Created.............. 1970
Professional Career..... Accountant
Political Career........ 1945 - 51 MP (Labour) for Manchester
            Blackley
            1957 - 70 MP (Labour) for Gloucester
            1964 - 70 Chief Secretary to the Treasury
            1982 - 88 Leader of Social Democratic
            Party, House of Lords

Dickinson, Baron (Richard Claverins Hyett Dickinson)

Type of Peerage .... Life
Political Allegiance..... Cross Bench
Succeeded........... 1943
Born............... 26th March 1926

MEMBERS OF THE HOUSE OF LORDS

Digby, Baron (Edward Henry Kenelm Digby)

Type of Peerage	Hereditary
Political Allegiance	Conservative
Succeeded	1964
Born	24th July 1924 in London
Educated	Eton College
	Trinity College, Oxford
Professional Career	1966 - 77 Chairman, Royal Agricultural Society of the Commonwealth
	1972 - 79 Deputy Chairman, South West Economic Planning Council
	1970 - 91 Director, Beazer plc
	1984 - Lord Lieutenant of Dorset
	1984 - 95 Chairman, Dorset Magistrates Courts Committee
	1986 - 91 Director, Gifford-Hill (Dallas)
	1986 - 91 Director, Kier International and Gifford-Hill Inc
	1990 - 97 Director, PACCAR (UK) Ltd
Political Career	1962 - 69 Member, Dorchester Rural District Council
	1966 - 81 Member, Dorset County Council (Vice Chairman from 1974)
Subject Interests	Local government, Magistrates' courts
Recreational Interests . . .	Skiing, Shooting
Correspondence Address . .	Minterne, Dorchester, Dorset, DT2 7AU
	Tel: (01300) 341370 Fax: (01300) 341747

Dilhorne, Viscount (John Mervyn Manningham-Buller)

Type of Peerage	Hereditary
Political Allegiance	Conservative
Succeeded	1980
Born	28th February 1932 in London
Professional Career	1950 - 57 Officer, Coldstream Guards
	1957 - 65 Brown Fleming and Murray, Chartered Accountants
	1965 - 67 Senior International Auditor and Taxation Manager
	1967 - 68 Stuart South, Taxation Adviser
	1968 - 69 Sales Director, Stewart Smith
	1969 - 71 Managing Director, Clarkson de Falbe
	1970 - 74 Managing Director, Stewart Smith
	1979 - Barrister
Subject Interests	Housing, Landlord and tenant law
Recreational Interests . . .	Singing, Skiing, Rugby, Shooting, Fishing

Dixon, Baron (Rt Hon Donald Dixon)

Type of Peerage	Life
Political Allegiance	Labour
Created	1997
Born	6th March 1929 in Jarrow
Educated	Elementary School, Jarrow
Professional Career	1943 - 79 Ship's Carpenter
	1997 - Deputy Lieutenant, Tyne and Wear
Political Career	1979 - 97 MP (Labour) for Jarrow
	1983 - 87 Opposition Whip, House of Commons
	1987 - 96 Opposition Deputy Chief Whip, House of Commons
Subject Interests	Housing, Local government, Trade unions, Shipping
Recreational Interests . . .	Football, Boxing, Reading
Correspondence Address . .	1 Hillcrest, Jarrow, Tyne and Wear, NE32 4DP
	Tel: (0191) 489 7635
	House of Lords, Westminster, London, SW1A 0PW
	Tel: (0171) 219 4129

Dixon-Smith, Baron (Robert William Dixon-Smith)

Type of Peerage	Life
Political Allegiance	Conservative
Born	30th September 1934 in Braintree, Essex
Created	1993
Educated	Oundle School, Northamptonshire
	Writtle College, Essex
Professional Career	1958 - Farmer
	1974 - 85 Chairman of Governors, Writtle College
	1985 - 93 Chairman of Governors, Anglia Polytechnic University
Political Career	1965 - 93 Member, Essex County Council (Chairman 1986 - 89)
	1980 - 93 Member, Association of County Councils (Chairman 1992 - 93)
	1994 - Member, Select Committee on Science and Technology, House of Lords
Subject Interests	Agriculture, Local government, Environment
Recreational Interests . . .	Golf, Shooting, Fishing
Correspondence Address . .	Lyons Hall, Braintree, Essex, CM7 9SH
	Tel: (01376) 326834 Fax: (0171) 352 9724

Donaldson of Lymington, Baron (Rt Hon John Francis Donaldson)

Type of Peerage	Life
Political Allegiance	Cross Bench
Born	6th October 1920 in London
Created	1988
Educated	Charterhouse School
	Trinity College, Cambridge
Professional Career	1946 - 66 Barrister (QC 1961)
	1966 - 79 High Court Judge
	1979 - 82 Lord Justice of Appeal
	1982 - 92 Master of the Rolls
Subject Interests	Administration of justice, Financial law, Shipping
Recreational Interests . . .	Sailing
Correspondence Address . .	House of Lords, Westminster, London, SW1A 0PW
	Tel and Fax: (0171) 588 6610

Donegall, Marquess (Dermot Richard Craud Chichester LVO)

Type of Peerage	Hereditary
Political Allegiance	Conservative
Succeeded	1975
Born	18th April 1916 in London
Educated	Harrow School
	Royal Military Academy, Sandhurst
Correspondence Address . .	Dunbrody Park, Arthurstown, County Wexford, Ireland

MEMBERS OF THE HOUSE OF LORDS

Donoughmore, Earl of
(Richard Michael John Hely-Hutchinson)

Type of Peerage . . . . Hereditary
Political Allegiance . . . . . Conservative
Succeeded 1981
Born . . . . 8th August 1927 in London
Educated . . . . Winchester College
New College, Oxford
Professional Career . . . . . 1952 - 53 St Mary's Hospital Paddington,
then Westminster Children's Hospital
1954 - 56 Officer, Royal Army
Medical Coprs
1957 - 66 Chairman and Managing Director,
Perdio Electronics Ltd
1967 - 74 WR Grace and Co (New York)
1986 - 97 Chairman, Hodder Headline plc
Subject Interests . . . . Small businesses
Recreational Interests . . . Fishing, Horseracing, Shooting
Correspondence Address . . Manor House, Bampton, Oxford, OX18 2LQ
Tel: (01993) 850231 Fax: (01993) 851334

Donoughue, Baron (Bernard Donoughue)

Type of Peerage . . . . Life
Political Allegiance . . . . . Labour
Succeeded 1985
Born . . . . 8th September 1934 in Ashton,
Northamptonshire
Educated . . . . Northampton Grammar School
Lincoln College, Oxford
Nuffield College, Oxford
Harvard University, USA
Professional Career . . . . . 1963 - 74 Senior Lecturer, London School
of Economics
1979 - 81 Development Director,
Economist Intelligence Unit
1981 - 82 Assistant Editor, The Times
1982 - 91 Investment Manager in City
Political Career . . . . 1974 - 79 Senior Policy Adviser to
successive Prime Ministers
(Rt Hon Harold Wilson MP and
Rt Hon James Callaghan MP)
1991 - 97 Opposition Spokesman on
Treasury, then Energy and National
Heritage, House of Lords
1997 - Parliamentary Secretary, Ministry of
Agriculture, Fisheries and Food
Subject Interests . . . . Arts, Sports, Finance
Recreational Interests . . . Horseracing, Music, Theatre, Literature
Correspondence Address . . House of Lords, Westminster,
London, SW1P 0AW
Tel: (0171) 219 5979
71 Ebury Mews East, London, SW1W 9QA
Tel: (0171) 730 7332

Dormand of Easington, Baron (John Donkin Dormand)

Type of Peerage . . . . Life
Political Allegiance . . . . . Labour
Created 1987
Born . . . . 27th August 1919 in Haswell, County
Durham
Educated . . . . Bede College, Durham
Loughborough College
St Peter's Hall, Oxford
Professional Career . . . . . 1963 - 70 District Education Officer,
Easington Council
Political Career . . . . 1970 - 87 MP (Labour) for Easington
1974 - 79 Government Whip,
House of Commons
1981 - 87 Chairman, Parliamentary
Labour Party
Subject Interests . . . . Education, Coal industry, Regional policy,
Film industry, Local government
Recreational Interests . . . Music, Sport and Films

Dormer, Baron (Geoffrey Henry Dormer)

Type of Peerage . . . . Hereditary
Political Allegiance . . . . . None
Born . . . . 13th May 1920 in London
Succeeded 1995
Educated . . . . Eton College
Trinity College, Cambridge
Professional Career . . . . . 1939 - 46, 1970 - 71 RNVR Officer
1960 - 70 RNR Officer
Subject Interests . . . . Navy
Recreational Interests . . . Sailing, Gardening
Correspondence Address . . Yew Tree Cottage, Dittisham, Dartmouth,
Devon, TQ6 0EX
Tel: (01803) 722272

Dowding, Baron

Type of Peerage . . . . Hereditary
Political Allegiance . . . . . Cross Bench
Succeeded 1992
Born . . . . 18th February 1948

Downe, Viscount (John Christian George Dawnay)

Type of Peerage . . . . Hereditary
Political Allegiance . . . . . None
Succeeded 1965
Born . . . . 18th January 1935 in Wykeham, North
Yorkshire

MEMBERS OF THE HOUSE OF LORDS

Downshire, Marquess of (Arthur Robin Ian Hill)
Type of Peerage . . . . Hereditary
Political Allegiance . . . . . Conservative
Succeeded 1989
Born . . . . 10th May 1929 in London
Educated . . . . Eton College
Professional Career . . . . . 1959 - 60 Audit Clerk, Mellors Basden & Co
         (Accountants)
         1960 - 63 Clerk, Gerrard and Reid Ltd
         (Discount Brokers)
         1963 - Senior Partner, Clifton Castle Farms
Political Career . . . . 1965 - 74 Member, Bedale Rural
         District Council
         1965 - 74 Chairman, Bedale, Thirsk and
         Malton Conservative Association
         1995 - President, Lagan Valley
         Conservative Association
Subject Interests . . . . Landowning, Conservation, Northern Ireland
Recreational Interests . . . Shooting, Travel
Correspondence Address . . Clifton Castle, Ripon, North
         Yorkshire, HG4 4AB
         Tel: (01765) 689611/(0171) 581 1903
         Fax: (01765) 689974

Drogheda, Earl of (Henry Dermot Ponsonby Moore)
Type of Peerage . . . . Hereditary
Political Allegiance . . . . . Cross Bench
Succeeded 1989
Born . . . . 14th January 1937 in London

Dubs of Battersea, Baron (Alfred Dubs)
Type of Peerage . . . . Life
Political Allegiance . . . . . Labour
Created 1994
Born . . . . December 1932 in Prague, Czechoslovakia
Educated . . . . London School of Economics
Professional Career . . . . . Local Government Officer
         1988 - 94 Director, Refugee Council
         1994 - 97 Deputy Chairman, Broadcasting
         Standards Council
Political Career . . . . 1979 - 83 MP (Labour) for Battersea South
         1983 - 87 MP (Labour) for Battersea
         1997 - Parliamentary Secretary,
         Northern Ireland Office
Subject Interests . . . . Civil liberties, Penal reform, National Health
         Service, Ireland, Human rights, Race
         relations/Immigration
Recreational Interests . . . Walking
Correspondence Address . . House of Lords, Westminster,
         London, SW1A 0PW
         Tel: (0171) 219 3590 Fax: (0171) 219 2082

Ducie, Earl of (David Leslie Morton)
Type of Peerage . . . . Hereditary
Without Writ of Summons
Succeeded 1991
Born . . . . 20th September 1951

Dudley, Earl of (William Humble David Ward)
Type of Peerage . . . . Hereditary
Political Allegiance . . . . . Conservative
Succeeded 1969
Born . . . . 5th January 1920 in Westminster, London
Professional Career . . . . . 1939 - 45 Adjurant 10th Royal Hussars
         1942 - 43 ADC to the Viceroy of India
         1949 - 70 Director, Baggerige Brick
         Company
         1950 - 70 Director, British Federal Welder
         and Machine Company
Political Career . . . . 1972 - 74 Member/Chairman, European
         Committee on Economics and Regional
         Policy, House of Lords
Subject Interests . . . . Economics, Environment

Dudley, Baroness (Barbara Amy Felicity Hamilton)
Type of Peerage . . . . Hereditary
On Leave Of Absence
Succeeded 1972
Born . . . . 23rd April 1907 in Kempsey, Worcestershire
Recreational Interests . . . Artist

Dulverton, Baron (Gilbert Michael Hamilton Willis)
Type of Peerage . . . . Hereditary
Political Allegiance . . . . . Cross Bench
Succeeded 1992
Born . . . . 2nd May 1944

Dundee, Earl of (Alexander Henry Scrymgeour)
Type of Peerage . . . . Hereditary
Political Allegiance . . . . . Conservative
Succeeded 1983
Born . . . . 5th June 1949
Political Career . . . . 1986 - 89 Government Whip,
         (Lord in Waiting)

Dundonald, Earl of (Iain Alexander Douglas Blair Cochrane)
Type of Peerage . . . . Hereditary
Political Allegiance . . . . . Conservative
Succeeded 1985
Born . . . . 17th February 1961 in London
Educated . . . . Wellington College, Berkshire
         Royal Agricultural College, Cirencester
Professional Career . . . . . 1985 - 97, Chairman, Jarrett Securities
         1996 - 97 Managing Director, Anglo Pacific
         Resources plc
Subject Interests . . . . Scottish Affairs, Marine Environment,
         Agriculture, Forestry, Country Matters,
         Information Technology, Alcohol/Licensing
         Matters
Recreational Interests . . . Walking, Sailing, Skiing, Fishing and
         Shooting
Correspondence Address . . Lochnell Castle, Ledaig, Argyll, PA37 1QT
         Tel: (01631) 720580

MEMBERS OF THE HOUSE OF LORDS

Dunleath, Baron (Brian Henry Mulholland)

Type of Peerage	Hereditary
Without Writ of Summons	
Succeeded	1997
Born	25th September 1950
Educated	Eton College
	Royal Agricultural College, Cirencester
Professional Career	1972 - 85 Marketing Manager, Matthew Clark Group Plc
	1985 - 91 Director, Lanyon Developments Ltd
	1991 - 94 Administrator, Belle Isle Estates
	1994 - Director, Dunleath Estates Ltd
Parliamentary Interests	Countryside, Housing
Recreational Interests	Shooting, Fishing, Gardening
Correspondence Address	The Estate Office, Ballywalter Park, Ballywalter, Newtownards, Northern Ireland, BT22 2PA
	Tel: (012477) 58264/58203
	Fax: (012477) 58818

Dunmore, Earl of (Malcolm Kenneth Murray)

Type of Peerage	Hereditary
Without Writ of Summons	
Succeeded	1995
Born	17th September 1946

Dunn, Baroness (Lydia Selina Dunn DBE)

Type of Peerage	Life
Political Allegiance	Cross Bench
Born	29th February 1940 in Hong Kong
Created	1990
Professional Career	1976 - 85 Member, Hong Kong Legislative Council
	1982 - 88 Member, Hong Kong Executive Council
	1983 - 91 Chairman, Hong Kong Trade Development Council
	1984 - 93 Member, Hong Kong/US Trade Development Council
	1985 - 88 Senior Member, Hong Kong Legislative Council
	1988 - 95 Chairman, Hong Kong/Japan Business Co-operation Committee
	1992 - 96 Deputy Chairman, Hong Kong and Shanghai Banking Corporation
	1992 - Deputy Chairman, HSBC Holdings plc
	1993 - 95 Chairman, Lord Wilson Heritage Trust
	1996 - Executive Director, John Swire and Sons
Political Career	1976 - 88 Member, Hong Kong Legislative Council
	1982 - 95 Member, Hong Kong Executive Council
Subject Interests	Trade, Economics, Hong Kong and Asian affairs
Recreational Interests	Study of Antiquities

Dunrossil, Viscount (John William Morrison)

Type of Peerage	Hereditary
Political Allegiance	Cross Bench
Succeeded	1961
Born	22nd May 1926 in London
Educated	Fettes College, Oriel College, Oxford
Professional Career	1944 - 48 Pilot, RAFVR
	1951 - 88 HM Diplomatic Service
	1978 - 82 High Commissioner to Fiji, Nauru, Tuvalu
	1982 - 83 High Commission to Barbados, Grenada, St Lucia (and other West Indian States)
	1983 - 88 Governor General and C in C, Bermuda
	1994 - Lord Lieutenant, Western Isles
Subject Interests	Foreign affairs, Dependent Territories, Constitutional, Scotland
Recreational Interests	Country life, Reading, Music
Correspondence Address	Dunrossil House, Clachan Sands, Lochmaddy, North Uist, Western Isles, Scotland, HS6 5AY
	Tel: (01876) 500213 Fax: (01876) 500411

Durham, Bishop of (Rt Rev Bishop Anthony Michael Turnbull)

Type of Peerage	Bishop
Born	27th December 1935 in Wombwell, Yorkshire
Entered Lords	1994
Educated	Ilkley Grammar School
	Keble College, Oxford
	St John's College, Durham
Professional Career	1961 - 61 Curate, Middleton
	1961 - 65 Curate and Lecturer, Luton
	1965 - 69 Chaplain to Archbishop of York
	1969 - 76 Rector of Heslington and Chaplain, University of York
	1976 - 84 Chief Secretary, Church Army
	1984 -88 Archdeacon of Rochester
	1988 - 94 Bishop of Rochester
	1994 - Bishop of Durham
Subject Interests	Overseas Aid, Employment, Environment, the North East
Recreational Interests	Cricket, Family life, Walking
Correspondence Address	Auckland Castle, Bishop Auckland, Co Durham, DL14 7NR
	Tel: (01388) 602576 Fax: (01388) 605264
	Web: http://www.durham.anglican.org

Dysart, Countess of (Rosamund Agnes Greaves)

Type of Peerage	Hereditary
Without Writ of Summons	
Succeeded	1975
Born	15th February 1914

Dynevor, Baron (Richard Charles Uryan Rhys)

Type of Peerage	Hereditary
Political Allegiance	None
Succeeded	1962
Born	19th June 1935 in London
Educated	Eton College
	Magdalene College, Cambridge
Parliamentary Interests	Welsh affairs, the Arts
Recreational Interests	Welsh history, Travel

MEMBERS OF THE HOUSE OF LORDS

E

Eames, Baron (Most Rev Robert Henry Alexander Eames)

Type of Peerage	Life
Political Allegiance	Cross Bench
Created	1995
Born	27th April 1937 in Belfast
Educated	Methodist College, Belfast
	Queen's University, Belfast
	Trinity College, Dublin
Professional Career	1960 - 63 Research Scholar, Law School, Queen's University, Belfast
	1963 - 66 Curate, Bangor, Down
	1966 - 74 Rector of Gilnahirk, Belfast
	1970 - 72 Domestic Chaplain to Bishop of Down
	1974 - 75 Rector of St Mark's, Dundela, Belfast
	1975 - 80 Bishop of Derry and Raphoe
	1980 - 86 Bishop of Down and Dromore
	1986 - Archbishop of Armagh and Primate of all Ireland
Subject Interests	Northern Ireland, Legal matters, Health, Education
Recreational Interests	Sailing, Sport, Reading
Correspondence Address	See House, Cathedral Close, Armagh, BT6 7EE
	Tel: (01861) 527144/522851
	Fax: (01861) 527823
	E-mail: archbishop@armagh.anglican.org.
	Church House, Abbey Street, Armagh
	Tel: (01861) 527144 Fax: (01861) 527823
Personal Staff	Mrs Elizabeth Gibson-Harries
	Tel: (01252) 232909/(01846) 652288

Eatwell, Baron (John Leonard Eatwell)

Type of Peerage	Life
Political Allegiance	Labour
Created	1992
Born	2nd February 1945 in Swindon, Wiltshire
Educated	Headlands Grammar School, Swindon
	Queens' College, Cambridge
	Harvard University
Professional Career	1968 - 69 Teaching Fellow, Harvard University
	1969 - 70 Research Fellow, Queens' College, Cambridge
	1970 - 96 Fellow, Director of Studies and Lecturer in Economics, Trinity College, Cambridge
	1975 - 77 Lecturer, Economics and Politics, Cambridge University
	1982 - 96 Visiting Professor of Economics, New School for Social Research, New York
	1993 - Chairman, Crusaid
	1997 - President, Queens' College, Cambridge
	1997 - Chairman, British Screen Finance Ltd
	1997 - Chairman, Institute for Public Policy Research
Political Career	1985 - 92 Economic Adviser to the Leader of Opposition (Rt Hon Neil Kinnock MP)
	1993 -97 Opposition Spokesman on Treasury and Economic Affairs, House of Lords
Subject Interests	Economic affairs, the Arts
Recreational Interests	Rugby Union, Classical and contemporary dance
Correspondence Address	Queens' College, Cambridge, CB3 9ET
	Tel: (01223) 335532/335556
	Fax: (01223) 335555
	E-mail: president@quns.ac.cam.uk
Personal Staff	Mrs Josephine Brown *(Personal Assistant)*
	Tel: (01223) 335556

Ebury, Baron (Francis Egerton Grosvenor)

Type of Peerage	Hereditary
Political Allegiance	None
Succeeded	1957
Born	8th February 1934

Eccles, Viscount (Rt Hon David McAdam Eccles CH KCVO)

Type of Peerage	Hereditary (First Creation)
Political Allegiance	Conservative
Created	1964 (First Created Baron 1962)
Born	18th September 1904 in London
Professional Career	1967 - 70 Chairman, Anglo-Helleric League
	1973 - 78 Chairman, British Library Board
	1974 - 78 President, World Crafts Council
Political Career	1943 - 62 MP (Conservative) for Chippenham
	1951 - 54 Minister of Works
	1954 - 57 Minister of Education
	1957 - 59 President of the Board of Trade
	1959 - 62 Minister of Education
	1962 - 64 Paymaster General (Minister for the Arts)

Eccles of Moulton, Baroness (Diana Catherine Eccles)

Type of Peerage	Life
Political Allegiance	Conservative
Created	1990
Born	4th October 1933
Educated	St James's School, West Malvern
	Open University
Professional Career	1963 - 77 Partner, Gray Design Associates
	1981 - 87 Vice Chairman, National Council of Voluntary Organisations
	1987 - Member, Teeside Urban Development Corporation
	1988 - 93 Chairman, Ealing District Health Authority
	1993 - Chairman, Ealing, Hammersmith and Hounslow Health Authority
Correspondence Address	Moulton Hall, Richmond, North Yorkshire, DL10 6QH
	Tel: (01325) 377227
	6 Barton Street, Westminster, London, SW1P 3NG
	Tel: (0171) 222 7559

MEMBERS OF THE HOUSE OF LORDS

Eden of Winton, Baron (Rt Hon John Benedict Eden)

Type of Peerage . . . . Life
Political Allegiance . . . . . Conservative
Created 1983
Born . . . . 15th September 1925 in London
Professional Career . . . . . 1953 - Vice President, International
                     Tree Foundation
                     1969 - 71 President, Independent Schools
                     Association
                     1974 - 86 Vice President, National Chamber
                     of Trade
                     1974 - Chairman, Lady Eden Schools Ltd
                     1982 - Chairman, Wonder World plc
                     1986 - 94 Chairman, Royal Armouries
                     1987 - 92 Chairman, Gamlestaden plc
                     1990 - Chairman, British Lebanese
                     Association
Political Career . . . . 1954 - 83 MP (Conservative)
                     for Bournemouth West
                     1968 - 70 Opposition Front Bench
                     Spokesman on Power, House of Commons
                     1970 Minister of State,
                     Ministry of Technology
                     1970 - 72 Minister for Industry, Department
                     of Trade and Industry
                     1972 - 74 Minister of Post and
                     Telecommunications
                     1976 - 79 Chairman, Select Committee on
                     European Legislation, House of Commons
                     1979 - 83 Chairman, Select Committee on
                     Home Affairs, House of Commons
Correspondence Address . . 41 Victoria Road, London, W8 5RH
                     Tel: (0171) 938 4805 Fax: (0171) 938 4805

Edinburgh, Duke of (HRH, the Prince Philip)

Type of Peerage . . . . Hereditary (First Creation)
Political Allegiance . . . . . Cross Bench
Created 1947
Born . . . . 10th June 1921

Effingham, Earl of (David Mowbray Algernon Howard)

Type of Peerage . . . . Hereditary
Political Allegiance . . . . . Cross Bench
Succeeded 1996
Born . . . . 29th April 1939 in Middlesex
Educated . . . . Fettes College, Edinburgh
Professional Career . . . . . 1962 - 90 Royal Navy
                     1992 - Royal British Legion
Recreational Interests . . . Horseracing, Fishing, Shooting
Subject Interests . . . . Defence, Maritime, Voluntary sector and
                     charities

Eglinton and Winton, Earl of (Archibald George Montgomerie)

Type of Peerage . . . . Hereditary
Political Allegiance . . . . . None *(Not currently active in House)*
Succeeded 1966
Born . . . . 27th August 1939 in Scotland
Educated . . . . Eton College
Professional Career . . . . . 1957 - 72 Grieveson Grant, Stockbrokers
                     (Partner from 1964)
                     1972 - 92 Director, Gerrard and National
                     (Deputy Chairman from 1980)
                     1989 - 95 Chairman, Gerrard Vivian Gray
Correspondence Address . . Balhomie, Cargill, Perth, PH2 6DS
                     Tel and Fax: (01250) 883222

Egmont, Earl of (Frederick George Moore Percival)

Type of Peerage . . . . Hereditary
Political Allegiance . . . . . None
Succeeded 1932
Born . . . . 14th April 1914

Eldon, Earl of (John Joseph Nicholas Scott)

Type of Peerage . . . . Hereditary
Political Allegiance . . . . . Cross Bench
Succeeded 1976
Born . . . . 24th April 1937

Elgin and Kincardine, Earl of (Andrew Douglas Alexander Thomas Bruce KT)

Type of Peerage . . . . Hereditary
Political Allegiance . . . . . Conservative
Succeeded 1968
Born . . . . 17th February 1924

Elibank, Lord (Alan Erskine-Murray)

Type of Peerage . . . . Hereditary
Political Allegiance . . . . . Conservative
Succeeded 1973
Born . . . . 31st December 1923 in Cape Town,
                     South Africa
Educated . . . . Bedford School
                     Peterhouse College, Cambridge
Professional Career . . . . . 1949 - 55 Barrister
                     1955 - 80 Shell International Petroleum Co
                     1981 - 86 Personnel Consultant, Deminex
                     UK Oil and Gas
Correspondence Address . . Flat 80, Pier House, Cheyne Walk,
                     London, SW3 5HX

MEMBERS OF THE HOUSE OF LORDS

Elis-Thomas, Baron (Dafydd Elis Elis-Thomas)

Type of Peerage	Life
Political Allegiance	Cross Bench
Created	1992
Born	18th October 1946
Educated	Ysgol Dyffryn Conwy
	University College, North Wales
Professional Career	1970 Research Worker, Board of
	Celtic Studies
	1971 Tutor in Welsh Studies, Coleg Harlech
	1993 - Chairman, Welsh Language Board
Political Career	1974 - 83 MP (Plaid Cymru) for Merionnydd
	1983 - 92 MP (Plaid Cymru) Merionnydd
	Nant Conwy
	1984 - 91 President, Plaid Cymru

Ellenborough, Baron (Richard Edward Cecil Law)

Type of Peerage	Hereditary
Political Allegiance	Conservative
Succeeded	1945 (as a minor)
Born	14th January 1926

Elles, Baroness (Diana Louie Elles)

Type of Peerage	Life
Political Allegiance	Conservative
Created	1972
Born	19th July 1921 in Bedford
Educated	Glendower School, London
	Cour Dupanloup, Paris
	University College, London
Professional Career	Barrister
	1974 - 75 Member, UN Sub Commission on
	Discrimination and Protection of
	Minorities
Political Career	1973 - 75 Delegate, European Parliament
	1973 - 79 Chairman, Conservative Party
	International Office
	1973 - 79 International Chairman,
	European Union of Women
	1975 - 79 Opposition Spokesman, Foreign
	and European Affairs, House of Lords
	1979 - 89 Member of the European
	Parliament, Thames Valley
	1982 - 87 A Vice-President, European
	Parliament
	1987 - 89 Chairman, Legal Affairs
	Committee, European Parliament
	1995 - Vice Chairman, Association of
	Conservative Peers
Subject Interests	Human rights, Europe, Foreign affairs
Recreational Interests	Opera, Reading, Crosswords
Correspondence Address	75 Ashley Gardens, London, SW1P 1HG
	Tel: (0171) 828 0175 Fax: (0171) 931 0046
Personal Staff	Miss Cherry Clarke *(Assistant)*
	Tel: (01444) 417120

Elliott of Morpeth, Baron (Robert William Elliott DL)

Type of Peerage	Life
Political Allegiance	Conservative
Born	11th December 1920 in Morpeth,
	Northumberland
Created	1985
Educated	King Edward VI Grammar School, Morpeth
Political Career	1957 - 83 MP (Conservative) for Newcastle-
	upon-Tyne North
	1963 - 64 Assistant Government Whip,
	House of Commons
	1964 - 70 Opposition Whip,
	House of Commons
	1970 - 74 Vice-Chairman,
	Conservative Party
	1972 - 83 Chairman, Select Committee on
	Agriculture, House of Commons
	1990 - Deputy Speaker and Deputy
	Chairman of Committees, House of Lords
Subject Interests	Regional affairs
Recreational Interests	Country life
Correspondence Address	Hindley Hall, Stocksfield,
	Northumberland, NE43 7RY
	Tel: (01661) 844031
	19 Laxford House, Cundy Street,
	London, SW1V 9JR
	Tel: (0171) 730 7619

Elphinstone, Baron (Alexander Mountstuart Elphinstone)

Type of Peerage	Hereditary
Without Writ of Summons	(as a minor)
Succeeded	1994
Born	15th April 1980 in Dundee, Scotland
Educated	Eton College
Correspondence Address	Whitberry House, Tyninghame, Dunbar, East
	Lothian, EH42 1XL
	Tel: (01620) 860882 Fax: (01620) 861414

MEMBERS OF THE HOUSE OF LORDS

Elton, Baron (Rodney Elton TD)

Type of Peerage	Hereditary
Political Allegiance	Conservative
Succeeded	1973
Born	2nd March 1930 in Headington, Oxford
Educated	Eton College
	New College, Oxford
Professional Career	1954 - 62 Farming
	1967 - 69 Assistant Master, Loughborough Grammar School
	1969 - 72 Lecturer, Bishop Lonsdale College, Derby
	1973 - 79 Director, Overseas Exhibition Services Ltd
	1987 - Deputy Chairman, Andry Montgomery Ltd
	1987 Chairman, Enquiry into Discipline in Schools
	1988 - 90 Chairman, FIMBRA
	1990 - 93 Chairman, Intermediate Treatment Fund
	1993 - Chairman, Divert Trust
Political Career	1979 - 81 Parliamentary Secretary, Northern Ireland Office
	1981 - 82 Parliamentary Secretary, Department of Health and Social Security
	1982 - 85 Parliamentary Secretary, then Minister of State, Home Office
	1985 - 86 Minister of State, Department of the Environment
	1997 - Deputy Chairman of Committees, House of Lords
Subject Interests	Home affairs, Education
Recreational Interests	Painting

Ely, Bishop of (Rt Rev Stephen Whitefield Sykes)

Type of Peerage	Bishop
Entered Lords	1996
Born	1939
Educated	St John's College, Cambridge
Professional Career	1964 - 74 Fellow and Dean, St John's College Cambridge
	1974 - 85 Professor of Divinity, Durham University
	1985 - 90 Regius Professor of Divinity and Fellow, St John's College, Cambridge
	1990 - Bishop of Ely
Address for Correspondent	The Bishop's House, Ely, Cambridge, CB7 4DW
	Tel: (01353) 662749 Fax: (01353) 669477

Ely, Marquess of (Charles John Tottenham)

Type of Peerage	Hereditary
Succeeded	1969
Born	30th May 1913

Elystan-Morgan, Baron (Dafydd Elystan Morgan)

Type of Peerage	Life
On Leave Of Absence	
Created	1981
Born	7th December 1932
Educated	University College of Wales, Aberystwyth
Professional Career	Barrister
	1983 - 87 Recorder
	1987 - Circuit Judge
Political Career	1966 - 74 MP (Labour) for Cardiganshire
	1968 - 70 Parliamentary Secretary, Home Office

Emerton, Baroness (Audrey Caroline Emerton)

Type of Peerage	Life
Political Allegiance	Cross Bench
Created	1997
Born	10th September 1935 in Tunbridge Wells
Educated	Tunbridge Wells County Grammar School for Girls
	St George's Hospital, London
	Battersea College of Technology
Professional Career	1974 - 91 Regional Director of Nursing, South East Thames Regional Health Authority
	1985 - 93 Chairman, United Kingdom Central Council for Nursing and Midwifery and Health Visiting
	1988 - 96 Chief Nursing Officer then Chief Officer (Nursing and Social Care), St John's Ambulance
	1992 - Chairman, Nurses Welfare Service
	1993 - Chairman, Brighton Healthcare NHS Trust
	1995 - Lay Member, General Medical Council
Subject Interests	Health and social care, Ethics
Recreational Interests	Walking, Travel
Correspondence Address	Carlton House, 3 Strettitt Gardens, Tonbridge, Kent, TN12 5ES
	Tel: (01622) 872659 Fax: (01622) 873241
	also (01273) 664905

MEMBERS OF THE HOUSE OF LORDS

Emslie, Rt Hon Baron (George Carlyle Emslie QC)
Type of Peerage . . . . Life
Political Allegiance . . . . . Cross Bench
Created 1980
Born . . . . 6th December 1919 in Glasgow, Scotland
Educated . . . . The High School of Glasgow
University of Glasgow
Professional Career . . . . . 1948 - 70 Advocate, Scotland (QC 1957)
1963 - 66 Sheriff of Perth and Angus
1965 - 70 Dean of the Faculty of Advocates
1970 - 72 Senator of the College of Justice
1972 - 89 Lord President of the Court of
Session and Lord Justice-General
Subject Interests . . . . Law
Recreational Interests . . . Golf
Correspondence Address . . 47 Heriot Row, Edinburgh, EH3 6EX
Tel: (0131) 225 3657

Enniskillen, Earl of (Andrew John Galbraith Cole)
Type of Peerage . . . . Hereditary
Political Allegiance . . . . . Cross Bench
Succeeded 1989
Born . . . . 28th April 1942 in Woking, Surrey
Educated . . . . Eton College
Professional Career . . . . . 1960 - 65 Irish Guards
1966 - 69 Manager, Narok Ranch Ltd
1969 - 79 Managing Director, Sudbird
Aviation Ltd
1979 - 82 Managing Director, Kenya
Airways Ltd
1982 - Managing Director, Mundui
Estate Ltd
1984 - Chairman, Lake Naivasha Riparian
Owners Association
1991 - Managing Director, Africa Air
Rescue Health Services
Subject Interests . . . . Aviation, Environment

Erne, Earl of (Henry George Victor John Crichton)
Type of Peerage . . . . Hereditary
Political Allegiance . . . . . Conservative
Succeeded . . . . 1940 (as a minor)
Born . . . . 9th July 1937

Erroll, Earl of (Merlin Sereld Victor Gilbert Hay)
Type of Peerage . . . . Hereditary
Political Allegiance . . . . . Cross Bench
Succeeded 1978
Born . . . . 20th April 1948 in Edinburgh
Educated . . . . Eton College
Trinity College, Cambridge
Professional Career . . . . . 1981 - 94 Proprietor, Erroll Computer
Consultants
1994 - 95 Group Director, Applications and
Development, Giro Vend Holdings Ltd
1995 Chairman, Cost Reduction
Consultants Ltd
1995 - Partner, Hayway Partners (Marketing)
Parliamentary Interests . . Science and Technology, Scotland,
Environment, Countryside Territorial Army
Recreational Interests . . . Country Pursuits
Correspondence Address . . Woodbury Hall, Sandy,
Bedfordshire, SG19 2HR
Tel: (01767) 650251 Fax: (01767) 651553

Erroll of Hale, Baron (Rt Hon Frederich James Erroll)
Type of Peerage . . . . Hereditary (First Creation)
Political Allegiance . . . . . Conservative
Created 1964
Born . . . . 27th May 1914
Political Career . . . . 1945 - 64 MP (Conservative) for Altrincham
and Sale
1955 - 56 Parliamentary Secretary, Ministry
of Supply
1956 - 58 Parliamentary Secretary,
Board of Trade
1958 - 59 Economic Secretary to
the Treasury
1959 - 61 Minister of State, Board of Trade
1961 - 63 President of the Board of Trade
1961- 64 Minister of Power

Esher, Viscount (Lionel Gordon Baliol Brett CBE)
Type of Peerage . . . . Hereditary
On Leave Of Absence
Succeeded 1963
Born . . . . 18th July 1913

Essex, Earl (Robert Edward De Vere Capell)
Type of Peerage . . . . Hereditary
Political Allegiance . . . . . Cross Bench
Succeeded 1989
Born . . . . 13th January 1920 in Petersfield, Hampshire
Educated . . . . Woking School
Professional Career . . . . . 1934 - 38 Sainsburys
1939 - 45 RAF
1946 - 70 Civil Service
1970 - 83 Grocer
Recreational Interests . . . Gardening, Art
Correspondence Address . . 2 Novak Place, Torrisholme, Morecambe,
Lancashire, LA4 6PG
Tel: (01524) 421725

Evans of Parkside, Baron (John Evans)
Type of Peerage . . . . Life
Political Allegiance . . . . . Labour
Created 1997
Born . . . . 19th October 1930 in Aylesham, Kent
Educated . . . . Jarrow Central School
Professional Career . . . . . 1952 - 55 Engineer, Merchant Navy
1955 - 65, 1968 - 74 Marine Fitter,
Shipbuilding/Ship Repair Industries
Political Career . . . . 1962 - 74 Member, Hebburn
District Council
1965 - 68 Secretary/Agent Jarrow
Constituency Labour Party
1973 - 74 Member, South Tyneside
Metropolitan Council
1974 - 83 MP (Labour) for Newton
1975 - 78 Member of the European
Parliament
1976 - 78 Chairman, Regional and
Transport Committee
1978 - 79 Government Whip,
House of Commons
1979 - 80 Opposition Whip,
House of Commons
1980 - 83 PPS to Leader of the Opposition
(Rt Hon Michael Foot MP)
1982 - 96 Member, Labour Party National
Executive (Chairman 1991 - 92)
1983 - 97 MP (Labour) for St Helens North
1983 - 88 Shadow Employment Spokesman,
House of Commons
Subject Interests . . . . Employment, Local government, Transport,
Energy, Trade and industry
Correspondence Address . . House of Lords, Westminster,
London, SW1A 0PW
Tel: (0171) 219 6541

MEMBERS OF THE HOUSE OF LORDS

Ewing of Kirkford, Baron (Harry Ewing)

Type of Peerage	Life
Political Allegiance	Labour
Created	1992
Born	20th January 1931 in Kirkford, Scotland
Political Career	1971 - 74 MP (Labour) for Falkirk and Stirling Burghs
	1974 - 79 Parliamentary Secretary, Scottish Office
	1974 - 83 MP (Labour) for Stirling, Falkirk and Grangemouth
	1979 - 83 Opposition Spokesman on Scottish Affairs, House of Commons
	1983 - 92 MP (Labour) for Falkirk East
	1983 - 86 Opposition Spokesman on Trade and Industry, House of Commons
	1987 - 96 Joint Chairman, Scottish Constitutional Convention
Subject Interests	Scottish affairs, Constitutional reform, Transport and Disability
Recreational Interests . . .	Gardening

Exeter, Bishop of (Rt Rev Hewlett Thompson)

Type of Peerage	Bishop
Entered Lords	1990
Born	14th August 1929 in Hove, Sussex
Educated	Aldenham School
	Trinity Hall, Cambridge
	Cuddesdon Theological College
Professional Career	1954 - 59 Curate, St Matthew's, Northampton
	1959 - 66 Vicar, St Augustine's, Wisbech
	1966 - 74 Vicar, St Saviour's, Folkestone
	1974 - 85 Bishop of Willesden
	1985 - Bishop of Exeter
Subject Interests	English History
Recreational Interests . . .	Walking, Gardening, Music, Reading
Correspondence Address . .	The Palace, Exeter, EX1 1HY
	Tel: (01392) 72362 Fax: (01392) 430923

Exeter, Marquess of (Michael William Anthony Cecil)

Type of Peerage	Hereditary
Political Allegiance	Cross Bench
Succeeded	1988
Born	1st September 1935 in Kamloops, Canada
Educated	Eton College
Professional Career	1957 - 82 Director/President, British Columbia Branch International Charity
	1988 - 96 Chair, then Trustee, Council of International Charity
	1992 - 96 Trustee of Council of International Charity
Subject Interests	Ecology/Environment, Complementary Healing Practices
Recreational Interests . . .	Hiking, Kayaking, Cross-country Skiing
Correspondence Address . .	RR3 Kelsey C21, Sechelt, British Columbia, Canada, VON 3AO
	Tel: 00-1-604-885-6461
	Fax: 00-1-604-885-7656
	also c/o Tessa Maskell, The Courtyard, Mickleton, Gloucestershire, GL55 6SF
	Tel: (01386) 438525 Fax: (01386) 438525
Personal Staff	Ms Tessa Maskell *(Secretary)*

Exmouth, Viscount (Paul Edward Pellow)

Type of Peerage	Hereditary
Political Allegiance	Cross Bench
Succeeded	1970
Born	8th October 1940

Ezra, Baron (Derek Ezra MBE)

Type of Peerage	Life
Political Allegiance	Liberal Democrat
Created	1983
Born	23th February 1919 in Australia
Educated	Monmouth School
	Magdalene College, Cambridge
Professional Career	1947 - 82 National Coal Board (Chairman from 1971)
	1979 - 89 Chairman, then President, Keep Britain Tidy Group
	1982 - Various Energy Companies (Chairman/Director etc)
	1983 - 86 President, British Standards Institution
	1985 - President, Economic Research Council
	1987 - 92 President, Institute of Trading Standards Administration
Political Career	1996 - Liberal Democrat Spokesman on Economic Affairs and Energy, House of Lords
Subject Interests	The Economy, Europe, Energy
Correspondence Address . .	House of Lords, Westminster, London, SW1A 0PW
	Tel: (0171) 219 3180/3932750
	Fax: (0171) 259 9738
	also Tel: (0171) 393 2750

MEMBERS OF THE HOUSE OF LORDS

F

Fairfax of Cameron, Baron (Nicholas John Albert Fairfax)

Type of Peerage . . . . Hereditary
Political Allegiance . . . . . Conservative
Succeeded . . . . 1964 (as a minor)
Born . . . . 4th January 1956

Fairhaven, Baron (Ailwyn Henry George Broughton)

Type of Peerage . . . . Hereditary
Political Allegiance . . . . . Conservative
Succeeded 1973
Born . . . . 16th November 1936 in London
Educated . . . . Eton College
Royal Military Academy, Sandhurst
Professional Career . . . . . 1958 - 71 Officer, Royal Horse Guards
1985 - 89 Senior Steward, Jockey Club
1989 - Chairman, Animal Health Trust
1995 - Chairman, National Horseracing
Museum
Subject Interests . . . . Racing, the Arts
Correspondence Address . . Anglesey Abbey, Cambridge, CB5 9EJ
Tel: (01223) 811746 Fax: (01223) 813154

Falconer of Thoroton, Baron (Charles Leslie Falconer QC)

Type of Peerage . . . . Life
Political Allegiance . . . . . Labour
Created 1997
Born . . . . 19th November 1951 in Edinburgh
Educated . . . . Glenalmond College
Queen's College, Cambridge
Professional Career . . . . . 1974 - 97 Barrister (1991 QC)
1997 - Solicitor General
Correspondence Address . . Attorney General's Chambers, 9 Buckingham
Gate, London, SW1E 6JP
Tel: (0171) 828 7155 Fax: (0171) 233 7194
House of Lords, Westminster,
London, SW1A 0PW
Tel: (0171) 219 3517 Fax: (0171) 222 6376
Personal Staff . . . . Ms Deborah Hermer (*Private Secretary*)
Tel: (0171) 233 5629

Falkender, Baroness (Marcia Matilda Falkender CBE)

Type of Peerage . . . . Life
Political Allegiance . . . . . Labour
Created 1974
Born . . . . March 1932
Educated . . . . Northampton High School
Queen Mary College, University of London
Political Career . . . . 1956 - 83 Private and Political Secretary to
Rt Hon Harold Wilson MP
(including when Leader of Opposition and
Prime Minister)

Falkland, Viscount (Lucius Edward William Plantagenet Cary)

Type of Peerage . . . . Hereditary
Political Allegiance . . . . . Liberal Democrat
Succeeded 1984
Born . . . . 8th May 1935 in London
Educated . . . . Wellington College
Political Career . . . . 1987 - Liberal Democrat Deputy Chief
Whip, House of Lords
1995 - Liberal Democrat Spokesman on
Culture, Media and Sport Culture, House
of Lords
Subject Interests . . . . Alcohol and drugs, Pre-School learning,
Transport, Film and Television
Recreational Interests . . . Cinema, Racing, Golf, Motorcycling
Correspondence Address . . Liberal Democrat Whips Office, House of
Lords, Westminster, London, SW1A 0PW
Tel: (0171) 219 3230 Fax: (0171) 219 2377

Falmouth, Viscount (George Hugh Boscawen)

Type of Peerage . . . . Hereditary
Political Allegiance . . . . . Conservative
Succeeded 1962
Born . . . . 31st October 1919

Fanshawe of Richmond, Baron (Anthony Henry Fanshawe Royle KCMG)

Type of Peerage . . . . Life
Political Allegiance . . . . . Conservative
Created 1983
Born . . . . 27th March 1927 in London
Educated . . . . Harrow School
Professional Career . . . . . 1975 - Vice President,
Franco-British Council
1980 - 83 Chairman, Wilkinson Sword
Group
1993 - 97 Chairman, Sedgwick Group
Political Career . . . . 1959 - 83 MP (Conservative) for Richmond
1967 - 70 Opposition Whip,
House of Commons
1970 - 74 Parliamentary Secretary, Foreign
and Commonwealth Office
1979 - 84 Vice Chairman, Conservative
Party Organisation (also Chairman of
International Office)
Correspondence Address . . The Chapter Manor, South Cerney,
Gloucestershire, GL7 5TN

Faringdon, Baron (Charles Michael Henderson)

Type of Peerage . . . . Hereditary
Political Allegiance . . . . . Cross Bench
Succeeded 1977
Born . . . . 3rd July 1937 in London
Educated . . . . Eton College
Trinity College, Cambridge
Professional Career . . . . . 1968 - 95 Partner, Cazenove & Co
1980 - Chairman, Witan Investment plc
1980 - Management Board, Institute of
Cancer Research
1994 - Chairman, Royal Commission on
Historic Monuments of England
Subject Interests . . . . Arts, Health, Trees
Recreational Interests . . . Blood sports, Gardens, Ballet
Correspondence Address . . 28 Brompton Square, London, SW3 2AD
Tel: (0171) 589 0724 Fax: (0171) 589 0724

MEMBERS OF THE HOUSE OF LORDS

Farrington of Ribbleton, Baroness (Josephine Farrington)

Type of Peerage . . . .
Political Allegiance . . . . . Labour
Created 1994
Born . . . . 29th June 1940
Political Career . . . . 1977 - 97 Member, Lancashire
 County Council
 1987 - 94 Leader, Labour Group,
 Association of County Councils
 1995 - 97 Opposition Whip, House of Lords
 1997 - Government Whip
 (Baroness in Waiting)

Feldman, Baron (Basil Feldman)

Type of Peerage . . . . Life
Political Allegiance . . . . . Conservative
Created 1995
Born . . . . 23rd September 1926 in London
Educated . . . . Grocers School, London
Professional Career . . . . . 1978 - 85 Chairman, Clothing Economic
 Development Committee
 1983 - Chairman, Better Made in Britain
 Campaign
 1985 - 93 Director, Young Entrepreneurs
 Fund
Political Career . . . . 1976 - 85 Chairman, Conservative Party,
 Greater London
 1981 - Variously President, Vice President,
 Chairman and Treasurer, National Union
 of Conservative Party
 (Treasurer since 1996)
Subject Interests . . . . Industry, Import substitution, Inward
 investment, Tourism, the Arts, Sport
Recreational Interests . . . Golf, Tennis, Theatre, Opera, Concerts,
 Reading, Travel
Personal Staff . . . . Ms Sheila Hale *(Personal Assistant)*
 Tel: (0171) 493 3178

Ferrers, Earl (Rt Hon Robert Washington Shirley)

Type of Peerage . . . . Hereditary
Political Allegiance . . . . . Conservative
Succeeded 1954
Born . . . . 8th June 1929 in London
Political Career . . . . 1962 - 64, 1964 - 67, 1971 - 74 Government
 Whip, (Lord in Waiting)
 1964 - 67 Opposition Whip, House of Lords
 1974 Parliamentary Secretary, Ministry of
 Agriculture, Fisheries and Food
 1976 - 79 Joint Deputy Leader of the
 Opposition, House of Lords
 1979 - 83, 1988 - 97 Deputy Leader,
 House of Lords
 1979 - 83 Minister of State, Ministry of
 Agriculture, Fisheries and Food
 1988 - 94 Minister of State, Home Office
 1994 - 95 Minister of State, Department of
 Trade and Industry
 1995 - 97 Minister of State, Department of
 the Environment
Subject Interests . . . . Agriculture, Home affairs, Trade,
 Environment
Recreational Interests . . . Shooting, Music and Travel
Correspondence Address . . Ditchingham Hall, Bungay,
 Suffolk, NR35 2LE
 Tel: (01508) 482 250

Feversham, Baron (Charles Antony Peter Duncombe)

Type of Peerage . . . . Hereditary
Political Allegiance . . . . . Cross Bench
Educated . . . . Eton College
 Middle Temple
Born . . . . 3rd January 1945 in Andover, Hampshire
Succeeded 1963
Professional Career . . . . . 1964 - Journalist, Farmer and Landowner
 1969 - 76 Chairman, Standing Conference
 Regional Arts Associations
 1969 - 80 Chairman, Yorkshire Arts
 Association (also President, 1987- 90)
 1981 - Chairman of Trustees, Yorkshire
 Sculpture Park
 1984 - President, Yorkshire Local Councils
 Association
 1986 - President, National Association of
 Local Councils
Subject Interests . . . . The Arts, Agriculture, Tourism, Local
 government
Recreational Interests . . . Country Sports, Gardening, Astronomy
Correspondence Address . . Duncombe Park, Helmsley, York, YO6 5EB
 Tel: (01439) 770213 Fax: (01439) 771114

Fife, Duke of (James George Alexander Bannerman Carnegie)

Type of Peerage . . . . Hereditary
Political Allegiance . . . . . None
Born . . . . 23rd September 1929 in London
Succeeded 1959
Educated . . . . Gordonstoun School
Professional Career . . . . . 1948 - 50 Served Scots Guards, Malaya
 1950 - Landowner and Farmer

Fisher of Kilverstone, Baron (John Vavasseur Fisher)

Type of Peerage . . . . Hereditary
Political Allegiance . . . . . Conservative
Succeeded 1955
Born . . . . 24th July 1921 in Thetford, Norfolk
Educated . . . . Stowe School
 Trinity College, Cambridge
Subject Interests . . . . Farming, the Countryside
Recreational Interests . . . Gardening, Forestry
Correspondence Address . . Marklyr, Rushlake Green, Heathfield,
 East Sussex, TN21 9PN
 Tel: (01435) 830270

Fisher of Rednal, Baroness (Doris Mary Gertrude Fisher)

Type of Peerage . . . . Life
Political Allegiance . . . . . Labour
Created 1976
Born . . . . 13th September 1919 in Birmingham
Political Career . . . . 1952 - 70 Member, Birmingham
 City Council
 1970 - 74 MP (Labour) for Birmingham
 Ladywood
Subject Interests . . . . Housing, Young people, Aged
Correspondence Address . . 60 Jacoby Place, Priory Road,
 Birmingham, B5 7UW

MEMBERS OF THE HOUSE OF LORDS

Fitt, Baron (Gerard Fitt)
Type of Peerage . . . . Life
Political Allegiance. . . . . None
Created. 1983
Born. . . . . 9th April 1926
Political Career. . . . . . . 1958 - 81 Councillor, then Alderman,
    Belfast Corporation
    1962 - 72 Member, Northern Ireland
    Parliament
    1966 - 83 MP (Social Democratic and
    Labour Party) for Belfast West
    1970 - 79 Leader, Social Democratic and
    Labour Party
    1973 - 75 Member, Northern Ireland
    Assembly
    1974 Deputy Chief Executive, Northern
    Ireland Executive

FitzWalter, Baron (Fitzwalter Brook Plumptre)
Type of Peerage . . . . Hereditary
Succeeded. 1953
Born. . . . . 15th January 1914 in Barberton,
    South Africa
Professional Career . . . . . Farmer and Landowner

Flather, Baroness (Shreela Flather)
Type of Peerage . . . . Life
Political Allegiance. . . . . Conservative
Created. 1990
Educated . . . . University College, London
Professional Career . . . . . Lawyer and Teacher
    1968 - 78 Secretary/Organiser, Maidenhead
    Ladies' Asian Club
    1991 - 94 Vice-Chairman, Refugee Council
    1996 - Chairman, Alcohol Education and
    Research Council
Political Career. . . . . . . 1976 - 91 Member, Royal Borough of
    Windsor and Maidenhead Committee
    (Mayor 1986 - 87)
    1978 - 89 Member, Conservative Women's
    National Committee
    1979 - 83 Executive Member, Anglo-Asian
    Conservative Association
Recreational Interests . . . Travel, Cinema, Swimming

Flowers, Baron (Brian Hilton Flowers)
Type of Peerage . . . . Life
Political Allegiance. . . . . Cross Bench
Created. 1979
Born. . . . . 13th September 1924 in Blackburn,
    Lancashire
Professional Career . . . . . 1958 - 72 Langworthy Professor of Physics,
    University of Manchester
    1973 - 76 Chairman, Royal Commission on
    Environmental Pollution
    1973 - 85 Rector, Imperial College of
    Science and Technology
    1985 - 90 Vice-Chancellor,
    University of London
    1994 - Chancellor, Manchester University

Foley, Baron (Adrian Gerald Foley)
Type of Peerage . . . . Hereditary
Succeeded. . . . . 1927 (as a minor)
Born. . . . . 9th August 1923 in London

Fookes, Baroness (Janet Evelyn Fookes DBE)
Type of Peerage . . . . Life
Political Allegiance. . . . . Conservative
Created. 1997
Born. . . . . 21st February 1936 in London
Educated . . . . Hastings and St Leonards Ladies College
    Hastings High School for Girls
    Royal Holloway College, University of
    London
Professional Career . . . . . 1958 - 70 School Teacher
Political Career. . . . . . . 1960 - 61, 1963 - 70 Member, Hastings
    County Borough Council
    1970 - 74 MP (Conservative) for Merton
    and Morden
    1974 - 97 MP (Conservative) for Plymouth
    Drake
    1992 -97 Deputy Speaker and Second
    Deputy Chairman of Ways and Means,
    House of Commons
Subject Interests. . . . . . . Penal affairs, Mental health, Defence,
    Animal welfare, Equal opportunities,
    Housing
Recreational Interests . . . Swimming, Gardening, Theatre, Keep fit
Correspondence Address. . House of Lords, Westminster,
    London, SW1A 0PW
    Tel: (0171) 219 5353
    Fax: (0171) 219 5979
Personal Staff. . . . . Mrs Naomi Lane *(Secretary)*
    Tel: (01424) 424108

Foot of Buckland Monachorum, Baron
  (John Mackintosh Foot)
Type of Peerage . . . . Life
Political Allegiance. . . . . Liberal Democrat
Created. 1967
Born. . . . . 17th February 1909 in Plymouth, Devon
Educated . . . . Bembridge School, Isle of Wight
    Balliol College, Oxford
Professional Career . . . . . 1934 - 39, 1945 - 95 Solicitor, Foot and
    Bowden, Plymouth
Subject Interests. . . . . . . Law, Penal Reform and the Environment
Correspondence Address. . Yew Tree, Crapstone, Yelverton,
    Devon, PL20 7PJ
    Tel: (01822) 853417

Forbes, Lord (Nigel Ivan Forbes KBE)
Type of Peerage . . . . Hereditary
Political Allegiance. . . . . Conservative
Succeeded. 1953
Born. . . . . 19th February 1918 in London
Educated . . . . Harrow School
    Royal Military College, Sandhurst
Professional Career . . . . . 1938 - 46 Grenadier Guards
    1947 - 48 Military Assistant, High
    Commissioner for Palestine
    1961 - 73 Chairman, Don District
    River Board
    1964 - 74 Deputy Chairman, Tennant
    Caledonian Breweries
    1975 - Chairman, Rolawn Ltd
Political Career. . . . . . . 1958 - 59 Minister of State, Scottish Office
Subject Interests. . . . . . . Agriculture, Forestry, Scottish affairs
Recreational Interests . . . Photography, Wildlife, Conservation, Travel
Correspondence Address. . Balforbes, Alford,
    Aberdeenshire, AB33 8DR
    Tel: (01975) 562516 Fax: (01975) 562898
    Also Tel: (01975) 562524 *(Secretary)*

MEMBERS OF THE HOUSE OF LORDS

Forester, Baron (George Cecil Brook Weld Forester)

Type of Peerage	Hereditary
Political Allegiance	Conservative
Succeeded	1977
Born	20th February 1938 in London
Educated	Eton College
	Royal Agricultural College, Cirencester
Subject Interests	Rural enterprise, Farming, Wildlife
Recreational Interests	Fishing, Silviculture, Fine arts, Tourism, Shooting
Correspondence Address	Willey Park, Broseley, Shropshire, TF12 5JJ
	Tel: (01952) 882133 Fax: (01952) 883680
Personal Staff	Mrs Alison Castle *(Personal Assistant)*

Forres, Baron (Alistair Stephen Grant Williamson)

Type of Peerage	Hereditary
Has Not Taken The Oath	
Political Allegiance	Cross Bench
Succeeded	1978
Born	16th May 1946

Forte, Baron (Charles Forte)

Type of Peerage	Life
Political Allegiance	Conservative
Created	1982
Born	26th November 1908 in Monforte Italy
Educated	Aloa Academy
	Dumfries College
	Mamiani, Rome
Professional Career	Hotelier and Caterer
	1970 - 96 Variously Chairman, Deputy Chairman, Chief Executive and President, Trust House Forte
Subject Interests	Literature, Music, Fishing, Golf
Personal Staff	Mrs Sarah Sybova *(Personal Assistant)*
	Tel: (0171) 235 6244

Fortescue, Earl (Charles Hugh Richard Fortescue)

Type of Peerage	Hereditary
Political Allegiance	Conservative
Succeeded	1993
Born	10th May 1951 in London
Educated	Eton College

Forteviot, Baron (John James Evelyn Dewar)

Type of Peerage	Hereditary
Political Allegiance	Conservative
Succeeded	1993
Born	5th April 1938 in London
Educated	Eton College
Subject Interests	Scotland, Africa, Farming, Country pursuits
Recreational Interests	Fishing, Shooting, Birdwatching, Photography
Correspondence Address	Aberdalgie House, Perth, PH2 0QD
	Tel: (01738) 625596 Fax: (01738) 622633

Fraser of Carmyllie, Baron (Rt Hon Peter Lovat Fraser QC)

Type of Peerage	Life
Political Allegiance	Conservative
Created	1989
Born	29th May 1945
Professional Career	1969 Called to the Scottish Bar (QC 1982)
Political Career	1979 - 83 MP (Conservative) Angus South
	1982 - 89 Solicitor General for Scotland
	1983 - 87 MP (Conservative) for Angus East
	1989 - 92 Lord Advocate
	1992 - 95 Minister of State, Scottish Office
	1995 - 97 Minister of Energy, Department of Trade and Industry
	1997 - Deputy Leader of Opposition, House of Lords (and Spokesman on Trade and Industry)

Freeman, Baron (Rt Hon Roger Norman Freeman)

Type of Peerage	Life
Political Allegiance	Conservative
Created	1997
Born	27th May 1942 in Neston, Cheshire
Educated	Whitgift School, Croydon
	Balliol College, Oxford
Professional Career	1965 - 69 Articled with Binderhamlyn and Co, Chartered Accountants
	1969 - Member, then Fellow, Institute of Chartered Accountants
	1969 - 83 Partner, Lehman Brokers, Investment Bankers, New York, USA
	1997 - Partner, Coopers and Lybrand, Chartered Accountants
Political Career	1983 - 97 MP (Conservative) for Kettering
	1986 - 88 Parliamentary Secretary for Armed Forces, Ministry of Defence
	1988 - 90 Parliamentary Secretary, Department of Health
	1990 - 94 Minister of State, Department of Transport
	1994 - 95 Minister of State, Ministry of Defence
	1995 - 97 Chancellor of the Duchy of Lancaster and Minister for Public Service
Subject Interests	Transportation, Aerospace, Information Technology

Freyberg, Baron (Valerian Bernard Freyberg)

Type of Peerage	Hereditary
Political Allegiance	Cross Bench
Born	15th December 1970 in London
Succeeded	1993
Educated	Eton College
	Camberwell College of Art
Professional Career	Sculptor
Subject Interests	Visual arts
Recreational Interests	Bees, Music

MEMBERS OF THE HOUSE OF LORDS

G

Gage, Viscount (Henry Nicolas)

Type of Peerage . . . . Hereditary
Political Allegiance . . . . . Conservative
Succeeded 1993
Born . . . . 9th April 1934
Educated . . . . Eton College
               Christ Church, Oxford
Subject Interests . . . . Countryside Issues, Housing/Homelessness,
               Asylum and immigration
Recreational Interests . . . Country Pursuits
Correspondence Address . . Firle Place, Firle, Near Lewes,
               East Sussex, BN8 6LP
               Tel: (01273) 858535 Fax: (01273) 858188
Personal Staff . . . . Mrs Brig Davies (*Secretary*)

Gainford, Baron (Joseph Edward Pease)

Type of Peerage . . . . Hereditary
Political Allegiance . . . . . Conservative
Succeeded 1971
Born . . . . 25th December 1921 in London
Educated . . . . Eton College
               Gordonstoun School
               University College London
               Open University
Professional Career . . . . . 1947 - 58 Surveyor (Hunting Aerosurveys,
               then Directorate of Colonial Surveys and
               Soil Mechanics Ltd)
               1958 - 78 Local Government Officer
               (London County Council, then Greater
               London Council)
               1973 United Kingdom Delegate to the
               United Nations
Subject Interests . . . . Transport, Education, Defence,
               Local government
Recreational Interests . . . Music, Association football, Cricket, Chess
Correspondence Address . . Swallowfield, 1 Dedmere Court, Marlow,
               Buckinghamshire, SL7 1PL
               Tel: (01628) 484679

Gainsborough, Earl of (Anthony Gerard Edward Noel)

Type of Peerage . . . . Hereditary
Political Allegiance . . . . . Cross Bench
Succeeded . . . . 1927 (as a minor)
Born . . . . 24th October 1923 in London
Professional Career . . . . . 1970 - 80 Chairman, Board of Management,
               Hospital of St John and St Elizabeth, London
Political Career . . . . 1974 - 80 President, Association of
               District Councils
Correspondence Address . . Horn House, Exton Park, Oakham,
               Leicestershire, LE15 7QU
               Tel: (01780) 460772

Gallacher, Baron (John Gallacher)

Type of Peerage . . . . Life
Political Allegiance . . . . . Labour
Created 1982
Born . . . . 7th May 1920
Professional Career . . . . . Chartered Secretary
               1963 - 67 Secretary, International
               Co-operative Alliance
               1974 - 83 Parliamentary Secretary,
               Co-operative Union
Political Career . . . . 1989 - 92 Principal Opposition Spokesman
               on Agriculture, House of Lords

Galloway, Earl of (Randolph Keith Reginald Stewart)

Type of Peerage . . . . Hereditary
Political Allegiance . . . . . Conservative
Succeeded 1979
Born . . . . 14th October 1928
Professional Career . . . . . 1946 Agriculture
               1947 -54 Gardener
               1959 - 62 Market Gardener
               1962 - 70 Interior Decorator
               1970 - 74 Community Gardener
Recreational Interests . . . Cycling, Walking, Painting, Drawing,
               Writing

Gardner of Parkes, Baroness (Rachel Trixie Anne Gardner)

Type of Peerage . . . . Life
Political Allegiance . . . . . Conservative
Born . . . . 17th July 1927
Created 1981
Educated . . . . Monte Sant Angelo College, Sydney
               East Sydney Technical College
               University of Sydney
Professional Career . . . . . 1954 - 90 Dental Surgeon
               1993 - Chairman, Suzy Lamplugh Trust
               1994 - Chairman, Royal Free Hampstead
               NHS Trust
Political Career . . . . 1968 - 78 Member, Westminster
               City Council
               1970 - 73, 1977 - 86 Member (for Havering
               then Enfield Southgate)
               Greater London Council
Subject Interests . . . . Housing, Health, Social services, Energy,
               Transport, Employment
Recreational Interests . . . Family, Gardening, Travel, Historic
               buildings, Frogs and toads
Correspondence Address . . House of Lords, Westminster,
               London, SW1A 0PW
               Tel: (0171) 219 6611 Fax: (0171) 219 5979

MEMBERS OF THE HOUSE OF LORDS

Garel-Jones, Baron (Rt Hon Tristan Garel-Jones)

Type of Peerage . . . . Life
Political Allegiance . . . . . Conservative
Created 1997
Born . . . . 28th February 1941 in South Wales
Educated . . . . King's School, Canterbury
Madrid University
Political Career . . . . 1979 - 97 MP (Conservative) for Watford
1982 Assistant Government Whip
1982 - 89 Government Whip,
House of Commons
1989 - 90 Deputy Government Chief Whip,
House of Commons
1990 - 93 Minister of State, Foreign and
Commonwealth Office
Subject Interests . . . . Europe, Latin America
Recreational Interests . . . Collecting books and contemporary art

Geddes of Rolvenden, Baron (Euan Michael Ross Geddes)

Type of Peerage . . . . Hereditary
Political Allegiance . . . . . Conservative
Succeeded 1975
Born . . . . 3rd September 1937 in Kent
Educated . . . . Rugby School
Gonville and Caius College, Cambridge
Harvard Business School
Professional Career . . . . . Company Director
Political Career . . . . 1996 - Chairman, European Communities
Sub-Committee on Energy, Industry and
Transport
Subject Interests . . . . Shipping, Anglo-Sino relations, Hong Kong,
South East Asia, Nationality/Immigration,
Energy
Recreational Interests . . . Music, Golf, Bridge, Gardening
Correspondence Address . . House of Lords, Westminster,
London, SW1A 0PW
Tel: (0171) 219 6400 Fax: (0171) 219 6715

Geraint, Baron (Geraint Wyn Howells)

Type of Peerage . . . . Life
Political Allegiance . . . . . Liberal Democrat
Created 1992
Born . . . . 15th April 1925
Educated . . . . Ardwyn Grammar School
Professional Career . . . . . Farmer
1977 - 87 Chairman, Wool Producers of
Wales Ltd
Political Career . . . . 1974 - 83 MP (Liberal) for Cardigan
1983 - 92 MP (Liberal, then Liberal
Democrat) for Ceredigion and
Pembroke North,
Deputy Speaker and Deputy Chairman of
Committees, House of Lords

Gerard, Baron (Anthony Robert Hugo Gerrard)

Type of Peerage . . . . Hereditary
Political Allegiance . . . . . Cross Bench
Succeeded 1992
Born . . . . 3rd December 1949

Gibson, Baron (Richard Patrick Tallentyre Gibson)

Type of Peerage . . . . Life
Political Allegiance . . . . . Cross Bench
Created 1975
Born . . . . 5th February 1916 in London
Educated . . . . Eton College
Magdalen College, Oxford
Professional Career . . . . . 1972 - 77 Chairman, Arts Council of
Great Britain
1977 - 86 Chairman, National Trust
1978 - 83 Chairman, Pearson plc
Subject Interests . . . . Arts, the Environment
Recreational Interests . . . Music, Gardening, Architecture
Correspondence Address . . 4 Swan Walk, London, SW3 4JJ
Tel and Fax: (0171) 351 0344

Gibson-Watt, Baron (Rt Hon James David Gibson-Watt MC)

Type of Peerage . . . . Life
Political Allegiance . . . . . Conservative
Created 1979
Born . . . . 11th September 1918 in Llandrindod Wells
Educated . . . . Eton College
Trinity College, Cambridge
Political Career . . . . 1956 - 74 MP (Conservative) for Hereford
1959 - 61 Government Whip,
House of Commons
1970 - 74 Minister of State, Welsh Office
Correspondence Address . . Doldowlod, Llandrindod Wells,
Powys, LD1 6HF
Tel: (01597) 860208

Gifford, Baron (Anthony Maurice Gifford QC)

Type of Peerage . . . . Hereditary
Political Allegiance . . . . . Labour
Succeeded 1961
Born . . . . 1st May 1940 in London
Professional Career . . . . . 1966 - 91 Barrister at Law (QC 1982)
1990 - Attorney at Law, Jamaica
Subject Interests . . . . Human rights
Correspondence Address . . 21 Church Street, Kingston, Jamaica

MEMBERS OF THE HOUSE OF LORDS

Gilbert, (Rt Hon Dr John William Gilbert)
Type of Peerage . . . . Life
Political Allegiance . . . . . Labour
Created 1997
Born . . . . 5th April 1927 in London
Educated . . . . Merchant Taylor's School
              St John's College, Oxford
              New York University
Political Career . . . . 1970 - 74 MP (Labour) for Dudley
              1974 - 97 MP (Labour) for Dudley East
              1972 - 74 Opposition Spokesman on
                Treasury Affairs, House of Commons
              1974 - 75 Financial Secretary to the
                Treasury
              1975 - 76 Minister for Transport,
                Department of Environment
              1976 - 79 Minister of State,
                Ministry of Defence
              1997 - Minister of State, Ministry of Defence

Gillmore of Thamesfield, Baron (David Howe Gillmore GCMG)
Type of Peerage . . . . Life
Political Allegiance . . . . . Cross Bench
Created 1996
Born . . . . 16th August 1934 in Swindon, Wiltshire
Educated . . . . Trent College
              King's College, Cambridge
Professional Career . . . . . 1958 - 60 Reuters Ltd
              1960 -65 Polypapier S A Paris
              1965 - 69 School Master, Wilson's
                Grammar School
              1970 - 94 HM Diplomatic Service
              1972 - 75 British Embassy Moscow
              1975 - 78 Counsellor, UK Delegation,
                Vienna
              1979 - 81 Head of Defence Department,
                Foreign and Commonwealth Office
              1981 - 83 Assistant Secretary, Foreign and
                Commonwealth Office
              1983 - 86 British High Commissioner,
                Malaysia
              1986 - 90 Deputy Secretary, Foreign and
                Commonwealth Office
              1991 - 94 Permanent Secretary and Head of
                HM Diplomatic Service, Foreign and
                Commonwealth Office
              1995 - Senior Adviser, BZW Ltd
              1997 - Vice Chairman, Vickers plc
Subject Interests . . . . International affairs, Education
Recreational Interests . . . Music, Exercise
Correspondence Address . . House of Lords, Westminster,
              London, SW1A 0PW
              Tel: (0181) 780 1394

Gilmour of Craigmillar, Baron
  (Rt Hon Ian Hedworth John Little Gilmour)
Type of Peerage . . . . Life
Political Allegiance . . . . . Conservative
Created 1992
Born . . . . 8th July 1926 in London
Professional Career . . . . . 1944 - 47 Grenadier Guards
              1952 Barrister at Law
              1954 - 59 Editor, The Spectator
Political Career . . . . 1962 - 74 MP (Conservative) for
                Norfolk Central
              1970 - 71 Parliamentary Secretary, (Army)
                Ministry of Defence
              1971 - 72 Minister of State for Defence
                Procurement, Ministry of Defence
              1974 - 75 Chairman, Conservative
                Research Department
              1974 - 92 MP (Conservative) for Chesham
                and Amersham
              1975 - 79 Opposition Defence Spokesman,
                House of Commons
              1979 - 81 Lord Privy Seal and Deputy
                Foreign Secretary
Correspondence Address . . The Ferry House, Old Isleworth,
              Middlesex, TW7 6BD
              Tel: (0181) 560 6769

Gisborough, Baron (Thomas Richard John Long Chaloner)
Type of Peerage . . . . Hereditary
Political Allegiance . . . . . Conservative
Succeeded 1951
Born . . . . 1st July 1927
Educated . . . . Eton College
              Royal Agricultural College
Subject Interests . . . . Farming, Defence, Law and Order
Recreational Interests . . . Skiing, Shooting, Fishing, Bridge, Piano,
              Tennis. Stalking, Walking
Correspondence Address . . Gisborough House,
              North Yorkshire, TS14 6PT
              Tel: (01287) 632002
              also House of Lords Tel: (0171) 219 3198

Gladwin of Clee, Baron (Derek Oliver Gladwin CBE)
Type of Peerage . . . . Life
Political Allegiance . . . . . Labour
Created 1994
Born . . . . 6th June 1930 in Cleethorpes,Grimsby
Educated . . . . Wintringham Grammar School, Grimsby
              Ruskin College, Oxford
              London School of Economics
Professional Career . . . . . 1946 - 52 Railway Clerk and Fish Dock
                Worker, Grimsby
              1956 - 90 District and National Officer, then
                Southern Regional Secretary, General and
                Municipal Workers Union (GMB)
              1963 - 70 National Industrial Officer,
                GMB Union
              1970 - 90 Southern Regional Secretary,
                GMB
              1979 - Chairman, Governing Council,
                Ruskin College, Oxford
              1986 - 88 Member, Trades Union Congress
                General Council
Political Career . . . . 1973 - 90 Chairman, Labour Party
                Conference Arrangements Committee
              1994 - 96 Co-ordinator, Trade Union
                Political Fund Campaign
Subject Interests . . . . Industrial relations, Labour law, Economics,
              Training, Adult education
Correspondence Address . . 2 Friars Rise, Woking, Surrey, GU22 7JL
              also House of Lords Tel: (0171) 219 6382
              Fax: (0171) 219 2082

MEMBERS OF THE HOUSE OF LORDS

Gladwyn, Baron (Miles Gladwyn Jebb)

Type of Peerage	Hereditary
Political Allegiance	Cross Bench
Succeeded	1996
Born	3rd March 1930 in London
Educated	Eton College
	Magdalen College, Oxford
Professional Career	1960 - 83 Senior Management,
	BOAC/British Airways
Subject Interests	Conservation, Countryside access, Aviation,
	Foreign affairs
Recreational Interests	Walking
Correspondence Address	E1 Albany, Piccadilly, London, W1V 9RH
	Tel: (0171) 734 1100

Glanusk, Baron (Christopher Russell Bailey TD)

Type of Peerage	Hereditary
Political Allegiance	None
Succeeded	1997
Born	18th March 1942 in Crickhowell
Educated	Eton College
	Clare College, Cambridge
Professional Career	1964 - 66 Design Engineer, English
	Electric Leo Ltd
	1966 - 78 Design Engineer/Product
	Marketing Manager, Ferranti Ltd
	1978 - 83 International Product Marketing
	Manager, Bestobell Mobrey Ltd
	1984 - 86 Principal Sales Engineer, STC
	Telecommunications Ltd
	1986 - 97 General Manager, Autocar
	Electrical Equipment Co Ltd
	1997 - General Manager, Wolfram Research
	Europe Ltd
Correspondence Address	51 Chertsey Road, Chobham, Woking,
	Surrey, GU24 8PD
	Tel: (01276) 856380/
	(01993) 883400 (Ext 39)

Glasgow, Earl of (Patrick Robin Archibald Boyle)

Type of Peerage	Hereditary
Political Allegiance	Liberal Democrat
Succeeded	1984
Born	30th July 1939 in London
Educated	Eton College
	Sorbonne, Paris
Professional Career	1958 - 60 National Service, RNR
	1960 - 68 Assistant Director, Film Industry
	1968 - 70 Producer/Director,
	(Documentaries) Yorkshire Television
	1970 - 80 Freelance Producer/Director
	(Documentaries)
	1976 - 97 Owner/Manager, Kelburn
	Country Centre
	1984 - 97 Landowner/Manager,
	Kelburn Estate
	1995 - Deputy Lieutenant, Ayrshire
Subject Interests	Theatre, Opera, Cinema, Television,
	Performing arts, Media, Tourism
Recreational Interests	Skiing, Tennis
Correspondence Address	Kelburn, Fairlie, Ayrshire, KA29 0BE
	Tel: (01475) 568685 Fax: (01475) 568121

Glenamara of Glenridding, Baron (Rt Hon Edward Watson Short CH)

Type of Peerage	Life
Political Allegiance	Labour
Created	1977
Born	17th December 1912 in Warcop, Cumbria
Educated	Bede College, Durham
Political Career	1951 - 76 MP (Labour) for
	Newcastle-upon-Tyne Central
	1955 - 62 Opposition Whip,
	House of Commons
	1962 - 64 Opposition Deputy Chief Whip,
	House of Commons
	1964 - 66 Government Chief Whip,
	House of Commons
	1966 - 68 Postmaster General
	1968 - 70 Secretary of State for Education
	and Science
	1972 - 76 Deputy Leader of the
	Labour Party
	1974 - 76 Lord President of the Council and
	Leader, House of Commons
Recreational Interests	Painting

Glenarthur, Baron (Simon Mark Arthur)

Type of Peerage	Hereditary
Political Allegiance	Conservative
Succeeded	1976
Born	7th October 1944 in Mauchline, Scotland
Educated	Eton College
Professional Career	1963 - 75 Army Officer
	(10th Royal Hussars)
	1976 - 82 Captain, British Airways
	Helicopters Ltd
	1989 - Consultant, British Aerospace Plc
	1989 - 96 Senior Executive, Hanson Plc
	1990 - Chairman, St Mary's Hospital
	Paddington NHS Trust
	1992 - Chairman, British Helicopters
	Advisory Board
	1994 - Deputy Chairman, Hanson Pacific
	1996 Chairman, European Helicopters
	Association
	1997 - Chairman, International Federation
	of Helicopter Associations
Political Career	1982 - 83 Government Whip,
	(Lord in Waiting)
	1983 - 85 Parliamentary Secretary,
	Department of Health and Social Security
	1985 - 86 Parliamentary Secretary,
	Home Office
	1986 - 87 Minister of State, Scottish Office
	1987 - 89 Minister of State, Foreign and
	Commonwealth Office
Subject Interests	Foreign affairs, Aviation, Defence, Scotland,
	Health, Penal affairs
Recreational Interests	Fieldsports, Gardening, Choral singing,
	Photography, Barometers
Correspondence Address	PO Box 11012, Banchory, AB31 6ZJ
	Tel: (01330) 844467 Fax: (01330) 844465
	E-mail: glenarth@rsc.co.uk

MEMBERS OF THE HOUSE OF LORDS

Glenconner, Baron (Colin Christopher Paget Tennant)
Type of Peerage . . . . Hereditary
Political Allegiance . . . . . Liberal Democrat
Succeeded 1983
Born . . . . 1st December 1926

Glendevon, Baron (Julian John Somerset Hope)
Type of Peerage . . . . Hereditary
Without Writ of Summons
Succeeded 1996
Born . . . . 6th March 1950

Glendyne, Baron (Robert Nivison)
Type of Peerage . . . . Hereditary
Political Allegiance . . . . . Conservative
Succeeded 1967
Born . . . . 27th October 1926

Glentoran, Baron (Thomas Robin Valerian Dixon CBE)
Type of Peerage . . . . Hereditary
Political Allegiance . . . . . Conservative
Succeeded 1995
Born . . . . 21st April 1935 in London
Educated . . . . Eton College
Grenoble, France
Professional Career . . . . . 1954 - 67 Grenadier Guards
1967 - 71 Kodak Ltd
1971 - Managing Director, Redland (NI) Ltd
1994 - Millennium Commissioner
Correspondence Address . . Drumadarragh House, Ballyclare,
County Antrim, BT39 0TA
Tel and Fax: (01960) 340222

Gloucester, Bishop of (Rt Rev David Edward Bentley)
Type of Peerage . . . . Bishop
Political Allegiance . . . . . None
Born . . . . 7th August 1935
Educated . . . . Great Yarmouth Grammar School
Leeds University
Westcott House, Cambridge
Professional Career . . . . . 1960 - 62 Curate, St Ambrose, Bristol
1962 - 66 Curate, Holy Trinity and St Mary,
Guildford
1966 - 73 Rector, Headley, Bordon
1973 - 86 Rector, Esher
1986 - 93 Bishop of Lynn
1993 - Bishop of Gloucester
Correspondence Address . . Bishopscourt, Pitt Street,
Gloucester, GL1 2BQ
Tel: (01452) 524598 Fax: (01452) 310025

Gloucester, Duke of (HRH Prince Richard)
Type of Peerage . . . . Hereditary
Political Allegiance . . . . . Cross Bench
Succeeded 1974
Born . . . . 26th August 1944

Goff of Chieveley, Baron
(Rt Hon Robert Lionel Archibald Goff DCL, FBA)
Type of Peerage . . . . Life (Law Lord)
Political Allegiance . . . . . Cross Bench
Born . . . . 12th November 1926 in Alyth, Scotland
Created 1986
Educated . . . . Eton College
New College, Oxford
Professional Career . . . . . 1951 - 55 Fellow, Lincoln College, Oxford
1956 - 75 Barrister (QC 1966)
1975 - 82 High Court Judge
1982 - 85 Lord Justice of Appeal
1986 - Lord of Appeal in Ordinary (Senior
Law Lord since 1996)
Correspondence Address . . Lords of Appeal Office, House of Lords,
Westminster, London, SW1A 0PW
Tel: (0171) 219 3202 Fax: (0171) 219 6156

Goodhart, Baron (William Howard Goodhart QC)
Type of Peerage . . . . Life
Political Allegiance . . . . . Liberal Democrat
Created 1997
Born . . . . 18th January 1933 in London
Educated . . . . Eton College
Trinity College, Cambridge
Harvard Law School
Professional Career . . . . . 1960 - Barrister (QC 1979)
Political Career . . . . 1995 - Vice Chairman, Liberal Democrat
Policy Committee
Subject Interests . . . . Human rights
Correspondence Address . . 11 Clarence Terrace, London, NW1 4RD
Tel: (0171) 262 1319 Fax: (0171) 723 5851
3 New Square, Lincolns Inn,
London, WC2A 3RS
Tel: (0171) 405 5577 Fax: (0171) 404 5032
E-mail: law@threenewsquare.demon.co.uk

Gordon of Strathblane, Baron (James Stuart Gordon CBE)
Type of Peerage . . . . Life
Political Allegiance . . . . . Labour
Born . . . . 17th May 1936 in Glasgow
Created 1997
Educated . . . . St. Aloysius' College
Glasgow University
Professional Career . . . . . 1965 - 73 Political Editor, Scottish
Television
1973 - 96 Managing Director, Radio Clyde
1981 - 90 Member, Scottish Development
Agency
1991 - 96 Chief Executive, Scottish Radio
Holdings
1991 - 97 Director, Melody Radio
1996 - Director, Johnstone Press plc
1996 - Director, Aim Trust
1997 - Member, Scottish Tourist Board
Subject Interests . . . . Tourism, Broadcasting, Scotland
Recreational Interests . . . Skiing, Golf, Genealogy
Correspondence Address . . Scottish Radio Holdings, Clydebank,
Glasgow, C81 2RX
Tel: (0141) 565 2202 Fax: (0141) 565 2322
Deil's Craig, Strathblane, Glasgow, G63 9ET

MEMBERS OF THE HOUSE OF LORDS

Gorell, Baron (Timothy John Radcliffe Barnes)

Type of Peerage	Hereditary
Political Allegiance	Cross Bench
Succeeded	1963
Born	2nd August 1927 in London
Educated	Eton College
	New College, Oxford
Professional Career	1951 - 59 Barrister, (Chancery Bar)
	1959 - 84 Senior Executive, Royal
	Dutch/Shell Group
Recreational Interests	Skiing, Sailing, Golf, Painting
Correspondence Address	4 Roehampton Gate, London, SW15 5JS
	Tel: (0181) 876 5522

Gormanston, Viscount (Jenico Nicholas Dudley Preston)

Type of Peerage	Hereditary
Political Allegiance	Conservative
Succeeded	1940 (as a minor)
Born	19th December 1939 in Andover, Hampshire
Educated	Downside School
	St Martin's School of Art, London
Subject Interests	Fine Arts
Recreational Interests	Reading, Travelling
Correspondence Address	Dalmeny House, 9 Thurloe Place,
	London, SW7 2RY

Goschen, Viscount (Giles John Harry Goschen)

Type of Peerage	Hereditary
Political Allegiance	Conservative
Succeeded	1977 (as a minor)
Born	16th November 1965
Political Career	1992 - 94 Government Whip
	(Lord in Waiting)
	1994 - 97 Parliamentary Secretary,
	Department of Transport

Gosford, Earl of
(Charles David Nicholas Alexander John Sparrow Acheson)

Type of Peerage	Hereditary
Political Allegiance	Cross Bench
Succeeded	1966
Born	13th July 1942

Gough, Viscount (Shane Hugh Maryon Gough)

Type of Peerage	Hereditary
Political Allegiance	Cross Bench
Succeeded	1951 (as a minor)
Born	26th August 1941

Gould of Potternewton, Baroness (Joyce Brenda Gould)

Type of Peerage	Life
Political Allegiance	Labour
Created	1993
Born	29th October 1932 in Leeds
Educated	Roundhay High School, Leeds
	Bradford Technical College
Professional Career	President, British Epilepsy Association
	1997 - Member, Government Commission on
	Electoral Systems
Political Career	1969 - 75 Assistant Regional Organiser and
	Women's Officer, Yorkshire, Labour Party
	1975 - 85 Assistant National Agent and
	Chief Women's Officer, Labour Party
	1985 - 93 Director of Organisation,
	Labour Party
	1994 - 97 Opposition Whip, House of Lords
	1997 Government Whip,
	(Baroness in Waiting)
Recreational Interests	Sport, Theatre, Cinema, Reading
Correspondence Address	Flat1, 5 Foulser Road, London, SW17 8UE
	Tel and Fax: (0181) 672 0641
	6 St Johns Mews, Bristol Road,
	Brighton, BN2 1BN
	Tel and Fax: (01273) 607474

Gowrie, Earl
(Rt Hon Alexander Patrick Greysteil Hore-Ruthven)

Type of Peerage	Hereditary
Political Allegiance	Conservative
Succeeded	1945
Born	26th November 1939
Professional Career	1994 - 98 Chairman, Arts Council
	of England
Political Career	1971 - 74 Government Whip,
	(Lord in Waiting)
	1971 - 79 Opposition Spokesman on
	Economic Affairs, House of Lords
	1979 - 81 Minister of State, Department of
	Employment
	1981 - 83 Minister of State,
	Northern Ireland Office
	1983 - 85 Minister for the Arts
	1984 - 85 Chancellor of the Duchy of
	Lancaster

Grade, Baron (Lew Grade)

Type of Peerage	Life
Political Allegiance	Cross Bench
Created	1976
Born	25th December 1906 in Tokmak, Russia
Professional Career	1943 - 55 Joint Managing Director, Lew and
	Leslie Grade Ltd
	1955 - 62 Managing Director, ITC
	1955 - 70 Deputy Managing Director, then
	Managing Director/Chairman,
	Chief Executive, ATV
	1969 - 82 Chairman, Stoll Moss Theatres Ltd
	1973 - 82 Chairman and Chief Executive,
	Associated Communications Corporation
	1977 - 82 President, ATV Network Ltd
	1982 - 85 Chairman/Chief Executive,
	Embassy Communications
	International Ltd
	1985 - Chairman/Chief Executive, Grade
	Enterprises Ltd
	1995 - Life Chairman, ITC
	Entertainment Group
Subject Interests	Entertainment industry
Recreational Interests	Reading, Cinema, Theatre, Sport
Correspondence Address	34 Grosvenor Street, London, W1X 9FG
	Tel: (0171) 409 1925 Fax: (0171) 408 2042

MEMBERS OF THE HOUSE OF LORDS

Grafton, Duke of (Hugh Denis Charles Fitzroy KG)

Type of Peerage . . . . Hereditary
Political Allegiance . . . . . Conservative
Succeeded 1970
Born . . . . 3rd April 1919

Graham of Edmonton, Baron (Thomas Edward Graham)

Type of Peerage . . . . Life
Political Allegiance . . . . . Labour
Created 1983
Born . . . . 26th March 1925 in Newcastle-upon-Tyne
Educated . . . . Co-operative College
    Open University
Professional Career . . . . . 1939 - 52 Newcastle Co-operative Society
    1952 - 53 Organiser, National Federation of
        Young Co-operatives
    1953 - 62 Education Secretary, Enfield
        Highway Co-operative
    1962 - 67 Organiser, Co-operative Union
    1997 - Chairman, UK Co-operative Council
Political Career . . . . 1967 - 74 National Secretary,
        Co-operative Party
    1974 - 83 MP (Labour and Co-op) for
        Enfield, Edmonton
    1976 - 79 Government Whip,
        House of Commons
    1979 - 81 Opposition Whip,
        House of Commons
    1981 - 83 Opposition Environment
        Spokesman, House of Commons
    1983 - 90 Opposition Whips, House of Lords
    1990 - 97 Opposition Chief Whip,
        House of Lords
Subject Interests. . . . . Environment, Sport, Travel
Correspondence Address . . House of Lords, Westminster,
    London, SW1A 0PW
    Tel: (0171) 219 6704/4991
    2 Clerks Piece, Loughton, Essex
    Tel: (0181) 508 9801

Granard, Earl of (Peter Arthur Edward Hastings Forbes)

Type of Peerage . . . . Hereditary
Political Allegiance . . . . . Conservative
Succeeded 1992
Born . . . . 15th March 1957

Grantchester, Baron (Christopher John Suenson-Taylor)

Type of Peerage . . . . Hereditary
Political Allegiance . . . . . Labour
Succeeded 1995
Born . . . . 8th April 1951 in London

Grantley, Baron (Richard William Brinsley Norton)

Type of Peerage . . . . Hereditary
Political Allegiance . . . . . Cross Bench
Succeeded 1995
Born . . . . 30th January 1956 in London
Educated . . . . Ampleforth College
    New College, Oxford
Professional Career . . . . . 1977 - 81 Conservative Party Research
        Department,
    1981 - 97 Director, Morgan Grenfell
        International Ltd and Director,
        Deutsche Morgan Grenfell
    1997 - Director, Project and Export Finance,
        HSBC Investment Bank plc
Political Career . . . . 1982 - 86 Councillor, Royal Borough of
        Kensington and Chelsea
    1997 Leader, UK Independence Party,
        House of Lords
Recreational Interests . . . Bridge
Correspondence Address . . 8 Halsey Street, London, SW3 2QH
    Tel and Fax: (0171) 589 7531

Granville, Earl of (Granville George Fergus Leveson Gower)

Type of Peerage . . . . Hereditary
Without Writ of Summons
Succeeded 1996
Born . . . . 10th September 1959

Gray, Baron (Angus Diarmid Ian Campbell-Gray)

Type of Peerage . . . . Hereditary
Political Allegiance . . . . . Conservative
Succeeded . . . . 1946 (as a minor)
Born . . . . 3rd July 1931

Gray of Contin, Baron (Rt Hon James Hector Northcy Gray)

Type of Peerage . . . . Life
Political Allegiance . . . . . Conservative
Created 1983
Born . . . . 28th June 1927 in Inverness
Professional Career . . . . . 1945 - 48 Queen's Own Cameron
        Highlanders
    1948 - 69 Director, Family and Other
        Private Companies
Political Career . . . . 1970 - 83 MP (Conservative) for Ross and
        Cromarty
    1971 - 74 Government Whip,
        House of Commons
    1975 - 79 Opposition Spokesman on Energy,
        House of Commons
    1979 - 83 Minister of State, Department
        of Energy
    1983 - 86 Minister of State, Scottish Office
        (also Government Spokesman on Energy,
        House of Lords)
Subject Interests. . . . . Energy, Industry, Scotland

MEMBERS OF THE HOUSE OF LORDS

Greene of Harrow Weald, Baron
(Sidney Francis Greene CBE)

Type of Peerage . . . . Life
Political Allegiance . . . . . Labour
Created 1975
Born . . . . 12th February 1910 in London
Professional Career . . . . . 1957 - 75 General Secretary, National Union
    of Railwaymen
Subject Interests . . . . Transport

Greenhill, Baron (Malcolm Greenhill)

Type of Peerage . . . . Hereditary
Without Writ of Summons
Succeeded 1989
Born . . . . 5th May 1924

Greenhill of Harrow, Baron
(Denis Arthur Greenhill GCMG, OBE)

Type of Peerage . . . . Life
Political Allegiance . . . . . Cross Bench
Created 1974
Born . . . . 7th November 1913 in South Woodford,
    Essex
Educated . . . . Bishops Stortford College
    Christ Church, Oxford
Professional Career . . . . . 1946 - 73 HM Diplomatic Service
    1955 - 57 Member, UK Delegation to NATO
    1957 - 59 Counsellor, Singapore
    1959 - 64 Counsellor, then Minister,
    Washington DC
    1964 - 69 Assistant, then Deputy Secretary,
    Foreign Office
    1969 - 73 Permanent Secretary and Head of
    Diplomatic Service, Foreign and
    Commonwealth Office
    1973 - 78 Director, British Petroleum
    1973 - 82 Member, Security Commission
Subject Interests . . . . Railways, Foreign affairs
Correspondence Address . . 25 Hamilton House, Vicarage Gate,
    London, W8 4HL
    Tel: (0171) 937 8362

Greenway, Baron (Ambrose Charles Drexel Greenway)

Type of Peerage . . . . Hereditary
Political Allegiance . . . . . Cross Bench
Succeeded 1975
Born . . . . 21st May 1941 in Edenbridge
Professional Career . . . . . 1967 - Marine Photographer
    1975 Marine Historian
    1986 - 88 Editor, Bond Street Magazine
    1986 - 90 Deputy Editor, Freight Forwarding
    1991 - 94 President, World Ship Society
    1994 - President, Cruise Europe
Subject Interests . . . . Maritime affairs, Shipping, Navigation,
    Sailing, Inland waterways, Photography
Recreational Interests . . . Sailing, Swimming

Greenwood, Viscount (David Henry Hamar Greenwood)

Type of Peerage . . . . . . Hereditary
Has Not Taken The Oath/ On Leave of Absence
Succeeded 1948
Born . . . . 30th October 1914

Gregson, Baron (John Gregson)

Type of Peerage . . . . Life
Political Allegiance . . . . . Labour
Created 1975
Born . . . . 29th January 1924
Educated . . . . Birchfield Road School, Withington,
    Manchester
Professional Career . . . . . 1939 - 94 Fairey Engineering Ltd
    (Managing Director 1978 - 94)
    1976 - 94 Director, (Non-Executive)
    British Steel plc
    1981 - Chairman, BNFL Expert Panel
    1984 - President, Defence Manufacturers
    Association
    1985 - Chairman, Waste Management
    Industry Training and Advisory Board
    1989 - Director (Non Executive)
    Innvotech Ltd
    1992 - 95 Director, (Non-Executive)
    National Rivers Authority
    1994 - 96 President, Environmental
    Industries Commission
    1995 - Non-Executive Director, OSC Process
    Engineering Ltd
    1997 - Chairman, Advisory Council, RMCS
    Shrivenham
    1997 - Chairman of the Onyx
    Environmental Trust
Political Career . . . . President, Labour Finance and
    Industry Group
    Member, Select Committee on Science and
    Technology, House of Lords
Recreational Interests . . . Mountaineering, Skiing, Sailing, Gardening
Correspondence Address . . 12 Rosemont Road, Richmond,
    Surrey, TW10 6QL
    Tel: (0181) 948 2244 Fax: (0181) 948 3388

Grenfell of Kilvey, Baron
(Julian Pascoe Francis St Leger Grenfell)

Type of Peerage . . . . Hereditary
Political Allegiance . . . . . Labour
Succeeded 1976
Born . . . . 23rd May 1935 in London
Educated . . . . Eton College
    King's College, Cambridge
Professional Career . . . . . 1965 - 95 The World Bank (various posts)
Political Career . . . . 1996 - Member, European Communities
    Sub-Committee on Economic,
    Financial Affairs, Trade and External
    Relations, House of Lords
    1997 - Member, UK Delegation to Council
    of Europe
Subject Interests . . . . European Affairs, Defence, Trade and
    development
Correspondence Address . . 24 Rue Chaptal, Paris 75009, France
    Tel: 00 33 1 487 40855
    Fax: 00 33 1 487 40855

MEMBERS OF THE HOUSE OF LORDS

Gretton, Baron (John Lysander Gretton)

Type of Peerage . . . . Hereditary
Without Writ of Summons
Succeeded . . . . 1989 (as a minor)
Born . . . . 17th April 1975

Grey, Earl of (Richard Fleming George Charles Grey)

Type of Peerage . . . . Hereditary
Political Allegiance . . . . . Liberal Democrat
Succeeded 1963
Born . . . . 5th March 1939

Grey of Codnor, Baron (Richard Henry Cornwall-Leigh)

Type of Peerage . . . . Hereditary
Political Allegiance . . . . . None
Succeeded 1996
Born . . . . 14th May 1936

Grey of Naunton, Baron
   (Ralph Francis Alnwick Gray GCMG, GCVO)

Type of Peerage . . . . Life
Political Allegiance . . . . . Cross Bench
Created 1968
Born . . . . 15th April 1910

Gridley, Baron (Richard David Arnold Gridley)

Type of Peerage . . . . Hereditary
Political Allegiance . . . . . Liberal Democrat
Succeeded 1996
Born . . . . 22nd August 1956 in Penang, Malaya
Educated . . . . Monkton Combe School, Bath
                              Portsmouth Polytechnic
                              University of Brighton
Professional Career . . . . . 1981 - 92 Construction Industry
                              1994 - Lecturer, South Downs College of
                                 Further Education
Subject Interests . . . . Education, Construction Industry
Recreational Interests . . . Mountain biking, Sailing, Environment,
                              Wildlife
Correspondence Address . . 79 Purbrook Gardens, Waterlooville,
                              Hampshire, PO7 5LE

Griffiths, Baron (Rt Hon William Hugh Griffiths MC)

Type of Peerage . . . . Life (Former Law Lord)
Political Allegiance . . . . . Cross Bench
Created 1985
Born . . . . 26th September 1923
Professional Career . . . . . 1942 - 46 Officer, Welsh Guards
                              1949 - Barrister (QC 1964)
                              1962 - 70 Recorder
                              1968 - 69 Treasurer, Bar Council
                              1971 - 80 High Court Judge,
                                 (Queen's Bench Division)
                              1980 - 85 Lord Justice of Appeal
                              1985 - 93 Lord of Appeal in Ordinary
                              1985 - 92 Chairman, Security Commission
Political Career . . . . 1995 - Chairman, Sub-Committee on Lords'
                              Interests, House of Lords

Griffiths of Fforestfach, Baron (Brian Griffiths)

Type of Peerage . . . . Life
Political Allegiance . . . . . Conservative
Created 1991
Born . . . . 27th December 1941 in Swansea
Educated . . . . London School of Economics
Political Career . . . . 1985 - 90 Head of Prime Minister's Policy
                              Unit (under Rt Hon Margaret
                              Thatcher MP)

Grimston of Westbury, Baron
   (Robert Walter Sigismund Grimston)

Type of Peerage . . . . Hereditary
Political Allegiance . . . . . Conservative
Succeeded 1979
Born . . . . 14th June 1925

Grimthorpe, Baron (Christopher John Beckett OBE)

Type of Peerage . . . . Hereditary
Political Allegiance . . . . . Conservative
Succeeded 1963
Born . . . . 16th September 1915 in London
Educated . . . . Eton College
Professional Career . . . . . 1934 - 68 Army Officer
                              1961 - 64 Brigadier, Royal Armoured Corps,
                                 HQ Western Command
                              1964 - 67 Deputy Commander,
                                 Malta and Libya
Recreational Interests . . . Horse sports
Correspondence Address . . Westow Hall, York, YO6 7NE

Guilford, Earl of (Edward Francis North)

Type of Peerage . . . . Hereditary
Political Allegiance . . . . . None
Succeeded . . . . 1949 (as a minor)
Born . . . . 22nd September 1933 in London

MEMBERS OF THE HOUSE OF LORDS

H

Habgood, Baron
(Rt Rev and Rt Hon John Stapylton Habgood)

Type of Peerage . . . . Life
Political Allegiance . . . . . Cross Bench
Created . . . . 1995 (previously in the House of Lords as Bishop/Archbishop 1973 - 95)
Born . . . . 23rd June 1927 in Stony Stratford
Educated . . . . Eton College
King's College, Cambridge
Professional Career . . . . . 1950 - 53 Demonstrator in Pharmacology, Cambridge
1954 - 56 Curate, St Mary Abbots, Kensington
1956 - 62 Vice-Principal, Westcott House, Cambridge
1962 - 67 Rector, St John's, Jedburgh
1967 - 73 Principal, Queen's College, Birmingham
1973 - 83 Bishop of Durham
1983 - 95 Archbishop of York
1996 - Chairman, UK Xenotransplantation Interim Regulatory Authority
Subject Interests . . . . Science, Theology, Ethics, Medicine
Recreational Interests . . . DIY, Painting
Correspondence Address . . 18 The Mount, Malton, North Yorkshire, YO17 0ND

Hacking, Baron (Douglas David Hacking)

Type of Peerage . . . . Hereditary
Political Allegiance . . . . . Conservative
Succeeded 1971
Born . . . . 17th April 1938 in London
Professional Career . . . . . 1964 - 75 Barrister at Law
1977 - Solicitor
1995 - Partner, Sonnensheins (Solicitors)
Subject Interests . . . . Law, European Union, International Arbitration
Recreational Interests . . . Running, Walking

Haddington, Earl of (John George Baillie-Hamilton)

Type of Peerage . . . . Hereditary
Political Allegiance . . . . . Conservative
Succeeded 1986
Born . . . . 21st December 1941

Haden-Guest, Baron (Christopher Haden-Guest)

Type of Peerage . . . . Hereditary
Political Allegiance . . . . . None
Succeeded 1996
Born . . . . 5th February 1948 in New York City
Educated . . . . Stockbridge School
New York University
Professional Career . . . . . Film Director, Actor, Musician
Subject Interests . . . . Environment
Recreational Interests . . . Fly fishing, Skiing

Haig, Earl (George Alexander Eugene Douglas Haig OBE)

Type of Peerage . . . . Hereditary
Political Allegiance . . . . . Conservative
Succeeded . . . . 1928 (as a minor)
Born . . . . 15th March 1918 at Kingston Hill
Educated . . . . Stowe School
Christ Church, Oxford
Camberwell School of Arts and Crafts
Professional Career . . . . . 1953 - 74 President, Scottish Craft Centre
1960 - 73 Chairman, Disablement Advisory Committee, South East Scotland
1979 - 86 President, Royal British Legion, Scotland (previously Chairman 1963 - 66)
1983 - 86 Chairman, Scottish National War Memorial
1987 - 96 President, Officers Association (Scottish Branch)
1988 - Associate, Royal Scottish Academy
Subject Interests . . . . Visual arts, Museums and galleries, Ex-service matters, Salmon fisheries, Landowning, Field sports, Heritage, Environment
Recreational Interests . . . Fishing, Landscape sketching, Music, Art galleries
Correspondence Address . . Bemersyde, Melrose, Roxburghshire, Scotland, TD6 9DP
Tel: (01835) 822762 Fax: (01835) 824104

Hailsham of Saint Marylebone, Baron
(Rt Hon Quintin McGarel Hogg KG, CH)

Type of Peerage . . . . Life
Political Allegiance . . . . . Conservative
Created . . . . 1970 (previously in House of Lords as Viscount Hailsham 1950 - 63, peerage then disclaimed)
Born . . . . 9th October 1907 in London
Educated . . . . Eton College
Christ Church, Oxford
Professional Career . . . . . 1931 - 38, 1961 - Fellow, All Souls College, Oxford
1932 Barrister (QC 1953)
1939 - 45 Officer, Rifle Brigade
1972 - Editor, Halsbury's Laws of England
Political Career . . . . 1938 - 50 MP (Conservative) for Oxford City
1945 Parliamentary Secretary for Air
1956 - 57 First Lord of the Admiralty
1957 - 59 Chairman, Conservative Party Organisation
1957 - 59, 1960 - 64 Lord President of the Council
1957 - 60 Deputy Leader, House of Lords
1957 Minister of Education
1959 - 60 Lord Privy Seal
1959 - 64 Minister for Science and Technology
1960 - 63 Leader, House of Lords
1963 - 70 MP (Conservative) for St Marylebone
1964 Secretary of State for Education and Science
1970 - 74, 1979 - 87 Lord Chancellor
Deputy Speaker, House of Lords
Correspondence Address . . Corner House, Heathview Gardens, London, SW15 3SZ
Tel: (0181) 788 2256

MEMBERS OF THE HOUSE OF LORDS

Halifax, Earl of (Charles Edward Peter Neil Wood)

Type of Peerage	Hereditary
Political Allegiance	Conservative
Succeeded	1980
Born	14th March 1944 in London
Educated	Eton College
	Christ Church, Oxford
Professional Career	1978 - 89 Director, Hambros Bank
	1985 - 96 Non-Executive Director, Yorkshire Post Newspapers
	1990 - 93 Non-Executive Director, East Yorkshire Health Authority
	1991 - 95 Non-Executive Director, Minster Sound Radio
	1993 - 96 Non-Executive Director, East Riding Health
Recreational Interests	Hunting, Shooting, Racing
Correspondence Address	Garrowby, York, YO4 1QD
	Tel: (01759) 368236 Fax: (01759) 368154

Halsbury, Earl of (John Anthony Hardinge Giffard)

Type of Peerage	Hereditary
Political Allegiance	Cross Bench
Succeeded	1943
Born	4th June 1908 in London
Educated	Eton College
Professional Career	1947 - 49 Research Director, Decca Record Co
	1949 - 59 Managing Director, National Research Development Corporation
	1951 - 65 Chairman, Science Museum Advisory Council
	1959 - 78 Consultant/Director, Distillers Co; also Head Wrightson Ltd, Joseph Lucas Industries
	1961 - 63 Chairman, Committee on Decimal Currency
	1962 - 77 Chairman, Management Committee, Institute of Cancer Research
	1966 - Chancellor, Brunel University
	1971 - 74 Chairman, Review Body on Doctors' and Dentists' Pay
Subject Interests	Chemistry, Medicine
Recreational Interests	Music, Literature, History
Correspondence Address	House of Lords, Westminster, London, SW1A 0PW
	Flat 4, Campden House, 29 Sheffield Terrace, London, W8 7NE
	Tel: (0171) 727 3125

Hambleden, Viscount (William Herbert Hambleden)

Type of Peerage	Hereditary
Political Allegiance	Conservative
Succeeded	1948 (as a minor)
Born	2nd April 1930 in London
Educated	Eton College
Professional Career	1949 - 50 Army, East African Rifles
	1984 - 86 World Wildlife Fund
Subject Interests	Environment, Horse Racing
Recreational Interests	Skiing, Shooting, Walking, Ballet
Correspondence Address	Dunsaller, Thorverton, Near Exeter, Devon, EX5 5JR
	Tel: (01392) 860239 Fax: (01392) 860769

Hambro, Baron (Charles Eric Alexander Hambro)

Type of Peerage	Life
Political Allegiance	Conservative
Created	1994
Born	24th July 1930 in London

Hamilton and Brandon, Duke of (Angus Alan Douglas-Hamilton)

Type of Peerage	Hereditary
Succeeded	1973
Political Allegiance	Cross Bench
Born	13th September 1938
Educated	Eton College
	Balliol College, Oxford
Professional Career	1956 - 67 RAF Senior Commercial Pilot
	1970 - 72 Test Pilot, Scottish Aviation
Subject Interests	Energy, Defence, Transport
Recreational Interests	Scottish History
Correspondence Address	Lennoxlove, Haddington, East Lothian, Scotland, EH41 4NZ
	Tel: (01620) 823720
	Archerfield Home Farm, by Dirleton, East Lothian, Scotland, EH39 5HQ
	Tel: (01620) 850364 Fax: (01620) 850298
	E-mail: diesel@archerfield.demon.co.uk

Hamilton of Dalzell, Baron (James Leslie Hamilton)

Type of Peerage	Hereditary
Political Allegiance	Conservative
Succeeded	1990
Born	11th February 1938 in London

Hampden, Viscount (Anthony David Brand)

Type of Peerage	Hereditary
Political Allegiance	Cross Bench
Succeeded	1975
Born	7th May 1937 in London
Educated	Eton College
Professional Career	1956 - 69 Lazard Brothers
	1970 - 82 Hoare Govett, Stockbrokers
	1984 - Glynde Estate
Correspondence Address	Glynde Place, Glynde, Lewes, BN8 6SX
	Tel: (01273) 858418 Fax: (01273) 858224

Hampton, Baron (Richard Humphrey Russell Pakington)

Type of Peerage	Hereditary
Political Allegiance	Liberal Democrat
Succeeded	1974
Born	25th May 1925 in London
Professional Career	1944 - 47 Observer in Fleet Air Arm, RNVR
	1971 - 73 Tansley Witt and Co, Chartered Accountants, Birmingham
Political Career	1977 - 87 Liberal Party Spokesman on Northern Ireland, House of Lords

MEMBERS OF THE HOUSE OF LORDS

Hamwee, Baroness (Sally Rachel Hamwee)
Type of Peerage . . . . Life
Political Allegiance . . . . . Liberal Democrat
Created 1991
Born . . . . 12th January 1947 in Manchester
Educated . . . . Manchester High School for Girls
　　　　　　　　　　　Girton College, Cambridge
Professional Career . . . . . Partner, Clintons Solicitors
　　　　　　　　　　　President, Town and County
　　　　　　　　　　　Planning Association
　　　　　　　　　　　1997 - Chairman, XFM Ltd
Political Career . . . . 1978 - Councillor, London Borough of
　　　　　　　　　　　Richmond upon Thames (Chair, Planning
　　　　　　　　　　　Committee 1983 - 87)
　　　　　　　　　　　1986 - 94 Chairman, London Planning
　　　　　　　　　　　Advisory Committee
　　　　　　　　　　　1991 - Liberal Democrat Spokesman on
　　　　　　　　　　　Environment, Local Government, Housing
　　　　　　　　　　　and Planning, House of Lords
Subject Interests . . . . Local Government, Planning, Housing
Correspondence Address . . House of Lords, Westminster,
　　　　　　　　　　　London, SW1A 0PW
　　　　　　　　　　　Tel: (0181) 878 1380 Fax; (0181) 392 9530

Hankey, Baron (Donald Robin Alers Hankey)
Type of Peerage . . . . Hereditary
Political Allegiance . . . . . Cross Bench
Succeeded 1996
Born . . . . 12th June 1938

Hanson, Baron (James Edward Hanson)
Type of Peerage . . . . Life
Political Allegiance . . . . . Conservative
Created 1983
Born . . . . 20th January 1922 in Huddersfield,
　　　　　　　　　　　Yorkshire
Professional Career . . . . . 1965 - 97 Chairman, Hanson plc and
　　　　　　　　　　　Hanson Transport Group

Hanworth, Viscount (David Stephen Jeffrey Pollock)
Type of Peerage . . . . Hereditary
Political Allegiance . . . . . Labour
Succeeded 1996
Born . . . . 16th February 1946

Hardie, Baron (Rt Hon Andrew Rutherford Hardie QC)
Type of Peerage . . . . Life
Political Allegiance . . . . . Labour
Created 1997
Born . . . . 8th January 1946 in Stirling
Educated . . . . St Modan's High School, Stirling
　　　　　　　　　　　Edinburgh University
Professional Career . . . . . 1971 - 72 Solicitor
　　　　　　　　　　　1973 - Advocate (QC 1985)
　　　　　　　　　　　1989 - 97 Treasurer then Dean, Faculty of
　　　　　　　　　　　Advocates
Political Career . . . . 1997 - Lord Advocate
Subject Interests . . . . Welfare of children,
　　　　　　　　　　　Environment and planning
Recreational Interests . . . Cricket, Family
Correspondence Address . . Lord Advocate's Chambers, 2 Carlton
　　　　　　　　　　　Gardens, London, SW1Y 5AA
　　　　　　　　　　　Tel: (0171) 210 1010 Fax: (0171) 210 1036
　　　　　　　　　　　Crown Office, 25 Chambers Street,
　　　　　　　　　　　Edinburgh, EH1 1LA
　　　　　　　　　　　Tel: (0131) 226 2626
Personal Staff . . . . Mr Jeff Gibbons (Private Secretary)
　　　　　　　　　　　Tel: (0171)210 1034

Harding of Petherton, Baron (John Charles Harding)
Type of Peerage . . . . Hereditary
Political Allegiance . . . . . Conservative
Succeeded 1989
Born . . . . 12th February 1928 in Long Ashton, Bristol
Educated . . . . Marlborough College
　　　　　　　　　　　Worcester College, Oxford
Professional Career . . . . . 1953 - 68 Regular Army Officer
　　　　　　　　　　　(11th Hussars)
　　　　　　　　　　　1969 - 90 Farmer
Subject Interests . . . . Economics, Housing, Farming, Defence,
　　　　　　　　　　　Education
Recreational Interests . . . Hunting, Horseracing
Correspondence Address . . Myrtle Cottage, Lamyatt,
　　　　　　　　　　　near Shepton Mallet, Somerset, BA4 6NP
　　　　　　　　　　　Tel: (01749) 812292

Hardinge, Viscount (Charles Henry Nicholas Hardinge)
Type of Peerage . . . . Hereditary
Political Allegiance . . . . . Cross Bench
Succeeded 1984
Born . . . . 25th August 1956

Hardinge of Penshurst, Baron (Julian Alexander Hardinge)
Type of Peerage . . . . Hereditary
Political Allegiance . . . . . None
Succeeded 1997
Born . . . . 23rd August 1945

Hardwicke, Earl of (Joseph Philip Sebastian Yorke)
Type of Peerage . . . . Hereditary
Political Allegiance . . . . . Conservative
Succeeded . . . . 1974 (as a minor)
Born . . . . 3th February 1971 in London

Hardy of Wath, Baron (Peter Hardy)
Type of Peerage . . . . Life
Political Allegiance . . . . . Labour
Born . . . . 17th July 1931 in South Yorkshire
Created 1997
Educated . . . . Wath upon Dearne Grammar School
　　　　　　　　　　　Westminster College, London
　　　　　　　　　　　Sheffield University
Professional Career . . . . . 1954 - 60 Assistant Teacher,
　　　　　　　　　　　South Yorkshire
　　　　　　　　　　　1957 - 62 Part Time Lecturer, Doncaster
　　　　　　　　　　　Technical College
　　　　　　　　　　　1960 - 70 Head of Department, then Head of
　　　　　　　　　　　Lower School, Mexborough
　　　　　　　　　　　Secondary School
Political Career . . . . 1960 - 70 Member, Wath upon Dearne
　　　　　　　　　　　Urban District Council
　　　　　　　　　　　(Chairman 1968 - 69)
　　　　　　　　　　　1970 - 83 MP (Labour) for Rother Valley
　　　　　　　　　　　1974 - 76 PPS to Secretary of State for
　　　　　　　　　　　the Environment
　　　　　　　　　　　(Rt Hon Anthony Crosland MP)
　　　　　　　　　　　1974 - 92 Chairman, Parliamentary Labour
　　　　　　　　　　　Party Energy Committee
　　　　　　　　　　　1976 - 77 PPS to Foreign Secretary
　　　　　　　　　　　(Rt Hon Anthony Crosland MP)
　　　　　　　　　　　1983 - 95 Leader, Labour Delegation to
　　　　　　　　　　　Council of Europe and WEU
　　　　　　　　　　　1983 - 97 MP (Labour) for Wentworth
　　　　　　　　　　　1993 - 79 Delegate, Conference on Security
　　　　　　　　　　　and Co-operation in Europe
Subject Interests . . . . Energy, Defence, Environment/Conservation
Recreational Interests . . . Wild life, Dogs
Correspondence Address . . 53 Sandygate, Wath upon Dearne,
　　　　　　　　　　　Rotherham, South Yorkshire, S63 7LU
　　　　　　　　　　　Tel: (01709) 874590
Personal Staff . . . . Lady Hardy (Personal Assistant)

MEMBERS OF THE HOUSE OF LORDS

Harewood, Earl of (George Henry Hubert Lascelles KBE)

Type of Peerage	Hereditary
Political Allegiance	None
Succeeded	1947
Born	7th February 1923 in London
Educated	Eton College
	King's College, Cambridge
Professional Career	1953 - 60 On staff of Royal Opera House, Covent Garden
	1958 - 74 Artistic Director, Leeds Festival
	1961 - 65 Artistic Director, Edinburgh Festival
	1963 - 72 President, English Football Association
	1966 - 76 Artistic Adviser, New Philharmonic Orchestra
	1972 - 95 Managing Director, then (from 1985) Chairman, English National Opera
	1985 - 96 President, British Board of Film Classification
	1986 - 88 Artistic Director, Adelaide Festival
Recreational Interests ...	Soccer, Cricket, Pictures, Sculpture
Correspondence Address ..	Harewood House, Leeds, LS17 9LG

Harlech, Baron (Francis David Ormsby Gore)

Type of Peerage	Hereditary
Political Allegiance	Conservative
Succeeded	1985
Born	13th March 1954

Harmar-Nicholls, Baron (Harmar Harmar-Nicholls)

Type of Peerage	Life
Political Allegiance	Conservative
Created	1974
Born	1st November 1912 in Staffordshire
Political Career	1950 - 74 MP (Conservative) for Peterborough
	1955 - 57 Parliamentary Secretary, Ministry of Agriculture, Fisheries and Food
	1957 - 60 Parliamentary Secretary, Ministry of Works
	1979 - 84 Member of the European Parliament (Conservative) for Manchester South
Recreational Interests ...	Theatre, Walking
Correspondence Address ..	Abbeylands, Weston, Staffordshire, ST18 0HX
	Tel: (01889) 270252

Harmsworth, Baron (Thomas Harold Raymond Harmsworth)

Type of Peerage	Hereditary
Political Allegiance	Conservative
Succeeded	1990
Born	20th July 1939 in London
Educated	Eton College
	Christ Church, Oxford
Professional Career	1962 - 74 Stockbroker
	1974 - 88 Civil Servant, Department of Health and Social Security
	1988 - Publisher
Subject Interests	Health, European Union, Local Government

Harrington, Earl of (William Henry Leicester Stanhope)

Type of Peerage	Hereditary
On Leave of Absence	
Succeeded	1929 (as a minor)
Born	24th August 1922

Harris, Baron (Anthony Harris)

Type of Peerage	Hereditary
Without Writ of Summons	
Succeeded	1996
Born	8th March 194

Harris of Greenwich, Baron (John Henry Harris)

Type of Peerage	Life
Political Allegiance	Liberal Democrat
Created	1974
Born	5th April 1930 in Harrow, Middlesex
Educated	Pinner County Grammar School, Middlesex
Professional Career	1970 - 74 On Staff of the Economist
	1979 - 82 Chairman, Parole Board for England and Wales
	1979 - Chairman of Executive Committee, Police Foundation
Political Career	1957 - 63 Member Harlow Council, Essex (Leader 1961 - 63)
	1959 - 62 Personal Assistant to Leader of the Opposition (Rt Hon Hugh Gaitskell MP)
	1962 - 64 Director of Publicity, Labour Party
	1964 - 65 Special Assistant to Foreign Secretary (Rt Hon Patrick Gordon Walker MP)
	1966 - 70 Special Assistant to Home Secretary, then to Chancellor of Exchequer, (Rt Hon Roy Jenkins MP)
	1974 - 79 Minister of State, Home Office (Labour Government)
	1988 - 94 Liberal Democrat Spokesman on House Affairs, House of Lords
	1995 - Liberal Democrat Chief Whip, House of Lords
Subject Interests	Criminal justice, Parliamentary reform, Police service
Recreational Interests ...	Cricket
Correspondence Address ..	House of Lords, Westminster, London, SW1A 0PW
	Tel: (0171) 219 3114

Harris of High Cross, Baron (Ralph Harris)

Type of Peerage	Life
Political Allegiance	Cross Bench
Created	1979
Born	10th December 1924 in London
Educated	Tottenham Grammar School
	Queen's College, Cambridge
Professional Career	1949 - 56 Lecturer, St Andrew's University
	1956 Leader Writer, Glasgow Herald
	1957 - General Director, then Chairman and (since 1990) President, Institute of Economic Affairs
Political Career	1989 - 91 Chairman, Bruges Group
Recreational Interests ...	Reading, Writing, Swimming, Pipe smoking

MEMBERS OF THE HOUSE OF LORDS

Harris of Peckham, Baron (Philip Charles Harris)

Type of Peerage . . . . Life
Political Allegiance . . . . . Conservative
Created 1996
Born . . . . 15th September 1942 in St Albans,
Hertfordshire
Educated . . . . Streatham Grammar School, London
Professional Career . . . . . 1964 - 88 Chairman, Harris Queensway
1988 - Chairman and Chief Executive,
Carpetright plc
Subject Interests . . . . Health, Education
Recreational Interests . . . Horseracing, Show jumping, Tennis
Correspondence Address . . 16 Cadogan Square, London, SW1X 0JU
Tel: (0171) 823 1657 Fax: (0171) 823 1678
Amberley House, New Road, Rainham,
Essex, RM13 8QN
Tel: (01708) 527730 Fax: (01708) 630970
Personal Staff . . . . Mrs Judy Willett *(Personal Assistant)*
Tel: (01708) 527730

Harrowby, Earl of (Dudley Danvers Granville Coutts Ryder TD)

Type of Peerage . . . . Hereditary
Political Allegiance . . . . . Conservative
Succeeded 1987
Born . . . . 20th December 1922 in London
Educated . . . . Eton College
Professional Career . . . . . 1949 - 89 Managing Director, then Deputy
Chairman, Coutts and Co
1953 - 60 Manager, Fulham and Kensington
Hospital Group
1965 - 73 Chairman of Management
Committee Institute of Psychiatry
1965 - 73 Chairman of Governors, Bethlem
and Maudsley Hospitals
1971 - 73 Chairman, Olympia Group Ltd
1973 - 88 Chairman, National Biological
Standards Board
1977 - 87 Chairman, International
Westminster Bank Ltd
1979 -81 Chairman, Orion Bank Ltd
1983 - 86 Chairman, Bentley
Engineering Co
1986 - 91 Chairman, Dowty Group plc
Political Career . . . . 1950 - 65 Member, Kensington Borough
Council (Chairman General Purposes
Committee 1957 - 59)
1965 - 71 Member, Kensington and Chelsea
Borough Council (Chairman, Finance
Committee (1968 - 71)
Correspondence Address . . 5 Tregunter Road, London, SW10 9LS
Tel: (0171) 373 9276
Also Tel and Fax: (0171) 370 0320
Sandon Hall, Sandon, Stafford, ST18 0BZ
Tel: (01889) 508392 Fax: (01889) 508338
Personal Staff . . . . Mrs Joyce Davies *(Secretary Administrator)*
Tel: (01889) 508392

Hartwell, Baron (William Michael Berry MBE, TD)

Type of Peerage . . . . Life
Political Allegiance . . . . . Cross Bench
Created . . . . 1968 (succeeded as Viscount Camrose 1995
but disclaimed that peerage)
Born . . . . 18th May 1911
Professional Career . . . . . 1934 - 35 Editor, Sunday Mail (Glasgow)
1937 - 39 Managing Editor, Financial Times
1954 - 59 Chairman, Amalgamated
Press Ltd
1954 - 87 Chairman and Editor in Chief,
Daily Telegraph (also Sunday
Telegraph 1961 - 87)

Harvey of Tasburgh, Baron (Peter Charles Oliver Harvey)

Type of Peerage . . . . Hereditary
Political Allegiance . . . . . Conservative
Succeeded 1968
Born . . . . 28th January 1921

Haskel, Baron (Simon Haskel)

Type of Peerage . . . . Life
Political Allegiance . . . . . Labour
Created 1993
Born . . . . 9th October 1934 in Kaunas, Lithuania
Educated . . . . Salford College of Advanced Technology
Professional Career . . . . . 1973 - 97 Chairman, Perrotts Group
Political Career . . . . 1994 - 97 Opposition Whip and Spokesman
on Trade and Industry, House of Lords
1997 - Government Whip, (Lord in Waiting)
Recreational Interests . . . Music, Cycling

Haslam, Baron (Robert Haslam)

Type of Peerage . . . . Life
Political Allegiance . . . . . Conservative
Created 1990
Born . . . . 4th February 1923

Hastings, Baron (Edward Delaval Henry Astley)

Type of Peerage . . . . Hereditary
Political Allegiance . . . . . Conservative
Succeeded 1956
Born . . . . 14th April 1912 in Melton Constable
Professional Career . . . . . 1939 - 45 Coldstream Guards
1951 - 57 Farmer, Southern Rhodesia
Political Career . . . . 1961 - 62 Government Whip,
(Lord in Waiting)
1962 - 64 Parliamentary Secretary, Ministry
of Housing and Local Government
Subject Interests . . . . Agriculture, Disabilities (mental handicap
and epilepsy), the Arts, Europe
Correspondence Address . . Seaton Delaval Hall, Whitley Bay,
Northumberland, NE26 4QR
Tel: (0191) 237 0786

Hatherton, Baron (Edward Charles Littleton)

Type of Peerage . . . . Hereditary
Without Writ of Summons
Succeeded 1985
Born . . . . 24th May 1950

MEMBERS OF THE HOUSE OF LORDS

Hattersley, Baron (Rt Hon Roy Sydney George Hattersley)

Type of Peerage . . . . Life
Political Allegiance . . . . . Labour
Created 1997
Born . . . . 28th December 1932
Educated . . . . Sheffield City Grammar School
 Hull University
Political Career . . . . 1957 - 65 Member, Sheffield City Council
 1964 - 97 MP (Labour) for Birmingham
 Sparkbrook
 1967 - 69 Parliamentary Secretary,
 Department of Employment and
 Productivity
 1969 - 70 Minister of Defence for
 Administration
 1970 -74 Opposition Spokesman on Defence,
 then Education and Science
 1974 - 76 Minister of State, Foreign and
 Commonwealth Office
 1976 - 79 Secretary of State for Prices and
 Consumer Protection
 1979 - 80 Opposition Spokesman on
 Environment
 1980 - 83, 1987 - 92 Opposition Spokesman
 on Home Affairs
 1983 - 87 Opposition Spokesman on
 Treasury and Economic Affairs
 1983 - 92 Deputy Leader, Labour Party

Hawke, Baron (Edward George Hawke)

Type of Peerage . . . . Hereditary
Political Allegiance . . . . . Conservative
Succeeded 1992
Born . . . . 25th January 1950 in Altrincham
Educated . . . . Eton College
Professional Career . . . . . Chartered Surveyor

Hayhoe, Baron (Rt Hon Barney Hayhoe)

Type of Peerage . . . . Life
Political Allegiance . . . . . Conservative
Created 1992
Born . . . . 8th August 1925
Educated . . . . Borough Polytechnic
Professional Career . . . . . 1954 - 63 Inspector of Armaments
 1993 - 95 Chairman, Guy's and St Thomas's
 NHS Trust
Political Career . . . . 1944 - 54 Ministry of Supply
 1965 - 70 Conservative Research
 Department
 1970 - 92 MP (Conservative) for Heston and
 Isleworth then Brentford and Isleworth
 1979 - 81 Parliamentary Secretary (Army),
 Ministry of Defence
 1981 - 85 Minister of State, HM Treasury
 1985 - 86 Minister of State, Department of
 Health and Social Security
 (Minister for Health)
Correspondence Address . . 20 Wool Road, London, SW20 0HW
 Tel: (0181) 947 0037

Hayman, Baroness (Helene Valerie Hayman)

Type of Peerage . . . . Life
Political Allegiance . . . . . Labour
Created 1995
Born . . . . 26th March 1949 in Wolverhampton
Educated . . . . Wolverhampton Girls' High School
 Newnham College, Cambridge
Professional Career . . . . . 1974 Deputy Director, National Council for
 One Parent Families
 1988 - 92 Vice Chairman, Bloomsbury
 Health Authority, then Bloomsbury and
 Islington Health Authority
 1992 - 97 Chairman, Whittington Hospital
 NHS Trust
Political Career . . . . 1974 - 79 MP (Labour) for Welwyn and
 Hatfield
 1997 - Parliamentary Secretary, Department
 of Environment, Transport and the
 Regions
Subject Interests . . . . Health, Education

Hayter, Baron (George Charles Hayter Chubb KCVO, CBE)

Type of Peerage . . . . Hereditary
Political Allegiance . . . . . Cross Bench
Succeeded 1967
Born . . . . 25th April 1911 in Hale, Cheshire
Educated . . . . Leys School, Cambridge
 Trinity College, Cambridge
Professional Career . . . . . 1957 - 81 Chairman, Chubb and Son Ltd
 1964 - 82 Chairman, Kings Fund
 1965 - 67 Chairman, Royal Society of Arts
 1972 - 79 Chairman, EDC International
 Freight Movement
 1973 - 77 Chairman, British Securities
 Industries
Political Career . . . . 1983 - 96 A Deputy Speaker,
 House of Lords
Subject Interests . . . . The Arts, Security, Health
Correspondence Address . . Ashstead House, Farm Lane, Ashstead,
 Surrey, KT21 1LU
 Tel: (01372) 273476

Hazlerigg of Noseley, Baron (Arthur Grey Hazlerigg)

Type of Peerage . . . . Hereditary
On Leave Of Absence
Succeeded 1949
Born . . . . 24th February 1910 in London
Educated . . . . Eton College
 Trinity College, Cambridge
Professional Career . . . . . Chartered Surveyor
 1946 - 76 Partner, John German and Son
Subject Interests . . . . Agriculture, Estate Management and Sport
Recreational Interests . . . Cricket, Golf, Reading
Correspondence Address . . Noseley Hall, Leicester, LE7 9EH
 Tel: (0116) 259 6322

MEMBERS OF THE HOUSE OF LORDS

Head, Viscount (Richard Antony)
Type of Peerage . . . . Hereditary
Political Allegiance . . . . . Cross Bench
Succeeded 1983
Born . . . . 27th February 1937 in London
Professional Career . . . . . 1957 - 66 Officer, Lifeguards
1968 - 83 Trainer of Racehorses
1983 - Farmer
Subject Interests . . . . Racing, Environment
Recreational Interests . . . Golf, Shooting

Headfort, Marquess
(Thomas Geoffrey Charles Michael Taylor)
Type of Peerage . . . . Hereditary
Political Allegiance . . . . . Cross Bench
Succeeded 1960
Born . . . . 20th January 1932

Healey, Baron (Rt Hon Denis Winston Healey CH MBE)
Type of Peerage . . . . Life
Political Allegiance . . . . . Labour
Created 1992
Born . . . . 30th August 1917 in Mottingham, Kent
Educated . . . . Bradford Grammar School
Balliol College, Oxford
Professional Career . . . . . 1940 - 45 Royal Engineers
1993 - President, Birkbeck College
Political Career . . . . 1945 - 52 International Secretary,
Labour Party
1952 - 92 MP (Labour) for East Leeds
1964 - 70 Secretary of State for Defence
1974 - 79 Chancellor of the Exchequer
1980 - 83 Deputy Leader of the
Labour Party
1980 - 87 Opposition Spokesman, Foreign
and Commonwealth Affairs
Subject Interests . . . . Foreign Affairs, Domestic Economy, Arts,
Defence
Recreational Interests . . . Music, Photography, Painting, Gardening
Correspondence Address . . House of Lords, Westminster,
London, SW1A 0PW
Tel: (0171) 219 3155 Fax: (0171) 219 5979
Also Tel: (0171) 935 2267

Hemingford, Baron (Nicholas Herbert)
Type of Peerage . . . . Hereditary
Political Allegiance . . . . . Cross Bench
Succeeded 1982
Born . . . . 25th July 1934 in Watford, Hertfordshire
Educated . . . . Oundle School
Clare College, Cambridge
Professional Career . . . . . 1956 - 61 Reuters, London/Washington
1961 - 70 The Times, Washington
correspondent, then Middle East
correspondent and Deputy Features Editor
1970 - 74 Editor, Cambridge Evening News
1974 - 95 Editorial Director, then Deputy
Chief Executive, Westminster Press
Subject Interests . . . . Press freedom, the National Trust
Correspondence Address . . The Old Rectory, Hemingford Abbots,
Huntingdon, Cambridgeshire, PE18 9AN
Tel: (01480) 466234 Fax: (01480) 380275
E-mail: 100417.2524@compuserve.com

Hemphill, Baron (Peter Patrick Martyn-Hemphill)
Type of Peerage . . . . Hereditary
Political Allegiance . . . . . Conservative
Succeeded 1957
Born . . . . 5th September 1928 in Dublin
Educated . . . . Downside School
Brasenose College, Oxford
Correspondence Address . . Raford Kiltulla, Co Galway, Ireland

Henderson of Brompton, Baron
(Peter Gordon Henderson KCB)
Type of Peerage . . . . Life
Political Allegiance . . . . . Cross Bench
Created 1984
Born . . . . 16th September 1922 in London
Educated . . . . Stowe School
Magdalen College, Oxford
Correspondence Address . . 16 Pelham Street, London, SW7 2NG
Tel: (0181) 589 2047

Henley, Baron (Oliver Michael Robert Eden)
Type of Peerage . . . . Hereditary
Political Allegiance . . . . . Conservative
Succeeded 1977
Born . . . . 22nd November 1953
Educated . . . . Clifton College
Durham University
Professional Career . . . . . Barrister
Political Career . . . . 1989 Government Whip, (Lord in Waiting)
1989 - 93 Parliamentary Secretary,
Department of Social Security
1993 - 94 Parliamentary Secretary,
Department of Employment
1994 - 95 Parliamentary Secretary,
Ministry of Defence
1995 - 97 Minister of State, Department for
Education and Employment
1997 - Opposition Spokesman on Home
Affairs, House of Lords
Correspondence Address . . Scaleby Castle, Carlisle, CA6 4LN
Tel: (01228) 75404 Fax: (01228) 75077
House of Lords, Westminster,
London, SW1A 0PW
Tel: (0171) 219 3108

Henniker, Baron (John Patrick Edward Chandos
Henniker Major KCMG, CVO, MC)
Type of Peerage . . . . Hereditary
Political Allegiance . . . . . Cross Bench
Succeeded 1980
Born . . . . 19th February 1916 in London
Educated . . . . Stowe School
Trinity College, Cambridge
Professional Career . . . . . 1940 - 45 Army Officer (Major, Rifle
Brigade)
1946 - 68 HM Diplomatic Service
1946 - 48 Assistant Private Secretary to
Foreign Secretary (Rt Hon Ernest
Bevin MP)
1960 - 62 Ambassador to Jordan
1962 - 66 Ambassador to Denmark
1967 - 68 Assistant Secretary,
Foreign Office
1968 - 72 Director-General, British Council
Subject Interests . . . . Foreign affairs, Law and order, Environment
Recreational Interests . . . Shooting, Walking
Correspondence Address . . Red House, Thornham Magna, Eye,
Suffolk, IP23 8HH
Tel: (01379) 783336 Fax: (01379) 783793

MEMBERS OF THE HOUSE OF LORDS

Hereford, Bishop of (Rt Rev John Oliver)
Type of Peerage . . . . Bishop
Has Not Taken The Oath
Entered Lords 1997
Born . . . . 14th April 1935 in London
Educated . . . . Westminster School
                    Gonville and Caius College, Cambridge
                    Westcott House, Cambridge
Professional Career . . . . . 1964 - 68 Assistant Curate, Hilborough
                    Group Norfolk
                    1968 - 72 Chaplain and Assistant Master,
                    Eton College
                    1973 - 82 Team Rector, South Molton Team
                    Ministry, Devon
                    1982 - 85 Team Rector, Central Exeter
                    Team Ministry
                    1985 - 90 Archdeacon of Sherborne
                    1990 - Bishop of Hereford
Subject Interests . . . . Theology, Environment, Transport,
                    Architecture, Social issues,
                    (unemployment, poverty)
Recreational Interests . . . Railways, Motorcycling, Walking, Music
Correspondence Address . . The Palace, Hereford, HR4 9BN
                    Tel: (01432) 271355 Fax: (01432) 343047

Hereford, Viscount (Robert Milo Leicester Devereux)
Type of Peerage . . . . Hereditary
Political Allegiance . . . . . None
Succeeded . . . . 1952 (as a minor)
Born . . . . 4th November 1932

Herries, Lady (Anne Elizabeth Fitzalan Howard)
Type of Peerage . . . . Hereditary
Without Writ of Summons
Succeeded 1975
Born . . . . 12th June 1938
Note: Lady Herries is married to Lord Cowdrey of Tonbridge, but is a peeress in her own right.

Herschell, Baron (Rognvald Richard Farrer Herschell)
Type of Peerage . . . . Hereditary
On Leave Of Absence
Succeeded . . . . 1920 (as a minor)
Born . . . . 13th September 1923

Hertford, Marquess of (Hugh Edward Conway Seymour)
Type of Peerage . . . . Hereditary
Political Allegiance . . . . . Conservative
Succeeded 1940
Born . . . . 29th March 1930 in London
Educated . . . . Eton College
                    Royal Agricultural College, Cirencester
Professional Career . . . . . Owner and Manager of Ragley Estate
Subject Interests . . . . Agriculture
Recreational Interests . . . Fox hunting, Riding
Correspondence Address . . North Wing, Ragley Hall, Alcester,
                    Warwickshire, B49 5NJ

Hesketh, Baron
   (Rt Hon Thomas Alexander Fermor Hesketh KBE)
Type of Peerage . . . . Hereditary
Political Allegiance . . . . . Conservative
Succeeded . . . . 1955 (as a minor)
Born . . . . 28th October 1950

Heytesbury, Baron (Francis William Holmes à Court)
Type of Peerage . . . . Hereditary
Political Allegiance . . . . . None
Succeeded 1971
Born . . . . 8th November 1931

Higgins, Rt Hon Baron
   (Rt Hon Terence Langley Higgins KBE, DL)
Type of Peerage . . . . Life
Political Allegiance . . . . . Conservative
Created 1997
Born . . . . 18th January 1928 in London
Educated . . . . Alleyn's School, Dulwich
                    Gonville and Caius College, Cambridge
                    Yale University
Professional Career . . . . . 1960 - 64 Economics Adviser, Unilever
                    1976 - 84 Director, Warner Wright and
                    Rowland Groups
                    1980 - 92 Director, Lex Service plc
                    1991 - 97 Director, First Choice
                    Holidays plc
                    1992 - Chairman, Lex Service Pensions Ltd
Political Career . . . . 1964 - 97 MP (Conservative) for Worthing
                    1967 - 70 Opposition Spokesman on
                    Treasury and Economic Affairs
                    1970 - 72 Minister of State, HM Treasury
                    1972 - 74 Financial Secretary to the
                    HM Treasury
                    1974 - 76 Opposition Spokesman on Trade,
                    House of Commons
                    1980 - 83 Chairman, Select Committee on
                    Procedure, House of Commons
                    1983 - 92 Chairman, Select Committee on
                    Treasury and Civil Service,
                    House of Commons
                    1984 - 97 Chairman, House of Commons
                    Liaison Committee
                    1996 - 97 Chairman, Public Accounts
                    Committee, House of Commons
                    1997 - Opposition Spokesman on Social
                    Security and Treasury Matters, House of
                    Lords
Subject Interests . . . . Social security, Economic policy, Transport
Recreational Interests . . . Golf
Correspondence Address . . House of Lords, Westminster,
                    London, SW1A 0PW
                    Tel: (0171) 219 4164
                    Fax: (0171) 219 6012
                    Also Tel: (0181) 318 1481

Hill, Viscount (Anthony Rowland Clegg Hill)
Type of Peerage . . . . Hereditary
On Leave Of Absence
Succeeded 1974
Born . . . . 19th March 1931

MEMBERS OF THE HOUSE OF LORDS

Hill-Norton, Baron
(Admiral of the Fleet Peter John Hill-Norton GCB)

Type of Peerage . . . . Life
Political Allegiance . . . . . Cross Bench
Created 1979
Born . . . . 8th February 1915 in Germiston,
    South Africa
Educated . . . . Royal Naval College, Dartmouth
    Royal Naval College, Greenwich
Professional Career . . . . . 1928 - 77 Royal Navy (various ranks)
    1968 - 70 Vice Admiral
    1970 - 71 First Sea Lord and Chief of
    Naval Staff
    1971 - 73 Chief of Defence Staff
    1974 - 77 Chairman, NATO Military
    Committee
Subject Interests . . . . Defence, Country sports, UFOs
Recreational Interests . . . Country sports and pastimes
Correspondence Address . . Cass Cottage, Hyde, Fordingbridge,
    Hampshire, SP6 2QH

Hilton of Eggardon, Baroness (Jennifer Hilton QPM)

Type of Peerage . . . . Life
Political Allegiance . . . . . Labour
Created 1991
Born . . . . 12th January 1936 in Nicosia, Cyprus
Educated . . . . Bedales School
    Manchester University
Professional Career . . . . . 1956 - 90 Metropolitan Police (Commander
    from 1984, Head of Training 1988 - 90)
Political Career . . . . 1991 - 97 Opposition Spokesman on
    Environment, House of Lords
    (also Opposition Whip 1991 - 95)
    1995 - Chairman, European Communities
    Sub-Committee on Environment,
    Public Health and Consumer Protection
Subject Interests . . . . Environment, Home Affairs (especially
    Police and Prisons)
Recreational Interests . . . Foreign travel, History of art, Gardening
Correspondence Address . . House of Lords, Westminster,
    London, SW1A 0PW
    Tel: (0171) 219 3182

Hindlip, Baron (Charles Henry Allsopp)

Type of Peerage . . . . Hereditary
Political Allegiance . . . . . Conservative
Succeeded 1993
Born . . . . 5th August 1940

Hives, Baron (Matthew Peter Hives)

Type of Peerage . . . . Hereditary
Succeeded 1997
Born . . . . 25th May 1971

Hoffmann, Baron (Rt Hon Leonard Hubert Hoffmann)

Type of Peerage . . . . Life (Law Lord)
Political Allegiance . . . . . Cross Bench
Created 1995
Born . . . . 8th May 1934 in South Africa
Educated . . . . South African College School, Cape Town
    University of Cape Town
    Queen's College, Oxford
Professional Career . . . . . 1958 - 60 Advocate, South Africa
    1964 - Barrister, Gray's Inn (QC 1977)
    1980 - 85 Judge, Courts of Appeal, Jersey
    and Guernsey
    1985 - 92 High Court Judge, Chancery
    Division
    1989 - 92 Chairman, Council of Legal
    Education
    1992 - 95 Lord Justice of Appeal
    1995 - Lord of Appeal in Ordinary
    1995 - Chairman, European Communities
    Sub-Committee on Law and Institutions,
    House of Lords

Hogg, Baroness (Sarah Elizabeth Mary Hogg)

Type of Peerage . . . . Life
Political Allegiance . . . . . Conservative
Created 1995
Born . . . . 14th May 1946
Educated . . . . St Mary's Convent, Ascot
    Lady Margaret Hall, Oxford
Professional Career . . . . . 1967 - 81 The Economist (Editor 1977 - 81)
    1981 - 82 Economics Editor, Sunday Times
    1982 - 83 Presenter, Channel 4 News
    1984 - 86 Economics Editor, The Times
    1986 - 89 . . Business and City Editor,
    The Independent
    1989 - 90 Economics Editor,
    Daily and Sunday Telegraph
    1995 - Chairman, Foreign and Colonial
    Smaller Companies Trusts
    1997 - Chairman, London Economics
Political Career . . . . 1990 - 95 Head of Prime Minister's Policy
    Unit (Rt Hon John Major MP)
Correspondence Address . . London Economics, 66 Chiltern Street,
    London, W1M 1PR
    Tel: (0171) 446 8400 Fax: (0171) 446 8484
    E-mail: sarah@londecon.co.uk
Personal Staff . . . . Mrs Helen Lowe (*Personal Assistant*)
    Tel: (0171) 446 8466

MEMBERS OF THE HOUSE OF LORDS

Hogg of Cumbernauld, Baron (Norman Hogg)

Type of Peerage . . . . Life
Political Allegiance . . . . . Labour
Created 1997
Born . . . . 12th March 1938 in Aberdeen
Educated . . . . Ruthrieston Secondary School, Aberdeen
Professional Career . . . . . 1953 - 67 Local Government Officer
1967 - 79 District Officer, NALGO
(Scotland)
Political Career . . . . 1979 - 83 MP (Labour) for East
Dunbartonshire
1982 - 83 Opposition Whip,
House of Commons
1983 - 97 MP (Labour) for Cumbernauld
and Kilsyth
1983 - 87 Opposition Deputy Chief Whip,
House of Commons
1987 - 88 Opposition Spokesman on Scottish
Affairs, House of Commons
1992 - 97 Chairman, Labour Friends of
Israel
Subject Interests . . . . Scottish Affairs, Public Transport, Local
Government, Constitutional Affairs, Israel
and the Middle East
Recreational Interests . . . Music, Reading biographies
Correspondence Address . . House of Lords, Westminster,
London, SW1A 0PW
Tel: (0171) 588 1008
E-mail: normanhogg@compuserve.com
14 Sanday Road, Aberdeen AB15 6DT
Tel: (01224) 314860

Holderness, Baron (Rt Hon Richard Frederick Wood)

Type of Peerage . . . . Life
Political Allegiance . . . . . Conservative
Created 1979
Born . . . . 5th October 1920 in London
Educated . . . . Eton College
New College, Oxford
Political Career . . . . 1950 - 79 MP (Conservative) for Bridlington,
Yorkshire
1955 - 58 Parliamentary Secretary, Ministry
of Pensions and National Insurance
1958 - 59 Parliamentary Secretary,
Ministry of Labour
1959 - 63 Minister of Power
1963 - 64 Minister of Pensions and National
Insurance
1970 - 73 Minister for Overseas
Development
Subject Interests . . . . Territorial Army
Recreational Interests . . . Reading, Writing, Travel
Correspondence Address . . Flat Top House, Bishop Wilton,
York, YO4 1RY
Tel: (01759) 368266
House of Lords, Westminster,
London, SW1A 0PW
Tel: (0171) 225 2151

Hollenden, Baron (Gordon Hope Hope-Morley)

Type of Peerage . . . . Hereditary
On Leave Of Absence
Political Allegiance . . . . . Conservative
Succeeded 1977
Born . . . . 8th January 1914 in London
Educated . . . . Eton College
Professional Career . . . . . 1933 - 67 Director/Chairman,
I & R Morley Ltd
Recreational Interests . . . Gardening, Shooting
Correspondence Address . . Hall Place, Leigh, near Tonbridge,
Kent, TN11 8HH
Tel: (01732) 832256

Hollick of Nottinghill, Baron (Clive Richard Hollick)

Type of Peerage . . . . Life
Political Allegiance . . . . . Labour
Created 1991
Born . . . . 20th May 1945 in Southampton
Educated . . . . Taunton School, Southampton
University of Nottingham
Professional Career . . . . . 1967 - 70 Graduate Trainee, then Director,
Hambros Bank
1974 - 96 Managing Director, JH Vavasseur,
then MAI plc
1996 - Chief Executive, United News and
Media plc
Political Career . . . . 1997 - Special Adviser to the President of
the Board of Trade (Rt Hon Margaret
Beckett MP)
Subject Interests . . . . Media
Recreational Interests . . . Tennis, Walking, Countryside, Reading,
Cinema, Theatre
Correspondence Address . . House of Lords, Westminster,
London, SW1A 0PW
Tel; (0171) 921 5088 Fax; (0171) 921 5043
E-mail: clive@unm.om
Personal Staff . . . . Mrs Lee Maginnis *(Secretary)*

Hollis of Heigham, Baroness (Patricia Lesley Hollis)

Political Allegiance . . . . . Labour
Created 1990
Born . . . . 24th May 1941
Professional Career . . . . . 1967 - 88 Lecturer, then Reader and Senior
Fellow in Modern History, University of
East Anglia
1988 - 90 Dean, School of English and
American Studies, University of
East Anglia
Political Career . . . . 1968 - 91 Member, Norwich City Council
(Leader 1983 - 88)
1981 - 85 Member, Norfolk County Council
1990 - 97 Opposition Whip, House of Lords
1995 - 97 Opposition Spokesman on Social
Security, Local Government and Housing
House of Lords
1997 - Parliamentary Secretary, Department
of Social Security
Recreational Interests . . . Boating, Singing, Domesticity

MEMBERS OF THE HOUSE OF LORDS

Holme of Cheltenham, Baron (Richard Gordon Holme CBE)

Type of Peerage	Life
Political Allegiance	Liberal Democrat
Created	1990
Born	27th May 1936 in London
Educated	Royal Masonic School
	St John's College, Oxford
	Harvard Business School
Political Career	1966 - 67 Vice Chairman, Liberal Party Executive
	1980 - 81 President, Liberal Party
	1992 - Liberal Democrat Spokesman on Northern Ireland, House of Lords
	1992 - 1997 Chairman, Liberal Democrat General Election Campaign
Subject Interests	Northern Ireland, Economy, Constitution
Recreational Interests	Opera, Walking

HolmPatrick, Baron (Hans James David Hamilton)

Type of Peerage	Hereditary
Political Allegiance	Conservative
Succeeded	1991
Born	15th March 1955

Home, Earl of (David Alexander Cospatrick Douglas-Home CVO, CBE)

Type of Peerage	Hereditary
Political Allegiance	Conservative
Succeeded	1995
Born	20th November 1943 in Coldstream, Berwickshire
Professional Career	1986 - Chairman, Morgan Grenfell (Scotland) and (from 1987) Morgan Grenfell International Ltd
	1996 - Morgan Grenfell Co Ltd
Subject Interests	International trade
Recreational Interests	Outdoor sports

Hood, Viscount (Alexander Lambert Hood)

Type of Peerage	Hereditary
Political Allegiance	Conservative
Succeeded	1981
Born	11th March 1914 in Mortlake, Surrey
Educated	Royal Naval College, Dartmouth
	Trinity College, Cambridge
	Harvard Business School
Professional Career	Numerous Directorships
Correspondence Address	67 Chelsea Square, London, SW3 6LE
	Tel: (0171) 352 4952 Fax: (0171) 795 0398
	Loders Court, Bridport, Dorset, DT6 3RZ
	Tel: (01308) 422983

Hooper, Baroness (Gloria Dorothy Hooper)

Type of Peerage	Life
Political Allegiance	Conservative
Created	1985
Born	25th May 1939 in Southampton
Educated	Convent High School, Southampton
	Sadlers Wells Ballet School, London
	University of Southampton
	Universidad Central, Quito, Ecuador
Professional Career	1960 - 61 Assistant to Chief Registrar, John Lewis Partnership
	1961 - 62 Editor, Sweet and Maxwell, Law Publishers
	1962 - 67 Information and Publicity Officer, Winchester City Council
	1967 - 72 Articled Clerk and Solicitor, Taylor and Humbert
	1972 - 73 Legal Adviser, Slater Walker France SA
	1974 - 84 Partner, Taylor and Humbert
Political Career	1979 - 84 Member of the European Parliament (Conservative) for Liverpool
	1985 - 87 Government Whip, (Baroness in Waiting)
	1987 - 88 Parliamentary Secretary, Department of Education and Science
	1988 - 89 Parliamentary Secretary, Department of Energy
	1989 - 92 Parliamentary Secretary, Department of Health
	1993 - 97 Member, Parliamentary Delegations to Council of Europe and Western European Union
	1993 - Deputy Speaker and Deputy Chairman of Committees, House of Lords

Hooson, Baron (Hugh Emlyn Hooson QC)

Type of Peerage	Life
Political Allegiance	Liberal Democrat
Created	1979
Born	26th March 1925 in Denbigh, North Wales
Educated	Denbigh Grammar School
	University College of Wales, Aberystwyth
Professional Career	1949 - 96 Barrister (QC 1960)
	1967 - Chairman, Merioneth Quarter Sessions
	1971 - 93 Recorder of Crown Court
	1971 - 74 Leader, Wales and Chester Circuit
	1991 - Chairman, Severn River Crossing plc
	1995 - 96 Chairman, Laura Ashley (Holdings)
Political Career	1962 - 79 MP (Liberal) for Montgomery
	1966 - 79 Leader, Welsh Liberal Party
	1983 - 86 President, Welsh Liberal Party
Subject Interests	Constitution, Agriculture, Defence, United Nations, Welsh affairs
Recreational Interests	Reading, Walking
Correspondence Address	Summerfield Park, Llanidloes, Powys, SY18 6AQ
	Tel and Fax: (01686) 412298
	House of Lords, Westminster, London, SW1A 0PW
	Tel: (0171) 219 5226 Fax: (0171) 219 2377
Personal Staff	Mrs Calan McGreery *(Secretary)*
	Tel: (0171) 219 5226 and (01446) 760174

MEMBERS OF THE HOUSE OF LORDS

Hope of Craighead, Baron (Rt Hon James Arthur David Hope)

Type of Peerage . . . . Life (Law Lord)
Political Allegiance . . . . . Cross Bench
Created 1995
Born . . . . 27th June 1938 in Edinburgh
Educated . . . . Rugby School
St John's College, Cambridge
University of Edinburgh
Professional Career . . . . . 1965 - Advocate, Scotland (QC 1978)
1978 - 82 Advocate Depute
1986 - 89 Dean of the Faculty of Advocates
1989 - 96 Lord Justice General of Scotland
   and Lord President of the Court of Session
1996 - Lord of Appeal in Ordinary
Subject Interests . . . . Law and order, Scottish affairs
Recreational Interests . . . Ornithology, Walking and Music
Correspondence Address . . Law Lords Corridor, House of Lords,
Westminster, London, SW1A 0PW
Tel: (0171) 219 3202 Fax: (0171) 219 6156

Hothfield, Baron (Anthony Charles Sackville Hothfield)

Type of Peerage . . . . Hereditary
Political Allegiance . . . . . Conservative
Succeeded 1992
Born . . . . 21st October 1939 in Bath
Educated . . . . Eton College
Magdalene College, Cambridge
Professional Career . . . . . 1962 - 93 Civil Engineer
Subject Interests . . . . Civil Engineering, Cumbrian Issues
Recreational Interests . . . Tennis, Real tennis, Bridge, Golf

Howard de Walden, Baron (John Osmael Scott-Ellis TD)

Type of Peerage . . . . Hereditary
On Leave of Absence
Succeeded 1946
Born . . . . 27th November 1912

Howard of Penrith, Baron (Francis Philip Howard)

Type of Peerage . . . . Hereditary
On Leave of Absence
Succeeded 1939
Born . . . . 5th October 1905 in Rome
Educated . . . . Downside School
Trinity College, Cambridge
Professional Career . . . . . 1932 - 39 Barrister
1945 - 97 Farmer
Correspondence Address . . Dean Farm, Coln-St-Aldwyns, Cirencester,
Gloucestershire, CL7 5AX
Tel: (01285) 750220

Howe, Earl (Frederick Richard Penn Curzon)

Type of Peerage . . . . Hereditary
Political Allegiance . . . . . Conservative
Succeeded 1984
Born . . . . 29th January 1951 in London
Educated . . . . Rugby School
Christ Church, Oxford
Professional Career . . . . . 1973 - 87 Barclays Bank plc
   (Manager from 1982)
1987 - 90 Director, Adam and Co plc
1988 - 91 Director, Provident Life
   Association Ltd
Political Career . . . . 1991 - 92 Government Whip,
   (Lord in Waiting)
1992 - 95 Parliamentary Secretary, Ministry
   of Agriculture, Fisheries and Food
1995 -97 Parliamentary Secretary, Ministry
   of Defence
1997 - Opposition Spokesman on Health,
   House of Lords
Subject Interests . . . . Agriculture, Penal affairs, Defence
Recreational Interests . . . Music, Literature, Estate management
Correspondence Address . . House of Lords, Westminster,
London, SW1A 0PW
Tel: (0171) 219 5353 Fax: (0171) 219 1177

Howe of Aberavon, Baron
(Rt Hon Richard Edward Geoffrey Howe CH, QC)

Type of Peerage . . . . Life
Political Allegiance . . . . . Conservative
Created 1992
Born . . . . 20th December 1926 in Port Talbot,
Glamorgan
Educated . . . . Winchester College
Trinity Hall, Cambridge
Professional Career . . . . . 1952 Barrister (QC 1965)
1969 Chairman, Ely Hospital (Cardiff)
   Inquiry
1994 - Chairman, Framlington Russian
   Investment Fund
Political Career . . . . 1964 - 66 MP (Conservative) for Bebington
1965 - 66 Opposition Spokesman on Labour
   and Social Services
1970 - 74 MP (Conservative) for Reigate
1970 - 72 Solicitor General,
1972 - 74 Minister for Trade and Consumer
   Affairs
1974 - 92 MP (Conservative) for Surrey East
1974 - 79 Opposition Spokesman on Social
   Services, then on Treasury and Economic
   Affairs, House of Commons
1979 - 83 Chancellor of the Exchequer
1983 - 89 Foreign Secretary
1989 - 90 Deputy Prime Minister, Lord
   President of the Council and Leader of the
   House of Commons
Subject Interests . . . . Legal affairs, Foreign affairs, Economy,
Trade and industry
Correspondence Address . . House of Lords, Westminster,
London, SW1A 0PW
Tel: (0171) 236 0137 Fax: (0171) 248 3248

MEMBERS OF THE HOUSE OF LORDS

Howell, Baron (Rt Hon Denis Herbert Howell)

Type of Peerage	Life
Political Allegiance	Labour
Created	1992
Born	4th September 1923 in Birmingham
Educated	Handsworth Grammar School
Professional Career	1956 - 70 Football League Referee
	1971 - 83 President, APEX (trade union)
	1981 - 83 Chairman, Committee of Enquiry into Sports Sponsorship
	1997 - Chairman, Severn Trent Water Trust
Political Career	1946 - 56 Member, Birmingham City Council
	1955 - 59 MP (Labour) for Birmingham All Saints,
	1961 - 92 MP (Labour) for Birmingham Small Heath
	1964 - 70 Minister for Sport
	1964 - 69 Parliamentary Secretary, Department of Education (and Minister for Sport)
	1969 - 70 Minister of State, Department of Housing and Local Government (and Minister for Sport)
	1974 - 79 Minister of State, Department of the Environment (Minister for Sport)
	1979 - Vice President, European Movement
	1979 - 83, 1984 - 92 Opposition Spokesman on Environment, House of Commons
	1983 - 84 Opposition Spokesman on Home Affairs, House of Commons
	1993 - 94 Opposition Spokesman on Defence, House of Lords
Subject Interests	Sport, Health, Local government
Recreational Interests . . .	Sport, Theatre, Music
Correspondence Address . .	33 Moor Green Lane, Moseley, Birmingham, B13 8NE
	Tel: (0121) 249 5050 Fax: (0121) 249 5051

Howell of Guildford, Baron
(Rt Hon David Arthur Russell Howell)

Type of Peerage	Life
Political Allegiance	Conservative
Created	1997
Born	18th January 1936 in London
Professional Career	1997 - Advisory Director, SBC Warburg Ditton Read
Political Career	1961 - 62 Chairman, Bow Group
	1964 - 66 Director, Conservative Political Centre
	1966 - 97 MP (Conservative) for Guildford
	1970 - 72 Parliamentary Secretary, Civil Service Department
	1972 - 74 Minister of State, Northern Ireland Office
	1974 Minister of State, Department of Energy
	1979 - 81 Secretary of State for Energy
	1981 - 83 Secretary of State for Transport
	1987 - 97 Chairman, Select Committee on Foreign Affairs, House of Commons
Subject Interests	International finance, Foreign affairs
Recreational Interests . . .	Writing

Howick of Glendale, Baron (Charles Evelyn Banng)

Type of Peerage	Hereditary
Without Writ of Summons	
Succeeded	1973
Born	30th December 1937

Howie of Troon, Baron (William Howie)

Type of Peerage	Life
Political Allegiance	Labour
Created	1978
Born	2nd March 1924 in Troon, Ayrshire
Educated	Marr College, Troon
	Royal Technical College, Glasgow
Professional Career	1944 - 63 1970 - 73 Civil Engineer
	1970 - 73 Civil Engineer
	1973 - 95 Journalist and Publisher
Political Career	1963 - 70 MP (Labour) for Luton
	1964 - 68 Government Whip, House of Commons
Subject Interests	Construction industry
Recreational Interests . . .	Opera
Correspondence Address . .	34 Temple Fortune Lane, London, NW11 7UL
	Tel and Fax: (0181) 455 0492
	Fax: (0181) 455 0492

Hoyle of Warrington, Baron (Eric Douglas Harvey Hoyle)

Type of Peerage	Life
Political Allegiance	Labour
Created	1997
Born	17th February 1930 in Lancashire
Educated	Adlington School
	Horwich and Bolton Technical College
Professional Career	1946 - 51 Engineering Apprentice, British Rail, Horwich
	1951 - 53 Sales Engineer, AEI, Manchester
	1953 - 74 Sales Engineer and Marketing Executive, Charles Weston, Salford
	1983 - 95 President, ASTMS (trade union)
	1990 - 91 President, MSF (trade union)
Political Career	1974 - 79 MP (Labour) for Nelson and Colne
	1981 - 97 MP (Labour) for Warrington, then Warrington North
	1992 - 97 Chairman, Parliamentary Labour Party
	1997 - Government Whip, (Lord in Waiting)
Recreational Interests . . .	Sport, Cricket, Theatre, Reading, Walking
Correspondence Address . .	House of Lords, Westminster, London, SW1A 0PW
	Tel: (0171) 219 3196
	Also Tel: (01908) 571457
	Fax: (01908) 571394
Personal Staff	Ms Cassandra McNeil *(PA)*
	Tel: (01908) 571457

MEMBERS OF THE HOUSE OF LORDS

Hughes, Rt Hon Baron (Rt Hon William Hughes CBE)

Type of Peerage	Life
Political Allegiance	Labour
Created	1961
Born	22nd January 1911 in Dundee
Educated	Dundee Technical College
Professional Career	1948 - 60 Chairman, Eastern Regional Hospital Board, Scotland
	1960 - 64 Chairman, Glenrothe Development Corporation
	1975 - 82 Chairman, East Kilbride Development Corporation
	1976 - 80 Chairman, Royal Commission on Legal Services in Scotland
Political Career	1939 - 61 Member, Dundee Council (Lord Provost 1954 - 60)
	1964 - 69 Parliamentary Secretary, Scottish Office
	1969 - 70, 1974 - 75 Minister of State, Scottish Office
Subject Interests	Health, Local government, Scottish affairs
Recreational Interests . . .	Gardening
Correspondence Address . .	The Stables, Ross, Comrie, Perthshire, PH6 2TJ
	Tel: (01764) 670557

Hughes of Woodside, Baron (Robert Hughes)

Type of Peerage	Life
Political Allegiance	Labour
Created	1997
Born	3rd January 1932 in Pittenweem, Scotland
Educated	Robert Gordon's College, Aberdeen
	Benoni High School, Transvaal, South Africa
	Pietermaritzburg Technical College, South Africa
Professional Career	1949 - 53 Engineering Apprentice, South African Rubber Co
	1954 - 70 CF Wilson & Co, Engineer, Aberdeen (Chief Draftsman 1966 - 70)
	1976 - 94 Chairman, Anti-Apartheid Movement
	1994 - Chairman, Action for Southern Africa
Political Career	1961 - 69 Chairman, Aberdeen City Labour Party
	1962 - 71 Member, Aberdeen Council (Convenor, Health and Welfare Committee 1963 - 68)
	1970 - 97 MP (Labour) for Aberdeen North
	1974 - 75 Parliamentary Secretary, Scottish Office
	1983 - 84 Opposition Spokesman on Agriculture, House of Commons
	1985 - 88 Opposition Spokesman on Transport, House of Commons
Subject Interests	Health, Social work, Foreign affairs
Recreational Interests . . .	Golf, Fly fishing

Hunt, Baron (Henry Cecil Hunt KG, CBE, DSO)

Type of Peerage	Life
Political Allegiance	Liberal Democrat
Created	1966
Born	22nd June 1910 in Simla, India
Educated	Marlborough College
	Royal Military Academy, Sandhurst
Professional Career	1930 - 56 Army Officer
	1952 - 53 Leader, British Expedition to Mount Everest
	1953 - 55 Assistant Commandant, The Staff College
	1967 - 74 Chairman, Parole Board for England and Wales

Hunt of Kings Heath, Baron (Philip Alexander Hunt)

Type of Peerage	Life
Political Allegiance	Labour
Created	1997
Born	19th May 1949 in Old Windsor
Educated	City of Oxford High School
	Oxford School
	Leeds University
Professional Career	1972 - 74 Work Study Officer, Oxford Regional Health Board
	1974 - 75 Administrator, Nuffield Orthopedic Centre
	1975 - 78 Secretary, Edgware/Hendon Community Health Council
	1978 - 84 Assistant Secretary then Assistant Director, National Association of Health Authorities (NAHA)
	1984 - 96 Director, NAHA (from 1990, Director, National Association of Health Authorities and Trusts)
	1994 - Co Chairman, Association for Public Health
	1996 - 97 Chief Executive, NHS Confederation
	1997 - President, Family Planning Association
Subject Interests	Devolution, Health, Transport, Environment
Recreational Interests . . .	Music, Cycling, Swimming, Football
Correspondence Address . .	31 Ashfield Avenue, Kings Heath, Birmingham, B14 7AT
	Tel: (0121) 449 1615
	Fax: (0121) 449 1615

MEMBERS OF THE HOUSE OF LORDS

Hunt of Tanworth, Baron (John Joseph Benedict Hunt GCB)

Type of Peerage . . . . Life
Political Allegiance . . . . . Cross Bench
Created 1980
Born . . . . 23rd October 1919 in Minehead
Educated . . . . Downside School
                               Magdalene College, Cambridge
Professional Career . . . . . 1946 - 79 Civil Servant
                               (Cabinet Secretary, 1973 - 79)
                               1980 - 97 Chairman, Banque Nationale de
                               Paris plc
                               1985 - 90 Chairman, Prudential Corporation
                               1991 - 97 Chairman, BNP UK Holdings Ltd
Political Career . . . . 1993 - 96 Chairman, European Communities
                               Sub-Committee on Economic and
                               Financial Affairs, House of Lords
                               1995 - 96 Chairman, Select Committee on
                               Central and Local Government Relations,
                               House of Lords
Subject Interests . . . . Europe, Local Government
Recreational Interests . . . Gardening
Correspondence Address . . 8 Wool Road, London, SW20 0HW
                               Tel: (0181) 947 7640 Fax: (0181) 947 4879

Hunt of Wirral, Baron
(Rt Hon David James Fletcher Hunt MBE)

Type of Peerage . . . . Life
Has Not Taken The Oath
Political Allegiance . . . . . Conservative
Created 1997
Born . . . . 21st May 1942 in North Wales
Educated . . . . Liverpool College
                               Montpellier University, France
                               Bristol University
                               Guildford College of Law
Professional Career . . . . . 1968 - Partner, Beachcroft Stanleys (Senior
                               Partner since 1996)
                               1971 - 74 Chairman, British Youth Council
Political Career . . . . 1976 - 97 MP (Conservative) for Wirral,
                               then Wirral West
                               1978 - 82 Vice Chairman, then Chairman
                               Conservative Group for Europe (also Vice
                               President, 1984 - 87)
                               1981 - 84 Government Whip,
                               House of Commons
                               1983 - 85 Vice Chairman,
                               Conservative Party
                               1984 - 87 Parliamentary Secretary,
                               Department of Energy
                               1987 - 89 Government Deputy Chief Whip,
                               (Treasurer of H M Household)
                               1989 - 90 Minister of State, Department of
                               the Environment
                               1990 - 93 Secretary of State for Wales
                               1991 - President, Tory Reform Group
                               1993 - 94 Secretary of State for Employment
                               1994 - 95 Chancellor of the Duchy of
                               Lancaster and Minister for Public Service
Correspondence Address . . Beachcroft Stanleys, 20 Furnival Street,
                               London, EC4R 1BN
                               Tel: (0171) 894 6066 Fax; (0171) 894 6158
                               E-mail: djfh@beacheroft.co.uk

Huntingdon, Earl of
(William Edward Robin Hood Hasting Bass)

Type of Peerage . . . . Hereditary
Political Allegiance . . . . . Cross Bench
Succeeded 1990
Born . . . . 30th January 1948

Huntly, Marquess of (Granville Charles Gomer Gordon)

Type of Peerage . . . . Hereditary
Political Allegiance . . . . . Conservative
Succeeded 1987
Born . . . . 4th February 1944

Hurd of Westwell, Baron
(Rt Hon Douglas Richard Hurd CH, CBE)

Type of Peerage . . . . Life
Political Allegiance . . . . . Conservative
Created 1997
Born . . . . 8th March 1930 in Marlborough, Wiltshire
Educated . . . . Eton College
                               Trinity College, Cambridge
Professional Career . . . . . 1952 - 66 HM Diplomatic Service
                               1995 - Deputy Chairman, Nat West Markets
                               1997 - Chairman, British Invisibles
                               1997 - Chairman, Prison Reform Trust
Political Career . . . . 1966 - 68 Conservative Research
                               Department
                               1968 -70 Private Secretary to Leader of the
                               Opposition (Rt Hon Edward Heath MP)
                               1970 - 74 Political Secretary to the Prime
                               Minister (Rt Hon Edward Heath MP)
                               1974 - 97 MP (Conservative) for Mid Oxon,
                               then for Witney
                               1976 - 79 Opposition Spokesman on Europe
                               1979 - 83 Minister of State, Foreign and
                               Commonwealth Office
                               1983 - 84 Minister of State, Home Office
                               1984 - 85 Secretary of State for
                               Northern Ireland
                               1985 - 89 Home Secretary
                               1989 - 95 Foreign Secretary
Recreational Interests . . . Writing, Broadcasting
Correspondence Address . . NatWest Markets, 135 Bishopsgate,
                               London, EC2M 3VR
                               Tel: (0171) 375 8452/8453
                               Fax: (0171) 375 8054
                               House of Lords, Westminster,
                               London, SW1A 0PW
Personal Staff . . . . Mrs Julia Broad (*Private Secretary*)
                               Tel: (0171) 375 8452

M E M B E R S   O F   T H E   H O U S E   O F   L O R D S

Hussey of North Bradley, Baron (Marmaduke James Hussey)

Type of Peerage	Life
Political Allegiance	Conservative
Created	1996
Born	29th August 1923 in Woking, Surrey
Educated	Rugby
	Trinity College, Oxford
Professional Career	1967 - 70 Managing Director, Harmsworth Publications
	1971 - 80 Chief Executive and Managing Director, Times Newspapers Ltd
	1985 - Chairman, Royal Marsden Hospital
	1986 - 96 Chairman, BBC
Political Career	Member, European Communities Committee, House of Lords
Subject Interests	Health, Hospital administration, Media, Europe
Correspondence Address	Flat 15, 47 Courtfield Road, London, SW7 4DB
	Tel: (0171) 370 1414 Fax: (0171) 370 3009

**Hutchinson of Lullington, Baron
(Jeremy Nicolas Hutchinson QC)**

Type of Peerage	Life
Political Allegiance	Liberal Democrat
Created	1978
Born	28th March 1915 in London
Educated	Stowe School
	Magdalen College, Oxford
Professional Career	Barrister (QC 1961)
	1962 - 72 Recorder of Bath
Subject Interests	Art, Penal policy, Law
Correspondence Address	10 Blenheim Road, London, NW8 0LU
	Tel: (0171) 624 4363

Hutton, Baron (Rt Hon James Brian Edward Heath)

Type of Peerage	Life (Law Lord)
Political Allegiance	Cross Bench
Created	1997
Born	29th June 1931

Hylton, Baron (Raymond Hervey Jolliffe)

Type of Peerage	Hereditary
Political Allegiance	Cross Bench
Succeeded	1967
Born	13th June 1932 in London
Professional Career	1960 - 62 Assistant Private Secretary to the Governor-General of Canada
Subject Interests	Human rights, Penal affairs, Northern Ireland
Correspondence Address	Ammerdown, Radstock, Bath, Avon, BA3 5SH
	Tel: (0171) 219 5353 Fax: (0171) 219 5979

Hylton-Foster, Baroness (Audrey Pellew Hylton-Foster OBE)

Type of Peerage	Life
Political Allegiance	Cross Bench
Created	1965
Born	19th May 1908 in Simla, India
Educated	St Georges, Ascot
Professional Career	1960 - 83 President and Chairman, British Red Cross Society (London Branch)
Political Career	1974 - 95 Convenor of Cross Bench Peers
Correspondence Address	The Coach House, Tanhurst, Holmbury St Mary, Dorking, Surrey, RH5 6LU
	Tel: (01306) 711975

Note: Baroness Hylton-Foster is the widow of the former Speaker of the House of Commons, Sir Harry Hylton-Foster

MEMBERS OF THE HOUSE OF LORDS

I

Iddesleigh, Earl of (Stafford Henry Northcote)

Type of Peerage . . . . Hereditary
Political Allegiance . . . . . Cross Bench
Born . . . . 14th July 1932 in London
Succeeded 1970
Educated . . . . Downside School
Professional Career . . . . . 1982 - 92 Director, Television South
 West plc
 1983 - 88 Chairman, South West Region,
 TSB Bank
Subject Interests . . . . Countryside matters,
 Local government, Media
Correspondence Address . . Shillands House, Upton Pyne Hill, Exeter,
 Devon, EX5 5EB
 Tel: (01392) 258916

Ilchester, Earl of
(Maurice Vivian de Touffreville Fox-Strangways)

Type of Peerage . . . . Hereditary
Political Allegiance . . . . . Cross Bench
Succeeded 1970
Born . . . . 1st April 1920 in Egypt
Educated . . . . Kingsbridge School
Professional Career . . . . . 1936 - 76 RAF
 (retired as Group Captain, C Eng)
 1974 - 75 President, Society of Engineers
 1976 Director, Biggin Hill News
 1976 - 95 Vice-Chairman, Biggin Hill
 Airport Consultative Committee
 1984 - Managing Director, then
 Vice Chairman, County Border News Ltd
 1990 - President, Grant-Maintained Schools
 Foundation
Subject Interests . . . . Defence, Ex-Service welfare,
 Aviation technology
Recreational Interests . . . Outdoor pursuits,
 Passive enjoyment of the Arts
Correspondence Address . . Farley Mill, Westerham, Kent, TN16 1UB

Iliffe, Baron (Robert Peter Richard Iliffe)

Type of Peerage . . . . Hereditary
Political Allegiance . . . . . None
Succeeded 1996
Born . . . . 22nd November 1944

Inchcape, Earl of (Kenneth Peter Lyle Mackay)

Type of Peerage . . . . Hereditary
Political Allegiance . . . . . Conservative
Succeeded 1994
Born . . . . 23rd January 1943 in London
Educated . . . . Eton College
 City of London College
Professional Career . . . . . 1962 - 66 Army Officer
 (9/12th Royal Lancers)
 1966 - 70 Banking
 1970 - 85 Inchcape Group
 1985 - 97 Director, Tea Companies (India)
 1991 - Chairman, Duncan Macneill Group
Subject Interests . . . . Oil, Tea, Agriculture
Recreational Interests . . . Shooting, Fishing, Golf, Skiing, Travelling,
 Sports, Opera
Correspondence Address . . Manor Farm, Clyffe Pypard, Swindon,
 Wiltshire, SN4 7PY
 Tel: (01793) 731223 Fax: (01793) 731081
Personal Staff . . . . Ms Diana Forrest *(Personal Assistant)*
 Tel: (0171) 839 4848

Inchyra, Baron (Robert Charles Reneke Hoyer Millar)

Type of Peerage . . . . Hereditary
Political Allegiance . . . . . Cross Bench
Succeeded 1989
Born . . . . 4th April 1935 in London
Educated . . . . Eton College
 New College, Oxford
Professional Career . . . . . 1967 - 75 Local Director, Barclays Bank,
 Newcastle upon Tyne
 1976 - 81 Regional General Manager,
 Barclays Bank
 1982 - 86 Deputy Chairman,
 Barclays Bank Trust Co
 1986 - 88 General Manager and Director UK
 Financial Services, Barclays Bank
 1988 - 94 Director General,
 British Bankers Association
Subject Interests . . . . European affairs, Banking and financial services
Correspondence Address . . Rookley Manor, King's Somborne,
 Stockbridge, Hampshire, SO20 6QX
 Tel and Fax: (01794) 388319
 76 Holland Park, London, W11 3SL
 Tel and Fax: (0171) 221 2195

Inge, Baron (Field Marshal Peter Anthony Inge GCB)

Type of Peerage . . . . Life
Political Allegiance . . . . . Cross Bench
Created 1997
Born . . . . 5th August 1935 in Croydon
Educated . . . . Wrekin College
 Royal Military Academy, Sandhurst
Professional Career . . . . . Army Officer (Commissioned Green
 Howards 1956)
 1986 - 87 Director, Logistic Policy (Army)
 1987 - 89 Commander, 1st British Corps
 1989 - 92 Commander in Chief, BAOR and
 Commander, Northern Army Group
 1992 - 94 Chief of General Staff
 1994 - 97 Chief of the Defence Staff
Subject Interests . . . . Defence, Public service
Recreational Interests . . . Music, Cricket, Walking, History

Ingleby, Viscount (Martin Raymond Peake)

Type of Peerage . . . . Hereditary
Political Allegiance . . . . . Cross Bench
Succeeded 1966
Born . . . . 31st May 1926

Inglewood, Baron (William Richard Fletcher)

Type of Peerage . . . . Hereditary
Political Allegiance . . . . . Conservative
Succeeded 1989
Born . . . . 31st July 1951 in Carlisle, Cumbria
Educated . . . . Eton College
 Trinity College, Cambridge
 Cumbria College of Agriculture and Forestry
Professional Career . . . . . 1975 - Barrister
 1979 - Associate, Royal Institution of
 Chartered Surveyors
 1981 - Farmer and Landowner
Political Career . . . . 1989 - 94 Member of the European
 Parliament (Conservative),
 Cumbria and Lancashire North
 1989 - 94 Conservative Spokesman on
 Legal Affairs, European Parliament
 1992 - 94 Deputy Chief Whip, then
 Chief Whip, Conservative MEPs,
 European Parliament
 1994 - 95 Government Whip,
 (Lord in Waiting)
 1995 Deputy Government Chief Whip
 (Captain of the Yeomen of the Guard), House
 of Lords
 1995 -97 Parliamentary Secretary,
 Department of National Heritage
 1997 - Opposition Spokesman on
 Environment, House of Lords
 Deputy Speaker, House of Lords
Subject Interests . . . . Europe, Media, Arts, Agriculture,
 Regional policy, Tourism
Correspondence Address . . Hutton-in-the-Forest, Penrith, Cumbria, CA11 9TH
 Tel: (017684) 84500 Fax: (017684) 84571
Personal Staff . . . . Mrs Melanie Dawes *(Secretary)*
 Tel: (017684) 84500

MEMBERS OF THE HOUSE OF LORDS

Ingrow, Baron (John Aked Taylor OBE, TD)

Type of Peerage . . . . Life
Political Allegiance . . . . . Conservative
Created 1982
Born . . . . 15th August 1917 in Keighley, West
    Yorkshire
Professional Career . . . . . 1957 - 86 Member, Council of Magistrates
    Association
Political Career . . . . 1946 - 67 Member, Keighley Town Council
    (Chairman, Education Committee 1949 -
    61, Finance Committee 1961 - 67)
    1971 - 76 Chairman, Executive Committee
    of National Union of Conservative and
    Unionist Associations
    1981 - 82 President, National Union of
    Conservative and Unionist Associations
Subject Interests . . . . Local government

Inverforth, Baron (Andrew Peter Weir)

Type of Peerage . . . . Hereditary
Without Writ of Summons
Succeeded . . . . 1982 (as a minor)
Born . . . . 16th November 1966

Ironside, Baron (Edmund Oslac Ironside)

Type of Peerage . . . . Hereditary
Political Allegiance . . . . . Conservative
Succeeded 1959
Born . . . . 21st September 1924 in Camberley, Surrey
Educated . . . . Tonbridge School
Professional Career . . . . . 1943 - 52 Lieutenant, Royal Navy
    1952 - 59 Marconi Co
    1959 - 64 English Electric Computers
    1964 - 68 Cryosystems Ltd
    1964 - 84 International Research and
    Development Co
    1976 - 90 Vice President, Institute of
    Patentees and Inventors
    1984 - 89 Market Co-ordinator
    (Defence), NEI
    1989 - 95 Defence Consultant, Rolls-Royce
Political Career . . . . 1996 - Chairman, All Party
    Defence Study Group
Subject Interests . . . . Defence industry, Health
Correspondence Address . . Priory House, Old House Lane, Boxted,
    Colchester, Essex, CO4 5RB
    Tel: (01206) 272860

Irvine of Lairg, Baron
(Rt Hon Alexander Andrew Mackay Irvine)

Type of Peerage . . . . Life
Political Allegiance . . . . . Labour
Created 1987
Born . . . . 23rd June 1940 in Inverness
Educated . . . . Hutchesons Boys' Grammar School, Glasgow
    Glasgow University
    Christ's College, Cambridge
Professional Career . . . . . 1965 - 69 Lecturer, London
    School of Economics
    1967 - Barrister (1978 QC)
    1985 - 88 Recorder
    1987 - 97 Deputy High Court Judge
Political Career . . . . 1992 - 97 Shadow Lord Chancellor
    1997 - Lord Chancellor
Subject Interests . . . . Legal affairs, Home affairs,
    Constitutional affairs
Recreational Interests . . . Collecting art, Cinema, Theatre,
    Reading, Travel
Correspondence Address . . House of Lords, Westminster,
    London, SW1A 0PW
    Tel: (0171) 219 3232 Fax: (0171) 219 4711
Personal Staff . . . . Miss Jenny Rowe
    (Principal Private Secretary)

Islwyn of Casnewydd, Baron (Royston John Hughes DL)

Type of Peerage . . . . Life
Political Allegiance . . . . . Labour
Created 1997
Born . . . . 9th June 1925 in Pontllanfraith, Gwent
Educated . . . . Pontllanfraith County Grammar
    Ruskin College, Oxford
Political Career . . . . 1962 - 66 Member, Coventry County Council
    1966 - 83 MP (Labour) for Newport (Gwent)
    1982 - 84, 1991 - 97 Chairman,
    Welsh Grand Committee
    1983 - 97 MP (Labour) for Newport East
    1984 - 88 Opposition Front Bench
    Spokesman on Welsh Affairs,
    House of Commons
    1990 - 92 Treasurer, Inter Parliamentary
    Union
Subject Interests . . . . Industry, Transport
Recreational Interests . . . Rugby, Cricket
Correspondence Address . . Chapel Field, Chapel Lane, Abergavenny,
    Gwent, NP7 7BT
    Tel: (01873) 856502
    House of Lords, Westminster,
    London, SW1A 0PW

Iveagh, Earl of (Arthur Edward Rory Guinness)

Type of Peerage . . . . Hereditary
Political Allegiance . . . . . Cross Bench
Succeeded 1992
Born . . . . 10th August 1969 in Dublin
Educated . . . . Marlborough College
    Wye College, University of London
    Royal Agricultural College, Cirencester
Subject Interests . . . . St Helena and British Dependent Territories,
    Conservation, Farming, the Countryside
Recreational Interests . . . Cycling, Walking, Countryside pursuits,
    Sailing, Back-packing

MEMBERS OF THE HOUSE OF LORDS

J

Jacobs, Baron (David Anthony Jacobs)
Type of Peerage . . . . Life
Political Allegiance . . . . . Liberal Democrat
Created 1997
Born . . . . November 1931

Jakobovits of Regent's Park, Baron (Immanuel Jakobovits)
Type of Peerage . . . . Life
Political Allegiance . . . . . Cross Bench
Created 1988
Born . . . . 8th February 1921 in Konigsberg
Educated . . . . Etz Chaim Yeshivah
Jews' College
University College, London
Professional Career . . . . . 1941 - 49 Various Rabbinic Posts, London
1949 - 58 Chief Rabbi of Ireland
1958 - 67 Rabbi, Fifth Avenue Synagogue,
New York City
1967 - 91 Chief Rabbi of the United Hebrew
Congregations of Great Britain and the
Commonwealth
Subject Interests . . . . Medical Ethics, Israel, Family, Education
Recreational Interests . . . Reading, Travelling, Family
Correspondence Address . . 44A Albert Road, London, NW4 2SJ
Tel: (0181) 203 8667 Fax: (0181) 203 8826
Personal Staff . . . . Mrs Norma Pearlman *(Secretary)*

James of Holland Park, Baroness (Phyllis Dorothy White)
Type of Peerage . . . . Life
Political Allegiance . . . . . Conservative
Created 1991
Born . . . . 3rd August 1920 in Oxford
Educated . . . . Cambridge High School for Girls
Professional Career . . . . . Author (Crime Fiction)
1949 - 68 Administrator,
National Health Service
1968 - 79 Civil Servant (Home Office)
Subject Interests . . . . Literature, the Arts, Criminal Law,
Broadcasting
Recreational Interests . . . Writing, Television
Correspondence Address . . 58 Holland Park Avenue, London, W11 3QY
Tel and Fax: (0171) 229 2643
Personal Staff . . . . Ms Joyce McLennon *(Personal Assistant)*

Janner of Braunstone, Baron (Greville Ewen Janner QC)
Type of Peerage . . . . Life
Has Not Taken The Oath
Political Allegiance . . . . . Labour
Born . . . . 11th July 1928 in Cardiff
Created 1997
Educated . . . . Bishop's College School, Canada
St Paul's School
Trinity Hall, Cambridge
Harvard Law School
Professional Career . . . . . Barrister and Author (QC 1971)
Political Career . . . . 1970 - 74 MP (Labour) for Leicester
North West
1971 - 97 Chairman, Committee for
Release of Soviet Jewry
1974 - 97 MP (Labour) for Leicester West
1983 - 97 Joint Chairman, British Israel
Parliamentary Group
1987 - 97 Chairman, British Spanish
Parliamentary Group
1987 - 97 Secretary, All Party
War Crimes Group
1992 - 96 Chairman, Select Committee on
Employment, House of Commons
Subject Interests . . . . Employment, Foreign affairs,
the Middle East
Recreational Interests . . . Family, Magic
Correspondence Address . . House of Lords, Westminster,
London, SW1A 0PW
Tel and Fax: (0171) 222 2864
also Tel: (0171) 976 8443
Personal Staff . . . . Mrs Maureen Gold *(Secretary)*
Tel: (0171) 222 2863

Jauncey of Tullichettle, Baron (Rt Hon Charles Eliot Jauncey)
Type of Peerage . . . . Life (Former Law Lord)
Political Allegiance . . . . . Cross Bench
Created 1988
Born . . . . 8th May 1925 in Edinburgh, Scotland
Educated . . . . Radley College
Christ Church, Oxford
Glasgow University
Professional Career . . . . . 1949 - Advocate, Scotland (QC 1963)
1979 - 88 Senator, College of Justice,
Scotland
1988 - 96 Lord of Appeal in Ordinary
Recreational Interests . . . Fishing, Shooting, Genealogy, Bicycling
Correspondence Address . . Tullichettle, Comrie, Perthshire, PH6 2HU
Tel: (01764) 670349

Jay of Paddington, Baroness (Margaret Ann Jay)
Type of Peerage . . . . Life
Political Allegiance . . . . . Labour
Created 1992
Born . . . . 18th November 1939
Professional Career . . . . . 1988 - 92 Director, National Aids Trust
Political Career . . . . 1994 -97 Opposition Spokesman on Health,
House of Lords
1997 - Minister of State, Department of
Health and Deputy Leader,
House of Lords

Jeffreys, Baron (Christopher Henry Mark Jeffreys)
Type of Peerage . . . . Hereditary
Political Allegiance . . . . . Conservative
Succeeded 1986
Born . . . . 22nd May 1957 in London
Educated . . . . Eton College
Air Marseille, France
Professional Career . . . . . 1976 - 85 Futures Broker, Wallace Brothers
1985 - 90 Futures Broker, GNI Ltd
1992 - 98 Stockbroker, Raphael Zorn
Hemsly Ltd
1998 Director, Raphael Asset Management
Subject Interests . . . . City
Recreational Interests . . . Field sports, Gardening, Sailing
Correspondence Address . . The Corner House, Sewstern, Grantham,
Lincs, NG33 5RF
Tel: (01476) 861454
c/o Raphael Zorn Hemsly Ltd, Cheapside
House, 138 Cheapside, London, EC2 6BJ
Tel: (0171) 776 1500 Fax: (0171) 776 1551

Jeger, Baroness (Lena May Jeger)
Type of Peerage . . . . Life
Political Allegiance . . . . . Labour
Created 1979
Born . . . . 19th November 1915
Professional Career . . . . . 1936 - 49 Civil Servant
Political Career . . . . 1945 - 59 Member,
St Pancras Borough Council
1953 - 59, 1964 - 74 MP (Labour) for
Holborn and St Pancras South
1968 - 80 Member, National Executive
Committee, Labour Party (Chairman 1980)
1974 - 79 MP (Labour) for Camden,
Holborn and St Pancras South

MEMBERS OF THE HOUSE OF LORDS

Jellicoe, Earl (Rt Hon George Patrick John
Rushworth Jellicoe KBE, DSO, MC, FRS**)**
Type of Peerage . . . . Hereditary
Political Allegiance . . . . . Conservative
Succeeded 1935
Born . . . . 4th April 1918 in Hatfield, Hertfordshire
Educated . . . . Winchester College
 Trinity College, Cambridge
Political Career . . . . 1961 Government Whip, (Lord in Waiting)
 1961 - 62 Parliamentary Secretary, Ministry
 of Housing and Local Government
 1962 - 63 Minister of State, Home Office
 1963 - 64 First Lord of the Admiralty
 1964 Minister of Defence for the Royal Navy
 1967 - 70 Deputy Leader of the Opposition,
 House of Lords
 1970 - 73 Lord Privy Seal, Leader of the
 House of Lords and Minister,
 Civil Service Department
Subject Interests . . . . Defence, Foreign affairs, Environment,
 Research, Education
Recreational Interests . . . Skiing, Riding
Correspondence Address . . Tidcombe Manor, Marlborough,
 Wiltshire, SN8 3SL
 Tel: (01264) 731225

Jenkin of Roding, Baron
(Rt Hon Charles Patrick Fleeming Jenkin)
Type of Peerage . . . . Life
Political Allegiance . . . . . Conservative
Created 1987
Born . . . . 7th September 1926 in Edinburgh
Educated . . . . Clifton College, Bristol
 Jesus College, Cambridge
 Middle Temple, London
Professional Career . . . . . 1952 - 57 Barrister
 1957 - 70 Adviser, The Distillers Co Ltd
 1988 - 98 Chairman,
 Friends Provident Life Office
 1990 - 96 President, British Urban
 Regeneration Association
 1991 - 97 Chairman, Forest Healthcare
 NHS Trust
 1991 - 98 Supervisory Board, Achmea
 NV (Netherlands)
 1992 - Adviser, National Economic
 Research Associates
 1993 - International Advisory Board,
 Marsh and McLennan Group
 1997 - Chairman, Foundation for
 Science and Technology
Political Career . . . . 1964 - 87 MP (Conservative) for
 Wanstead and Woodford
 1965 - 70 Opposition Spokesman on
 Treasury, Trade and Economics,
 House of Commons
 1970 - 72 Financial Secretary, HM Treasury
 1972 - 74 Chief Secretary, HM Treasury
 1974 Minister for Energy
 1974 - 76 Opposition Spokesman on Energy,
 House of Commons
 1976 - 79 Opposition Spokesman on Health
 and Social Security, House of Commons
 1979 - 81 Secretary of State for Health and
 Social Security
 1981 - 83 Secretary of State for Industry
 1983 - 85 Secretary of State for the
 Environment
 1997 Member, Select Committee on Science
 and Technology, House of Lords
Subject Interests . . . . Health, Environment, Financial services,
 Science and technology, Energy, the
 Disabled, Japan
Recreational Interests . . . Reading, Sailing, Gardening
Correspondence Address . . House of Lords, Westminster,
 London, SW1A 0PW
 Tel: (0171) 219 6966
 E-mail: jenkinp@parliament.uk

Jenkins of Hillhead, Baron (Rt Hon Roy Harris Jenkins OM**)**
Type of Peerage . . . . Life
Political Allegiance . . . . . Liberal Democrat
Created 1987
Born . . . . 11th November 1920 in South Wales
Educated . . . . Abersychan Grammar School
 University College of Wales, Cardiff
 Balliol College, Oxford
Professional Career . . . . . 1954 - 64 Adviser, then Director Financial
 Operations, John Lewis Partnership
 1977 - 81 President, European Commission
Political Career . . . . 1948 - 50 MP (Labour) for Central
 Southwark
 1950 - 76 MP (Labour) for Birmingham
 Stechford
 1964 - 65 Minister of Aviation
 1965 - 67 Home Secretary
 1967 - 70 Chancellor of the Exchequer
 1970 - 72 Deputy Leader, Labour Party
 1974 - 76 Home Secretary
 1982 - 83 Leader, Social Democratic Party
 1982 - 87 MP (Social Democratic Party)
 for Glasgow Hillhead
 1988 - 97 Leader, Liberal Democrat Peers

Jenkins of Putney, Baron (Hugh Gater Jenkins)
Type of Peerage . . . . Life
Political Allegiance . . . . . Labour
Created 1981
Born . . . . 27th July 1908 in Enfield, Middlesex
Educated . . . . Enfield Grammar School
Professional Career . . . . . 1930 - 40 Assistant Superintendent,
 Prudential Assurance Co
 1941 - 46 RAF (Flight Lieutenant,
 Fighter Command)
 1947 - 50 Research and Publicity Officer,
 National Union of Bank Employees
 1950 - 64 Assistant General Secretary,
 British Actors' Equity Association
 1964 - Variously Chairman, Vice President
 and (from 1996) President, Theatres
 Advisory Council
 1977 - Variously Deputy Chairman, Director
 and Consultant, Theatres Trust (Joint Life
 President from 1995)
 1979 - Chairman, then Vice President,
 Campaign for Nuclear Disarmament
Political Career . . . . 1959 - 65 Member, London County Council
 1964 - 79 MP (Labour) for Putney
 1974 - 76 Minister for the Arts
Subject Interests . . . . Nuclear disarmament, the Arts, Media,
 Constitution
Recreational Interests . . . Theatre, Arts, Reading, Writing, Radio and
 television, Music
Correspondence Address . . 75 Kenilworth Court, Lower Richmond
 Road, Putney, London, SW15 1EN
 Tel: (0181) 788 0371
 Tel: (0171) 219 6706 Fax: (0171) 219 5979

MEMBERS OF THE HOUSE OF LORDS

Jersey, Earl of (George Francis Child Villiers)

Type of Peerage . . . . Hereditary
On Leave of Absence
Succeeded . . . . 1923 (as a minor)
Born . . . . 15th February 1910 in London

Johnston of Rockport, Baron (Charles Collier Johnston TD)

Type of Peerage . . . . Life
Political Allegiance . . . . . Conservative
Created 1987
Born . . . . 4th March 1915 in Portadown, Northern
Ireland
Educated . . . . Tonbridge School
Professional Career . . . . . 1938 - 46 Army Officer
1948 - 76 Managing Director, Standex
International (also Chairman 1951 - 77)
1980 Member, Royal Commission
(Official Observers at Zimbabwe Election)
1982 - 95 Chairman, Thames and Kennet
Marina Ltd
1983 Chairman, Standex Holdings
1986 Chairman, James Burn International
Political Career . . . . 1971 - 81 Vice Chairman, then Chairman,
Executive Committee, National Union of
Conservative and Unionist Associations
1982 - 87 Conservative Party Treasurer
1983 - 86 Chairman, Conservative
Friends of Israel
1986 - 87 President, National Union
Conservative and Unionist Associations
Recreational Interests . . . Politics, Travelling, Gardening
Correspondence Address . . The Dower House, Marston, Devizes,
Wiltshire, SN10 5SN
Tel: (01380) 725782

Joicey, Baron (James Michael Joicey)

Type of Peerage . . . . Hereditary
Political Allegiance . . . . . Cross Bench
Succeeded 1993
Born . . . . 28th June 1953 in London
Educated . . . . Eton College
Christ Church, Oxford
Professional Career . . . . . 1976 - 81 Language Teacher
1982 - 96 Translator for Agricultural
Services
1983 Farmer/Landowner
Subject Interests . . . . Rural economy
Recreational Interests . . . Ornithology, Morris Minors, Travel
Correspondence Address . . East Flodden, Wooler,
Northumberland, NE71 6JF
Tel: (01668) 216271

Jopling, Baron (Rt Hon Thomas Michael Jopling)

Type of Peerage . . . . Life
Political Allegiance . . . . . Conservative
Created 1997
Born . . . . 10th December 1930 in Ripon, Yorkshire
Educated . . . . Cheltenham College
King's College, Newcastle
Professional Career . . . . . Farmer
Political Career . . . . 1964 - 83 MP (Conservative) for
Westmorland
1971 - 74 Government Whip,
House of Commons
1974 - 79 Opposition Spokesman on
Agriculture, House of Commons
1974 - 79, 1987 - 97 Vice Chairman,
Commonwealth Parliamentary Association
1979 - 83 Government Chief Whip,
House of Commons
1983 - 97 MP (Conservative) for
Westmorland and Lonsdale
1983 - 87 Minister of Agriculture,
Fisheries and Food
1991 - 92 Chairman, Select Committee on
Sittings of the House of Commons

Judd, Baron (Frank Ashcroft Judd)

Type of Peerage . . . . Life
Political Allegiance . . . . . Labour
Created 1991
Born . . . . 28th March 1935 in Sutton, Surrey
Educated . . . . City of London School
London School of Economics
Professional Career . . . . . 1960 - 66 Secretary General,
International Voluntary Service
1979 - 80 Associate Director, International
Defence and Aid Fund for Southern Africa
1980 - 85 Director of Voluntary Service
Overseas
1985 - 91 Director, Oxfam
1996 President, YMCA
1997 - Chairman Trustees, International
Alert
Political Career . . . . 1966 - 74 MP (Labour) for Portsmouth West
1970 - 72 PPS to the Leader of the
Opposition (Rt Hon Harold Wilson MP)
1972 - 74 Opposition Spokesman on
Royal Navy
1974 - 79 MP (Labour) for Portsmouth North
1974 - 76 Parliamentary Secretary
(for Royal Navy), Ministry of Defence
1976 - 77 Minister of State for
Overseas Development
1977 - 79 Minister of State, Foreign and
Commonwealth Office
1991 - 97 Opposition Spokesman variously
on Foreign Affairs, Defence, Education
and Overseas Development, House of Lords
Correspondence Address . . House of Lords, Westminster,
London, SW1A 0PW
Tel: (0171) 219 3205 Fax: (0171) 219 5979

MEMBERS OF THE HOUSE OF LORDS

K

Keith of Castleacre, Baron (Kenneth Alexander Keith)

Type of Peerage . . . . Life
Political Allegiance . . . . . Conservative
Created 1980
Born . . . . 30th August 1916 in Norfolk
Educated . . . . Rugby School
Professional Career . . . . . 1962 - 65 Chairman, Philip Hill Higginson
    Erlangers Ltd
    1964 - 71 Vice-Chairman, British European
    Airways
    1965 - 70 Deputy Chairman and
    Chief Executive, Hill Samuel
    1965 - 70 Chairman, Economic Planing
    Committee for East Anglia
    1972 - 80 Chairman and Chief Executive,
    Rolls-Royce
    1974 - 87 Vice Chairman, then Chairman,
    Beecham Group
    1977 - 85 Director, Standard Telephone and
    Cables Ltd
    1982 - 90 Chairman, Arlington Securities
    1985 - 89 Chairman, Standard Telephone
    and Cables Ltd
    1989 - 94 President, British Standards
    Institution
    1989 - 92 President, Royal Society for
    Prevention of Accidents
Recreational Interests . . . Farming, Shooting, Golf
Correspondence Address . . The Wicken House, Castle Acre,
    King's Lynn, Norfolk, PE32 2BP
    Tel: (01760) 755225 Fax: (01760) 755327
    E-mail: wicken@c-acre.u-net.com

Keith of Kinkel, Baron (Rt Hon Henry Shanks Keith)

Type of Peerage . . . . Life (Former Law Lord)
Political Allegiance . . . . . Cross Bench
Created 1977
Born . . . . 7th February 1922 in Edinburgh
Educated . . . . Edinburgh Academy
    Magdalen College, Oxford
    Edinburgh University
Professional Career . . . . . 1950 Advocate, Scotland (QC 1962)
    1951 Barrister (Gray's Inn)
    1970 - 71 Sheriff Principal of Roxburgh,
    Berwick and Selkirk
    1971 - 76 Senator of the College of Justice,
    Scotland
    1977 - 96 Lord of Appeal in Ordinary

Kelvedon, Baron (Rt Hon Henry Paul Guinness Channon)

Type of Peerage . . . . Life
Political Allegiance . . . . . Conservative
Created 1997
Born . . . . 9th October 1935 in London
Professional Career . . . . . 1959 - 97 MP (Conservative) for
    Southend West
    1967 - 70 Opposition Spokesman on
    The Arts
    1970 Parliamentary Secretary, Ministry of
    Housing and Local Government
    1970 - 72 Parliamentary Secretary,
    Department of the Environment
    1972 Minister of State,
    Northern Ireland Office
    1972 - 74 Minister of State,
    Department of the Environment
    1974 Opposition Spokesman on
    Consumer Affairs
    1974 - 75 Opposition Spokesman on the
    Environment
    1979 - 81 Minister of State,
    Civil Service Department
    1981 - 83 Minister of State,
    Department of Education and Science
    (Minister for the Arts)
    1983 - 86 Minister of State,
    Department of Trade and Industry
    1986 - 87 Secretary of State for Trade and
    Industry
    1987 - 89 Secretary of State for Transport

Kemsley, Viscount (Geoffrey Lionel Berry Kemsley)

Type of Peerage . . . . Hereditary
Political Allegiance . . . . . Conservative
Succeeded 1968
Born . . . . 29th June 1909
Educated . . . . Marlborough College
    Magdalen College, Oxford
Professional Career . . . . . 1938 - 59 Deputy Chairman,
    Kemsley Newspapers Ltd
    1949 - 51, 1959 - 61 Master Spectacle
    Makers' Company
Political Career . . . . 1943 - 45 MP (Conservative) for
    Buckingham
Correspondence Address . . Thorpe Lubenham, Market Harborough,
    Leicestershire

Kenilworth, Baron (John Randley Siddeley)

Type of Peerage . . . . Hereditary
Political Allegiance . . . . . Conservative
Succeeded 1981
Born . . . . 16th June 1954

Kennedy of The Shaws, Baroness (Helena Ann Kennedy QC)

Type of Peerage . . . . Life
Political Allegiance . . . . . Labour
Created 1997
Born . . . . 12th May 1950
Educated . . . . Holyrood Secondary School, Glasgow
    Council of Legal Education
Professional Career . . . . . 1972 - Barrister (QC 1991)

MEMBERS OF THE HOUSE OF LORDS

Kennet, Baron (Wayland Hilton Young)

Type of Peerage . . . . Hereditary
Political Allegiance . . . . . Labour
Succeeded 1960
Born . . . . 2nd August 1923 in London
Educated . . . . Stowe School
      Trinity College, Cambridge
Professional Career . . . . . Author
      1970 - 74 Chairman, Advisory Committee on
        Oil Pollution
      1971 - 72 Chairman, Campaign for
        Preservation of Rural England
Political Career . . . . 1966 - 70 Parliamentary Secretary, Ministry
        of Housing and Local Government
      1971 - 74 Opposition Spokesman on Foreign
        Affairs and Science, House of Lords
      1978 - 79 Member (Labour) European
        Parliament
      1981 - 83 Social Democratic Party
        Chief Whip, House of Lords
      1981 - 90 Social Democratic Party Spokesman
        on Foreign Affairs and Defence,
        House of Lords

Kensington, Baron (Hugh Ivor Edwards)

Type of Peerage . . . . Hereditary
On Leave Of Absence
Succeeded 1981
Born . . . . 24th November 1933

Kenswood, Baron (John Michael Howard Whitfield)

Type of Peerage . . . . Hereditary
Without Writ of Summons
Succeeded 1963
Born . . . . 6th April 1930

Kent, Duke of
(HRH Prince Edward George Nicholas Paul Patrick)

Type of Peerage . . . . Hereditary
Political Allegiance . . . . . Cross Bench
Succeeded . . . . 1942 (as a minor)
Born . . . . 9th October 1935

Kenyon, Baron (Lloyd Tyrell-Kenyon)

Type of Peerage . . . . Hereditary
Political Allegiance . . . . . Conservative
Succeeded 1993
Born . . . . 13th July 1947
Educated . . . . Eton College
      Magdalene College, Cambridge
Subject Interests . . . . Local government, Rural affairs, Wales
Recreational Interests . . . Gardening, Shooting
Correspondence Address . . Gredington, Whitchurch,
      Shropshire, SY13 3DH
      Tel: (01948) 830305 Fax: (01948) 830673

Kershaw, Baron (Edward John Kershaw)

Type of Peerage . . . . Hereditary
Political Allegiance . . . . . None
Succeeded 1962
Born . . . . 12th May 1936

Keyes, Baron (Roger George Bowlby Keyes)

Type of Peerage . . . . Hereditary
Political Allegiance . . . . . Conservative
Succeeded 1945
Born . . . . 14th March 1919 in Dover, Kent
Educated . . . . King's Mead School, Seaford
      Royal Naval College, Dartmouth
Professional Career . . . . . 1932 - 35 Royal Naval College, Dartmouth
      1935 - 38 Cadet and Midshipman,
        Royal Navy
      1936 - 49 Served at Sea
      1950 - Director of Companies
      1952 - 66 Farmer
      1966 - 71 Proprietor of LWO Schools
Subject Interests . . . . Defence, Foreign affairs
Recreational Interests . . . Travel, Yachting, Reading, Historical
      research, Do It Yourself and carpentry
Correspondence Address . . East Farleigh House, Lower Road, East
      Farleigh, Maidstone, Kent, ME15 0JW
      Tel: (01622) 726295 Fax: (01622) 721471

Kilbracken, Baron (John Raymond Godley DSC)

Type of Peerage . . . . Hereditary
Political Allegiance . . . . . Labour
Succeeded 1950
Born . . . . 17th October 1920 in London
Educated . . . . Eton College
      Balliol College, Oxford
Professional Career . . . . . 1940 - 45 Pilot, Fleet Air Arm
        (Lieutenant-Commander)
      1947 - Author and Journalist
      1950 - Landowner and Farmer
Subject Interests . . . . Family Law, Ireland, Kurds
Recreational Interests . . . Chess, Cricket, Rowing, Birdwatching
Correspondence Address . . Killegar, Cavan, Ireland
      Tel: (00353) 49 34309
      House of Lords, Westminster,
      London, SW1A 0PW
      Tel: (0171) 219 5353 Fax; (0171) 219 5979

Killanin, Baron (Michael Morris MBE, TD)

Type of Peerage . . . . Hereditary
Political Allegiance . . . . . Cross Bench
Succeeded . . . . 1927 (as a minor)
Born . . . . 30th July 1914

Killearn, Baron (Victor Miles George Aldous Lampson)

Type of Peerage . . . . Hereditary
Political Allegiance . . . . . Conservative
Succeeded 1996
Born . . . . 9th September 1941 in Egypt
Educated . . . . Eton College
Professional Career . . . . . 1960 - 66 HM Forces,
        Commission in Scots Guards
      1966 - 67 Chase Manhattan Bank
      1968 Partner, Cazenove & Co
Subject Interests . . . . Armed Forces, Asia, Australasia, Field
      sports
Recreational Interests . . . Shooting, Fishing
Correspondence Address . . c/o Cazenove & Co, 12 Tokenhouse Yard,
      London, EC2R 7AN
      Tel: (0171) 588 2828

MEMBERS OF THE HOUSE OF LORDS

Kilmarnock, Baron (Alistair Ivor Gilbert Boyd)
Type of Peerage . . . . Hereditary
Political Allegiance . . . . . Cross Bench
Succeeded 1975
Born . . . . 11th May 1927

Kilpatrick of Kincraig, Baron (Robert Kilpatrick)
Type of Peerage . . . . Life
Political Allegiance . . . . . Cross Bench
Created 1996
Born . . . . 29th July 1926 in Wemyss, Fife
Educated . . . . Buckhaven High School
University of Edinburgh
Professional Career . . . . . 1966 - 75 Professor of Therapeutics,
University of Sheffield
1971 - 74 Dean of Medicine,
University of Sheffield
1975 - 87 Chairman, Advisory
Committee on Pesticides
1975 - 89 Dean of Medicine,
University of Leicester
1989 - 95 President,
General Medical Council
1997 - President, British Medical
Association
Subject Interests . . . . Medicine, Health, Higher education
Recreational Interests . . . Golf, Walking in isolated places
Correspondence Address . . 12 Wester Coates Gardens,
Edinburgh, EH12 5LT
Tel: (0131) 337 7304

Kimball, Baron (Marcus Richard Kimball)
Type of Peerage . . . . Life
Political Allegiance . . . . . Conservative
Created 1985
Born . . . . 18th October 1928 in London
Educated . . . . Eton College
Trinity College, Cambridge
Professional Career . . . . . 1964 - 92 Chairman,
River Naver Fishing Board
1966 - 82 Chairman,
British Field Sports Society
1989 - 94 Chairman,
Firearms Consultative Committee
1991 - President, Olympia International
Showjumping
Political Career . . . . 1956 - 83 MP (Conservative) for
Gainsborough
Subject Interests . . . . Agriculture, Finance, Country sport
Recreational Interests . . . Hunting, Shooting, Fishing
Correspondence Address . . Great Easton Manor, Great Easton, Market
Harborough, Leicestershire, LE16 8TB
Tel: (01536) 770333

Kimberley, Earl of (John Wodehouse)
Type of Peerage . . . . Hereditary
Political Allegiance . . . . . Conservative
Succeeded . . . . 1941 (as a minor)
Born . . . . 12th May 1924 in London
Educated . . . . Eton College
Cambridge University
Political Career . . . . 1981 - 83 Chairman, Foreign Affairs
Committee, Monday Club
1981 - 94 Delegate to North Atlantic
Assembly
Subject Interests . . . . Defence, Field sports, Terrorism, Security,
Law and order
Recreational Interests . . . Fishing, Gardening, Bridge
Correspondence Address . . Hailstone House, Cricklade,
Wiltshire, SN6 6JP
Tel: (01793) 750344 Fax: (01793) 752078

Kindersley, Baron (Robert Hugh Molesworth Kindersley)
Type of Peerage . . . . Hereditary
Political Allegiance . . . . . Cross Bench
Succeeded 1975
Born . . . . 18th August 1929 in London
Educated . . . . Eton College
Trinity College, Oxford
Harvard Business School
Professional Career . . . . . 1959 - 89 Managing/Executive Director/Vice
Chairman, Lazard Brothers
1980 - 89 Chairman, Commonwealth
Development Corporation
1990 - 91 Chairman, Brent Walker
Subject Interests . . . . Complementary medicine
Recreational Interests . . . Skiing, Tennis, Shooting, Painting,
Gardening
Correspondence Address . . West Green Farm, Shipbourne,
Kent, TN11 9PU
Tel: (01732) 810293 Fax: (01732) 810799
Personal Staff . . . . Ms Lesley Nethercroft *(Secretary)*
Tel: (01732) 366315

King of Wartnaby, Baron (John Leonard King)
Type of Peerage . . . . Life
Political Allegiance . . . . . Conservative
Created 1983
Born 1918

Kingsdown, Rt Hon Baron (Robin Leigh-Pemberton KG)
Type of Peerage . . . . Life
Political Allegiance . . . . . Cross Bench
Created 1993
Born . . . . 5th January 1927 in Lenham, Kent
Educated . . . . St Peters Court, Broadstairs
Eton College
Trinity College, Oxford
Professional Career . . . . . 1954 - Barrister
1975 - 77 Chairman, Birmid Qualcast
1977 - 83 Chairman, National
Westminster Bank
1982 - Lord Lieutenant of Kent
1983 - 93 Governor of the Bank of England
Political Career . . . . 1961 - 77 Member, Kent County Council
(Chairman 1972 - 75)
Subject Interests . . . . Economics, Banking, Farming, Rural issues,
Local authorities
Recreational Interests . . . Country life, Family
Correspondence Address . . Hambros plc, 41 Tower Hill,
London, EC3N 4HA
Tel: (0171) 865 3955 Fax: (0171) 865 3985
Personal Staff . . . . Miss Gill Herriot *(Personal Assistant)*

MEMBERS OF THE HOUSE OF LORDS

Kingsland, Rt Hon Baron
    (Rt Hon Christopher James Prout TD QC)

Type of Peerage . . . . Life
Political Allegiance . . . . . Conservative
Created 1994
Born . . . . 1st January 1942 in London
Educated . . . . Sevenoaks School
    Manchester University
    Queen's College, Oxford
Professional Career . . . . . Barrister
    1966 - 69 The World Bank Group,
      Washington DC
    1969 - 79 Leverhulme Fellow and Lecturer
      in Law, University of Sussex
Political Career . . . . 1979 - 94 Member of the European
    Parliament (Conservative) for Shropshire
    and Stafford
    1983 - 87 Chief Whip, European Democratic
      Group, European Parliament
    1987 Chairman, Legal Affairs Committee
      European Parliament
    1987 - 94 Leader, Conservative MEPs in the
      European Parliament
    1987 - 92 Chairman, European Democratic
      Group, European Parliament
    1992 - 94 Vice-Chairman, European Peoples
      Party Group, European Parliament
    1997 Shadow Lord Chancellor
Subject Interests . . . . Constitutional law
Recreational Interests . . . Boating, Gardening, Musical comedy, Racing
Correspondence Address . . House of Lords, Westminster,
    London, SW1A 0PW
    17 Crescent Place, Town Walls, Shrewsbury,
    Shropshire, SY1 1TQ
    Tel: (01743) 232913
Personal Staff . . . . Mrs Helen Gillow *(Personal Assistant)*
    Tel: (01743) 232913

Kinloss, Lady (Beatrice Mary Grenville Freeman-Grenville)

Type of Peerage . . . . Hereditary
Political Allegiance . . . . . Cross Bench
Succeeded . . . . 1944 (as a minor)
Born . . . . 18th August 1922

Kinnoull, Earl of (Arthur William George Patrick Hay)

Type of Peerage . . . . Hereditary
Political Allegiance . . . . . Conservative
Succeeded . . . . 1938 (as a minor)
Born . . . . 26th March 1935

Kinross, Baron (Christopher Patrick Balfour)

Type of Peerage . . . . Hereditary
Political Allegiance . . . . . None
Succeeded 1985
Born . . . . 1st October 1949 in Edinburgh
Educated . . . . Eton College
    Edinburgh University
Professional Career . . . . . 1977 - 97 Partner, Shepherd and
      Wedderburn
    1997 - Partner, Taylor Kinross Legal
      Partnership
Recreational Interests . . . Shooting, Motorsport
Correspondence Address . . 11 Belford Place, Edinburgh, EH4 3DH
    Tel: (0131) 623 1997 Fax: (0131) 623 2323

Kintore, Earl of (Michael Canning William John Keith)

Type of Peerage . . . . Hereditary
Political Allegiance . . . . . Cross Bench
Succeeded 1989
Born . . . . 22nd February 1939

Kirkhill, Baron (John Farquharson Smith)

Type of Peerage . . . . Life
Political Allegiance . . . . . Labour
Created 1975
Born . . . . 7th May 1930 in Aberdeen
Professional Career . . . . . 1979 - 82 Chairman, North of Scotland
      Hydro-Electric Board
Political Career . . . . 1971 - 75 Lord Provost of Aberdeen
    1975 - 78 Minister of State, Scottish Office

Kirkwood, Baron (David Harvie Kirkwood)

Type of Peerage . . . . Hereditary
Political Allegiance . . . . . Liberal Democrat
Succeeded 1970
Born . . . . 24th November 1931 in Bristol
Educated . . . . Rugby School
    Trinity Hall, Cambridge
Professional Career . . . . . 1962 - 87 Lecturer and Senior Lecturer,
      Sheffield University
    1987 Metallurgical Consultant (and Honorary
      Senior Lecturer), Sheffield University
Subject Interests . . . . Higher education, Science and technology
Correspondence Address . . 56 Endcliffe Hall Avenue, Sheffield, S10 3EL
    Tel and Fax: (0114) 266 3107

MEMBERS OF THE HOUSE OF LORDS

Kitchener of Khartoum, Earl (Henry Herbert Kitchener)

Type of Peerage .... Hereditary
Political Allegiance ..... Conservative
Succeeded 1937
Born .... 24th February 1919 in Ringwould, Kent
Educated .... Winchester College
Trinity College, Cambridge
Professional Career ..... 1940 - 45 Major, Royal Signals
1946 - 81 Technical Officer, ICI, Cheshire
Subject Interests .... Voting systems, Complementary medicine,
Organic growing
Correspondence Address .. Westergate Wood, Eastergate, Chichester,
West Sussex, PO20 6SB
Tel and Fax: (01243) 543061

Knight of Collingtree, Baroness
(Joan Christabel Jill Knight DBE)

Type of Peerage .... Life
Political Allegiance ..... Conservative
Created 1997
Born .... 9th July 1927 in Bristol
Educated .... King Edward Grammar School, Birmingham
Political Career .... 1966 -97 MP (Conservative) for
Birmingham Edgbaston
1982 - 97 Chairman, Conservative
Health Committee
1983 - 97 Secretary, then Vice Chairman,
1922 Committee
1984 - 97 Chairman, Lords and Commons
Family and Child Protection Group
1994 - 97 Chairman, Executive Committee,
Inter Parliamentary Union
Subject Interests .... Health, Child welfare, Home Office,
Foreign affairs
Recreational Interests ... Theatre, Antique hunting, Tapestry, Singing
Correspondence Address .. House of Lords, Westminster,
London, SW1A 0PW
Tel: (0171) 219 6878

Knights, Baron (Philip Douglas Knights CBE, QPM)

Type of Peerage .... Life
Political Allegiance ..... Cross Bench
Created 1987
Born .... 3rd October 1920 in Ottershaw, Surrey
Educated .... King's School, Grantham
Police Staff College
Professional Career ..... 1937 - 59 Lincolnshire Constabulary
1959 - 63 Assistant Chief Constable,
Birmingham City Police
1963 - 66 Deputy Commandant,
Police Staff College
1966 - 72 Assistant Chief Constable then
Deputy Chief Constable, Birmingham
City Police
1972 - 74 Chief Constable, Sheffield and
Rotherham Constabulary
1974 - 75 Chief Constable,
South Yorkshire Police
1975 - 85 Chief Constable,
West Midlands Police
Subject Interests .... Policing, Law and order,
Local government affairs
Recreational Interests ... Sport, Music, Theatre and Reading

Knollys, Viscount (David Francis Dudley Knollys)

Type of Peerage .... Hereditary
Political Allegiance ..... Conservative
Succeeded 1966
Born .... 12th June 1931

Knutsford, Viscount (Michael Holland-Hibbert)

Type of Peerage .... Hereditary
Political Allegiance ..... Conservative
Succeeded 1986
Born .... 27th December 1926 in Oxford
Educated .... Eton College
Trinity College, Cambridge
Professional Career ..... 1950 - 86 Regional Director, Barclays Bank
1965 - National Trust (Member variously of
Executive Committee, Council and
Finance Committee)
Subject Interests .... Arts, Music, English architecture,
Countryside, Heritage
Recreational Interests ... Field sports
Correspondence Address .. Broadclyst House, Exeter, Devon, EX5 3EW
Tel: (01392) 461244

MEMBERS OF THE HOUSE OF LORDS

L

Laing of Dunphail, Baron (Hector Laing)

Type of Peerage . . . . Life
Political Allegiance . . . . . Conservative
Created 1991
Born . . . . 12th May 1923 in Edinburgh
Educated . . . . Loretto School, Musselburgh
    Jesus College, Cambridge
Professional Career . . . . . 1964 - 85 Managing Director, United
    Biscuits (Chairman 1972 - 90, Life President
    since 1990)
    1973 - 91 Director, Bank of England
    1977 - 79 Chairman, Food and Drink
    Industries Council
    1982 - 90 Chairman, Scottish
    Business in the Community
    1987 - 91 Chairman, Business in the
    Community
    1991 - 94 President, Institute of
    Business Ethics
    1992 - 94 President, Trident Trust
Political Career . . . . 1988 - 93 Treasurer, Conservative Party
Recreational Interests . . . Walking, Gardening
Correspondence Address . . High Meadows, Windsor Road, Gerrards
    Cross, Buckinghamshire, SL9 8ST
    Tel: (01753) 882437 Fax: (01753) 885106
Personal Staff . . . . Mrs Helen Tiedman *(Secretary)*
    Tel: (01258) 817891

Lambert, Viscount (Michael Joan Lambert)

Type of Peerage . . . . Hereditary
Without Writ of Summons
Succeeded 1989
Born . . . . 29th September 1912

Lane, Baron (Rt Hon Geoffrey Dawson Lane)

Type of Peerage . . . . . . Life (Former Law Lord)
Political Allegiance . . . . . Cross Bench
Created 1979
Born . . . . 17th July 1918
Educated . . . . Shrewsbury School
    Trinity College, Cambridge
Professional Career . . . . . 1946 Barrister (QC 1962)
    1963 - 66 Recorder of Bedford
    1966 - 74 High Court Judge,
    Queen's Bench Division
    1974 - 79 Lord Justice of Appeal
    1979 - 80 Lord of Appeal in Ordinary
    1980 - 92 Lord Chief Justice of England

Lane of Horsell, Baron (Peter Stewart Lane)

Type of Peerage . . . . Life
Political Allegiance . . . . . Conservative
Created 1990
Born . . . . 29th January 1925 in Woking, Surrey
Educated . . . . Sherborne School, Dorset
Professional Career . . . . . 1950 - 92 Partner, then Senior Partner,
    Binder Hamlyn (Chartered Accountants)
    1985 - 95 Chairman, Brent International
    1985 - 97 Deputy Chairman, More O'Ferrall
    1993 - 96 Chairman, Nuffield Hospitals
    1994 - 96 Chairman, Automated Security
    (Holdings)
Political Career . . . . 1981 - 84 Vice-Chairman, then Chairman,
    National Union of Conservative
    Associations (Vice-President since 1984)
Subject Interests . . . . Finance
Correspondence Address . . Rossmore Pond Road, Woking,
    Surrey, GU22 0SY
    Tel: (01483) 761858 Fax: (01483) 770993

Lang of Monkton, Baron (Rt Hon Ian Bruce Lang)

Type of Peerage . . . . Life
Created 1997
Born . . . . 27th June 1940 in Glasgow
Created 1997
Educated . . . . Rugby School
    Sidney Sussex College, Cambridge
Political Career . . . . 1979 - 97 MP (Conservative) for Galloway
    then Galloway and Upper Nithsdale
    1981 - 86 Government Whip,
    House of Commons
    1986 Parliamentary Secretary,
    Department of Employment
    1986 - 87 Parliamentary Secretary,
    Scottish Office
    1987 - 90 Minister of State, Scottish Office
    1990 - 95 Secretary of State for Scotland
    1995 - 97 President of the Board of Trade

Lansdowne, Marquess of (George John Charles Mercer Nairne Petty-Fitzmaurice)

Type of Peerage . . . . Hereditary
Political Allegiance . . . . . None
Succeeded 1944
Born . . . . 27th November 1912 in London
Political Career . . . . 1958 - 62 Parliamentary Secretary,
    Foreign Office
    1962 - 64 Minister of State for Colonial
    Affairs and Commonwealth Relations

Latham, Baron (Dominic Charles Latham)

Type of Peerage . . . . Hereditary
On Leave of Absence
Succeeded 1970
Born . . . . 20th September 1954

Latymer, Baron (Hugo Nevill Money-Coutts)

Type of Peerage . . . . Hereditary
Political Allegiance . . . . . None
Succeeded 1987
Born . . . . 1st March 1926

Lauderdale, Earl of (Patrick Francis Maitland)

Type of Peerage . . . . Hereditary
Political Allegiance . . . . . Conservative
Succeeded 1968
Born . . . . 17th March 1911
Professional Career . . . . . 1939 - 41 Balkans and Danubian
    Correspondent, The Times
    1941 - 43 War Correspondent,
    News Chronicle
Political Career . . . . 1951 - 59 MP (Unionist/Independent
    Conservative) for Lanark
    1974 - 79 Chairman, European Communities
    Sub-Committee on Energy and Transport
    1980 Vice-Chairman, Parliamentary Group
    for Energy Strategies

MEMBERS OF THE HOUSE OF LORDS

Lawrence, Baron (David John Downer Laurence)
Type of Peerage . . . . Hereditary
Political Allegiance . . . . . Cross Bench
Succeeded 1968
Born . . . . 4th September 1937

Lawson of Blaby, Baron (Rt Hon Nigel Lawson)
Type of Peerage . . . . Life
Political Allegiance . . . . . Conservative
Created 1992
Born . . . . 11th March 1932
Educated . . . . Westminster School
                    Christ Church, Oxford
Professional Career . . . . . 1956 - 60 Editorial Staff, Financial Times
                    1961 - 63 City Editor, Sunday Telegraph
                    1966 - 70 Editor, The Spectator
                    1990 - Chairman, Central Europe Trust Co
                    1990 - Director, Barclays Bank
Political Career . . . . 1963 - 64 Special Assistant to Prime
                      Minister (Rt Hon Sir Alec Douglas
                      Home MP)
                    1973 - 74 Special Adviser,
                      Conservative Party HQ
                    1974 - 92 MP (Conservative) for Blaby
                    1976 - 77 Opposition Whip,
                      House of Commons
                    1977 - 79 Opposition Spokesman on
                      Treasury and Economic Affairs,
                      House of Commons
                    1979 - 81 Financial Secretary, HM Treasury
                    1981 - 83 Secretary of State for Energy
                    1983 - 89 Chancellor of the Exchequer

Layton, Baron (Geoffrey Michael Layton)
Type of Peerage . . . . Hereditary
Political Allegiance . . . . . Conservative
Succeeded 1989
Born . . . . 18th July 1947

Leathers, Viscount (Christopher Graeme Leathers)
Type of Peerage . . . . Hereditary
Political Allegiance . . . . . Cross Bench
Succeeded 1996
Born . . . . 31st August 1941 in Esher, Surrey
Educated . . . . Rugby School
                    Open University
Professional Career . . . . . 1961 - 84 Manager, Wm Cory and Son
                    1984 - 86 Chief Executive, Mostyn Docks
                    1986 - 88 Transport Consultant
                    1988 - Civil Servant, Department of
                    Transport
Subject Interests . . . . Surface transport, Emergency planning,
                    Homelessness
Recreational Interests . . . Walking, Grandchildren
Correspondence Address . . Lime Cottage, High Street, Burwash,
                    Etchingham, East Sussex, TN19 7EL
                    Tel: (01435) 882530

Leconfield and Egremont, Baron
(John Max Henry Sawen Wyndham)
Type of Peerage . . . . Hereditary
Political Allegiance . . . . . Conservative
Succeeded 1972
Born . . . . 21st April 1948

Leicester, Bishop (Rt Rev Thomas Frederick Butler)
Type of Peerage . . . . Bishop
Entered Lords 1996
Born . . . . 5th March 1940 in Birmingham
Educated . . . . University of Leeds
                    College of the Resurrection, Mirfield
Professional Career . . . . . 1964 - 66 Curate, St Augustine's, Wisbech
                    1966 - 68 Curate, St Saviour's, Folkestone
                    1968 - 73 Lecturer and Chaplain,
                      University of Zambia
                    1973 Acting Dean, Lusaka Cathedral,
                      Zambia
                    1973 - 80 Chaplain to University of
                      Kent at Canterbury
                    1980 - 85 Archdeacon of Northolt
                    1985 - 91 Bishop of Willesden
                    1991 - Bishop of Leicester
                    1995 - Chairman, Board of Mission,
                      General Synod of Church of England
Recreational Interests . . . Walking, Running, Reading
Correspondence Address . . Bishop's Lodge, 10 Springfield Road,
                    Leicester, LE2 3BD
                    Tel: (0116) 270 8985

Leicester, Earl of (Edward Douglas Coke)
Type of Peerage . . . . Hereditary
Political Allegiance . . . . . Cross Bench
Succeeded 1994
Born . . . . 6th May 1936 in Harare, Zimbabwe
Educated . . . . St Andrew's College, Grahamstown, S Africa
Subject Interests . . . . Countryside, Built environment, Farming,
                    Forestry, Defence, Transport
Recreational Interests . . . Shooting, Fishing, Walking, Reading
Correspondence Address . . Holkham, Wells-next-the-Sea,
                    Norfolk, NR23 1AB
                    Tel: (01328) 710227 Fax: (01328) 711707
Personal Staff . . . . Mrs Marilyn Franklin *(Secretary)*

Leigh, Baron (John Piers Leigh)
Type of Peerage . . . . Hereditary
Political Allegiance . . . . . Conservative
Succeeded 1979
Born . . . . 11th September 1935

Leighton of Saint Mellons, Baron (John Leighton Seager)
Type of Peerage . . . . Hereditary
Without Writ of Summons
Succeeded 1963
Born . . . . 11th January 1922

Leinster, Duke of (Gerald FitzGerald)
Type of Peerage . . . . Hereditary
On Leave of Absence
Succeeded 1976
Born . . . . 27th May 1914 in London

MEMBERS OF THE HOUSE OF LORDS

Lester of Herne Hill, Baron (Anthony Paul Lester QC)

Type of Peerage	Life
Political Allegiance	Liberal Democrat
Created	1993
Born	3rd July 1936 in London
Educated	City of London School
	Trinity College, Cambridge
	Harvard Law School
Professional Career	1963 - Barrister (QC 1975)
Political Career	1974 - 76 Special Adviser to
	Home Secretary (Roy Jenkins)
Subject Interests	Constitutional reform, Protection of human
	rights, Freedom of expression, Equality
	without discrimination
Recreational Interests	Golf, Walking
Correspondence Address	18-20 Outer Temple, 222 Strand,
	London, WC2 1BA
	Tel: (0171) 353 4612 Fax: (0171) 353 4696
	E-mail: Anthony_Lester@compuserve.com
	2 Hare Court, Temple, London, EC4 7BH
	Tel: (0171) 583 1770 Fax; (0171) 583 9269
Personal Staff	Ms Stephanie Mehanna (*Secretary*)

Leven and Melville, Earl of (Alexander Robert Leslie Melville)

Type of Peerage	Hereditary
Without Writ of Summons	
Political Allegiance	Conservative
Succeeded	1947
Born	13th May 1924 in London
Educated	Eton College
Professional Career	1942 - 52 Coldstream Guards
Recreational Interests	Shooting, Skiing, Fishing
Correspondence Address	Glenferness House, Nairn,
	Scotland, IV12 5VP
	Tel: (01309) 651202

Levene of Portsoken, Baron (Peter Keith Levene KBE)

Type of Peerage	Life
Political Allegiance	Cross Bench
Created	1997
Born	8th December 1941 in Pinner
Educated	City of London School
	University of Manchester
Professional Career	1963 - 85 Managing Director, then
	Chairman, United Scientific Holdings plc
	1985 - 91 Chief of Defence Procurement,
	Ministry of Defence
	1991 - 94 Deputy Chairman, Wasserstein
	Perella and Co Ltd
	1993 - 94 Chairman, Docklands Light
	Railway Ltd
	1993 - 96 Chairman, Canary Wharf Ltd
	1996 - Senior Adviser,
	Morgan Stanley and Co Ltd
Political Career	1991 - 95 Adviser variously to Secretary of
	State for Environment, Chancellor of
	Exchequer and President of Board of Trade
	1992 - 97 Prime Minister's Adviser on
	Efficiency (to Rt Hon John Major MP)
Subject Interests	Defence, Public administration, Transport
Recreational Interests	Skiing, Watching football
Correspondence Address	25 Cabot Square, London, E14 4QA
	Tel: (0171) 513 5419 Fax: (0171) 513 4680
	E-mail: levenep@ms.com
Personal Staff	Ms Elizabeth Crichton (*Personal Assistant*)

Leverhulme, Viscount (Philip William Bryce Lever KG, TD)

Type of Peerage	Hereditary
Political Allegiance	Conservative
Succeeded	1949
Born	1st July 1915 in Thornton Hough, Cheshire
Educated	Eton College
	Trinity College, Cambridge
Professional Career	Advisory Director, Unilever Ltd
	1949 - 90 Lord Lieutenant, City and
	County of Chester
	1980 - 94 Chancellor, Liverpool University
Subject Interests	Horseracing, Horse breeding
Recreational Interests	Shooting, Fishing
Correspondence Address	Thornton Manor, Thornton Hough,
	Wirral, L63 1JB
	Tel: (0151) 336 4834 and (0151) 336 1108
	Fax: (0151) 353 0265
	Flat 6, Kingston House East, Prince's Gate,
	Kensington, London, SW7 1LJ
Personal Staff	Mrs Irene Pugh (*Private Secretary*)
	Tel: (0151) 336 1108

Levy, Baron (Rt Hon Michael Abraham Levy)

Type of Peerage	Life
Has Not Taken The Oath	
Political Allegiance	Labour
Created	1997
Born	11th July 1944 in London
Educated	Hackney Downs Grammar School
Professional Career	1966 - 69 Principal, M Levy and Co
	(Chartered Accountants)
	1969 - 73 Partner, Wagner Prager Levy and Co
	1973 - 88 Chairman, Magnet Group of
	Companies
	1988 - 92 Chairman, D and J Securities Ltd
	1992 - 97 Chairman, M and G Records Ltd
	1992 - Chairman, Chase Music Ltd and
	Wireart Ltd
Subject Interests	Voluntary sector, Social welfare, Education
Recreational Interests	Tennis, Swimming
Correspondence Address	Chase House, Nan Clarks Lane,
	London, NW7 4HH
	Tel: (0171) 487 5394 Fax: (0171) 486 7919
	Also Tel: (0181) 959 2161
	Fax: (0181) 906 4765
Personal Staff	Mrs Joan Cobb (*PA/Researcher*)
	Tel: (0171) 487 5174

MEMBERS OF THE HOUSE OF LORDS

**Lewin, Baron (Admiral of the Fleet
Terence Thornton Lewin KG, GCB, LVO, DSC)**

Type of Peerage . . . . Life
Political Allegiance . . . . . Cross Bench
Created 1982
Born . . . . 19th November 1920 in Dover, Kent
Educated . . . . Judd School, Tonbridge
Royal Naval College, Greenwich
Professional Career . . . . . 1969 - 70 Assistant Chief of Naval Staff
1970 - 71 Second in Command,
Far East Fleet
1971 - 74 Vice Chief of Naval Staff
1974 - 75 Commander in Chief, Fleet
1975 - 77 Commander in Chief,
Naval Home Command
1977 - 79 Chief of Naval Staff and
First Sea Lord
1979 - 82 Chief of Defence Staff
1988 - 95 Chairman of Trustees,
National Maritime Museum
Subject Interests . . . . Defence, Museums, Heritage

Lewis of Newnham, Baron (Jack Lewis)

Type of Peerage . . . . Life
Political Allegiance . . . . . Cross Bench
Created 1989
Born . . . . 13th February 1928 in Barrow
Educated . . . . Barrow Grammar School
University of London
Professional Career . . . . . 1954 - 56 Lecturer, University of Sheffield
1956 - 57 Lecturer, Imperial College,
London
1957 - 61 Lecturer/Reader,
University College London
1961 - 67 Professor of Chemistry,
Manchester University
1967 - 70 Professor of Chemistry,
University College, London
1970 - 95 Professor of Chemistry,
Cambridge University
1975 - Warden, Robinson College,
Cambridge
1986 - 92 Chairman, Royal Commission on
Environmental Pollution
Subject Interests . . . . Chemistry, Education, Environment
Recreational Interests . . . Music, Walking
Correspondence Address . . Robinson College, Grange Road,
Cambridge, CB3 9AN
Tel: (01223) 339120 Fax: (01223) 339962
Personal Staff . . . . Mrs Denise Prosser *(Secretary)*
Tel: (01223) 339122

Lichfield, Bishop of (Rt Rev Keith Norman Sutton)

Type of Peerage . . . . Bishop
Entered Lords 1989
Born . . . . 23rd June 1934 in London
Educated . . . . Jesus College, Cambridge
Professional Career . . . . . 1959 - 62 Curate, St Andrew's, Plymouth
1962 - 67 Chaplain, St John's College,
Cambridge
1968 - 72 Tutor/Chaplain, Bishop Tucker
College, Mukono, Uganda
1973 - 78 Principal, Ridley Hall, Cambridge
1978 - 83 Bishop of Kingston-upon-Thames
1984 - Bishop of Lichfield
Subject Interests . . . . Russian literature, Third World issues
Recreational Interests . . . Baroque Music, Walking, Travel in France
and Africa
Correspondence Address . . Bishop's House, 22 The Close, Lichfield,
Staffordshire, WS13 7LG

Lichfield, Earl of (Thomas Patrick John Anson)

Type of Peerage . . . . Hereditary
Political Allegiance . . . . . Conservative
Succeeded 1960
Born . . . . 25th April 1939
Professional Career . . . . . Photographer

Lilford, Baron (George Vernon Powys)

Type of Peerage . . . . Hereditary
On Leave Of Absence
Succeeded . . . . 1949 (as a minor)
Born . . . . 8th January 1931

Limerick, Earl of (Patrick Edmund Pery KBE)

Type of Peerage . . . . Hereditary
Political Allegiance . . . . . Conservative
Succeeded 1967
Born . . . . 12th April 1930 in London
Educated . . . . Eton College
New College, Oxford
Professional Career . . . . . 1979 - 83 Chairman, British Overseas
Trade Board
1983 - 87 Vice-Chairman then Deputy
Chairman, Kleinwort Benson Ltd
1983 - Chairman, City of London
Polytechnic/London Guildhall University
1989 - Chairman, Pirelli UK plc
1992 - Chairman, AMP Asset
Management plc
1993 - 97 Chairman, De La Rue plc
Political Career . . . . 1972 - 74 Parliamentary Secretary,
Department of Trade and Industry
Subject Interests . . . . Trade/Trade promotion, Education
Recreational Interests . . . Mountaineering, Skiing, Gardening
Correspondence Address . . Pirelli UK plc, 11 Berkeley Street,
London, W1X 6BU
Tel: (0171) 355 5085 Fax: (0171) 355 5066
Personal Staff . . . . Mrs Jasmine Boxall *(Personal Assistant)*

MEMBERS OF THE HOUSE OF LORDS

Lincoln, Bishop of (Rt Rev Robert Maynard Hardy)
Type of Peerage . . . . Bishop
Entered Lords 1993
Born . . . . 5th October 1936 in Wakefield
Educated . . . . Queen Elizabeth Grammar School, Wakefield
                    Clare College, Cambridge
Professional Career . . . . . 1962 - 65 Curate, All Saints and Martyrs,
                    Langley, Manchester
                    1965 - 72 Fellow and Chaplain,
                    Selwyn College, Cambridge
                    1972 - 75 Vicar, All Saints, Borehamwood
                    1975 - 80 Priest in Charge, St Botolph,
                    Aspley Guise
                    1980 - 87 Bishop of Maidstone
                    1984 - Bishop to HM Prisons
                    1987 - Bishop of Lincoln
Subject Interests . . . . Penal affairs, Rural economy
Recreational Interests . . . Gardening, Walking, Reading
Correspondence Address . . Bishop's House, Eastgate, Lincoln, LN2 1QQ
                    Tel: (01522) 534701 Fax: (01522) 511095

Lincoln, Earl of (Edward Horace Fiennes-Clinton)
Type of Peerage . . . . Hereditary
Without Writ of Summons
Succeeded 1988
Born . . . . 23rd February 1913

Lindsay, Earl of (James Randolph Lindesay-Bethune)
Type of Peerage . . . . Hereditary
Political Allegiance . . . . . Conservative
Succeeded 1989
Born . . . . 19th November 1955
Educated . . . . Eton College
                    University of Edinburgh
Professional Career . . . . . Landscape Architect and Environmental
                    Consultant
                    1992 - 95 Chairman, The Landscape
                    Foundation
                    1995 - President, International Tree
                    Foundation
                    1997 - Chairman, Assured British Meat
Political Career . . . . 1995 Government Whip, (Lord in Waiting)
                    1995 - 97 Parliamentary Secretary,
                    Scottish Office
Subject Interests . . . . Scotland, Environment, Agriculture,
                    Forestry, Culture, Arts

Lindsay of Birker, Baron (James Francis Lindsay)
Type of Peerage . . . . Hereditary
Political Allegiance . . . . . Cross Bench
Succeeded 1995
Born . . . . 29th January 1945 in Yenan, China
Educated . . . . Geelong Grammar School, Australia
                    Bethesa-Chevy Chase Senior High School,
                    Maryland, USA
                    University of Keele
                    University of Liverpool
Professional Career . . . . . 1972 - Australian Foreign Service
                    1996 - Deputy High Commissioner, Australian
                    High Commission, Nairobi, Kenya
Subject Interests . . . . Foreign relations, International development,
                    Environment issues, Human rights
Recreational Interests . . . Hiking, Mountaineering
Correspondence Address . . Australian High Commission, Box 39341,
                    Nairobi, Kenya
                    E-mail: mukinduri@form-net.com

Lindsey and Abingdon, Earl of (Richard Henry Rupert Bertie)
Type of Peerage . . . . Hereditary
Political Allegiance . . . . . Conservative
Succeeded 1964
Born . . . . 28th June 1931 in Johannesburg,
                    South Africa
Professional Career . . . . . 1958 - 92 Insurance Broker and
                    Underwriting Agent, Lloyds
Subject Interests . . . . Defence, Insurance, Southern Africa
Correspondence Address . . Gilmilnscroft House, Sorn, Mauchline,
                    Ayrshire, KA5 6ND

Linklater of Butterstone, Baroness (Veronica Linklater)
Type of Peerage . . . . Life
Political Allegiance . . . . . Liberal Democrat
Created 1997
Born . . . . 15th April 1943 in Perthshire
Educated . . . . Cranborne Chase School
                    Sorbonne, Paris
                    University of Sussex
                    University of London
Professional Career . . . . . 1967 - 68 Child Care Officer, London
                    Borough of Tower Hamlets
                    1971 - 77 Co Founder, Visitors Centre,
                    Pentonville Prison
                    1981 - 82 Project Organiser, Winchester
                    Prison, Prison Reform Trust
                    1983 - Founder/Administrator/Consultant,
                    then Trustee, The Butler Trust
Recreational Interests . . . Music, Theatre, Gardening
Correspondence Address . . 5 Drummond Place, Edinburgh, EH3 6PH
                    Tel: (0131) 557 5705 Fax: (0131) 557 9757
Personal Staff . . . . Mrs Sue Moorhouse *(Secretary)*

Linlithgow, Marquess of (Adrian John Charles Hope)
Type of Peerage . . . . Hereditary
Political Allegiance . . . . . None
Succeeded 1987
Born . . . . 1st July 1946

Listowel, Earl of (Francis Michael Hare)
Type of Peerage . . . . Hereditary
Without Writ of Summons
Succeeded 1997
Born . . . . 28th June 1964

Liverpool, Earl of (Edward Peter Bertram Savile Foljambe)
Type of Peerage . . . . Hereditary
Political Allegiance . . . . . Conservative
Succeeded 1969
Born . . . . 14th November 1944

Lloyd of Berwick, Baron (Anthony John Leslie Lloyd)
Type of Peerage . . . . Life (Law Lord)
Political Allegiance . . . . . Cross Bench
Created 1993
Born . . . . 9th May 1929
Educated . . . . Eton College
                    Trinity College, Cambridge
Professional Career . . . . . 1955 - Barrister (QC 1967)
                    1969 - 77 Attorney General to HRH
                    The Prince of Wales
                    1975 - 94 Chairman, Glyndebourne
                    Arts Trust
                    1978 - 84 Judge High Court,
                    (Queen's Bench Division)
                    1984 - 93 Lord Justice of Appeal
                    1985 - Vice-Chairman, then (since 1992)
                    Chairman, Security Commission
                    1993 - Lord of Appeal in Ordinary
Recreational Interests . . . Music, Carpentry

THE GUIDE TO
THE HOUSE
OF LORDS

MEMBERS OF THE HOUSE OF LORDS

Lloyd of Highbury, Baroness (June Kathleen Lloyd DBE)

Type of Peerage . . . . Life
Political Allegiance . . . . . Cross Bench
Created 1996
Born . . . . 1st January 1928

Lloyd-George of Dwyfor, Earl (Owen Lloyd George)

Type of Peerage . . . . Hereditary
Political Allegiance . . . . . Cross Bench
Succeeded 1968
Born . . . . 28th April 1924

Lloyd-Webber, Baron (Andrew Lloyd Webber)

Type of Peerage . . . . Life
Political Allegiance . . . . . Conservative
Created 1997
Born . . . . 22nd March 1948
Educated . . . . Westminster School
    Magdalen College, Oxford
    Royal College of Music
Professional Career . . . . . Composer

Lockwood, Baroness (Betty Lockwood)

Type of Peerage . . . . Life
Political Allegiance . . . . . Labour
Created 1978
Born . . . . 22nd January 1924 in Dewsbury, Yorkshire
Educated . . . . Dewsbury Technical College
    Ruskin College, Oxford
Professional Career . . . . . 1975 - 83 Chairman, Equal Opportunities
    Commission
    1983 - 89 President, Birkbeck College
    1983 - 92 Council Member, Advertising
    Standards Authority
    1988 - 97 Pro Chancellor then Chancellor,
    University of Bradford
    1995 - Chairman, National Coal Mining
    Museum
Political Career . . . . 1952 - 67 Yorkshire Regional Women's
    Organiser, Labour Party
    1967 - 75 National Women's Officer,
    Labour Party
    1989 - 92 Chairman, European Communities
    Sub-Committee on Social and Consumer
    Affairs, House of Lords
    1990 - 92 Member, Council of Europe
    Deputy Speaker and Deputy Chairman of
    Committees, House of Lords
Subject Interests . . . . Equal opportunities, Higher education, Arts,
    Heritage, Preservation of countryside
Recreational Interests . . . Opera, Theatre, Gardening, Yorkshire Dales
Correspondence Address . . House of Lords, Westminster,
    London, SW1A 0PW
    Tel: (0171) 219 3148

Lofthouse of Pontefract, Baron (Geoffrey Lofthouse)

Type of Peerage . . . . Life
Political Allegiance . . . . . Labour
Created 1997
Born . . . . 18th December 1925 in Featherstone, West
    Yorkshire
Educated . . . . Leeds University
Professional Career . . . . . 1939 - 78 Coal Mining Industry
Political Career . . . . 1978 - 97 MP (Labour) for Pontefract and
    Castleford
    1988 - 92 Chairman, Labour Group of
    Yorkshire MPs
    1992 - 97 Deputy Speaker,
    House of Commons
Subject Interests . . . . Local government, Energy, Sport
Recreational Interests . . . Rugby League, Football, Cricket
Correspondence Address . . 67 Carleton Crest, Pontefract, WF8 2QR
    Tel and Fax: (01977) 704275
Personal Staff . . . . Mrs Jane Robinson
    Tel: (01977) 792459

Londesborough, Baron (Richard John Denison)

Type of Peerage . . . . Hereditary
Political Allegiance . . . . . None
Succeeded . . . . 1968 (as a minor)
Born . . . . 2nd July 1959

**London, Bishop of
(Rt Rev and Rt Hon Richard John Carew Chartres)**

Type of Peerage . . . . Bishop
Entered Lords 1995
Born . . . . 11th July 1947
Educated . . . . Hertford Grammar School
    Trinity College, Cambridge
    Cuddesden Theological College
Professional Career . . . . . 1973 - 75 Assistant Curate,
    St Andrew's, Bedford
    1975 - 80 Bishop's Domestic Chaplain,
    St Albans
    1980 - 84 Chaplain to Archbishop of
    Canterbury
    1984 - 92 Vicar, St Stephen with
    St John, Westminster
    1992 - 95 Bishop of Stepney
    1995 - Bishop of London
Correspondence Address . . The Old Deanery, Dean's Court,
    London, EC4V 5AA
    Tel: (0171) 248 6233

**Londonderry, Marquess of
(Alexander Charles Robert Vane-Tempest-Stewart)**

Type of Peerage . . . . Hereditary
Without Writ of Summons
Succeeded . . . . 1955 (as a minor)
Born . . . . 7th September 1937

Long, Viscount (Richard Gerard Long CBE)

Type of Peerage . . . . Hereditary
Political Allegiance . . . . . Conservative
Succeeded 1967
Born . . . . 30th January 1929 in London
Political Career . . . . 1974 - 79 Opposition Whip, House of Lords
    1979 - 97 Government Whip,
    (Lord in Waiting)

MEMBERS OF THE HOUSE OF LORDS

Longford, Earl of (Rt Hon Francis Aungier Pakenham KG)

Type of Peerage . . . . Hereditary (First Creation, as Baron
Packenham)

Political Allegiance . . . . . Labour

Created . . . . 1945 (Succeeded to Earldom of
Longford, 1961)

Born . . . . 5th October 1905 in London

Educated . . . . Eton College
New College, Oxford

Professional Career . . . . . 1932 - 46, 1952 - 64 Christ Church, Oxford
1941 - 44 Assistant to Sir William Beveridge
1955 - 63 Chairman, National Bank Ltd
1968 - 71 Chairman, National Youth
Employment Council
1970 - 80 Chairman, Sidgwick and Jackson

Political Career . . . . 1930 - 32 Conservative Party Economic
Department
1946 - 47 Parliamentary Secretary,
War Office
1947 - 48 Chancellor of the
Duchy of Lancaster
1948 - 51 Minister of Civil Aviation
1951 First Lord of the Admiralty
1964 - 68 Leader, House of Lords
1964 - 65, 1966 - 68 Lord Privy Seal
1965 - 66 Secretary of State for the Colonies

Subject Interests . . . . Social questions, especially penal questions

Lonsdale, Earl of (James Hugh William Lowther)

Type of Peerage . . . . Hereditary

Political Allegiance . . . . . Conservative

Succeeded 1953

Born . . . . 3rd November 1922

Lothian, Marquess of (Peter Francis Walter Kerr KCVO)

Type of Peerage . . . . Hereditary

Political Allegiance . . . . . Conservative

Succeeded . . . . 1940 (as a minor)

Born . . . . 8th September 1922 in Melbourne,
Derbyshire

Educated . . . . Ampleforth College
Christ Church, Oxford

Professional Career . . . . . 1976 - 86 Chairman, Scottish Council,
British Red Cross Society

Political Career . . . . 1960 - 63 PPS to the Foreign Secretary
(Earl of Home)
1962 - 63, 1972 - 73 Government Whip,
(Lord in Waiting)
1964 Parliamentary Secretary,
Ministry of Health
1970 - 72 Parliamentary Secretary,
Foreign and Commonwealth Office

Correspondence Address . . Ferniehirst Castle, Jedburgh,
Scotland, TD8 6NX
Tel: (01835) 862872

Loudoun, Countess (Barbara Huddleston Abney-Hastings)

Type of Peerage . . . . Hereditary

Political Allegiance . . . . . Cross Bench

Succeeded 1960

Born . . . . 3rd July 1919

Lovat, Baron (Simon Fraser)

Type of Peerage . . . . Hereditary

Without Writ of Summons

Succeeded . . . . 1994 (as a minor)

Born . . . . 13th February 1977 in London

Educated . . . . Harrow School
Edinburgh University

Professional Career . . . . . 1996 - Edinburg University

Subject Interests . . . . The Highlands of Scotland

Correspondence Address . . 31 St Leonards Terrace, London, SW3 4QG
Tel: (0171) 730 3018 Fax: (0171) 730 3141

Lovelace, Earl of (Peter Axel William Locke King)

Type of Peerage . . . . Hereditary

Political Allegiance . . . . . Cross Bench

Succeeded . . . . 1964 (as a minor)

Born . . . . 26th November 1951

Lovell-Davis, Baron (Peter Lovell-Davis)

Type of Peerage . . . . Life

Political Allegiance . . . . . Labour

Created 1974

Born . . . . 8th July 1924 in Margate, Kent

Educated . . . . King Edward VI Grammar School, Stratford-
on-Avon
Jesus College, Oxford

Professional Career . . . . . 1950 - 70 Managing Director,
Central Press Features Ltd
1970 - 74 Chairman, Features Syndicate Ltd
Davis and Harrison Ltd
1983 - 90 Chairman, Lee Cooper
Licensing Services Ltd
1986 - Chairman, Pettifor Morrow and
Associates Ltd

Political Career . . . . 1962 - 74 Adviser to Labour Party/
Government on Communications
1974 - 75 Government Whip,
(Lord in Waiting)
1975 - 76 Parliamentary Secretary,
Department of Energy

Subject Interests . . . . Aviation, Industrial archaeology, Energy,
Health matters, European Union, Media

Correspondence Address . . 80 North Road, London, N6 4AA
Tel: (0181) 348 3919 Fax: (0171) 384 1590

Lucan, Earl of (Richard John Bingham)

Type of Peerage . . . . Hereditary

Without Writ of Summons

Succeeded 1964

Born . . . . 18th December 1934

Note: The Earl of Lucan has been missing since 1974.

Lucas of Chilworth, Baron (Michael William George Lucas)

Type of Peerage . . . . Hereditary

Political Allegiance . . . . . Conservative

Succeeded 1967

Born . . . . 26th April 1926

Professional Career . . . . . 1980 - 83 President,
Institute of Transport Administration

Political Career . . . . 1983 - 84 Government Whip,
(Lord in Waiting)
1984 - 87 Parliamentary Secretary,
Department of Trade and Industry

Subject Interests . . . . Central/East European affairs, Transport,
Road safety, Sport, Industry

MEMBERS OF THE HOUSE OF LORDS

Lucas of Crudwell and Dingwall, Baron
(Ralph Matthew Palmer)

Type of Peerage . . . . Hereditary
Political Allegiance . . . . . Conservative
Succeeded 1991
Born . . . . 7th June 1951 in London
Educated . . . . Eton College
          Balliol College, Oxford
Professional Career . . . . . Chartered Accountant
          1976 - 88 SF Warburg & Co Ltd
Political Career . . . . 1994 - 97 Government Whip
          (Lord in Waiting)
          1997 - Opposition Spokesman on International
          Development, House of Lords
Subject Interests . . . . Finance, Industry, Education,
          Social Security
Recreational Interests . . . Gardening, Fishing
Correspondence Address . . E-mail: lucasr@parliament.uk
Note: The above is sometimes addressed simply as Lord Lucas.

Ludford, Baroness (Sarah Ann Ludford)

Type of Peerage . . . . Life
Political Allegiance . . . . . Liberal Democrat
Created 1997
Born . . . . 14th March 1951
Professional Career . . . . . Barrister and European Affairs Consultant
Political Career . . . . 1991 - Member, Islington London
          Borough Council

Luke, Baron (Arthur Charles St John Lawson Johnston)

Type of Peerage . . . . Hereditary
Political Allegiance . . . . . Conservative
Succeeded 1996
Born . . . . 13th January 1933 in London
Educated . . . . Eton College
          Trinity College, Cambridge
Professional Career . . . . . Fine Art Dealer
Political Career . . . . 1965 - 70 Member, Bedfordshire
          County Council
          1997 - Opposition Whip, House of Lords
Subject Interests . . . . Arts, Agriculture, Defence,
          History, Field sports
Recreational Interests . . . Field sports
Correspondence Address . . House of Lords, Westminster,
          London, SW1A 0PW
          Tel; (0171) 219 3703
          Odell Manor, Bedfordshire, MK43 7BB
          Tel: (01234) 720416

Lyell, Baron (Charles Lyell)

Type of Peerage . . . . Hereditary
Political Allegiance . . . . . Conservative
Succeeded . . . . 1943 (as a minor)
Born . . . . 27th March 1939
Political Career . . . . 1974 - 79 Opposition Whip, House of Lords
          1979 - 84 Government Whip,
          (Lord in Waiting)
          1984 - 89 Parliamentary Secretary,
          Northern Ireland Office
          Deputy Speaker and Deputy Chairman of
          Committees, House of Lords

Lytton, Earl of (John Peter Michael Scawen Lytton)

Type of Peerage . . . . Hereditary
Political Allegiance . . . . . Cross Bench
Succeeded 1985
Born . . . . 7th June 1950 in Minehead, Somerset
Educated . . . . Downside School
          College of Estate Management,
          University of Reading
Professional Career . . . . . 1975 - 81 Valuer, Inland Revenue
          Valuation Office
          1982 - 86 Associate Partner, Permutt
          Brown and Co, Surveyors
          1986 - 87 Valuer, Cubitt and West
          1988 - Principal, John Lytton and Co,
          Chartered Surveyors
          1994 - Chairman, Leasehold Franchisement
          Advisory Service
Subject Interests . . . . Environment, Property taxation, Rural land
          use management, Planning, Forestry
Recreational Interests . . . Reading, Family history, Rural estate
          management, Gardening, Country sports
Correspondence Address . . Estate Office, Newbuildings Place, Shipley,
          Horsham, West Sussex, RH13 7JQ
          Tel: (01403) 741650 Fax: (01403) 741744
          E-mail: lyttonjpm@parliament.uk

Lyveden, Baron (Ronald Cecil Vernon)

Type of Peerage . . . . Hereditary
Without Writ of Summons
Succeeded 1973
Born . . . . 10th April 1915

MEMBERS OF THE HOUSE OF LORDS

M

McAlpine of West Green, Baron (Robert Alistair McAlpine)

Type of Peerage . . . . Life
Political Allegiance . . . . . None
Created 1984
Born . . . . 14th May 1942 in London
Educated . . . . Stowe School
Professional Career . . . . . 1958 - 95 Sir Robert McAlpine and Sons Ltd
Political Career . . . . 1975 - 90 Treasurer, Conservative Party
    (also Deputy Chairman 1979 - 83)

MacAndrew, Baron (Christopher Anthony Colin MacAndrew)

Type of Peerage . . . . Hereditary
Political Allegiance . . . . . Conservative
Succeeded 1989
Born . . . . 16th February 1945

Macaulay of Bragar, Baron (Donald Macaulay QC)

Type of Peerage . . . . Life
Political Allegiance . . . . . Labour
Created 1989
Born . . . . 14th November 1933 in Clydebank
Educated . . . . University of Glasgow
Professional Career . . . . . Advocate, Scotland (QC 1975)

McCarthy, Baron (William Edward John McCarthy)

Type of Peerage . . . . Life
Political Allegiance . . . . . Labour
Created 1976
Born . . . . 30th July 1925 in London
Educated . . . . Holloway County School
    Ruskin College, Oxford
    Merton College, Oxford
    Nuffield College, Oxford
Professional Career . . . . . 1960 - 64, 1970 - 94 Research Fellow,
    Nuffield College, Lecturer in Industrial
    Relations
    1965 - 68 Research Director, Royal
    Commission on Trade Unions and
    Employers Associations
    1973 - 86 Chairman, Railway Staff
    National Tribunal
    1974 - Member, ACAS Arbitration Panel
    1996 - Member, Civil Service Arbitration
    Tribunal
Political Career . . . . 1968 - 70 Senior Economic Adviser,
    Department of Employment and
    Productivity
    1975 - 79 Senior Industrial Relations
    Advisor, Department of Health and
    Social Security
    1979 - 97 Opposition Spokesman on
    Employment, House of Lords
Subject Interests . . . . Industrial relations, Labour law, and
    Economics, Culture, Media
Recreational Interests . . . Theatre, Ballet, Opera, Gardening
Correspondence Addresses 4 William Orchard Close, Headington,
    Oxford, OX3 9DR
    Tel and Fax: (01865) 72016
    Nuffield College, Oxford, OX1 1NF
    Tel: (01865) 278500

Macclesfield, Earl of (Richard Timothy George Mansfield Parker)

Type of Peerage . . . . Hereditary
Political Allegiance . . . . . Cross Bench
Succeeded 1992
Born . . . . 31st May 1943 in Oxford

McCluskey, Baron (John Herbert McCluskey)

Type of Peerage . . . . Life
Political Allegiance . . . . . Cross Bench
Created 1976
Born . . . . 12th June 1929 in Glasgow
Educated . . . . Holy Cross Academy, Edinburgh
    Edinburgh University
Professional Career . . . . . 1955 - Advocate, Scotland (QC 1967)
    1964 - 71 Advocate-Depute
    1972 - 74 Chairman, Medical Appeals
    Tribunal for Scotland
    1984 - Senator of College of Justice in
    Scotland
    1985 - 94 Chairman, Scottish Association
    for Mental Health
Political Career . . . . 1974 - 79 Solicitor General for Scotland
    1979 - 84 Labour Spokesman on Scottish
    Legal Affairs, House of Lords
Subject Interests . . . . Scottish law
Recreational Interests . . . Tennis, Swimming, Theatre
Correspondence Address . . 5 Lansdowne Crescent,
    Edinburgh, EH12 5EQ
    Tel: (0131) 225 2595 Fax: (0131) 225 8213

McColl of Dulwich, Baron (Ian McColl CBE)

Type of Peerage . . . . Life
Political Allegiance . . . . . Conservative
Created 1989
Born . . . . 6th January 1933
Educated . . . . Hutcheson's Grammar School, Glasgow
    St Paul's School, London
    Guy's Hospital, London
Professional Career . . . . . 1957 - 67 Junior Doctor
    1957 - 67 Various Hospital Appointments
    1967 - 71 Recorder in Surgery and
    Sub-Dean St Bartholomew's Hospital
    1971 - Consultant Surgeon, Guy's Hospital
    (Director of Surgery since 1985)
    1971 Professor of Surgery,
    University of London
    1984 - 96 Chairman, Government Working
    Party on Supply on Artificial Limbs and
    Wheelchairs
    1991 - 94 President, Society for Minimally
    Invasive Surgery
Political Career . . . . 1994 - 97 PPS (House of Lords) to the
    Prime Minister, (Rt Hon John Major MP)
    1997 - An Opposition Spokesman on Health,
    House of Lords
    Deputy Speaker and Deputy Chairman of
    Committees, House of Lords
Subject Interests . . . . Health, Environment, Universities
Recreational Interests . . . Forestry
Correspondence Address . . House of Lords, Westminster,
    London, SW1A 0AA
    Tel: (0171) 219 5141
    E-mail: .McColli@Parliament.uk.
    Also Tel: (0171) 955 4466
    Fax: (0171) 403 0212
    E-mail: imccoll@udms.as.uk
Personal Staff . . . . Mrs Josephine Paterson *(PA)*
    Tel: (0171) 955 4466

MEMBERS OF THE HOUSE OF LORDS

McConnell of Lisburn, Baron (Rt Hon Brian McConnell)

Type of Peerage	Life
Political Allegiance	Cross Bench (also Ulster Unionist)
Created	1995
Born	25th November 1922 in Belfast
Educated	Sedbergh School
	Queen's University, Belfast
Professional Career	1948 - 63 Barrister, Northern Ireland
	1958 - 63 Counsel to Northern Ireland Attorney General MP (Unionist) for South Antrim, Northern Ireland Parliament
	1968 - 81 President, Industrial Court of Northern Ireland
Political Career	1951 - 68 MP (Unionist) for South Antrim, Northern Ireland Parliament
	1963 - 68 Minister of Home Affairs, Northern Ireland
Subject Interests	Northern Ireland
Correspondence Address	50A Glenavy Road, Lisburn, Northern Ireland, BT28 3UT
	Tel: (01846) 663432

Macdonald of Gwaenysgor, Baron (Gordon Ramsay MacDonald)

Type of Peerage	Hereditary
Without Writ of Summons	
Succeeded	1966
Born	16th October 1915

Macfarlane of Bearsden, Baron (Norman Somerville MacFarlane KT)

Type of Peerage	Life
Political Allegiance	Conservative
Created	1991
Born	5th March 1926

McFarlane of Llandaff, Baroness (Jean Kennedy McFarlane)

Type of Peerage	Life
Political Allegiance	Cross Bench
Created	1979
Born	1st April 1926 in Cardiff
Professional Career	1950 - 51 Staff Nurse, St Bartholomew's Hospital
	1953 - 59 Health Visitor, Cardiff
	1960 - 69 Royal College of Nursing (various posts) Senior Lecturer, then (from 1974) Professor and Head of Department
	1969 - 71 Director of Education and Research, Institute of Advance Nursing Education
	1971 - 88 Professor and Head of Department of Nursing, University of Manchester
	1980 - 83 Chairman, English Board for Nursing, Midwifery and Health Visiting
Subject Interests	Health, Education
Recreational Interests	Music, Photography, Walking

McGowan, Baron (Harry Duncan Cory McGowan)

Type of Peerage	Hereditary
Political Allegiance	None
Succeeded	1996
Born	20th July 1938

McIntosh of Haringey, Baron (Andrew Robert McIntosh)

Type of Peerage	Life
Political Allegiance	Labour
Created	1982
Born	30th April 1933 in London
Educated	Haberdashers' Aske's Hampstead School
	Royal Grammar School, High Wycombe
	Jesus College, Oxford
	Ohio State University
Professional Career	1963 - 68 Member, Hornsey Borough Council, then Haringey Borough Council
	1973 - 83 Member, Greater London Council (Leader of Opposition 1980 - 81)
	1965 - 97 Variously Managing Director, Chairman and Deputy Chairman, IFF Research
	1974 - 80 Chairman, Association for Neighbourhood Councils
	1983 Chairman, SVP (UK) Ltd
	1988 - Principal, Working Men's College
	1995 - President, Market Research Society (Editor of Journal 1963 - 67, Chairman 1972 - 73)
Political Career	1983 - 97 Opposition Spokesman variously Industry, Education, Science, Environment and Home Affairs, House of Lords
	1992 - 97 Deputy Leader of Opposition, House of Lords
	1997 - Government Deputy Chief Whip, House of Lords (Captain of the Yeomen of the Guard)
	Deputy Chairman of Committees, House of Lords
Recreational Interests	Cooking, Reading, Music
Correspondence Address	House of Lords, Westminster, London, SW1A 0PW
	Tel: (0171) 219 3131/6782
	Fax: (0171) 219 6837
	E-mail: mcintoshar@parliament.uk
Personal Staff	Ms Jill Baronti *(Secretary)*
	Tel: (0171) 219 3131

MEMBERS OF THE HOUSE OF LORDS

Mackay of Ardbrecknish, Baron
(Rt Hon John Jackson Mackay)

Type of Peerage . . . . Life
Political Allegiance . . . . . Conservative
Created 1991
Born . . . . 15th November 1938 in Lochgilphaed,
Argyll
Educated . . . . Dunoon Grammar School
Campbeltown Grammar School
University of Glasgow
Jordanhill College of Education
Professional Career . . . . . 1972 - 79 Principal Teacher of Mathematics,
Oban High School
1990 - 93 Chairman, Seafish Industry
Authority
Political Career . . . . 1969 - 74 Member, Oban Town Council
1979 - 87 MP (Conservative) for Argyll, then
Argyll and Bute
1982 - 87 Parliamentary Secretary,
Scottish Office
1987 - 90 Chief Executive, Scottish
Conservative Office
1993 Government Whip, (Lord in Waiting)
1994 Parliamentary Secretary,
Department of Transport
1994 - 97 Minister of State,
Department of Social Security
1997 Opposition Spokesman on Constitution,
Scotland, and Treasury
Subject Interests . . . . Treasury, Economics, Constitution, Scotland,
Fishing, Agriculture, Health, Social Security
Recreational Interests . . . Angling
Correspondence Address . . House of Lords, Westminster,
London, SW1A 0PW
Tel: (0171) 219 5870

Mackay of Clashfern, Baron
(Rt Hon James Peters Hymers Mackay QC)

Type of Peerage . . . . Life
Political Allegiance . . . . . Conservative
Created 1979
Born . . . . 2nd July 1927 in Edinburgh, Scotland
Educated . . . . George Heriot's School, Edinburgh
Edinburgh University
Trinity College, Cambridge
Professional Career . . . . . 1948 - 50 Lecturer in Mathematics,
St Andrews University
1955 - 65 Advocate, Scotland (QC 1965)
1972 - 74 Sheriff Principal, Renfrew and
Argyll
1976 - 79 Dean, Faculty of Advocates
1976 - 79 Member, Scottish Law
Commission
1984 - 85 Judge of the Supreme Courts of
Scotland
1985 - 87 Lord of Appeal in Ordinary
1991 - Chancellor, Herriot Watt University
Political Career . . . . 1979 - 84 Lord Advocate
1987 - 97 Lord Chancellor
Subject Interests . . . . Law, Religion, Childrens' affairs,
Constitutional affairs
Recreational Interests . . . Walking, Travel

Mackay of Drumadoon, Baron
(Rt Hon Donald Sage Mackay QC)

Type of Peerage . . . . Life
Political Allegiance . . . . . Conservative
Entered Lords 1995
Born . . . . 30th January 1946 in Aberdeen
Educated . . . . George Watson's Boys College, Edinburgh
University of Edinburgh
University of Virginia
Professional Career . . . . . 1971 - 76 Solicitor
1976 - Advocate, Scotland (QC 1987)
1989 - 95 Member, Criminal Injuries
Compensation Board
Political Career . . . . 1995 - 96 Solicitor General for Scotland
1996 - 97 Lord Advocate
1997 - Opposition Front Bench Spokesman
on Legal Affairs and Scotland,
House of Lords
Subject Interests . . . . Legal, Constitutional affairs, Scottish affairs
Recreational Interests . . . Golf, Isle of Arran
Correspondence Address . . 39 Hermitage Gardens,
Edinburgh, EH10 6AZ
Tel: (0131) 447 1412 Fax: (0131) 447 9863

Mackenzie-Stuart, Baron (Alexander John Mackenzie-Stuart)

Type of Peerage . . . . Life
Political Allegiance . . . . . Cross Bench
Created 1988
Born . . . . 18th November 1924
Educated . . . . Fettes College, Edinburgh
Sidney Sussex College, Cambridge
University of Edinburgh
Professional Career . . . . . 1951 - Advocate, Scotland (QC 1963)
1957 - 63 Standing Junior Counsel,
Inland Revenue, Scotland
1971 - 72 Sheriff Principal, Aberdeen,
Kincardine and Banff
1972 Senator, College of Justice, Scotland
1973 - 84 Judge, Court of Justice
European Communities
1984 - 88 President of the Court of Justice,
European Communities
Subject Interests . . . . European law, Legal history
Correspondence Address . . 7 Randolph Cliff, Edinburgh, EH3 7TZ
Tel: (0131) 225 1089
Le Garidel, Gravieres,
07140 Les Vans, France
Tel: 00 33 475 373529
Fax: 00 33 475 85063

MEMBERS OF THE HOUSE OF LORDS

Mackie of Benshie, Baron
(George Yull Mackie CBE, DSO, DFC)

Type of Peerage . . . . Life
Political Allegiance . . . . . Liberal Democrat
Created 1974
Born . . . . 10th July 1919 in Aberdeenshire
Educated . . . . Aberdeen Grammar School
　　　　　　　　　　　　　Aberdeen University
Professional Career . . . . . 1939 - 45 RAF, Bomber Command
　　　　　　　　　　　　　1945 - 89 Farmer
　　　　　　　　　　　　　1966 - 84 Chairman, Caithness Glass Ltd
　　　　　　　　　　　　　1975 - 84 Chairman, Caithness Pottery Co
　　　　　　　　　　　　　1986 - Chairman, Benshie Cattle Co
　　　　　　　　　　　　　1986 - Chairman, Land and Timber
　　　　　　　　　　　　　　Services Co
　　　　　　　　　　　　　1981 - 83 Rector, Dundee University
Political Career . . . . 1964 - 66 MP (Liberal) for Caithness and
　　　　　　　　　　　　　　Sutherland
　　　　　　　　　　　　　1965 - 70 Chairman, Scottish Liberal Party
　　　　　　　　　　　　　　(also President 1983 - 88)
　　　　　　　　　　　　　1986 - 97 Member, Delegation to Council of
　　　　　　　　　　　　　　Europe and Western European Union
　　　　　　　　　　　　　1989 - Liberal Democrat Spokesman on
　　　　　　　　　　　　　　Agriculture and Scottish Affairs,
　　　　　　　　　　　　　　House of Lords
Subject Interests . . . . Agriculture, Environment
Recreational Interests . . . Golf, Social life
Correspondence Address . . Benshie Cottage, Oathlaw by Forfar,
　　　　　　　　　　　　　Angus, DD8 3PQ
　　　　　　　　　　　　　Tel: (01307) 850376

Mackintosh of Halifax, Viscount (John Clive Mackintosh)

Type of Peerage . . . . Hereditary
Political Allegiance . . . . . Conservative
Succeeded 1980
Born . . . . 9th September 1958 in Norfolk
Educated . . . . The Leys School, Cambridge
　　　　　　　　　　　　　Oriel College, Oxford
Professional Career . . . . . 1992 - Chartered Accountant, Partner,
　　　　　　　　　　　　　　Price Waterhouse
Subject Interests . . . . Economy, Taxation, Financial Services,
　　　　　　　　　　　　　Youth, Sport
Recreational Interests . . . Cricket, Golf , Shooting, Bridge
Correspondence Address . . House of Lords, Westminster,
　　　　　　　　　　　　　London, SW1A 0PW
　　　　　　　　　　　　　Tel: (0171) 939 3000 Fax; (0171) 939 4298

MacLaurin of Knebworth, Baron (Ian Charter MacLaurin)

Type of Peerage . . . . Life
Political Allegiance . . . . . Conservative
Created 1996
Born . . . . 30th March 1937 in Blackheath, Kent
Educated . . . . Malvern College
Professional Career . . . . . 1959 - Tesco plc (Managing Director
　　　　　　　　　　　　　　1973 - 83, Deputy Chairman 1983 - 85,
　　　　　　　　　　　　　　Chairman since 1985)
　　　　　　　　　　　　　1996 - Chairman, England and Wales
　　　　　　　　　　　　　　Cricket Board
Subject Interests . . . . Cricket, Sport
Recreational Interests . . . Golf
Correspondence Address . . 14 Great College Street, London, SW1P 3RX
　　　　　　　　　　　　　Tel: (0171) 233 2203 Fax: (0171) 233 0438

Maclay, Baron (Joseph Paton Maclay)

Type of Peerage . . . . Hereditary
On Leave of Absence
Political Allegiance . . . . . Conservative
Succeeded 1969
Born . . . . 11th April 1942 in Kilmacolm, Scotland
Educated . . . . Winchester College
　　　　　　　　　　　　　Sorbonne University
Professional Career . . . . . 1970 - 83 Managing Director, Denholm
　　　　　　　　　　　　　　Maclay Co Ltd
　　　　　　　　　　　　　1975 - 83 Managing Director,
　　　　　　　　　　　　　　Triport Ferries Ltd
　　　　　　　　　　　　　1991 - 93 Marketing Director,
　　　　　　　　　　　　　　Denholm Ship Management Ltd
　　　　　　　　　　　　　1994 - Director, Altnamara Shipping plc
Subject Interests . . . . Shipping
Correspondence Address . . Duchal, Kilmacolm,
　　　　　　　　　　　　　Renfrewshire, PA13 4RS
　　　　　　　　　　　　　Tel: (01505) 822255 Fax: (01505) 873485

MacLehose of Beoch, Baron
(Crawford Murray MacLehose KT, GBE, KGMG, KCVO)

Type of Peerage . . . . Life
Political Allegiance . . . . . Cross Bench
Created 1982
Born . . . . 16th October 1917 in Glasgow

Macleod of Borve, Baroness (Evelyn Hester Macleod)

Type of Peerage . . . . Life
Political Allegiance . . . . . Conservative
Created 1971
Born . . . . 19th February 1915 in Easton, Suffolk
Educated . . . . Lawnside, Malvern
Professional Career . . . . . 1967 Co-Founder, Crisis at Christmas
　　　　　　　　　　　　　1972 - 77 Chairman, National Gas
　　　　　　　　　　　　　　Consumer Council
　　　　　　　　　　　　　1973 - 85 President, National Association of
　　　　　　　　　　　　　　the Leagues of Hospital Friends
　　　　　　　　　　　　　1976 - President, National Association of
　　　　　　　　　　　　　　Widows
Subject Interests . . . . Road safety, Law and order, Music,
　　　　　　　　　　　　　Hospitals
Recreational Interests . . . Gardening
Correspondence Address . . Luckings Farm, Coleshill,
　　　　　　　　　　　　　Amersham, HP7 0LS
　　　　　　　　　　　　　Tel: (01494) 725158

Note: Baroness Macleod is the widow of the former Chancellor of the Exchequer Rt Hon Iain MacLeod.

MEMBERS OF THE HOUSE OF LORDS

McNair, Baron (Duncan James McNair)

Type of Peerage	Hereditary
Political Allegiance	Liberal Democrat
Succeeded	1989
Born	26th June 1947 in London
Educated	Bryanston School, Dorset
	Gloucester Technical College
Professional Career	1994 - Chairman, Unitax Association
	1996 - Chairman, Emission Control Systems UK
	1996 - Member of Executive Committee, Council for Human Rights and Religious Freedom
Subject Interests	Human rights, Religious liberty, Education, Environment, Drug rehabilitation
Correspondence Address	House of Lords, Westminster, London, SW1A 0PW
	Tel: (0171) 219 3227 Fax: (0171) 219 5979
	E-mail: mcnairdj@parliament.uk

McNally, Baron (Tom McNally)

Type of Peerage	Life
Political Allegiance	Liberal Democrat
Entered Lords	1995
Born	20th February 1943 in Thornton, near Blackpool
Professional Career	1966 - 67 Vice President, National Union of Students
	1983 - 84 Public Affairs Adviser, GEC
	1985 - 87 Director General, Retail Consortium
	1987 - 93 Head of Public Affairs, Hill and Knowlton
	1993 - 96 Director, Public Affairs, Shandwick Consultants
	1993 - 96 Head of Public Affairs, Shandwick Consultants
	1996 - Vice Chairman, Shandwick Consultants
Political Career	1966 - 67 Assistant General Secretary, Fabian Society
	1967 - 74 Researcher then (from 1969) International Secretary, Labour Party
	1974 - 76 Political Adviser to the Foreign Secretary (Rt Hon James Callaghan MP)
	1976 - 79 Head of Prime Minister's Political Office, (Rt Hon James Callaghan MP)
	1979 - 83 MP (Labour, then Social Democratic Party) for Stockport South
	1997 - Liberal Democrat Spokesman on Home Affairs, House of Lords
Subject Interests	Tourism, Europe affairs, Foreign affairs, Trade and industry
Recreational Interests	Sport, Political Biographies

Macpherson of Drumochter, Baron (James Gordon Macpherson)

Type of Peerage	Hereditary
Political Allegiance	Conservative
Succeeded	1965
Born	22nd January 1924
Educated	Loretto School
	Wells House, Malvern
Professional Career	1964 - 96 Chairman and Managing Director, Macpherson Train and Co Ltd and associated companies
	1972 - Chairman/Patron, British Importers Confederation
	1973 - Chairman, A J Macpherson and Co Ltd (Bankers)
Subject Interests	Scotland, Landowning, Farming
Recreational Interests	Fishing, Shooting, Bridge, Gardening
Correspondence Address	Kyllachy, Tomatin, Invernessshire, IV13 7YA
	(01808) 511212 Fax: (01808) 511469

Maddock, Baroness (Diana Margaret Maddock)

Type of Peerage	Life
Political Allegiance	Liberal Democrat
Created	1997
Born	19th May 1945 in Croydon
Educated	Brockenhurst Grammar School
	Shenstone College of Education, Bromsgrove
	Portsmouth Polytechnic
Professional Career	1966 - 76 Teacher (Western Park Girls' School Southampton; then Stockholm University and Anglo Continental School of English, Bournemouth)
Political Career	1987 - 93 Member, Southampton City Council
	1993 - 97 MP (Liberal Democrat) for Christchurch
	1993 - 97 Liberal Democrat Spokesman on Housing, Women and Family, House of Lords
Subject Interests	Housing, Local Government, Education, Energy efficiency, Matters relating to older people
Recreational Interests	Travel, Music, Theatre, Reading
Correspondence Address	House of Lords, Westminster, London, SW1A 0PW
	Tel: (0171) 219 5353 Pager: 01399 724676

Mallalieu, Baroness (Ann Mallalieu QC)

Type of Peerage	Life
Political Allegiance	Labour
Created	1991
Born	27th November 1945
Professional Career	Barrister (QC 1988)
	1985 - 93 Recorder
	1993 - Chairman, Independent Council of Ombudsman for Corporate Estate Agents
Political Career	1992 - 97 Opposition Spokesman on Home and Legal Affairs, House of Lords
Recreational Interests	Sheep, Hunting, Horseracing, Poetry

MEMBERS OF THE HOUSE OF LORDS

Malmesbury, Earl of (William James Harris TD)

Type of Peerage	Hereditary
Political Allegiance	Conservative
Succeeded	1950
Born	19th November 1907 in Christchurch
Educated	Eton College
	Trinity College, Cambridge
Professional Career	1936 - Professional Associate, Surveyors
	Institution
	1958 - 64 Personal Liaison Officer to
	Ministry of Agriculture,
	(South East Region)
	1966 - 74 Official Verderer of The New
	Forest
Subject Interests	Agriculture, Forestry, Water, Reserve Forces
Recreational Interests . . .	Sailing, Travelling, Music, Training and
	working labradors
Correspondence Address . .	The Ford, Greywell, Hook,
	Hampshire, RG29 1DS
	Tel: (01256) 703223/702033

Malvern, Viscount (Ashley Kevin Godfrey Higgins)

Type of Peerage	Hereditary
Without Writ of Summons	
Succeeded	1978
Born	26th October 1949

Manchester, Bishop of (Rt Rev Christopher John Mayfield)

Type of Peerage	Bishop
Political Allegiance	None
Entered Lords	1997
Born	18th December 1935
Educated	Sedbergh School
	Gonville and Caius College, Cambridge
	Linacre House, Oxford
Professional Career	1963 - 71 Curate then Lecturer, St Martin
	in-the-Bull Ring, Birmingham
	1967 - 71 Chaplain, Children's Hospital,
	Birmingham
	1971 - 80 Vicar of Luton
	1979 - 85 Archdeacon of Bedford
	1985 - 93 Bishop of Wolverhampton
	1993 - Bishop of Manchester
Correspondence Address . .	Bishopscourt, Bury New Road,
	Manchester, M7 4LE
	Tel: (0161) 792 2096

Manchester, Duke of (Angus Charles Drogo Montagu)

Type of Peerage	Hereditary
Political Allegiance	Cross Bench
Succeeded	1985
Born	9th October 1938

Mancroft, Baron (Benjamin Lloyd Stormont Mancroft)

Type of Peerage	Hereditary
Political Allegiance	Conservative
Succeeded	1987
Born	16th May 1957

Manners, Baron (John Robert Cecil Manners)

Type of Peerage	Hereditary
Political Allegiance	Conservative
Succeeded	1972
Born	13th February 1923
Educated	Eton College
	Trinity College, Oxford
Correspondence Address . .	Sabines, Avon, Christchurch,
	Dorset, BH23 7BQ
	Tel: (01425) 672317

Mansfield, Earl of (William David Mungo James Murray)

Type of Peerage	Hereditary
Political Allegiance	Conservative
Succeeded	1971
Born	7th July 1930 in London
Educated	Eton College
	Christ Church, Oxford
Professional Career	1958 - 71 Barrister
	1985 - 95 First Crown Estate Commissioner
Political Career	1973 - 75 Member, Delegation to the
	European Parliament
	1979 - 83 Minister of State, Scottish Office
	1983 - 84 Minister of State,
	Northern Ireland Office
Correspondence Address . .	Scone Palace, Perth, PH2 6BE
	Tel: (01738) 552308 Fax: (01738) 552588
	16 Thorburn House, Kinnerton Street,
	London SW1X 8EX
	Tel and Fax: (0171) 235 7645
Personal Staff	Mrs Sarah Healy
	(Personal Assistant/Secretary)
	Tel: (01738) 552308

Manton, Baron (Rupert Eric Joseph Robert Watson)

Type of Peerage	Hereditary
Political Allegiance	Conservative
Succeeded	1968
Born	22nd January 1924 in Compton Verney,
	Warwickshire
Educated	Eton College
	Royal Military College, Sandhurst
Professional Career	1942 - 56 Regular Officer, Army
	1963 - 94 York Race Course
	1968 - Member, Jockey Club
	1968 - 75 Member, Horse Race Betting
	Levy Board
	1970 - Director, Thirsk Race Course
	1982 - 85 Senior Steward, Jockey Club
	1985 - 92 Chairman, York Race Committee
Political Career	1962 - 72 Independent District Councillor
Subject Interests	Agriculture, Horseracing and Administration
Recreational Interests . . .	Field sports, Bridge
Correspondence Address . .	Houghton Hall, Sancton,
	Yorkshire, YO4 3RE
	Tel: (01430) 873234

MEMBERS OF THE HOUSE OF LORDS

Mar, Countess of (Margaret of Mar)

Type of Peerage . . . . Hereditary
Political Allegiance . . . . . Cross Bench
Succeeded 1975
Born . . . . 19th September 1940 in Nairobi, Kenya
Educated . . . . County Grammar School for Girls,
Lewes, Sussex
Professional Career . . . . . 1959 - 62 Clerical Officer, Ministry of
Pensions and National Insurance
1963 - 69 Nursing Auxiliary, Bromsgrove
Cottage Hospital
1969 - 82 Sales Superintendent,
Post Office/British Telecom
1985 - Lay Member, Immigration
Appeal Tribunal
Political Career . . . . 1997 - A Deputy Chairman of Committees,
House of Lords
Subject Interests . . . . Toxic chemicals in the environment,
Farming, Health
Recreational Interests . . . Gardening, Goat keeping, Cheese making,
DIY, Reading
Correspondence Address . . St Michael's Farm, Great Witley,
Worcester, WR6 6JB
Tel: (01299) 896608

Mar and Kellie, Earl of (James Thorne Erskine)

Type of Peerage . . . . Hereditary
Political Allegiance . . . . . Liberal Democrat
Succeeded 1993
Born . . . . 10th March 1949 in Edinburgh
Educated . . . . Eton College
Moray House College of Education
Inverness College
Professional Career . . . . . 1971 - 73 Youth and Community Worker,
Edinburgh
1973 - 87 Social Work, (Sheffield then
Grampian and Highland Regions)
1989 - 91 Builder, Kincardine on Forth
1991 - 93 Project Worker, SACRO, Falkirk
1996 Chairman, Strathclyde Tram Inquiry
Subject Interests . . . . National Heritage, Devolution, Social Policy,
Criminal Justice, Public Transport
Recreational Interests . . . Hill walking, Canoeing, Sailing, Railways,
Alloa Tower
Correspondence Address . . Erskine House, Clackmannan,
Scotland, FK10 4JF
Tel and Fax: (01259) 212438
House of Lords, Westminster,
London, SW1A 0PW
Tel: (0171) 219 3563 Fax: (0171) 219 5979

Marchamley, Baron (William Francis Whiteley)

Type of Peerage . . . . Hereditary
Without Writ of Summons
Succeeded 1994
Born . . . . 27th July 1968

Marchwood, Viscount (David George Staveley Penny)

Type of Peerage . . . . Hereditary
Political Allegiance . . . . . Conservative
Succeeded 1979
Born . . . . 22nd May 1936 in London
Educated . . . . Winchester College
Professional Career . . . . . 1958 - 85 Cadbury Schweppes Group
(various positions)
1985 Deputy, then Managing Director,
Moet and Chandon (London) Ltd
(Chairman since 1997)
Subject Interests . . . . Sport, European affairs
Recreational Interests . . . Racing, Cricket, Shooting, Skiing, Real
tennis
Correspondence Address . . 5 Buckingham Mews, London, SW1E 6NR
Tel: (0171) 235 9411 Fax: (0171) 235 6937
Also Tel: (0171) 828 2678
Filberts, Aston Tirrold, Near Didcot,
Oxfordshire, OX11 9DG
Tel: (01235) 850386

Margadale, Baron (James Ian Morrison TD)

Type of Peerage . . . . Hereditary
Political Allegiance . . . . . None
Succeeded 1996
Born . . . . 17th July 1930

Margesson, Viscount (Frances Vere Hampden Margesson)

Type of Peerage . . . . Hereditary
On Leave Of Absence
Succeeded 1965
Born . . . . 17th April 1922

Marks of Broughton, Baron (Michael Marks)

Type of Peerage . . . . Hereditary
Political Allegiance . . . . . Cross Bench
Succeeded 1964
Born . . . . 27th August 1920 in London
Subject Interests . . . . Arts, Environment

Marlborough, Duke of (John George Vanderbilt Henry Spencer Churchill)

Type of Peerage . . . . Hereditary
Political Allegiance . . . . . Conservative
Succeeded 1972
Born . . . . 13th April 1926

MEMBERS OF THE HOUSE OF LORDS

Marlesford, Baron (Mark Shuldham Schreiber)

Type of Peerage .... Life
Political Allegiance ..... Conservative
Created 1991
Born .... 11th September 1931 in London
Educated .... Eton College
Trinity College, Cambridge
Professional Career ..... 1976 - 91 Lobby Correspondent,
The Economist
1991 - Independent Director,
Times Newspaper Holdings
1993 - Chairman, Council for the Protection
of Rural England
Political Career .... 1963 - 70 Conservative Research
Department
1970 - 74 Special Adviser to Government
1974 - 75 Special Adviser to Leader of the
Opposition (Rt Hon Edward Heath MP)
Subject Interests .... Economics, Hong Kong, the Environment,
Countryside, Home Office, and Facilities
for cycling
Recreational Interests ... Chairman, Council for the Protection of
Rural England
Correspondence Address .. House of Lords, Westminster,
London, SW1A 0PW
Tel: (0171) 219 5480 Fax: (0171) 219 5979

Marsh of Mannington, Baron (Rt Hon Richard William Marsh)

Type of Peerage .... Life
Political Allegiance ..... Cross Bench
Created 1980
Born .... 14th March 1928 in Swindon, Wiltshire
Educated .... Ruskin College, Oxford
Professional Career ..... 1970 - 75 Chairman, British Railways Board
1975 - 88 Chairman, Newspaper Publishers
Association
1977 - 81 Chairman, Allied Medical Group
1980 - 84 Deputy Chairman, then Chairman,
TV AM
1986 - Chairman, Laurention Financial
Services Group
1990 - Chairman, China and Eastern
Investment Trust
Political Career .... 1959 - 71 MP (Labour) for Greenwich
1964 - 65 Parliamentary Secretary,
Ministry of Labour
1965 - 66 Parliamentary Secretary,
Ministry of Technology
1966 - 68 Minister of Power
1968 - 69 Minister of Transport
Subject Interests .... Financial services, Pensions, the
Far East
Correspondence Address .. House of Lords, Westminster,
London, SW1A 0PW
Tel: (0171) 834 8770

Martonmere, Baron (John Stephen Robinson)

Type of Peerage .... Hereditary
Political Allegiance ..... Cross Bench
Succeeded 1989
Born .... 19th July 1963

Masham of Ilton, Baroness (Susan Lilian Primrose Swinton)

Type of Peerage .... Life
Political Allegiance ..... Cross Bench
Created 1970
Born .... 14th April 1935 in Lyth, Caithness, Scotland
Educated .... Heathfield School, Ascot
London Polytechnic
Professional Career ..... Voluntary Social Work
1963 - 88 President, Red Cross Society
1963 - 94 Board Member, Wetherby Young
Offenders Institution
1973 - 85 Member, Peterlee and Newton
Aycliffe New Town Corporation
1975 - 82 President, Chartered Society of
Physiotherapy
1982 - 90 Member, Yorkshire Regional
Health Authority
1990 - 96 Member, North Yorkshire, FHSA
Subject Interests .... Health, Disability, AIDS, Drug Abuse,
Penal Affairs
Recreational Interests ... Breeding Highland Ponies, Swimming,
Gardening
Correspondence Address .. Dykes Hill House, Masham, Ripon, North
Yorkshire, HG4 4NS
Tel: (01765) 689241 Fax: (01765) 689596
46 Westminster Gardens, Marsham Street,
London, SW1P 4JG
Tel: (0171) 834 0700 Fax: (0171) 834 6126
E-mail flat46@westgard.co.uk
Personal Staff .... Mrs Sally Craig *(Secretary)*
Tel: (01765) 689241
*Note: Baroness Masham is married to the Earl of Swinton, but holds the
life peerage in her own right.*

Mason of Barnsley, Baron (Rt Hon Roy Mason)

Type of Peerage .... Life
Political Allegiance ..... Labour
Created 1987
Born .... 18th July 1924 in Royston, Yorkshire
Educated .... Carlton and Royston Elementary Schools
London School of Economics
Professional Career ..... 1938 - 53 Miner
1989 - 92 Member, National Rivers
Authority
Political Career .... 1953 - 87 MP (Labour) for Barnsley, then
Barnsley Central
1960 - 64 Opposition Spokesman on
Defence and Post Office
1964 - 67 Minister of State (Shipping),
Board of Trade
1967 - 68 Minister for Defence Equipment,
Ministry of Defence
1968 Postmaster General
1968 - 69 Minister of Power
1969 - 70 President of the Board of Trade
1970 - 74 Opposition Spokesman on Trade,
House of Commons
1974 - 76 Secretary of State for Defence
1976 - 79 Secretary of State for Northern
Ireland
1979 - 81 Opposition Spokesman on
Agriculture, House of Commons
Subject Interests .... Coal industry, Human rights, Northern
Ireland, Defence, Pollution
Recreational Interests ... Fly fishing, Golf, Tie designing, Philately

MEMBERS OF THE HOUSE OF LORDS

Massereene and Ferrard, Viscount
(John David Clotworthy Whyte-Melville Foster Skeffington)

Type of Peerage	Hereditary
Political Allegiance.....	Conservative
Succeeded...........	1993
Born...............	3rd June 1940 in Devon
Educated	Millfield School
	Institute Monte Rosa
Professional Career.....	1961 - 64 1970 - Stockbroker
	1964 - 70 Motor Trade
Subject Interests.......	Industry, Field sports, European Union
Recreational Interests ...	Shooting, Stalking, Vintage cars

May, Baron (Michael St John May)

Type of Peerage	Hereditary
Political Allegiance.....	Conservative
Succeeded...........	1950 (as a minor)
Born...............	26th September 1931

Mayhew of Twysden, Rt Hon Baron
(Patrick Barnabas Burke Mayhew QC)

Type of Peerage	Life
Political Allegiance.....	Conservative
Created.............	1997
Born...............	11th September 1929 in Cookham, Berkshire
Educated	Tonbridge School
	Balliol College, Oxford
Professional Career.....	1955 - Barrister (QC 1972)
Political Career.......	1974 - 97 MP (Conservative) for
	Tunbridge Wells
	1979 - 81 Parliamentary Secretary,
	Department of Employment
	1981 - 83 Minister of State, Home Office
	1983 - 87 Solicitor General
	1987 - 92 Attorney General
	1992 - 97 Secretary of State for
	Northern Ireland

Meath, Earl of (Anthony Windham Normand Brabazon)

Type of Peerage	Hereditary
On Leave Of Absence	
Succeeded...........	1949
Born...............	3rd November 1910 in London
Educated	Eton College
	Royal Military Academy, Sandhurst
Professional Career.....	Farmer and Forester, Killruddery Estate
Subject Interests.......	Farming, Forestry
Recreational Interests ...	Fishing
Correspondence Address..	Killruddery, Bray, Co Wicklow,Ireland

Melchett, Baron (Peter Robert Henry Mond)

Type of Peerage	Hereditary
On Leave of Absence	
Succeeded...........	1973
Born...............	24th February 1948 in London
Educated	Eton College
	Pembroke College, Cambridge
	Keele University
Professional Career.....	1975 - 76 Chairman, Working Party on
	Pop Festivals
	1979 - 85 Chairman, Community Industry
	1979 - 87 Chairman, Wildlife Link
	1981 - 84 President, Ramblers Association
	1986 - 88 Chairman, Greenpeace UK
	1989 - Executive Director, Greenpeace UK
	1995 - Chairman, Greenpeace Japan
Political Career.......	1974 - 75 Government Whip, (Lord in
	Waiting)
	1975 - 76 Parliamentary Secretary,
	Department of Industry
	1976 - 79 Minister of State,
	Northern Ireland Office
Subject Interests.......	Environment, Animal rights, Countryside
Correspondence Address..	House of Lords, Westminster,
	London, SW1A 0PW
	Tel: (0171) 865 8161

Mellish, Rt Hon Baron (Rt Hon Robert Joseph Mellish)

Type of Peerage	Life
Political Allegiance.....	None
Created.............	1985
Born...............	March 1913
Professional Career.....	1938 - 46 Official, Transport and General
	Workers Union
	1981 - 85 Deputy Chairman, London
	Dockland Development Corporation
Political Career.......	1946 - 82 MP (Labour then Independent)
	Bermondsey, then Rotherhithe, then
	Southwark Bermondsey
	1964 - 67 Parliamentary Secretary,
	Ministry of Housing and Local
	Government
	1967 - 69 Minister of Public
	Building and Works
	1969 - 70, 1974 - 76 Government
	Chief Whip, House of Commons
	1970 - 74 Opposition Chief Whip,
	House of Commons

Melville, Viscount (Robert David Ross Dundas)

Type of Peerage	Hereditary
Political Allegiance.....	Conservative
Succeeded...........	1972
Born...............	28th May 1937 in Melville Castle, Lasswade,
	Midlothain
Educated	Wellington College, Berkshire
Recreational Interests ...	Golf, Chess, Fishing
Correspondence Address..	Wey House, Norton Fitzwarren, Taunton,
	Somerset, TA4 1BT
	Tel: (01823) 337391

MEMBERS OF THE HOUSE OF LORDS

Menuhin, Baron (Yehudi Menuhin OM, KBE)
Type of Peerage .... Life
Political Allegiance..... Cross Bench
Created.............. 1993
Born............... 22nd April 1916 in New York
Educated .... Private
Professional Career..... 1950 - Violinist and Conductor
Subject Interests........ Music, Education, Human rights and
responsibilities
Correspondence Address.. SYM Music Co Ltd, PO Box 6160,
London, SW1W 0XJ
Personal Staff........ Mrs Vera Lamport *(Private Secretary)*

Merlyn-Rees, Baron (Rt Hon Merlyn Merlyn-Rees)
Type of Peerage .... Life
Political Allegiance..... Labour
Created.............. 1992
Born............... 18th December 1920 in Cilfynydd, Mid
Glamorgan
Educated .... Harrow Weald Grammar School
Goldsmiths College, University of London
London School of Economics
Professional Career..... 1949 - 60 Teacher, Harrow Weald Grammar
School
1961 - 63 Lecturer, Luton College of
Technology
1990 - President, Video Standards Council
1993 - Director, Leeds City Development
Corporation
1994 - Chancellor, University of Glamorgan
Political Career........ 1963 - 92 MP (Labour) for Leeds South
1964 PPS to Chancellor of Exchequer
(Rt Hon James Callaghan MP)
1965 - 68 Parliamentary Secretary,
Ministry of Defence
1968 - 70 Parliamentary Secretary,
Home Office
1972 - 74 Opposition Spokesman on
Northern Ireland, House of Commons
1974 - 76 Secretary of State for
Northern Ireland
1976 - 79 Home Secretary
1979 - 83 Opposition Spokesman on
Home Affairs, then Energy,
House of Commons
Subject Interests........ Home affairs, Northern Ireland, Education
Recreational Interests ... Reading

Merrivale, Baron (John Henry Edmond Duke)
Type of Peerage .... Hereditary
Political Allegiance..... Conservative
Succeeded........... 1951
Born............... 27th January 1917

Mersey, Viscount (Richard Maume Clive Bigham)
Type of Peerage .... Hereditary
Political Allegiance..... Conservative
Succeeded........... 1979
Born............... 8th July 1934

Meston, Baron (James Meston QC)
Type of Peerage .... Hereditary
Political Allegiance..... Liberal Democrat
Succeeded........... 1984
Born............... 10th February 1950 in Berkshire
Educated .... Wellington College
St Catharine's College, Cambridge
Leicester University
Professional Career..... 1973 - Barrister (QC 1996)
1997 - Recorder
Subject Interests........ Law, Family, Children
Correspondence Address.. Queen Elizabeth Building, Temple,
London, EC4Y 9BS
Tel: (0171) 797 7837

Methuen, Baron (Robert Alexander Holt Methuen)
Type of Peerage .... Hereditary
Political Allegiance..... Liberal Democrat
Succeeded........... 1964
Born............... 22nd July 1931 in Corsham, Wiltshire
Educated .... Shrewsbury School
Trinity College, Cambridge
Professional Career..... 1957 - 94 Electrical Engineer
(Westinghouse, then IBM and
Rolls-Royce)
Subject Interests........ Industrial archaeology, Transport,
Information Technology, Arts
Recreational Interests ... Horse Riding, Walking

Middleton, Baron (Michael Willoughby MC)
Type of Peerage .... Hereditary
Political Allegiance..... Conservative
Succeeded........... 1970
Born............... 1st May 1921 in Settrington,
Nr Malton, Yorkshire
Educated .... Eton College
Trinity College, Cambridge
Political Career........ 1989 - 96 Chairman, European Communities
Sub-Committee on Agriculture, Fisheries
and Food, House of Lords
Subject Interests........ Agriculture, Countryside, Local government,
Defence, European Union
Correspondence Address.. Birdsall House, Malton,
North Yorkshire, YO17 9NR
Tel: (01944) 768206

Midleton, Viscount (Alan Henry Brodrick)
Type of Peerage .... Hereditary
Political Allegiance..... Cross Bench
Succeeded........... 1989
Born............... 4th August 1949

Milford, Baron (Hugo John Laurence Philipps)
Type of Peerage .... Hereditary
On Leave of Absence
Succeeded........... 1993
Born............... 27th August 1929

Milford Haven, Marquess of (George Ivor Louis Mountbatten)
Type of Peerage .... Hereditary
Political Allegiance..... Conservative
Succeeded........... 1970 (as a minor)
Born............... 6th June 1961

MEMBERS OF THE HOUSE OF LORDS

Miller of Hendon, Baroness (Doreen Miller MBE)

Type of Peerage	Life
Political Allegiance	Conservative
Created	1993
Born	13th June 1933 in London
Educated	Brondesbury and Kilburn High School
	London School of Economics
Professional Career	1970 - Justice of the Peace
	1971 - 88 Chairman and Managing Director,
	Universal Beauty Club Ltd
	1985 - 88 Chairman and Executive Director,
	the 300 Group
	1987 - Chairman, Women Into Public Life
	Campaign
	1990 - 94 Crown Agent
	1990 - 94 Chairman, Barnet Family Health
	Services Authority
	1997 - Chairman, National Association of
	Leagues of Hospital Friends
Political Career	1994 -97 Government Whip,
	(Baroness in Waiting)
	1997 - Opposition Whip, House of Lords
Subject Interests	Women's interests, Law and order, Health,
	Small businesses
Recreational interests	Reading, Football, Politics
Personal Staff	Mrs Cynthia Brown *(Secretary)*
	Tel: (0171) 935 3876

Mills, Viscount (Christopher Philip Roger Mills)

Type of Peerage	Hereditary
Political Allegiance	Conservative
Succeeded	1988
Born	20th May 1956
Professional Career	1980 - 89 Biologist, Salmon Research Trust
	of Ireland
	1989 - 96 National Rivers Authority
	(Technical Assistant, then Manager, North
	West Area and Thames Area)
	1996 - Area Manager, Environment Agency
	(Thames Region)
Subject Interests	Environment, Fisheries
Recreational Interests	Fly fishing, Antiques, Wine

Milne, Baron (Rt Hon George Douglas Milne TD)

Type of Peerage	Hereditary
Political Allegiance	Cross Bench
Succeeded	1948
Born	10th February 1909 in Lichfield
Educated	Winchester College
	New College, Oxford
Professional Career	Chartered Accountant
	1954 - 73 Partner, Arthur Young,
	McClelland Moore and Co
	1973 - 87 Director, London and Northern
	Group plc (Deputy Chairman 1981)
Subject Interests	Company law and affairs, Economics,
	European Union
Recreational Interests	Art, Golf
Correspondence Address	33 Lonsdale Road, Barnes,
	London, SW13 9JP
	Tel: (0181) 748 6421

Milner of Leeds, Baron (Arthur James Michael Milner)

Type of Peerage	Hereditary
Political Allegiance	Labour
Succeeded	1967
Born	12th September 1923
Political Career	1971 - 74 Opposition Whip, House of Lords

Milverton, Baron (Rev Fraser Arthur Richard Richards)

Type of Peerage	Hereditary
Political Allegiance	Conservative
Succeeded	1978
Born	21st July 1930
Professional Career	1959 Curate, St George, Beckenham
	1959 - 60 Curate, St John the Baptist,
	Sevenoaks
	1960 - 63 Curate, St Nicholas,
	Great Bookham
	1963 - 67 Vicar, Okewood with Forest Green
	1967 - 93 Rector, Christian Malford with
	Sutton Berger and Tytherton Kellaways

Minto, Earl of (Gilbert Edward George Lariston Elliot-Murray-Kynynmound OBE)

Type of Peerage	Hereditary
Political Allegiance	Cross Bench
Succeeded	1975
Born	19th June 1928

Mishcon, Baron (Victor Mishcon)

Type of Peerage	Life
Political Allegiance	Labour
Created	1978
Born	14th August 1915 in London
Educated	City of London School
Professional Career	Solicitor
	1937 - 92 Senior Partner, Victor Mishcon
	and Co, then Misdicon de Reya
	(Consultant since 1992)
Political Career	1983 - 92 Opposition Spokesman on
	Home Affairs and Legal Affairs
Subject Interests	Legal affairs, Home affairs
Recreational Interests	Theatre, Music
Correspondence Address	House of Lords, Westminster,
	London, SW1A 0PW
	Fax: (0171) 404 2371

Molloy, Baron (William John Molloy)

Type of Peerage	Life
Political Allegiance	Labour
Created	1981
Born	26th October 1918
Educated	University College of Wales, Swansea
Professional Career	1947 - 52 Editor, Civil Service Review
Political Career	1954 - 66 Member, Fulham Borough Council
	(Leader 1959 - 62), then Hammersmith
	and Fulham Council
	1964 - 79 MP (Labour) for Ealing North
	1976 - 79 Member of the European
	Parliament

MEMBERS OF THE HOUSE OF LORDS

Molyneaux of Killead, Baron
(Rt Hon James Henry Molyneaux KBE)

Type of Peerage . . . . Life
Political Allegiance . . . . . Cross Bench
Created 1997
Born . . . . 27th August 1920 in Crumlin,
County Antrim
Educated . . . . Aldergrove School
Political Career . . . . 1970 - 97 MP (Ulster Unionist) for Antrim
South, then Lagan Valley
1979 - 95 Leader, Ulster Unionist Party
Subject Interests . . . . Mental health, Housing, Local government
Recreational Interests . . . Gardening, Music
Correspondence Address . . House of Lords, Westminster,
London, SW1A 0PW
41 Ballynadrentagh Road, Crumlin, County
Antrim, Northern Ireland, BT29 4AR
Tel: (01849) 422545

Monck, Viscount (Charles Stanley Monck)

Type of Peerage . . . . Hereditary
Without Writ of Summons
Succeeded 1982
Note: The above mentioned peer does not use his title.

Monckton of Brenchley, Viscount (Major-General
Gilbert Walter Riversdale Monckton CB, OBE, MC)

Type of Peerage . . . . Hereditary
Political Allegiance . . . . . Cross Bench
Succeeded 1965
Born . . . . 3rd November 1915 in Kent
Educated . . . . Harrow School
Trinity College, Cambridge
Professional Career . . . . . 1939 - 67 Army Officer
1963 - 65 Chief of Staff HQ, British Army on
the Rhine
Recreational Interests . . . Archaeology
Correspondence Address . . Runhams Farm, Harrietsham, Maidstone,
Kent, ME17 1NJ
Tel: (01622) 850313

Moncreiff, Baron (Harry Robert Wellwood Moncreiff)

Type of Peerage . . . . Hereditary
Succeeded 1942
On Leave of Absence
Born . . . . 4th February 1915

Monk Bretton, Baron (John Charles Dodson)

Type of Peerage . . . . Hereditary
Political Allegiance . . . . . Conservative
Succeeded . . . . 1933 (as a minor)
Born . . . . 17th July 1924

Monkswell, Baron (Gerard Collier)

Type of Peerage . . . . Hereditary
Political Allegiance . . . . . Labour
Succeeded 1984
Born . . . . 28th January 1947 in London
Educated . . . . George Heriots School, Edinburgh
North East Essex Technical College and
School of Art, Colchester
Portsmouth Polytechnic
Slough College of Technology
Professional Career . . . . . 1972 - 89 Product Quality Engineer, then
Service Administration Manager, Massey
Ferguson
Political Career . . . . 1989 - 94 Member, Manchester City Council
Recreational Interests . . . Swimming, Reading, Movies
Correspondence Address . . House of Lords, Westminster,
London, SW1A 0PW
Tel: (0171) 219 3455
Also Tel: (0171) 793 1082 / (0161) 881 3887

Monro, Baron (Rt Hon Hector Seymour Peter Monro)

Type of Peerage . . . . Life
Political Allegiance . . . . . Conservative
Created 1997
Born . . . . 4th October 1922 in Edinburgh
Educated . . . . Canford School
King's College, Cambridge
Professional Career . . . . . 1941 - 54 Royal Air Force, then Royal
Auxiliary Air Force
1976 - 77 President, Scottish Rugby Union
1984 - 90 President, Auto Cycle Union
1985 - 92 President, National Small Bore
Rifle Association
Political Career . . . . 1964 - 97 MP (Conservative) for Dumfries
1966 - 70 Opposition Whip,
House of Commons
1970 - 71 Government Whip,
House of Commons
1971 - 74 Parliamentary Secretary, Scottish
Office (Minister of Health and Education)
1974 - 79 Opposition Spokesman on Sport
1979 - 81 Parliamentary Secretary,
Department of Environment (with
responsibility for Sport)
1992 - 95 Parliamentary Secretary, Scottish
Office (Minister of Agriculture and
Environment)
Subject Interests . . . . Scotland, Sport, Agriculture, Defence,
Aviation
Recreational Interests . . . Country sports, Golf, Rugby, Vintage Cars,
Flying
Correspondence Address . . Williamwood, Kirtlebridge,
Lockerbie, DG11 3LN
Tel: (01461) 500213

Monson, Baron (John Monson)

Type of Peerage . . . . Hereditary
Political Allegiance . . . . . Cross Bench
Succeeded 1958
Born . . . . 3rd May 1932

MEMBERS OF THE HOUSE OF LORDS

Montagu of Beaulieu, Baron
(Edward John Barrington Douglas-Scott-Montagu)

Type of Peerage .... Hereditary
Political Allegiance ..... Conservative
Succeeded .... 1929 (as a minor)
Born .... 20th October 1926 in London
Educated .... Eton College
New College, Oxford
Professional Career ..... 1952 - Founder, Montagu Motor Museum
(National Motor Museum from 1972)
1956 - 79 Editor and Publisher, Veteran and
Vintage Magazine
1973 - 78 Founder President, Historic
Houses Associations
1978 - 81 President, European Union of
Historic House Associations
1980 - 83 President, Fédération
Internationale des Véhicules Anciens
1982 - 84 President, Museums Association
1983 - 92 Chairman, Historic Buildings and
Monuments Commission (English
Heritage)
1994 - Chairman, British Educational Travel
Trust
President, Federation of British Historic
Vehicle Clubs, Historic Commercial
Vehicle Society and Disabled Drivers
Motor Club
Subject Interests .... Tourism, Motoring and transport,
Environment
Correspondence Address .. Palace House, Beaulieu,
Hampshire, SO42 7ZN
Tel: (01590) 612345 Fax: (01590) 612623
Flat 11, Wyndham House, 24 Bryanston
Square, London, W1H 7FJ
Tel: (0171) 262 2603 Fax; (0171) 724 3262
Personal Staff .... Mrs Jill Lindemere *(Personal Assistant)*
Tel: (01590) 612345

Montagu of Oxford, Rt Hon Baron
(Michael Jacob Montague CBE)

Type of Peerage .... Life
Political Allegiance ..... Labour
Succeeded 1997
Born .... 10th March 1932 in London
Educated .... High Wycombe Royal Grammar School
Magdalen College School, Oxford
Professional Career ..... 1959 Founder, Gatehill Beco Ltd
1965 - 91 Chairman, Valor
(from 1987 Yale and Valor)
1967 Founder, Hospitality Hotels
(Cyprus, Hawaii)
1979 - 84 Chairman, English Tourist Board
1983 - 85 President, British Association of
Industrial Editors
1984 - 87 Chairman, National Consumer
Council
1991 - 93 Chairman, Henley Festival Ltd
1992 Chairman, Montague Multinational Ltd
(from 1997 Acorn Assets Ltd)
1995 Chairman, Superframe plc
1994 - 97 Member, Millennium Commission
Correspondence Address .. House of Lords, Westminster,
London, SW1A 0PW
Tel: (0181) 575 8484 Fax: (0181) 575 0622
Personal Staff .... Mrs Jeanne Poole *(Personal Assistant)*

Monteagle of Brandon, Baron (Gerald Spring Rice)

Type of Peerage .... Hereditary
Political Allegiance ..... Conservative
Succeeded 1946
Born .... 5th July 1926

Montgomery of Alamein, Viscount
(David Bernard Montgomery CBE)

Type of Peerage .... Hereditary
Political Allegiance ..... Conservative
Succeeded 1976
Born .... 18th August 1928 in Camberley, Surrey
Educated .... Winchester College
Trinity College, Cambridge
Professional Career ..... 1950 - 62 Manager, Shell International
1962 - 74 Director, Yardley International
1974 - Managing Director, Terimar Services
(Overseas Trade Consultancy)
Political Career .... 1992 - Representative, Parliamentary
Assembly, Organisation for Security and
Co-operation in Europe
Subject Interests .... Latin America, Consumer affairs
Correspondence Address .. 54 Cadogan Square, London, SW1X 0JW
Tel: (0171) 589 8747 Fax: (0171) 589 5020

Montrose, Duke of (James Graham)

Type of Peerage .... Hereditary
Political Allegiance ..... Conservative
Succeeded 1992
Born .... 6th April 1935 in Salisbury, Rhodesia
Subject Interests .... Agriculture, Environment, Europe,
Commonwealth

Moore of Lower Marsh, Baron
(Rt Hon John Edward Michael Moore)

Type of Peerage .... Life
Political Allegiance ..... Conservative
Created 1992
Born .... 26th November 1937
Educated .... London School of Economics
Professional Career ..... 1961 - 65 Banking and Stockbroking,
Chicago
1975 - 79 Chairman, Dean Witter
International
1990 - Chairman, Monitor Europe
1991 - Chairman, Credit Suisse Asset
Management
Political Career .... 1971 - 74 Councillor, London Borough of
Merton
1974 - 92 MP (Conservative) for Croydon
Central
1975 - 79 Vice Chairman,
Conservative Party
1979 -83 Parliamentary Secretary,
Department of Energy
1983 - 86 Economic Secretary, then
Financial Secretary, HM Treasury
1986 - 87 Secretary of State for Transport
1987 - 88 Secretary of State for Social
Services
1988 - 89 Secretary of State for Social
Security

MEMBERS OF THE HOUSE OF LORDS

Moore of Wolvercote, Baron
(Rt Hon Philip Brian Cecil Moore GCB, GCVO, CMG)

Type of Peerage	Life
Political Allegiance	Cross Bench
Created	1986
Born	6th April 1921 in Lucknow, India
Professional Career	1940 - 45 RAF, Bomber Command
	1947 - 60 Home Civil Service, Admiralty
	1960 - 65 Deputy UK High Commissioner, Singapore
	1965 - 66 Chief of Public Relations, Ministry of Defence
	1966 - 77 Assistant, then (from 1972) Deputy Private Secretary to HM the Queen
	1977 - 86 Private Secretary to HM the Queen
Subject Interests	Defence, Education, Churches, Foreign and Commonwealth affairs

Moran, Baron (Richard John McMoran Wilson KCMG)

Type of Peerage	Hereditary
Political Allegiance	Cross Bench
Succeeded	1977
Born	22nd September 1924 in London
Educated	Eton College
	King's College, Cambridge
Professional Career	1943 - 45 RNVR
	1945 - 84 HM Diplomatic Service
	1965 - 68 Counsellor, British Embassy, South Africa
	1968 - 73 Head of West Africa Department, Foreign and Commonwealth Office
	1973 - 76 Ambassador to Hungary
	1976 - 81 Ambassador to Portugal
	1981 - 84 High Commissioner to Canada
	1988 - 95 Vice Chairman, Atlantic Salmon Trust
	1992 - 95 Chairman, Wildlife and Countryside Link
Subject Interests	Conservation, Fisheries, Europe

Moray, Earl (Douglas John Stuart)

Type of Peerage	Hereditary
Political Allegiance	Conservative
Succeeded	1974
Born	13th February 1928 in South Africa
Educated	Hilton College, Natal
	Trinity College, Cambridge
Professional Career	1974 - Chairman and Director, Moray Estates Development Co Ltd
Subject Interests	Agriculture, Forestry
Recreational Interests	Vintage and Classic Cars
Correspondence Address	Doune Park, Doune, Perthshire, FK16 6HA
	Tel: (01786) 841333

Morley, Earl of (John St Aubyn Parker)

Type of Peerage	Hereditary
Political Allegiance	Conservative
Succeeded	1962
Born	29th May 1923 in London
Educated	Eton College
Professional Career	1942 - 67 Officer, Armed Forces
	1970 - 96 Farmer and Company Director

Morris, Baron (Michael David Morris)

Type of Peerage	Hereditary
Without Writ of Summons	
Succeeded	1975
Born	9th December 1937

Morris of Castle Morris, Baron (Brian Robert Morris)

Type of Peerage	Life
Political Allegiance	Labour
Created	1990
Born	4th December 1930 in Cardiff
Educated	Cardiff High School
	Worcester College, Oxford
Professional Career	1958 - 65 Lecturer, University of Reading
	1965 - 71 Lecturer, then Senior Lecturer, University of York
	1971 - 80 Professor of English Literature, Sheffield University
	1985 - 90 Chairman, Museums and Galleries Commission
	1993 - Chairman of Council, Prince of Wales Institute of Architecture
	1993 - Vice Chairman of Trustees, National Portrait Gallery
Political Career	1992 - 97 Opposition Deputy Chief Whip, House of Lords (also Spokesman on Education)
Subject Interests	Education and Culture (especially Higher Education, Museums and Galleries), Media, Sport
Recreational Interests	Music, Mountains, Museums
Correspondence Address	House of Lords, Westminster, London, SW1A 0PW
	Tel: (0171) 219 4414 Fax: (0171) 219 5979
	The Old Hall, Foolow, Hope Valley, Derbyshire, S32 5QR
	Tel and Fax: (01433) 631186
Personal Staff	Ms Corinne Brown *(Secretary)*
	Tel: (0171) 916 7580

Morris of Kenwood, Baron (Philip Geoffrey Morris))

Type of Peerage	Hereditary
Political Allegiance	Cross Bench
Succeeded	1954
Born	18th June 1928 in Sheffield
Educated	Loughborough College
Professional Career	Company Director (Retired)
	1967 - 98 Justice of the Peace
Recreational Interests	Golf
Correspondence Address	35 Fitzjohns Avenue, London, NW3 5JY
	Tel: (0171) 431 6332

MEMBERS OF THE HOUSE OF LORDS

Morris of Manchester, Baron (Rt Hon Alfred Morris)

Type of Peerage . . . . Life
Political Allegiance . . . . . Labour
Created 1997
Born . . . . 23rd March 1928
Educated . . . . Ruskin College, Oxford
                St Catherine's College, Oxford
                University of Manchester
Professional Career . . . . . 1954 - 56 Teacher and Lecturer, Manchester
                1956 - 64 Industrial Relations Officer,
                Electricity Supply Industry
Political Career . . . . 1964 - 97 MP (Labour and Co-op) for
                Manchester Wythenshaw
                1964 - 67 PPS to Minister of Agriculture,
                Fisheries and Food
                1968 - 70 PPS to Leader of the
                House of Commons
                1970 - 74 Opposition Spokesman on
                Social Services
                1974 - 79 Parliamentary Secretary,
                Department of Health and Social Security
                (Minister for the Disabled)
                1979 - 92 Opposition Spokesman for the
                Disabled
Subject Interests . . . . Disablement, Co-operative movement,
                Regional development, Airports, Technology
Recreational Interests . . . Tennis, Gardening, Chess, Snooker
Correspondence Address . . 20 Hitherwood Drive,
                London, SE19 1XB
                Tel: (0171) 219 5353 Fax: (0181) 670 6259
                Also Tel: (0171) 219 5353

Morton, Earl of (John Charles Sholto Douglas)

Type of Peerage . . . . Hereditary
Political Allegiance . . . . . Cross Bench
Succeeded 1976
Born . . . . 19th March 1927

Mostyn, Baron (Roger Edward Lloyd Lloyd-Mostyn MC)

Type of Peerage . . . . Hereditary
Political Allegiance . . . . . Conservative
Succeeded 1965
Born . . . . 17th April 1920 in London
Educated . . . . Eton College
                Royal Military Academy, Sandhurst
Correspondence Address . . Mostyn Hall, Mostyn, Flintshire,
                North Wales, CH8 9HN
                Tel: (01745) 560222

Mottistone, Baron (Captain David Peter Seely CBE)

Type of Peerage . . . . Hereditary
Political Allegiance . . . . . Conservative
Succeeded 1966
Born . . . . 16th December 1920 in London
Educated . . . . Royal Naval College, Dartmouth
Professional Career . . . . . 1941 - 67 Officer, Royal Navy
                1967 - 69 Director, Personnel and Training,
                Radio Rentals
                1969 - 75 Director, Distribution Industry
                Training Board
                1975 - 81 Director, Cake and Biscuit
                Alliance
                1981 - 83 Export Secretary, Biscuit, Cake,
                Chocolate and Confectionery Alliance
                1986 - 95 Lord Lieutenant, Isle of Wight
Subject Interests . . . . Isle of Wight, Food Processing, Industry,
                Electronics Industry, Mental Illness
Recreational Interests . . . Yachting
Correspondence Address . . The Old Parsonage, Mottistone,
                Isle of Wight, PO30 4EE
                Tel and Fax: (01983) 740264
                103 Collingwood House, Dolphin Square,
                London, SW1V 3NG
                Tel: (0171) 834 3712

Mount Edgcumbe, Earl of (Robert Charles Edgcumbe)

Type of Peerage . . . . Hereditary
Political Allegiance . . . . . Cross Bench
Succeeded 1982
Born . . . . 1st June 1939 in New Zealand
Educated . . . . Nelson College
Professional Career . . . . . 1960 - 82 Farm Manager
Subject Interests . . . . Farming
Recreational Interests . . . Classic and American cars
Correspondence Address . . Empacombe House, Cremyll, Mount
                Edgcumbe, Cornwall, PL10 0HZ
                Tel: (01752) 822311 Fax: (01752) 823379

Mountbatten of Burma, Countess
    (Patricia Edwina Victoria Knatchbull CBE)

Type of Peerage . . . . Hereditary
Political Allegiance . . . . . Cross Bench
Succeeded 1979
Born . . . . 14th February 1924 in London
Educated . . . . PNEU School, London
                New York City
Professional Career . . . . . 1971 - 97 Justice of the Peace
                1984 - Vice Lord Lieutenant, Kent
                Chairman, Sir Ernest Cassel Educational
                Trust
                Vice President of British Red Cross Society
                Chairman, Edwina Mountbatten Trust
Subject Interests . . . . Children, Penal reform
Correspondence Address . . Newhouse, Mersham, Ashford,
                Kent, TN25 6NQ
                Tel: (01233) 503636

Mountevans, Baron (Edward Patrick Broke Evans)

Type of Peerage . . . . Hereditary
Political Allegiance . . . . . Conservative
Succeeded 1974
Born . . . . 1st February 1943

MEMBERS OF THE HOUSE OF LORDS

Mountgarret, Viscount (Richard Henry Piers Butler)
Type of Peerage .... Hereditary
Political Allegiance ..... Conservative
Succeeded 1966
Born .... 8th November 1936

Mowbray and Stourton, Baron
(Charles Edward Stourton CBE)
Type of Peerage .... Hereditary
Political Allegiance ..... Conservative
Succeeded 1965
Born .... 11th March 1923

Moyne, Baron (Jonathan Bryan Guinness)
Type of Peerage .... Hereditary
Political Allegiance ..... Conservative
Succeeded 1992
Born .... 16th March 1930

Moynihan, Baron (Colin Berkeley Moynihan)
Type of Peerage .... Hereditary
Political Allegiance ..... Conservative
Succeeded 1997
Born .... 13th September 1955 in Ashtead, Surrey
Educated .... Monmouth School
University College, Oxford
Brasenose College, Oxford
Professional Career ..... 1977 - 83 Tate and Lyle Ltd (Assistant to
Chairman, then Marketing Development
Manager)
1982 - 87 Chief Executive, then Chairman,
Ridgways Tea and Coffee Merchants
1993 - Founding Partner, Colin Moynihan
Associates
1996 - Managing Director, Independent
Power Corporation
Political Career .... 1983 - 92 MP (Conservative) for
Lewisham East
1987 - 90 Parliamentary Secretary,
Department of Environment (Minister
for Sport)
1990 - 92 Parliamentary Secretary,
Department of Energy
1997 - Opposition Spokesman on Foreign
Affairs, House of Lords
Subject Interests .... Foreign affairs, Disabled Sport
Correspondence Address .. Prince Consort House, 27-29 Albert
Embankment, London, JE1 7TJ
Tel: (0171) 793 9595 Fax: (0171) 793 8777
E-mail: ipc.cma@dircon.co.uk
House of Lords, Westminster,
London, SW1A 0PW
Personal Staff .... Mrs Debbie Hornblo *(Personal Assistant)*

Moyola of Castledawson, Baron
(Rt Hon James Dawson Chichester-Clark)
Type of Peerage .... Life
Has Not Taken The Oath
Created 1971
Born .... 12th February 1923 in Castle Dawson,
Co Londonderry
Educated .... Eton College
Political Career .... 1960 - 73 MP (Unionist) for South Derry,
Northern Ireland Parliament
1963 - 68 Unionist Chief Whip,
Northern Ireland Parliament
1966 - 67 Leader of the House, Northern
Ireland Parliament
1967 - 69 Minister of Agriculture,
Northern Ireland
1969 - 71 Prime Minister, Northern Ireland
Subject Interests .... Agriculture, Northern Ireland
Recreational Interests ... Fishing
Correspondence Address .. Moyola Park, Castle Dawson, County
Londonderry, BT45 8ED
Tel: (01648) 468606 Fax: (01648) 468999
Note: Lord Moyola is not currently active in the House of Lords.

Munster, Earl of (Anthony Charles FitzClarence)
Type of Peerage .... Hereditary
Political Allegiance ..... Conservative
Succeeded 1983
Born .... 21st March 1926 in Woking, Surrey
Professional Career ..... 1957 - 69 Graphic Designer, Daily Mirror
Newspapers, then IPC Newspapers
1979 - 89 Stained Glass Conservator,
Burrell Collection, Glasgow, then Chapel
Studio Hertfordshire

Murray of Epping Forest, Baron (Rt Hon Lionel Murray OBE)
Type of Peerage .... Life
Political Allegiance ..... Labour
Created 1985
Born .... 2nd August 1922
Professional Career ..... 1947 - 84 Trades Union Congress (Head of
Economic Department 1954 - 69, Assistant
General Secretary 1969 - 73, General
Secretary 1973 - 84)

Murton of Lindisfarne, Baron
(Rt Hon Henry Oscar Merton OBE)
Type of Peerage .... Life
Political Allegiance ..... Conservative
Created 1979
Born .... 8th May 1914
Educated .... Uppingham School
Political Career .... 1964 - 79 MP (Conservative) for Poole
1971 - 73 Government Whip,
House of Commons
1973 - 74 Second, then First Deputy
Chairman, of Ways and Means,
House of Commons
1976 - 79 Deputy Speaker and Chairman of
Ways and Means, House of Commons
1981 - Deputy Chairman of Committees,
House of Lords
1983 - Deputy Speaker, House of Lords

Mustill, Baron (Rt Hon Michael John Mustill)
Type of Peerage .... Life (Former Law Lord)
Political Allegiance ..... Cross Bench
Created 1992
Born .... 10th May 1931
Professional Career ..... 1955 - Barrister (QC 1968)
1971 - 78 Chairman, Civil Service Appeal
Tribunal
1972 - 78 Crown Court Recorder
1978 - 85 High Court Judge, Queen's Bench
Division
1985 - 89 Chairman, Judicial Studies Board
1985 - 92 Lord Justice of Appeal
1992 - 97 Lord of Appeal in Ordinary

MEMBERS OF THE HOUSE OF LORDS

N

Napier and Ettrick, Rt Hon Baron
(Francis Nigel Napier GCVO)

Type of Peerage . . . . Hereditary
Political Allegiance . . . . . Cross Bench
Succeeded 1954
Born . . . . 5th December 1930
Educated . . . . Eton College
        Royal Military Academy, Sandhurst
Professional Career . . . . . 1948 - 60 Officer, Scots Guards
        1962 - 66 Deputy Ceremonial and Protocol
         Secretary, Commonwealth Relations Office
        1973 - Private Secretary, Comptroller and
         Equerry to HRH The Princess Margaret
Political Career . . . . 1970 - 71 Government Whip,
        (Lord in Waiting)
Correspondence Address . . Nottingham Cottage, Kensington Palace,
        London, W8 4PU

Napier of Magdâla, Baron (Robert Alan Napier)

Type of Peerage . . . . Hereditary
Political Allegiance . . . . . Cross Bench
Succeeded 1987
Born . . . . 6th September 1940
Educated . . . . Winchester College
        St John's College, Cambridge
Professional Career . . . . . 1962 - 66 Project Engineer, Northern
         Research and Engineering Corporation
         International
        1966 - 82 Director and Manager
         (various companies), Ocean Group
        1983 - 85 Chief Executive, Alexandra
         Towing Co Ltd
        1986 - 87 Port Director, Manchester Ship
         Canal Co
        1989 - 91 Director and General Manager,
         Port of Felixstowe International Ltd
        1992 - 94 Consultant, Sir William
         Halcrow and Partners Ltd
        1994 - Consultant, (Shipping and Ports)
Subject Interests . . . . Maritime, Shipping, Ports
Recreational Interests . . . Playing the cello, Dinghy Sailing,
        Trout fishing, Skiing
Correspondence Address . . The Coach House, Kingsbury Street,
        Marlborough, Wiltshire, SN8 1HU
        Tel and Fax: (01672) 512333
        E-mail: rob.napier@clara.net

Naseby, Baron (Rt Hon Michael Wolfgang Laurence Morris)

Type of Peerage . . . . Life
Political Allegiance . . . . . Conservative
Created 1997
Born . . . . 25th November 1936 in Bromley, Kent
Educated . . . . Bedford School
        St Catharine's College, Cambridge
Professional Career . . . . . 1964 - 79 Director Various Advertising
         Agencies
        1979 - 92 Owner, A.M. International
         Consultancy
        1997 - Owner, "Julius" International
         Consultants
Political Career . . . . 1968 - 72 Leader of Council,
         London Borough of Islington
        1974 - 97 MP (Conservative)
         Northampton South
        1983 - 91 Member, Council of Europe and
         Western European Union
        1992 - 97 Chairman of Ways and Means and
         Deputy Speaker, House of Commons
Subject Interests . . . . South East Asia, Financial services, NHS,
        Pharmaceutical industry, Exports, Arts,
        History, Energy
Recreational Interests . . . Tennis, Cricket, Golf, Shooting, Forestry,
        Victoria County history Project
Correspondence Address . . Caesar's Camp, Sandy,
        Bedfordshire, SG19 2AD
        Tel: (01767) 680388 Fax: (01767) 692099
        60a Cambridge Street, London, SW1V 4QG
        Tel: (0171) 834 0297

Nathan, Baron (Roger Carol Michael Nathan)

Type of Peerage . . . . Hereditary
Political Allegiance . . . . . Cross Bench
Succeeded 1963
Born . . . . 5th December 1922 in London
Educated . . . . Stowe School
        New College, Oxford
Professional Career . . . . . 1950 - 87 Partner, then Senior Partner,
         Herbert Oppenheimer Nathan & Vandyk
         (Solicitors)
        1988 - 92 Consultant, Denton Hall, Solicitors
Political Career . . . . 1983 - 87, 1982 - 92 Chairman, European
         Communities Sub-Committee on
         Environment, House of Lords
        1988 Chairman, European Communities
         Sub-Committee on European Companies,
         House of Lords
Subject Interests . . . . Environment, Charities, European Union
Correspondence Address . . Collyers Farm, Lickfold, Petworth,
        West Sussex, GU28 9DU
        Tel: (01798) 861284 Fax: (01798) 861619
        E-mail: 101523.1543@compuserve.com

MEMBERS OF THE HOUSE OF LORDS

Neill of Bladen (Patrick Neill QC)

Type of Peerage	Life
Political Allegiance	Cross Bench
Succeeded	1997
Born	8th August 1926
Educated	Highgate School
	Magdalen College, Oxford
Professional Career	1950 - 77 Fellow of All Souls, Oxford
	1951 Barrister (QC 1966)
	1974 - 75 Chairman, Bar Council
	1975 - 78 Recorder, Crown Court
	1977 - 95 Warden of All Souls, Oxford
	1978 - 83 Chairman, Press Council
	1978 - 85 Chairman, Council for the Securities Industry
	1986 - 87 Chairman, Department of Trade and Industry Inquiry into Regulatory Arrangements at Lloyds
	1988 - Independent Director, Times Newspapers Holdings
	1997 - Chairman, Committee on Standards on Public Life
Recreational Interests	Forestry, Music

Nelson, Earl of (Peter John Horatio Nelson)

Type of Peerage	Hereditary
Political Allegiance	Cross Bench
Succeeded	1981
Born	9th October 1941 in Sherborne, Dorset
Educated	St Joseph's College, Ipswich
	National Institute of Agriculture, Kesteven, Lincs
Subject Interests	Law and Order
Recreational Interests	DIY, Reading, Gardening

Nelson of Stafford, Baron (Henry Roy George Nelson)

Type of Peerage	Hereditary
Political Allegiance	Cross Bench
Succeeded	1995
Born	26th October 1943 in London
Educated	Ampleforth College
	King's College, Cambridge
Professional Career	1973 - 81 Manager, then Managing Director, RHP Bearings
	1983 - 85 Managing Director, Hopkinsons Ltd
	1985 - 86 Managing Director, (Industrial and Distribution) Division, Pegler-Hattersley plc
	1986 - 90 Managing Director, GSPK Group Ltd
	1991 - 92 Managing Director, Power Transmission Division, Fenner plc
	1993 - 97 Operations Director, TIB plc
Subject Interests	Manufacturing engineering industry, Agricultural industry, Small businesses
Correspondence Address	Eastlands, Tibthorpe, Driffield, East Yorkshire, YO25 9LD
	Tel: (01377) 229244 Fax: (01377) 229245
	E-mail: nofs@globalnet.co.uk

Netherthorpe, Baron (James Frederick Turney)

Type of Peerage	Hereditary
Political Allegiance	Cross Bench
Succeeded	1982
Born	7th January 1964

Newall, Baron (Rt Hon Francis Storer Eaton Newall)

Type of Peerage	Hereditary
Political Allegiance	Conservative
Succeeded	1963
Born	23rd June 1930 in Surrey
Educated	Eton College
	Royal Military Academy, Sandhurst
Professional Career	1948 - 61 Army Officer, (Captain, 11th Hussars)
	1967 - 72 Director of Public Relations, Schweppes (USA) Ltd
	1972 - 75 Company Director (Various Companies)
	1985 - Chairman, British Greyhound Racing Board
Political Career	1976 - 79 Opposition Whip, House of Lords
	1983 - Parliamentary Delegate, Council of Europe and Western European Union
Subject Interests	Defence, Europe, Romania, Travel
Recreational Interests	Tennis, Gardens, Trees
Correspondence Address	House of Lords, Westminster, London, SW1A 0PW
	Tel: (0171) 219 3208 Fax: (0171) 219 5979

Newby, Baron (Richard Mark Newby OBE)

Type of Peerage	Life
Political Allegiance	Liberal Democrat
Created	1997
Born	14th February 1953 in Rothwell, West Yorkshire
Educated	Rothwell Grammar School
	St Catherine's College, Oxford
Professional Career	1974 - 81 Staff of HM Customs and Excise
	1988 - 91 Director of Corporate Affairs, Rosehaugh plc
	1992 - Director, Matrix Communications Consultancy
Political Career	1981 - Secretary, Social Democratic Party Parliamentary Committee
	1981 - 88 National Secretary, Social Democratic Party
	1989 - Treasurer, Liberal Democratic Party (England)
	1995 - 97 Vice Chairman, Liberal Democrat General Election Campaign
Subject Interests	Economic policy
Recreational Interests	Football, Tennis, Cricket, Family, Reading
Correspondence Address	4 Rockwells Gardens, Dulwich Wood Park, London, SE19 1HW
	Tel: (0181) 244 5675 Fax: (0181) 670 4302
	Also Tel: (0171) 405 6655
	Fax: (0171) 405 6633
Personal Staff	Ms Charlotte Maxwell-Lyte (*Researcher*)

Newton, Baron (Richard Thomas Legh)

Type of Peerage	Hereditary
Political Allegiance	Conservative
Succeeded	1992
Born	11th January 1950

MEMBERS OF THE HOUSE OF LORDS

Newton of Braintree, Baron (Rt Hon Tony Newton KBE)

Type of Peerage	Life
Political Allegiance	Conservative
Succeeded	1997
Born	29th August 1937
Educated	Friends School, Saffron Walden
	Trinity College, Oxford
Political Career	1965 - 74 Conservative Research Department (Head of Economic Section, then Assistant Director)
	1974 - 97 MP (Conservative) for Braintree
	1979 - 82 Government Whip, House of Commons
	1982 - 86 Parliamentary Secretary, then Minister of State, Department of Social Security (also Minister for the Disabled)
	1986 - 88 Minister of State, Department of Health and Social Security (Minister for Health)
	1988 - 89 Chancellor of Duchy of Lancaster and Minister of Trade and Industry
	1989 - 92 Secretary of State for Social Security
	1992 - 97 Lord President of the Council and Leader of House of Commons

**Nicholls of Birkenhead, Baron
(Rt Hon Donald James Nicholls)**

Type of Peerage	Life (Law Lord)
Political Allegiance	Cross Bench
Created	1994
Born	25th January 1933 in Bebington, Cheshire
Educated	Birkenhead School
	Liverpool University
	Trinity Hall, Cambridge
Professional Career	1958 - Barrister (QC 1974)
	1983 - 86 High Court Judge, (Chancery Division)
	1986 - 91 Lord Justice of Appeal
	1991 - 94 Vice-Chancellor of the Supreme Court
	1994 - Lord of Appeal in Ordinary
Recreational Interests	Walking, History, Music

**Nicholson of Winterbourne, Baroness
(Emma Harriet Nicholson)**

Type of Peerage	Life
Political Allegiance	Liberal Democrat
Created	1997
Born	16th October 1941 in Oxford
Educated	St Mary's School, Wantage, Oxon
	Royal Academy of Music, London
Professional Career	1962 - 74 Computer Programmer, Analyst and Consultant
	1977 - 85 Director of Fund Raising, Save the Children Fund
Political Career	1983 - 87 Vice-Chairman, Conservative Party
	1987 - 97 MP (Conservative, then Liberal Democrat) for Devon and West Torridge

Nickson, Baron (David Wigley Nickson KBE DL)

Type of Peerage	Life
Political Allegiance	Conservative
Created	1994
Born	27th November 1929 in Eton
Educated	Eton College
	Royal Military Academy, Sandhurst
Professional Career	1961 - 85 WM Collins (Variously Director, Managing Director and Vice Chairman)
	1982 - 95 Deputy Chairman, then Chairman, Scottish and Newcastle plc
	1982 Chairman, Pan Books
	1983 - 85 Chairman, Countryside Commission for Scotland
	1986 - 88 President, CBI
	1989 - 93 Chairman, Scottish Development Agency, then Scottish Enterprise
	1989 - 95 Chairman, Top Salaries, then Senior Salaries Review Body
	1991 - Chairman, Clydesdale Bank
Recreational Interests	Fishing, Shooting, Birdwatching, Countryside
Correspondence Address	Clydesdale Bank plc, 30 St Vincent Place, Glasgow, G1 2HL
	Tel: (0141) 223 2002 Fax: (0141) 204 1527
	Renagour House, Aberfoyle, Stirling, FK8 3TF
	Tel: (01877) 382275 Fax; (01877) 382925

Nicol, Baroness (Olive Mary Wendy Nicol)

Type of Peerage	Life
Political Allegiance	Labour
Created	1983
Born	21st March 1923 in Cwmtillery, Gwent
Professional Career	1942 - 48 Civil Servant
Political Career	1972 - 82 Councillor, Cambridge City Council
	1983 - 89 Opposition Whip, then Opposition Deputy Chief Whip, House of Lords
	1983 - 92 Opposition Spokesman on Green Issues, House of Lords
	1988 - 89 Opposition Spokesman on Energy, House of Lords
	1995 - Deputy Speaker and Deputy Chairman of Committees, House of Lords
Subject Interests	Environment, Rural affairs, Retailing
Recreational Interests	Reading, Walking, Gardening
Correspondence Address	House of Lords, Westminster, London, SW1A 0PW
	Tel: (0171) 219 6705 Fax: (0171) 219 5979

Noel-Buxton, Baron (Martin Connal Noel-Buxton)

Type of Peerage	Hereditary
Political Allegiance	Conservative
Succeeded	1980
Born	8th December 1940 in Guildford
Professional Career	Solicitor
Subject Interests	Company, Commercial, Intellectual property Law; Alcohol and drug abuse

MEMBERS OF THE HOUSE OF LORDS

Nolan of Brasted, Baron (Rt Hon Michael Patrick Nolan)

Type of Peerage .... Life (Law Lord)
Political Allegiance ..... Cross Bench
Created 1994
Born .... 10th September 1928 in London
Educated .... Ampleforth College
Wadham College, Oxford
Professional Career ..... 1953 - Barrister (QC 1968)
1975 - 82 Crown Court Recorder
1982 - 90 High Court Judge,
(Queen's Bench Division)
1991 - 93 Lord Justice of Appeal
1994 - Lord of Appeal in Ordinary
1994 - 97 Chairman, Committee on
Standards in Public Life
1997 - Chancellor, Essex University
Subject Interests .... Standards of Conduct in Public Life
Recreational Interests ... Family, Gardening, Theatre, Travel
Correspondence Address .. House of Lords, Westminster,
London, SW1A 0PW
Tel: (0171) 219 3202 Fax: (0171) 219 6156

Norfolk, Duke of (Miles Francis Stapleton Fitzalan-Howard KG, GCVO, CB, CBE, MC)

Type of Peerage .... Hereditary
Political Allegiance ..... Conservative
Succeeded 1975
Born .... 21st July 1915 in London
Educated .... Ampleforth College
Christ Church, Oxford
Professional Career ..... Earl Marshal and Chief Butler of England
1937 - 67 Army Officer
1963 - 65 Major General, GOC 1st Division
1965 - 67 Director, Management and
Support Intelligence, then of Service
Intelligence, Ministry of Defence
1967 - 79 Director, Robert Fleming Bank
Correspondence Address .. 61 Clabon Mews, London, SW1X 0EQ
Tel: (0171) 584 3430
Arundel Castle, West Sussex, BN18 9AB
Tel: (01903) 882173 Fax: (01903) 884726

Normanby, Marquess of (Constantine Edmund Walter Phipps)

Type of Peerage .... Hereditary
Political Allegiance ..... Cross Bench
Succeeded 1994
Born .... 24th February 1954 in Whitby
Educated .... Eton College
Worcester College, Oxford
Correspondence Address .. 52 Tite Street, London, SW3 4JA
Personal Staff .... Mrs Annabel Stein *(Secretary)*

Normanton, Earl of (Shaun James Christian Welbore Ellis Agar)

Type of Peerage .... Hereditary
Political Allegiance ..... None
Succeeded 1968
Born .... 21st August 1945 in London
Educated .... Eton College
Recreational Interests ... Tennis, Skiing, Scuba diving
Correspondence Address .. Somerley, Ringwood, Hampshire, BH24 3PL
Tel: (01425) 473253 Fax: (01425) 478613

Norrie, Baron (George Willoughby Moke Norrie)

Type of Peerage .... Hereditary
Political Allegiance ..... Conservative
Succeeded 1976
Born .... 27th April 1936 in Bentley, Hampshire
Educated .... Eton College
Royal Military Academy, Sandhurst
Professional Career ..... 1956 - 70 Army Officer
1976 - Director (various companies)
1987 - President, British Trust for
Conservation Volunteers
1991 - Adviser, S Grundon (Waste) Ltd
Political Career .... 1988 - 92 European Communities
Committee, House of Lords
Subject Interests .... Environment, National Parks,
Swimming, Health
Recreational Interests ... Fishing, Golf
Correspondence Address .. House of Lords, Westminster,
London, SW1A 0PW
Tel: (0171) 219 5353 Fax: (0171) 219 5979
Personal Staff .... Mr Nick Herbert *(Researcher)*
Tel: (01279) 718280

Northampton, Marquess of (Spencer Douglas David Compton)

Type of Peerage .... Hereditary
Succeeded 1978
Born .... 2nd April 1946 in Northampton
Educated .... Eton College
Royal Agricultural College, Cirencester
Recreational Interests ... Freemasonry
Correspondence Address .. Compton Wynyates, Tysoe,
Warwickshire, CV35 0UD
Tel: (01295) 680629 Fax: (01295) 688107

Northbourne, Baron (Christopher George Walter James DL)

Type of Peerage .... Hereditary
Political Allegiance ..... Cross Bench
Succeeded 1982
Born .... 18th February 1926 in London
Educated .... Eton College
Magdalen College, Oxford
Professional Career ..... Chartered Surveyor
1975 - Chairman, Betteshanger Farms
1996 - Deputy Lieutenant, Kent
Subject Interests .... Education, Children, Disadvantaged
children, Families, Parenting, Agriculture,
Forestry, Land management
Recreational Interests ... Sailing, Gardening, Painting
Correspondence Address .. 11 Eaton Place, London, SW1
Tel: and Fax: (0171) 235 6224
Also Tel: (01304) 611277
Fax: (01304) 611128
Personal Staff .... Mrs Julia Purcell
Tel: (0171) 235 6224

MEMBERS OF THE HOUSE OF LORDS

Northbrook, Baron (Francis Thomas Baring)

Type of Peerage . . . . Hereditary
Political Allegiance . . . . . Conservative
Succeeded 1990
Born . . . . 21st February 1954

Northesk, Earl of (David John MacRae Carnegie)

Type of Peerage . . . . Hereditary
Political Allegiance . . . . . Conservative
Succeeded 1994
Born . . . . 3rd November 1954
Educated . . . . Eton College
                                 Brooke House, Market Harborough
                                 University College, London
Subject Interests . . . . IT, Education, Conservation, Constitution,
                                 the Rural resource
Recreational Interests . . . Gardening
Correspondence Address . . House of Lords, Westminster,
                                 London, SW1A 0PW
                                 Tel: (0171) 219 3597

Northfield, Baron (William Donald Chapman)

Type of Peerage . . . . Life
Political Allegiance . . . . . Labour
Created 1975
Born . . . . 25th November 1923 in Wath, Yorkshire
Professional Career . . . . . 1974 - 80 Chairman, Rural Development
                                 Commission
                                 1975 - 87 Chairman, Telford Development
                                 Corporation
                                 1979 - 81 Chairman, Enquiry into
                                 Agricultural Land
                                 1979 - 83 Special Adviser (Environment),
                                 European Commission
                                 1987 - 91 Chairman, Consortium
                                 Developments Ltd
Political Career . . . . 1949 - 53 General Secretary, Fabian Society
                                 1951 - 70 MP (Labour) for Birmingham
                                 Northfield

Northumberland, Duke of (Ralph George Algernon Percy)

Type of Peerage . . . . Hereditary
Political Allegiance . . . . . Cross Bench
Succeeded 1995
Born . . . . 16th November 1956 in Alnwick,
                                 Northumberland
Educated . . . . Eton College
                                 Christ Church, Oxford
Professional Career . . . . . 1980 - 95 Land Agent/Chartered Surveyor
Subject Interests . . . . Agriculture, Field sports, Rural economy
Recreational Interests . . . Tennis, Shooting, Fishing
Correspondence Address . . Alnwick Castle, Alnwick,
                                 Northumberland, NE66 1NQ
                                 Tel: (01665) 602456 Fax: (01665) 606122

Norton, Baron (James Nigel Arden Adderley)

Type of Peerage . . . . Hereditary
Political Allegiance . . . . . Cross Bench
Succeeded 1993
Born . . . . 2nd June 1947

Norwich, Bishop of (Rt Rev Peter John Nott)

Type of Peerage . . . . Bishop
Entered Lords 1991
Born . . . . 30th December 1933
Educated . . . . Bristol Grammar School
                                 Dulwich College
                                 Royal Military Academy, Sandhurst
                                 Fitzwilliam House, Cambridge
                                 Westcott House, Cambridge
Career . . . . 1961 - 64 Curate, Harpenden
                                 1964 - 69 Chaplain and Fellow,
                                 Fitzwilliam College
                                 1969 - 77 Rector of Beaconsfield
                                 1977 - 85 Bishop of Taunton
                                 1985 - Bishop of Norwich
Correspondence Address . . Bishop's House, Norwich, NR3 1SB
                                 Tel: (01603) 629001

Norwich, Viscount (John Julius Cooper cvo)

Type of Peerage . . . . Hereditary
On Leave Of Absence
Succeeded 1954
Born . . . . 15th September 1929 in London
Educated . . . . Eton College
                                 New College, Oxford
                                 University of Strasbourg
Professional Career . . . . . Writer and Broadcaster
                                 1952 - 64 HM Diplomatic Service
Subject Interests . . . . History, Art, Architecture, Music
Recreational Interests . . . Piano, Travel
Correspondence Address . . 24 Blomfield Road, London, W9 1AD
                                 Tel: (0171) 286 5050 Fax: (0171) 266 2561
Personal Staff . . . . Miss Marion Koenig *(Secretary)*

Nunburnholme, Baron (Ben Charles Wilson)

Type of Peerage . . . . Hereditary
Political Allegiance . . . . . None
Succeeded 1974
Born . . . . 16th July 1928

MEMBERS OF THE HOUSE OF LORDS

O

O'Cathain, Baroness (Detta O'Cathain)

Type of Peer . . . . Life
Political Allegiance . . . . . Conservative
Created 1991
Born . . . . 3rd February 1938 in Cork, Ireland
Educated . . . . Laurel Hill, Limerick, Ireland
University College, Dublin
Professional Career . . . . . 1962 - 66 Assistant Economist, Aer Lingus
1966 - 69 Group Economist, Tarmac plc
1969 - 72 Economic Adviser,
Rootes/Chrysler
1972 - 73 Senior Economist,
Carrington Viyella
1973 - 76 Director of Market Planning,
British Leyland
1976 - 81 Corporate Planning Executive,
Unigate plc
1981 - 89 Group Planning Executive, then
Managing Director, Milk Marketing Board
1990 - 95 Managing Director, Barbican
Centre, London
Parliamentary Interests . . Economy, Industry, Commerce, Europe,
Agriculture, Disabled, Countryside,
Ireland, Arts
Recreational Interests . . . Music, Reading, Walking, Gardening,
Swimming
Correspondence Address . . 121 Shakespeare Tower, Barbican,
London, EC2Y 8DR
Tel: (0171) 638 6443 Fax: (0171) 638 6443
Eglantine, Tower House Gardens,
Arundel, BN18 9RU
Tel and Fax: (01903) 883775
Also Tel: (0171) 219 0662
E-mail: ocathaind@parliament.uk

Ogmore, Baron (Gwilym Rees Rees-Williams)

Type of Peer . . . . Hereditary
Political Allegiance . . . . . Liberal Democrat
Succeeded 1976
Born . . . . 5th May 1931 in Penang, Malaya
Educated . . . . Mill Hill School

O'Hagan, Baron (Charles Towneley Strachey)

Type of Peer . . . . Hereditary
Political Allegiance . . . . . Conservative
Succeeded 1961
Born . . . . 6th September 1945 in London
Educated . . . . Eton College
New College, Oxford
Political Career . . . . 1973 - 75 Member of the European
Parliament (Independent)
1977 - 79 Junior Opposition Whip,
House of Lords
1979 - 94 Member of the European
Parliament (Conservative) for Devon
Correspondence Address . . The Old Rectory, Weare Giffard, Bideford,
Devon, EX39 4QP
Tel: (01237) 475947 Fax: (01237) 424077

Oliver of Aylmerton, Baron (Rt Hon Peter Raymond Oliver)

Type of Peer . . . . Life (Former Law Lord)
Political Allegiance . . . . . Cross Bench
Created 1986
Born . . . . 7th March 1921 in Cambridge
Educated . . . . The Leys, Cambridge
Trinity Hall, Cambridge
Professional Career . . . . . 1948 - 65 Barrister (QC 1965)
1974 - 80 Justice of the High Court
1980 - 86 Lord Justice of Appeal
1986 - 92 Lord of Appeal in Ordinary
Subject Interests . . . . Law
Recreational Interests . . . Gardening, Walking
Correspondence Address . . New Gate Cottage, 17 Ridgeway,
Wimbledon, London, SW19 4SF
Tel: (0181) 947 1679
The Canadas, Sandy Lane, West Runton,
Norfolk, NR27 9ND
Tel: (01263) 837493

O'Neill, Baron (Raymond Arthur Clanaboy O'Neill TD)

Type of Peer . . . . Hereditary
Political Allegiance . . . . . Conservative (also Alliance Party,
Northern Ireland)
Succeeded 1944
Born . . . . 1st September 1933 in London
Educated . . . . Eton College
Royal Agriculture College, Cirencester
Professional Career . . . . . 1972 - 76 Chairman, Ulster Countryside
Committee
1975 - 80 Chairman, Northern Ireland
Tourist Board
1984 - 86 President, Royal Ulster
Agricultural Society
1993 - Chairman, Northern Ireland
Museums Council
Subject Interests . . . . Agriculture, Forestry, Transport
Recreational Interests . . . Gardening, Walking, Railways, Vintage
motoring
Correspondence Address . . Shanes Castle, Antrim,
Northern Ireland, BT41 4NE
Tel: (01849) 463264 Fax: (01849) 468457
Also Tel: (01849) 428216

Onslow, Earl of (Michael William Copplestone Dillon Onslow)

Type of Peer . . . . Hereditary
Political Allegiance . . . . . Conservative
Succeeded 1971
Born . . . . 28th February 1938

MEMBERS OF THE HOUSE OF LORDS

Onslow of Woking, Baron (Rt Hon Cranley Onslow KCMG)

Type of Peer	Life
Political Allegiance	Conservative
Created	1997
Born	8th June 1926
Educated	Harrow School
	Oriel College, Oxford
Professional Career	1944 - 52 Army Officer
	1953 - 60 HM Diplomatic Service
	1983 - Chairman, Nautical Museums Trust
Political Career	1964 - 97 MP (Conservative) for Woking
	1972 - 74 Parliamentary Secretary, (Aerospace and Shipping), Department of Trade and Industry
	1974 - 76 Opposition Spokesman on Health and Social Security, then Defence
	1981 - 82 Chairman, Select Committee on Defence, House of Commons
	1982 - 83 Minister of State, Foreign and Commonwealth Office
	1984 - 92 Chairman, Conservative 1922 Committee

Oppenheim-Barnes, Baroness (Rt Hon Sally Oppenheim-Barnes)

Type of Peer	Life
Political Allegiance	Conservative
Created	1989
Born	26th July 1930 in Dublin
Educated	Sheffield High School
	Lowther College, North Wales
Professional Career	Social Worker, Inner London Education Authority
	1982 Chairman, Inquiry into Pedestrian Safety at Level Crossings
	1987 - 89 Chairman, National Consumer Council
Political Career	1970 - 87 MP (Conservative) for Gloucester
	1974 - 79 Opposition Spokesman on Prices and Consumer Protection, House of Commons
	1979 - 82 Minister of State (Consumer Affairs), Department of Trade
Subject Interests	Consumer affairs
Recreational Interests	Tennis, Bridge
Correspondence Address	12 Ulster Terrace, Regents Park, London, NW1 4PJ
	Tel and Fax: (0171) 935 3696
	Quietways, The Highlands, Painswick, Gloucestershire, GL6 6SL
Personal Staff	Mrs Patricia Sturman (*Personal Secretary*)
	Tel: (01895) 236667

Oram, Baron (Albert Edward Oram)

Type of Peer	Life
Political Allegiance	Labour
Created	1975
Born	13th August 1913 in Burgess Hill, Sussex
Professional Career	1978 - 81 Chairman, Co-operative Development Agency
Political Career	1946 - 55 Research Officer, Co-operative Party
	1955 - 74 MP (Labour and Co-op) for East Ham South
	1964 - 69 Parliamentary Secretary, Ministry of Overseas Development
	1976 - 78 Government Whip, (Lord in Waiting)
Subject Interests	Overseas development, Industrial democracy
Recreational Interests	Chess, Cricket, Football

Oranmore and Browne, Baron (Dominick Geoffrey Edward Browne)

Type of Peer	Hereditary
On Leave Of Absence	
Succeeded	1927
Born	21st October 1901 in Dublin
Educated	Eton College
	Christ Church, Oxford
Correspondence Address	52 Eaton Place, Belgravia, London, SW1X 8AL
Personal Staff	Mr Philip Townsend-Rose (*Private Secretary*)

Orkney, Earl of (Oliver Peter St John)

Type of Peer	Hereditary
Without Writ of Summons	
Succeeded	1998
Born	27th February 1938

Orme, Baron (Rt Hon Stanley Orme)

Type of Peer	Life
Political Allegiance	Labour
Created	1997
Born	5th April 1923 in Sale, Cheshire
Educated	National Council of Labour Colleges
	Workers Educational Association classes
Professional Career	Engineer
Political Career	1958 - 64 Member, Sale Borough Council
	1964 - 97 MP (Labour) for Salford West, then (from 1983) Salford East
	1974 - 76 Minister of State, Northern Ireland Office
	1976 Minister of State, Department of Health and Social Security
	1976 - 79 Minister for Social Security
	1979 - 87 Opposition Spokesman on Health and Social Security, then Industry and Energy
	1987 - 92 Chairman, Parliamentary Labour Party
Recreational Interests	Theatre, Opera, Cricket, Walking, Football
Correspondence Address	8 Northwood Grove, Sale, Cheshire, M33 3DZ
	Tel: (0161) 973 5341 Fax: (0161) 976 4070

MEMBERS OF THE HOUSE OF LORDS

Orr-Ewing, Baron (Charles Ian Orr-Ewing OBE)

Type of Peer . . . . Life
Political Allegiance . . . . . Conservative
Created 1971
Born . . . . 10th February 1912 in London
Professional Career . . . . . 1939 - 46 Served, RAFVR
(Wing Commander, 1941)
1946 - 48 BBC Television Outside
Broadcasts Manager
1969 - 70 President, Electronic
Engineering Association
1972 - 77 Chairman, Metrication Board
Political Career . . . . 1950 - 70 MP (Conservative) for
North Hendon
1957 - 59 Parliamentary Secretary,
Air Ministry
1959 - 63 Parliamentary and Financial
Secretary, then Civil Lord of the Admiralty
1980 - 86 Deputy Chairman,
Association of Conservative Peers
Recreational Interests . . . Tennis, Cricket, Skiing

Owen, Baron (Rt Hon David Anthony Llewellyn Owen CH)

Type of Peer . . . . Life
Political Allegiance . . . . . Cross Bench
Created 1992
Born . . . . 2nd July 1938 in Plymouth, Devon
Educated . . . . Bradfield College
Sidney Sussex College, Cambridge
Professional Career . . . . . 1964 - 68 Neurological and Psychiatric
Registrar, then Research Fellow,
St Thomas's Hospital, London
1990 - Chairman, Humanities
1995 - Chairman, Middlesex Holdings
1992 - 95 European Union Co-Chairman,
International Conference on former
Yugoslavia
Political Career . . . . 1966 - 92 MP (Labour, then Social
Democratic Party) for Plymouth Sutton
and Plymouth Devonport
1968 - 70 Parliamentary Secretary (Navy),
Ministry of Defence
1970 - 72 Opposition Spokesman on
Defence
1974 Parliamentary Secretary,
Department of Health and Social Security
1974 - 76 Minister of State (Health),
Department of Health and Social Security
1976 - 77 Minister of State, Foreign and
Commonwealth Office
1977 - 79 Foreign Secretary
1979 - 80 Opposition Spokesman on Energy
1981 - 82 Leader of Parliamentary
Committee (and Co-Founder) Social
Democratic Party
1982 - 83 Deputy Leader, Social Democratic
Party 1983 - 87, 1988 - 90
1983 - 87, 1988 - 90 Leader, Social
Democratic Party
Subject Interests . . . . International affairs
Correspondence Address . . House of Lords, Westminster,
London, SW1A 0PW
Tel: (01442) 872617 Fax: (01442) 876108
Personal Staff . . . . Mrs Maggie Smart *(Private Secretary)*

Oxford, Bishop of (Rt Rev Richard Douglas Harries)

Type of Peer . . . . Bishop
Entered Lords 1994
Born . . . . 2nd June 1936
Educated . . . . Wellington College
Selwyn College, Cambridge
Cuddesdon College, Oxford
Professional Career . . . . . 1963 - 69 Curate, Hampstead Parish Church
1966 - 69 Chaplain, Westfield College,
Hampstead
1969 - 72 Lecturer and Warden,
Wells Theological College
1971 - 72 Warden, Wells Theological
College
1972 - 81 Vicar, All Saints Fulham
1981 - 87 Dean, King's College, London
1987 - Bishop of Oxford
1996 - Chairman, Church of England Board
for Social Responsibility
Subject Interests . . . . Christian/Jewish relations, Social and
medical ethics, Arms control, Housing,
Homelessness
Recreational Interests . . . Walking, Theatre, Reading
Correspondence Address . . Diocesan Church House, North Hinksey,
Oxford, OX2 0NB
Tel: (01865) 208222 Fax: (01865) 790470

Oxford and Asquith, Earl of (Julian Edward George Asquith KCMG)

Type of Peer . . . . Hereditary
Political Allegiance . . . . . Cross Bench
Succeeded . . . . 1928 (as a minor)
Born . . . . 22nd April 1916

Oxfuird, Viscount (George Hubbard Makgill CBE)

Type of Peer . . . . Hereditary
Political Allegiance . . . . . Conservative
Succeeded 1986
Born . . . . 7th January 1934
Professional Career . . . . . 1964 - 92 Overseas Executive, Lansing
Bagnall Ltd
Political Career . . . . 1993 - Vice-Chairman, Association of
Conservative Peers
Deputy Speaker and Deputy Chairman of
Committees, House of Lords
Subject Interests . . . . Industry, Exports
Recreational Interests . . . Shooting, Fishing, Gardening

MEMBERS OF THE HOUSE OF LORDS

P

Palmer, Baron (Adrian Bailie Nottage Palmer)

Type of Peerage .... Hereditary
Political Allegiance ..... Cross Bench
Succeeded 1990
Born .... 8th October 1951 in Reading, Berkshire
Educated .... Eton College
Edinburgh University
Professional Career ..... Farmer
1974 - 77 Sales Manager, Huntley and
Palmers, (Belgium)
1994 - Chairman, Historic Houses
Association for Scotland
Subject Interests .... Agriculture, Heritage, Arts, Media
Recreational Interests ... Hunting, Shooting, Gardening
Correspondence Address .. Manderston, Duns, Berwickshire, TD11 3PP
Tel: (01361) 883450/882636
Fax: (01361) 882010
Personal Staff .... Mrs Julie Bareham *(Personal Assistant)*
Tel: (01361) 882636

Palumbo, Baron (Peter Garth Palumbo)

Type of Peerage .... Life
Political Allegiance ..... Conservative
Created 1991
Born .... 20th July 1935
Professional Career ..... 1989 - 94 Chairman,
Arts Council of Great Britain
1994 - Chairman, Serpentine Gallery

Park of Monmouth, Baroness
(Daphne Margaret Sybil Désirée Park CMG, OBE)

Type of Peerage .... Life
Political Allegiance ..... Conservative
Created 1990
Born .... 1st September 1921 in Claygate, Surrey
Educated .... Rosa Basset School
Somerville College, Oxford
Professional Career ..... 1948 - 79 HM Diplomatic Service
1980 - 89 Principal, Somerville College,
Oxford
1981 - 86 Member, British Library Board
1982 - 87 A Governor of the BBC
1986 - 92 Chairman, Legal Aid Advisory
Committee to Lord Chancellor
1989 - 94 Chairman, Royal Commission on
the Historical Monuments of England
1989 - 94 Member, Sheffield Development
Corporation
Subject Interests .... Defence, Foreign affairs, Higher education,
Broadcasting
Recreational Interests ... Conversation, Music

Parkinson, Baron (Rt Hon Cecil Edward Parkinson)

Type of Peerage .... Life
Political Allegiance ..... Conservative
Created 1992
Born .... 1st September 1931
Educated .... Royal Lancaster Grammar School
Emmanuel College, Cambridge
Political Career .... 1970 - 92 MP (Conservative) for Enfield
West, then (from 1974) for Hertfordshire
South and (1983) Hertsmere
1974 Assistant Government Whip, House of
Commons
1974 - 76 Opposition Whip, House of
Commons
1976 - 79 An Opposition Spokesman on
Trade, House of Commons
1979 - 81 Minister for Trade, Department of
Trade
1981 - 83 Paymaster General
1981 - 83, 1997 - Chairman, Conservative
Party
1982 - 83 Chancellor of the Duchy of
Lancaster
1983 Secretary of State for Trade and
Industry
1987 - 89 Secretary of State for Energy
1989 - 90 Secretary of State for Transport
1997 - Chairman of the Conservtive Party

Parmoor, Baron (Milo Cripps)

Type of Peerage .... Hereditary
Political Allegiance ..... None
Succeeded 1977
Born .... 18th June 1929

Parry, Baron (Gordon Samuel David Parry)

Type of Peerage .... Life
Political Allegiance ..... Labour
Created 1975
Born .... 30th November 1925
Professional Career ..... Writer and Broadcaster
1952 - 68 Teacher
1969 - 78 Warden, Pembroke Teachers'
Centre
1978 - 84 Chairman, Wales Tourist Board
1983 - 87 Chairman, British Cleaning
Council
1984 - Chairman, then President, Milford
Docks Company
1991 - 96 Chairman, Clean World
International

MEMBERS OF THE HOUSE OF LORDS

Patten, Baron (Rt Hon John Haggitt Charles Patten)
Type of Peerage . . . . Life
Political Allegiance . . . . . Conservative
Created 1997
Born . . . . 17th July 1945
Educated . . . . Wimbledon College
         Sidney Sussex College, Cambridge
Professional Career . . . . . 1969 - 79 University Lecturer and Fellow of
         Hertford College, Oxford
         1997 - Adviser, Charterhouse plc
Political Career . . . . 1979 - 97 MP (Conservative) for City of
         Oxford, then Oxford West and Abingdon
         1981 - 83 Parliamentary Secretary, Northern
         Ireland Office
         1983 - 85 Parliamentary Secretary,
         Department of Health and Social Security
         1985 - 87 Minister of State, Department of
         Environment
         1987 - 92 Minister of State, Home Office
         1992 - 94 Secretary of State for Education

Paul, Baron (Swraj Paul)
Type of Peerage . . . . Life
Political Allegiance . . . . . Labour
Created 1996
Born . . . . 18th February 1931 in Jalandhar, India
Educated . . . . Doaba College, Lahore
         Massachusetts Institute of Technology, USA
Professional Career . . . . . 1966 - 97 Chairman, Caparo Group Ltd
Subject Interests . . . . Industry
Recreational Interests . . . Reading, Current affairs
Correspondence Address . . Caparo House, 103 Baker Street,
         London, W1M 2LN
         Tel: (0171) 486 1417 Fax: (0171) 935 3242
Personal Staff . . . . Miss Elizabeth Allan *(Personal Assistant)*

Pearson of Rannoch, Baron
   (Malcolm Everard MacLaren Pearson)
Type of Peerage . . . . Life
Political Allegiance . . . . . Conservative
Created 1990
Born . . . . 20th July 1942 in Devizes, Wiltshire
Professional Career . . . . . 1964 Founder, Pearson Welsh Springer
         (Insurance Brokers)
         1970 - Chairman, PWS Group
         1983 - 92 Treasurer, Council for National
         Academic Awards
Recreational Interests . . . Fishing, Stalking, Golf

Peel, Earl (William James Robert Peel)
Type of Peerage . . . . Hereditary
Political Allegiance . . . . . Conservative
Succeeded 1969
Born . . . . 2nd October 1947 in London
Educated . . . . Ampleforth College
Subject Interests . . . . Agriculture, Environment
Recreational Interests . . . Fieldsports, Photography, Walking
Correspondence Address . . Kilgram Grange, Ripon, Yorkshire HG4 4PQ

Pembroke and Montgomery, Earl of
   (Henry George Charles Alexander Herbert)
Type of Peerage . . . . Hereditary
Political Allegiance . . . . . Conservative
Succeeded 1969
Born . . . . 19th May 1939

Pender, Baron (John Willoughby Denison-Pender)
Type of Peerage . . . . Hereditary
Political Allegiance . . . . . Conservative
Succeeded 1965
Born . . . . 6th May 1933 in London
Educated . . . . Eton College
Subject Interests . . . . Communications, Racing, Handicapped
         People
Recreational Interests . . . Golf, Gardening, Swimming, Walking
Correspondence Address . . North Court, Tilmanstone,
         Deal, Kent, CT14 0JP
         Tel: (01304) 611726

Penrhyn, Baron (Malcolm Frank Douglas-Pennant DSO)
Type of Peerage . . . . Hereditary
Political Allegiance . . . . . Conservative
Succeeded 1967
Born . . . . 11th July 1908 in Towcester,
         Northamptonshire
Educated . . . . Eton College
         Royal Military College, Sandhurst
Professional Career . . . . . 1929 - 58 Armed Forces

Perry of Southwark, Baroness (Pauline Perry)
Type of Peerage . . . . Life
Political Allegiance . . . . . Conservative
Created 1991
Born . . . . 15th October 1931 in Wolverhampton
Educated . . . . Wolverhampton Girls' High School
         Girton College, Cambridge
Professional Career . . . . . 1970 - 86 HM Inspector of School (Chief
         Inspector from 1981)
         1987 - 93 Vice-Chancellor, South Bank
         Polytechnic/University
         1993 - Chairman, DTI Export Group for
         Education and Training
         1994 - President, Lucy Cavendish College,
         Cambridge
         1997 Chairman, Advisory Panel on
         Citizen's Charter
Subject Interests . . . . International affairs, Education, Exports
         (trade and investment)
Recreational Interests . . . Walking, Music, Reading
Correspondence Address . . House of Lords, Westminster,
         London, SW1A 0PW
         Lucy Cavendish College,
         Cambridge, CB3 0BU
         Tel: (01223) 332192 Fax: (01223) 339056
         E-mail: Lee-presd@lists.cam.ac.uk

MEMBERS OF THE HOUSE OF LORDS

Perry of Walton, Baron
(Walter Laing Macdonald Perry OBE, FRSE, FRS)

Type of Peerage . . . . Life
Political Allegiance. . . . . Liberal Democrat
Created. 1979
Born. . . . . 16th June 1921 in Dundee, Scotland
Educated . . . . Ayr Academy
Dundee High School
St Andrews University
Professional Career . . . . . 1952 - 58 Director, Department of Biological Standard, National Institute of Medical Research
1958 - 68 Professor of Pharmacology, Edinburgh University (Vice Principal 1967 - 68)
1967 - 81 Vice-Chancellor, Open University
1979 - Chairman, then President, Videotel International
Political Career. . . . . . . 1981 - 83, 1988 - 89 Deputy Leader, Social Democratic peers, House of Lords
Member, Select Committee on Science and Technology
Subject Interests. . . . . . . Medicine, Pharmacology, Science, Higher education, Distance education, Shipping
Recreational Interests . . . Music, Golf
Correspondence Address . . 2 Cramond Road South, Edinburgh, EH4 6AD
Tel: (0131) 336 3666 Fax: (0131) 539 5666

Perth, Earl of (Rt Hon David John Drummond)

Type of Peerage . . . . Hereditary
Political Allegiance. . . . . Cross Bench
Succeeded. 1951
Born. . . . . 13th May 1907
Educated . . . . Downside College
Cambridge University
Political Career. . . . . . . 1957 - 62 Minister of State for Colonial Affairs

Peston, Baron (Maurice Harry Peston)

Type of Peerage . . . . Life
Political Allegiance. . . . . Labour
Created. 1987
Born. . . . . 19th March 1931
Professional Career . . . . . 1957 - 65 Reader in Economics, London School of Economics
1965 - 88 Professor of Economics, Queen Mary College, London University
1991 - Chairman, Pools Panel
1991 - Chairman, National Foundation for Educational Research
Political Career. . . . . . . 1966 - 70, 1972 - 73 Adviser to Select Committee, on Nationalised Industries, House of Commons
1974 - 75 Special Adviser to Secretary of State for Education (Rt Hon Reg Prentice MP)
1976 - 79 Special Adviser to the Secretary of State for Prices and Consumer Affairs (Rt Hon Roy Hattersley MP)
1987 - Principal Opposition Spokesman on Energy and Trade and Industry, House of Lords

Petre, Baron (John Patrick Lionel Petre)

Type of Peerage . . . . Hereditary
Political Allegiance. . . . . Cross Bench
Succeeded. 1989
Born. . . . . 4th August 1942 in Windsor, Berkshire
Educated . . . . Eton College
Trinity College, Oxford
Correspondence Address . . Writtle Park, Highwood, Chelmsford, Essex, CM1 3QF
Tel: (01245) 248242 Fax: (01245) 248979

Peyton of Yeovil, Rt Hon Baron (John Wynne William Peyton)

Type of Peerage . . . . Life
Political Allegiance. . . . . Conservative
Created. 1983
Born. . . . . 13th February 1919 in London
Educated . . . . Eton College
Trinity College, Oxford
Professional Career . . . . . 1974 - 90 Chairman, Texas Instruments
1984 - 91 Treasurer, Zoological Society of London
1987 - 91 Chairman, British Alcan Aluminium
Political Career. . . . . . . 1951 - 83 MP (Conservative) for Yeovil
1962 - 64 Parliamentary Secretary, Ministry of Power
1970 Minister of Transport
1970 - 74 Minister of Transport Industries
Correspondence Address . . 6 Temple West Mews, West Square, London, SE11 4TJ
Tel: (0171) 582 3611
The Old Malt House, Hinton St George, Somerset, TA17 8SE
Tel: (01460) 73618

Phillimore, Baron (Francis Stephen Phillimore)

Type of Peerage . . . . Hereditary
Political Allegiance . . . . Conservative
Succeeded. 1994
Born. . . . . 25th November 1944 in Tresco Abbey, Isles of Scilly
Educated . . . . Eton College
Trinity College, Cambridge
Professional Career . . . . . 1972 - Barrister
Subject Interests. . . . . . . Family law, Employment law, Land management and rural economy
Recreational Interests . . . Sailing, Shooting, Polo, Real Tennis, Venetian Rowing, Opera, Theatre, Travel
Correspondence Address . . Phillimore Cottage, 14 Phillimore Walk, London, W8 7SA
Tel: (0171) 938 1304 Fax: (0171) 938 1304
Also Tel: (0171) 797 7837
Fax: (0171) 353 5422

MEMBERS OF THE HOUSE OF LORDS

Phillips of Ellesmere, Baron (David Chilton Phillips)

Type of Peerage . . . . Life
Political Allegiance . . . . . Cross Bench
Created 1994
Born . . . . 7th March 1924 in Ellesmere, Shropshire
Educated . . . . Oswestry Boys' High School
      University College, Cardiff
Professional Career . . . . 1944 - 47 Radar Officer, RNVR
      1951 - 55 Fellow/Research Officer, National
      Research Council, Ottawa, Canada
      1956 - 66 Research Worker/MRC External
      Staff, Royal Institution, London
      1966 - 90 Professor of Molecular Biophysics,
      Oxford University and Professorial Fellow,
      Corpus Christi College
      1976 - 83 Biological Secretary and
      Vice-President, Royal Society
      1983 - 94 Chairman, Advisory Board for the
      Research Councils
Political Career . . . . 1997 - Chairman, Science and technology
      Committee, House of Lords
Subject Interests . . . . Science and technology, Higher education,
      Information Technology, Biotechnology
Recreational Interests . . . Theatre, History, Sport, Grandchildren
Correspondence Address . . 35 Addisland Court, Holland Villas Road,
      London, W14 8DA
      Tel: (0171) 602 0738 Fax: (0171) 602 5346
      E-mail: lord_phillips@compuserve.com
      Also Tel: (0171) 219 6020

Piercy, Baron (James William Piercy)

Type of Peerage . . . . Hereditary
Without Writ of Summons
Succeeded 1981
Born . . . . 19th January 1946

Pike, Baroness (Irene Mervyn Parnicott Pike DBE)

Type of Peerage . . . . Life
Political Allegiance . . . . . Conservative
Created 1974
Born . . . . 16th September 1918 in Castleford
Educated . . . . Humnanby Hall
      Reading University
Professional Career . . . . 1974 - 81 Chairman, WRVS
      1981 - 85 Chairman, Broadcasting
      Complaints Commission
Political Career . . . . 1955 - 57 Member, West Riding County
      Council
      1956 - 74 MP (Conservative) for Melton
      Leicestershire
      1959 - 63 Assistant Postmaster General
      1963 Parliamentary Secretary, Home Office
Recreational Interests . . . Walking, Gardening
Correspondence Address . . Hownam, Near Kelso,
      Roxburghshire, TD5 8AL

Pilkington of Oxenford, Baron (Rev Canon Peter Pilkington)

Type of Peerage . . . . Life
Political Allegiance . . . . . Conservative
Succeeded 1996
Born . . . . 5th September 1933 in Whitley Bay,
      Northumberland
Educated . . . . Dame Allans School, Newcastle-upon-Tyne
      Jesus College, Cambridge
Professional Career . . . . 1955 - 58 Schoolmaster, East Africa
      1959 - 62 Curate, Bakewell, Derbyshire
      1962 - 75 Schoolmaster and Housemaster,
      Eton College
      1975 - 86 Headmaster, King's School,
      Canterbury
      1986 - 92 High Master, St Paul's School,
      London
      1990 - 95 Member, Parole Board
      1992 - 96 Chairman, Broadcasting
      Complaints Commission
Political Career . . . . 1997 - Opposition Spokesman on Education
      and Employment, House of Lords
Subject Interests . . . . Education, Broadcasting, Penal Matters
Correspondence Address . . 30 Bourne Street, London, SW1W 8JJ
      Tel: (0171) 730 4883
      Oxenford House, Ilminster,
      Somerset, TA19 0PP

Pitkeathley, Baroness (Jill Elizabeth Pitkeathley)

Type of Peerage . . . . Life
Political Allegiance . . . . . Labour
Created 1997
Born . . . . 4th January 1940 in Guernsey
Educated . . . . Ladies College, Guernsey
      Bristol University
Professional Career . . . . 1962 - 70 Social Worker, Manchester,
      then Essex
      1970 - 81 Voluntary Services Co-ordinator,
      Berkshire
      1981 - 86 Senior Research Officer,
      National Consumer Council
      1986 - Chief Executive, Carers National
      Association
Subject Interests . . . . Social policy, Carers, Community care,
      Social Security
Recreational Interests . . . Gardening, Grandchildren
Correspondence Address . . House of Lords, Westminster,
      London, SW1A 0PW
      Tel: (0171) 490 8818
Personal Staff . . . . Mrs Betty Hall *(PA)*

MEMBERS OF THE HOUSE OF LORDS

Plant of Highfield, Baron (Raymond Plant)

Type of Peerage	Life
Political Allegiance	Labour
Created	1992
Born	19th March 1945 in Grimsby
Educated	Havelock School, Grimsby
	King's College, London University
	University of Hull
Professional Career	1967 - 79 Lecturer in Philosophy, Manchester University
	1979 - 94 Professor of Politics, Southampton University
	1994 - Master, St Catherine's College, Oxford
Political Career	1990 - 93 Chairman, Labour Party Working Party on Electoral Systems
	1992 - 96 Opposition Front Bench Spokesman on Home Affairs, House of Lords
Subject Interests	Home affairs, Social policy, Foreign affairs
Recreational Interests	Music, Theatre, Ornithology
Correspondence Address	Master's Lodgings, St Catherine's College, Oxford, OX1 3UJ
	Tel: (01865) 271762 Fax: (01865) 271767
Personal Staff	Mrs Margaret Lavercombe *(Secretary)*
	Tel: (01865) 271762

Platt of Writtle, Baroness (Beryl Catherine Platt CBE, DL)

Type of Peerage	Life
Political Allegiance	Conservative
Created	1981
Born	18th April 1923 in Leigh-on-Sea
Educated	Westcliff High School for Girls
	Girton College, Cambridge
Professional Career	1979 - 81 Vice Chairman, Technician Education Council
	1981 - 90 Member, Engineering Council
	1983 - 88 Chairman, Equal Opportunities Commission
	1993 - Chancellor, Middlesex University
	1995 - Chairman, Meteorological Office Advisory Committee
Political Career	1958 - 65 Member, Chelmsford Rural District Council
	1965 - 85 Member, Essex County Council (Chairman Education Committee)
	1971 - 80 Member, Science and Technology Committee, House of Lords
Recreational Interests	Cooking, Reading
Correspondence Address	Greenbury House, 46 Writtle Green, Essex, CM1 3DU
	Tel: (01245) 420337

Plowden, Rt Hon Baron (Edwin Noel Plowden)

Type of Peerage	Life
Has Not Taken The Oath	
Political Allegiance	Cross Bench
Created	1959
Born	6th January 1907 in Strachur, Scotland
Educated	Switzerland
	Pembroke College, Cambridge
Professional Career	1939 - 46 Civil Servant, Ministry of Economic Warfare, then Aircraft Production
	1945 - 46 Chief Executive and Member of Aircraft Supply Council
	1947 - 53 Chief Planning Officer and Chairman of Economic Planning Board (HM Treasury)
	1951 - 52 Vice-Chairman, Temporary Council Committee of NATO
	1953 - 54 Adviser on Atomic Energy Organisation
	1954 - 59 Chairman, Atomic Energy Authority
	1959 - 75 Chairman, Committees of Enquiry into Control of Public Expenditure (1959) Representational Services Overseas (1963), Aircraft Industry (1964), Electricity Supply Industry (1974)
	1959 - 79 Chairman, Various Committees of Enquiry
	1963 - 90 Chairman, then President, Tube Investments Ltd
	1976 - 81 Chairman, Police Complaints Board
	1979 - 82 Independent Chairman, Police Negotiating Board
	1981 - 89 Chairman, Top Salaries Review Body
Correspondence Address	Martels Manor, Dunmow, Essex, CM6 1NB
	Tel: (01371) 872141
Personal Staff	Ms Ann King *(Secretary)*
	Tel: (01628) 635710

MEMBERS OF THE HOUSE OF LORDS

Plumb, Baron (Charles Henry Plumb)

Type of Peerage . . . . Life
Political Allegiance . . . . . Conservative
Created 1987
Born . . . . 27th March 1925 in Warwickshire
Educated . . . . King Edward VI School, Nuneaton
Professional Career . . . . . 1970 - 79 President, National Farmers'
    Union
    1975 - 77 President, Committee des
    Organisations Professsionelles Agricoles
    1977 President, Royal Agricultural Society
    1979 - 82 President, International
    Federation of Agricultural Producers
    1987 - Chairman, International Agricultural
    Training Programme
    1995 - Chancellor, Coventry University
Political Career . . . . 1980 - 82 Chairman, Agriculture Committee,
    European Parliament
    1979 - MEP (Conservative) for The
    Cotswolds
    1982 - 87 Chairman, Democratic Group,
    European Parliament
    1987 - 89 President of the European
    Parliament
    1994 - 97 Vice-President, European Peoples
    Party
    1994 - 97 Leader, British Conservative
    Group, European Parliament
    1994 - Member, European Parliament
    Committee on Development and
    Co-operation
    1994 - Co-President, European
    Union/Africa, Caribbean and Pacific
    Joint Assembly
Subject Interests . . . . Agriculture, Rural affairs, Development and
    cooperation, Third World
Recreational Interests . . . Country pursuits
Correspondence Address . . Maxstoke, Coleshill, Warwickshire, B46 2QJ
    Tel: (01675) 463133 Fax: (01675) 464156
    E-mail: p.w@demon.co.uk
    2 Queen Anne's Gate, London, SW1H 9AA
    Tel: (0171) 227 4300 Fax: (0171) 222 0869
Personal Staff . . . . Mr Tod McClay *(Research Assistant)*
    Tel: + 32 2 284 5383

Plummer of St Marylebone, Baron
   (Arthur Desmond Herne Plummer)

Type of Peerage . . . . Life
Political Allegiance . . . . . Conservative
Created 1981
Born . . . . 25th May 1914 in London
Educated . . . . Hurstpierpoint College
    College of Estate Management
Professional Career . . . . . 1974 - 82 Chairman, Horserace Betting
    Levy Board
    1975 - 82 Chairman, National Stud
    1983 - 89 Chairman, National Employers
    Life Assurance
    1983 - 89 President, Metropolitan
    Association of Building Societies
    1983 - Chairman, then President,
    Portman Building Society
Political Career . . . . 1952 - 64 Member, St Marylebone
    Borough Council
    1960 - 65 Member, London County Council
    1964 - 76 Member, Greater London Council
    (Leader 1967 - 73)
    1964 - 76 Member, Inner London
    Education Authority
Subject Interests . . . . London Government, Building societies,
    Horseracing, Bloodstock, Betting
Recreational Interests . . . Swimming, Rugby Union, Horse Racing
Correspondence Address . . 4 The Lane, St John's Wood,
    London, NW8 0PN
    Tel: (0171) 935 4914 Fax: (0171) 224 3735

Plunket, Baron (Robin Rathmore Plunket)

Type of Peerage . . . . Hereditary
Political Allegiance . . . . . Conservative
Succeeded 1975
Born . . . . 3rd December 1925

MEMBERS OF THE HOUSE OF LORDS

Plymouth, Earl of (Other Robert Ivor Windsor-Clive)

Type of Peerage	Hereditary
On Leave Of Absence	
Political Allegiance	Conservative
Succeeded	1943
Born	9th October 1923 in London
Educated	Eton College
	Cambridge University
Professional Career	1942 - 46 Coldsteam Guards
	1949 - Farmer, Landowner and Quarryman
	1981 - 85 Chairman, Reviewing Committee
	on Export of Works of Art
Subject Interests	Farming, Quarrying, Art
Recreational Interests	Walking, Tennis, Sightseeing
Correspondence Address	The Stables, Oakly Park, Ludlow,
	Shropshire, SY8 2JW
	Tel: (01584) 856243

Poltimore, Baron (Mark Coplestone Bampfylde)

Type of Peerage	Hereditary
Political Allegiance	Conservative
Succeeded	1978
Born	8th June 1957 in London
Educated	Radley College
Professional Career	1987 - Director, Christie's
	(Head of 19th Century Pictures, 1988 - 97)
	1997 - Chairman, Christie's, Australia
Subject Interests	Art
Correspondence Address	c/o Christie's, 8 King Street,
	London, SW1Y 6QT
	Tel: (0171) 389 2430 Fax: (0171) 389 2411

Polwarth, Lord (Henry Alexander Hepburne-Scott TD)

Type of Peerage	Hereditary
Political Allegiance	Conservative
Succeeded	1944
Born	17th November 1916 in Edinburgh, Scotland
Educated	Eton College
	King's College, Cambridge
Professional Career	1955 - 72 Chairman, then President,
	Scottish Council
	(Development and Industry)
	1966 - 72 Governor, Bank of Scotland
	1968 - 72 Chairman, General Accident,
	Fire and Life Assurance Group
Political Career	1972 - 74 Minister of State, Scottish Office
Correspondence Address	Wellfield Parva, near Marshwood,
	Hawkchurch, Axminster, Devon, EX13 5UT

Ponsonby of Shulbrede, Baron
(Frederick Matthew Thomas Ponsonby)

Type of Peerage	Hereditary
Political Allegiance	Labour
Succeeded	1991
Born	27th October 1958 in London
Political Career	1990 - 94 Councillor, London Borough of
	Wandsworth
	1992 - 97 Opposition Spokesman on
	Education, House of Lords
Subject Interests	Education, Europe, Race

Poole of Aldgate, Baron (David Charles Poole)

Type of Peerage	Hereditary
Political Allegiance	Conservative
Succeeded	1993
Born	6th January 1945 in Welshpool
Educated	Gordonstoun School
	Christ Church College, Oxford
	INSEAD Fountainebleau
Professional Career	1978 - 87 Chief Executive, Capel Cure
	Myers
	1987 - 90 Chief Executive,
	Invest International
	1990 - 94 Director, James Capel
	1994 - Chief Executive, Ockham
	Holdings plc
Political Career	1992 - 94 Member, Prime Ministers' Policy
	Unit (under Rt Hon John Major MP)
Subject Interests	Pensions, City, Insurance
Recreational Interests	Sailing

Porter of Luddenham, Baron (George Porter OM)

Type of Peerage	Life
Political Allegiance	Cross Bench
Created	1990
Born	6th December 1920 in Stainforth, Yorkshire
Professional Career	1955 - 66 Professor of Chemistry, Sheffield
	University
	1966 - 85 Director, Royal Institution
	1985 - 90 President, The Royal Society
	1987 - Professor and (since 1990) Chairman,
	Centre for Photomolecular Sciences,
	Imperial College, London
Subject Interests	Science, Education
Recreational Interests	Sailing

Portland, Earl of (Timothy Charles Robert Noel Bentinck)

Type of Peerage	Hereditary
Political Allegiance	Cross Bench
Succeeded	1997
Born	1st June 1953 in Tasmania
Educated	Harrow School
	University of East Anglia
Professional Career	1978 - Actor
Subject Interests	Environment, Arts, Information Technology,
	the NSPCC
Recreational Interests	Computers, Music, House renovation, Skiing
Correspondence Address	3 Stock Orchard Crescent, London, N7 9SL
	Tel: (0171) 607 8814 Fax: (0171) 607 6746
	E-mail: bentinck@compuserve.com

MEMBERS OF THE HOUSE OF LORDS

Portman, Viscount (Edward Henry Berkeley Portman)

Type of Peerage . . . . Hereditary

Political Allegiance . . . . . Conservative

Succeeded 1967

Born . . . . 22nd April 1934 in London

Educated . . . . Canford

Royal Agricultural College, Cirencester

Professional Career . . . . . Farmer and Landowner

Recreational Interests . . . Hunting, Shooting, Fishing, Motoracing,

Music

Correspondence Address . . Clock Mill, Clifford,

Herefordshire, HR3 5HB

Tel: (01497) 831235 Fax: (01497) 831258

E-mail: lordportman@compuserve.com

46 Pont Street Mews, London, SW1 0AF

Tel: (0171) 581 3167 Fax: (0171) 823 9161

Portsmouth, Earl of (Quentin Gerard Carew Wallop)

Type of Peerage . . . . Hereditary

Political Allegiance . . . . . None

Succeeded 1984

Born . . . . 25th July 1954

Powerscourt, Viscount (Mervyn Niall Wingfield)

Type of Peerage . . . . Hereditary

Without Writ of Summons

Succeeded 1973

Born . . . . 3rd September 1935

Powis, Earl of (John George Herbert)

Type of Peerage . . . . Hereditary

Political Allegiance . . . . . Cross Bench

Succeeded 1993

Born . . . . 19th May 1952

Prentice, Baron (Rt Hon Reginald Ernest Prentice)

Type of Peerage . . . . Life

Political Allegiance . . . . . Conservative

Created 1992

Born . . . . 16th July 1923 in Thornton Heath, Surrey

Educated . . . . Whitgift School, Croydon

London School of Economics

Professional Career . . . . . 1942 - 46 Royal Artillery

1950 - 57 Assistant Legal Secretary,

Transport and General Workers Union

Political Career . . . . 1957 - 74 MP (Labour) for East Ham North

1964 - 66 Minister of State, Department of

Education and Science

(Labour Government)

1966 - 67 Minister of Public Building and

Works

1967 - 69, 1975 - 76 Minister for Overseas

Development

1972 - 74 Opposition Spokesman on

Employment

1974 - 79 MP (Labour, then Conservative)

for Newham North East

1974 - 75 Secretary of State for Education

1979 - 87 MP (Conservative) for Daventry

1979 - 81 Minister of State (Social Security),

Department of Health and Social Security

(Conservative Government)

Subject Interests . . . . Foreign affairs, Employment

Recreational Interests . . . Walking

Correspondence Address . . Wansdyke, Church Lane, Mildenhall,

Marlborough, Wiltshire, SN8 2LU

Tel: (01672) 515397

MEMBERS OF THE HOUSE OF LORDS

Prior, Baron (Rt Hon James Michael Leathes Prior)

Type of Peerage .... Life
Political Allegiance ..... Conservative
Created 1987
Born .... 11th October 1927 in Norwich, Norfolk
Educated .... Charterhouse School
Pembroke College, Cambridge
Professional Career ..... 1984 - Chairman, The General Electric
Co plc
1989 - 94 Chairman, Allders plc
1990 - Chairman, Royal Veterinary College
1990 - Chairman, Rural Housing Trust
1992 - 96 Chairman, East Anglian Radio plc
1996 - Chairman, Arab-British Chamber of
Commerce
Political Career .... 1959 - 83 MP (Conservative) for Lowestoft,
then Waveney
1965 - 70 Parliamentary Secretary to Leader
of Opposition (Rt Hon Edward Heath MP)
1970 - 72 Minister of Agriculture, Fisheries
and Food
1972 - 74 Lord President of the Council and
Leader of the House of Commons
1974 - 79 Opposition Spokesman on
Employment
1979 - 81 Secretary of State for Employment
1981 - 84 Secretary of State for
Northern Ireland
Recreational Interests ... Cricket, Tennis, Golf, Gardening, Philately
Correspondence Address .. House of Lords, Westminster,
London, SW1A 0PW
Tel: (0171) 493 8484 Fax: (0171) 409 0723
Personal Staff .... Miss E Muir *(Secretary)*
Tel: (0171) 493 8484

Prys-Davies, Baron (Gwilym Prys Prys-Davies)

Type of Peerage .... Life
Political Allegiance ..... Labour
Created 1982
Born .... 8th December 1923 in Oswestry
Professional Career ..... 1956 - 90 Solicitor
Political Career .... 1983 - 95 Opposition Spokesman variously
on Northern Ireland, Health, Wales,
House of Lords
Subject Interests .... Devolution, Northern Ireland, Welfare, Penal
reform, Rights of minorities

Puttnam, Baron (David Terence Puttnam CBE)

Type of Peerage .... Life
Political Allegiance ..... Labour
Created 1997
Born .... 25th February 1941 in London
Educated .... Minchenden Grammar School
Professional Career ..... 1958 - 66 Advertising Industry
1966 - 68 Photographers' agent
1968 - 86 Independent Film Producer
1986 - 88 Chairman and Chief Executive
Officer, Columbia Pictures
1988 - Independent Film Producer
1988 - 96 Chairman, National Film and
Television School
1988 - Chairman, International Television
Enterprises Ltd
Subject Interests .... Arts, Education, Training
Recreational Interests ... Reading
Correspondence Address .. 13/15 Queen's Gate Place Mews,
London, SW7 5BG
Tel: (0171) 581 0238 Fax: (0171) 584 1799
E-mail: d.puttnam@enigma.co.uk
Personal Staff .... Ms Felicity Gillespie *(Researcher)*
Tel: (0181) 581 0238

Pym, Baron (Rt Hon Francis Leslie Pym MC)

Type of Peerage .... Life
Political Allegiance ..... Conservative
Created 1987
Born .... 13th February 1922 in Penpergwm,
Abergavenny
Educated .... Eton College
Magdalene College, Cambridge
Professional Career ..... 1995 - Chairman, Diamond Cable
Communication plc
Political Career .... 1961 - 87 MP (Conservative) for
Cambridgeshire, then Cambridgeshire
South East
1962 - 64 Assistant Government Whip,
House of Commons
1964 - 70 Opposition Whip,
House of Commons
1970 - 73 Government Chief Whip,
House of Commons
1973 - 74 Secretary of State for
Northern Ireland, House of Commons
1974 - 76 Opposition Spokesman on
Agriculture, House of Commons
1976 - 78 Opposition Spokesman on
House of Commons Affairs and Devolution
1978 - 79 Opposition Spokesman on Foreign
Affairs, House of Commons
1979 - 81 Secretary of State for Defence
1981 - 83 Leader of the House of Commons
(also Chancellor of Duchy of Lancaster,
then Lord President of the Council)
Subject Interests .... Foreign Affairs, Parliamentary affairs
Recreational Interests ... Gardens
Correspondence Address .. Everton Park, Sandy,
Bedfordshire, SG19 2DE
Tel: (01767) 681640 Fax: (01767) 683129

MEMBERS OF THE HOUSE OF LORDS

Q

Queensberry, Marquess of (David Harrington Angus Douglas)

Type of Peerage . . . . Hereditary
On Leave Of Absence
Political Allegiance . . . . . Liberal Democrat
Succeeded 1954
Born . . . . 19th December 1929 in London
Educated . . . . Eton College
　　　　　　　　　　　 Central School of Art
　　　　　　　　　　　 North Staffordshire College of Technology
Professional Career . . . . . 1959 - 82 Professor of Ceramics,
　　　　　　　　　　　　 Royal College of Art
　　　　　　　　　　　 1964 - Partner, Queensberry Hunt Levein
　　　　　　　　　　　　 Design Consultants
Subject Interests . . . . Art, Design, Design education, Ceramics
Correspondence Address . . 19 Fermoy Road, London, W9 3NH
　　　　　　　　　　　 Tel: (0171) 724 3701
　　　　　　　　　　　 Also Tel: (0181) 968 9701
　　　　　　　　　　　 Fax: (0171) 723 0508

Quinton, Baron (Anthony Meredith Quinton)

Type of Peerage . . . . Life
Political Allegiance . . . . . Conservative
Created 1982
Born . . . . 22nd March 1925 in Gillingham, Kent
Professional Career . . . . . 1949 - 55 Fellow, All Souls College, Oxford
　　　　　　　　　　　 1957 - 78 Fellow, New College, Oxford
　　　　　　　　　　　 1978 - 87 President, Trinity College, Oxford
　　　　　　　　　　　 1985 - 90 Chairman of Board,
　　　　　　　　　　　　 British Library
Subject Interests . . . . Education, Arts, Media
Correspondence Address . . Mill House, Turville, Henley-on-Thames,
　　　　　　　　　　　 Oxfordshire, RG9 6QL
　　　　　　　　　　　 Tel: (01491) 638777 Fax: (01491) 638572

Quirk, Baron (Charles Randolph Quirk)

Type of Peerage . . . . Life
Political Allegiance . . . . . Cross Bench
Created 1994
Born . . . . 12th July 1920 on the Isle of Man
Educated . . . . Douglas High School
　　　　　　　　　　　 University College, London
　　　　　　　　　　　 Yale University, USA
Professional Career . . . . . 1954 - 60 Professor of English,
　　　　　　　　　　　　 University of Durham
　　　　　　　　　　　 1960 - 81 Professor of English,
　　　　　　　　　　　　 University of London
　　　　　　　　　　　 1981 - 85 Vice Chancellor,
　　　　　　　　　　　　 University of London
　　　　　　　　　　　 1985 - 89 President, British Academy
Subject Interests . . . . Linguistics, History of English, English
　　　　　　　　　　　 Grammar and lexicology
Recreational Interests . . . Music
Correspondence Address . . University College London, Gower Street,
　　　　　　　　　　　 London, WC1E 6BT
　　　　　　　　　　　 Tel: (0171) 387 7050 Fax: (0171) 916 2054

R

Radnor, Earl of (Jacob Pleydell-Bouverie)

Type of Peerage . . . . Hereditary
Political Allegiance . . . . . Conservative
Succeeded 1968
Born . . . . 10th November 1927 in the United Kingdom
Educated . . . . Harrow School
　　　　　　　　　　　 Trinity College, Cambridge
Professional Career . . . . . 1956 - Chairman, Longford Farms Ltd
　　　　　　　　　　　 1968 - Consultant, Trafalgar Fisheries
　　　　　　　　　　　 1972 - 77 Chairman, British Dyslexia
　　　　　　　　　　　　 Association
　　　　　　　　　　　 1972 - 94 President, Dyslexia Institute
Subject Interests . . . . Art, Environment, Farming, Fish farming,
　　　　　　　　　　　 Forestry, Country affairs, Dyslexia, South
　　　　　　　　　　　 America
Recreational Interests . . . Country pursuits

Raglan, Baron (FitzRoy John Somerset)

Type of Peerage . . . . Hereditary
Political Allegiance . . . . . Cross Bench
Succeeded 1964
Born . . . . 8th November 1927 in Usk, Monmouthshire
Educated . . . . Westminster School
　　　　　　　　　　　 Magdalen College, Oxford
　　　　　　　　　　　 Royal Agricultural College, Cirencester
Professional Career . . . . . 1970 - 74 Crown Estate Commissioner
Political Career . . . . 1975 - 77 Chairman, European Communities
　　　　　　　　　　　 Agriculture and Consumer Affairs
　　　　　　　　　　　 Sub-Committee, House of Lords

Ramsay of Cartvale, Baroness (Meta Ramsay)

Type of Peerage . . . . Life
Political Allegiance . . . . . Labour
Created 1996
Born . . . . 12th July 1936
Educated . . . . Hutcheson's Girls Grammar School
　　　　　　　　　　　 University of Glasgow
Professional Career . . . . . 1963 - 67 Manager, Fund for International
　　　　　　　　　　　 Student Co-operation
　　　　　　　　　　　 1969 - 91 HM Diplomatic Service
Political Career . . . . 1992 - 94 Foreign Policy Adviser to Leader
　　　　　　　　　　　 of Opposition (Rt Hon John Smith MP)
　　　　　　　　　　　 1998 - Government Whip,
　　　　　　　　　　　　 (Baroness in Waiting)

Randall of St Budeaux, Baron (Stuart Randall)

Type of Peerage . . . . Life
Political Allegiance . . . . . Labour
Created 1997
Born . . . . 22nd June 1938
Educated . . . . University College, Cardiff
Political Career . . . . 1983 - 97 MP (Labour) for Hull West
　　　　　　　　　　　 1985 - 87 Opposition Spokesman on
　　　　　　　　　　　　 Agriculture, Fisheries and Food,
　　　　　　　　　　　　 House of Commons
　　　　　　　　　　　 1987 - 92 Opposition Spokesman on
　　　　　　　　　　　　 Home Affairs, House of Commons

MEMBERS OF THE HOUSE OF LORDS

Ranfurly, Earl of (Gerald Francois Needham Knox)

Type of Peerage	Hereditary
Political Allegiance	Cross Bench
Succeeded	1988
Born	4th January 1929 in London
Professional Career	1947 - 60 Royal Naval Officer (retired as Lt Commander)
	1960 - 96 Stockbroker (Chairman, Brewin Dolphin Ltd 1988 - 94)

Rankeillour, Baron (Peter St Thomas More Henry Hope)

Type of Peerage	Hereditary
Political Allegiance	Conservative
Succeeded	1967
Born	29th May 1935
Professional Career	Farmer and Landowner
Correspondence Address	Achaderry House, Roy Bridge, West Invernesshire, Scotland, PH31 4AN
	Tel: (01397) 712206

Rathcavan, Baron (Hugh Detmar Torrens O'Neill)

Type of Peerage	Hereditary
Political Allegiance	Cross Bench
Succeeded	1994
Born	14th June 1939 in London
Educated	Eton College
Professional Career	1959 - 61 Captain, Irish Guards
	1961 - 64 J Henry Schroder Wagg & Co Ltd
	1965 - 68 Financial Editor, Irish Times
	1968 - 70 Industrial Correspondent, Financial Times
	1973 - Deputy Chairman, Lamont Holdings plc
	1989 - 94 Savoy Hotel Management Co
	1978 - 82 Deputy Chairman, IPEC Europe
	1979 - 94 Chairman, St Quentin Ltd
	1986 - 92 Chairman, Northern Ireland Airports Ltd
	1988 - 96 Chairman, Northern Ireland Tourist Board
	198- Chairman, FRX International Ltd
	1990 - 97 Director, Northern Bank Ltd
	1990 - Director, Old Bushmills Distillery Ltd
Political Career	Member, European Sub-Committee on Agriculture, Fisheries and Food, House of Lords
	Member, British-Irish Parliamentary Body
Subject Interests	Tourism, Transport, Agriculture, Economic and industrial issues
Recreational Interests	Travel, Food
Correspondence Address	14 Thurloe Place, London, SW7 2RZ
	Cleggan Lodge, Ballymena, County Antrim, BT43 7JW
	Tel: (01266) 862222/(0171) 584 5293
	Fax: (01266) 862000
	E-mail: rathcavan.cleggan@TIBUS.co

Rathcreedan, Baron (Christopher John Norton)

Type of Peerage	Hereditary
Political Allegiance	Cross Bench
Succeeded	1990
Born	3rd June 1949 in London
Educated	Wellington College
	Royal Agricultural College, Cirencester
Professional Career	1983 - 93 Partner, Hobsons, (Pedigree Livestock Auctioneers)
	1993 - 97 Partner, Norton and Brooksbank, Pedigree Livestock Auctioneers
Subject Interests	Agriculture, Horseracing
Correspondence Address	Stoke Common House, Purton Stoke, Swindon, Wiltshire, SN5 9LL
	Tel: (01793) 772492

Ravensdale, Baron (Nicholas Mosley MC)

Type of Peerage	Hereditary
Political Allegiance	Cross Bench
Succeeded	1966
Born	25th June 1923 in London
Professional Career	Writer
Correspondence Address	2 Gloucester Crescent, London, NW1 9DS
	Tel: (0171) 485 4514

Ravensworth, Baron (Arthur Waller Liddell)

Type of Peerage	Hereditary
On Leave of Absence	
Succeeded	1950
Born	25th July 1924

Rawlings, Baroness (Patricia Elizabeth Rawlings)

Type of Peerage	Life
Political Allegiance	Conservative
Created	1994
Born	27th January 1939 in London
Educated	Oakhall, Haslemere
	Le Manior, Lausanne
	Florence University
	University College, London
	London School of Economics
Professional Career	1959 - 61 Assessor, Children's Care Committee, London County Council
	1963 - 68 WNHR Nurse, Westminster Hospital
	1989 - 94 Member of the European Parliament (Conservative) for Essex South West
	1989 - 92 Deputy Whip, European Democratic Group, European Parliament
	1997 - Opposition Whip, House of Lords
Subject Interests	European legislation, Broadcasting, Heritage, Sport, Eastern and Central Europe (especially Bulgaria and Albania)
Recreational Interests	Music, Art, Architecture, Gardening, Travel, Skiing, Golf

MEMBERS OF THE HOUSE OF LORDS

Rawlinson of Ewell, Baron
(Rt Hon Peter Anthony Grayson Rawlinson QC)

Type of Peerage . . . . Life
Political Allegiance . . . . . Conservative
Created 1978
Born . . . . 26th June 1919 in Birkenhead, Cheshire
Educated . . . . Downside School
Christ's College, Cambridge
Professional Career . . . . . 1946 - 85 Barrister (QC 1959)
1960 - 62 Recorder of Salisbury
1975 - 76 Chairman of the Bar
1975 - 82 Leader, Western Circuit
1984 - 85 Treasurer, Inner Temple
Political Career . . . . 1955 - 78 MP (Conservative) for Epsom,
then Epsom and Ewell
1962 - 64 Solicitor General
1964 - 65, 1968 - 70 Opposition Spokesman
on Legal Affairs, House of Commons
1970 - 74 Attorney General
Recreational Interests . . . Painting
Correspondence Address . . East Wing, Wardour Castle, Tisbury,
Wiltshire, SP3 6RH
Tel: (01747) 871900 Fax: (01747) 871611
Personal Staff . . . . Ms Pauline Jane Henson *(Private Secretary)*
Tel: (01747) 861435

Rayleigh, Baron (John Gerald Strutt)

Type of Peerage . . . . Hereditary
Political Allegiance . . . . . Conservative
Succeeded 1988
Educated . . . . Eton College
Royal Agricultural College, Cirencester
Born . . . . 4th June 1960 in Hatfield Peverel, Essex
Professional Career . . . . . 1981 - 84 Lieutenant, 1st Welsh Guards
1988 - Chairman, Lord Rayleigh's
Dairies Ltd
Recreational Interests . . . Sport, Horticulture

Rayne, Baron (Max Rayne)

Type of Peerage . . . . Life
Political Allegiance . . . . . Cross Bench
Created 1976
Born . . . . 8th February 1918
Professional Career . . . . . 1960 - Chairman, London Merchant
Securities Ltd
1967 - 75 Chairman, London Festival
Ballet Trust
1967 - 72 Deputy Chairman,
British Lion Films
1971 - 88 Chairman, National Theatre Board
1979 Founder Member, Motability
1984 - 95 Deputy Chairman, then Chairman,
First Leisure Corporation plc
1987 - Vice President, Yehudi Menuhin
School

Rayner, Baron (Derek George Rayner)

Type of Peerage . . . . Life
On Leave Of Absence
Created 1983
Born . . . . 30th March 1926
Educated . . . . City College, Norwich
Selwyn College, Cambridge
Professional Career . . . . . 1971 - 72 Chief Executive, Procurement
Executive, Minister of Defence
1973 - 91 Managing Director and
(from 1984 - Chairman, Marks and
Spencer plc)
1978 - 80 Deputy Chairman, Civil Service
Pay Board
Political Career . . . . 1979 - 83 Adviser to Prime Minister
(Rt Hon Margaret Thatcher MP) on
Efficiency in Government

Razzall, Baron (Edward Timothy Razzall CBE)

Type of Peerage . . . . Life
Political Allegiance . . . . . Liberal Democrat
Created 1997
Born . . . . 12th June 1943 in London
Educated . . . . St Paul's School
Worcester College, Oxford
Professional Career . . . . . 1968 - 95 Solicitor/Partner, Frere Cholmeley
Bischoff (Solicitors)
1995 - Partner, Argonaut Associates
(Corporate Financiers)
Political Career . . . . 1974 - Member, London Borough of
Richmond (Deputy Leader 1983 - 96)
1988 - Treasurer, Liberal Democrats
1990 - 94 President, Association of Liberal
Democrat Councillors
Correspondence Address . . House of Lords, Westminster,
London, SW1A 0PW
Tel: (0171) 976 1233 Fax; (0171) 976 1833
Personal Staff . . . . Mrs Danelle Filce *(Personal Assistant)*

Rea, Baron (John Nicolas Rea)

Type of Peerage . . . . Hereditary
Political Allegiance . . . . . Labour
Succeeded 1981
Born . . . . 6th June 1928 in London
Educated . . . . Belmont Hill School, Massachusetts, USA
Dauntsey's School, Wiltshire
University College Hospital Medical School
Professional Career . . . . . 1946 - 48 National Service,
Suffolk Regiment
1954 - 57 Junior Hospital Doctor
1957 - 62, 1968 - 93 General
Practitioner, NHS
1962 - 65 Research Fellow in Paediatrics,
Lagos, Nigeria
1966 - 68 Lecturer, Social Medicine,
St Thomas's Hospital
Political Career . . . . 1992 - 97 Opposition Spokesman on Health
and Overseas Development, House of
Lords
Subject Interests . . . . Health, Human Rights, International
Development
Recreational Interests . . . Music, Gardening, Outdoor activities
Correspondence Address . . 11 Anson Road, London, N7 0RN
Tel and Fax: (0171) 607 0546
1 Littledene Colleges, Glynde,
East Sussex, BN8 6LA
Tel: (01273) 858322

MEMBERS OF THE HOUSE OF LORDS

Reading, Marquess of (Simon Charles Henry Rufus Isaacs)

Type of Peerage . . . . Hereditary
Political Allegiance . . . . . Conservative
Succeeded 1980
Born . . . . 18th May 1942 in Sutton, Surrey
Educated . . . . Eton College
Professional Career . . . . Management Consultant
Correspondence Address . . Jaynes Court, Bisley,
 Gloucestershire, GL6 7BE
 Tel: (01452) 770121 Fax: (01452) 770626

Reay, Baron (Hugh William McKay)

Type of Peerage . . . . Hereditary
Political Allegiance . . . . . Conservative
Succeeded 1963
Born . . . . 19th July 1937

Redesdale, Baron (Rupert Bertram Mitford)

Type of Peerage . . . . Hereditary
Political Allegiance . . . . . Liberal Democrat
Succeeded 1991
Born . . . . 18th July 1967 in London
Educated . . . . Highgate School
 Newcastle University
Political Career . . . . 1993 - Liberal Democrat Spokesman on
 Overseas Development, House of Lords
Subject Interests . . . . Overseas Development
Correspondence Address . . House of Lords, Westminster,
 London, SW1A 0PW
 Tel: (0171) 219 3438 Fax: (0171) 219 2082
 E-mail: redesdaler@parliament.uk

Rees of Goytre, Baron
 (Rt Hon Peter Wynford Innes Rees QC)

Type of Peerage . . . . Life
Political Allegiance . . . . . Conservative
Created 1987
Born . . . . 9th December 1926 in Camberley, Surrey
Educated . . . . Stowe School
 Christ Church, Oxford
Professional Career . . . . . 1953 - Barrister (QC 1969)
 1985 - Chairman, Leopold Joseph Holdings
 1987 - Chairman, Duty Free Confederation
 1990 - 95 Chairman, General Cable Ltd
 1990 - 92 Chairman, Westminster
 Industrial Brief
 1991 - 95 Chairman, General Mobile
 Communications
 1992 - Chairman, Quadrant Group
Political Career . . . . 1970 - 74 MP (Conservative) for Dover
 1983 - 87 for Dover and Deal
 1979 - 81 Minister of State, HM Treasury
 1981 - 83 Minister for Trade, Department of
 Trade and Industry
 1983 - 85 Chief Secretary, HM Treasury
Correspondence Address . . 39 Headfort Place, London, SW1X 7DE
 Tel: (0171) 235 6919

Rees-Mogg, Baron (William Rees-Mogg)

Type of Peerage . . . . Life
Political Allegiance . . . . . Cross Bench
Created 1988
Born . . . . 14th July 1928 in Somerset
Educated . . . . Charterhouse
 Balliol College, Oxford
Professional Career . . . . . 1967 - 81 Editor, The Times
 1981 - 86 Vice Chairman, BBC Governors
 1982 - 89 Chairman, Arts Council of
 Great Britain
 1988 - 93 Chairman,
 Broadcasting Standards Council
Correspondence Address . . 17 Pall Mall, Westminster,
 London, SW1Y 5NB
 Tel: (0171) 930 3088 Fax: (0171) 839 4509
Personal Staff . . . . Mrs Jennifer Mitchell *(Personal Assistant)*

Remnant, Baron (James Wogan Remnant)

Type of Peerage . . . . Hereditary
Political Allegiance . . . . . Conservative
Succeeded 1967
Born . . . . 23rd October 1930 in London
Educated . . . . Eton College
Professional Career . . . . . 1958 - 89 Partner, then Managing Director
 and Chairman, Touche Ross
Correspondence Address . . Bear Ash, Hare Hatch, Reading, RG10 9XR
 Tel: (0118) 940 2639

Rendell of Babergh, Baroness (Ruth Barbara Rendell CBE)

Type of Peerage . . . . Life
Educated . . . . Loughton County High School
Political Allegiance . . . . . Labour
Created 1997
Born . . . . 17th February 1930
Professional Career . . . . . Writer (Crime Novelist)

Renfrew of Kaimsthorn, Baron (Andrew Colin Renfrew)

Type of Peerage . . . . Life
Political Allegiance . . . . . Conservative
Created 1991
Born . . . . 25th July 1937 in Stockton-on-Tees
Educated . . . . St Alban's School
 St John's College, Cambridge
Professional Career . . . . . 1965 - 72 Lecturer in Prehistory and
 Archaeology, Sheffield University
 1972 - 81 Professor of Archaeology,
 Southampton University
 1981 - Disney Professor of Archaeology,
 University Cambridge
 1981 - 86 Fellow, St. John's College,
 Cambridge
 1986 - Fellow, Jesus College, Cambridge
 (Master 1986 - 97)
 1991 - Director, McDonald Institute for
 Archaelogical Research
Political Career . . . . 1995 - Chairman, House of Lords Library
 and Computing Sub-Committee
Subject Interests . . . . Education, Foreign affairs
Recreational Interests . . . Contemporary art, Sculpture
Correspondence Address . . McDonald Institute for Archeological
 Research, Downing Street,
 Cambridge, CB2 3ER
 Tel: (01223) 333538 Fax: (01223) 333536
 5a Chaucer Road, Cambridge, CB2 3ER
Personal Staff . . . . Miss Sheila Nightingale *(Secretary)*
 Tel: (01223) 333538

MEMBERS OF THE HOUSE OF LORDS

Rennell, Baron (John Adrian Tremayne Rodd)

Type of Peerage	Hereditary
Political Allegiance	Conservative
Succeeded	1978
Born	28th June 1935

Renton, Baron
(Rt Hon David Lockhart-Mure Renton KBE, TD QC)

Type of Peerage	Life
Political Allegiance	Conservative
Created	1979
Born	12th August 1908 in Dartford, Kent
Educated	Oundle School
	University College, Oxford
Professional Career	1933 - 54 Junior Barrister
	1954 - QC
	1933 - Barrister (QC 1954)
	1963 - 71 Recorder of Rochester, then of Guildford
	1971 - 73 Member, Royal Commission on Constitution
	1978 - 88 Chairman, then President, Mencap
	1980 - President, Statue Law Society
Political Career	1945 - 68 MP (National Liberal then Conservative) for Huntingdonshire
	1955 - 58 Parliamentary Secretary, Ministry of Power
	1958 - 62 Parliamentary Secretary then Minister of State, Home Office
	1968 - 79 Conservative MP for Huntingdonshire
	1973 - 75 Chairman, Committee on the Preparation of Legislation
	1982 - 88 Deputy Speaker, House of Lords
Subject Interests	Constitutional issues, Legislative drafting, Mental handicap, Environment, Defence, Law and order
Recreational Interests	Gardening, Shooting, Lawn Tennis
Correspondence Address	Moat House, Abbots Ripton, Huntingdon, PE17 2PE
	Tel: (01487) 773227
	16 Old Buildings, Lincoln's Inn, London, WC2A 3TL
	Tel: (0171) 242 8986

Renton of Mount Harry, Baron
(Rt Hon Ronald Timothy Renton)

Type of Peerage	Life
Political Allegiance	Conservative
Created	1997
Born	28th May 1932 in London
Political Career	1974 - 97 MP (Conservative) for Mid Sussex
	1984 - 87 Parliamentary Secretary, then Minister of State, Foreign and Commonwealth Office
	1987 - 89 Minister of State, Home Office
	1989 - 90 Government Chief Whip, House of Commons
	1990 - 92 Minister of State, Privy Council Office (Minister for the Arts)

Renwick, Baron (Harry Andrew Renwick)

Type of Peerage	Hereditary
Political Allegiance	Conservative
Succeeded	1973
Born	10th October 1935 in Kingston-upon-Thames, Surrey
Subject Interests	Technology, Special educational needs

Renwick of Clifton, Baron (Robin William Renwick KCMG)

Type of Peerage	Life
Political Allegiance	Labour
Created	1997
Born	13th December 1937 in York
Educated	St Paul's School
	Jesus College, Cambridge
	Sorbonne, Paris
Political Career	1963 - 95 HM Diplomatic Service
	1978 - 80 Head of Rhodesia Dept, Foreign and Commonwealth Office
	1981 - 84 Head of Chancery, Washington
	1984 - 87 Assistant Under-Secretary, Foreign and Commonwealth Office
	1987 - 91 Ambassador to South Africa
	1991 - 95 Ambassador to United States
	1995 - Director, Robert Fleming Holdings
	1996 - Chairman, Fluor Daniel Ltd
	1996 - Chairman, Save and Prosper Group
Correspondence Address	Robert Fleming and Co, 25 Copthall Avenue, London, E2R 7DR
	Tel: (0171) 638 5858

Revelstoke, Baron (John Baring)

Type of Peerage	Hereditary
Without Writ of Summons	
Succeeded	1994
Born	2nd December 1934

MEMBERS OF THE HOUSE OF LORDS

Richard, Rt Hon Baron (Ivor Seward Richard QC)

Type of Peerage	Life
Political Allegiance	Labour
Created	1990
Born	30th May 1932 in Ammanford, Carmarthenshire
Educated	St Michael's School, Bryn, Llanelli
	Cheltenham College
	Pembroke College, Oxford
Professional Career	1955 - Barrister (QC 1971)
	1974 - 79 UK Permanent Representative to the United Nations
	1981 - 84 Member, European Commission
	1985 - 97 Chairman, World Trade Centre, Wales Ltd
	1987 - 91 Chairman, British United Nations Association
Political Career	1964 - 74 Labour MP for Barons Court
	1966 - 69 PPS to Secretary of State for Defence (Rt Hon Denis Healey MP)
	1969 - 70 Parliamentary Secretary (Army), Ministry of Defence
	1970 - 74 Opposition Spokesman on Broadcasting, Ports, Telecommunications, then Foreign Affairs, House of Commons
	1990 - 92 Opposition Spokesman on Home Affairs, House of Lords
	1992 - 97 Leader of the Opposition, House of Lords
	1997 - Lord Privy Seal and Leader of the House of Lords
Subject Interests	Foreign affairs, Europe
Correspondence Address	House of Lords, Westminster, London, SW1A 0PW
	Tel: (0171) 219 3200 Fax: (0171) 219 3051
	Also Tel: (0171) 270 0491
	Fax: (0171) 270 0491
Personal Staff	Mr Damien Welfare
	Ms Marianne Morris *(Special Advisers)*
	Tel: (0171) 219 6224/4991

Richardson, Baron (John Samuel Richardson LVO)

Type of Peerage	Life
Political Allegiance	Cross Bench
Created	1979
Born	16th June 1910 in Sheffield
Educated	Charterhouse
	Trinity College, Cambridge
	St Thomas's Hospital
Professional Career	1946 - 75 Physician, St Thomas's Hospital
	1957 - 80 Consulting Physician, Metropolitan Police
	1966 - 70 President, International Society of Internal Medicine
	1967 - 72 Chairman, Joint Consultants Committee
	1969 - 71 President, Royal Society of Medicine
	1970 - 71 President, British Medical Association
	1972 - 80 Chairman, Council for Post Graduate Medical Education (England and Wales)
	1973 - 80 President, General Medical Council
Subject Interests	Medicine
Correspondence Address	Windcutter Lee, Ilfracombe, EX34 8LW
	Tel: (01271) 863198

Richardson of Duntisbourne, Baron (Rt Hon Gordon William Humphreys Richardson KG)

Political Allegiance	Cross Bench
Created	1983
Born	25th November 1915 in London
Professional Career	1962 - 72 Chairman, J Henry Schroder Wagg
	1972 - 73 Chairman, Industrial Development Advisory Board
	1973 - 83 Governor, Bank of England
	1986 - 95 Chairman, Morgan Stanley International Inc
Correspondence Address	c/o Morgan Stanley, 25 Cabot Square, Canary Wharf, London, E14 4QA
	Tel: (0171) 425 8004

Richmond Lennox and Gordon, Duke of (Charles Henry Gordon-Lennox)

Type of Peerage	Hereditary
Political Allegiance	Cross Bench
Succeeded	1989
Born	19th September 1929 in London
Professional Career	1949 - 50 2nd Lieutenant, KRRC, 60th Rifles
	1956 - Chartered Accountant
	1959 - 64 Financial Controllers Department, Courtaulds Ltd, Coventry
	1965 - Chairman, Dexam International (Holdings) Ltd of Haslemere
	1964 - 68 Director of Industrial Studies, William Temple College
	1965 - 68 Member West Midlands Regional Economic Planning Council
	1969 - Chairman, Goodwood Group of Companies
	1975 - 78 Chairman, Historic Houses Association, South East Region
	1975 - 82 Hon Treasurer, Historic Houses Association
	1985 - Chancellor, Sussex University
	1987 - 89 Chairman, Ajax Insurance (Holdings) Ltd of Liphook
	1990 - Lord Lieutenant of West Sussex

MEMBERS OF THE HOUSE OF LORDS

Ridley, Viscount (Matthew White Ridley KG, GCVO, TD)

Type of Peerage	Hereditary
Political Allegiance	Cross Bench
Succeeded	1964
Born	29th July 1925 in London
Educated	Eton College
	Balliol College, Oxford
Professional Career	1943 - 64 Armed Forces (Colonel, Northumberland Hussars, 1961 - 64)
	1987 - 92 Chairman, Northern Rock Building Society
	1989 - University of Newcastle
Subject Interests	Reserve Forces, Defence, Universities
Recreational Interests	Dendrology, Fishing, Shooting
Correspondence Address	Blagdon, Seaton Burn, Newcastle-upon-Tyne, NE13 6DD
	Tel: (01670) 789236

Ripon, Bishop of (Rt Rev David Nigel De Lorentz Young)

Type of Peerage	Bishop
Entered Lords	1984
Born	2nd September 1931 in Poona, India
Educated	Wellington College
	Balliol College, Oxford
Professional Career	1955 - 59 Research Mathematician, Plessey Co
	1959 - 62 Curate of All Hallows, Allerton, Liverpool
	1962 - 63 Curate, St Mark's, St John's Wood
	1963 - 67 CMS Missionary in Sri Lanka
	1967 - 70 Lecturer in Buddhist Studies, Manchester University
	1970 - 75 Vicar, Burwell, Cambridgeshire
	1975 - 77 Archdeacon of Huntingdon
	1977 - Bishop of Ripon
	1994 - Chairman, Church of England Board of Education
Subject Interests	Education, Immigration and Asian affairs
Recreational Interests	Fell walking, Sailing, Tennis
Correspondence Address	Bishop Mount, Ripon, North Yorkshire, HG4 5DP
	Tel: (01765) 602045 Fax: (01765) 600758

Ritchie of Dundee, Baron (Harold Malcolm Ritchie)

Type of Peerage	Hereditary
Political Allegiance	Liberal Democrat
Succeeded	1978
Born	29th August 1919

Riverdale, Baron (Robert Arthur Balfour)

Type of Peerage	Hereditary
On Leave Of Absence	
Succeeded	1957
Born	1st September 1901 in Sheffield
Educated	Oundle School
Professional Career	1949 - 69 Managing Director/Chairman, Arthur Balfour and Co Ltd
Recreational Interests	Sailing, Shooting, Stalking, Fishing
Correspondence Address	Ropes, Grindleford, Near Sheffield, S30 1HX
	Tel: (01433) 630408

Rix, Baron (Brian Norman Roger Rix CBE)

Type of Peerage	Life
Political Allegiance	Cross Bench
Created	1992
Born	27th January 1924 in Cottingham, East Yorkshire
Educated	Bootham School, York
Professional Career	1942 - 79 Actor/Manager
	1980 - Secretary-General, then (from 1988) Chairman, MENCAP
	1997 - Chancellor, University of East London
Subject Interests	Theatre, Learning Disabilities, Cricket, Higher Education, Charities, Amateur Radio
Recreational Interests	Theatre, Gardening, After-Dinner Speaking, Cricket
Correspondence Address	House of Lords, Westminster, London, SW1A 0PW
	Tel: (0171) 219 5353
	Mencap, 123 Golden Lane, London, EC1Y 0RT
	Tel: (0171) 454 0454/(0181) 879 7748
	Fax: (0181) 879 7748
Personal Staff	Ms Banks *(Personal Assistant)*
	Tel: (0171) 696 5614

Robens of Woldingham, Baron (Rt Hon Alfred Robens)

On Leave Of Absence	
Created	1961
Born	15th December 1910
Educated	Manchester Secondary School
Political Career	1945 - 60 MP (Labour) for Wansbeck then Blyth
	1947 - 51 Parliamentary Secretary, Minister of Fuel and Power
	1951 Minister of Labour and National Service

MEMBERS OF THE HOUSE OF LORDS

Roberts of Conwy, Baron (Rt Hon Ieuan Wyn Pritchard)

Political Allegiance	Conservative
Created	1997
Born	10th July 1910
Educated	Harrow School
	University College, Oxford
Professional Career	1952 - 54 Sub Editor, Liverpool Daily Post
	1954 - 57 News Assistant, BBC
	1957 - 68 Producer, then Welsh Controller, TWW Ltd
	1969 Programme Executive, Harlech TV
Political Career	1970 - 97 MP for Conway, then Conwy
	1979 - 74 PPS to Secretary of State for Wales (Rt Hon Peter Thomas MP)
	1974 - 79 Opposition Spokesman on Welsh Affairs, House of Commons
	1979 - 94 Parliamentary Secretary, then Minister of State, Welsh Office

Robertson of Oakridge, Baron (William Ronald Robertson)

Type of Peerage	Hereditary
Political Allegiance	Cross Bench
Succeeded	1974
Born	8th December 1930 in Beaconsfield Buckinghamshire
Educated	Hilton College, Natal
	Charterhouse
	Army Staff College, Camberley
Professional Career	1949 - 69 Armed Forces (Royal Scots Greys)
	1972 - 95 Member, London Stock Exchange
	1985 - 86 Master, Salters Company
Subject Interests	Abortion, Euthanasia, Prisons, Human Rights, Religious Education
Recreational Interests	History
Correspondence Address	House of Lords, Westminster, London, SW1A 0PW
	Tel: (01305) 257612

Roborough, Baron (Henry Massey Lopes)

Type of Peerage	Hereditary
Political Allegiance	Cross Bench
Succeeded	1992
Born	2nd February 1940

Robson of Kiddington, Baroness (Inga-Stina Robson)

Type of Peerage	Life
Political Allegiance	Liberal Democrat
Created	1974
Born	20th August 1919 in Stockholm, Sweden
Educated	Sweden
Professional Career	1939 - 43 Swedish Foreign Office, then Ministry of Information
	1970 - 84 Chairman, Board of Governors, Queen Charlotte's and Chelsea Hospital
	1974 - 82 Chairman, South-West Thames Regional Health Authority
Political Career	1968 - 70 President, Women's Liberal Federation
	1970 - 71 President, Liberal Party Organisation
	1971 - 77 Chairman, Liberal Party Environment Panel
	1990 - Liberal Democrat Spokesman on Health, House of Lords
Subject Interests	Health, Agriculture
Correspondence Address	The Dower House, Kiddington, Woodstock, Oxford, OX20 1BU
	Tel: (01608) 677398

Rochdale, Viscount (St John Durival Kemp)

Type of Peerage	Hereditary
Without Writ of Summons	
Succeeded	1976
Born	15th January 1938

Rochester, Baron (Foster Charles Lowry Lamb)

Type of Peerage	Hereditary
Political Allegiance	Liberal Democrat
Succeeded	1955
Born	7th June 1916 in Kingswood, Surrey
Educated	Mill Hill School
	Jesus College, Cambridge
Professional Career	1939 - 46 Armed Forces (Captain, 23rd Hussars)
	1946 - 72 ICI (Personnel Manager)
	1973 - 86 Pro-Chancellor, Keele University
Subject Interests	Industrial relations, Employment, Training
Recreational Interests	Rugby, Cricket, Golf, Walking
Correspondence Address	The Hollies, Hartford, Northwich, Cheshire, CW8 1PG
	Tel: (01606) 74733

Rockley, Baron (John Hugh Cecil)

Type of Peerage	Hereditary
Political Allegiance	Conservative
Succeeded	1976
Born	5th April 1934

MEMBERS OF THE HOUSE OF LORDS

Rodger of Earlsferry, Baron (Rt Hon Alan Ferguson Rodger)

Type of Peerage . . . . Hereditary
Created 1992
Born . . . . 18th September 1944 in Glasgow
Professional Career . . . . . 1970 - 72 Fellow of New College, Oxford
       1974 - Advocate, Scotland (QC 1985)
       1985 - 88 Advocate Depute
       1995 - 96 Senator, College of Justice
       1996 - Lord President of the Court of Session
       1989 - 92 Solicitor General for Scotland
       1992 - 95 Lord Advocate
       1995 - 96 Senator of College of Justice in Scotland
       1996 - Lord Justice, General of Scotland and Lord President of the Court of Session
Subject Interests . . . . Law
Recreational Interests . . . Walking and Reading

**Rodgers of Quarry Bank, Baron
(Rt Hon William Thomas Rodgers)**

Type of Peerage . . . . Life
Political Allegiance . . . . . Liberal Democrat
Created 1992
Born . . . . 28th October 1928 in Liverpool
Educated . . . . Quarry Bank High School, Liverpool
       Magdalen College, Oxford
Professional Career . . . . . 1953 - 60 General Secretary, Fabian Society
       1987 - 94 Director-General, Royal Institute of British Architects
       1995 - Chairman, Advertising Standards Authority
Political Career . . . . 1962 - 74 MP (Labour, then Social Democratic Party) for, Stockton-on-Tees/Teeside, Stockton
       1964 - 67 Parliamentary Secretary, Department of Economic Affairs
       1967 - 68 Parliamentary Secretary, Foreign Office
       1968 - 69 Minister of State, Board of Trade
       1969 - 70 Minister of State, Treasury
       1974 - 83 Labour MP for Teeside, Stockton
       1974 - 76 Minister of State, Ministry of Defence
       1976 - 79 Secretary of State for Transport
       1981 - 83 Liberal Democrat MP for Teeside, Stockton
       1982 - 87 Vice-President, SDP
       1994 - Liberal Democrat Spokesman on Home Office Affairs, House of Lords
       1998 - Leader, Liberal Democrats, House of Lords

Rodney, Baron (George Bridges Rodney)

Type of Peerage . . . . Hereditary
Political Allegiance . . . . . Conservative
Succeeded 1992
Born . . . . 3rd January 1953

Rogers of Riverside, Baron (Richard George Rogers)

Type of Peerage . . . . Life
Political Allegiance . . . . . Labour
Created 1996
Born . . . . 23rd July 1933 in Florence, Italy
Educated . . . . Architectural Association
       Yale University
Professional Career . . . . . Architect
       1978 - Chairman, Richard Roger Architects Ltd
       1984 - 88 Chairman, Board of Trustees, Tate Gallery
       1994 - 97 Vice Chairman, Arts Council of Great Britain; Chairman, National Tenants Resource Centre; Chairman, Architecture Foundation
Subject Interests . . . . Urban planning, Architecture, Culture, Environment
Recreational Interests . . . Tennis, Travel, Food
Correspondence Address . . Richard Rogers Partnership, Thames Wharf Studios, Rainville Road, London, W6 9HA
       Tel: (0171) 385 1235 Fax: (0171) 385 8409
       45 Royal Avenue, London, SW3 4QE
       Tel: (0171) 730 4887 Fax: (0171) 730 5606
Personal Staff . . . . Ms Jo Murtagh (*Personal Assistant*)
       Tel: (0171) 385 1235

MEMBERS OF THE HOUSE OF LORDS

Roll of Ipsden, Baron (Eric Roll KCMG, CB)

Type of Peerage	Life
Political Allegiance	Cross Bench
Created	1977
Born	1st December 1907 in Austria
Educated	University of Birmingham
Professional Career	1935 - 39 Professor of Economics and Commerce, University College, Hull
	1941 - 46 Deputy Head, British Food Mission to North America
	1946 - 47 Assistant Secretary, Ministry of Food
	1948 Under Secretary, HM Treasury (Central Economic Planning Staff)
	1952 Deputy Head, UK Delegation to NATO
	1953 - 57 Under Secretary, then (1959 - 61) Deputy Secretary Ministry of Agriculture, Fisheries and Food
	1957 - 59 Executive Director, International Sugar Council
	1961 - 63 Deputy Leader, UK Delegation for Negotiations with EEC
	1964 - 66 Permanent Secretary, Department of Economic Affairs
	1968 - 77 Director, Bank of England
	1974 - 84 Chancellor, Southampton University
	1974 - 87 Chairman then President, Mercury Securities Ltd
	1974 - 95 Chairman, then President, S G Warburg Group
	1995 - Senior Adviser, SBC Warburg
Recreational Interests	Reading
Correspondence Address	1 Finsbury Avenue, London, EC2M 2PP Tel: (0171) 568 2477 Fax: (0171) 568 00500
Personal Staff	Mrs Trudi Paulie *(Personal Assistant)*

Rollo, Lord (Eric John Stapylton Rollo)

Type of Peerage	Hereditary
Without Writ of Summons	
Succeeded	1947
Born	3rd December 1915 in Englefield Green, Surrey

Romney, Earl of (Michael Henry Marsham)

Type of Peerage	Hereditary
Political Allegiance	Conservative
Succeeded	1975
Born	22nd November 1910 in Rougham, Norfolk
Educated	Sherborne School
Professional Career	1932 - 39, 1945 - 63 Resident Land Agent, Lord O'Neill's Estate
	1939 - 45 Armed Forces (Major, Royal Artillery)
Subject Interests	Northern Ireland, Church of England, Agriculture, Forestry
Recreational Interests	Foxhunting
Correspondence Address	Wensum Farm, West Rudham, King's Lynn, Norfolk, PE31 8SZ Tel: (01485) 538249

Rootes, Baron (Nicholas Geoffrey Rootes)

Type of Peerage	Hereditary
Without Writ of Summons	
Succeeded	1992
Born	12th July 1951

Rosebery, Earl of (Neil Archibald Primrose)

Type of Peerage	Hereditary
Political Allegiance	None
Succeeded	1974
Born	11th February 1929

Rosslyn, Earl of (Peter St Clair Erskine)

Political Allegiance	Cross Bench
Succeeded	1977 (as a minor)
Born	31st March 1958

Rossmore, Baron (William Warner Westenra)

Type of Peerage	Hereditary
On Leave Of Absence	
Succeeded	1958
Born	14th February 1931

Rothermere, Viscount (Vere Harold Esmond Harmsworth)

Type of Peerage	Hereditary
Political Allegiance	None
Succeeded	1978
Born	27th August 1925 in London
Educated	Eton College Kent School, Conneticut, USA
Professional Career	1948 - 51 Anglo Canadian Paper Mill, Quebec
	1951 - 70 Associated Newspapers Ltd
	1970 - 78 Chairman, Associated Newspapers Ltd
	1978 - Chairman, Daily Mail and General Trust plc
Subject Interests	Media
Recreational Interests	Reading, Painting, Sailing, Walking
Correspondence Address	Chairman's Office, Daily Mail, Northcliffe House, 2 Derry Street, Kensington, London, W8 5TT Tel: (0171) 938 6610 Fax: (0171) 939 0043 E-mail: lord.rothermere@assocnews.co.uk
Personal Staff	Ms Kathleen Campbell *(Personal Assistant)* Tel: (0171) 938 6612

MEMBERS OF THE HOUSE OF LORDS

Rotherwick, Baron (Herbert William Kayzer)

Type of Peerage	Hereditary
Political Allegiance	Conservative
Succeeded	1996
Born	12th March 1954 in London
Educated	Harrow School
	Royal Military Academy, Sandhurst
Subject Interests	Aviation, Defence, Countryside
Recreational Interests . . .	Aviation, Conservation
Correspondence Address . .	House of Lords, Westminster,
	London, SW1A 0PW
	Tel: (01385) 992500
	Also Tel: (01608) 810207
	Fax: (01608) 811252
	E-mail: rotherwickr@
	cornburypark.demon.co.uk
Personal Staff	Ms Linda Tilson (*Personal Assistant*)
	Tel: (01608)811276

Rothes, Earl of (Ian Lionel Malcolm Leslie)

Type of Peerage	Hereditary
On Leave Of Absence	
Political Allegiance	None
Succeeded	1975
Born	10th May 1932 in London
Educated	Eton College

Rothschild, Baron (Nathaniel Charles Jacob Rothschild)

Type of Peerage	Hereditary
Political Allegiance	Cross Bench
Succeeded	1990
Born	29th April 1936

Rowallan, Baron (John Polson Cameron Corbett)

Type of Peerage	Hereditary
Political Allegiance	Conservative
Succeeded	1993
Born	8th March 1947 in Glasgow
Educated	Eton College
	Royal Agricultural College, Cirencester
Professional Career	Chartered Surveyor
	1977 - 90 Farmer
	1980 - Commentator at Equestrian Events
	1990 - 97 Director, Rowallan Group of
	Companies
Subject Interests	Devolution, Farming, Equine industry,
	Mental illness
Recreational Interests . . .	Showjumping, Skiing
Correspondence Address . .	House of Lords, Westminster,
	London, SW1A 0PW
	Tel: (0171) 219 3129 Fax: (0171) 219 2772

Roxburghe, Duke of (Guy David Innes-Ker)

Type of Peerage	Hereditary
Political Allegiance	Conservative
Succeeded	1974
Born	18th November 1954 in Edinburgh
Educated	Eton College
	Royal Military Academy, Sandhurst
	Magdalene College, Cambridge
Professional Career	1977 - Chairman, Roxburghe Estates
Subject Interests	Agriculture, Fishing, Horseracing, Scotland
Recreational Interests . . .	Golf, Fishing, Skiing, Tennis
Correspondence Address . .	Roxburghe Estate Office, Kelso,
	Roxburghshire, TD5 7SF
	Tel: (01573) 223333 Fax: (01573) 226056
Personal Staff	Miss Anne Chassels (*Secretary*)

Rugby, Baron (Robert Charles Maffey)

Type of Peerage	Hereditary
Political Allegiance	Cross Bench
Succeeded	1990
Born	4th May 1951 in London

Runcie, Baron (Rt Rev and Rt Hon Robert Alexander Kennedy Runcie MC)

Political Allegiance	Cross Bench
Created	1991 (previously in House of Lords as
	Bishop/Archbishop)
Born	2nd October 1921 in Liverpool
Educated	Merchant Taylors' School, Crosby
	Brasenose College, Oxford
	Westcott House, Cambridge
Professional Career	1939 - 46 Armed Forces (Scots Guards)
	1950 - 52 Curate, All Saints, Gosforth
	1953 - 56 Chaplain and Vice Principal,
	Westcott House, Cambridge
	1956 - 60 Dean, Trinity Hall, Cambridge
	1960 - 70 Principal, Cuddesdon Theological
	College
	1970 - 80 Bishop of St Albans
	1980 - 91 Archbishop of Canterbury
Subject Interests	History, Interfaith concerns
Recreational Interests . . .	Opera, Cricket
Correspondence Address . .	26A Jennings Road, St Albans, AL1 4PD
	Tel and Fax: (01727) 848021
Personal Staff	Mrs Frances Charlesworth
	(*Personal Assistant*)
	Tel: (01727) 836820

MEMBERS OF THE HOUSE OF LORDS

Runciman of Doxford, Viscount
    (Walter Garrison Runciman CBE)

Type of Peerage . . . . Hereditary
Political Allegiance . . . . . Cross Bench
Succeeded 1989
Born . . . . 10th November 1934 in London
Educated . . . . Eton College
        Trinity College, Cambridge
Professional Career . . . . . 1953 - 55 National Service
        1971 - Fellow, Trinity College, Cambridge
        1976 - Chairman, Walter Runciman plc,
          then (from 1990) Runciman
          Investments Ltd
        1986 - 87 President, General Council of
          British Shipping
        1990 - Deputy Chairman, Securities and
          Investments Board
        1991 - Chairman, Andrew Weir and Co Ltd
        1991 - 93 Chairman, Royal Commission on
          Criminal Justice

Russell, Earl (Conrad Sebastian Robert Russell)

Type of Peerage . . . . Hereditary
Political Allegiance . . . . . Liberal Democrat
Succeeded 1987
Born . . . . 15th April 1937 in Midhurst, Sussex
Educated . . . . Eton College
        Merton College, Oxford
Professional Career . . . . . 1960 - 79 Lecturer/Reader in History,
          Bedford College, University of London
         1979 - 84 Professor of History, Yale
          University, USA
        1984 - 90 Professor of British History,
          University College, London
        1990 - Professor, King's College, London
Political Career . . . . 1989 - Liberal Democrat Spokesman on
          Social Security, House of Lords
Subject Interests . . . . Social Security, Constitutional issues,
          Home affairs

Russell of Liverpool, Baron (Simon Gordon Jared Russell)

Type of Peerage . . . . Hereditary
Political Allegiance . . . . . Cross Bench
Succeeded 1981
Born . . . . 30th August 1982

Russell-Johnston, Baron (David Russel Russell-Johnston)

Type of Peerage . . . . Life
Created 1997
Born . . . . 28th July 1932
Educated . . . . Portree High School
        Edinburgh University
Political Career . . . . 1964 - 97 MP (Liberal, then Liberal
          Democrat) for Inverness, then Inverness
          Nairn and Lochabe
        1970 - 88 Chairman, then Leader,
          Scottish Liberal Party
        1988 - 92 Deputy Leader, Social and
          Liberal Democrats
        1988 - 94 President, Scottish
          Liberal Democrats
        1988 - 97 Liberal Democrat Spokesman on
          Foreign Affairs, European Community
          Affairs, House of Commons

Rutland, Duke of (Charles John Robert Manners CBE)

Type of Peerage . . . . Hereditary
On Leave Of Absence
Succeeded 1940
Born . . . . 28th May 1919

Ryder of Eaton Hastings, Baron (Don Ryder)

Type of Peerage . . . . Life
On Leave Of Absence
Created 1975
Born . . . . 16th September 1916

Ryder of Warsaw, Baroness (Sue Ryder CMG, OBE)

Political Allegiance . . . . . Cross Bench
Created 1979
Born . . . . 3rd July 1923
Educated . . . . Benenden School
Professional Career . . . . . Founder, Sue Ryder Foundation for Sick and
        Disabled

Ryder of Wensam, Baron (Rt Hon Richard Andew Ryder OBE)

Political Allegiance . . . . . Conservative
Created 1997
Born . . . . 4th February 1949
Educated . . . . Radley College
        Magdalene College, Cambridge
Political Career . . . . 1975 - 81 Political Secretary to Leader of
          Opposition, then Prime Minister (Rt Hon
          Margaret Thatcher MP)
        1983 - 97 MP (Conservative) for Mid Norfolk
        1986 - 88 Assistant Government Whip,
          House of Commons
        1988 - 89 Parliamentary Secretary, Ministry
          of Agriculture, Fisheries and Food
        1989 - 90 Economic Secretary, HM Treasury
        1990 Paymaster General
        1990 - 95 Government Chief Whip,
          House of Commons

MEMBERS OF THE HOUSE OF LORDS

S

Saatchi, Baron (Maurice Saatchi)

Type of Peerage . . . . Life
Political Allegiance . . . . . Conservative
Created 1996
Born . . . . 21st June 1946 in Baghdad, Iraq
Educated . . . . London School of Economics
Professional Career . . . . . 1970 Co Founder, Saatchi and Saatchi
Co (Chairman 1985 - 94)
1995 - Chairman, Megaolmedia plc
1995 - Partner, M and C Saatchi Agency
Correspondence Address . . M and C Saatchi, 36 Golden Square,
London, W1R 4EE
Tel: (0171) 543 4510/4513
Fax: (0171) 543 4502
E-mail: maurices@mcsaatch.com
Personal Staff . . . . Mr James Stuart *(Personal Assistant)*
Tel: (0171) 543 4510
Mrs Camilla Graham *(Secretary)*
Tel: (0171) 543 4513

Sackville, Baron (Lionel Bertrand Sackville-West)

Type of Peerage . . . . Hereditary
Political Allegiance . . . . . Conservative
Succeeded 1965
Born . . . . 30th May 1913 in London
Educated . . . . Winchester College
Magdalen College, Oxford
Subject Interests . . . . Forestry and Estate Management
Recreational Interests . . . Forestry planting, Reading, Music
Correspondence Address . . Knole, Sevenoaks, Kent, TN15 0RP
Tel: (01732) 455694

Sainsbury, Baron (Alan John Sainsbury)

Type of Peerage . . . . Life
Created 1962
Born . . . . 13th August 1902
Professional Career . . . . . 1956 - Chairman, then President,
J Sainsbury plc

Sainsbury of Preston Candover, Baron (John Davan Sainsbury KG)

Type of Peerage . . . . Life
Political Allegiance . . . . . Conservative
Created 1989
Born . . . . 2nd November 1927 in London
Educated . . . . Stowe School
Worcester College, Oxford
Professional Career . . . . . 1967 - 69 Vice-Chairman, then Chairman
and President, J Sainsbury plc
1987 - 91 Chairman, Royal Opera House
1993 - 97 President, British Retail
Consortium
1994 - Chairman, Board of Trustees,
Dulwich Picture Gallery
1995 - Chairman of Governors, Royal Ballet
Subject Interests . . . . Commerce, the Arts
Correspondence Address . . Stamford House, Stamford Street,
London, SE1 9LL
Tel: (0171) 695 6663 Fax: (0171) 695 7581
Personal Staff . . . . Ms Mary Cozens *(Secretary)*
Tel: (0171) 695 6661

Sainsbury of Turville, Baron (David John Sainsbury)

Type of Peerage . . . . Life
Political Allegiance . . . . . Labour
Created 1997
Born . . . . 24th October 1940 in Montreal, Canada
Educated . . . . Eton College
Kings College, Cambridge
Columbia University, New York
Professional Career . . . . . 1973 - Variously Financial Director, Deputy
Chairman, Chief Executive and (from
1992) Chairman, J Sainsbury plc
1984 - 93 Chairman, Savacentre Ltd
1991 - Chairman, London Business School
Subject Interests . . . . Economy, Industry, Education
Correspondence Address . . Chairman's Office, J Sainsbury plc,
Stamford House, Stamford Street,
London, SE1 9LL
Tel: (0171) 695 6362 Fax: (0171) 695 6279
Personal Staff . . . . Miss Gloria Turner *(Secretary)*
Tel: (0171) 695 6362

Saint Albans, Duke of (Murray de Vere Beauclerk)

Type of Peerage . . . . Hereditary
Political Allegiance . . . . . Conservative
Succeeded 1988
Born . . . . 19th January 1939

St Aldwyn, Earl (Michael Henry Hicks Beach)

Type of Peerage . . . . Hereditary
Political Allegiance . . . . . Conservative
Succeeded 1992
Born . . . . 7th February 1950 in Oxford
Professional Career . . . . . 1975 - 78 Self-employed in Brazil
1979 - 94 ED&F Management Group
1994 - Managing Director, International
Fund Marketing (UK) Ltd
Correspondence Address . . Williamstrip Park, Coln St Aldwyns,
Cirencester, GL7 5AT

St Davids, Viscount (Colwyn Jestyn John Phillips)

Type of Peerage . . . . Hereditary
Political Allegiance . . . . . Conservative
Succeeded 1991
Born . . . . 30th January 1939
Political Career . . . . 1992 - 94 Government Whip, (Lord in
Waiting)
Deputy Speaker and Deputy Chairman of
Committees, House of Lords

St Germans, Earl of (Peregnne Nicholas Elliot)

Type of Peerage . . . . Hereditary
Political Allegiance . . . . . Conservative
Succeeded 1988
Born . . . . 2nd January 1941

St Helens, Baron (Richard Frances Hughes Young)

Type of Peerage . . . . Hereditary
Political Allegiance . . . . None
Succeeded 1980
Born . . . . 4th November 1945

MEMBERS OF THE HOUSE OF LORDS

St John of Bletso, Baron (Anthony Tudor St John)

Type of Peerage	Hereditary
Political Allegiance	Cross Bench
Succeeded	1978
Born	16th May 1957 in London
Educated	Diocesan College, Cape Town
	Cape Town University
	University of South Africa
	London University
Professional Career	1982 - Solicitor, South Africa
	1983 - 85 Adviser/Auditor, Shell (SA)
	1985 - 89 Oil Analyst, County NatWest
	Securities
	1991 - Consultant, Merrill Lynch
	International
	1994 - Non Executive Chairman,
	Eurotrust International SA
	1995 - Chairman of Governing Board,
	Certification International
Political Career	1996 - Vice Chairman, All Party
	Parliamentary South Africa Group
	1996 - Member, European Communities
	Sub-Committee on Finance, Trade and
	External Affairs
	1997 - Member of House of Lords Library
	and Computers Sub-Committee
Subject Interests	Foreign affairs, (particularly Southern
	Africa), Environment, Deregulation,
	Financial services
Recreational Interests	Golf, Tennis, Skiing, Bridge
Correspondence Address	House of Lords, Westminster,
	London, SW1A 0PW
	Tel and Fax: (0171) 730 9922
	E-mail: astj@enterprise.net

St John of Fawsley, Baron
(Rt Hon Norman Antony Francis St John-Stevas)

Type of Peerage	Life
Political Allegiance	Conservative
Created	1987
Born	18th May 1929
Educated	Ratcliffe College
	Fitzwilliam College, Cambridge
Political Career	1964 - 87 MP (Conservative) for Chelmsford
	1972 - 73 Parliamentary Secretary, then
	Minister of State, Department of Education
	and Science
	1974 - 78 Opposition Spokesman on
	Education, Science and Arts
	1978 - 79 Shadow Leader of the House
	(of Commons)
	1979 - 81 Chancellor of the Duchy of
	Lancaster and Leader of the House of
	Commons and Minister for the Arts

Saint Levan, Baron (John Francis Arthur St Aubyn DSC)

Type of Peerage	Hereditary
Political Allegiance	Conservative
Succeeded	1978
Born	23rd February 1919 in London
Educated	Eton College
	Trinity College, Cambridge
Professional Career	1948 - Solicitor
Subject Interests	Conservation, Law, Farming
Recreational Interests	Sailing
Correspondence Address	St Michael's Mount, Marazion,
	Cornwall, TR17 0HT

Saint Oswald, Baron (Derek Edward Anthony Winn)

Type of Peerage	Hereditary
Political Allegiance	Conservative
Succeeded	1984
Born	9th July 1919 in London

St Vincent, Viscount (Ronald George James Jervis)

Type of Peerage	Hereditary
On Leave Of Absence	
Succeeded	1940
Born	3rd May 1905

Salisbury, Bishop of (Rt Rev David Stafforth Stancliffe)

Type of Peerage	Bishop
Political Allegiance	None
Born	1st October 1942
Educated	Westminster School
	Trinity College, Oxford
	Cuddesdon Theological College
Professional Career	1967 - 70 Assistant Curate,
	St Bartholomews, Armley, Leeds
	1970 - 77 Chaplain, Clifton College, Bristol
	1977 - 82 Canon of Portsmouth Cathedral,
	Diocesan
	1982 - 93 Provost of Portsmouth
	1993 - Bishop of Salisbury
	1993 - Chairman, Church of England
	Liturgical Commission
Correspondence Address	South Canonry, Salisbury,
	Wiltshire, SP1 2ER
	Tel: (01722) 334031

Salisbury, Marquess of (Robert Edward Peter Cecil)

Type of Peerage	Hereditary
Political Allegiance	Conservative
Succeeded	1972
Born	24th October 1916
Political Career	1950 - 54 MP (Conservative) for
	Bournemouth West

Saltoun of Abernethy, Lady (Flora Marjory Fraser)

Type of Peerage	Hereditary
Political Allegiance	Cross Bench
Succeeded	1979
Born	18th October 1930 in Edinburgh
Educated	St Mary's School, Wantage
Subject Interests	Scottish affairs, Forestry, Children

Samuel, Viscount (David Herbert Samuel CBE)

Type of Peerage	Life
Political Allegiance	Cross Bench
Succeeded	1997
Born	8th July 1922

Sandberg, Baron (Michael Graham Ruddock Sandberg CBE)

Type of Peerage	Life
Political Allegiance	Liberal Democrat
Created	1997
Born	31st May 1927

M E M B E R S   O F   T H E   H O U S E   O F   L O R D S

Sanderson of Bowden, Baron (Charles Russell Sanderson DL)

Type of Peerage	Life
Political Allegiance	Conservative
Created	1985
Born	30th April 1933 in Melrose, Scotland
Educated	Glenalmond College
	Bradford University
Professional Career	1958 - 87 Partner, Sanderson Wool and Yarn Merchants
	1983 - 87 Chairman, Edinburgh Financial Trust
	1983 - 87 Chairman, Shire Investment Trust
	1991 - Chairman, Harwick Cashmere Co
	1991 - Chairman, Scottish Mortgage and Trust plc
	1996 - Deputy Chairman, Clydesdale Bank
Political Career	1981 - 86 Chairman, National Union of Conservative Associations
	1987 - 90 Minister of State, Scottish Office
	1990 - 93 Chairman, Scottish Conservative Party
Subject Interests	Scottish affairs, Rural matters, Fishing, Agriculture
Recreational Interests	Golf, Fishing
Correspondence Address	Beckettsfield, Bowden, Melrose, Scotland, TD6 0ST
	Tel: (01835) 822271 Fax: (01835) 823272
Personal Staff	Mrs Helen Leishman *(Secretary)*
	Tel: (01835) 822271

Sandford, Baron (Rev John Cyril Edmondson DSC)

Type of Peerage	Hereditary
Political Allegiance	Conservative
Succeeded	1959
Born	22nd December 1920 in Goring-on-Thames
Educated	Eton College
	Dartmouth College
	Westcott House, Cambridge
Professional Career	1939 - 56 Royal Navy Commander
	1958 - 70 Priest, Parish of St Nicholas, Harpenden
	1974 - 84 President, Council for Environmental Education
	1977 - 89 Director, Ecclesiastical Insurance Office
	1980 - 86 President, Association of District Councils
	1981 - 89 Chairman, Standing Conference of London and South East Planning Authorities
	1982 - 88 Chairman, Redundant Churches Committee
	1982 - 89 Church Commissioner
Political Career	1966 - 70 Opposition Whip, House of Lords
	1970 - 73 Parliamentary Secretary, Department of Environment
	1973 - 74 Parliamentary Secretary, Department of Education and Science
Subject Interests	Defence, Theology, Heritage, Farming, Forestry, Social services, Local government, Youth training, Disability
Recreational Interests	Scrabble, Birdwatching
Correspondence Address	27 Ashley Gardens, Ambrosden Avenue, London, SW1P 1QD
	Tel: (0171) 834 5722
Personal Staff	Lady Catharine Sandford *(Secretary)*

Sandhurst, Baron (Terence Mansfield)

Type of Peerage	Hereditary
Political Allegiance	Cross Bench
Succeeded	1964
Born	4th September 1920 in Edinburgh
Educated	Harrow School
Subject Interests	Channel Islands, RAF, Civil Aviation
Recreational Interests	Golf
Correspondence Address	La Voliere, Les Ruisseaux, St Brelade, Jersey, JE3 8DD
	Tel and Fax: (01534) 46040

Sandwich, Earl of (John Edward Hollister Montagu)

Type of Peerage	Hereditary
Political Allegiance	Cross Bench
Succeeded	1995
Born	11th April 1943 in London
Educated	Eton College
	Trinity College, Cambridge
Professional Career	1974 - 86 Information and Research Officer, Christian Aid
	1982 - Joint Administrator, Mapperton Estate, Dorset
	1986 - 88 Freelance Journalist
	1986 - 92 Editorial Consultant, Save the Children, Fund Care International,
Subject Interests	International development, Asylum and immigration, Education
Correspondence Address	House of Lords, Westminster, London, SW1A 0PW
	Tel: (0171) 223 0997 Fax: (0171) 978 4535

Sandys, Baron (Richard Michael Oliver Hill)

Type of Peerage	Hereditary
Political Allegiance	Conservative
Succeeded	1961
Born	21st July 1931
Political Career	1974 Government Whip, (Lord in Waiting)
	1974 - 79 Opposition Whip, House of Lords
	1979 - 82 Deputy Government Chief Whip, House of Lords (Captain of the Yeomen of the Guard)

Savile, Baron (George Halifax Lumley-Savile)

Type of Peerage	Hereditary
Political Allegiance	Conservative
Succeeded	1931 (as a minor)
Born	24th January 1919 in London
Educated	Eton College
Subject Interests	Agriculture, Rural housing
Recreational Interests	Classical music
Correspondence Address	Gryce Hall, Shelley, Huddersfield, West Yorkshire, HD8 8LP
	Tel: (01484) 602774

MEMBERS OF THE HOUSE OF LORDS

Saville of Newdigate, Baron (Rt Hon Mark Oliver Saville)

Type of Peerage	Life (Law Lord)
Political Allegiance	Cross Bench
Created	1997
Born	20th March 1936
Professional Career	Barrister (QC 1975)
	1985 - 93 High Court Judge (Queen's Bench Division)
	1994 - 97 Lord Justice of Appeal
	1997 - Lord of Appeal in Ordinary

Saye and Sele, Baron (Nathaniel Thomas Allen Fiennes)

Type of Peerage	Hereditary
On Leave Of Absence	
Succeeded	1968
Born	22nd September 1920 in London
Educated	Eton College
Professional Career	1952 - 97 Chartered Surveyor (Partner, Laws and Fiennes)
	1967 - 90 Chairman, Ernest Cook Trust
	1980 - 87 Regional Director, Lloyds Bank
Subject Interests	Countryside, Heritage
Correspondence Address	Broughton Castle, Banbury, Oxfordshire, OX15 5EB
	Tel: (01295) 262624

Scanlon of Davyhulme, Baron (Hugh Parr Scanlon)

Type of Peerage	Life
Political Allegiance	Labour
Created	1979
Born	20th April 1913 in Melbourne, Australia
Educated	National Council of Labour Colleges
Professional Career	1947 - 78 Divisional Organiser, Member of Executive Council and (from 1967) President, Amalgamated Engineering Union
	1968 - 78 Member, TUC General Council
	1974 - 78 President, Metalworkers Federation
	1975 - 82 Chairman, Engineering Industry Training Board
	1976 - 82 Board Member, British Gas Corporation
Subject Interests	Education, Training
Recreational Interests	Swimming, Gardening, Golf
Correspondence Address	23 Seven Stones Drive, Broadstairs, Kent, CT10 1TW
	Tel: (01843) 867064

Scarbrough, Earl of (Richard Aldred Lumley)

Type of Peerage	Hereditary
Political Allegiance	None
Succeeded	1969
Born	5th December 1932 in London
Educated	Eton College
	Magdalen College, Oxford
Professional Career	1996 - Lord Lieutenant of South Yorkshire
Correspondence Address	Sandbeck Park, Maltby, Rotherham, S66 8PF
	Tel: (01302) 742210 Fax: (01302) 750090

Scarman, Baron (Rt Hon Leslie George Scarman OBE)

Type of Peerage	Life (Former Law Lord)
Political Allegiance	Cross Bench
Created	1977
Born	29th July 1911 in Streatham, London
Educated	Radley College
	Brasenose College, Oxford
Professional Career	1936 - Barrister (QC 1957)
	1961 - 73 High Court Judge
	1965 - 73 Chairman, Law Commission
	1973 - 76 Chairman, Council of Legal Education
	1973 - 77 A Lord Justice of Appeal
	1976 - 81 Vice Chairman, English National Opera
	1977 - 86 Lord of Appeal in Ordinary
	1981 - 89 President, Royal Institute of Public Administration
	1984 - President, Constitutional Reform Centre
Subject Interests	Law reform, Constitutional reform, Human rights, Social services

Scarsdale, Viscount (Francis John Nathaniel Curzon)

Type of Peerage	Hereditary
Political Allegiance	None
Succeeded	1977
Born	28th July 1924 in London
Professional Career	1943 - 47 Captain, Scots Guards
	1948 - 64 Shell International Petroleum Co
	1969 - 77 Estate Manager, Kedleston Estate
Recreational Interests	Racing, Photography, Shooting, Piping

Scotland of Asthoil, Baroness (Patricia Janet Scotland QC)

Type of Peerage	Life
Political Allegiance	Labour
Created	1997
Educated	University of London
Professional Career	1977 - Barrister (QC 1991)
	1994 - Member, Millennium Commission

Seafield, Earl of (Ian Derek Francis Ogilvie-Grant)

Type of Peerage	Hereditary
Political Allegiance	Conservative
Succeeded	1969
Born	20th March 1939 in London
Educated	Eton College
	Royal Agricultural College, Cirencester
Subject Interests	Agriculture, Forestry, Defence
Recreational Interests	Countryside pursuits
Correspondence Address	Old Cullen, Cullen, Buckie, Banffshire, Scotland, AB56 2XW
	Tel: (01542) 840221

MEMBERS OF THE HOUSE OF LORDS

Seccombe, Baroness (Joan Anna Dalziel Seccombe DBE)
Type of Peerage . . . . Life
Political Allegiance . . . . . Conservative
Created 1991
Born . . . . 3rd May 1930
Educated . . . . St Martin's School, Solihull
Political Career . . . . 1979 - 81 Member, West Midlands County
          Council
          1981 - 84 Chairman, Conservative Women's
            National Committee
          1984 - 88 Vice-Chairman, then Chairman,
            National Union Associations
          1988 - Vice Chairman, Conservative Party
            (with special responsibility for women)
          1997 - Opposition Whip, House of Lords

Sefton of Garston, Baron (William Henry Sefton)
Type of Peerage . . . . Life
Political Allegiance . . . . . Labour
Created 1978
Born . . . . 5 August 1915
Educated . . . . Duncombe Road School, Liverpool
Professional Career . . . . 1974 - 85 Chairman, then Vice Chairman,
            Warrington and Runcorn Development
            Corporation
          1975 - 89 Chairman, North West Economic
            Planning Council
Political Career . . . . 1953 - 74 Member, Liverpool City Council
            (Leader 1964)
          1974 - 77 Chairman and Leader, Merseyside
            County Council
          1977 - 79 Leader of the Opposition,
            Merseyside County Council

Selborne, Earl of (John Roundell Palmer KBE, FRS)
Type of Peerage . . . . Hereditary
Political Allegiance . . . . . Conservative
Succeeded 1971
Born . . . . 24th March 1940 in Somerset
Educated . . . . Eton College
          Christ Church, Oxford
Professional Career . . . . . 1983 - 89 Chairman, Agricultural and
            Food Research Council
          1991 - 97 Chairman, Joint Nature
            Conservation Committee
Political Career . . . . 1991 - 93 Chairman European Communities
          Sub Committee on Agriculture, Fisheries
          and Food, House of Lords
          1993 - Member, Royal Commission on
            Environmental Pollution
          1993 - 97 Chairman, Select Committee on
            Science and Technology, House of Lords
          1996 - Chancellor, Southampton University
Subject Interests . . . . Nature conservation, Environmental issues,
          Agriculture, Higher education
Correspondence Address . . Temple Manor, Selborne, Alton,
          Hampshire, GU34 3LR
          Tel: (01420) 476003 Fax: (01420) 475878
          E-mail: selbornejr@parliament.uk

Selby, Viscount (Edward Thomas William Gully)
Type of Peerage . . . . Hereditary
Political Allegiance . . . . . None
Succeeded 1997
Born . . . . 21st September 1967

Selkirk of Douglas, Baron
    (Rt Hon James Alexander Douglas-Hamilton QC)
Type of Peerage . . . . Life
Political Allegiance . . . . . Conservative
Created 1997
Born . . . . 31st July 1942 in Strathaven, Lancashire
Educated . . . . Eton College
          Balliol College, Oxford
          Edinburgh University
Professional Career . . . . . Advocate, Scotland
Political Career . . . . 1974 - 97 MP (Conservative) for
            Edinburgh West
          1977 - 79 Opposition Whip,
            House of Commons
          1979 - 81 Government Whip,
            House of Commons
          1987 - 97 Parliamentary Secretary,
            Minister of State, Scottish Office
Subject Interests . . . . Scottish issues, Environment, Heritage,
          Health, Education, Housing, Transport
Recreational Interests . . . Golf, History, Forestry
Correspondence Address . . House of Lords, Westminster,
          London, SW1A 0PW
Lord Selkirk of Douglas previously disclaimed the Earldom of Selkirk for his lifetime, but now sits in the House of Lords by virtue of a separately created life peerage.

Selsdon, Baron (Malcolm McEacharn Mitchell-Thomson)
Type of Peerage . . . . Hereditary
Political Allegiance . . . . . Conservative
Succeeded 1963
Born . . . . 27th October 1937 in London
Professional Career . . . . . 1972 - 76 C T Bowring Group
          1976 - 90 Midland Bank Group
          1990 - President, British Exporters
            Association
Subject Interests . . . . Foreign affairs, Trade and industry, Defence
Recreational Interests . . . Squash, Tennis, Lawn tennis, Skiing, Sailing

Sempill, Baron (James William Stuart Whitemore Sempill)
Type of Peerage . . . . Hereditary
Political Allegiance . . . . . Cross Bench
Succeeded 1995
Born . . . . 25th February 1949 in London
Professional Career . . . . . 1981 - 92 Manager/Director Various
            Companies, South Africa
          1992 - 95 Director, Scottish and Newcastle
Subject Interests . . . . Scottish education, Whiskey industry,
          Scottish devolution, South Africa
Recreational Interests . . . Watching rugby, Walking, Painting

MEMBERS OF THE HOUSE OF LORDS

Serota of Hampstead, Baroness (Beatrice Serota DBE)

Type of Peerage . . . . Life
Political Allegiance . . . . . Labour
Created 1967
Born . . . . 15th September 1919 in London
Educated . . . . John Howard School
　　　　　　　　　　London School of Economics
Professional Career . . . . . 1941 - 46 Administrative Civil Servant
　　　　　　　　　　1970 - 73 Director of Studies, London
　　　　　　　　　　　School of Economics
　　　　　　　　　　1974 - 82 Chairman, Commission for Local
　　　　　　　　　　　Administration (Local Government
　　　　　　　　　　　Ombudsman)
Political Career . . . . 1945 - 49 Member, Hampstead Borough
　　　　　　　　　　　Council
　　　　　　　　　　1954 - 65 Member, London County Council
　　　　　　　　　　1965 - 67 Member, Greater London Council
　　　　　　　　　　1968 - 69 Government Whip (Baroness in
　　　　　　　　　　　Waiting)
　　　　　　　　　　1969 - 70 Minister of State (Health),
　　　　　　　　　　　Department of Health and Social Security
　　　　　　　　　　1986 - 92 Principal Deputy Chairman of
　　　　　　　　　　　Committees and Chairman of European
　　　　　　　　　　　Communities Select Committee,
　　　　　　　　　　　House of Lords
　　　　　　　　　　1996 - Member, Select Committee on
　　　　　　　　　　　Public Service, House of Lords
　　　　　　　　　　　Deputy Speaker and Deputy Chairman of
　　　　　　　　　　　Committees, House of Lords
Subject Interests . . . . Social Services, Local Government, Public
　　　　　　　　　　administration, Europe
Recreational Interests . . . Gardening, Needlepoint
Correspondence Address . . The Coach House, 15 Lyndhurst Terrace,
　　　　　　　　　　London, NW3 5QA
　　　　　　　　　　House of Lords, Westminster,
　　　　　　　　　　London, SW1A 0PW
　　　　　　　　　　Tel: (0171) 219 3176 Fax: (0171) 219 5979

Sewel, Baron (John Buttifant Sewel CBE)

Type of Peerage . . . . Life
Political Allegiance . . . . . Labour
Created 1995
Born . . . . 15th January 1946
Political Career . . . . 1994 - 95 Member, Scottish Constitutional
　　　　　　　　　　　Commission
　　　　　　　　　　1997 - Parliamentary Secretary,
　　　　　　　　　　　Scottish Office

Shaftesbury, Earl of (Anthony Ashley Cooper)

Type of Peerage . . . . Hereditary
Political Allegiance . . . . . Conservative
Succeeded 1961
Born . . . . 22nd May 1938

Shannon, Earl of (Richard Bentinck Boyle)

Type of Peerage . . . . Hereditary
Political Allegiance . . . . . Cross Bench
Succeeded 1963
Born . . . . 23rd October 1924 in Octacumund, India
Professional Career . . . . . 1942 - 53 Irish Guards
　　　　　　　　　　1954 - 69 Director, Various Industrial
　　　　　　　　　　　Companies
　　　　　　　　　　1966 - 74 President, Architectural Metal
　　　　　　　　　　　Craftsmen's Association
　　　　　　　　　　1969 - 85 Director, Committee of Directors
　　　　　　　　　　　of Research Associations
　　　　　　　　　　1971 - 86 Secretary/Treasurer, Federation of
　　　　　　　　　　　European Industrial Co-operative
　　　　　　　　　　　Research Organisations
　　　　　　　　　　1977 - 83 Chairman, Foundation for
　　　　　　　　　　　Science and Technology
Political Career . . . . 1968 - 78 Deputy Speaker and Deputy
　　　　　　　　　　　Chairman of Committees, House of Lords
Subject Interests . . . . Trans-Caucasus, Industrial research, Science
　　　　　　　　　　and technology

Sharples, Baroness (Pamela Sharples)

Type of Peerage . . . . Life
Political Allegiance . . . . . Conservative
Created 1973
Born . . . . 11th February 1923 in Sunningdale,
　　　　　　　　　　Berkshire
Educated . . . . Southover Manor, Lewes
　　　　　　　　　　Florence and Zurich
Professional Career . . . . . 1941 - 46 WAAF
　　　　　　　　　　1982 - 93 Director, TVS
Subject Interests . . . . Small Businesses, Prisoner's Wives, Cheque
　　　　　　　　　　book Journalism
Recreational Interests . . . Golf, Tennis, Gardening, Walking
Correspondence Address . . 60 Westminster Gardens, Marsham Street,
　　　　　　　　　　London, SW1P 4JG
　　　　　　　　　　Tel and Fax: (0171) 821 1875
　　　　　　　　　　Also Tel: (01747) 8529
Baroness Sharples is the widow of the former Conservative Minister and
Governor of Burmuda, Sir Richard Sharples.

Shaughnessy, Baron (William Graham Shaughnessy)

Type of Peerage . . . . Hereditary
Political Allegiance . . . . . Cross Bench
Succeeded . . . . 1938 (as a minor)
Born . . . . 28th March 1922 in Montreal, Canada
Professional Career . . . . . 1981 - Director, Canada-UK Chamber of
　　　　　　　　　　Commerce
Subject Interests . . . . Delegated legislation, Commonwealth and
　　　　　　　　　　foreign affairs

MEMBERS OF THE HOUSE OF LORDS

Shaw of Northstead, Baron (Michael Norman Shaw)

Type of Peerage	Life
Political Allegiance	Conservative
Created	1994
Born	9th October 1920 in Leeds
Educated	Sedbergh School
Professional Career	1945 - 78 Chartered Accountant
Political Career	1960 - 64 MP (Conservative) for Brighouse and Spenborough
	1966 - 92 MP (Conservative) for Scarborough and Whitby
Subject Interests	Finance, Europe
Correspondence Address	Duxbury Hall, Liversedge, West Yorkshire, WF15 7NR
	Tel: (01924) 402270

Shawcross, Baron
(Rt Hon Hartley William Shawcross GBE QC)

Type of Peerage	Life
Political Allegiance	Cross Bench
Created	1959
Born	4th February 1902 in Giessen, Germany
Professional Career	1925 Barrister (QC 1939)
	1945 Chief Prosecutor for UK, Nuremberg War Crime Trials
	1950 - 67 UK Member, Court of Arbitration, The Hague
	1952 - 57 Chairman, Bar Council
	1961 - 62 Chairman, Royal Commission on the Press
	1969 - 80 Chairman, Panel on Takeovers and Mergers
Political Career	1945 - 58 MP (Labour) for St Helens
	1945 - 51 Attorney General
	1951 President of the Board of Trade
Recreational Interests	Sailing

Shepherd, Baron (Rt Hon Malcolm Newton Shepherd)

Type of Peerage	Hereditary
Political Allegiance	Labour
Succeeded	1952
Born	29th September 1918 in Blackburn, Lancashire
Political Career	1962 - 64 Opposition Chief Whip, House of Lords (Captain of the Gentlemen at Arms)
	1964 - 67 Government Chief Whip, House of Lords (and Deputy Leader, House of Lords 1968 - 70)
	1967 - 70 Minister of State, Foreign Office
	1970 - 74 Deputy Leader of the Opposition, House of Lords
	1974 - 78 Lord Privy Seal and the Leader of House of Lords
Subject Interests	Procedure
Recreational Interests	Golf

Sheppard of Didgemere, Baron (Allen John George Sheppard)

Type of Peerage	Life
Political Allegiance	Conservative
Created	1994
Born	25th December 1932 in Forest Gate, London
Educated	Ilford County High School
	London School of Economics
Professional Career	1958 - 75 Various Posts, Motor Industry (Ford, then Chrysler and British Leyland)
	1992 - Chairman, London First
	1993 - Chairman, McBride plc
	1994 - Chairman, Group Trust plc
	1995 - Co-Chairman, London Pride Partnership
	1995 - Chairman, Prince's Trust Administrative Council
	1996 - Chairman, GB Railways plc
	1996 - Chairman, Unipart Group plc
	1975 - 96 Director/Chief Executive/Chief Executive, then Chairman, Grand Metropolitan
Political Career	1992 - Member, Conservative Party Board of Management
Subject Interests	London
Recreational Interests	Gardens, Reading, Red Setter dogs
Correspondence Address	20 Cockspur Street, London, SW1Y 5BL
	Tel: (0171) 930 3445 Fax: (0171) 930 7808
Personal Staff	Ms Brenda Cook *(Secretary)*

Sherfield, Baron (Christopher James Makins)

Type of Peerage	Hereditary
Without Writ of Summons	
Succeeded	1996
Born	23rd July 1942

MEMBERS OF THE HOUSE OF LORDS

Shore of Stepney, Baron (Rt Hon Peter David Shore)

Type of Peerage . . . . Life
Political Allegiance . . . . . Labour
Created 1997
Born . . . . 20th May 1924 in Great Yarmouth, Norfolk
Educated . . . . Quarry Bank High School, Liverpool
King's College, Cambridge
Professional Career . . . . . Political Economist
Political Career . . . . 1959 - 64 Head of Research, Labour Party
Head Office
1964 - 97 MP (Labour) for Stepney, then
Stepney and Poplar, then Bethnal Green
and Stepney
1965 - 66 PPS to Prime Minister,
(Rt Hon Harold Wilson MP)
1966 - 67 Parliamentary Secretary,
Ministry of Technology
1967 Parliamentary Secretary,
Department of Economic Affairs
1967 - 69 Secretary of State for
Economic Affairs
1969 - 70 Minister without Portfolio and
Deputy Leader of the House of Commons
1971 - 74 Opposition Spokesman on
European Affairs, House of Commons
1974 - 76 Secretary of State for Trade
1976 - 79 Secretary of State for Environment
1979 - 80 Opposition Spokesman on Foreign
Affairs, House of Commons
1980 - 83 Opposition Spokesman on
Treasury and Economic Affairs, House of
Commons
1983 - 84 Opposition Spokesman on Trade
and Industry, House of Commons
1984 - 87 Shadow Leader of the
House of Commons
1994 - Member, Committee on Standards in
Public Life
Subject Interests . . . . Europe
Recreational Interests . . . Swimming, Cinema

**Shrewsbury, Earl of (Charles Henry,
John Benedict Crofton Chetwynd Chetwynd-Talbot)**

Type of Peerage . . . . Hereditary
Political Allegiance . . . . . Cross Bench
Succeeded 1980
Born . . . . 18th December 1952 in Stafford
Educated . . . . Harrow School
Professional Career . . . . . 1984 - 93 Director and Deputy Chairman,
Britannia Building Society
1992 - 97 President, Building Societies
Association
1996 - President, British Institute of
Innkeeping
Subject Interests . . . . Agriculture, Commerce and industry, Horses
and horseracing
Recreational Interests . . . Field sports
Correspondence Address . . Wanfield Hall, Kingstone, Uttoxeter,
Staffordshire, ST14 8QT
Tel: (01889) 500275
E-mail: eof@wanfield.u-net.com

**Shuttleworth, Baron
(Charles Geoffrey Nicholas Kay-Shuttleworth)**

Type of Peerage . . . . Hereditary
Political Allegiance . . . . . Conservative
Succeeded 1975
Born . . . . 2nd August 1948
Educated . . . . Eton College
Professional Career . . . . . 1977 - 96 Partner, Burton, Barnes and
Vigess (Chartered Surveyors)
1990 - Chairman, Rural Development
Commission
1994 - 96 Chairman, National and Provincial
Building Society
1996 - Deputy Chairman, Abbey
National plc

Sidmouth, Viscount (John Tonge Anthony Pellew Addington)

Type of Peerage . . . . Hereditary
Political Allegiance . . . . . Cross Bench
Succeeded 1976
Born . . . . 3rd October 1914

Sieff of Brimpton, Baron (Joseph Marcus Sieff OBE)

Type of Peerage . . . . Life
Political Allegiance . . . . . None
Succeeded 1980

Silsoe, Baron (David Malcolm Trustram Eve QC)

Type of Peerage . . . . Hereditary
On Leave Of Absence
Succeeded 1976
Born . . . . 2nd May 1930 in London
Educated . . . . Winchester College
Christ Church, Oxford
Columbia University, New York
Professional Career . . . . . 1955 - Barrister (QC 1972)
Correspondence Address . . 2 Mitre Court Buildings, Temple,
London, EC4Y 7BX

Simon, Viscount (Jan David Simon)

Type of Peerage . . . . Hereditary
Political Allegiance . . . . . Labour
Succeeded 1993
Born . . . . 20th July 1940 in London
Educated . . . . Westminster School
Southampton University
Sydney Technical College
Subject Interests . . . . Road transport, Road safety, Australia,
Disabled people, Merchant Navy

MEMBERS OF THE HOUSE OF LORDS

Simon of Glaisdale, Baron
(Rt Hon Jocelyn Edward Salis Simon)

Type of Peerage . . . . Life (Former Law Lord)
Political Allegiance . . . . . Cross Bench
Created 1971
Born . . . . 15th January 1911 in London
Educated . . . . Gresham's School, Holt
     Trinity Hall, Cambridge
Professional Career . . . . . 1934 - Barrister (KC 1951)
     1962 - 71 President, Probate, Divorce and
       Admiralty Division, High Court
     1971 - 77 Lord of Appeal in Ordinary
Political Career . . . . 1951 - 62 MP (Conservative) for
     Middlesborough West
     1957 - 58 Parliamentary Secretary,
       Home Office
     1958 - 59 Financial Secretary, HM Treasury
     1959 - 62 Solicitor General

Simon of Highbury, Baron (David Alec Gwyn Simon)

Type of Peerage . . . . Life
Political Allegiance . . . . . Labour
Created 1997
Born . . . . 24th July 1939 in London
Educated . . . . Christ's Hospital
     Gonville and Caius, Cambridge
Professional Career . . . . . 1961 - 97 Various Management Posts,
     British Petroleum (Managing Director
     1985 - 92, Chief Executive 1992 - 95,
     Chairman, 1995 - 97)
Political Career . . . . 1997 - Minister of State, Department of
     Trade and Industry
Subject Interests . . . . Industry, Commerce, Europe
Recreational Interests . . . Golf, Music, Reading, Watching sport

Simon of Wythenshawe, Baron (Roger Simon)

Type of Peerage . . . . Hereditary
Without Writ of Summons
Succeeded 1960
Born . . . . 16th October 1913 in Manchester
Educated . . . . Gresham's School
     Gonville and Caius College, Cambridge
Correspondence Address . . Oakhill, Chester Avenue,
     Richmond, Surrey, TW10 6NP
Note: The above mentioned peer does not use his title.

Simpson of Dunkeld, Baron (George Simpson)

Type of Peerage . . . . Life
Political Allegiance . . . . . Labour
Created 1997
Born . . . . 2nd July 1942 in Dundee
Educated . . . . Morgan Academy, Dundee
     Abertay University, Dundee
Professional Career . . . . . 1988 - 92 Chief Executive/Chairman,
     Rover Group
     1992 - 94 Deputy Chief Executive,
     British Aerospace
     1994 - 96 Chief Executive, Lucas
     Industries plc
     1996 - Managing Director, GEC plc
Subject Interests . . . . Trade and industry, Education, Training
Recreational Interests . . . Golf

Sinclair of Cleeve, Baron
(John Laurence Robert Sinclair cvo)

Type of Peerage . . . . Hereditary
Without Writ of Summons
Succeeded 1985
Born . . . . 6th January 1953

Sinha, Baron (Anindo Kumar Sinha)

Type of Peerage . . . . Hereditary
Without Writ of Summons
Succeeded 1992
Born . . . . 18th May 1930

Skelmersdale, Baron (Roger Bootle-Wilbraham)

Type of Peerage . . . . Hereditary
Political Allegiance . . . . . Conservative
Succeeded 1973
Born . . . . 2nd April 1945 in Cove, Farnborough,
     Hampshire
Political Career . . . . 1981 - 86 Government Whip,
     (Lord in Waiting)
     1986 - 87 Parliamentary Secretary,
     Department of Environment
     1987 - 89 Parliamentary Secretary,
     Department of Health and Social Security,
     then Department of Social Security
     1989 - 90 Parliamentary Secretary,
     Northern Ireland Office
     Deputy Speaker and Chairman of
     Committees, House of Lords
Subject Interests . . . . Energy, Privatised industries, Post office,
     Northern Ireland
Recreational Interests . . . Walking, Bridge, Gardening

Skidelsky of Tilton, Baron
(Robert Jacob Alexander Skidelsky)

Type of Peerage . . . . Life
Political Allegiance . . . . . Conservative
Created 1991
Born . . . . 25th April 1939 in Harbin, Manchuria
Educated . . . . Brighton College
     Jesus College, Oxford
Professional Career . . . . . 1965 - 68 Research Fellow, Nuffield
     College, Oxford
     1968 - 70 Research Fellow, British Academy
     1970 - 76 Associate Professor, John Hopkins
     University, Washington DC
     1976 - 78 Head of History, Philosophy and
     European Studies, North London
     Polytechnic
     1978 - Professor of International Studies,
     then of Political Economy (since 1990),
     Warwick University
     1991 - Chairman, Social Market Foundation
Political Career . . . . Opposition Spokesman on Media, Culture
     and Sport, House of Lords
Subject Interests . . . . Economic policy, Education, Social policy,
     Globalisation
Recreational Interests . . . Opera, Tennis, Conversation
Correspondence Address . . Tilton House, Firle, East Sussex, BN8 6LL
     Tel: (01323) 811570 Fax: (01323) 811017
     E-mail: rskidelsky@smf.couk
     Social Market Foundation, 11 Tufton Street,
     London, SW1P 3QB
     Tel: (0171) 222 7060 Fax: (0171) 222 0310
Personal Staff . . . . Miss Sara Lander *(Personal Assistant)*
     Tel: (0171) 222 7060

MEMBERS OF THE HOUSE OF LORDS

Sligo, Marquess of (Jeremy Ulick Browne)

Type of Peerage . . . . Hereditary
Without Writ of Summons
Succeeded 1991
Born . . . . 4th June 1939

Slim, Viscount (John Douglas Slim OBE)

Type of Peerage . . . . Hereditary
Political Allegiance . . . . . Cross Bench
Succeeded 1970
Born . . . . 20th July 1927
Professional Career . . . . . 1945 - 72 Armed Forces
1971 - President, Burma Star Association
1978 - 84 Chairman, British-Australia
Society (Vice President since 1988)
Subject Interests . . . . Foreign affairs, Defence, Exports,
Veterans' affairs

Slynn of Hadley, Baron (Rt Hon Gordon Slynn)

Type of Peerage . . . . Life (Law Lord)
Political Allegiance . . . . . Cross Bench
Created 1992
Born . . . . 17th February 1930
Professional Career . . . . . 1956 - Barrister (QC 1974)
1971 - 76 Recorder of Hereford
1974 - 76 Leading Counsel to the Treasury
1976 - 81 High Court Judge (Queens Bench
Division)
1978 - 81 President, Employment Appeal
Tribunal
1981 - 92 An Advocate General, then Judge,
European Community Court of Justice,
Luxembourg
1992 - Lord of Appeal in Ordinary
Parliamentary Career . . . 1996 - Chairman, Committee on the Public
Service, House of Lords

Smith, Baron (Rodney Smith KBE)

Type of Peerage . . . . Life
Political Allegiance . . . . . Cross Bench
Created 1978
Born . . . . 10th May 1914 in London
Educated . . . . Westminster School
St Thomas's Hospital
Professional Career . . . . . 1973 - 77 President/Consultant Surgeon,
Royal College of Surgeons
1978 - 80 President, Royal Society of
Medicine
Subject Interests . . . . Medicine and surgery
Recreational Interests . . . Bridge, Painting, All sports
Correspondence Address . . Dower Cottage, Marlow Common, Marlow,
Bucks, SL7 2QP
Tel: (01628) 485189

Smith of Clifton, Baron (Trevor Arthur Smith)

Type of Peerage . . . . Life
Political Allegiance . . . . . Liberal Democrat
Created 1997
Born . . . . 14th June 1937
Educated . . . . London School of Economics
Professional Career . . . . . 1960 - 62 Researcher, Acton Society Trust
1962 - 67 Lecturer in Politics, University of
Hull
1967 - 91 Lecturer, then Professor, Political
Studies, Queen Mary College, London
(also Senior Vice Principal 1989 - 91)
1991 - Vice-Chancellor, University of Ulster
Subject Interests . . . . Political science, Education, Constitutional
matters, Health, Tourism, Opera, Northern
Ireland, European Union
Recreational Interests . . . Watercolour painting
Correspondence Address . . University House, University of Ulster,
Coleraine, Co Londonderry, BT52 1SA
Tel: (01265) 324329 Fax: (01265) 324901
E-mail: tasmith@ulst.ac.uk
Personal Staff . . . . Mrs Margaret Connolly *(Personal Assistant)*
Tel: (01265) 324329

Smith of Gilmorehill, Baroness (Elizabeth Margaret Smith)

Type of Peerage . . . . Life
Political Allegiance . . . . . Labour
Created 1995
Born . . . . 4th June 1940 in Ayr, Scotland
Educated . . . . Hutchesons' Girls Grammar School, Glasgow
University of Glasgow
Professional Career . . . . . 1995 - Member, Press Complaints
Commission
Subject Interests . . . . Culture/Heritage, Foreign affairs especially
Former Soviet Union
Recreational Interests . . . Family life
Correspondence Address . . House of Lords, Westminster,
London, SW1P 0PW
Tel: (0171) 219 4437/5418
Fax: (0171) 219 0984
*Baroness Smith is the widow of the former Leader of the Labour Party,
Rt Hon John Smith MP.*

Snowdon, Earl of
(Antony Charles Robert Armstrong-Jones GCVO)

Type of Peerage . . . . Hereditary (First Creation)
Political Allegiance . . . . . Cross Bench
Created 1961
Born . . . . 7th March 1930 in London
Educated . . . . Sandroyd School, Dorset
Eton College
Jesus College, Cambridge
Professional Career . . . . . 1950 - Photographer
1961 - Design Council, Sunday Times and
Sunday Times Magazine, Design
Magazine, Telegraph Magazine,
Vogue Magazine, Vanity Fair
Subject Interests . . . . Problems facing disabled people, Design for
disabled people
Correspondence Address . . 22 Launceston Place, London, W8 5RL
Tel: (0171) 937 9293 Fax: (0171) 938 1727
Personal Staff . . . . Mrs Hannah Christopherson
(Personal Assistant)

MEMBERS OF THE HOUSE OF LORDS

Somerleyton, Baron (Savile William Francis Crossley KCVO)
Type of Peerage . . . . Hereditary
Succeeded 1959
Born . . . . 17th September 1928 in London
Educated . . . . Eton College
Royal Agricultural College, Cirencester
Professional Career . . . . . Farmer
1978 - 91 Lord in Waiting to HM the Queen
1994 - 97 Director, Essex and Suffolk Water
Subject Interests . . . . Conservation
Recreational Interests . . . Hunting, Shooting
Correspondence Address . . Somerleyton Hall, Somerleyton, Lowestoft,
Suffolk, NR32 5QQ
Tel: (01502) 730308 Fax: (01502) 732143
Personal Staff . . . . Mrs Fiona Clark *(Private Secretary)*
Tel: (01502) 730224

Somers, Baron (Philip Sebastian Somers Cocks)
Type of Peerage . . . . Hereditary
Political Allegiance . . . . . Conservative
Succeeded 1995
Born . . . . 4th January 1948 in Rome
Educated . . . . Craig-y-Parc School, Cardiff
Subject Interests . . . . History
Recreational Interests . . . Music, particularly opera
Correspondence Address . . 19 Kempson Road, London, SW6 4PX
Tel: (0171) 736 7000
Note: The above mentioned peer is not at present active in the House of Lords.

Somerset, Duke of (John Michael Edward Seymour)
Type of Peerage . . . . Hereditary
Political Allegiance . . . . . Cross Bench
Succeeded 1984
Born . . . . 30th December 1952 in Bath
Educated . . . . Eton College
Subject Interests . . . . Rural affairs, Foreign affairs, Defence
Recreational Interests . . . Walking
Correspondence Address . . House of Lords, Westminster,
London, SW1A 0PW
Tel: (01803) 866633 Fax: (01807) 866626

Soper, Baron (Rev Donald Oliver Soper)
Type of Peerage . . . . Life
Political Allegiance . . . . . Labour
Created 1965
Born . . . . 31st January 1903 in London
Educated . . . . Haberdashers Aske's School, London
St Catharine's College, Cambridge
Wesley House, Cambridge
Professional Career . . . . . Methodist Minister
1926 - 29 Minister, Bermondsey,
South London
1929 - 36 Superintendent Methodist
Minister, Islington Central Hall, North
London
1936 - 78 Superintendent Methodist
Minister, Kingsway Hall, London
1974 - 78 Chairman, Shelter
Subject Interests . . . . Peace and pacifism, Social welfare,
Homelessness, Animal welfare,
Alcohol addiction
Recreational Interests . . . Music, Watching sport, Open air speaking
Correspondence Address . . 19 Thayer Street, London, W1M 5LJ
Tel: (0171) 935 6179
Personal Staff . . . . Miss Kathleen Humphreys *(Secretary)*

Soulbury, Viscount (James Herwald Ramsbotham)
Type of Peerage . . . . Hereditary
Political Allegiance . . . . . Cross Bench
Succeeded 1971
Born . . . . 21st March 1915

Soulsby of Swaffham Prior, Baron
(Ernest Jackson Lawson Soulsby)
Type of Peerage . . . . Life
Political Allegiance . . . . . Conservative
Created 1990
Born . . . . 23rd June 1926 in Haltwistle
Educated . . . . Queen Elizabeth Grammar School, Penrith
University of Edinburgh
Professional Career . . . . . 1949 - 52 Veterinary Officer, City of
Edinburgh
1952 - 54 Lecturer, Bristol University
1954 - 64 Lecturer, Cambridge University
1964 - 78 Professor of Parasitology,
Pennsylvania University, USA
1978 - 93 Professor of Animal Pathology,
Cambridge University
Political Career . . . . Member, Science and Technology Select
Committee, House of Lords
Subject Interests . . . . Animal welfare, Veterinary medicine,
Agriculture, Third world development, and
Higher education
Recreational Interests . . . Gardening and Travel
Correspondence Address . . Old Barn House, 25 High Street, Swaffham
Prior, Cambridge, CB5 0LD
Tel and Fax: (01638) 741304

Southampton, Baron (Charles James Fitzroy)
Type of Peerage . . . . Hereditary
Political Allegiance . . . . . None
Succeeded 1989
Born . . . . 12th August 1928

Southwell, Bishop of (Rt Rev Patrick Burnet Harris)
Type of Peerage . . . . Bishop
Entered Lords 1995
Born . . . . 30th September 1934 in Watford
Educated . . . . St Albans School
Keble College, Oxford
Clifton Technical College, Bristol
Professional Career . . . . . 1960 - 63 Curate, St Ebbe's, Oxford
1963 - 73 Missionary, South American
Missionary Society
1970 - 73 Archdeacon of Salta, Argentina
1973 - 80 Bishop of Northern Argentina
1981 - 85 Rector of Kirkheaton, Wakefield
1986 - 88 Secretary, Partnership for World
Mission
1988 - Bishop of Southwell
Subject Interests . . . . Developing countries, Refugees/Asylum,
disability, Latin-America
Recreational Interests . . . South American Indian culture, Music,
Harvesting
Correspondence Address . . Bishop's Manor, Southwell,
Nottingham, NG25 0JR
Tel: (01636) 812112 Fax: (01636) 815401
E-mail: bishop.southwell@john.316.com

MEMBERS OF THE HOUSE OF LORDS

Spencer, Earl of (Charles Edward Maurice Spence)
Type of Peerage . . . . Hereditary
Political Allegiance . . . . . None
Succeeded 1992
Born . . . . 20th May 1964

Spens, Baron (Patrick Michael Rex Spens)
Type of Peerage . . . . Hereditary
Political Allegiance . . . . . Cross Bench
Succeeded 1984
Born . . . . 27th July 1942 in Muree, India
Educated . . . . Rugby School
Corpus Christi College, Cambridge
Professional Career . . . . . 1965 - 69 Accountant, Roller Wise Fisher
and Co
1969 - 82 Director, Morgan Grenfell and
Co Ltd
1982 - 87 Managing Director, Henry
Ansbacher and Co Ltd
1987 - 91 Managing Director, Castlecrest
Investments Ltd
1991 - 98 Principal, Patrick Spens and Co,
Chartered Accountants
Subject Interests . . . . City, Finance, Justice
Recreational Interests . . . Philately
Correspondence Address . . Gould, Frittenden, Kent, TN17 2DT
Tel: (01580) 852272 Fax: (01580) 852475

Stafford, Baron (Francis Melfort William Fitzherbert)
Type of Peerage . . . . Hereditary
Political Allegiance . . . . . Conservative
Succeeded 1986
Born . . . . 13th March 1954 in Rhynie, Scotland
Educated . . . . Ampleforth College
Reading University
Royal Agricultural College, Cirencester
Professional Career . . . . . 1985 - 94 Non-Executive Director,
Tarmac Industrial Products
1992 - Director, Staffordshire Land Bank
Trust
1997 - Director, Staffordshire
Environmental Fund
Subject Interests . . . . Agriculture
Recreational Interests . . . Cricket, Golf, Field sports
Correspondence Address . . Swynnerton Park, Stone,
Staffordshire, ST15 0QE
Tel: (01782) 796334 Fax: (01782) 796661

Stair, Earl of (John David James Dalrymple)
Type of Peerage . . . . Hereditary
Political Allegiance . . . . . None
Succeeded 1996
Born . . . . 4th September 1961

Stallard, Baron (Albert William Stallard)
Type of Peerage . . . .
Political Allegiance . . . . . Labour
Created 1983
Born . . . . 5th November 1921
Professional Career . . . . . 1965 - 70 Technical Training Officer
Political Career . . . . 1953 - 59 Member, St Pancras Metropolitan
Borough Council
1965 - 70 Member, Camden London
Borough Council
1970 - 83 MP (Labour) for St Pancras North
1976 - 79 Government Whip, House of
Commons

Stamp, Baron (Trevor Charles Bosworth Stamp)
Type of Peerage . . . . Hereditary
Political Allegiance . . . . . Cross Bench
Succeeded 1987
Born . . . . 18th September 1935 in London
Professional Career . . . . . 1974 - Consultant Lecturer, Physician and
Director, Department of Bone and Mineral
Metabolism, Royal National Orthopaedic
Hospital
Subject Interests . . . . Medical ethics, Education, Sport
Recreational Interests . . . Music, Contract Bridge, Tennis

Stanley of Alderley, Baron (Thomas Henry Oliver Stanley)
Type of Peerage . . . . Hereditary
Political Allegiance . . . . . Conservative
Succeeded 1971
Born . . . . 28th September 1927 in London
Educated . . . . Wellington College, Berkshire
Moulton Institute of Agriculture
Professional Career . . . . . 1954 - Farmer
1986 - 95 Chairman, RNLI Fund Raising
Committee
Subject Interests . . . . Agriculture, Rural Affairs
Recreational Interests . . . Sailing, Fishing, Skiing
Correspondence Address . . Trysglwyn Fawr, Amlwch,
Anglesey, LL68 9RF
Tel: (01407) 830364 Fax: (01407) 832626

Steel of Aikwood, Baron
(Rt Hon David Martin Scott Steel KBE)
Type of Peerage . . . . Life
Political Allegiance . . . . . Liberal Democrat
Created 1997
Born . . . . 31st March 1938 in Kirkcaldy, Scotland
Educated . . . . Prince of Wales School, Nairobi, Kenya
George Watson's College, Edinburgh
University of Edinburgh
Professional Career . . . . . Journalist and Broadcaster
1966 - 70 President, Anti-Apartheid
Movement (GB)
1969 - 73 Chairman, Scottish Advisory
Council, Shelter
1971 - 75 Member, British Council of
Churches
1982 - 85 Rector, Edinburgh University
1995 - 97 Chairman, Countryside Movement
1997 - President, Medical Aid for
Palestinians
Political Career . . . . 1962 - 64 Assistant Secretary, Scottish
Liberal Party
1965 - 83 MP (Liberal/Liberal Democrat) for
Roxburgh, Selkirk and Peebles, then
Tweedale, Ettrick and Lauderdale
1966 - 70 President, Anti-Apartheid
Movement
1970 - 75 Liberal Party Chief Whip,
House of Commons
1976 - 88 Leader, Liberal Party
1988 - 94 Liberal Democrat Spokesman on
Foreign affairs
1994 - 96 President, Liberal International
1997 - Deputy Leader of Liberal Democrats,
House of Lords
Subject Interests . . . . Foreign affairs, (especially Africa and
Middle East) Scottish Parliament
Recreational Interests . . . Angling, Classic car rallying
Correspondence Address . . House of Lords, Westminster,
London, SW1A 0PW
Tel: (0171) 219 4433 Fax: (0171) 219 1174
Personal Staff . . . . Mr Jeremy Purvis (*Personal Assistant*)

MEMBERS OF THE HOUSE OF LORDS

Sterling of Plaistow, Baron (Jeffrey Maurice Sterling CBE)

Type of Peerage . . . . Life
Political Allegiance . . . . . Conservative
Created 1991
Born . . . . 27th December 1934 in London
Professional Career . . . . . 1955 - 57 Paul Schweder and Co
1957 - 62 G Eberstadt and Co
1962 - 64 Finance Director, General
Guarantee Corporation
1964 - 69 Managing Director,
Gula Investments Ltd
1969 - 85 Chairman, Sterling Guarantee
Trust plc
1983 - Chairman, P & O Steam Navigation
Company
1990 - 91 President, General Council of
British Shipping
1992 - 94 President, European Community
Shipowners Associations
Political Career . . . . 1982 - 90 Special Adviser to the Secretary of
State for Industry/ Trade and Industry
Recreational Interests . . . Music, Swimming, Tennis

Stevens of Ludgate, Baron (David Robert Stevens)

Type of Peerage . . . . Life
Political Allegiance . . . . . Conservative
Created 1987
Born . . . . 26th May 1936

Stewartby, Baron (Rt Hon Bernard Harold Ian Halley Stewart)

Type of Peerage . . . . Life
Political Allegiance . . . . . Conservative
Created 1992
Born . . . . 10th August 1935 in London
Educated . . . . Haileybury
Jesus College, Cambridge
Professional Career . . . . . 1963 - 83 Manager/Director, Brown Shipley
and Co
1990 - Chairman, The Throgmorton Trust plc
1993 - 97 Member, Financial Services
Authority
1993 - Deputy Chairman, Standard
Chartered plc
1995 - Deputy Chairman, Angerstein
Underwriting Trust plc
Political Career . . . . 1974 - 92 MP (Conservative) for Hitchin,
then North Hertfordshire
1979 - 82 PPS to Chancellor of Exchequer
(Rt Hon Geoffrey Howe MP)
1983 - 83 Parliamentary Secretary, Ministry
of Defence
1983 - 87 Economic Secretary, HM Treasury
1987 - 88 Minister of State (for Armed
Forces), Ministry of Defence
1988 - 89 Minister of State, Northern
Ireland Office
Subject Interests . . . . Finance, International affairs, Defence
Recreational Interests . . . History, Cricket, Real tennis

Steyn, Baron (Rt Hon Johan Steyn)

Type of Peerage . . . . Life (Law Lord)
Political Allegiance . . . . . Cross Bench
Created 1995
Born . . . . 15th August 1932 in Stellenbosch, South
Africa
Educated . . . . Jan van Riebeck School, Cape Town
University of Stellenbosch, South Africa
University College, Oxford
Professional Career . . . . . 1958 - Barrister, South Africa
1973 - Barrister, England (QC 1979)
1985 - 91 High Court Judge, Queen's
Bench Division
1987 - 88 Chairman, Race Relations
Committee of the Bar
1989 - 91 Presiding Judge, Northern Circuit
1990 - 94 Chairman, Advisory Committee on
Arbitration Law
1992 - 95 Lord Justice of Appeal
1993 - 96 Chairman, Lord Chancellor's
Advisory Committee on Legal Education
and Conduct
1995 - Lord of Appeal in Ordinary
Correspondence Address . . House of Lords, Westminster,
London, SW1A 0PW
Tel: (0171) 219 3202

Stockton, Earl of (Alexander Daniel Alan Macmillan)

Type of Peerage . . . . Hereditary
Political Allegiance . . . . . Conservative
Succeeded 1986
Born . . . . 10th October 1943 in Oswestry, Shropshire
Educated . . . . Eton College
University of Paris
Strathclyde University
Professional Career . . . . . 1963 - 65 Sub-Editor, Glasgow Herald
1965 - 68 Foreign Correspondent,
Daily Telegraph
1968 - 70 Chief European Correspondent,
Sunday Telegraph
1970 - Macmillan Publishing Ltd (Chairman
1985 - 90, President since 1990)
Subject Interests . . . . Education, Training, Copyright,
Broadcasting, Media, Defence
Recreational Interests . . . Shooting, Reading, Conversation
Correspondence Address . . Macmillan Publishers Ltd, 25 Eccleston
Place, London, SW1W 9NF
Tel: (0171) 881 8000 Fax: (0171) 881 8073
Personal Staff . . . . Ms Linda Ferguson (PA)

Stodart of Leaston, Rt Hon Baron (James Anthony Stodart)

Type of Peerage . . . . Life
Political Allegiance . . . . . Conservative
Created 1981
Born . . . . 6th June 1916 in Exeter
Political Career . . . . 1959 - 74 MP (Conservative) for
Edinburgh West
1963 - 64 Parliamentary Secretary,
Scottish Office
1966 - 69 Opposition Spokesman on Scottish
and Agricultural Affairs
1970 - 72 Parliamentary Secretary, then
Minister of State, Ministry of Agriculture,
Fisheries and Food
Subject Interests . . . . Agriculture, Fishing, Local government

MEMBERS OF THE HOUSE OF LORDS

Stoddart of Swindon, Baron (David Leonard Stoddart)

Type of Peerage	Life
Political Allegiance	Labour
Created	1983
Born	4th May 1926
Educated	St Clement Danes School
	Henley Grammar School
Professional Career	1944 - 46 Self-employed businessman
	1947 - 49 Railway Clerk
	1949 - 51 Hospital Clerk
	1951 - 70 Clerical Worker, Power Station
Political Career	1954 - 72 Member, Reading County Borough Council
	1970 - 83 MP (Labour) for Swindon
	1975 - 77 Government Whip, House of Commons
	1983 - 88 Opposition Whip and Spokesman on Energy, House of Lords
Recreational Interests	Gardening, Music
Correspondence Address	Sintra, 37a Bath Road, Reading, Berkshire, RG1 6HL
	Tel: (0118) 957 6726

Stokes, Baron (Donald Gresham Stokes)

Type of Peerage	Life
Political Allegiance	Cross Bench
Created	1969
Born	22nd March 1914 in London
Educated	Blundell's School
	Harris Institute of Technology, Preston
Professional Career	1946 - 73 Manager/Director/Chairman/Managing Director, Leyland Motor Corporation
	1966 - 68 Chairman, EDC for Electronics Industry
	1967 - 75 Vice Chairman, Engineering Employers Federation
	1969 - 71 Deputy Chairman, Industrial Re-organisation Corporation
	1973 - 79 Chairman and Chief Executive, then President, British Leyland Motor Corporation
	1979 - 81 Consultant, Leyland Vehicles
	1981 - 90 Chairman Dutton Fershaw Motor Group
	1981 - 90 Chairman, Jack Barclay Ltd
Subject Interests	Motor industry
Recreational Interests	Yachting
Correspondence Address	Branksome Cliff, Westminster Road, Poole, Dorset, BH13 6JW
	Tel: (01202) 763088

Stone of Blackheath, Baron (Andrew Zelig Stone)

Type of Peerage	Life
Political Allegiance	Labour
Succeeded	1997
Born	7th September 1942
Educated	Cardiff High School
Professional Career	1966 - Marks and Spencer (Joint Managing Director since 1994)
	1991 - Chairman, British Overseas Trade Board Group for Israel

Strabolgi, Baron (David Montague de Burgh Kenworthy)

Type of Peerage	Hereditary
Political Allegiance	Labour
Succeeded	1953
Born	1st November 1914 in Devonport
Educated	Gresham's School, Holt
	Chelsea School of Art
Professional Career	1958 - 74, 1979 - 87 (Chairman 1986 - 87) Director, Bolton Building Society
Political Career	1970 - 74 Opposition Whip, House of Lords
	1974 - 79 Deputy Chief Government Whip, House of Lords (Captain of Yeoman of the Guard)
	1979 - 85 Opposition Spokesman on the Arts, House of Lords
	1986 - A Deputy Speaker and Deputy Chairman of Committees, House of Lords
Subject Interests	National Heritage, Environment
Recreational Interests	Music, Travel
Correspondence Address	House of Lords, Westminster, London, SW1A 0PW
	Tel: (0171) 219 5353 Fax: (0171) 219 5979

Stradbroke, Earl of (Robert Keith Rous)

Type of Peerage	Hereditary
Political Allegiance	None
Succeeded	1983
Born	25th March 1937 in London
Educated	Harrow School
Professional Career	Salesman and Real Estate Developer
Subject Interests	Aboriginal arts, Rock paintings, Conservation, Solar energy
Correspondence Address	MT Fyans Station, RSD Darlington, Victoria, Australia, 3271

Strafford, Earl of (Thomas Edmund Byng)

Type of Peerage	Hereditary
Political Allegiance	Cross Bench
Succeeded	1984
Born	26th September 1936 in London
Educated	Eton College
	Clare College, Cambridge
Professional Career	Nurseryman and River Keeper
Subject Interests	Drugs, Forestry, Water
Recreational Interests	Gardening, Walking, Travelling
Correspondence Address	Apple Tree Cottage, Easton, Near Winchester, SO21 1EF
	Tel and Fax: (01962) 779467
	E-mail: StraffordJ@aol.com

Strang, Baron (Colin Strang)

Type of Peerage	Hereditary
Without Writ of Summons	
Succeeded	1978
Born	12th June 1922

MEMBERS OF THE HOUSE OF LORDS

Strange, Baroness (Jean Cherry Drummond)

Type of Peerage . . . . Hereditary

Political Allegiance . . . . . Conservative

Succeeded 1986

Born . . . . 17th December 1928 in London

Educated . . . . Oxenfoord Castle School, Ford, Midlothian

St Andrew's University

Cambridge University

Professional Career . . . . . 1966 - Owner Managing Director, Megginch

Estate, Castle Gardens

1990 - President, War Widows Association

of Great Britain

Subject Interests . . . . Defence, Foreign affairs, Conservation,

Heritage, Children, Animals

Correspondence Address . . House of Lords, Westminster,

London, SW1A 0PW

Tel: (0171) 219 5353

Megginch Castle, Errol,

Perthshire, PH2 7SW

Tel: (01821) 642222 Fax: (01821) 642708

Strathalmond, Baron (William Robertson Fraser)

Type of Peerage . . . . Hereditary

Political Allegiance . . . . . Cross Bench

Succeeded 1976

Born . . . . 22nd July 1947

Strathcarron, Baron
(David William Anthony Blyth Macpherson)

Type of Peerage . . . . Hereditary

Political Allegiance . . . . . Conservative

Succeeded 1945

Born . . . . 23rd January 1924 in London

Educated . . . . Eton College

Jesus College, Cambridge

Professional Career . . . . Motor Industry (Various Aspects)

Political Career . . . . 1992 - Chairman, All Party Parliamentary

Motorcycle Group

Subject Interests . . . . Transport, Motorcycling

Recreational Interests . . . Motorcycling, Sailing

Correspondence Address . . 22 Rutland Gate, London, SW7 1BB

Tel and Fax: (0171) 584 1240

Otterwood, Beaulieu, Hampshire, SO42 7YS

Tel: (01590) 612334

Strathclyde, Baron (Rt Hon Thomas Galloway
Dunlop du Roy de Blicquy Galbraith)

Type of Peerage . . . . Hereditary

Political Allegiance . . . . . Conservative

Succeeded 1985

Born . . . . 22nd February 1960 in Glasgow

Educated . . . . Wellington College

University of East Anglia

Université d'Aix-en-Provence

Professional Career . . . . . 1982 - 88 Insurance, Bain Clarkson Ltd

Political Career . . . . 1988 - 89 Government Whip,

Lord in Waiting

1989 - 90 Parliamentary Secretary,

Department of Employment

1990, 1992-93 Parliamentary Secretary,

Department of Environment

1990 - 92 Parliamentary Secretary,

Scottish Office

1993 - 94 Minister of State, Department of

Trade and Industry

1994 - 97 Government Chief Whip, House of

Lords (Captain of the Gentlemen at Arms)

1997 - Opposition Chief Whip,

House of Lords

Deputy Speaker and Deputy Chairman of

Committees, House of Lords

Correspondence Address . . House of Lords, Westminster,

London, SW1A 0PW

Tel: (0171) 219 5353

Strathcona and Mount Royal, Baron
(Donald Euan Palmer Howard)

Type of Peerage . . . . Hereditary

Political Allegiance . . . . . Conservative

Succeeded 1959

Born . . . . 26th November 1923 in London

Educated . . . . Eton College

Trinity College, Cambridge

McGill University, Montreal

Professional Career . . . . . 1965 - 70 Chairman, Tallon Ltd

1966 - 72 Chairman, Kelston Engineering

1981 - 91 Director, Computing Devices Co

1982 - President, Falkland Islands Trust

1995 - Chairman, Coastal Forces

Heritage Trust

Political Career . . . . 1972 - 73 Government Whip,

(Lord in Waiting)

1973 - 73 Parliamentary Secretary

(for RAF), Ministry of Defence

1974 - 79 Opposition Spokesman on

Defence and Energy, House of Lords (also

Deputy Leader of Opposition from 1976)

1979 - 81 Minister of State, Ministry of

Defence

Subject Interests . . . . Defence, Energy, Housing, Maritime affairs

Recreational Interests . . . Gardening, Sailing, Music

Correspondence Address . . 16 Henning Street, London, SW11 3DR

Tel: (0171) 223 2885

Colonsay House, Isle of Colonsay,

Argyll, PA61 7YU

Tel: (01951) 200301 Fax: (01951) 200369

MEMBERS OF THE HOUSE OF LORDS

Stratheden and Campbell, Baron (Donald Campbell)

Type of Peerage . . . . Hereditary
Political Allegiance . . . . . Cross Bench
Succeeded 1987
Born . . . . 4th April 1934

Strathmore and Kinghorne, Earl of
(Michael Fergus Bowes Lyon)

Type of Peerage . . . . Hereditary
Political Allegiance . . . . . Conservative
Succeeded 1987
Born . . . . 7th June 1957 in London
Political Career . . . . 1989 - 91 Government Whip,
      (Lord in Waiting)
      1991 - 94 Government Deputy Chief Whip,
      (Captain of the Yeomen of the Guard)
Subject Interests . . . . Defence, Agriculture, Home Office

Strathspey, Baron (James Patrick Trevor Grant)

Type of Peerage . . . . Hereditary
Without Writ of Summons
Succeeded 1992
Born . . . . 9th September 1943

Stuart of Findhorn, Viscount (David Randolph Moray Stuart)

Type of Peerage . . . . Hereditary
On Leave Of Absence
Succeeded 1959
Born . . . . 20th June 1924 in London
Educated . . . . Eton College
      Royal Agricultural College, Cirencester
Professional Career . . . . . 1952 - Chartered Surveyor
Correspondence Address . . Findhorn, Forres, Moray, IV36 0YE

Sudeley, Baron (Merlin Charles Sainthill Hanbury-Tracy)

Type of Peerage . . . . Hereditary
Political Allegiance . . . . . Conservative
Succeeded . . . . 1941 (as a minor)
Born . . . . 17th June 1939 in London
Educated . . . . Eton College
      Worcester College, Oxford
Subject Interests . . . . Arts, Church of England, Bankruptcy
Recreational Interests . . . Conversation
Correspondence Address . . 25 Melcombe Court, Dorset Square,
      London, NW1 6EP
      Tel: (0171) 258 0351

Suffield, Baron (Anthony Philip Harbord-Hamond MC)

Type of Peerage . . . . Hereditary
Political Allegiance . . . . . Conservative
Succeeded 1951
Born . . . . 19th June 1922 in London
Educated . . . . Eton College
Professional Career . . . . . 1942 - 61 Armed Forces (Major,
      Coldstream Guards)
Recreational Interests . . . Sailing, Painting, Country pursuits
Correspondence Address . . Gardeners Cottage, Gunton Park, Hanworth,
      Norfolk, NR11 7HL
      Tel: (01263) 768423

Suffolk and Berkshire, Earl of (Michael John James George Robert Howard)

Type of Peerage . . . . Hereditary
Political Allegiance . . . . . Conservative
Succeeded . . . . 1941 (as a minor)
Born . . . . 27th March 1935

Sutherland, Duke of (John Sutherland Egerton TD)

Type of Peerage . . . . Hereditary
Political Allegiance . . . . . None
Succeeded 1944
Born . . . . 10th May 1915

Sutherland, Countess of (Elizabeth Millicent Sutherland)

Type of Peerage . . . . Hereditary
Succeeded 1963
Born . . . . 30th March 1921 in London
Educated . . . . Queen's College, Harley Street, London
Subject Interests . . . . Preservation of Historic Houses, Monuments,
      Gardens, Rural Buildings
Recreational Interests . . . Reading, Travelling
Correspondence Address . . House of Tongue, Lairg, Sutherland,
      Scotland, IV27 4XH
      Tel: (01847) 611209
      39 Edwardes Square, London, W8 6HH
      Tel: (0171) 603 0659

Swansea, Baron (John Hussey Hamilton Vivian)

Type of Peerage . . . . Hereditary
Political Allegiance . . . . . Cross Bench
Succeeded . . . . 1934 (as a minor)
Born . . . . 1st January 1925

MEMBERS OF THE HOUSE OF LORDS

Swaythling, Baron (David Charles Samuel Montagu)

Type of Peerage . . . . Hereditary

Political Allegiance . . . . . Conservative

Succeeded 1990

Born . . . . 6th August 1928 in London

Educated . . . . Eton College

Trinity College, Cambridge

Professional Career . . . . . 1954 - 73 Director, then Chairman and Chief

Executive, Samuel Montagu and Co Ltd

1974 - 79 Chairman and Chief Executive,

Orion Bank Ltd

1981 - 87 Director, then Deputy Chairman,

J Rothschild Holdings plc

1988 - Chairman, Rothmans International

Recreational Interests . . . Racing, Theatre, Opera

Correspondence Address . . 15 Hill Street, London, W1X 7FB (Office)

Tel: (0171) 491 4366 Fax: (0171) 493 0562

14 Craven Hill Mews, Devonshire Terrace,

London, W2 3DY

Tel: (0171) 724 7860

Symons of Vernham Dean, Baroness
(Elizabeth Conway Symons)

Type of Peerage . . . . Life

Political Allegiance . . . . . Labour

Created 1996

Born . . . . 14th April 1951 in Liverpool

Educated . . . . Putney High School for Girls

Girton College, Cambridge

Professional Career . . . . . 1974 - 77 Administration Trainee,

Civil Service

1977 - 88 Assistant Secretary, Inland

Revenue Staff Federation

1989 - 96 General Secretary, Association of

First Division Civil Servants

Political Career . . . . 1997 - Parliamentary Secretary, Foreign and

Commonwealth Office

Subject Interests . . . . Foreign Affairs, Government Issues,

Employment and Trade Union issues

Recreational Interests . . . Family and friends, Gardening, Reading

Swinfen, Baron (Roger Mynors Swinfen Eady)

Type of Peerage . . . . Hereditary

Political Allegiance . . . . . Conservative

Succeeded 1977

Born . . . . 14th December 1938 in London

Educated . . . . Westminster School

Royal Military Academy, Sandhurst

Professional Career . . . . . Chartered Surveyor

Subject Interests . . . . Disability, Defence

Sysonby, Baron (John Frederick Ponsonby)

Type of Peerage . . . . Hereditary

Without Writ of Summons

Succeeded . . . . 1956 (as a minor)

Born . . . . 5th August 1945

Swinton, Earl of (David Yarburgh Cunliffe-Lister)

Type of Peerage . . . . Hereditary

Political Allegiance . . . . . Conservative

Succeeded 1972

Born . . . . 21st March 1937 in London

Educated . . . . Winchester College

Royal Agricultural College, Cirencester

Political Career . . . . 1961 - 74 Member, North Riding County

Council Yorkshire

1973 - 77 Member, North Yorkshire County

Council

1982 - 86 Government Deputy Chief Whip,

House of Lords (Captain of the Yeomen of

the Guard)

Recreational Interests . . . Shooting

Correspondence Address . . Dykes Hill House, Masham, Ripon,

North Yorkshire, HG4 4NS

Tel: (01765) 689241 Fax: (01765) 689596

46 Westminster Gardens, Marsham Street,

London, SW1P 4JG

Tel: (0171) 834 0700

MEMBERS OF THE HOUSE OF LORDS

T

Tankerville, Earl of (Peter Grey Bennet)

Type of Peerage . . . . Hereditary
Without Writ of Summons
Political Allegiance . . . . . Non-Partisan
Succeeded 1980
Born . . . . 18th October 1956 in San Francisco,
California
Educated . . . . Oberlin College Conservatory, Ohio
San Francisco State University
Correspondence Address . . 139 Olympic Way,
San Francisco, CA 94131, USA
Tel: (00 1415) 826 6639

Tanlaw, Baron (Simon Brooke Mackay)

Type of Peerage . . . . Life
Political Allegiance . . . . . Cross Bench
Created 1971
Born . . . . 30th March 1934 in London
Educated . . . . Eton College
Trinity College, Cambridge
Professional Career . . . . 1967 - 71 Managing Director, Inchape and Co
1971 - 74 Chairman, Thwaites and Reed Ltd
1973 - Chairman and Managing Director,
Fandstan Group
Political Career . . . . 1971 - 92 Liberal Spokesman on Energy and
Transport, House of Lords
Subject Interests . . . . Horology, Radio astronomy, Railways and
Public transport
Recreational Interests . . . Country Pursuits
Correspondence Address . . 31 Brompton Square, Knightsbridge,
London, SW3 2AE
Tel: (0171) 225 0848 Fax: (0171) 581 3295

Taverne, Baron (Dick Taverne QC)

Type of Peerage . . . . Life
Political Allegiance . . . . . Liberal Democrat
Created 1996
Born . . . . 18th October 1928 im Sumatra, Indonesia
Educated . . . . Charterhouse
Balliol College, Oxford
Professional Career . . . . 1955 - (QC 1965)
1971 - 83 Director, then Chairman, Institute
for Fiscal Studies
1983 - 87 Chairman, Public Policy Centre
1987 - Founder, Prima Europe Ltd (later
Chairman and, since 1993, President)
1989 - Chairman, OLIM Convertible Trust plc
1994 - Deputy Chairman, Central European
Growth Fund
Political Career . . . . 1962 - 74 MP (Labour then Democratic
Labour) for Lincoln
1966 - 68 Parliamentary Secretary,
Home Office
1968 - 69 Minister of State, HM Treasury
1969 - 70 Financial Secretary, HM Treasury
1970 - 72 Chairman, General
Sub-Committee, Public Exp Committee
Subject Interests . . . . EMU, Economy, Tax, Industry, Pensions in
Europe and UK, Law reform, (especially
Legal Aid/Drug abuse/prevention/treatment
Recreational Interests . . . Sailing
Correspondence Address . . 60 Cambridge Street, London, SW1V 4QQ
Tel: (0171) 828 0166
Prima Europe, 14 Soho Square,
London, W1V 5FB
Tel: (0171) 287 6676 Fax: (0171) 287 8139

Taylor of Blackburn, Baron (Thomas Taylor CBE)

Type of Peerage . . . . Life
Political Allegiance . . . . . Labour
Created 1978
Born . . . . 10th June 1929 in Blackburn, Lancashire
Professional Career . . . . . 1977 Chairman, Government Enquiry into
Management and Government of Schools
1977 - 80 Chairman, Electricity Consumers
Council for North West and Member,
Norweb Board
Political Career . . . . 1954 - 76 Member, Blackburn Council
(Sometime Leader)

Taylor of Gryfe, Baron (Thomas Johnston Taylor)

Type of Peerage . . . . Life
Political Allegiance . . . . . Labour
Created 1967
Born . . . . 27th April 1912 in Glasgow
Educated . . . . Bellahousten Academy, Glasgow
Professional Career . . . . . 1970 - 76 Chairman, Forestry Commission
1965 - 70 President, Scottish Co-operative
Wholesale Society
1968 - 80 Member, British Railways Board
(Chairman, Scottish Railways Board,
1971 - 80)
1971 - 74 Member, Scottish Economic
Council
1973 - 85 Chairman, Morgan Grenfell
(Scotland) Ltd
Subject Interests . . . . Forestry, Railways, Scottish affairs,
Economy, Overseas aid
Recreational Interests . . . Golf
Correspondence Address . . 33 Seagate, Kingsbarns,
St Andrews, Fife, KY16 8SR
Tel: (01334) 880430

Taylor of Warwick, Baron (John David Beckett Turner)

Type of Peerage . . . . Life
Political Allegiance . . . . . Conservative
Created 1996
Born . . . . 21st September 1952 in Birmingham
Educated . . . . Moseley Grammar School
University of Keele
Inns of Court School of Law
Professional Career . . . . . 1978 - Barrister
1990 - 92 Consultant, Lowe Bell
Communications Ltd
1992 - Producer/Presenter, BBC TV and
BBC Radio
1994 - 96 Director of Communications,
City Technology Colleges Trust
1997 - Chairman, Warwick Consulting
International Ltd
Subject Interests . . . . Legal system, Media, Business
Recreational Interests . . . Soccer, Cricket, Singing, Drama

MEMBERS OF THE HOUSE OF LORDS

Tebbit, Baron (Rt Hon Norman Beresford Tebbit CH)

Type of Peerage . . . . Life
Political Allegiance . . . . . Conservative
Created 1992
Born . . . . 29th March 1931 in Enfield, Middlesex
Educated . . . . Edmonton County Grammar School
Professional Career . . . . . 1947 - 49 Journalist, Financial Times
1949 - 51 Commissioned RAF Pilot
1951 - 53 Publishing
1953 - 70 Airline Pilot
1987 - 96 Director, British Telecom and Director, BET
1987 - Director, Sears (Holdings)
1989 - Director, Spectator (1828) Ltd
1995 - Columnist, The Sun, then (from 1997) The Mail on Sunday
Political Career . . . . 1970 - 92 MP (Conservative) for Epping then (from 1974) for Chingford
1979 - 81 Parliamentary Secretary, Department of Trade
1981 Minister of State, Department of Industry
1981 - 83 Secretary of State for Employment
1983 - 85 Secretary of State for Trade and Industry
1985 - 87 Chancellor of the Duchy of Lancaster, Chairman of the Conservative Party
Subject Interests . . . . Aviation, Europe
Recreational Interests . . . Gardening, Shooting
Correspondence Address . . House of Lords, Westminster, London, SW1A 0PW
Tel: (0171) 219 6929 Fax: (0171) 245 5946
Personal Staff . . . . Mrs Beryl Goldsmith *(PA)*

Tedder, Baron (Robin John Tedder)

Type of Peerage . . . . Hereditary
Without Writ of Summons
Succeeded 1994
Born . . . . 6th April 1955

Temple of Stowe, Earl
 (Walter Grenville Algernon Temple-Gore-Langton)

Type of Peerage . . . . Hereditary
Political Allegiance . . . . . Cross Bench
Succeeded 1988
Born . . . . 2nd October 1924 in Victoria, British Columbia, Canada
Educated . . . . Pangbourne College
Professional Career . . . . . 1959 - 86 Antique Dealer
Subject Interests . . . . History, Arts
Recreational Interests . . . Golf
Correspondence Address . . The Cottage, Easton, Winchester, Hampshire, SO21 1EH
Tel: (01962) 779300

Templeman, Baron (Rt Hon Sydney William Templeman)

Type of Peerage . . . . Life (Former Law Lord)
Political Allegiance . . . . . Cross Bench
Created 1982
Born . . . . 3rd March 1920 in London
Educated . . . . Southall Grammar School
St John's College, Cambridge
Professional Career . . . . . 1947 - Barrister (QC 1964)
1972 - 78 High Court Judge (Chancery Division)
1978 - 82 Lord Justice of Appeal
1982 - 94 Lord of Appeal in Ordinary
Correspondence Address . . "Mellowstone", Rosebank Crescent, Exeter, Devon, EX4 6EJ
Tel: (01392) 499912

Tenby, Viscount (William Lloyd-George)

Type of Peerage . . . . Hereditary
Political Allegiance . . . . . Cross Bench
Succeeded 1983
Born . . . . 7th November 1927 in London

Tennyson, Baron (Rt Hon Mark Aubrey Tennyson DSC)

Type of Peerage . . . . Hereditary
Political Allegiance . . . . . Cross Bench
Succeeded 1992
Born . . . . 28th March 1920 in London
Educated . . . . The Royal Naval College, Dartmouth
Professional Career . . . . . 1939 - 60 Royal Navy, (Retired as Commander)
Correspondence Address . . 304 Grosvenor Square, Duke Road, Rondesbosch - 7700, Cape Town, South Africa

Terrington, Baron (James Allen David Woodhouse)

Type of Peerage . . . . Hereditary
Political Allegiance . . . . . Cross Bench
Succeeded 1961
Born . . . . 30th December 1915

Teviot, Baron (John Charles Kerr)

Type of Peerage . . . . Hereditary
Political Allegiance . . . . . Conservative
Succeeded 1968
Born . . . . 16th December 1934

Teynham, Baron (John Christoper Ingham Roper-Curzon)

Type of Peerage . . . . Hereditary
Political Allegiance . . . . . Conservative
Succeeded 1972
Born . . . . 25th December 1928

MEMBERS OF THE HOUSE OF LORDS

Thatcher, Baroness (Rt Hon Margaret Hilda Thatcher LG, OM)

Type of Peerage . . . . Life
Political Allegiance . . . . . Conservative
Created 1992
Born . . . . 13th October 1925 in Grantham,
Lincolnshire
Educated . . . . Kesteven and Grantham Girls' School
Somerville College, Oxford
Professional Career . . . . . 1947 - 51 Research Chemist
1954 Barrister
1992 - Chancellor, University of
Buckingham
Political Career . . . . 1959 - 92 MP (Conservative) for Finchley
1961 - 64 Parliamentary Secretary, Ministry
of Pensions and National Insurance
1965 - 70 Opposition Spokesman on
Housing and Land, then Treasury Affairs
and Education
1970 - 74 Secretary of State for Education
and Science
1974 - 75 Opposition Spokesman on
Environment, House of Commons
1975 - 79 Leader of the Opposition
1979 - 90 Prime Minister

Thomas of Gresford, Baron (Martin Thomas OBE, QC)

Type of Peerage . . . . Life
Political Allegiance . . . . . Liberal Democrat
Created 1996
Born . . . . 13th March 1937 in Wrexham
Educated . . . . Grove Park Grammar School, Wrexham
Peterhouse School, Cambridge
Professional Career . . . . . 1961 - 66 Solicitor
1966 - 68 Lecturer in Law
1968 - Barrister (QC 1979)
1985 - Deputy High Court Judge
Subject Interests . . . . Law Reform, Civil and Criminal Justice
System, Wales, Scotland, Home Affairs,
Fishing, Sport
Recreational Interests . . . Rugby, Football, Rowing, Golf, Music,
Fishing
Correspondence Address . . House of Lords, Westminster,
London, SW1A 0PW
Tel: (0171) 219 3453
E-mail: lordthomas@compuserve.com
Glasfryn, Gresford, Wrexham,
Clwyd, LL12 8RG
Tel: (01978) 852205 Fax: (01978) 855078

Thomas of Gwydir, Baron
(Rt Hon Peter John Mitchell Thomas QC)

Type of Peerage . . . . Life
Political Allegiance . . . . . Conservative
Created 1987
Born . . . . 31st July 1920 in Llanrwst, North Wales
Educated . . . . Epworth College, Rhyl
Jesus College, Oxford
Professional Career . . . . . 1947 - Barrister (QC 1965)
1974 - 88 Recorder of the Crown Court
Political Career . . . . 1951 - 66 MP (Conservative) for Conway
1956 - 61 Parliamentary Secretary, Ministry
of Labour
1961 - 64 Parliamentary Secretary then
Minister of State, Foreign Office
1964 - 66 Opposition Spokesman on Foreign
Affairs and Law, House of Commons
1970 - 87 MP (Conservative) for Hendon
South
1970 - 72 Chairman, Conservative Party
Organisation
1970 - 74 Secretary of State for Wales
1974 - 75 President, National Union of
Conservative and Unionist Associations
Subject Interests . . . . Foreign affairs, Welsh affairs, Law

Thomas of Macclesfield, Rt Hon Baron
(Terence James Thomas CBE)

Type of Peerage . . . . Life
Political Allegiance . . . . . Labour
Created 1997
Born . . . . 19th October 1937 in Carmarthen, Dyfed
Educated . . . . Queen Elizabeth Grammar School,
Carmarthen
Bath University School of Management
Insead, France
Professional Career . . . . . 1971 - 73 Research Manager/National Sales
Manager, Joint Credit Card Co
1973 - 83 Marketing Manager/Joint General
Manager, Co-operative Bank plc
1984 - 88 Managing Director, Unity Trust
Bank and Director, Co-operative Bank
1988 - 97 Managing Director, Co-operative
Bank plc
Subject Interests . . . . Co-operation, North West, Corporate ethics,
Ecology
Recreational Interests . . . Reading, Rugby
Correspondence Address . . 51 Willowmead Drive, Prestbury,
Cheshire, SK10 4DD
Tel: (01625) 828092 Fax: (01625) 820079
House of Lords, Westminster,
London, SW1A 0PW
Mobile: 0410 975704

Thomas of Swynnerton, Baron (Hugh Swynnerton Thomas)

Type of Peerage . . . . Life
Political Allegiance . . . . . Liberal Democrat
Created 1981
Born . . . . 21st October 1931

MEMBERS OF THE HOUSE OF LORDS

Thomas of Walliswood, Baroness
(Susan Petronella Thomas OBE)

Type of Peerage . . . . Life
Political Allegiance . . . . . Liberal Democrat
Created 1994
Born . . . . 20th December 1935 in London
Educated . . . . Cranborne Chase School
Lady Margaret Hall, Oxford
Professional Career . . . . . 1975 - 78 Chief Executive, British Clothing
Industries' Council of Europe
Political Career . . . . 1985 - 97 Member, Surrey County Council
1993 - Vice Chairman, Surrey County
Council
1994 - Liberal Democrat Spokesman on
Transport, House of Lords
Subject Interests . . . . Environment, Poverty, Gender equality,
Education, Health, Structure of
government/constitutional reform
Recreational Interests . . . Gardening, Theatre, Ballet, Travel
Correspondence Address . . 7 Old Palace Yard, London, SW1P 3JY
Tel: (0171) 219 3599 Fax: (0171)219 2082
Personal Staff . . . . Mrs Susan Vincent

Thomson of Fleet, Baron (Kenneth Roy Thomson)

Type of Peerage . . . . Hereditary
Without Writ of Summons
Succeeded 1976
Born . . . . 1st September 1923

Thomson of Monifieth, Rt Hon Baron
(George Morgan Thomson KT)

Type of Peerage . . . . Life
Political Allegiance . . . . . Liberal Democrat
Created 1977
Born . . . . 16th January 1921 in Dundee, Scotland
Educated . . . . Grove Academy, Dundee
Professional Career . . . . . 1973 - 77 Member of European Commission
(responsibility for Regional Policy)
1977 - 80 First Crown Estate Commissioner
1977 - 80 Chairman, Advertising Standards
Authority
1981 - 88 Chairman, Independent
Broadcasting Authority
1985 - Chairman, Vallie and Income
Investment Trust
1988 - 91 Deputy Chairman, Woolwich
Equitable Building Society
1989 - 91 Chairman, European Television
and Film Forum
1990 - 93 Suzy Lamplugh Trust
1994 - 97 Member, Committee on Standards
in Public Life
Political Career . . . . 1952 - 72 MP (Labour) for Dundee East
1964 - 66 Minister of State, Foreign Office
1966 - 67 Chancellor of the Duchy of
Lancaster
1966 - 68 Secretary of State for
Commonwealth Affairs
1968 - 69 Minister without Portfolio
1969 - 70 Chancellor of the Duchy of
Lancaster
1970 - 72 Opposition Spokesman on
Defence (Labour), House of Commons
1990 - 97 Liberal Democrat Spokesman on
Foreign Affairs and Broadcasting,
House of Lords
1998 - Chairman, Scottish Peers Association
Correspondence Address . . House of Lords, Westminster,
London, SW1A 0PW
Tel: (01622) 880656 Fax: (01622) 880588
Personal Staff . . . . Mrs Glenis Malone *(Secretary)*
Tel: (01622) 880588

Thurlow, Baron
(Francis Edward Hovel-Thurlow-Cumming-Bruce)

Type of Peerage . . . . Hereditary
Political Allegiance . . . . . Cross Bench
Succeeded 1971
Born . . . . 9th March 1912 in Barnet, Hertfordshire
Educated . . . . Shrewsbury School
Trinity College, Cambridge
Professional Career . . . . . 1937 - 64 Civil Servant, Dominions Office,
then Commonwealth Office (various posts
in UK and abroad)
1959 - 63 UK High Commissioner,
New Zealand
1964 - 67 UK High Commissioner, Nigeria
1968 - 72 Governor of the Bahamas
Correspondence Address . . 102 Leith Mansions, Grantully Road,
London, W9 1LJ
Tel: (0171) 289 9664 Fax: (0171) 289 9664

Thurso, Viscount (John Archibald Sinclair)

Type of Peerage . . . . Hereditary
Political Allegiance . . . . . Liberal Democrat
Succeeded 1995
Born . . . . 10th September 1953 in Thurso
Educated . . . . Eton College
Westminster Technical College
Professional Career . . . . . 1978 - 81 Reception Manager, Claridges
1981 - 85 General Manager, Hotel Lancaster
Hotel, Paris
1985 - 92 Operations Director and General
Manager, Cliveden, Bucks
1992 - 95 Chief Executive, Cranfel
Holdings Ltd
1995 - Managing Director, Fitness and
Leisure Ltd
Subject Interests . . . . Tourism, Management education, Business
Recreational Interests . . . Country pursuits
Correspondence Address . . Fitness and Leisure Holdings Ltd, New
Court, Wigginton, Tring,
Hertfordshire, HP23 6HY
Tel and Fax: (01442) 291291

Tollemache, Baron (Timothy John Edward Tollemache)

Type of Peerage . . . . Hereditary
Political Allegiance . . . . . Conservative
Succeeded 1975
Born . . . . 13th December 1939 in Norwich

MEMBERS OF THE HOUSE OF LORDS

Tombs, Baron (Francis Leonard Tombs)

Type of Peerage .... Life
Political Allegiance..... Cross Bench
Created.............. 1991
Born................ 17th May 1924 in Walsall
Educated .... Elmore Green School, Walsall
Birmingham College of Technology
London University
Professional Career..... 1974 - 77 Chairman, South of Scotland
Electricity Board
1977 - 80 Chairman, Electricity Council
1980 - 83 Chairman, Weir Group plc
1982 - 89 Chairman, T & N plc
1985 - 92 Chairman, Rolls-Royce plc
1994 - Chairman, Old Mutual South
Africa Trust
Subject Interests........ Engineering, Nuclear power, Environment,
Higher education
Recreational Interests ... Music
Correspondence Address.. Honington Lodge, Honington,
Shipston-on-Stour, CV36 5AA

Tope, Baron (Graham Norman Tope CBE)

Type of Peerage .... Life
Political Allegiance..... Liberal Democrat
Created.............. 1994
Born................ 30th November 1943 in Plymouth
Educated .... Whitgift School, Croydon
Professional Career..... 1970 - 72 Company Secretary,
Air Products Ltd
1975 - 90 Deputy General Secretary,
Voluntary Action Camden
Political Career........ 1971 - 75 Vice-Chairman, then President,
National League of Young Liberals
1972 - 74 MP (Liberal) for Sutton and
Cheam
1974 - Councillor, London Borough of Sutton
(Leader since 1986)
1994 - Member, European Union Committee
of the Regions
1994 - Liberal Democrat Spokesman on
Education, House of Lords
1996 - Vice Chairman, Association of
London Government
Subject Interests........ Education, Local government, London, the
Environment, Europe
Correspondence Address.. Leadership Office, London Borough of
Sutton, St Nicholas Way, Sutton, SM1 1EA
Tel: (0181) 770 5410 Fax: (0181) 770 5414
E-mail: grahamtope.sutton@dial.pipex.com
88 The Gallop, Sutton, Surrey, SM2 5SA
Tel and Fax: (0181) 770 7269

Tordoff, Baron (Geoffrey Johnson Tordoff)

Type of Peerage .... Life
Political Allegiance..... Liberal Democrat
Created.............. 1981
Born................ 11th October 1928
Educated .... Manchester Grammar School
Manchester University
Political Career........ 1976 - 79 Chairman, Liberal Party
(also President 1983 - 84)
1983 - 84 President, Liberal Party
1983 - 88 Liberal Deputy Chief Whip, then
Chief Whip, House of Lords
1988 - 94 Liberal Democrat Chief Whip,
House of Lords
1994 - Principal Deputy Chairman of
Committees and Chairman European
Communities Select Committee,
House of Lords
Deputy Speaker, House of Lords
Subject Interests....... Europe
Correspondence Address.. House of Lords, Westminster,
London, SW1A 0PW
Tel: (0171) 219 6613

Torphichen, Baron (James Andrew Douglas Sandilands)

Type of Peerage .... Hereditary
Political Allegiance..... Conservative
Succeeded........... 1975
Born................ 27th August 1946

Torrington, Viscount (Timothy Howard St George Byng)

Type of Peerage .... Hereditary
Political Allegiance..... Conservative
Succeeded........... 1961
Born................ 13th July 1943 in Durban, South Africa
Educated .... Harrow School
St Edmund Hall, Oxford
Professional Career..... 1975 - 86 Managing Director,
Anvil Petroleum Plc
1987 - 93 Director, Flextech Plc
1994 - Managing Director, Heritage
Oil and Gas Ltd
Subject Interests........ Energy, Overseas development, Foreign
affairs
Recreational Interests ... Shooting, Fishing
Correspondence Address.. Great Hunts Place, Owslebury. Winchester,
Hampshire, SO21 1JL
Tel: (01962) 777234
Fax: (01967) 777242

MEMBERS OF THE HOUSE OF LORDS

Townshend, Marquess
(George John Patrick Dominic Townshend)

Type of Peerage . . . . Hereditary
Political Allegiance . . . . . Conservative
Succeeded . . . . 1921 (as a minor)
Born . . . . 13th May 1916 in London
Professional Career . . . . . 1950 - 86 Vice-Chairman, Norwich Union
Fire Insurance Society
1950 - 86 Vice-Chairman, Norwich Union
Life Insurance Society
1954 - 87 Chairman, Norfolk Agricultural
Station
1957 - Chairman, Raynham Farm Co Ltd
1958 - 86 Chairman, Anglia Television Ltd
1964 - 96 Director, London Merchant
Securities plc
1975 - 87 Chairman, AP Bank Ltd
1976 - 86 Chairman, Anglia Television
Group Ltd
1981 - 86 Director, Norwich Union
Holdings plc

Trefgarne, Baron (Rt Hon David Garro Trefgarne)

Type of Peerage . . . . Hereditary
Political Allegiance . . . . . Conservative
Succeeded 1960
Born . . . . 31st March 1941 in Llandrindod Wells,
Wales
Political Career . . . . 1977 - 79 Opposition Whip, House of Lords
1979 - 81 Government Whip,
(Lord in Waiting)
1981 Parliamentary Secretary,
Department of Trade
1981 - 82 Parliamentary Secretary, Foreign
and Commonwealth Office
1982 - 83 Parliamentary Secretary,
Department of Health and Social Security
1983 - 85 Parliamentary Secretary, then
Minister of State, Ministry of Defence
1989 - 90 Minister of State, Department of
Trade and Industry
Subject Interests . . . . Defence, Trade, Industry, Foreign affairs
Recreational Interests . . . Photography

Trenchard, Viscount (Hugh Trenchard)

Type of Peerage . . . . Hereditary
Political Allegiance . . . . . Conservative
Succeeded 1987
Born . . . . 12th March 1951 in London
Educated . . . . Eton College
Trinity College, Cambridge
Professional Career . . . . . 1986 - 96 Director, Kleinwort Benson Ltd
1994 - 95 Director, Japan Securities Dealers
Association, also Vice-Chairman,
European Business Community in Japan
1996 - Director, Robert Fleming and Co
Political Career . . . . 1986 - 88 Chairman, Conservatives Abroad
in Japan
1997 - Vice-Chairman, British-Japanese
Parliamentary Group
Subject Interests . . . . Japan, Financial markets
Correspondence Address . . Standon Lordship, Ware, Hertfordshire,
SG11 1PR
Tel: (01920) 823785 Fax: (01920) 823802
c/o Robert Fleming and Co Ltd,
25 Copthall Avenue, London, EC2R 7DR
Tel: (0171) 382 8764 Fax: (0171) 382 8761
E-mail: hugh.trenchard@flemings.com

Trevethin and Oaksey, Baron
(John Geoffrey Tristram Lawrence Oaksey OBE)

Type of Peerage . . . . Hereditary
Political Allegiance . . . . . Conservative
Succeeded 1971
Born . . . . 21st March 1929 in London
Educated . . . . Eton College
New College, Oxford
Yale Law School
Professional Career . . . . . Racing Correspondent and Television
Commentator
Subject Interests . . . . Racing, Horses, Flying
Recreational Interests . . . Riding, Skiing, Hunting
Correspondence Address . . Hill Farm, Oaksey, Malmesbury,
Wiltshire, SN16 9HS
Tel: (01666) 577303 Fax: (01666) 577962
Lord Trevethin and Oaksey is know as Lord Oaksey.

Trevor, Baron (Mark Charles Hill Trevor)

Type of Peerage . . . . Hereditary
Political Allegiance . . . . . None
Succeeded 1997
Born . . . . 8th January 1970

Trumpington, Baroness (Rt Hon Jean Alys Barker)

Type of Peerage . . . . Life
Political Allegiance . . . . . Conservative
Created 1980
Born . . . . 23rd October 1922 in London
Educated . . . . Privately
Political Career . . . . 1963 - 73 Member, Cambridge City Council
(Mayor 1971 - 72)
1973 - 75 Member, Cambridgeshire County
Council
1983 - 85, 1992 - 97 Government Whip,
(Baroness in Waiting)
1985 - 87 Parliamentary Secretary,
Department of Health and Social Security
1987 - 92 Parliamentary Secretary, then
Minister of State, Ministry of Agriculture,
Fisheries and Food
Subject Interests . . . . Farming, Horticulture, Heritage, Foreign
Affairs, Arts, Sports
Recreational Interests . . . Racing, Bridge, Cookery, Golf, Antique
hunting, Needlepoint
Correspondence Address . . House of Lords, Westminster,
London, SW1A 0PW
Tel: (0171) 219 6255
October Cottage, Town Croft, Hartfield, W
Sussex, TN7 4AD
Tel: (01892) 770014
36 Cyril Mansions, Prince of Wales Drive,
London, SW11 4HP
Tel: (0171) 720 4071

MEMBERS OF THE HOUSE OF LORDS

Tryon, Baron (Anthony George Merrik Tryon)

Type of Peerage	Hereditary
Political Allegiance.....	Cross Bench
Succeeded...........	1976
Born...............	26th May 1940
Professional Career.....	1976 - 83 Director, Lazard Brothers and Co Ltd
	1977 - 78 Chairman, English and Scottish Investors Ltd
Subject Interests.......	Countryside, Wildlife, Conservation, Firearms, Financial services
Recreational Interests ...	Shooting, Fishing

Tugendhat, Baron (Christopher Samuel Tugendhat)

Type of Peerage	Life
Political Allegiance.....	Conservative
Created.............	1993
Born...............	23rd February 1937
Professional Career.....	1960 - 70 Feature and Leader Writer, Financial Times
	1977 - 85 Member, European Commission (Vice President from 1981)
	1986 - 91 Chairman, Civil Aviation Authority
	1991 - Chairman, Abbey National plc
	1996 - Chairman, Blue Circle Industries plc
Political Career........	1970 - 76 MP (Conservative) for the City of London and Westminster South

Turner of Camden, Baroness (Muriel Winifred Turner)

Type of Peerage	Life
Political Allegiance.....	Labour
Created.............	1985
Born...............	18th September 1927 in London
Professional Career.....	1970 - 87 Assistant General Secretary, ASTMS (trade union)
	1979 - 87 Member, Occupational Pensions Board
	1982 - 88 Member, Equal Opportunities Commission
Political Career........	1986 - 96 Opposition Spokesman on Employment and Social Security, House of Lords
	Deputy Chairman of Committees, House of Lords
Subject Interests.......	Employment, Social Security, Financial services, Pension provision, Industrial law

Tweeddale, Marquess of (Edward Douglas John Hay)

Type of Peerage	Hereditary
Political Allegiance.....	Cross Bench
Succeeded...........	1979
Born...............	6th August 1947

Tweedsmuir, Baron (William James de L'Aigle Buchan)

Type of Peerage	Hereditary
Political Allegiance.....	Cross Bench
Succeeded...........	1996
Born...............	10th January 1916 in London
Educated	Eton College
	New College, Oxford
Correspondence Address..	West End House, Hornton, Banbury, Oxon, OX15 6DA
	Tel: (01295) 670608

U

Ullswater, Viscount
(Rt Hon Nicholas James Christopher Lowther)

Type of Peerage	Hereditary
Political Allegiance.....	Conservative
Succeeded...........	1949 (as a minor)
Born...............	9th June 1942
Political Career.......	1989 - 90 Government Whip, (Lord in Waiting)
	1990 - 93 Parliamentary Secretary, Department of Employment
	1993 - 94 Government Chief Whip, House of Lords (Captain of the Gentlemen at Arms)
	1994 - 95 Minister of State, Department of the Environment

MEMBERS OF THE HOUSE OF LORDS

V

Varley, Baron (Rt Hon Eric Varley)

Type of Peerage .... Life
Political Allegiance ..... Labour
Created 1990
Born .... 11th August 1932
Educated .... Ruskin College, Oxford
Political Carrer .... 1964 - 86 MP (Labour) for Chesterfield
1967 - 68 Assistant Government Whip,
House of Commons
1968 - 69 PPS to Prime Minister
(Rt Hon Harold Wilson MP)
1974 - 75 Secretary of State for Energy
1975 - 79 Secretary of State for Industry
1979 - 83 Opposition Spokesman on
Employment
1981 - 83 Treasurer, Labour Party

Vaux of Harrowden, Baron (John Hugh Philip Gilbey)

Type of Peerage .... Hereditary
Political Allegiance ..... Conservative
Succeeded 1977
Born .... 4th August 1915

Vernon, Baron (John Lawrance Vernon)

Type of Peerage .... Hereditary
On Leave of Absence
Succeeded 1963
Born .... 1st February 1923
Educated .... Eton College
Magdalen College, Oxford

Verulam, Earl of (John Duncan Grimston)

Type of Peerage .... Hereditary
Political Allegiance ..... None
Succeeded 1973
Born .... 21st April 1951

Vestey, Baron (Samuel George Armstrong Vestey)

Type of Peerage .... Hereditary
Political Allegiance ..... Conservative
Succeeded .... 1954 (as a minor)
Born .... 19th March 1941 in Guildford, Surrey
Educated .... Eton College
Professional Career ..... 1965 - 94 Director, Union International Plc
1991 - 95 Chairman, Meat Training Council
1995 - 97 Chairman, Vestey Group Ltd
Subject Interests .... Racing, Field sports, South America
Recreational Interests ... Racing, Foxhunting, Shooting
Correspondence Address .. Stowell Park, Northleach,
Gloucestershire, GL54 3LE
Tel: (01285) 720247 Fax: (01285) 720714

Vincent of Coleshill, Baron
(Field-Marshal Richard Frederick Vincent GBE, KCB, DSO)

Type of Peerage .... Life
Political Allegiance ..... Cross Bench
Created 1996
Born .... 23rd August 1931 in London
Educated .... Aldenham School
Royal Military College of Science
Royal College of Defence Studies
Professional Career ..... 1952 - 96 Armed Forces
1980 - 83 Commandant, Royal Military
College of Science
1983 - 87 Master General of the Ordnance
1987 - 91 Vice Chief of the Defence Staff
1991 - 92 Chief of the Defence Staff
1993 - 96 Chairman, Military Committee,
NATO
1996 - Chairman, Hunting Defence Ltd
1996 - Chairman, Imperial College of
Science, Technology and Medicine
1996 - Vice President, Defence
Manufacturers Association
Subject Interests .... Defence policy and strategy,
Defence manufacturing, Education
Recreational Interests ... Reading, Travel
Correspondence Address .. House of Lords, Westminster,
London, SW1A 0PW
Hunting Defence Ltd, Reddings Wood,
Ampthill, Bedfordshire
Tel: (01525) 841000
Personal Staff .... Brigadier Peter Painter
(Regimental Secretary)
Tel: (0181) 781 3031

Vinson of Roddam Dene, Baron (Nigel Vinson)

Type of Peerage .... Life
Political Allegiance ..... Conservative
Created 1985
Born .... 27th January 1931 in Nettlestead, Kent
Educated .... Pangbourne College
Professional Career ..... 1952 - 72 Chairman/Founder, Plastic
Coatings Ltd
Political Career .... 1971 - 89 Chairman, then President,
Industrial Participation Association
1980 - 90 Chairman, Rural Development
Commission
1989 - 96 Chairman, Institute of Economic
Affairs
1990 - Deputy Chairman, Electra
Investment Trust
Subject Interests .... Finance, Economics, Pensions, Deregulation,
Rural affairs
Recreational Interests ... Fine Art, Crafts
Correspondence Address .. 34 Kynance Mews, London, SW7 4QR
Tel: (01668) 217230 Fax: (01668) 217356

Vivian, Baron (Nicholas Crespigny Laurence Vivian)

Type of Peerage .... Hereditary
Political Allegiance ..... Conservative
Succeeded 1991
Born .... 11th December 1935 in London
Professional Career ..... 1954 - 90 Armed Forces (Brigadier 1987)
1984 - 87 Deputy Commander, Land Forces
and Chief of Staff, Cyprus

MEMBERS OF THE HOUSE OF LORDS

W

Waddington, Baron
(Rt Hon David Charles Waddington GCVO, QC)

Type of Peerage . . . . Life
Political Allegiance . . . . . Conservative
Created 1990
Born . . . . 2nd August 1929 in Burnley, Lancashire
Educated . . . . Sedbergh School, North Yorkshire
Hertford College, Oxford
Professional Career . . . . . 1953 - Barrister (QC 1971)
Political Career . . . . 1968 - 74 MP (Conservative) for Nelson and
Colne
1979 - 90 MP (Conservative) for Clitheroe,
then Ribble Valley
1979 - 81 Government Whip, House of
Commons
1981 - 83 Parliamentary Secretary,
Department of Employment
1983 - 87 Minister of State, Home Office
1987 - 89 Government Chief Whip,
House of Commons
1989 - 90 Home Secretary
1990 - 92 Lord Privy Seal and Leader of the
House of Lords
1992 - 97 Governor of Burmuda
Parliamentary Interests . . Law, Constitution, Crime and punishment
Recreational Interests . . . Golf
Correspondence Address . . Stable House, Sabden, Near Clitheroe,
Lancashire, BB7 9DY
Tel and Fax: (01282) 771070
Flat 4, 39 Chester Way, London, SE11 4UR
Tel: (0171) 820 9338 Fax: (0171) 219 6448

Wade of Chorlton, Baron (William Oulton Wade)

Type of Peerage . . . . Life
Political Allegiance . . . . . Conservative
Created 1990
Born . . . . 24th December 1932 in Chester
Educated . . . . Birkenhead School
Queens University, Belfast
Professional Career . . . . . Farmer, Cheese Master and Company
Director
1982 - 84 Chairman, Cheese Export Council
1984 - 88 Member, Food From Britain
Council
1993 - Chairman, Cheshire Historic
Churches Trust
1994 - President, Energy from Waste
Political Career . . . . 1976 - 81 Chairman, North West Area
Conservative Association
1982 - 90 Joint Treasurer, Conservative
Party
Subject Interests . . . . Rural economy, Technology, Food and
agriculture
Recreational Interests . . . Reading, Shooting
Correspondence Address . . House of Lords, Westminster,
London, SW1A 0PW
Tel: (0171) 219 5499
Personal Staff . . . . Mrs Patricia Fea *(Personal Assistant)*
Tel: (0171) 219 6365

Wakefield, Bishop of (Rt Rev Nigel Simeon McCulloch)

Type of Peerage . . . . Bishop
Political Allegiance . . . . . None
Entered Lords 1997
Born . . . . 17th January 1942 in Liverpool
Educated . . . . Liverpool College
Selwyn College, Cambridge
Cuddesdon College, Oxford
Professional Career . . . . . 1966 - 70 Curate, Ellesmere Port, Chester
1970 - 75 Chaplain and Director of Studies
in Theology, Christ's College, Cambridge
1973 - 78 Diocesan Missioner, Norwich
1978 - 86 Rector, St Thomas and
St Edmund, Salisbury
1979 - 86 Archdeacon of Sarum
1986 - 92 Bishop of Taunton
1992 - Bishop of Wakefield
1997 - Lord High Almoner
Subject Interests . . . . Evangelism, Church in community,
Media, Africa
Recreational Interests . . . Music, Lake District
Correspondence Address . . Bishop's Lodge, Woodthorpe Lane,
Wakefield, WF2 6JL
Tel: (01924) 255349 Fax: (01924) 250202

Wakeham, Baron (Rt Hon John Wakeham)

Type of Peerage . . . . Life
Political Allegiance . . . . . Conservative
Created 1992
Born . . . . 22nd June 1932
Educated . . . . Charterhouse
Professional Career . . . . . Chartered Accountant
Political Career . . . . 1974 - 92 MP (Conservative) for Maldon,
then for Colchester South and Maldon
1979 - 81 Assistant Government Whip,
House of Commons
1981 - 82 Parliamentary Secretary,
Department of Industry
1982 - 83 Minister of State, HM Treasury
1983 - 87 Government Chief Whip,
House of Commons
1987 - 89 - Lord Privy Seal, then President
of the Council and Leader of the House of
Commons
1989 - 92 Secretary of State for Energy
1992 - 94 Lord Privy Seal and Leader of the
House of Lords
Subject Interests . . . . Finance, Business and taxation, Energy,
Agriculture, Europe
Recreational Interests . . . Farming, Sailing, Racing, Reading
Correspondence Address . . House of Lords, Westminster,
London, SW1A 0PW
Tel: (0171) 353 1248

MEMBERS OF THE HOUSE OF LORDS

Wakehurst, Baron (John Christopher Loder)

Type of Peerage . . . . Hereditary
Political Allegiance . . . . . Conservative
Succeeded 1970
Born . . . . 23rd September 1925 in London
Educated . . . . Eton College
The King's School, Sydney, Australia
Trinity College, Cambridge
Professional Career . . . . . 1950 - Barrister
1973 - 84 Chairman, Continental Illinois Ltd
1980 - 96 Chairman, Anglo and Overseas
Trust plc
1985 - 90 Chairman, Philadelphia
National Ltd
1991 - 95 Chairman, Morgan Grenfell
Equity Income Trust plc
Subject Interests . . . . Photography
Correspondence Address . . Trillinghurst Oast, Goudhurst,
Kent, TN1Y 1HL

Waldegrave, Earl (James Sherbrooke Waldegrave)

Type of Peerage . . . . Hereditary
Political Allegiance . . . . . Conservative
Succeeded 1995
Born . . . . 8th December 1940

Wales, Prince of (HRH Prince Charles Philip Arthur George)

Type of Peerage . . . . Hereditary (Duke of Cornwall and Rothesay)
Political Allegiance . . . . . Cross Bench
Succeeded . . . . 1952 (Created Prince of Wales 1958)
Born . . . . 14th November 1948

Walker of Doncaster, Baron (Rt Hon Harold Walker)

Type of Peerage . . . . Life
Political Allegiance . . . . . Labour
Created 1997
Born . . . . 12th July 1927 in Manchester
Educated . . . . Manchester College of Technology
Political Career . . . . 1967 - 68 Government Whip,
House of Commons
1968 - 70 Parliamentary Secretary,
Department of Employment
1970 - 74, 1979 - 83 Opposition Front
Bench Spokesman on Employment,
House of Commons
1974 - 79 Parliamentary Secretary, then
Minister of State, Department of
Employment
1983 - 92 Chairman of Ways and Means and
Deputy Speaker, House of Commons
Subject Interests . . . . Occupational health and safety, Industrial
relations, Manpower policy
Recreational Interests . . . Gardening, Reading
Correspondence Address . . 15 Grosvenor Hill, Wimbledon, SW19 4SA
Tel: (0181) 946 8560

Walker of Worcester, Baron
(Rt Hon Peter Edward Walker MBE)

Type of Peerage . . . . Life
Political Allegiance . . . . . Conservative
Created 1992
Born . . . . 25th March 1932 in Harrow, Middlesex
Educated . . . . Latymer Upper School, London
Professional Career . . . . . 1990 - 96 Director, British Gas
1991 - Chairman, Thornton and Co
1992 - Chairman, Cornhill Insurance
1992 - Chairman, English Partnerships
1997 - Chairman, Kleinwort Benson
Political Career . . . . 1958 - 60 Chairman, Young Conservatives
1961 - 92 MP (Conservative) for Worcester
1963 - 64 PPS to Leader of the
House of Commons
1964 - 70 Opposition Spokesman in
Economics/Finance, then Transport and
Housing/ Local Government
1970 - 72 Secretary of State for the
Environment
1974 - 75 Opposition Spokesman on Trade
and Industry, then Defence
1972 - 74 Secretary of State for Trade and
Industry
1979 - 83 Minister of Agriculture,
Fisheries and Food
1983 - 87 Secretary of State for Energy
1987 - 90 Secretary of State for Wales
Correspondence Address . . 12 Cowley Street, London, SW1P 3LZ
Tel: (0171) 222 9695 Fax: (0171) 799 2294
Personal Staff . . . . Miss Sue Cornford (Secretary)
173 Sandycombe Road, Kew, TW9 2EN
Tel: (0181) 948 5995

Wallace of Coslany, Baron (George Douglas Wallace)

Type of Peerage . . . . Life
Political Allegiance . . . . . Labour
Created 1974
Born . . . . 18th April 1906 in Cheltenham,
Gloucestershire
Professional Career . . . . . 1970 -86 Member, War Graves Commission
1974 - 77 Vice Chairman, Greenwich and
Bexley Area Health Authority
Political Career . . . . 1945 - 50 MP (Labour) for Chislehurst
1964 - 74 MP (Labour) for Norwich North
1977 - 79 Government Whip,
(Lord in Waiting)
Correspondence Address . . 44 Shuttle Close, Sidcup, Kent, DA15 8EP
Tel: (0181) 300 3634

MEMBERS OF THE HOUSE OF LORDS

Wallace of Saltaire, Baron (William John Lawrence)

Type of Peerage	Life
Political Allegiance	Liberal Democrat
Created	1995
Born	12th March 1941 in Leicester
Educated	St Edward's School, Oxford
	King's College, Cambridge
	Nuffield College, Oxford
	Cornell University, USA
Professional Career	1967 - 77 Lecturer in Government, Manchester University
	1978 - 90 Director of Studies, Royal Institute of International Affairs, London
	1990 - 95 Walater F Hallstein Fellow, St Anthony's College, Oxford
	1995 - Reader in International Relations, London School of Economics
Political Career	1996 - Liberal Democrat Defence Spokesman, House of Lords
Subject Interests	Europe, Foreign affairs

Walpole, Baron (Robert Horatio Walpole)

Type of Peerage	Hereditary
Political Allegiance	Cross Bench
Succeeded	1989
Born	8th December 1938 in Norwich
Educated	Eton College
	Kings College, Cambridge
Professional Career	1977 - 87 Chairman, Norwich School of Art
	1981 - 88 Chairman, Textile Conservation Centre
	1982 - 88 Chairman, East Anglian Tourist Board
Political Career	1970 - 81 Member, Norfolk County Council
Subject Interests	Agriculture, Arts, Tourism
Correspondence Address	Mannington Hall, Norwich, Norfolk, NR11 7BB
	Tel: (01263) 584175 Fax: (01263) 761214
	E-mail: walpolerh@parliament.uk

Walsingham, Baron (John de Grey MC)

Type of Peerage	Hereditary
Succeeded	1965
Born	21st February 1925 in Wandsworth, London
Professional Career	1942 - 47 Royal Artillery
	1950 Foreign Office
	1950 - 54 Royal Artillery
	1954 - 56 SAS
	1956 - 58 Parachute Brigade
	1958 - 60 Royal Military College of Science
	1960 - 63 Royal Artillery
	1963 - 65 Commando Brigade
	1965 - 67 Ministry of Defence
	1968 - Company Director
Subject Interests	Finance, Europe

Walton of Detchant, Baron (John Nicholas Walton)

Type of Peerage	Life
Political Allegiance	Cross Bench
Created	1989
Born	16th September 1922 in Rowlands Gill, County Durham
Educated	Alderman Wraith Grammar School, Spennymore, County Durham
	Medical School, King's College, University of Durham
Professional Career	1947 - 49 Service in RAMC
	1958 - 83 Consultant Neurologist, Newcastle University Hospitals
	1968 - 83 Professor of Neurology, Newcastle University (also Dean of Medicine 1971 - 81)
	1980 - 82 President, British Medical Association
	1982 - 89 President, General Medical Council
	1983 - 89 Warden, Green College, Oxford
	1984 - 86 President, Royal Society of Medicine
	1989 - 97 President, World Federation of Neurology
	1991 - 96 Chairman, Hamlyn Foundation National Commission in Education
Political Career	1993 - 94 Chairman, Select Committee on Medical Ethics, House of Lords
Subject Interests	Medicine, Neuroscience, Education
Recreational Interests	Cricket, Golf, Reading, Music
Correspondence Address	13 Norham Gardens, Oxford, OX2 6PS
	Tel: (01865) 512492 Fax: (01865) 51249
	The Old Piggery, Detchant, Belford, Northumberland, NE70 7PQ
	Tel: (01668) 213374 Fax: (01668) 213012
	Northview, 20 Tanners Lane, Burford, Oxon, OX18 4NB
	Tel: (01993) 823263 Fax: (01993) 0823854
Personal Staff	Miss Rosemary Allan *(Secretary)*
	Tel: (01865) 512492

Wardington of Alnmouth, Baron (Christopher Henry Beaumont Pease)

Type of Peerage	Hereditary
Political Allegiance	Conservative
Succeeded	1950
Born	22nd January 1924 in London
Educated	Eton College
Professional Career	Stockbrocker
	1989 - 96 Chairman, Friends of the British Library
Subject Interests	Antiquarian books
Correspondence Address	Wardington Manor, Banbury, Oxford, OX17 1SW
	Tel: (01295) 750202 Fax: (01295) 750805
	29 Moore Street, London, SW3 2QW
	Tel: (0171) 584 5245

MEMBERS OF THE HOUSE OF LORDS

Warnock, Baroness (Helen Mary Warnock DBE)

Type of Peerage	Life
Political Allegiance	Cross Bench
Created	1985
Born	14th April 1924 in Winchester, Hampshire
Educated	St Swithun's School, Winchester
	Lady Margaret Hall, University of Oxford
Professional Career	1949 - 66 Fellow and Tutor in Philosophy, St Hugh's College, Oxford
	1966 - 72 Headmistress, Oxford High School
	1972 - 76 Research Fellow, Lady Margaret Hall, Oxford
	1974 - 78 Chairman, Committee of Enquiry into Special Education
	1976 - 85 Senior Research Fellow, St Hugh's Oxford
	1982 - 84 Chairman, Committee of Enquiry into Human Fertilisation and Embryology
	1985 - 92 Mistress, Girton College, Cambridge
Subject Interests	Education, Medical ethics, Broadcasting, Environment, Wildlife
Recreational Interests	Music, Gardening
Correspondence Address	House of Lords, Westminster, London, SW1A 0PW
	3 Church Street, Great Bedwyn, Wiltshire, SN8 3PE
	Tel: (01672) 870214

Waterford, Marquess of (John Hubert de la Poer Beresford)

Type of Peerage	Hereditary
Political Allegiance	Conservative
Succeeded	1934 (as a minor)
Born	14th July 1933 in London
Professional Career	1951 - 53 Royal Horse Guards
	1954 - Estate Management
Recreational Interests	Riding, Climbing, Shooting

Watson of Invergowrie, Baron (Michael Goodall Watson)

Type of Peerage	Life
Political Allegiance	Labour
Succeeded	1997
Born	1st May 1949
Professional Career	1974 - 77 Development Officer (East Midlands), Workers Educational Association
	1977 - 89 Official, ASTMS, then MSF (trade union)
Political Career	1987 - 97 MP (Labour) for Glasgow Central

Waverley, Viscount (John Desmond Forbes Anderson)

Type of Peerage	Hereditary
Political Allegiance	Cross Bench
Succeeded	1990
Born	31st October 1949

Weatherill, Baron (Rt Hon Bruce Bernard Weatherill)

Type of Peerage	Life
Political Allegiance	Cross Bench
Created	1992
Born	25th November 1920 in Sunningdale, Berkshire
Educated	Malvern College
Professional Career	1940 - 46 Armed Forces (Captain, Indian Army)
	1946 - 70 Managing Director, Bernard Weatherill Ltd
Political Career	1964 - 92 MP for Croydon North East (Conservative till 1983)
	1967 - 70 An Opposition Whip, House of Commons
	1970 - 71 A Government Whip, House of Commons
	1971 - 72 Government Whip, Vice-Chamberlain, HM Household
	1972 - 73 Government Whip, Comptroller, HM Household
	1973 - 74 Government Deputy Chief Whip, House of Commons
	1974 - 79 Opposition Deputy Chief Whip, House of Commons
	1979 - 83 Chairman of Ways and Means and Deputy Speaker, House of Commons
	1983 - 92 Constituency MP for Croydon North East
	1983 - 92 Speaker of the House of Commons
	1995 - Convenor of Cross Bench Peers
Subject Interests	Constitutional matters, Commonwealth, Overseas development
Recreational Interests	Golf, Tennis
Correspondence Address	House of Lords, Westminster, London, SW1A 0PW
	Tel: (0171) 219 2224 Fax: (0171) 219 5979
Personal Staff	The Hon Fiona Rippon *(Secretary)*
	Tel: (0171) 219 4059

Wedderburn of Charlton, Baron (Kenneth William Wedderburn QC)

Type of Peerage	Life
Political Allegiance	Labour
Created	1977
Born	13th April 1927 in London
Professional Career	1952 - 64 Lecturer in Law, Cambridge University (Fellow of Clare College)
	1953 Barrister (QC 1990)
	1964 - 92 Professor of Commercial Law, London School of Economics
	1989 - 95 President, Institute Employment Rights
Subject Interests	Employment, Education
Recreational Interests	Charlton Athletic FC

Wedgwood, Baron (Piers Anthony Weymouth Wedgwood)

Type of Peerage	Hereditary
Political Allegiance	Conservative
Succeeded	1970
Born	20th Septeber 1954

MEMBERS OF THE HOUSE OF LORDS

Weidenfeld, Baron (Arthur George Weidenfeld)

Type of Peerage	Life
Political Allegiance	Cross Bench
Created	1976
Born	13th September 1919 in Vienna
Educated	Piaristen Gymnasium
	Vienna University and Diplomatic Academy
Professional Career	1939 - 46 BBC (Monitoring Service, then
	News Commentator, Overseas Service)
	1948 - Chairman, Weidenfeld and Nicolson
Subject Interests	Foreign affairs, Europe, the Middle East,
	Atlantic Alliance, Arts, Broadcasting
Recreational Interests	Opera, Travel
Correspondence Address	Orion House, Supper Street, Martin's Lane,
	London, WC2H 9EA
	Tel: (0171) 520 4411 Fax: (0171) 240 4822
	Flat 23, 9 Chelsea Embankment,
	London, SW3 4LE
	Tel: (0171) 351 0042 Fax: (0171) 352 8095
Personal Staff	Mrs Pat Kinsman *(PA)*

Weinstock, Baron (Arnold Weinstock)

Type of Peerage	Life
Political Allegiance	Cross Bench
Created	1980
Born	29th July 1924 in London
Educated	London School of Economics
Professional Career	1963 - 97 Managing Director, General
	Electric Co
Recreational Interests	Music, Racing/breeding horses
Correspondence Address	7 Grosvenor Square, London, W1X 9LA
	Tel: (0171) 493 8484

Weir, Viscount (William Kenneth James Weir)

Type of Peerage	Hereditary
Political Allegiance	Conservative
Succeeded	1976
Born	9th November 1933 in Glasgow, Scotland
Educated	Eton College
	Trinity College, Cambridge
Professional Career	1957 - Executive, then Director and (from
	1973 Chairman, Weir Group
	1971 - Director, St James Place Capital
	1972 - 76 Director, British Steel Corporation
	1972 - 84 Director, Bank of England
	1996 - Chairman, BICC plc
Subject Interests	Scottish constitutional affairs,
	Trade and industry, Overseas economies,
	Life assurance
Recreational Interests	Shooting, Golf, Fishing
Correspondence Address	Weir Group plc, Cathcart, Glasgow
	Tel: (0141) 637 7111 Fax: (0141) 637 2221
	Rodinghead, Mauchline, Ayrshire, KA5 5TR
	Tel: (01563) 884233
Personal Staff	Mrs Isabel Grieve *(Secretary)*
	Tel: (0141) 637 7111

Wellington, Duke of (Arthur Valerian Wellesley KG, LVO, DBE, MC)

Type of Peerage	Hereditary
Political Allegiance	Cross Bench
Succeeded	1972
Born	2nd July 1915 in Rome
Educated	Eton College
	New College, Oxford
Professional Career	1938 - 67 Armed Forces (retired as
	Brigadier)
	1964 - 67 Defence Attaché, Madrid
Subject Interests	Agriculture, Forestry, The Army, Military
	history
Recreational Interests	Fishing, Shooting
Correspondence Address	Stratfield Saye House, Basingstoke,
	Hampshire, RG27 0AS
	Tel: (01256) 882218 Fax: (01256) 882698
Personal Staff	Mrs Molly Ball *(Personal Secretary)*
	Tel: (01256) 882218

Wemyss and March, Earl of (Francis David Charteris KT)

Type of Peerage	Hereditary
Political Allegiance	Conservative
Succeeded	1937
Born	19th January 1912 in London
Educated	Eton College
	Balliol College, Oxford
Professional Career	1937 - 44 Assistant District Commissioner,
	Basutoland
	1967 - 89 Lord Lieutenant of East Lothian
Subject Interests	Conservation
Correspondence Address	Gosford House, Longniddry,
	East Lothian, EN32 0PX
	Tel: (01875) 870200

Westbury, Baron (David Alan Bethell CBE, MC, DL)

Type of Peerage	Hereditary
Political Allegiance	Conservative
Succeeded	1961
Born	16th July 1922 in London
Educated	Harrow School
	Royal Military College, Sandhurst
Correspondence Address	House of Lords, Westminster,
	London, SW1A 0PW
	Tel: (0171) 352 7911
	8 Ropers Orchard, Danvers Street,
	London, SW3 5AX

Westminster, Duke of (Gerald Cavendish Grosvenor OBE, TD)

Type of Peerage	Hereditary
Succeeded	1979
Born	22nd December 1951
Professional Career	Landowner
	1981 - 93 Director, Claridges Hotel
	1982 - Director, Mauher Sound Ltd
	1989 - Director, Grosvenor Estate Holdings
Recreational Interests	Shooting, Fishing, Scuba diving

MEMBERS OF THE HOUSE OF LORDS

Westmorland, Earl of (Anthony David Francis Henry Fane)

Type of Peerage . . . . Hereditary
Political Allegiance . . . . . Cross Bench
Succeeded 1993
Born . . . . 1st August 1951 in London
Educated . . . . Eton College
Professional Career . . . . . 1994 - Director, Philips International
Auctioneers
Subject Interests . . . . Sport, Environment
Recreational Interests . . . Travel, Reading
Correspondence Address . . 31 Langton Street, London, SW10 0JL
Tel: (0171) 629 6602

Westwood, Baron (William Gavin Westwood)

Type of Peerage . . . . Hereditary
Without Writ of Summons
Succeeded 1991
Born . . . . 30th January 1944 in Newcastle-upon-Tyne
Professional Career . . . . . 1962 - 66 Articled Clerk, Coopers and
Lybrand
1968 - 70 Accountant
1970 - 90 Financial Director

Whaddon, Baron (John Derek Page)

Type of Peerage . . . . Life
Political Allegiance . . . . . Labour
Created 1978
Born . . . . 14th August 1927 in Sale, Cheshire
Educated . . . . St Bede's College, Manchester
Political Career . . . . 1964 - 70 MP (Labour) for King's Lynn
Subject Interests . . . . Eastern Europe

Wharncliffe, Earl of (Richard Alan Montagu Stuart Wortley)

Type of Peerage . . . . Hereditary
Without Writ of Summons
Succeeded 1987
Born . . . . 26th May 1953

Wharton, Baroness (Myrtle Olive Felix Robertson)

Type of Peerage . . . . Hereditary
Political Allegiance . . . . . Cross Bench
Succeeded 1990
Born . . . . 20th February 1934 in London
Educated . . . . Herschel School for Girls, Claremont, South
Africa
Subject Interests . . . . Media, Animal welfare, South Africa
Recreational Interests . . . Photography, Opera
Correspondence Address . . 9 Gipsy Lane, London, SW15 5RG
Tel: (0181) 876 8300 Fax: (0181) 392 1262

White, Baroness (Eirene Lloyd White)

Type of Peerage . . . . Life
Political Allegiance . . . . . Labour
Created 1970
Born . . . . 7th November 1909 in Belfast
Educated . . . . St Paul's Girls School
Somerville College, Oxford
Professional Career . . . . . 1933 - 37 Official, Ministry of Labour
1941 - 45 Political Correspondent,
Manchester Evening News
Political Career . . . . 1947 - 53, 1958 - 72 Member, Labour Party
National Executive Committee (Chairman
1968 - 69)
1950 - 70 Labour MP for East Flint
1964 - 66 Parliamentary Secretary,
Colonial Office
1966 - 67 Minister of State, Foreign Office
1967 - 70 Minister of State, Welsh Office
1974 - 81 Member, Royal Commission on
Environmental Pollution
1979 - 82 Chairman, European Committees
Committee and Principal Deputy
Chairman of Committees, House of Lords
1979 - 89 Deputy Speaker, House of Lords

Whitelaw, Viscount (Rt Hon William Stephen Ian Whitelaw KT, CH MC)

Type of Peerage . . . . Hereditary (First Creation)
Political Allegiance . . . . . Conservative
Created 1983
Born . . . . 28th June 1918
Educated . . . . Winchester College
Trinity College, Cambridge
Political Career . . . . 1955 - 83 MP (Conservative) for Penrith and
the Border
1957 - 58 PPS for Chancellor of Exchequer
1959 - 62 Government Whip,
House of Commons
1962 - 64 Parliamentary Secretary,
Ministry of Labour
1964 - 70 Opposition Chief Whip,
House of Commons
1970 - 72 Lord President of the Council and
Leader of the House of Commons
1972 - 73 Secretary of State for Northern
Ireland
1973 - 74 Secretary of State for Employment
1974 - 75 Chairman of the Conservative
Party
1975 - 79 Opposition Spokesman on Home
Affairs and Deputy Leader of Opposition,
House of Commons
1979 - 83 Home Secretary
1983 - 88 Lord President of the Council and
Leader of the House of Lords

MEMBERS OF THE HOUSE OF LORDS

Whitty, Baron (John Lawrence Whitty)

Type of Peerage	Life
Political Allegiance.....	Labour
Created..............	1996
Born...............	15th June 1943
Educated	Latymer Upper School, Hammersmith
	St John's College, Cambridge
Professional Career.....	1965 - 70 Civil Servant, Ministry of
	Aviation/Technology
	1970 - 73 Economic Dept, Trades Union
	Congress
	1973 - 85 Research and Political Officer,
	GMWU (Trade Union)
Political Career.......	1985 - 94 General Secretary, Labour Party
	1997 - Government Whip, House of Lords
Subject Interests.......	European affairs, Employment, Environment,
	Education
Recreational Interests ...	Theatre, History, Cinema
Correspondence Address..	Government Whips Office, House of Lords,
	Westminster, London, SW1A 0PW
	Tel: (0171) 219 3118/3131
	Fax: (0171) 219 6837
	61 Bimport, Shaftesbury, Dorset, SP7 8AZ
	Tel: (01747) 854619

Wigoder, Baron (Thomas Wigoder QC)

Type of Peerage	Life
Political Allegiance.....	Liberal Democrat
Created..............	1974
Born...............	12th February 1921
Political Career.......	1977 - 84 Liberal Chief Whip,
	House of Lords

Wigram, Baron (George Neville Clive Wigram MC)

Type of Peerage	Hereditary
Political Allegiance.....	Conservative
Born...............	2nd August 1915 in Ascot
Professional Career.....	1936 - 57 Grenadier Guards
	1946 - 49 Military Secretary to Governor
	General, New Zealand
	1967 - 74 Governor of Westminster Hospital
	1957 - 96 Local Government, Lieutenancy,
	Magistry and Involvement in Diocesan,
	County, District and Parish Affairs
Subject Interests.......	Agriculture, Defence

Wilberforce, Baron (Rt Hon Richard Orme Wilberforce)

Type of Peerage	Life (Law Lord)
Political Allegiance.....	Cross Bench
Created..............	1964
Born...............	11th March 1907 in India
Educated	Winchester College
	New College, Oxford
Professional Career.....	1932 Barrister (QC 1954)
	1932 - 46 Armed Forces (Brigadier)
	1946 - 47 Under Secretary, Control Office,
	Germany/Austria
	1961 - 64 High Court Judge (Chancery
	Division)
	1964 - 82 Lord of Appeal in Ordinary
	1966 - 88 Chairman, Executive Council,
	International Law Association
Subject Interests.......	Slavery, Human rights, International law,
	Taxation
Recreational Interests ...	Music, Opera, Horseracing
Correspondence Address..	8 Cambridge Place, London, W8 5PB

Wilcox, Baroness (Judith Ann Wilcox)

Type of Peerage	Life
Political Allegiance.....	Conservative
Created..............	1996
Born...............	31st October 1940
Educated	St Mary's School, Wantage
	Plymouth Polytechnic
Professional Career.....	1979 - 84 Financial Director, Capstan Foods
	1984 - 89 Chairman, Channel Foods
	1990 - 96 Chairman, National Consumer
	Council
	1991 - Board Member, Automobile
	Association
	1997 - Director, Carpetright plc
	1997 - Director, Cadbury Schweppes plc
	President, National Federation of
	Consumer Groups
	President, Institute of Trading Standards
	Administration
Subject Interests.......	Consumer affairs/protection,
	Fishing industry, Food
Recreational Interests ...	Sailing, Walking, Fishing, Calligraphy
Correspondence Address..	17 Great College Street, London, SW1P 3RX
	Tel: (0171) 222 1319 Fax: (0171) 976 7087
	E-mail: wilcoxj@parliament.uk

MEMBERS OF THE HOUSE OF LORDS

Williams of Crosby, Baroness
(Rt Hon Shirley Vivien Teresa Brittain Williams)

Type of Peerage . . . . Life
Political Allegiance . . . . . Liberal Democrat
Born . . . . 27th July 1930 in London
Created 1993
Educated . . . . St Paul's Girls School
　　　　　　　　　　　　Talbot Heath School
　　　　　　　　　　　　Somerville College, Oxford
　　　　　　　　　　　　Columbia University, New York
Professional Career . . . . . 1988 - Professor of Elective Politics,
　　　　　　　　　　　　Harvard University, USA
Political Career . . . . 1960 - 64 General Secretary, Fabian Society
　　　　　　　　　　　　1964 - 79 MP (Labour) for Hitchin then
　　　　　　　　　　　　Hertford and Stevenage
　　　　　　　　　　　　1966 - 67 Parliamentary Secretary,
　　　　　　　　　　　　Ministry of Labour
　　　　　　　　　　　　1966 - 69 Minister of State, Department of
　　　　　　　　　　　　Education and Science
　　　　　　　　　　　　1969 - 70 Minister of State, Home Office
　　　　　　　　　　　　1970 - 74 Opposition Spokesman on Social
　　　　　　　　　　　　Services, Home Affairs then Prices and
　　　　　　　　　　　　Consumer Protection
　　　　　　　　　　　　1974 - 76 Secretary of State for Prices and
　　　　　　　　　　　　Consumer Protection
　　　　　　　　　　　　1976 - 79 Secretary of State, Education and
　　　　　　　　　　　　Science and Paymaster General
　　　　　　　　　　　　1981 - 83 MP (Social Democratic Party) for
　　　　　　　　　　　　Crosby
　　　　　　　　　　　　1981 - 88 President, Social Democratic
　　　　　　　　　　　　Party
　　　　　　　　　　　　1995 - Member, European Communities
　　　　　　　　　　　　Select Committee, House of Lords
Subject Interests . . . . Europe, Foreign affairs, Employment policy
Recreational Interests . . . Hill walking, Swimming, Music
Correspondence Address . . House of Lords, Westminster,
　　　　　　　　　　　　London, SW1A 0PW
　　　　　　　　　　　　Tel: (0171) 219 5850 Fax: (0171) 219 2082
Personal Staff . . . . Mrs Carol Savage *(Assistant)*

Williams of Elvel, Baron
(Charles Cuthbert Powell Williams CBE)

Type of Peerage . . . . Life
Political Allegiance . . . . . Labour
Created 1985
Born . . . . 9th February 1933
Educated . . . . Westminster School
　　　　　　　　　　　　Christ Church, Oxford
Political Career . . . . 1986 - 97 Opposition Spokesman on Trade
　　　　　　　　　　　　and Industry, Energy, Defence and
　　　　　　　　　　　　Environment, House of Lords
　　　　　　　　　　　　1989 - 92 Deputy Leader of the Opposition,
　　　　　　　　　　　　House of Lords
Correspondence Address . . House of Lords, Westminster,
　　　　　　　　　　　　London, SW1A 0PW
　　　　　　　　　　　　Tel: (0171) 219 6054

Williams of Mostyn, Baron (Gareth Wyn Williams QC)

Type of Peerage . . . . Life
Political Allegiance . . . . . Labour
Created 1992
Born . . . . 5th February 1941 in North Wales
Educated . . . . Rhyl Grammar School
　　　　　　　　　　　　Queen's College, Cambridge
Professional Career . . . . . 1965 Barrister (QC 1978)
　　　　　　　　　　　　1986 Deputy High Court Judge
　　　　　　　　　　　　1991 - 92 Chairman, Bar Council
　　　　　　　　　　　　1994 - Chancellor, University of Wales
Political Career . . . . 1992 - 97 Principal Opposition Spokesman
　　　　　　　　　　　　on Northern Ireland, Legal and Home
　　　　　　　　　　　　Affairs
　　　　　　　　　　　　1997 - Parliamentary Secretary, Home Office

Willoughby de Broke, Baron (Leopold David Verney)

Type of Peerage . . . . Hereditary
Political Allegiance . . . . . Conservative
Succeeded 1986
Born . . . . 14th September 1938
Educated . . . . Le Rosey
　　　　　　　　　　　　New College, Oxford

Willoughby De Eresby, Baroness
(Nancy Jane Marie Heathcote-Drummond-Willoughby)

Type of Peerage . . . . Hereditary
Political Allegiance . . . . . Cross Bench
Succeeded 1994
Born . . . . 1st December 1934 in London
Professional Career . . . . . 1978 - 92 Save the Children Fund,
　　　　　　　　　　　　Overseas Committee
　　　　　　　　　　　　1994 - Trustee, National Portrait Gallery
Correspondence Address . . Grimsthorpe, Bourne,
　　　　　　　　　　　　Lincolnshire, PE10 0LZ

Wilson, Baron (Patrick Maitland Wilson)

Type of Peerage . . . . Hereditary
Without Writ of Summons
Succeeded 1964
Born . . . . 14th September 1915

MEMBERS OF THE HOUSE OF LORDS

Wilson of Tillyorn, Baron (David Clive Wilson GCMG)

Type of Peerage	Life
Political Allegiance	Cross Bench
Created	1992
Born	14th February 1935 in Alloa, Scotland
Educated	Trinity College, Glenalmond
	Keble College, Oxford
	School of Oriental and African Studies,
	University of London
Professional Career	1958 - 68, 1974 - 92 HM Diplomatic Service
	1963 - 65 Second, then First Secretary,
	Peking
	1971 - 81 Political Adviser, Hong Kong
	1981 - 84 Head, South European
	Department, Foreign and Commonwealth
	Office
	1984 - 87 Assistant Under Secretary,
	Foreign and Commonwealth Office
	1987 - 92 Governor of Hong Kong
	1993 - Chairman, Scottish Commerce,
	British Council
	1993 - Chairman, Scottish
	Hydro-Electric plc
	1997 Chancellor, University of Aberdeen
Subject Interests	Hong Kong, South East Asia, Scotland
Recreational Interests	Hill walking
Correspondence Address	Scottish Hydro-Electric plc,
	10 Dunkeld Road, Perth, PH1 5WA
	Tel: (01738) 455201 Fax: (01738) 455201
Personal Staff	Mrs Anne MacLehose *(Secretary)*
	Tel; (01738) 455202

Wilton, Earl of (Seymour William Arthur John Egerton

Type of Peerage	Hereditary
Succeeded	1927 (as minor)
Born	29th May 1921

Wimborne, Viscount (Ivor Mevyn Vigors Guest)

Type of Peerage	Hereditary
Political Allegiance	Cross Bench
Succeeded	1994
Born	19th September 1968 in London
Educated	Eton College
Correspondence Address	5 Wetherby Gardens, London, SW5 0JN
	Tel: (0171) 373 2120

Winchester, Bishop of (Rt Rev Michael Charles Scott-Joynt)

Type of Peerage	Bishop
Entered Lords	1995
Born	15th March 1943 in Bromley, Kent
Educated	Bradfield College, Berkshire
	King's College, Cambridge
	Cuddesdon College, Oxford
Career	1967 - 72 Tutor and Curate of
	Cuddesdon, Oxford
	1972 - 75 Team Vicar, Newbury
	1975 - 81 Priest in Charge then Rector,
	Bicester Area Team Ministry
	1982 - 87 Canon Residentiary and Director
	of Ordinands, St Albans
	1987 - 95 Bishop of Stafford
	1995 - Bishop of Winchester
Subject Interests	Uganda, Rwanda, Malaysia, Pensioners,
	Homeless, Penal affairs,
	Education, Ethics of public life
Recreational Interests	Walking, Soccer, Opera
Correspondence Address	Wolvesey, Winchester, SO23 9ND
	Tel: (01962) 854050 Fax: (01962) 842376

Winchester, Marquess of (Nigel George Paulet

Type of Peerage	Hereditary
Succeeded	1968
Born	23rd December 1941

Winchilsea and Nottingham, Earl of
(Christopher Denys Stormont Finch Hatton)

Type of Peerage	Hereditary
Political Allegiance	Liberal Democrat
Succeeded	1950
Born	17th November 1936 in London
Educated	Gordonstoun School
Subject Interests	Western Sahara, Police (UK International),
	Licenced taxi trade
Recreational Interests	Jazz, Photography, Travel
Correspondence Address	House of Lords, Westminster,
	London, SW1A 0PW
	Tel: (0171) 219 6225/5353
	Fax: (0171) 219 2377
Personal Staff	Mr Ian Allan *(Researcher)*

Windlesham, Baron
(Rt Hon David James George Hennesey CVO)

Type of Peerage	Hereditary
Political Allegiance	Conservative
Succeeded	1962
Born	28th January 1932
Political Career	1970 - 72 Minister of State, Home Office
	1972 - 73 Minister of State,
	Northern Ireland Office
	1973 - 74 Lord Privy Seal and Leader of the
	House of Lords

MEMBERS OF THE HOUSE OF LORDS

Winston, Baron (Robert Maurice Lipson Winston)
Type of Peerage . . . . Life
Political Allegiance . . . . . Labour
Created 1995
Born . . . . 15th July 1940
Educated . . . . St Paul's School
London Hospital Medical College
Professional Carrer . . . . . 1978 - Consultant Obstetrician and
Gynaecologist, Hammersmith Hospital
1982 - Reader, then (1987) Professor of
Fertility Studies, Royal Postgraduate
Medical School

Wise, Baron (John Clayton Wise)
Type of Peerage . . . . Hereditary
Political Allegiance . . . . . Conservative
Succeeded 1968
Born . . . . 11th June 1923

Wolfson, Baron (Leonard Gordon Wolfson)
Type of Peerage . . . . Life
Political Allegiance . . . . . Conservative
Created 1985
Born . . . . 11th November 1927

Wolfson of Sunningdale, Baron (David Wolfson)
Type of Peerage . . . . Life
Political Allegiance . . . . . Conservative
Created 1991
Born . . . . 9th November 1935

Wolverton, Baron (Christopher Richard Glynn)
Type of Peerage . . . . Hereditary
Political Allegiance . . . . . Cross Bench
Succeeded 1988
Born . . . . 5th October 1938

Woolf, Baron (Rt Hon Harry Kenneth Woolf)
Type of Peerage . . . . Life (Law Lord)
Political Allegiance . . . . . Cross Bench
Created 1992
Born . . . . 2nd May 1933
Educated . . . . Fettes College
University College, London
Professional Career . . . . . 1956 -Barrister
1972 - 79 Recorder, Crown Court
1979 - 86 High Court Judge, Queen's Bench
Division
1986 - 92 Lord Justice of Appeal
1992 - 96 Lord of Appeal in Ordinary
1996 - Master of the Rolls
Correspondence Address . . Royal Courts of Justice, London, WC2A 2LL

Woolton, Earl of (Simon Frederick Marquis)
Type of Peerage . . . . Hereditary
Political Allegiance . . . . . Conservative
Succeeded . . . . 1969 (as a minor)
Born . . . . 24th May 1958 in London
Subject Interests . . . . Countryside, Environment, Scotland, Sport

Wraxall, Baron (George Richard Lawley Gibbs)
Type of Peerage . . . . Hereditary
Political Allegiance . . . . . Conservative
Succeeded . . . . 1931 (as a minor)
Born . . . . 16th May 1928 in London
Educated . . . . Eton College
Royal Military Academy, Sandhurst
Professional Career . . . . . 1946 - 53 RMAS and Coldstream Guards
Subject Interests . . . . Forestry, Farming
Recreational Interests . . . Shooting, Gardening, Reading
Correspondence Address . . Tyntesfield, Wraxall, Bristol, BS19 1NU
Tel: (01275) 462923 Fax: (01275) 463771

Wrenbury, Baron (Rev John Burton Buckley)
Type of Peerage . . . . Hereditary
Political Allegiance . . . . . Cross Bench
Succeeded . . . . 1940 (as a minor)
Born . . . . 18th June 1927 in London
Professional Career . . . . . 1948 - 74 Partner, Freshfields, Solicitors
1974 - 90 Partner, Thomson Snell and
Passmore, Solicitors
1990 - Curate, Dallington, Brightling,
Mountfield and Netherfield
1990 Ordained Deacon
1991 - Priest

Wright of Richmond, Baron
(Patrick Richard Henry Wright GCMG)
Type of Peerage . . . . Life
Political Allegiance . . . . . Cross Bench
Created 1994
Born . . . . 28th June 1931 in Reading, Berkshire
Professional Career . . . . . 1955 - 91 HM Diplomatic Service
Subject Interests . . . . Foreign affairs

Wrottesley, Baron
(Clifton Hugh Lancelot de Verdon Wrottesley)
Type of Peerage . . . . Hereditary
Political Allegiance . . . . . Conservative
Succeeded 1977
Born . . . . 10th August 1968 in Dublin
Educated . . . . Eton College
Edinburgh University
Professional Career . . . . . 1989 - 91 Chairman and Sales Director,
Edinburgh Publications Ltd
1992 - 95 Armed Forces (Captain, Grenadier
Guards)
1996 - Director of Operations, Savoy Knight
Yachts Intl Ltd
Subject Interests . . . . Political, constitutional and electoral reform,
Media, Sport, Information Technology
Recreational Interests . . . Sports

Wyfold, Baron (Hermon Robert Fleming Hermon-Hodge)
Type of Peerage . . . . Hereditary
On Leave Of Absence
Succeeded 1942
Born . . . . 26th June 1915

Wynford, Baron (Robert Samuel Best MBE)
Type of Peerage . . . . Hereditary
Political Allegiance . . . . . Conservative
Succeeded 1943
Born . . . . 5th January 1917

MEMBERS OF THE HOUSE OF LORDS

Y

Yarborough, Earl of (Charles John Pelham)
Type of Peerage . . . . Hereditary
Political Allegiance . . . . . Conservative
Succeeded 1991
Born . . . . 5th November 1963 in London
Correspondence Address . . Brocklesby Park, Habrough,
Lincolnshire, DN37 8PL

York, Archbishop of
(Most Rev and Rt Hon David Michael Hope)
Type of Peerage . . . . Bishop
Entered Lords 1990
Born . . . . 14th April 1940 in Wakefield
Educated . . . . Queen Elizabeth Grammar School,
Wakefield
University of Nottingham
Linacre College, Oxford
Professional Career . . . . . 1965 - 67, 1968 -70 Assistant Curate,
St John's Tuebrook, Liverpool
1967 - 68 Priest in Charge, Church of
Resurrection, Bucharest
1970 - 74 Vicar, St Andrew's, Orford,
Warrington
1974 - 82 Principal, St Stephen's House,
Oxford
1982 - 85 Vicar, All Saints, Margaret Street,
London
1985 - 91 Bishop of Wakefield
1991 - 95 Bishop of London
1995 - Archbishop of York
Subject Interests . . . . Eastern Europe, Housing/Homelessness,
Employment/Unemployment
Recreational Interests . . . Walking, Music, Cinema, Photography
Correspondence Address . . Bishopthorpe Palace, Bishopthorne,
York, YO2 1QE
Tel: (01904) 707021 Fax: (01904) 709204
E-mail: office@bishopthorpe.u-net.com

York, Duke of (HRH Prince Andrew Albert Edward Christian)
Type of Peerage . . . . Hereditary (First Creation)
Political Allegiance . . . . . Cross Bench
Created 1986
Born . . . . 19th February 1960

Young, Baroness (Rt Hon Janet Mary Young)
Type of Peerage . . . . Life
Political Allegiance . . . . . Conservative
Created 1971
Born . . . . 23rd October 1926
Political Career . . . . 1972 - 73 Government Whip,
(Baroness in Waiting)
1973 - 74 Parliamentary Secretary,
Department of Environment
1979 - 81 Minister of State, Department of
Education and Science
1981 - 82 Chancellor of the Duchy of
Lancaster
1981 - 83 Leader of the House of Lords
(also Chancellor of Duchy of Lancaster
then Lord Privy Seal)
1983 - 87 Minister of State, Foreign and
Commonwealth Office

Young of Dartington, Baron (Michael Young)
Type of Peerage . . . . Life
Political Allegiance . . . . . Labour
Created 1978
Born . . . . 9th August 1915

Young of Graffham, Baron (Rt Hon David Ivor Young)
Type of Peerage . . . . Life
Political Allegiance . . . . . Conservative
Created 1984
Born . . . . 27th February 1932 in London
Educated . . . . Christ College, Finchley
University College London
Professional Career . . . . . 1955 - 95 Solicitor, Malcolm Slowe,
Piccadilly
1956 - 61 Executive Chairman,
The Great Universal Stores Ltd
1961 - 70 Chairman, Eldon Wall Ltd
1974 - 80 Chairman, Manufacturers Hanover
Property Services
1976 - 82 Chairman, Greenwood Homes
1982 - 84 Chairman, Manpower Services
Commission
1990 - 95 Chairman, Cable and Wireless plc
1996 - Chairman, Young Associates Ltd
Political Career . . . . 1979 - 82 Special Adviser, Department of
Trade and Industry (also Department of
Education 1981 - 82)
1984 - 85 Minister without Portfolio
1985 - 87 Secretary of State for Employment
1985 - 89 Secretary of State for Trade and
Industry
1989 - 90 Deputy Chairman, Conservative
Party
Subject Interests . . . . Telecommunications, Technology,
Interactive services
Recreational Interests . . . Music, Book collecting, Photography
Correspondence Address . . Young Associates Ltd, Harcourt House,
19 Cavendish Square, London, W1M 9AB
Tel: (0171) 447 8800 Fax: (0171) 447 8849
E-mail: young@youngassoc.com
Personal Staff . . . . Ms Andrea Poole *(PA)*
Tel: (0171) 447 8810

MEMBERS OF THE HOUSE OF LORDS

Young of Old Scone, Baroness (Barbara Scott Young)

Type of Peerage . . . . Life
Political Allegiance . . . . . Labour
Created 1997
Born . . . . 8th April 1948 in Perth, Scotland
Educated . . . . Perth Academy
Edinburgh University
Strathclyde University
Political Career . . . . 1971 - 90 Health Service Administrator
1985 - 90 District General Manager,
Parkside Health Authority
1991 - Chief Executive, Royal Society for
Protection of Birds
1998 - Chairman, English Nature
Subject Interests . . . . Environment, Conservation, Agriculture,
Health, Homelessness
Recreational Interests . . . Cinema, Gardening
Correspondence Address . . c/o RSPB, The Lodge,
Bedfordshire, SG19 2DL
Tel: (01767) 680551

Younger of Leckie, Rt Hon Viscount
(George Kenneth Hotson Younger KT, KCVO, TD)

Type of Peerage . . . . Hereditary
Political Allegiance . . . . . Conservative
Succeeded . . . . 1997 (Previously created life Peer as Baron
Younger of Prestwich 1992)
Born . . . . 22nd September 1931 in Stirling
Educated . . . . Winchester College
New College, Oxford
Professional Career . . . . . 1958 - 64 Director, George Younger and
Sons Ltd, Alloa
1964 - 70 Director, Charrington Vintners
1990 - Chairman, Siemens Plessey
Electronic Systems
1991 - Chairman, Royal Bank of Scotland
Group
Political Career . . . . 1964 - 92 MP (Conservative) for Ayr
1965 - 67 Opposition Whip
1970 - 74 Parliamentary Secretary
(Development), Scottish Office
1974 - 74 Ministry of State, Ministry of
Defence
1974 - 75 Chairman, Conservative
Party in Scotland
1979 - 86 Secretary of State for Scotland
1986 - 89 Secretary of State for Defence
1987 - 88 President, National Union of
Conservative and Unionist Associations
Subject Interests . . . . Defence, Scotland, Arts
Recreational Interests . . . Tennis, Golf, Sailing, Music
Correspondence Address . . Leckie, Garcunnock, Stirling, FK8 3BN
Tel: (01786) 860274 Fax: (01786) 860559

Z

Zetland, Marquess of (Lawrence Mark Dundas)

Type of Peerage . . . . Hereditary
Political Allegiance . . . . . Conservative
Succeeded 1989
Born . . . . 28th December 1937 in London
Subject Interests . . . . Horseracing, Leisure
Correspondence Address . . Aske, Richmond,
North Yorkshire, DL10 5HY
Tel: (01748) 823222 Fax: (01748) 823252

Zouche of Haryngworth, Baron (James Assheton Frankeland)

Type of Peerage . . . . Hereditary
Political Allegiance . . . . . Conservative
Succeeded 1965
Born . . . . 23rd February 1943

PEERS – LANGUAGES SPOKEN

Notes: (i) Peers were asked to supply details of languages spoken by them to such a level that they could be interviewed on the radio or television in that language.

(ii) This is not an exhaustive list.

(iii) The following abbreviations are used to denote the various titles of members of the House of Lords.

Bs ....Baroness	Bp.............................Bishop	C ....Countess
D..........................Duke	E ....Earl	L................................Baron/Lord
Ly ....Lady	M................................Marquess	V ....Viscount

Afrikaans
St John of Bletso, L

Dutch
Birmingham, Bp
St John of Bletso, L
Steyn, L
Taverne, L

French
Ackner, L
Alexander of Weedon, L
Armstrong of Ilminster, L
Astor of Hever, L
Baillieu, L
Baldwin of Bewdley, E
Bath, M
Beloff, L
Biddulph, L
Birkett, L
Brain, L
Bridport, V
Briggs, L
Brooke and Warwick, E
Butterfield, L
Cadman, L
Carlisle, E
Carnarvon, E
Carver, L
Castle of Blackburn, Bs
Chalker of Wallasey, Bs
Colgrain, L
Cox, Bs
David, Bs
De Ramsey, L
Derwent, L
Dormer, L
Dunleath, L
Dunrossil, V
Elles, Bs
Erroll, E
Ezra, L
Falkland, V
Faringdon, L
Feldman, L
Fortescue, E

Gainford, L
Garel-Jones, L
Gibson, L
Gillmore of Thamesfield, L
Gladwyn, L
Glasgow, E
Glentoran, L
Gorel, L
Gormanston, V
Grade, L
Grenfell, L
Haig, E
Halsbury, E
Hardinge pf Penshurst, L
Harewood, E
Harmsworth of Egham, L
Healey, L
Hereford, Bp
Hill-Norton, L
Hilton of Eggardon, Bs
Hood, V
Hooper, Bs
Hothfield, L
Howard of Penrith, L
Hunt, L
Hurd of Westwell, L
Inchape, E
Inglewood, L
Janner of Braunstone, L
Joicey, L
Kingsland, L
Lester of Herne Hill, L
Levene of Portsoken, L
Limerick, E
Linklater of Butterstone, Bs
McIntosh of Haringey, L
Mackenzie-Stuart, L
Malmesbury, E
Manton, L
Marchwood, V
Marlesford, L
Menuhin, L
Milne, L
Montague of Beaulieu, L
Moynihan, L
Naseby, L
Newall, L
Nicholson of Winterbourne, Bs

Norfolk, D
Normanby, M
Northbourne, L
Norwich, V
O'Hagan, L
O'Neill, L
Oranmore and Browne, L
Palmer, L
Perry of Southwark, Bs
Phillimore, L
Pitkeathley, Bs
Polwarth, L
Poole, L
Portland, E
Portman, V
Rawlings, Bs
Rea, L
Rees, L
Renfrew of Kaimsthorn, L
Renton, L
Renwick, L
Rogers of Riverside, L
Roll of Ipsden, L
Rowallan, L
St John of Bletso, L
Saltoun, L
Sanderson of Bowden, L
Sandwich, E
Sharples, Bs
Simon of Glaisdale, L
Simon of Highbury, L
Steel, L
Stockton, E
Strange, Bs
Strathclyde, L
Sudeley, L
Sutherland, C
Swaythling, L
Taylor of Warwick, L
Tennyson, L
Thomas of Walliswood, Bs
Thurlow, L
Thurso, V
Trumpington, Bs
Tweedsmuir, L
Wallace of Coslany, L
Weidenfeld, L
Weinstock, L

PEERS – LANGUAGES SPOKEN

Wellington, D
Wemyss and March, E
Westmorland, E
Whitty, L
Wilberforce, L
Williams of Crosby, L
Williams of Elvel, L
Wrottesley, L
York, Abp
Younger of Leckie, V

Estonian
Carlisle, E
German
Ackner, L
Baldwin of Bewdley, E
Birkett, L
Birmingham, Bp
Chalker of Wallasey, Bs
Dahrendorf, L
Feldman, L
Gainford, L
Gibson, L
Grade, L
Grenfell, L
Haig, E
Harewood, E
Healey, L
Hereford, Bp
Hunt, L
Inglewood, L
Joicey, L
Levene of Portsoken, L
Menuhin, L
Milne, L
Norfolk, D
Portland, E
Renfrew of Kaimsthorn, L
Renton, L
Roll of Ipsden, L
St John of Bletso, L
Sandwich, E
Simon of Glaisdale, L
Simon of Highbury, L
Taylor of Gryfe, L
Weidenfeld, L

Greek
Renfrew of Kaimsthorn, L

Gujarati
Dholakia, L

Hebrew
Jakobovits, L
Janner of Braunstone, L

Hindi
Bagri, L
Dholakia, L
Paul, L

Indonisian
Brooke and Warwick, E

Italian
Bridges, L
Bridport, V
Elles, Bs
Gainford, L
Gibson, L
Gormanston, V
Grenfell, L
Harewood, E
Healey, L
Howard of Penrith, L
Menuhin, L
Portman, V
Rawlings, Bs
Rees, L
Renton, L
Rogers of Riverside, L
Weidenfeld, L
Wemyss and March, E

Japanese
Trenchard, V

Malay
Gorrell, L

Mandarin
Wilson of Tillyorn, L

Norwegian
Elton, L
Robson of Kiddington, Bs

Portuguese
Joicey, L
Wrottesley, L

Romanian
York, Abp

Russian
Baillieu, L
Cox, Bs

Spanish
Derwent, L
Garel-Jones, L
Gorell, L
Hartsbury, E
Hardinge, L
Hill-Norton, L
Hooper, Bs
Janner of Braunstone, L
Joicey, L
Kingsland, L
Lindsay of Birker, L
Marlesford, L
Menuhin, L
Montgomery of Alamein, V
Rawlings, Bs
Rea, L
Southwell, Bp
Thomas of Walliswood, Bs
Warwick, E
Weidenfeld, L
Wellington, D
Westmorland, E
Wrottesley, L

Swahili
Alport, L
Steel, L

Swedish
Robson of Kiddington, Bs

Urdu
Abinger, L
Bagot, L
Weatherill, L

Welsh
Cledwyn of Penrhos, L
Thomas of Gresford, L
Williams of Mostyn, L

PUBLISHED BOOKS BY MEMBERS OF THE HOUSE OF LORDS

Notes: (i) The following abbreviations are used to denote the various titles of members of the House of Lords:

Abp ....*Archbishops*	*Bs* ....*Baroness*	*Bp* ....*Bishop*
C ....*Countess*	*D* ....*Duke*	*E* ....*Earl*
L ....*Baron/Lord*	*Ly* ....*Lady*	*M* ....*Marquess*
V ....*Viscount*		

(ii) Peers were asked to supply details of books written by them.

Author	Title of Publication	Date Published
Aberdare, L.	The Story of Tennis	1959
	The Willis Faber Book of Tennis and Rackets	
Aberdeen and Temair, M	A Slight Touch of Safari	1953
Acton, L	To Go Free: A Treasury of Iowa's Legal Heritage (Joint Author)	1995
Alexander of Weedon, L.	The Voice of the People: A Constitution for Tomorrow	1997
Alport, L	Kingdoms in Partnership	1937
	Hope in Africa	1952
	The Sudden Assignment	1965
Alton of Liverpool, L	What Kind of Country?	1987
	Whose Choice Anyway?	1988
	Faith in Britain	1991
	Signs of Contradiction	1996
	Life After Death	1997
	The Virtuous Citizen	1998
Anglesey, M.	The Capel Letters 1814–1817	1955
	One-Leg: the Life and Letters of 1st Marquess of Anglesey	1961
	Sergeant Pearman's Memoirs	1968
	"Little Hodge"	1971
	A History of the British Cavalry 1816–1919 (8 vols)	1973-97
Annan, L.	Leslie Stephen	1952 (2nd edn 1984)
	The Intellectual Aristocrat in Studies in Social History (ed JH Plumb)	1956
	Roxburgh of Stowe	1966
	Our Age	1990
	Changing Enemies	1995
Archer of Sandwell, L	The Queen's Courts	1957
	Social Welfare and the Citizen	1957
	Communism and the Law	1960
	Freedom at Stake	1961
	Purpose in Socialism (Joint Author)	
Archer of Weston-Super-Mare, L	Not a Penny More, Not a Penny Less	1975
	Shall We Tell the President	1977
	Kane and Abel	1979
	A Quiver Full of Arrows	1980
	The Prodigal Daughter	1982
	Honour Among Thieves	1983
	First Among Equals	1984
	As the Crow Flies	1991
	Twelve Red Herrings	1994
	The Proprietors	1996
	The Fourth Estate	1996
	The Eleventh Commandment	1998

PUBLISHED BOOKS BY MEMBERS OF THE HOUSE OF LORDS

Author	Title of Publication	Date Published
Ashley of Stoke, L	Journey into Silence	1972
	Acts of Defiance	1993
Bagot, L	Skis in India	1942
Baker of Dorking, L	London Lines	
	I Have No Gun But I Can Spit	
	The Faber Book of English History in Verse	
	Unauthorised Versions: Poems and their Parodies	
	The Faber Book of Conservatism	
	The Turbulent Years	
	The Prime Ministers: An Irreverent Political History in Cartoons	
	Kings and Queens: An Irreverent Cartoon History of British Monarchy	1996
	The Faber Book of War Poetry	1996
Balfour of Inchrye, L	Famous Diamonds	1987 (3rd edn 1997)
Barnett, L	Inside the Treasury	1982
Bath, M	The Carrycot	1972
	Lord Weymouth's Murals	1974
	The King is Dead	1976
	Pillars of the Establishment	1980
Beaumont of Whitley, L	Modern Religious Verse	1965
	The Liberal Cookbook	1972
	New Christian Reader	1974
	The Selective Ego: The Diaries of James Agate	1976
	Where Shall I Place My Cross	1984
	The End of the Yellowbrick Road	1997
Beloff, L	The Federalist	1948 (2nd edn 1987)
	Mankind and his Story	1948
	The Debate on the American Revolution	1949 (2nd edn 1989)
	On the Track of Tyranny	1959
	Imperial Sunset	1969 (2nd edn 1988)
	The Intellectual in Politics	1970
	The Government of the United Kingdom	1980 (2nd edn 1985)
	War and Welfare 1914–1945	1984
	An Historian in the 20th Century	1992
	Britain and European Union	1996
Biffin, L	Inside the House of Commons	1989
Birmingham, Bp	The Phenomenon of Christian Belief	1970
	Documents in Early Christian Thought	1975
	Their Lord and Ours	1982
	The Church and the State	1984
	Dropping the Bomb	1985
	Reconciling Memories	1988
	Communion and Episcopacy	1988
	Liturgy for a New Century	1991

PUBLISHED BOOKS BY MEMBERS OF THE HOUSE OF LORDS

Author	Title of Publication	Date Published
Blackstone, Bs.	Students in Conflict, LSE in 1967	1970
	A Fair State: The Provision of Pre-School Education	1971
	The Academic Labour Market: Economic and Social Aspects of a Profession	1974
	Educational Policy and Educational Inequality	1982
	Disadvantage and Education	1982
	Testing Children: Standardised Testing in Local Education	1983
	Authorities and Schools Response to Adversity	1983
	Inside the Think Tank: Advising the Cabinet 1971–83	1988
Blake, L	The Private Papers of Douglas Haig	1952
	The Unknown Prime Minister	1955
	Disraeli	1966
	The Office of Prime Minister	1975
	The Conservative Opportunity	1976
	A History of Rhodesia	1977
	Disraeli's Grand Tour	1982
	The Decline of Power 1915–64	1985
	Churchill (Ed with Roger Jonis)	1993
	A Conservative Party from Peel to Major	1997
Blaker, L	Coping with the Soviet Union	1978
	Small is Dangerous: Micro States in a Macro World	1984
Blease, L	Trade Unions in Ireland	1983
Borrie, L	The Consumer, Society and the Law (Joint Author)	1981 (4th edn)
	The Development of Consumer Law and Policy	1984
	Commercial Law	1986 (6th edn)
	The Law of Contempt (Joint Author)	1996 (3rd edn)
Boyd-Carpenter, L	Way of Life	1987
Briggs, L	Victorian People	1954
	History of Broadcasting in the UK (5 Vols)	1961-94 (new edn 1995)
	Victorian Cities	1963
	Victorian Things	1988
	A Social History of England	1994
Butterfield, L	On Burns	1953
	Tolbutamide after 10 Years	1967
	Priorities in Medicine	1968
	International Directory of Medicine and Biology	1986
Callaghan of Cardiff, L	A House Divided: The Dilemma of Northern Ireland	1973
	Time and Chance	1987
Campbell of Alloway, L	Restrictive Trade Practices and Monopolies	1956 (supplement 1973)
	Common Market Law (3 Vols)	1964 (supplement 1975)
	Restrictive Trading Agreements in the Common Market	1964 (supplement 1965)
	Industrial Relations Act 1971	1971
	Trade Unions and the Individual	1980
	EC Competition Law	1980
Campbell of Croy, L	Disablement, Prospects and Problems in the United Kingdom	1981

PUBLISHED BOOKS BY MEMBERS OF THE HOUSE OF LORDS

Author	Title of Publication	Date Published
Canterbury, Abp	I Believe in Man	1975
	God Incarnate	1976
	The Great Acquittal (Joint Author)	1980
	The Church in the Market Place	1984
	The Meeting of the Waters	1985
	The Gate of Glory	1986
	The Message of the Bible	1986
	The Great God Robbery	1989
	I Believe	1991
	Sharing a Vision	1993
	Spiritual Journey	1994
	My Journey, Your Journey (With Others)	1996
Carr of Hadley, L	One Nation	1951
	Change is Our Ally	1953
	A Responsible Society	1959
Carrington, L	Reflect on Things Past	1988
Carver, L	Second to None	1954
	El Alamein	1962
	Tobruk	1964
	The War Lords	1976
	Harding of Petherton	1978
	The Apostles of Mobility	1979
	War Since 1945	1980
	A Policy for Peace	1982
	The Seven Ages of the British Army	1984
	Dilemmas of the Desert War	1986
	Twentieth Century Warriors	1987
	The British Army in the Twentieth Century	1988
	Out of Step: Memoirs	1989
	Tightrope Walking: British Defence Policy Since 1945	1992
Castle of Blackburn, Bs	Castle Diaries 74–76	1980
	Castle Diaries 64–74	1984
	Sylvia and Christabel Pankhurst	1987
	The Castle Diaries 64–76	1987
	Fighting all the Way	1993
Chalfont, L	Montgomery of Alamein	1976
	Waterloo, A Battle of Three Armies	1979
	Star Wars, Suicide or Survival	1985
	Defence of the Realm	1987
	By God's Will	1989
Chalker of Wallasey, Bs	We're Richer Than We Think	1979
	Africa: Turning the Tide	1989
Chapple, L	Sparks Fly	1984
Chelmsford, V	L is for Linnet	1992
Cledwyn of Penrhos, L	Conditions: A Island of St Helena	1998
Clyde, L	Armour on Valuation (Joint Editor)	1961-85

PUBLISHED BOOKS BY MEMBERS OF THE HOUSE OF LORDS

Author	Title of Publication	Date Published
Cocks of Hartcliffe, L.	Labour and the Benn Factor	1989
Coggan, L	Paul: Portrait of a Revolutionary	1984
	The Sacrament of the Word	1987
	Cuthbert Bardsley	1989
	The Voice from the Cross	1993
	The Servant-Son	1995
Cooke of Thordon, L	Portrait of a Professional	1969
	The Laws of New Zealand	1995
Cox, Bs	A Sociology of Medical Practice (Joint Editor)	1975
	The Right to Learn	1982
	Sociology: A Guide for Nurses, Midwives and Health Visitors	1983
	Trajectories of Despair: Misdiagnosis and Maltreatment of Soviet Orphans	1991
	Ethnic Cleansing in Progress: War in Nagorno Karabakh (Co Author)	1993
	Made to Care: The Case for Residential and Village Communities for People with a Mental Handicap (with M Pearson)	1995
Cranbrook, E	A Tropical Rainforest	1994
Crathorne, L	Edouard Vuillard	1967
	Tennant's Stalk (Co Author)	1973
	A Present from Crathorne (Co Author)	1989
	Cliveden: The Place and the People	1995
Crickhowell, L	Opera House Lottery	1997
Cromartie, E	Rock and Hill Climbs in Skye	1978
	Selected Rock and Hill Climbs in Skye	1997
Cudlipp, L	Publish and be Damned	1955
	At Your Peril	1962
	Walking on the Water	1976
	The Prerogative of the Harlot	1980
Cumberlege, Bs	Neighbourhood Nursing – A Focus for Care	1986
	Changing Childbirth	1993
Cunliffe, L	Office Buildings (Co Author)	1962
	Tomorrow's Office (Co Author)	1996
Dacre of Glanton, L	Archbishop Laud	1940
	The Last Days of Hitler	1947
	Religion, the Reformation and Social Change	1967
	The Philby Affair	1968
	Princes and Artists	1976
	Hermit of Peking	1976
	Renaissance Essays	1985
	Catholics, Anglicans and Puritans	1987
	From Counter-Reformation to Glorious Revolution	1992

PUBLISHED BOOKS BY MEMBERS OF THE HOUSE OF LORDS

Author	Title of Publication	Date Published
Dahrendorf, L	Marx in Perspective	1953
	Class and Class Conflict	1959
	Society and Democracy in Germany	1966
	Essays in the Theory of Society	1968
	The New Library	1975
	The Modern Social Conflict	1988
	Reflections on the Revolution in Europe	1990
	LSE: A History of the London School of Economics 1895–1995	1995
	After 1989. Morals, Revolution and Civil Society	1997
Denham, L	The Man Who Lost His Shadow	1979
	Two Thyrdes	1983
	Fox Hunt	1988
Denning, L	Freedom Under the Law	1949
	The Changing Law	1953
	The Road to Justice	1955
	The Discipline of Law	1979
	The Due Process of Law	1979
	The Family Story	1981
	What Next in the Law	1982
	The Closing Chapter	1983
	Landmarks in the Law	1984
	Leaves From My Library	1986
Deramore, L	Winged Promises	1996
	Still Waters	1996
Donoughue, L	British Politics and American Revolution	1963
	The People into Politics (Joint Author)	1966
	Herbert Morrison (Co Author)	1973
	Prime Minister	1987
Drogheda, E	The Dream Come True: Great Houses of Los Angeles	1980
	Royal Gardens	1982
	Stately Homes of Britain	1982
	Washington, Houses of the Capital	1982
	The English Room	1984
	The Englishwoman's House	1984
	The Englishman's Room	1986
	The Gardens of Queen Elizabeth, the Queen Mother	1988
Dubbs of Battersea, L	Lobbying: An Insiders Guide to the Parliamentary Process	1989
Dunn, Bs	In the Kingdom of the Blind	1983
Durham, Bp	God's Front Line	1978
	Parish Evangelism	1980
Eames, L	Quiet Revolution: Irish Disestablishment	1970
	Through Suffering	1973
	Through Lent	1984
	Chains to be Broken	1992

PUBLISHED BOOKS BY MEMBERS OF THE HOUSE OF LORDS

Author	Title of Publication	Date Published
Eatwell, L	An Introduction to Modern Economics (Joint Author)	1973
	Whatever Happened to Britain	1982
	Keynes' Economics and the Theory of Value and Distribution (Co Edited)	1983
	The New Palgrave: A Dictionary of Economics (Co Edited)	1987
	The World of Economics (Co Edited)	1991
	The New Palgrave Dictionary of Money and Finance (Co Edited)	1992
	Transformation and Integration: Shaping the Future of Central and Eastern Europe (Co Author)	1995
	Global Unemployment: Loss of Jobs in the 90s (Edited)	1996
	Not "Just Another Accession": The Political Economy of EU Enlargement to the East (Co Author)	1997
Eccles, V	By Safe Hand: Letters of Sybil and David Eccles	1939
	Half-Way to Faith	1966
	Life and Politics: A Moral Diagnosis	1967
	On Collecting	1968
Elles, Bs	Human Rights of Aliens	1980
	Rights of Non Citizens (UN Special Report)	1984
	Legal Aspects of Maestricht	1995
	European Union and World Trade Law	1996
Exeter, M	Rising Tide of Change	1986
	Living at the Heart of Creation	1990
Ezra, L	Coal and Energy	1978
	The Energy Debate	1983
Feldman, L	Constituency Campaigning	1977
	Some Thoughts on Job Creation	1984
Feversham, L	A Wolf in Tooth	1967
	Great Yachts	1970
Flowers, L	Properties of Matter	1970
	An Introduction to Numerical Methods in C++	1995
Forte, L	Forte	1986
Freeman, L	Professional Practices	1968
	Fair Deal for Water	1985
	NHS, Reforms	1990
	Democracy in the Digital Age	1997
Gainford, L	Calvary and St Benedict	1985
Gifford, L	Where's the Justice?	1985
	Broadwater Farm Inquiry	1986
	Liverpool 8 Inquiry	1989
Gillmour of Thamesfield, L	A Way from Exile	1967

PUBLISHED BOOKS BY MEMBERS OF THE HOUSE OF LORDS

Author	Title of Publication	Date Published
Gilmour of Craigmillar, L.	The Body Politic	1969
	Inside Right: A Study of Conservatism	1977
	Britain Can Work	1983
	Riots, Risings and Revolution	1992
	Dancing with Dogma	1992
Gladwyn, L	Thames Valley Heritage Walk	1983
	Guide to South Downs Way	1984
	Walkers	1986
	Guide to Thames Path	1988
	Anthology of East Anglia	1993
	Guide to Colleges of Oxford	1992
	Suffolk	1995
	Diaries of Cynthia Gladwyn	1996
Glenamara, L	Education in a Changing World	1971
	Birth to Five	1974
	I Knew My Place	1983
	Whip to Wilson	1989
Goff of Chieveley, L	Law of Restitution (Co Author)	1966
Goodhart, L	Specific Performance	1996
Gould of Potternewton, Bs	Women and Health	1979
Gowrie, E	A Postcard from Don Giovanni	1972
	The Genius of British Painting	1975
	The Conservative Opportunity	1976
	Derek Hill: An Appreciation	1987
Grade, L	Still Dancing	1987
Greenhill, L	More by Accident	1992
Greenway, L	Soviet Merchant Ships	1976
	Comecon Merchant Ships	1978
	A Century of Cross-Channel Passenger Ferries	1980
	A Century of North Sea Passenger Steamers	1986
Grenfell, L	Margot	1984
Griffiths of Fforestfach, L	The Creation of Wealth	1984
	Monetarism in the United Kingdom	1984
	Morality and the Market Place	1989
Habgood, L	Religion and Science	1964
	A Working Faith	1980
	Church and Nation in a Secular Age	1983
	Confessions of a Conservative Liberal	1988
	Making Sense	1993
	Faith and Uncertainty	1997
Haddington, E	Glenkiln	1993

PUBLISHED BOOKS BY MEMBERS OF THE HOUSE OF LORDS

Author	Title of Publication	Date Published
Hailsham of Saint Marylebone, L	The Law of Arbitration	1935
	One Year's Work	1944
	The Law and Employers' Liability	1944
	The Times We Live In	1944
	Making Peace	1944
	The Left was Never Right	1945
	The Purpose of Parliament	1946
	Case for Conservatism	1947
	The Law of Monopolies, Restrictive Practices and Resale Price Maintenance	1956
	The Conservative Case	1959
	Interdependence	1961
	Science and Politics	1963
	The Devil's Own Song	1968
	The Door Wherein I Went	1975
	Elective Directorship	1976
	The Dilemma of Democracy	1978
	A Sparrow's Flight	1990
	On the Constitution	1992
	Values: Collapse and Cure	1994
Hamilton and Brandon, D	Maria 'R'	1991
Hampden, V	Henry and Eliza	1982
	A Glimpse of Glynde	1997
Hardy of Wath, L	A Lifetime of Badgers	1975
Harewood, E	Kobbé's Complete Opera Book	1953 (4th edn 1997)
	The Tongs and the Bones	1981
	Kobbés Illustrated Opera Book	1989
Healey, L	Healey's Eye	1980
	The Time of My Life	1989
	My Secret Planet	1992
	Denis Healey's Yorkshire Dales	1995
Hemingford, L	Jews and Arabs in Conflict	1969
	Press Freedom: The Lifeblood of Democracy (Editor)	1975
	Press Freedom in Britain (Co Author)	1991
Hereford, Bp	The Church and Social Order	1968
Hill-Norton, L	No Soft Options	1978
	Sea Power	1981
Hilton of Eggardon, Bs	The Gentle Arm of the Law	1968
	Individual Development and Social Experience	1975

PUBLISHED BOOKS BY MEMBERS OF THE HOUSE OF LORDS

Author	Title of Publication	Date Published
Holme of Cheltenham, L	Partners in one Nation	1982
	The People's Kingdom	1986
	1688–1988: Time for a New Constitution	1988
Howe of Aberavon, L	Conflict of Loyalty	1994
Howell, L	Soccer Referee	1969
	Made in Birmingham	1990
Howell of Guildford, L	Freedom and Capita	1980
	Blind Victory	1986
Howie of Troon, L	Trade Unions and the Professional Engineer	1977
	Trade Unions in Construction	1981
	Thames Tunnel to Channel Tunnel	1987
Hunt, L	The Ascent of Everest	1953
	The Red Snows	1959
	Life is Meeting	1978
Hurd of Westwell, L	Truth Game	1962
	The Arrow War	1967
	Send Him Victorious (Co Author)	1968
	The Smile on the Face of the Tiger (Co Author)	1969
	Scotch on the Rocks (Co Author)	1971
	Vote to Kill	1975
	An End of Promises	1979
	War Without Frontiers (Co Author)	1982
	Palace of Enchantments (Co Author)	1985
	The Search for Peace	1997
Ironside, L	High Road to Command	1973
Jakobovits, L	Jewish Medical Ethics	1959 (4th edn 1975)
	Journal of a Rabbi	1966
	Zionism in My Life	1984
	Authorised Daily Prayer-Book	1990
	Dear Chief Rabbi	1995
James of Holland Park, Bs	Cover her Face	1962
	A Mind to Murder	1963
	Unnatural Causes	1967
	Shroud for a Nightingale	1971
	The Maul and the Pear Tree	1971
	An Unsuitable Job for a Woman	1972
	The Black Tower	1975
	Death of an Expert Witness	1977
	Innocent Blood	1980
	The Skull Beneath the Skin	1982
	A Taste for Death	1986
	Devices and Desires	1989
	The Children of Men	1992
	Original Sin	1994
	A Certain Justice	1997
Jay of Paddington, Bs	Battered	1986
	How Rich Can We Get	1995

PUBLISHED BOOKS BY MEMBERS OF THE HOUSE OF LORDS

Author	Title of Publication	Date Published
Jenkins of Hillhead, L	Purpose and Policy	1947
	Mr Attlee: An Interim Biography	1948
	New Fabian Essays	1952
	Pursuit of Progress	1953
	Mr Balfour's Poodle	1954
	Sir Charles Dilke: A Victorian Tragedy	1958
	The Labour Case	1959
	Asquith	1964
	Hugh Gaitskell: a Memoir	1964
	Essays and Speeches	1967
	Afternoon on the Potomac?	1972
	What Matters Now	1972
	Nine Men of Power	1975
	European Diary	1977
	Partnership of Principle	1985
	Truman	1986
	Baldwin	1987
	Gallery of Twentieth Century Portraits	1988
	A Life at the Centre	1991
	Portraits and Miniatures	1993
	Gladstone	1995
Jenkins of Putney, L	The Culture Gap	1979
	Rank and File	1980
Kennet, L	The Italian Left	1949
	The Deadweight	1951
	Now or Never	1953
	Old London Churches	1956
	The Montesi Scandal	1957
	Still Alive Tomorrow	1958
	Strategy for Survival	1959
	The Profumo Affair	1963
	Eros Denied	1965
	Thirty-Four Articles	1965
	Existing Mechanisms of Arms Control	1965
	Preservation	1972
	The Futures of Europe	1976
	The Rebirth of Britain	1982
	London's Churches	1986
	Northern Lazio	1990
	Parliaments and Screening	1995
Keyes, L	Outrageous Fortune: The Tragedy of Leopold III of the Belgians	1984
	Un Règne Brisé	1985
	Echec au Roi	1986
	Een Beproeft Koning	1986
	Complot Tegende Koning	1987

PUBLISHED BOOKS BY MEMBERS OF THE HOUSE OF LORDS

Author	Title of Publication	Date Published
Kilbracken, L	Even for an Hour	1940
	Tell Me the Next One	1950
	The Master Forger	1951
	Letters from Early New Zealand	1951
	A Peer Behind the Curtain	1959
	Shamrocks and Unicorns	1962
	Van Meegeren	1967
	Bring Back My Stringbag	1979
	The Easy Way to Bird Recognition	1982
	The Easy Way to Tree Recognition	1983
	The Easy Way to Wild Flower Recognition	1984
Kingsland, L	Market Socialism in Yugoslavia	1985
	Vols 8, 51 and 52 (Contribution) Halsbury's Laws of England (4th Edition)	1986
Lauderdale, E	European Dateline	1945
	Task for Giants	1957
Lawson of Blaby, L	The Power Game	1976
	The View from No 11: Memoirs from a Tory Radical	1992
Lester of Herne Hill, L	Justice in the American South	1964
	Shawcross and Beaumont on Air Law	1964 (3rd edn)
	Race and Law	1972
	Constitutional Law and Human Rights	1996
Lichfield, Bp	The People of God	1984
Lofthouse, L	A Very Miner MP	1986
Longford, E	Born to Believe	1953
	Causes of Crime	1958
	The Idea of Punishment	1961
	Five Lives	1964
	Humility	1969
	Eamon de Valera	1970
	The Grain of Wheat	1974
	Abraham Lincoln	1974
	Jesus Christ	1974
	Kennedy	1976
	St Francis of Assisi	1978
	Nixon	1980
	Ulster	1981
	Pope John Paul II	1982
	Diary of a Year	1982
	Eleven at No. 10	1984
	One Man's Faith	1984
	The Search for Peace	1985
	The Bishops	1986
	Saints	1987
	A History of the House of Lords	1989
	Suffering and Hope	1990
	Punishment and the Punished	1991
	Prisoner or Patient	1992
	Young Offenders	1993
	Avowed Intent	1995
	Epilogue	1996
Lytton, E	The Party Wall Act Explained (With Others)	1996

PUBLISHED BOOKS BY MEMBERS OF THE HOUSE OF LORDS

Author	Title of Publication	Date Published
McAlpine of West Green, L	The Servant	1992
	Journal of a Collector	1994
	Letter to a Young Politician	1995
	Once a Jollybagman	1996
	The New Machlavelli	1997
McCarthy, L	The Closed Shop British Industry	1964
	Shop Stewards in British Industry	1966
	Management by Agreement	1973
	Change in Trade Unions	1981
	Strikes in Post War Britain	1983
	Trade Unions	1985
	Employment Relations Audits	1990
	Legal Intervention in Industrial Relations	1992
	New Labour at Work	1997
McCluskey, L	Law, Justice and Democracy	1987
	Criminal Appeals	1992
McColl of Dulwich, L	Intestinal Absorption in Man	1976
	Talking to Patients	1982
	NHS Data Book	1986
McFarlane of Llandaff, Bs	The Proper Study of the Nurse	1970
McIntosh of Haringey, L	Industry and Employment in the Inner City	1979
	Employment Policy in UK and US	1980
	Women and Work	1981
Mackay of Clashfern, L	Armour on Valuation for Rating	1960
Mackenzie-Stuart, L	European Communities and the Rule of Law	1977
	A French King at Holyrood	1995
Marks of Broughton, L	The Prince of the Golden Apple	1975
Masham of Ilton, Bs	The World Walks By	1986
Melchett, L	The Countryside We Want	1987
Menuhin, L	Unfinished Journey	1977
	Life Class	1986
	The Music of Man	1980
	The Violin	1996
Merlyn-Rees, L	Public Sector in the Mixed Economy	1982
	Northern Ireland: A Personal Perspective	1986
Miller of Hendon, Bs	Lets Make Up	1975

PUBLISHED BOOKS BY MEMBERS OF THE HOUSE OF LORDS

Author	Title of Publication	Date Published
Montagu of Beaulieu, L	The Motoring Montagus	1959
	Lost Causes of Motoring	1960
	Jaguar: A Biography	1961
	The Gordon Bennett Races	1963
	Rolls of Rolls-Royce	1966
	The Gilt and the Gingerbread	1967
	Lost Causes of Motoring: Europe (2 Vols)	1969-71
	More Equal than Others	1970
	History of the Steam	1971
	The Horseless Carriage	1975
	Royalty on the Road	1976
	Behind the Wheel	1977
	Early Days on the Road	1980
	Home James	1982
	The British Motorist	1987
	English Heritage	1987
	The Daimler Century	1995
Montgomery of Alamein, V	The Lonely Leader (Co Author)	1994
Moran, L	CB: A Life of Sir Henry Campbell-Bannerman	1973
	Fairfax	1985
Morris of Castle Morris, L	John Cleveland: A Bibliography of his Poems	1967
	The Poems of John Cleveland	1967
	New Mermaid Critical Commentaries I–III	1969
	Mary Quant's London	1973
	Ritual Murder	1980
	Harri Webb	1993
Naseby, L	Helping the Exporter	1967
	Marketing Below the Line	1970
	The Disaster of Direct Labour	1978
Nicholson of Winterbourne, Bs	Why Does the West Forget	1993
	Secret Society Inside and Outside the Conservative Party	1996
Normanby, M	Careful with the Sharks	1985
	Among thin Ghosts	1989

PUBLISHED BOOKS BY MEMBERS OF THE HOUSE OF LORDS

Author	Title of Publication	Date Published
Norwich, V	Mount Athos	1966
	The Normans in the South	1967
	Sahara	1968
	The Kingdom in the Sun	1970
	Great Architecture of the World	1975
	A History of Venice Vol 1 (2 vols)	1977-81
	Britain's Heritage	1982
	The Italian World	1983
	The Architecture of South England	1985
	Fifty Years of Glyndebourne	1985
	A Taste for Travel	1985
	Byzantium, the Early Centuries	1988
	Venice, a Traveller's Companion	1990
	The Oxford Illustrate Encyclopedia of the Arts	1990
	Byzantium: the Apogee	1991
	Byzantium: Decline and Fall	1995
Oram, L	Changes in China	1987
Orr-Ewing, L	Lords and Commons Cricket 1850–1988	1989
Owen, L	The Politics of Defence	1972
	In Sickness and in Health: The Politics of Medicine	1976
	Human Rights	1978
	Face the Future	1981
	A Future that Will Work	1984
	A United Kingdom	1986
	Our NHS	1988
	Time to Declare	1991
	Seven Ages Poetry Anthology	1992
	Balkan Odyssey	1995
Oxford, Bp.	Prayers of Hope	1975
	Turning to Prayer	1978
	Prayers of Grief and Glory	1979
	Being a Christian	1981
	Should Christians Support Guerillas	1982
	The Authority of Divine Love	1983
	Praying Round the Clock	1983
	Prayer and the Pursuit of Happiness	1985
	Morning has Broken	1985
	Christianity and War in a Nuclear Age	1986
	C S Lewis: the Man and his God	1987
	Christ is Risen	1988
	Is There a Gospel for the Rich?	1992
	Art and the Beauty of God	1993
	The Real God	1994
	Questioning Belief	1995
Paul, L	Indira Gandhi	1984
Perry of Walton, L	Open University	1976
	Introduction to Distance Education	1987
Peyton of Yeovil, L	Without Benefit of Laundry	1997

PUBLISHED BOOKS BY MEMBERS OF THE HOUSE OF LORDS

Author	Title of Publication	Date Published
Pitkeathley, Bs	It My Duty Isn't it?	1989
	Only Child	1994
	Age Gap Relationships	1996
Plant of Highfield, L	Community and Ideology	1974
	Political Philosophy and Social Welfare	1981
	Hegel	1983
	Philosophy, Politics and Citizenship	1984
	Conservative Capitalism in Britain and the List	1990
	Modern Political Thought	1992
Plowden, L	An Industrialist in the Treasury: The Post War Years	1989
Plummer of St Marylebone, L	Time for Change in Great London	1966
	Report to London	1970
	Planning and Participation	1973
Poltimore, L	Popular 19th Century Painting	1986
Poole, L	European Money Puzzle (Co Author)	1972
Porter of Luddenham, L	Chemistry for the Modern World	1962
	Chemistry in Microtime	1996
Prentice, L	Right Turn	1978
Prior, L	The Right Approach to the Economy	1977
	A Balance of Power	1986
Prys-Davies, L	A Central Welsh Council	1963
	Y Ffermwr a'r Gyfraith	1967
	Llafur Blynyddoedd	1991
Pym, L	The Politics of Consent	1984
	Sentimental Journey	1998
Quinton, L	The Nature of Things	1973
	The Politics of Imperfection	1976
	Francis Bacon	1980
	Thoughts and Thinkers	1982
Quirk, L	Comprehensive Grammar of the English Language	1985
	Student's Grammar of the English Language	1990
	English in Use	1993
	Grammatical and Lexical Variance	1995
Ravensdale, L	Impossible Object	1968
	Hopeful Monsters	1990
	Efforts at Truth	1994
	Children of Darkness and Light	1996

PUBLISHED BOOKS BY MEMBERS OF THE HOUSE OF LORDS

Author	Title of Publication	Date Published
Rawlinson of Ewell, L	A Price Too High	1989
	The Jesuit Factor	1990
	The Columbia Syndicate	1991
	Hatred and Contempt	1992
	His Brother's Keeper	1993
	Indictment for Murder	1994
Rea, L	Learning Teaching	1980
Rees-Mogg, L	The Reigning Error: the Crisis of Word Inflation	1974
	An Humbler Heaven	1977
	How to Buy Rare Books	1985
	Picnics on Vesuvius: Steps Towards the Millennium (Co Author)	1992
	Blood in the Streets	1988
	The Great Reckoning	1991
Renfrew of Kaimsthorn, L	The Emergence of Civilisation: The Cyclades and the Aegean in the 3rd Millennium BC	1972
	Before Civilisation: Prehistoric Europe	1973
	Archaeology and Language	1987
	The Cycladic Spirit	1992
Richard, L	Europe or the Open Sea	1971
	We, the British	1983
Richardson, L	The Practice of Medicine	1960 (2nd edn)
	Connective Tissue Disorders	1963
	Anticoagulant Prophylaxis and Treatment	1965
	British Encyclopedia of Medicinal Practice	1969
Riverdale, L	Squeeze the Trigger Gently	1991
	A Life, A Sail, A Changing Sea	1995
Rix, L	My Farce from my Elbow	1974
	Farce about Face	1989
	Tour de Farce	1992
	Life in the Farce Lane	1995
	Gullible's Travails	1996
Rodger of Earlsferry, L	Owners and Neighbours in Roman Law	1972
	The Law of Scotland	1995 (10th edn)
Rodgers of Quarry Bank, L	Hugh Gaitskell 1906–63	1964
	The People into Parliament	1966
	The Politics of Change	1982
	Government and Industry	1986
Rogers of Riverside, L	Cities for a Small Planet	

PUBLISHED BOOKS BY MEMBERS OF THE HOUSE OF LORDS

Author	Title of Publication	Date Published
Roll of Ipsden, L	An Early Experiment in Industrial Organisation	1930
	Spotlight on Germany	1933
	About Money	1934
	Elements of Economic Theory	1935
	Organised Labour	1938
	The British Commonwealth at War	1943
	A History of Economic Thought	1954
	The Combined Food Board	1957
	The World After Keynes	1968
	The Uses and Abuses of Economics	1978
	The Mixed Economy	1982
	Crowded Hours	1985
	Where Die We Go Wrong	1995
Runcie, L	Cathedral and City: St Albans Ancient and Modern	1978
	Season of the Spirit	1983
	Windows on to God	1983
	One Light for One World	1988
	Authority in Crisis? An Anglican Response	1988
	The Unity We Seek	1989
Runciman of Doxford, V	Plato's Later Epistemology	1962
	Social Science and Political Theory	1963
	Relative Deprivation and Social Justice	1966
	A Critique of Max Weber's Philosophy of Social Science	1972
	A Treatise on Social Theory (3 Vols)	1983-97
	Confessions of a Reluctant Therapist	1989
	The Social Animal	1998
Russell, E	The Causes of the English Civil War	1990
	The Fall of the British Monarchies 1637–1642	1991
	Academic Freedom	1993
Sainsbury of Turville, L	Government and Industry – A New Partnership	1981
	Wealth Creation and Jobs	1987
St John of Fawsley, L	Obscenity and the Law	1956
	Walter Bagehot	1959
Saint Levan, L	Illustrated History of St Michael's Mount	1979
Saltoun of Abernethy, Ly	Lady Saltoun's Favourite Fish Dishes	1981
	Lady Saltoun's Favourite Puddings	1994
	Clan Fraser	1997
Sandwich, E	Book of the World	1971
	Prospects for Africa's Children	1990
	Children at Crisis Point	1992
	Namaste India	1995
Selkirk of Douglas, L	Motive for a Mission	1971
	Roof of the World	1983
	The Truth About Rudolf Hess	

PUBLISHED BOOKS BY MEMBERS OF THE HOUSE OF LORDS

Author	Title of Publication	Date Published
Shawcross, L	Life Sentence	1995
Sheppard of Didgemere, L	Your Business Matters	1958
	Maximum Leadership	1995
Simon of Glaisdale, L	Change is Our Ally	1954
	Rule of Law	1955
	The Church and the Law of Nullity of Marriage	1955
Skidelsky, L	Politicians and the Slump	1967
	English Progressive Schools	1969
	Oswald Mosley	1975
	J M Keynes 1883–1920 (Vol 1)	1983
	J M Keynes 1920–1937 (Vol 2)	1992
	The World After Communism	1995
Smith of Clifton, L	Town Councillors (Co Author)	1966
	Anti-Politics	1971
	Direct Action and Democratic Politics (Co Editor)	1971
	The Politics of the Corporate Economy	1979
	The Fixers (Co Author)	1997
Snowdon, E	London	1958
	Malta	1958
	Private View	1965
	Assignments	1972
	A View of Venice	1972
	The Sack of Bath	1972
	Inchcape Review	1977
	Pride of the Shires	1979
	Personal View	1979
	Tasmanian Essay	1981
	Sittings	1983
	Israel: A First View	1986
	My Wales	1986
	Skills 1983–87	1987
	Public Appearances 1987–91	1991
	Wild Fruit	1997
	Snowden on State	1996
	Wild Flowers	1998
Soper, L	All His Grace	1957
	Advocacy of the Gospel	1961
	Tower Hill 12:30	1963
	A Flame with Faith	1963
	Christian Politics	1977
	Calling for Action	1984

PUBLISHED BOOKS BY MEMBERS OF THE HOUSE OF LORDS

Author	Title of Publication	Date Published
Soulsby of Swaffham Prior, L	Clinical Veterinary Parasitology	1965
	Helminths, Arthropods and Protozoa of Domestic Animals	1982
	Parasite Immunity	1987
	Zoonoses	1998
Spens, L	The QE II Waterloo 'Castle' High Values 1955–67	1990
Steel, L	No Entry	1969
	A House Divided	1980
	Scotland's Border Country (Co Author)	1985
	The Time Has Come (Co Author)	1987
	Mary Stuart's Scotland (Co Author)	1987
	Against Goliath	1989
Stewartby, L	The Scottish Coinage	1955
	Coinage in Tenth-Century England (Co-Author)	1989
Stodart of Leaston, L	Lord of Abundance	1962
Strange, Bs	Love from Belinda	1960
	Lalage in Love	1962
	Creatures Great and Small	1968
	Love is For Ever	1990
	The Remarkable Life of Victoria Drummond Marine Engineer	1994
Strathcarron, L	Motoring for Pleasure	1964
Sudeley, L	The Sudeleys – Lords of Toddington (Co Author)	1987
Taverne, L	Future of the Left	1974
	Pension Time Born in Europe	1995
	Pensions in Europe	1997
Taylor of Blackburn, L	A New Partnership for Our Schools	1977
Tebbit, L	Upwardly Mobile	1988
	Unfinished Business	1990
Tope, L	Liberals and the Community	1974
Trevethin and Oaksey, L	History of Steeplechasing	1967
	The Story of Mill Reef	1974
	Oaksey on Racing	1991
Tugendhat, L	Oil: The Biggest Business	1968
	The Multinationals	1971
	Making Sense of Europe	1986
	Options for British Foreign Policy in the 1990s (Co Author)	1988

PUBLISHED BOOKS BY MEMBERS OF THE HOUSE OF LORDS

Author	Title of Publication	Date Published
Tweedsmuir, L	Kumari	1955
	Helen All Alone	1961
	The Blue Pavilion	1966
	John Buchan: A Memoir	1982
	Letters to John Masefield	1983
	The Rags of Time	1990
Vinson, L	Personal Portable Pensions for All	1982
	Take Upon Retiring	1997
Wakefield, Bp	A Gospel to Proclaim	1992
	Barriers to Belief	1995
Walker of Worcester, L	The Ascent of Britain	1977
	Trust the People	1987
	Staying Power	1991
Wallace of Saltaire, L	Foreign Policy Process in Britain	1976
	The Transformation of Western Europe	1990
	Regional Integration: the West European Experience	1994
	Policy Making in the European Union	1996
Walsingham, L	75 MM MIAI GunDrill for Daisy Chain Parachute Dropping	1948
Walton of Detchant, L	Subarachroid Haemorrhage	1956
	Polymyosits (Co Author)	1958
	Essentials of Neurology	1989
	Introduction to Clinical Neuroscience	1983
	Skeletal Muscle Pathology (Co Author)	1992
	The Spice of Life	1993
	Brain's Diseases of the Nervous System	1993
	Disorders of Voluntary Muscle (Editor)	1994
	Oxford Medical Companion (Joint Editor)	1994
Warnock, Bs	Ethics since 1900	1960
	The Philosophy of J-P Sartre	1965
	Existentialist Ethics	1966
	Existentialism	1970
	Imagination	1976
	Schools of Thought	1977
	What Must We Teach	1978
	Education: A Way Forward	1979
	A Question of Life	1984
	An Intelligent Person's Guide to Ethics	1986
	Memory	1987
	A Common Policy for Education	1988
	Universities: Knowing our Minds	1989
	The Uses of Philosophy	1992
	Imagination and Time	1994
	Women Philosophers	1996
	A Policy for Small Business	1998
Weatherill, L	Acorns to Oaks	1967

PUBLISHED BOOKS BY MEMBERS OF THE HOUSE OF LORDS

Author	Title of Publication	Date Published
Wedderburn of Charlton, L.	The Worker and the Law	1986
	Employment Rights in Britain and Europe	1991
	Labour Law and Freedom	1995
	Economic Torts	1995
Weidenfeld, L	The Göbbels Experiment	1943
	Remembering My Good Friends	1994
White, Bs	The Ladies of Gregynog	1985
Whitelaw, V	The Whitelaw Memoirs	1989
Wilberforce, L	Monopolies and Restrictive Practices	1956
Williams of Crosby, Bs	Politics is for People	1981
	Youth Without Work	1983
	A Job to Live	1985
	Snakes and Ladders	1996
Williams of Mostyn, L	Law Reform For All	1996
York, Abp	Leonine Sacramentary	1971
	Friendship with God	1989
	Living the Gospel	1993
Young of Dartington, L	Family and Kinship in East London	1957
	The Rise of the Meritocracy	1958
	Family and Class in a London Suburb	1960
	Innovation and Research in Education	1965
	Learning Begins at Home	1968
	Forecasting and the Social Sciences	1968
	The Symmetrical Family	1973
	The Poverty Report	1974-75
	Mutual Aid in a Selfish Society	1979
	Distance Teaching for the Third World	1980
	The Elmhirsts of Dartington: The Creation of an Utopian Community	1982
	Revolution from Within: Co-operatives and Co-operation in British Industry	1983
	Social Scientist as Innovator	1984
	The Meronamic Society	1988
	The Rhythms of Society	1988
	Life After Work: The Arrival of the Ageless Society	1991
	Your Head in Mine	1994
Young of Graffham, L	The Enterprise Years: A Businessman in the Cabinet	1990

PEERS – DIRECTORSHIPS

Note: (i) The following list is not exhaustive some additional information on peers' directorships can be found in the
section entitled Members of the House of Lords at page 88 et seq
(ii) The following abbreviations are used to denote the various titles of members of the House of Lords.

Bs.....................Baroness	*C.....................Countess*	*D.....................Duke*
E.....................Earl	*L.....................Baron/Lord*	*Ly.....................Lady*
M.....................Marquess	*V.....................Viscount*	

(iii) This is not an exhaustive list.

Member of the House of Lords	Company/Organisation	Position
Ackner, L	City Disputes Panel	Director
Aldenham, L	Montclare Shipping Co Ltd	Director
Alexander of Weedon, L	BCH Property Ltd	Director
	National Westminster Bank plc	Chairman
	Total SA (France)	Director
	Trevitt Properties Ltd	Director
	Tyrolese (394) Ltd	Director
Alton, L	Banner Financial Services	Director
	Merseyside Council Voluntary Service	Director
	The People's Trust	Director
Amherst of Hackney, L	Short Sea Europe plc	Director
Amos, Bs	Amos Fraser Bernard	Director
Ampthill, L	Express Newspapers plc	Deputy Chairman
Armstrong of Ilminster, L	Bank of Ireland	Director
	Forensic Investigative Associates plc	Chairman
	IAM Gold Ltd	Director
Astor, V	Cladeto plc	Director
	Prestburt plc	Director
	Trocadero plc	Director
Avebury, L	CL Projects Ltd	Director
Baden Powell, L	Fieldguard Ltd	Director
Bagri, L	Bagri Foundation	Chairman
	London Metal Exchange Limited	Chairman
	Metdist Group	Chairman
Baillieu, L	Anthony Baillieu and Associates (Hong Kong) Ltd	Director
Baker of Dorking, L	Bell Cablemedia plc	Director
	Hanson plc	Director
	Millennium Chemicals Inc	Director
	Waveler Corporation	Director
Barnett, L	Education Broadcasting Services Trust Ltd	Director
	Mercury Recycling Ltd	Director
	Origin (UK) Ltd	Director
Bath, M	Longleat Enterprises	Director

PEERS – DIRECTORSHIPS

Member of the House of Lords	Company/Organisation	Position
Beaverbrook, L	Beaverbrook Racing Ltd	Chairman
	Highwayone Corporation Ltd	Chairman
Bellwin, L	Bellwin Associates Ltd	Director
	Programme Publications Ltd	Director
	Stewart Title (UK) Ltd	Director
Biffen, L	Glynwed International	Director
	J Bibby and Sons	Director
Birkett, L	British School for Performing Arts	Director
	CAARE	Director
	Childrens Film and TV Foundation	Director
	Hatton Foundation	Director
	IMS Prussia Cove	Director
	International Shakespeare Globe Centre	Director
	Lottery Promotion Co	Director
	Park Lane Group	Director
	Theatres Advisory Council	Director
Blyth of Rowington, L	Anixter International Inc (USA)	Director
	The Boots Company plc	Deputy Chairman and Chief Executive
Boardman, L	Editorial Board Nottingham Evening Post	Director
Borrie, L	Mirror Group plc	Director
	Newspaper Publishing plc	Director
	Telewest Communications plc	Director
	Three Valleys Water plc	Director
	Woolwich plc	Director
Boyne, V	Burwarton Estates Company	Director
Brabazon of Tara, L	Aurigny Aviation Holdings Ltd	Director
	Exeter Group (C.I.) Ltd	Director
Brabourne, L	The BAFTA Endowment Ltd	Director
	B Securities	Chairman
	Brabourne Films Ltd	Director
	Britwell Books Ltd	Director
	The Copyright Promotions Group plc	Director
	Emberdove Ltd	Chairman
	G W Films Ltd	Chairman
	Hatch Video Ltd	Director
	H Securities	Director
	HMB Services Ltd	Director
	Kenilworth Film Productions Ltd	Director
	Leontyne Films Ltd	Director
	Mersham Productions Ltd	Chairman
	The National Film School Distribution Co Ltd	Director
	Warnham Residential Rentals Ltd	Director
Brain, L	Council of the Royal Photographic Society	Member
	Court of the Worshipful Company of Weavers	Member

PEERS – DIRECTORSHIPS

Member of the House of Lords	Company/Organisation	Position
Bridges, L	Pontis Caffe Deli Ltd	Director
	South Eastern Recovery Assured Home II, III and IV	Director
Bridport, V	Alger International	Director
	Bridport and Cie	Director
	Camollie Associates	Director
	New Europe Fund	Director
Broadbridge, L	The Angel Improvement Trust	President
	Everyman, The Worshipful Company of Goldsmiths	President
	The Islington Society	President
Brookeborough, V	Basel International (Jersey)	Chairman
	Green Park Healthcare Trust	Non-Executive Director
Buckinghamshire, E	The Russian Pension Trust	Director
	Watson Wyatt Partners	Partner
	Watson Wyatt Trustees Ltd	Director
	Watson Wyatt World Wide	Partner
Butterfield, L	Cemorc Ltd	Director
	Hawks Club	Director
	Hughes Hall	Director
Cadogan, E	Cadogan Developments Ltd	Director
	Cadogan Estates (Agricultural Holdings) Ltd	Director
	Cadogan Estates International Ltd	Director
	Cadogan Estates Ltd	Director
	Cadogan Estates Management Ltd	Director
	Cadogan Group Ltd	Director
	Cadogan Group Management Ltd	Director
	Cadogan Holdings Company	Director
	Chelsea Securities 'B' Ltd	Director
	Chelsea Land Developments Ltd	Director
	Chelsea Land Ltd	Director
	Eagle Star Insurance Company Ltd	Director
	Jockey Club Estates Ltd	Director
	Livermere Investment Ltd	Director
	Merlix Air Ltd	Director
	Oakley Investments Ltd	Director
	The Royal Masonic School for Girls	Director
Carlisle of Bucklow, E	Manchester and London Investment Trust plc	Director
Carrington, L	Christie's International plc	Director
	The Telegraph plc	Director
Chadlington, L	Halifax plc	Non-Executive Director
	Shandwick International plc	Chairman
Chalfont, L	Marlborough Stirling Group plc	Chairman
	Southern Mining Corporation	Chairman
	Television Corporation plc	Director

PEERS – DIRECTORSHIPS

Member of the House of Lords	Company/Organisation	Position
Chalker of Wallasey, Bs	Baygen Power Group Ltd.	Non Executive Director
	Capital Shopping Centres plc	Non Executive Director
Charteris of Amisfield, L	Leeds Castle Foundation	Director
	Prayer Book Society	Chairman
	The Rank Foundation	Director
Churston, L	Cadogan Estates	Director
Clark of Kempston, L	W G Clark (Properties) Ltd	Director
	R C Glaze Properties Ltd	Director
Cledwyn of Penrhos, L	Anglesey Aluminium	Director
	Holyhead Towing Company Ltd	Director
Clyde, L	Westminster Mansions (Holdings) Ltd	Director
	20 - 46 Westminster Mansions Ltd	Director
Cobbold, L	Close Brothers Group plc	Director
	Lytton Enterprises Ltd	Director
	39 Production Co Ltd	Director
	University of Hertfordshire	Director
Colgrain, L	Alexander and Berendt Ltd	Director
Colwyn, L	Cortecs plc	Director
	Dental Protection Ltd	Chairman
	Lord Colwyn Organisation	Director
	Medical Protection Society Ltd	Director
	Nicky Colwyn Associates	Director
	Project Hope	Director
Cottesloe, L	Radcliffe Trust Nominees	Chairman
	Thomas Tapling and Co Ltd	Chairman
Cowdrey of Tonbridge, L	Bilton plc	Non-Executive Director
Cox, Bs	Audrey Sakhazor Foundation	Non-Executive Director
	PWS Holdings plc	Non-Executive Director
Crathorne, L	Cliveden plc	Director
	Woodhouse Securities	Director
Crickhowell, L	Anglesey Mining plc	Vice Chairman
	Associated British Ports Holdings plc	Director
	HTV Group plc	Chairman
	ITNET Limited	Chairman
Cromartie, E	Dervish Mine Clearance	Director
	Ross and Cromarty Footpath Trust	Director
Cumberlege, Bs	MJM Healthcare Solutions	Executive Director
Cunliffe, L	Exhibition Consultants Ltd	Director

PEERS – DIRECTORSHIPS

Member of the House of Lords	Company/Organisation	Position
Dahrendorf, L	Bankgesellschaff Berlin (UK) plc	Director
Darcy de Knayth, Bs	The Grange	Director
	Ipsea	Director
	Skill	Director
	Tristar	Director
Daresbury, L	Aintree Racecourse Company Limited	Chairman
	Daresbury Dairy Farm Limited	Director
	Daresbury Properties Ltd	Chairman
	Grand National Steeplechase Limited	Director
	The Greenalls Group plc	Director
Davies, L	Cardiff Theatrical Services Ltd	Director
	EOBC Ltd	Director
	Llandinam Developers Ltd	Director
	Wales National Opera Ltd	Director
	Welsh Millennium Centre	Director
Derby, E	Culverin Consortium Ltd	Director
	Embankment Properties Ltd	Director
	Embankment Properties (Management) Ltd	Director
	Embankment Properties (Trading) Ltd	Director
	Fleming Private Asset Management Ltd	Director
	Fleming Private Fund Management Ltd	Director
	Fleming Private Nominees Ltd	Director
	The Haydock Park Racecourse Co Ltd	Director
	Knowsley Chamber of Industry and Commerce	President
	Knowsley Salads Ltd	Chairman
	Monlostan Nominees Ltd	Director
	Robert Fleming and Company Limited	Director
Derwent, L	Foreign and Colonial (Pacific) Investment Trust	Director
	Hutchison Whampoa (Europe) Ltd	Director
	Orange plc	Director
	Port of Felixstowe Ltd	Director
	Scarborough Building Society	Director
Donaldson of Lymington, L	Financial Law Panel Ltd	Chairman
Downshire, M	Meadowhead Ltd	Director
Dunleath, L	Dunleath Estates Ltd	Director
Dunrossil, V	Bank of Bermuda	Director
	International Registry Inc	Director
Eatwell, L	Anglia Television Group Ltd	Non-Executive Director
	Arts Theatre Trust, Cambridge	Director
	British Screen Finance Ltd	Chairman
	Cambridge Econometrics Ltd	Non-Executive Director
	Extemporary Dance Theatre	Chairman
	Securities and Futures Authority	Director

PEERS – DIRECTORSHIPS

Member of the House of Lords	Company/Organisation	Position
Eglinton, E	Charities Investment Managers Ltd	Director
	Dunedin Income Growth Investment Trust	Director
	Dunedin Worldwide Investment Trust	Director
	Edinburgh Investment Trust	Director
Elliott of Morpeth, L	Lyonnaise des Eaux Euro	Vice-Chairman
	Telewest (North East) Ltd	Chairman
Elton, L	Andry Montgomery Ltd	Director
Emerton, Bs	Brighton Healthcare NHS Trust	Chairman
Erroll, E	Moncreiffe and Co plc	Director
Ezra, L	Energy and Technical Services Group plc	Director
	Sheffield Heat and Power Ltd	Director
Falkland, V	Northern League Investment Services Ltd	Director
Faringdon, L	Witar Investment plc	Director
Feversham, L	Yorkshire Sculpture Park	Chairman of Trustees
Forbes, L	Rolawn Ltd	Director
Forester, L	Broseley Hospital Trust	Director
	Callkilo	Director
	Linley Farms	Director
	Pett Hamett	Director
	Sipolilo Estates	Director
	Telford Drive	Director
Fortescue, E	Christie Manson Woods Ltd	Director
Gardner of Parkes, Bs	Plan International UK	Chairman
Geddes, L	AES Electric Ltd	Director
	Parasol Portrait Photography Ltd	Director
	Regional Airports Ltd	Director
Gibson, L	Fine Art Travel Cowdray Trust	Director
Gillmore of Thamesfield, L	The Prudential Corporation plc	Director
	Vickers plc	Director
Gisborough, L	Gisborough Hall Hotel	Director
Glenarthur, L	European Helicopter Association	Chairman
	International Federation of Helicopter Associations	Chairman
	St Mary's NHS Trust	Chairman
	Whirly Bird Services Ltd	Director
Gordon of Strathblane, L	Clydeport SC	Director
	Johnstone Press	Director
	Radar Holdings	Director

PEERS – DIRECTORSHIPS

Member of the House of Lords	Company/Organisation	Position
Grade, L	Alberto-Culver (UK) Ltd	Director
	Euro-Disney SCA	Director
	Grade Enterprises Ltd.	Director
	The Grade Company Ltd	Director
	The Grade Organisation	Director
	ITC Entertainment Group	Chairman
	Supervisory Board of Euro Disney SCA, Paris	Director
Grantley, L	Egan Associates International Ltd	Director
	Order of St John Homes Trust	Director
Grenfell, L.	Worldaware (Development NGO)	Director
Grimthorpe, L	Jockey Club	Director
Hamwee, Bs	Xfm Ltd	Chairman
Harris of Peckham, L.	Carpetright plc	Director
	C W Harris Properties.	Director
	Great Universal Stores	Director
	Harris Ventures Ltd	Director
	Harveys Furnishing Group Ltd	Director
Hazlerigg, L	Dunstervile Allen Property Co.	Director
Hogg, Bs	The Energy Group	Non-Executive Director
	Foreign and Colonial Smaller Companies Trust	Chairman
	GKN.	Non-Executive Director
	National Provident Institution	Non-Executive Director
	3i Group plc	Non-Executive Director
Hollick, L	Anglia Television Ltd	Director
	Bringing Up Baby Ltd.	Director
	Channel 5 Television Group Ltd	Director
	Garban LLC	Director
	GHL Investments Ltd	Director
	The London School of Economics and Political Science	Director
	United News and Media plc	Director
	Village Roadshow Ltd	Director
Hooper, Bs	Tablet Publishing Co Ltd.	Non-Executive Director
	Winterthur Life UK Ltd.	Non-Executive Director
	Medical Defence Union Ltd.	Non-Executive Director
	Smith Kline Beecham plc	Non-Executive Director
	Morgan Grenfell Latin American Companies Trust plc	Non-Executive Director
Howe, E	Trident Trust.	Director
Howell, L	Birmingham Cable Corporation Ltd	Director
	Wembley Stadium Ltd.	Director
Howell of Guildford, L.	John Laing Investment Ltd	Non-Executive Director
	Monks Investment Trust	Non-Executive Director

PEERS – DIRECTORSHIPS

Member of the House of Lords	Company/Organisation	Position
Howie of Troon, L	PMS Publications Ltd	Director
	Structural Engineers Trading Organisation Ltd	Director
Hughes, L	Comrie (Dispensary) Ltd	Chairman
Hurd of Westwell, L	National Westminster Bank plc	Director
Hussey of North Bradley, L	Cadweb	Director
	MAID	Director
	Ruffer Investment Management	Director
Inchcape, E	Assam Company	Director
	Duncan MacNeill	Director
	Glenapp Estate Company	Director
	Gray Dowes Travels	Director
	Inchcape Family Investments	Director
	Saracen Power	Director
Inchyra, L	Johnson Fry European Utilities Trust plc	Non Executive Chairman
	Witan Investments Company plc	Non-Executive Director
Inglewood, L	CN Group	Director
Jeffreys, L	Raphael Asset Management	Director
Joplings, L	Oxley Development Ltd	Director
Keith of Castleacre, L	Wicken Farms Ltd	Director
	Wicken Farms Weasenham	Director
Kindersley, L	Maersk UK	Director
	Maersk India	Director
Kingsdown, L	Hambros plc	Director
	Foreign and Colonial Investment Trust plc	Director
Kinross, L	Musketeers Rifle and Pistol Club Ltd	Director
	Ramsay Dinnis Ltd	Director
	Scottish Land Rover Owners Club Ltd	Director
Kitchnener, E	Henry Doubleday Research Association	Director
	Wholefood Trust	Director
	Wholefood Ltd	Director
Knight of Collingtree, Bs	Computeach	Director
Levy, L	Chase Music Ltd	Director
	Jewish Care	Director
	Jewish Care Community Foundation	Director
	Stepney Jewish Clubs and Settlement	Director
	Wireart Ltd	Director
Levene of Portsoken, L	The Haymarket Group Ltd	Director
Linklater of Butterstone, Bs	Maggie Keswick Jencks Caring Centres	Director
	Butterstone Ltd	Director

PEERS – DIRECTORSHIPS

Member of the House of Lords	Company/Organisation	Position
Lucas of Crudwell, L	Intercredit Ltd	Director
Lytton, E	Leasehold Advisory Service	Chairman
McAlpine of West Green, L	Development Securities	Director
	Waddington Galleries	Director
McColl of Dulwich, L	National Back Pain Assoication	Director
	Mildmay Mission Hospital	Director
	Dulwich College Preparatory School Trust	Director
	Mercy Ships UK Ltd	Director
Maclay, L	Altnamara Shipping plc	Director
	Glasgow Aged Seaman Relief Fund	Director
	Glasgow Shipowners Benevolent Association	Director
	Northern Lighthouse Board	Commissioner
Macpherson of Drumochter, L	Union Castle Travel	Chairman
Mansfield, E	Edinburgh US Tracker Trust	Director
	General Accident	Director
Manton, L	Thirsk Racecourse	Director
Mar and Kellie, E	Clackmanshire Enterprise	Director
	Clackmanshire Heritage Trust	Director
Marchwood, V	Hennessy (UK) Ltd	Director
	Moet and Chandon (London) Ltd	Chairman
	Parfums Christian Dior (UK) Ltd	Vice Chairman
	Ruinart (UK) Ltd	Director
Marlesford, L	Baring Taiwan Fund Ltd	Director
	Times Newspapers Holdings Ltd	Director
Marsh, L	British Income Growth Trust plc	Director
	Imperial Life Canada (Toronto)	Director
Massereene and Ferrard, V	Atkin Grant and Lang Gunmakers	Chairman
	Pyman Bell and Co Ltd	Director
	R M Walkden and Co Ltd	Chairman
	Shirlstar Container Transport Ltd	Director
Menuhin, L	SYM Music Co	Director
Merlyn-Rees, L	Video Standards Council	President
Middleton, L	The Birdsall Estates Co Ltd	Director

PEERS – DIRECTORSHIPS

Member of the House of Lords	Company/Organisation	Position
Montagu of Beaulieu, L	Arab-British Chamber of Commerce	Director
	Beaulieu River Management Ltd	Chairman
	Buildings at Risk Trust	Director
	Commodore International Travel	Director
	Corkwise Ltd	Director
	Crag Automotive Ltd	Chairman
	Mayflower Theatre Trust	Director
	Montague Ventures Ltd	Chairman
	Southern Tourist Board	Director
	United Management Systems plc	Chairman
	Ventures Consultancy Ltd	Director
	Vintage Tyre Supplies Ltd	Director
	Wire Guild of the United Kingdom	Director
Montgomery of Alamein, V	Baring Puma Fund	Director
	Terimar Services Ltd	Director
Mount Edgcumbe, E	Grenill Properties	Director
Moynihan, L	Independent Power Corporation	Director
	Ranger Rowan	Director
Naseby, L	Tunbridge Wells Equitable Friendly Society	Director
Nelson, L	Select Detail Ltd	Director
	Tritech Ltd	Director
	TIB plc	Director
Newall, L	GCP Ltd	Director
	Liberty International Holdings plc	Director
	MPA Ltd	Director
Newby, L	Matrix Communications Consultancy Ltd	Director
	Reform Publications Ltd	Director
Normanton, E	Somerley Aggregates	Director
Norrie, L	Hilliers (Fairfield) Newbery	Director
	MPA (UK) Ltd	Director
Northbourne, L	Betteshanger Farms Ltd	Director
	Betteshanger Investments Ltd	Director
	Betteshanger Properties Ltd	Director
	Northbourne Park School Ltd	Director
Northumberland, D	Albury Estate Fisheries Ltd	Director
	Burncastle Farming Co Ltd	Director
	Crescent Farming Co Ltd	Director
	Hotspur Investments plc	Director
	Hotspur Productions Ltd	Director
	Lovaine Trust Company Ltd	Director
	Northumberland Out of School Initiative	Director
	Percy Farming Co Ltd	Director
	Percy Northern Estates Ltd	Director
	Percy Southern Estates Ltd	Director
	Syon Park Ltd	Director
	Trading Enterprises Albury Ltd	Director

PEERS – DIRECTORSHIPS

Member of the House of Lords	Company/Organisation	Position
O'Cathain, Bs	Arundel Festival Society	Director
	BNP UK (Holdings) plc	Director
	British Airways plc	Director
	East Sussex Water	Director
	South East Water	Director
	Sinfonia 21	Director
	Tesco plc	Director
	Thistle Hotels plc	Director
O'Neill, L	Romney, Hythe and Dymchurch Railway Co	Director
	Shanes Castle Estates Co	Director
	Shanes Developments Ltd	Director
Oppenheim-Barnes, Bs	HFC Bank	Non-Executive Director
Paul, L	Caparo Group Ltd	Director
	Caparo Industries plc	Director
	Indo British Association	Director
Perry of Walton, L	Educational Broadcasting Trust	Director
	Open University Foundation	Director
	Research Defence Society	President
	William Harvey Research Institute	Director
Plumb, L	Midland Marks	Director
Plummer of St Marylebone, L	Purton Property Co Ltd	Director
	Regional Funding Co Ltd	Director
	Speen Property Trust Ltd	Director
Poole, L	Ockham Holdings plc	Director
Prentice, L	EW Fact plc	Director
Prior, L	GEC	Director
Puttman, L	Anglia Television plc	Director
	Enigma Productions Ltd	Director
	International Television Enterprises Ltd	Director
	Oxygen 107-9 FM Ltd	Director
	Survival Anglia Ltd	Director
	Village Roadshow plc	Director
Pym, L	Christie Brockbank Shipton Ltd	Director
	Diamond Cable Communications plc	Director
	The Landscape Foundation	Director
	St Andrew's (Ecumenical) Trust	Director
Queensberry, M	Highland Stoneware Ltd	Director
	Royal Academy Enterprises Ltd	Director
Rathcreedan, L	Bath Racecourse Company	Chairman
Rawlinson of Ewell, L	The Telegraph Group Ltd	Director

PEERS – DIRECTORSHIPS

Member of the House of Lords	Company/Organisation	Position
Rayleigh, L	Lord Rayleigh's Farms Ltd	Director
	Eastern Data Processing Ltd	Director
Razzall, L	Bachmann Group Ltd	Director
	C and B Publishing plc	Director
	Caza plc	Director
	Milner Estates plc	Director
	Star Mining Corporation	Director
Rees-Mogg, L	General Electric Company	Director
	IBC Group plc	Director
	The Private Bank and Trust Company	Director
	St James's Place Capital plc	Director
Renwick, L	British Airways	Director
	Billiton plc	Director
	Canal Plus	Director
	Fluor Corporation,	Director
	Fluor Daniel	Chairman
	Liberty International	Director
	Richemont	Director
	Robert Fleming Holdings	Director
	Save and Prosper	Chairman
Rix, L	Brian Rix Enterprises	Voluntary Director
	Elephant Productions Ltd	Voluntary Director
	Mencap City Insurance Services Ltd	Voluntary Director
	Mencap City Foundation	Voluntary Director
	United Chariteis Ethical Trust Advisory Board	Voluntary Director
Rogers of Riverside, L	Architecture Foundation	Chairman of Trustees
	Building Experiences Trust	Trustee
	London First	Director
	Médecins du Monde	Trustee
	Member United Nations Architect's Committee	Director
	National Tenants Resource Centre	Chairman of Trustees
	Richard Rogers Architects Ltd	Director
	Richard Rogers Partnership Ltd	Director
	Richard Rogers and Partners Ltd	Director
	Richard Rogers Partnership Japan	Director
	Richard Rogers GMBH	Director
	River Cafe	Director
	Thames Wharf Studios Ltd	Director
	Thames Wharf Management Services Ltd	Director
Rothermere, V	Daily Mail and General Trust plc	Chairman
	Euromoney Publications plc	Joint President
	Reuters Founders Share Company Ltd	Non-Executive Director
Rowallan, L	Rowallan Activity Centre	Director
	Rowallan Holdings	Director
	Rowallan Ltd	Director
	Turner Dandas	Director

PEERS – DIRECTORSHIPS

Member of the House of Lords	Company/Organisation	Position
Roxburghe, D	Chance Holdings	Director
	Floors Stud Company	Director
	Franklin Hotels	Director
	Golf Course Management (Hillingdon) Ltd	Director
	Irvine Robertson Wines	Director
	Kelso Races Ltd	Director
	Quintus Group	Director
Runciman of Doxford, V	Andrew Weir and Co Ltd	Chairman
	Financial Services Authority	Deputy Chairman
	Runciman Investments Ltd	Chairman
Saathci, L	Josephine Hart Productions Ltd	Director
	Maurice Saatchi Associates Ltd	Director
	London School of Economics and Political Science	Director
	London First Centre	Director
	Storesurvey Ltd	Director
	Hatzone Ltd	Director
	Graduate Appointments Services Ltd	Director
	Forward Publishing Ltd	Director
	Megalomeida plc	Director
	The Net Channel Ltd	Director
	Net Search Ltd	Director
	Net Job Ltd	Director
	Net Care Ltd	Director
	Net TV Ltd	Director
	Net Home Ltd	Director
	Net Car Ltd	Director
	M & C Saatchi Ltd	Director
	M & C Saatchi Worldwide Ltd	Director
	Loot Ltd	Director
St John of Bletso, L	Bell Technology Group	Director
	Eurotrust International	Non-Executive Chairman
	London Science Park	Chairman
Sainsbury of Turville, L	Giant Food	Director
	Sainsbury's Bank plc	Director
Saint Levan, L	ETS Ltd	Director
	Godolphin Company Ltd	Director
Sanderson of Bowden, L	Clydesdale Bank	Deputy Chairman
	Hawick Cashmere Co	Chairman
	Morrison Construction plc	Director
	National Australia Bank Europe	Director
	Scottish Mortgage Trust plc	Chairman
	United Auctions plc	Director
	Watson and Philip plc	Director
Selborne, E	Agricultural Mortgage Corporation plc	Director
	Lloyds TSB Group plc	Director
Selkirk of Douglas, L	Douglas-Hamilton Ltd	Director

PEERS – DIRECTORSHIPS

Member of the House of Lords	Company/Organisation	Position
Sheppard of Didgemere, L	Didgemere Consultants Ltd	Chairman
	Didgemere Forms Ltd	Chairman
	GB Railways plc	Non-Executive Chairman
	Group Trust plc	Non Executive Chairman
	High-Point Rendel	Director
	London Waste Action Ltd	Director
	McBride plc	Non-Executive Chairman
	Robert McBride Group Pension Fund Trustees Ltd	Director
	Unipart Group of Companies plc	Chairman
Shrewsbury, E	Banafix Ltd	Director
	Bayliss and Cooke Ltd	Director
Simpson of Dunkeld, L	ICI plc	Director
	Pilkington plc	Director
Skidelsky, L	Social Market Foundation	Chairman
Smith of Clifton, L	Government and Opposition Ltd	Director
	Irish Peace Institute Ltd	Director
	Joseph Rowntree Reform Trust Ltd	Director
	Opera Northern Ireland Ltd	Director
	Taste of Ulster Ltd	Director
Smith of Gilmorehill, Bs	Morgan Grenfell (Scotland) Ltd	Director
Snowdon, E	Armstrong Jones	Director
Stafford, L	Hanley Economic Building Society	Non-Executive Director
	St George's Hospital	Non-Executive Director
	Staffordshire Environmental Fund	Director
	Staffordshire Land Bank Trust	Director
Steel, L	Border Television plc	Director
	General Mediterranean Holdings (Luxemourg)	Director
	International Institute for Democracy and Rectorial Assistance(Stockholm)	Director
	One Planet Partnership Ltd	Director
Stewartby, L	Angerstein Underwriting Trust plc	Deputy Chairman
	Standard Chartered plc	Deputy Chairman
	The Throgmorton Trust plc	Chairman
Stockton, E	Digital Drum Ltd	Director
	Macmillan College CTC	Director
	Merchant Taylors Enterprises plc	Director
	St John's School	Director
	Townleigh Farm Ltd	Director
	Thrussell Ltd	Director
Strathcarron, L	Kent International Airport plc	Director
	Kirchoff (UK) Ltd	Director
	Seabourne World Express Group plc	Director

PEERS – DIRECTORSHIPS

Member of the House of Lords	Company/Organisation	Position
Sutherland, C	Dunrobin Castle Ltd	Director
Swaythling, L.	Chelsfield plc	Director
	Rothmans International BV	Chairman
Tanlaw, L.	Fandstan Ltd	Chairman
Taverne, L.	Axa Equity and Law	Director
	Central European Growth Fund plc	Director
Tebbit, L.	Sears plc	Director
	The Spectator (1828) Ltd.	Director
Thomas of Gresford, L.	Independent Radio for North Wales and Cheshire	Director
	Marcher Sound Ltd	Chairman
Thomas of Macclesfield, L.	FI Group Shareholders Trust	Chairman
	Stanley Leisure plc	Non-Executive Director
	Venture Technic Cheshire	Chairman
Thomson of Monifieth, L	Value and Income Trust.	Chairman
Thurlow, L.	Sealeisure (UK) Ltd	Director
Thurso, V	Anthon Mosiman Ltd	Director
	Fitness and Leisure Holdings Ltd	Managing Director
	Profile Ltd	Director
	Royal Olympic Cruise Lines	Director
	Savoy Group plc	Director
	Thurso Fisheries Ltd.	Director
	Walker Green Bank plc	Director
Tope, L	Association of Metropolitan Authorities (Properties) Ltd.	Director
	Community Investors Ltd	Director
	Local Government International Bureau.	Director
Torrington, V	Baltic Mills Ltd	Director
	Heritage Oil and Gas Ltd	Director
Trenchard, V	Endsleigh Fishing Club Ltd.	Director
	The Japan Society.	Director
	Robert Fleming and Co Ltd.	Director
Trevethin and Oaksey, L	Axom Racing Syndicates.	Director
	HTV West.	Director
Vestey, L	Racecourse Holdings Trust Ltd	Director
	The Steeple Chase Company	Director
	Vestey Group Ltd	Director

PEERS – DIRECTORSHIPS

Member of the House of Lords	Company/Organisation	Position
Vincent, L	Defence Manufacturers Association	Vice-President
	Hunting-BRAE	Director
	Hunting Defence Ltd	Director
	Hunting Engineering Ltd.	Director
	Imperial College of Science, Technology and Medicine	Director
	MoDeM Consortium	Director
	Officers' Pension Society	Vice-President
	Royal Artillery Museums Ltd	Director
	Vickers Defence Systems	Director
Wakeham, L	Britsol and West plc	Non-Executive Director
	British Horseracing Board	Director
	Carlton Club	Chairman
	Enron Corporation	Non-Executive Director
	GamCare	President
	Genner Holdings Ltd	Chairman
	Horserace Totalisator Board	Non-Executive Director
	Kalon Group plc	Director
	Michael Page Group plc	President
	N M Rothschild and Sons Ltd	Non-Executive Director
	Press Complaints Commission	Director
	Vosper Thornycroft Holdings plc	Chairman
Walker of Worcester, L.	Cornhill Insurance plc	Chairman
	Kleinwort Benson Group plc	Chairman
	London International Future and Options Exchange	Non-Executive Director
	Tate and Lyle plc	Non-Executive Director
	Walpole, L	Peter Beales Roses Director
Weatherill, L	Bernard Weatherill Ltd	President
	Industry and Parliament Trust	Chairman of Trustees
	The Parliamentary Channel	Chairman
Weidenfeld, L	Global Asset Management	Director
	Orion Publishing Company	Director
	Stella AG (Stuttgart)	Director
Weir, V	BICC plc	Director
	Canadian Pacific Ltd	Director
	St James Place Capital plc	Director
	Weir Group plc	Chairman
Westmorland, E	Phillips International Auctioneers	Director
Whaddon, L	Cambridge Chemicals (International) Ltd.	Director
	Champbridge Ltd	Director
	Crac Group Ltd.	Director
	Daltrade Ltd.	Director
	Slorimpex-Rind Ltd	Director

PEERS – DIRECTORSHIPS

Member of the House of Lords	Company/Organisation	Position
Wilcox, Bs.	Automobile Association Ltd	Director
	Carpetright plc	Director
	Cadbury Schweppes plc	Director
	Fanum Ltd	Director
	Institute of Food, Research	Director
	St Marys School, Wantage Trust	Director
Willoughby de Eresby, Bs	Ancaster Estates	Director
	Grimsthorpe and Drummond Castle Trust	Director
	Tay Salmon Fisheries	Director
Wilson of Tillyorn, L	Martin Currie Pacific Trust	Director
Wrottesley, L	Savoy Knight Yachts International	Director
Young of Graffham, L.	Anglo Hong Kong Trust UK Council	Director
	Annes Gate Property plc	Director
	CDT Holdings plc	Director
	Chelsea Land Development Corporation plc	Director
	Directfour Ltd	Director
	Educational Low-Priced Sponsored Texts	Director
	European Land and Property Corporation (KC and UMDS) plc	Director
	European Land (Four SS) Ltd	Director
	European Land (KC and UMDS PFI) Developments Ltd	Director
	Gresham Street Corporation plc	Director
	Havering Riverside Corporation plc	Director
	Jewish Care	Director
	Jewish Care Community Foundation	Director
	Luton International Development Corporation plc	Director
	NBA Quality Systems Ltd	Director
	New Village Properties plc	Director
	Paddington Basin Developments Ltd	Director
	Powerdesk plc	Director
	The Prince of Wales Business Leaders Forum 2552695	Director
	Second Opinion Investments Ltd	Director
	Southside Land Corporation plc	Director
	The South Bank Foundation Ltd	Director
	UK Lotteries Ltd	Director
	White City (Shepherd's Bush) General Partners Ltd	Director
	Whitehall Corporation plc	Director
	Whitehall Investors Ltd	Director
	Young Associations Ltd	Director
Younger of Leckie, V	Royal Bank of Scotland Group	Director/Chairman
	Scottish Equitable Life Assurance	Director
	Siemens Plesse Electronic Systems	Chairman
Zetland, M.	Catterick Race Course Co	Director
	International Racecourse Management Ltd	Director
	Redcar Race Co Ltd	Chairman

PEERS – CONSULTANTS AND PARLIAMENTARY ADVISERS

Notes: (i) The following abbreviations are used to denote the various titles of members of the House of Lords.

Bs ....Baroness	C ....Countess	D ....Duke
E ....Earl	L...............................Baron/Lord	Ly ....Lady
M................................Marquess	V.............................Viscount	

(ii) This is not an exhaustive list.

Member of the House of Lords	Company/Organisation
Alton of Liverpool, L	Jubilee Campaign
Baker of Dorking, L	Cable and Wireless Communication ICL plc
Balfour of Inchrye, L	I Hennig & Co
Bassam of Brighton, L	Capita KPMG
Birkett, L	British Phonographic Industry
Blaker, L	Ashley Business Consultants
Butterfield, L	Animals in Medicines Research Information Centre Howard Foundation International Centre for Organisational Management Yakult Ltd (Japan)
Carrington, L	Chime Communications
Chalfont, L	Atlantic Research Corporation
Chalker of Wallasey, Bs	World Bank Washington
Clark of Kempston, L	Life Insurance Association Tate and Lyle
Cornwallis, L	GS Hall and Co
Elles, Bs	Vanbael and Bellis (Law Firm, Brussels)
Exeter, M	The Fieldworks Institute (Founding Partner)
Glenarthur, L	Imperial Tobacco Group plc
Howell, L	Denis Howell Consultants Severn Trent Water Trust
Marsh, L	Taidei Corporation (Tokyo)
McColl of Dulwich, L	Hon Consultant to the British Army
Mottistone, L	Biscuit Cake, Chocolate and Confectionery Alliance
Moynihan, L	CMA Thames Embankment Ltd

PEERS – CONSULTANTS AND PARLIAMENTARY ADVISERS

Member of the House of Lords	Company/Organisation
Naseby, L	Council for Responsible Nutrition Forum Holdings Ltd
Norrie, L	S W Grundon Waste
Perry of Walton, L	Board of Editors Encyclopedia Britannia Videotel International
Phillips of Ellesmere, L	Celltech plc
Prentice, L	Air Call plc City College of Higher Education
Quirk, L	Addison Wesley Longman Linguaphone Wolfson Foundation
Rowallan, L	Southgate Retail Parks Ltd
St John of Bletso, L	Merrill Lynch
Shewsbury, E	PMI Ltd
Snowdon, E	Thomas Goode and Co Ltd
Steel of Aikwood, L	Stationary Office (Scotland)
Tebbit, L	JCB Excavators Ltd
Trenchard, V	Koei Co Ltd, Japan
Walton of Detchant, L	Royal Society of Medicine Press
Weidenfeld, L	Bertelsmann Foundation Quandt Foundation Burda Medien
Wemyss and March, E	Wemyss and March Estates
Williams of Crosby, Bs	European Job Competition

ADDENDUM

The information in this book is, as far as possible, correct at 1st March 1998. Since that date the deaths have been announced of:

Lord Donaldson of Kingsbridge (Life Peer, Liberal Democrat).
Lord Howell (Life Peer, Labour)
Baroness Lestor of Eccles (Life Peer, Labour)

The following new life peerages were announced in the 1998 New Years Honours List; but the recipients had not yet been introduced to the House of Lords:

Sir Robin Butler KCB, CVO (Formerly Secretary to the Cabinet and Head of the Home Civil Service)
Sir Ron Dearing CB (Formerly Chairman of the Post Office and Chairman of the National Committee of Enquiry into Higher Education)
Paul Hamlyn CBE (Publisher)
Rt Rev David Sheppard (Formerly Bishop of Liverpool)

In the Queen's Birthday Honours of June 1998 the following were awarded life peerages:

Richardson, Reverend Kathleen Margaret	Moderator, Free Churches Council
Burns, Sir Terence	Permanent Secretary, HM Treasury
Laming, Sir William Herbert	Chief Social Services Inspector, Department of Health
Marshall, Sir Colin	Chairman, British Airways

In a list of working peers published in June 1998 the following were awarded life peerages:

Ahmed, Nazir	Business Development Manager	Labour
Alli, Waheed	Managing Director, Planet 24 Productions Ltd	Labour
Bach, William	Barrister	Labour
Bell, Sir Timothy	Chairman, Chime Communications plc	Conservative
Bragg, Melvyn	Writer, Presenter and Editor, South Bank Show, ITN	Labour
Brookman, David	General Secretary, Iron and Steel Trades Confederation	Labour
Buscombe, Peta	Vice-Chairman, Conservative Party and Councillor, South Oxfordshire District Council	Conservative
Christopher, Anthony	Chairman, Trades Union Fund Managers Ltd	Labour
Clarke, Anthony	Former Deputy General Secretary, Union of Postal Workers	Labour
Clement-Jones, Timothy	Solicitor, Management and Public Affairs Consultant	Liberal Democrat
Crawley, Christine	Member of the European Parliament for Birmingham East	Labour
Evans, David	Chairman, Centurion Press Group	Labour
Goudie, Mary	Independent Public Affairs Consultant	Labour
Harris, Toby	Leader, Haringey Borough Council	Labour
Haskins, Christopher	Chairman, Northern Foods	Labour
Lamont, Rt Hon Norman	Director, Jupiter Asset Management	Conservative
Mackenzie, Brian	Lately Chief Superintendent, Durham Constabulary	Labour
Miller, Sue	Former Liberal Democrat Leader, South Somerset District Council	Liberal Democrat
Norton, Professor Philip	Professor of Government and Director of Centre for Legislative Studies, University of Hull	Conservative
Phillips, Andrew OBE	Solicitor	Liberal Democrat
Sawyer, Thomas	General Secretary, Labour Party	Labour
Sharp, Margaret	Senior Research Fellow, Science Policy Research Unit, Sussex University	Liberal Democrat
Thornton, Glenys	Freelance Public Affairs Consultant	Labour
Tomlinson, John	Member of the European Parliament for Birmingham West	Labour
Uddin, Polla	Total Quality Management Manager, London Borough of Tower Hamlets	Labour
Warner, Norman	Senior Policy Adviser to Rt Hon Jack Straw MP	Labour
White, Paul	Farmer, Leader, Conservative Group, Essex County Council	Conservative